Rabbis and Revolution

STANFORD STUDIES IN JEWISH HISTORY AND CULTURE

EDITED BY *Aron Rodrigue and Steven J. Zipperstein*

Rabbis and Revolution

The Jews of Moravia
in the Age of Emancipation

Michael Laurence Miller

STANFORD UNIVERSITY PRESS

STANFORD, CALIFORNIA

Stanford University Press
Stanford, California

This book has been published with the assistance of the Lucius
N. Littauer Foundation and Institute for Israel and Jewish
Studies at Columbia University.

Printed in the United States of America on acid-free, archival-
quality paper

Library of Congress Cataloging-in-Publication Data

Miller, Michael Laurence.
  Rabbis and revolution : the Jews of Moravia in the age of
emancipation / Michael Laurence Miller.
     p. cm. — (Stanford studies in Jewish history and culture)
  Includes bibliographical references and index.
  ISBN 978-0-8047-7056-9 (cloth : alk. paper)
  ISBN 978-0-8047-9971-3 (pbk. : alk. paper)
  ISBN 978-0-8047-7652-3 (electronic)
  1. Jews—Czech Republic—Moravia—History—19th cen-
tury. 2. Judaism—Czech Republic—Moravia—History—19th
century. 3. Moravia (Czech Republic)—Ethnic relations—
Political aspects—History—19th century. 4. Austria—History—
Revolution, 1848–1849—Influence. I. Title. II. Series: Stanford
studies in Jewish history and culture.
  DS135.C96M665 2011
  943.72'004924—dc22
                                    2010021731

Typeset by Bruce Lundquist in 10.5/14 Galliard

To William S. Miller (1909–2010), "grandpa fefufnik,"
in loving memory

זכר עולם
לאיש ישר ונדיב לב
שלום זאב בן ישראל מענדל ושרה רבקה

Contents

Illustrations

Maps

Figures

Acknowledgments

Twenty years have passed since Czechoslovakia's Velvet Revolution. At the time, I was an aspiring Egyptologist, more interested in the Twenty-Second Dynasty than the Habsburg dynasty, more proficient in Middle Egyptian and Hieratic than Czech or German, and able to find El-Amarna on a map of the ancient Near East more quickly than Moravia on a map of nineteenth-century Europe. For me, like many of my generation, the fall of the iron curtain opened a world of possibility that had been unimaginable when I started high school and irresistible when I graduated college. In the summer of 1991, my mother and I planned a ten-day trip to Prague with hopes of experiencing the post-Communist euphoria firsthand. Many years later, long after the euphoria has died down, my own journey continues, and to almost everyone's surprise, I have spent twelve of the last eighteen years in Central Europe, mostly in Budapest, but also in Prievidza, Vienna, and Brno.

My decision to focus on the Jews of the Habsburg monarchy was undoubtedly influenced by the year I spent teaching in two of its successor states. Had I taught English in Poland or Lithuania—instead of Czechoslovakia and Hungary—I probably would have written a very different book. Surely no one would have found it strange for a Litvak like me to write about the world of my ancestors from Szulborze Kozy, Oshmiany, and Pinsk. By fluke or by fate, I have written instead about the forebears of Sigmund Freud, Gustav Mahler, Arnold Schoenberg, Stefan Zweig, Edmund Husserl, Anna Ticho, Peter Salzman, and John F. Kerry. For much of the period covered by this book, Hungary was an El Dorado for Moravian Jews, attracting young men who wished to escape the restrictive Familiants Laws of 1726–27. Fittingly and unwittingly, I followed in their footsteps, finishing this book among the surviving remnant of Naschers, Pullitzers, Boskowitzes, Austerlitzes, and Leipniks, whose surnames attest to Moravian ancestry.

This book grew out of my studies at New York's Columbia University, where I had the honor to study under Yosef Hayim Yerushalmi ז"ל, Michael F. Stanislawski, and István Deák and the privilege to study alongside Nils Roemer, David Wachtel, and Marina Rustow. I learned from all of them and appreciate the encouragement they have given me over the years. I am saddened that Yosef Yerushalmi, a great historian and a marvelous teacher, will not be able to read my book in its final version.

No one deserves more credit for inspiring me to research Moravian Jewry than Michael K. Silber of the Hebrew University of Jerusalem, whose guidance and expertise have made this a better book and me a better historian. My topic emerged during our lengthy discussions on the Jews of the Habsburg monarchy, and I thank him for being a *moreh*, *madrikh*, *ḥavruta*, and *ḥaver*.

It is my pleasure to thank here the many colleagues from whom I received help and inspiration while researching and writing this book: Bradley Abrams, Gerson Bacon, Iveta Cermanová, Marie Crhová, Maria Diemling, Michal Frankl, Zvi Gitelman, Eagle Glassheim, William Godsey, Louise and Dieter Hecht, Maoz Kahana, Hillel J. Kieval, Rudolf Klein, Rebekah Klein-Pejšová, John D. Klier ז"ל, Pawel Maciejko, Rachel Manekin, Natan Meir, Ezra Mendelsohn, Marsha Rozenblit, Ismar Schorsch, Dimitry Shumsky, Nancy Sinkoff, Shaul Stampfer, Luděk Štipl, Zsuzsa Toronyi, Scott Ury, Kati Vörös, Kalman Weiser, and Carsten Wilke. I would also like to thank friends and colleagues at Central European University, who have a share in this book: Erika Belko, Hanoch Ben-Yami and Vered Glickman, Victor Karády, Mária M. Kovács, Szabolcs Pogonyi, Markian Prokopovych, Matthias Riedl, and especially András Kovács.

I owe particular thanks to those who generously funded my research and writing over the past years: the Center for Israel and Jewish Studies at Columbia University, the Jacob K. Javits Fellowship Program, the Memorial Foundation for Jewish Culture, the National Foundation for Jewish Culture, and the Wexner Graduate Foundation. I appreciate the support of the Leslie and Vera Keller Foundation Fellowship, which funded my recent sojourn in Jerusalem and enabled me to put the finishing touches on this book. I owe additional thanks to the Lucian N. Littauer Foundation and the Institute for Israel and Jewish Studies at Columbia University for helping to fund the book's publication. I wrote much of this book while teaching at Central European University, and I thank the university for offering an environment so conducive to research.

I am indebted to the directors and staffs of the archives and libraries who provided materials for my research: Allgemeines Verwaltungsarchiv, Vienna; Archiv města Brna, Brno; Archiv města Olomouce, Olomouc; Archiv města Prostějova, Prostějov; Central Archives for the History of the Jewish People, Jerusalem; Central European University Library, Budapest; Columbia University Libraries, New York; Haus-, Hof-, und Staatsarchiv, Vienna; Hebrew Union College, Cincinnati; Institute for the Research of Diaspora Jewry, Bar-Ilan University, Ramat-Gan; Jewish National and University Library, Jerusalem; Jewish Theological Seminary of America, New York; Jüdisches Museum, Vienna; Leo Baeck Institute, New York; Moravská zemská knihovna, Brno; Moravský zemský archiv, Brno; Národní Archiv Praha, Prague; New York Public Library, New York; Országos rabbiképző intézet, Budapest; Österreichische Nationalbibliothek, Vienna; Státní okresní archiv Třebíč; Wiener Stadt- und Landesbibliothek, Vienna; and Židovské Muzeum Praha, Prague. I would like to single out Jerry Schwarzbard, head of special collections at the library of the Jewish Theological Seminary; Haddasah Assouline, director of the Central Archives for the History of the Jewish People; and the kind archivist at the Moravský zemský archiv, who sometimes bent the rules for me.

I owe special thanks to Norris Pope, Sarah Crane Newman, Carolyn Brown, and Mimi Braverman at Stanford University Press for their patience, professionalism, flexibility, and attention to detail. It has been a pleasure working with them.

I am indebted to the many people whose friendship and support gave me strength during the many "stations" of this book, including Doris Felkl, Robert Schiestl, Edward Serotta, and Guido Tiefenthaler in Vienna; the Salzman family in Brno; Michal Goldberg, Joram Ronel, Yaron and Mazi Schrötter, and Gil Yaron in Jerusalem (in its broadest sense); and Larry Koffler, Josh Prager, and Shai Held in New York. A very special thanks to Cara Stern, a caring friend and a careful reader. I am saddened that David Ertel ז"ל will not have the chance to read this book, which never could have been finished without his help.

My nieces, Chelsea and Eliza, helped me keep things in perspective just by being their adorable and curious selves. Thanks to them and to Andrew Tabachnick and Leona Miller, who both became part of my family after my initial discovery of Moravia.

Words can hardly express the gratitude I feel toward my family for their love, patience, and understanding: my parents, Irvin Miller and Linda Miller; and my sister, Margo, whose friendship and inexhaustible moral support sustained me through the most difficult stages of writing (and rewriting).

I also thank my grandfather, William Samuel Miller. He was born when Moravia was still a Habsburg crown land, and I feel privileged to have had him in my life until recently. I dedicate this book to his loving memory.

BUDAPEST, HUNGARY
MARCH 2010

A Note on Language, Place Names, and Currency

In Bohemia, Moravia, and Austrian Silesia—the former Habsburg territories that now constitute the Czech Republic—almost all cities, towns,
and villages had German and Czech names; some had Polish, Slovak,
Hungarian, Latin, and Hebrew/Yiddish names as well. In this book, I
have chosen to use German names, except in the cases of Vienna, Prague,
and other geographic locations for which there is a standard English-
language name. The choice of German is not intended to privilege one
nation (or national narrative) over the other but merely reflects the general linguistic preferences of Moravia's Jews in the period covered by this
book. Referring to Nikolsburg as Mikulov or Gross-Meseritsch as Velké
Meziříčí might correspond to current usage, but it would misrepresent
the Jewish topography of nineteenth-century Moravia. Similarly, I use
Pressburg instead of Bratislava or Pozsony when referring to the capital
of today's Slovakia. The Czech and Hebrew/Yiddish names of Moravia's
Jewish communities can be found in Appendixes 1 and 2.

I refer to Bohemia, Moravia, and Austrian Silesia as the Bohemian
Lands or the Lands of the Bohemian Crown, rather than using the
anachronistic Czech Lands. Nevertheless, I sometimes use the term
Germany to refer to the lands that were later incorporated into the German Empire in 1871.

I have transliterated Hebrew words in accordance with the *Jewish
Quarterly Review*'s general scheme of transliteration.

During the period covered by this book, the gulden—also known xv
as the florin (fl.)—was the official currency of the Habsburg monarchy.
From 1754 to 1857, the gulden comprised 60 kreuzer (kr.); from 1857 to
1892, it comprised 100 kreuzer. In 1892, the gulden was replaced by the
krone.

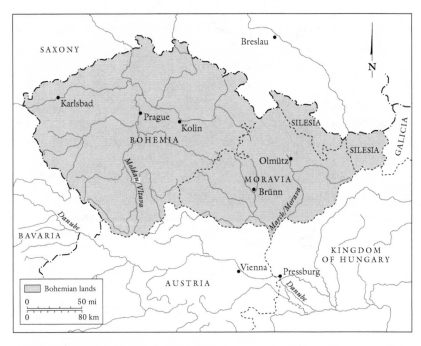

Map 1. The Bohemian Lands around 1840.

Introduction

Writing in the 1940s, as the "world of yesterday" was slipping irretrievably beyond his grasp, Stefan Zweig reached into the recesses of his memory to conjure up an image of Jewish haute bourgeois society in fin-de-siècle Central Europe. Zweig was born and bred in Vienna, but like many of his Jewish and non-Jewish contemporaries, he could trace his immediate ancestry back to the "provinces" of the Habsburg monarchy. As he recalled in his memoirs:

> My father's family came from Moravia. There the Jewish communities lived in small country towns on friendly terms with the peasants and the petty bourgeoisie. They were entirely free both of the sense of inferiority and of the smooth pushing impatience of the Galician or Eastern Jews. Strong and powerful, owing to their life in the country, they went their way quietly and surely, as the peasants of their homeland strode over the fields. Early emancipated from their orthodox religion, they were passionate followers of the religion of the time, "progress," and in the political era of liberalism they supported the most esteemed representatives in parliament. When they moved from their home to Vienna, they adapted themselves to the higher cultural sphere with phenomenal rapidity, and their personal rise was organically bound up with the general rise of the times.[1]

More a bucolic flight of fancy than a historically accurate rendering of the past, Zweig's romanticized vision of Jewish life in the Moravian countryside probably says more about his own state of mind than it does about the experiences of his Moravian Jewish forebears. Nevertheless, he correctly points to the "small country towns" as the locus of Moravian Jewish life not only in his grandparents' generation but also in the preceding ones.

Neither urban nor rural, these small country towns were large enough to support the richly embroidered fabric of Jewish life yet small enough to endow the individual Jewish communities with a distinct—and sometimes idiosyncratic—character of their own. Like children in a schoolyard, many of the communities had nicknames that drew attention to their most striking features. Austerlitz was known as the white town (*weisse Stadt*) because of its distinct chalk-covered houses, but the nicknames that stuck to other Jewish communities (and their inhabitants) often revealed more colorful attributes.[2] The inhabitants of Nikolsburg, Moravia's largest Jewish community, were known as proud ones (*gavsonim*) because of their celebrated talmudic scholars.[3] In contrast, the inhabitants of Holleschau were known as idiots (*naronim*), a kind of Moravian counterpart to Poland's legendary "fools of Chelm."[4] In Prossnitz, where the Sabbatian heresy had made inroads in the seventeenth and eighteenth centuries, the inhabitants were known as *Schepsen*, a derogatory term for the followers of the false messiah, Shabbetai Tsvi.[5] Triesch was known as Little Berlin (*Klein-Berlin*) because the Berlin-based Haskalah (Jewish Enlightenment) found many adherents in this small Moravian town in the first half of the nineteenth century.[6]

When Moravia came under Habsburg rule in 1526, its Jewish population was already concentrated in small and medium-size noble towns—a pattern of settlement that would characterize Moravian Jewry until the middle of the nineteenth century. This pattern, which emerged after the fifteenth- and sixteenth-century expulsions from Moravia's royal free towns, meant that no single Jewish community could claim to be the undisputed center of Moravian Jewry. Unlike neighboring Bohemia, where Prague eclipsed all the other Jewish communities, Moravia had several dozen Jewish communities that could vie with one another in economic, religious, and demographic terms. Nikolsburg, seat of the Moravian chief rabbinate and home to 10% of Moravia's Jewish population, was celebrated as a "city and mother in Israel" (*'ir va-em be-yisrael*), but Prossnitz, which was Moravia's second largest Jewish community, could certainly compete. Known as Jerusalem of the Hana (plains), Prossnitz was an illustrious center of rabbinic learning and by the beginning of the nineteenth century Moravia's wealthiest Jewish community. Still, Nikolsburg and Prossnitz were not alone. Other Moravian communities, such as Boskowitz, Leipnik, Holleschau, and Trebitsch, not only had sizable Jewish communities but also boasted yeshivas that attracted students from neighboring Bohemia, Hungary, Poland, and Germany.

Compared with its neighbors—Bohemia, Hungary, the German lands, and the Polish-Lithuanian Commonwealth—the uniqueness of Moravia's settlement pattern becomes apparent. In the eighteenth century, more than half of Bohemia's 30,000 Jews resided in Prague, and the rest were dispersed in roughly 800 "small villages and market towns."[7] Prague was a "city and mother in Israel," but in the Bohemian countryside, most localities were too small to even sustain a Jewish community. In this respect, Bohemia resembled Germany, where, up until the second half of the nineteenth century, the Jewish population was scattered across hundreds of tiny towns and villages, many of them unable to support a rabbi or ritual slaughterer.[8] Similarly, in the eighteenth century, most of Hungary's 15,000 Jews lived in "small clusters of families in isolated villages," a pattern that continued well into the nineteenth century.[9]

Only the Polish-Lithuanian Commonwealth could compare with Moravia, but even in this case the sheer size of the Jewish population (and of the Polish-Lithuanian Commonwealth) meant that Jewish settlement patterns differed by an order of magnitude. In 1754, only 20,000 Jews lived in Moravia,[10] compared with 750,000 living in the Polish-Lithuanian Commonwealth in 1764. At the time, the Polish-Lithuanian Commonwealth was home to more than half the Jews of the world, and the Lublin region alone had more Jews than all of Moravia.[11] In Poland-Lithuania, as in Moravia, the majority of Jews lived in small noble-owned "country towns," but the size and character of the towns in Poland-Lithuania differed considerably from those in Moravia. In Poland-Lithuania, a "substantial majority" of Jews lived in communities of 500 or more, and at least 16 communities had more than 2,000 Jews each; Brody, the largest community, had 8,600 Jews.[12] In Moravia, by contrast, only the 3,000-strong Nikolsburg community had more than 2,000 Jews, and the vast majority of Moravia's Jews lived in 52 medium-size communities that numbered 500 Jews or less. Unlike their counterparts in large swaths of Germany, Hungary, and rural Bohemia, Moravia's Jewish communities were large enough to support rabbis, ritual slaughterers, ritual baths, synagogues, and—in many cases—yeshivas; but nowhere could they compare with Poland-Lithuania, where "a significant proportion" of Jews lived in towns, or shtetls, with a Jewish majority.[13]

Like Polish-Lithuanian Jewry, Moravian Jewry had a highly developed supracommunal organization, called the Council of the Land (va'ad ha-medinah), which helped draw together the individual Jewish communities as a single cohesive whole. Germany, Alsace, and rural Bohemia also had supracommunal organizations, but these Landjuden-schaften (as they were called) were emblematic of the "atomized" Jewish life in these lands, where Jewish settlements were so scattered and so small that they had to share a rabbi, circumciser, ritual slaughterer, and a single supracommunal framework just to meet the basic requirements of Jewish law.[14] In contrast, Poland-Lithuania's Council of the Four Lands and Moravia's Council of the Land were emblematic of the complex and entangled Jewish life in territories where sizable Jewish communities vied with one another for importance and the supracommunal organization had to weigh the collective interests of Polish-Lithuanian (or Moravian) Jewry against the fierce independence of the individual Jewish communities. In other words, while the Landjudenschaften emerged in territories without Jewish communities of great significance, the Councils of the Land emerged in territories where multiple Jewish communities competed with one another for primacy.

In Moravia, the statutes of the Council of the Land were drafted to ensure that no single Jewish community could lord over the others. The Council was to meet every three years, but never were two consecutive assemblies to be held in the same community (or even in the same administrative district).[15] Between 1650 and 1748, the Council met twenty-three times in eleven different communities, but never did it meet in Nikolsburg or Prossnitz, Moravia's two largest Jewish communities.[16] For Nikolsburg, this is particularly noteworthy, because this community of "proud ones" could make a strong case for being the center of Moravian Jewry. In effect, the decentralized supracommunal structure helped ensure that Nikolsburg (and Prossnitz) would remain, at best, first among equals.

The Sum of Its Parts: The Jews and Jewish Communities of Moravia

The paramount importance of Moravia's individual Jewish communities has presented historians of Moravian Jewry with a singular challenge. Whereas some scholars have latched on to the Moravian chief rabbinate or the Council of the Land as expressions of a Moravian Jewish collectivity, most have preferred to examine Moravian Jewry through the prism of a single community, quite often their own. One of the earliest such studies, Moritz Duschak's "Towards a History of the Jews of Moravia" (1861), deals exclusively with Duschak's native town of Triesch.[17] Even the most comprehensive work on the subject, Hugo Gold's *Jews and Jewish Communities of Moravia in the Past and Present* (1929), shies away from the term *Moravian Jewry* and focuses instead on individual Jewish communities (and Jews). Of the eighty-four articles in Gold's anthology, the overwhelming majority are local histories of Moravian Jewish communities, large and small.

Moravian Jewish historiography flourished during five distinct periods. The first stage (1851–1880) centered around Leopold Löw (1811–1875), a Moravian-born rabbi, scholar, and publicist who served various Hungarian communities (Nagykanizsa, Pápa, and Szeged) between 1841 and 1875. Löw wrote groundbreaking articles on the Moravian chief rabbinate and the Moravian Jewish Enlightenment, and his scholarly journal, *Ben Chananja* (Szeged, 1858–1867), published a number of local histories written by Moritz Duschak (1815–1890), Gerson Wolf (1823–1892), and Nehemiah Brüll (1843–1891), all of whom were born and educated in Moravia. Wolf published documents from the Viennese archives in *Ben Chananja*, and in 1880 (after Löw's death), he also published the statutes for Moravia's Council of the Land, which had originally been translated into German for Empress Maria Theresa.[18]

Wolf's activities presaged the next stage (1895–1908), which witnessed the publication of primary sources and personal recollections dealing with the Jews of Moravia. In 1895, the liberal politician, Moravian patriot, and amateur historian Christian d'Elvert (1803–1896) published the first comprehensive history of the Jews of Moravia and Austrian Silesia.[19] Elvert was not Jewish, but he considered the Jewish experience to be part and parcel of Moravian history. In his effort to document Moravia's Jewish history, he made extensive use of the provincial archives in his native Brünn, bringing many important primary sources to light. In the same year, Isaac Hirsch Weiss (1815–1905), a Moravian-born scholar of rabbinic Judaism, published a Hebrew autobiography in which he reminisced about the dynamic rabbinic culture that characterized the Moravia of his youth.[20] Weiss possessed a keen historical sense, and his memoir is unquestionably the most important personal account of Moravian Jewish life in the nineteenth century. At roughly the same time, Weiss's younger contemporary, Emanuel Baumgarten (1828–1908), published a number of Hebrew manuscripts that shed light on Moravia's more distant past,[21] and Dr. Rabbi Adolf Frankel-Grün (1847–1916) published highly detailed histories of the Jewish communities in Kremsier (where he was rabbi) and Ungarisch-Brod (where he was born).[22]

In 1906, Gottlieb Bondy, a Jewish industrialist in Prague, and Franz Dworsky, director of the Bohemian archives, published a two-volume source collection that documented Jewish life in Bohemia, Moravia, and Silesia from 906 to 1620.[23] Dworsky's foreword stressed the ancient, uninterrupted history of Jewish settlement in these territories, a point that was underscored by the caption on the first document: "Jews resided in Bohemia and Moravia already in ancient times."[24] This work served as the basis for a source collection on Moravian Jewry, which was published in 1935 by Bertold Bretholz (1862–1936), an archivist in Brünn and a specialist on medieval Moravia.[25]

Bretholz's work was published during the third stage (1918–1938), which constituted the most productive period of research on the Jews of the Bohemian Lands. During this stage, which was coterminous with the First Czechoslovak Republic, scholarly activity centered around the Society for the History of the Jews in the Czechoslovak Republic (Gesellschaft für die Geschichte der Juden in der čechoslovakischen Republik) in Prague and the Jewish Book and Art Publisher (Jüdischer Buch- und Kunstverlag) in Brünn. The society put out the scholarly journal *Jarhbuch der Gesellschaft für die Geschichte der Juden in der čechoslovakischen Republik* (1929–1938), which published articles—often of monograph length—on all aspects of Jewish life in the Bohemian Lands. (In 1935, it also launched a book series, but Bertold Bretholz's source collection was the only work to be published.) In 1929, the Brünn-based Jüdischer Buch- und Kunstverlag published Gold's *Jews and Jewish Communities of Moravia in the Past and Present*, which still remains the standard work on Moravian Jewry.[26] Hugo Gold, the Viennese-born head of the Jüdischer Buch- und Kunstverlag, edited this volume and subsequently founded the *Zeitschrift für die Geschichte der Juden in der Tschechoslowakei* (1930–1938), a quarterly journal devoted to "research on [this] hitherto disregarded and then strongly neglected field of Jewish local history."[27] Gold's *Zeitschrift* and the society's *Jahrbuch* published numerous articles on Moravian Jewry, most notably by the Prossnitz-born economic historian Bernhard Heilig (1902–1943).

After the destruction of Czechoslovak Jewry, the motto of Gold's *Zeitschrift* ("Out of the past, for the present and future") held little relevance for Moravia's decimated Jewish population. Gold had emigrated to Palestine in 1940, but many of his contributors (and readers) met more tragic fates. Heilig, for example, died in the Łodz ghetto in 1943. Not surprisingly, the fourth stage in Moravian Jewish historiography (1945–1989) reflects the new reality. Much of the literature in the immediate postwar decades was published in Israel or the United States and aimed to preserve the memory and legacy of the destroyed Jewish communities. A lengthy paean to Nikolsburg was published in Jerusalem in 1950, followed by a critical edition of Moravia's supracommunal statutes in 1951 and a critical edition of Nikolsburg's communal statutes in 1961.[28] Beginning in 1968, the New York–based Society for the History of Czechoslovak Jews published a three-volume work, *The Jews of Czechoslovakia*, which, in the plaintive words of its preface, "is a survey of a tragically concluded chapter."[29] In a similar vein, Hugo Gold, by then in Tel Aviv, published his *Memorial Book for Moravia's Jewish Communities*, a final epilogue to his 1929 volume, providing updated details on the tragic fate of Moravia's Jewish communities.[30]

In this period, there were some continuities with the prewar historiographic tradition. In 1965, the Jewish Museum in Prague began publishing *Judaica Bohemiae*, an annual journal that was conceived as the successor to *Jarhbuch der Gesellschaft für die Geschichte der Juden in der čechoslovakischen Republik*.[31] Ruth Kestenberg-Gladstein (1910–2002), who had contributed to the penultimate volume of the interwar *Jahr-*

buch, also wrote for *Judaica Bohemiae* in the 1960s, establishing a personal link between the two publications.[32] After the rise of Nazism in her native Germany, Kestenberg-Gladstein had found refuge in Prague (1933–1938), where she began her lifelong research on the Jews of Bohemia and Moravia. In 1969, by then in Israel, she published a trailblazing monograph on the Jewish Enlightenment in the Bohemian Lands, which remains the most important work published in the four decades following the Holocaust.[33] (In the late 1980s, the American historian Hillel J. Kieval picked up the mantle and wrote a number of now classic studies, primarily on the Jews of Bohemia.)[34]

The fifth stage of Moravian Jewish historiography (1989–present), which begins with the Velvet Revolution, has produced synthetic works, such as Tomáš Pěkný's *History of the Jews in Bohemia and Moravia*, and popular guidebooks, such as Jiří Fiedler's *Jewish Sights in Bohemia and Moravia*. Most of the original research, however, has been conducted on a small scale by the archivists, laypeople, and local historians who have been sharing their findings since 1994 at the annual "Židé a Morava" (Jews and Moravia) conference in Kroměříž (Kremsier), Czech Republic.[35] Two of these historians have written monographs on individual Jewish communities, in effect reviving the genre that characterized Moravian Jewish historiography at its inception.[36]

In the current work I set aside the communal history approach, choosing instead to view Moravian Jewry as a cohesive whole, the sum of its many complex parts. Based on a wide variety of sources from archives in the Czech Republic, Austria, Israel, and the United States, in this book I take a comparative approach to Moravian Jewry, examining its distinctiveness in an effort to shed light on a range of religious, ideological, political, and socioeconomic challenges that transformed Central European Jewry. Surprisingly, for a Jewish population that produced cultural giants, such as Sigmund Freud, Gustav Mahler, and Edmund Husserl, as well as renowned scholars of Judaism, such as Moritz Steinschneider, Leopold Löw, Adolf Jellinek, and Isaac Hirsch Weiss, there has been precious little research and not a single scholarly monograph on this subject.

In this book, I examine the Jews of Moravia during the Age of Emancipation, a period that is framed by the emancipation of French Jewry in 1790–91 and the subsequent emancipation of Russian Jewry in 1917.

The Jews of Moravia, like the Jews in the rest of the Habsburg monarchy, were initially emancipated during the Revolution of 1848 (and then again in 1867); the momentous events of 1848–49 were a turning point in the social, political, religious, and demographic development of Moravian Jewry, and as such, the Revolution of 1848 also serves as the fulcrum of this book. In the first chapters I examine the origins and development of Moravian Jewry from the Middle Ages onward, focusing on the compact and cohesive constellation of Jewish communities that remained intact until the Revolution of 1848. Until then, Moravian Jewry was characterized by its dense settlement pattern, relatively uniform socioeconomic status, high degree of communal self-government, and a venerable supracommunal organization with a chief rabbi at its head. Moravian Jewry tended to be uniformly settled in noble-owned villages, some of which had large populations but none of which could compare to such metropolises as Prague, Vienna, or Pest. Nikolsburg, the largest of Moravia's fifty-two Jewish communities and the seat of the chief rabbinate, was perhaps "first among equals," but it could not compare with Jewish communities situated in imperial or provincial capitals.

The Jewish communities were beset by residential and occupational restrictions and, more significantly, by the Familiants Laws of 1726–27, which allowed only firstborn Jewish males to marry. A constant source of communal strife and discord, these "pharaonic" Familiants Laws were sometimes circumvented through conversions to Christianity but more often through emigration to neighboring Hungary. In effect, these laws served to siphon off Moravia's young and disenchanted men, removing precisely the demographic group that was most likely to seek solace, hope, or rebellion in Hasidism or Haskalah, two characteristic responses to modernity among the Jews of Central and Eastern Europe. This may explain why Hasidism failed to take root in Moravia and why both the Haskalah and the Reform movement were tamed in this Habsburg province. In fact, until the middle of the nineteenth century, Moravia was the only place in Europe where a network of German-Jewish schools (a hallmark of the Haskalah) and a thriving cluster of renowned yeshivas coexisted in harmony. Prossnitz was not only a center of traditional Jewish learning but also a center of the conservative "rabbinic Haskalah" and of moderate religious and educational reform.

The Familiants Laws and other restrictions placed artificial limitations on even the most natural of human urges and not surprisingly served as regular catalysts for the perennial discord that came to characterize Jewish communal life in Moravia in the first half of the nineteenth century. This discord was relieved temporarily during the Revolution of 1848, which provided a rare opportunity for the Jews of Moravia to coalesce around a common goal (Jewish emancipation) and a common leader (Samson Raphael Hirsch).

Hirsch, who served as Moravia's chief rabbi from 1847 to 1851, assumes a central place in the middle chapters of this book. Previous scholars have focused on Hirsch's subsequent tenure in Frankfurt-am-Main (1851–1888), which was marked by a militant and uncompromising defense of Orthodoxy. Hirsch's brief yet industrious sojourn in Moravia—which is crucial for gaining a full understanding of his later militancy—has received scant attention. German-born Hirsch came to Moravia with an almost messianic hope of unifying its Jews and guiding them into the Age of Emancipation with their traditional Jewish observance intact. After a frustrating four years in Moravia—including a prominent role in the Revolution of 1848—he departed for Frankfurt, convinced that unity was no longer a possibility as far as religious and communal affairs were concerned.

The Revolution of 1848 ushered in a new age of freedom, but it also precipitated demographic, financial, and social transformations that emerged precisely when the Czech-German conflict began to dominate public life in Moravia. In the final chapters of this book I examine these transformations—most notably the self-liquidation of small-town Jewry through migration to Vienna, Brünn, and other previously off-limits cities—and place them in the context of the virulent (and sometimes violent) nationality conflict. In these chapters I pay particular attention to unique features of the Moravian Jewish landscape—such as the political Jewish communities (*politische Judengemeinden*) and the network of German-Jewish schools—that helped preserve a Jewish "national" identity yet made Moravian Jewry all the more vulnerable to the vagaries of the nationality conflict. Indeed, the cautious embrace of Zionism was a way out of this conflict, but it was also a continuation of Moravian Jewry's distinctive role as mediator—and often tamer—of the major ideological movements that pervaded Central Europe in the "long nineteenth century."

One
From Přemyslids to Habsburgs
Moravian Jewry in the "Land of Canaan"

During the Age of Emancipation, Moravian Jewry experienced the transformation—and disruption—of religious, communal, and demographic patterns that had become deeply entrenched as far back as the Middle Ages. I examine the development of these patterns here, beginning with the eleventh and twelfth centuries, when Jews were first documented in Moravia, and continuing into the late eighteenth century, when Moravia had become an important center of Jewish learning. Moravia was also known as a place of Jewish suffering because of the harsh residential and occupational restrictions, onerous taxation, and, above all, the Familiants Laws. These restrictions helped shape Moravian Jewry's reputation—and self-image—as the most oppressed Jewish population in the Habsburg realm.

A center of rabbinic learning, Moravia was home to a constellation of renowned yeshivas that attracted students and rabbis from neighboring Bohemia, Hungary, Galicia, Lower Austria, and beyond. As an important node in the interconnected network of Central and Eastern European Jewish communities, Moravia's inhabitants were continuously exposed to religious, educational, and ideological trends, some finding greater reception than others. In the seventeenth and eighteenth centuries, for example, Sabbatianism (and then Frankism) made considerable inroads in Moravia, particularly in the communities of Holleschau, Prossnitz, and Kojetein. In the eighteenth century, however, Hasidism never found a foothold in Moravia, despite its considerable success in neighboring Galicia and Hungary. I examine these religious movements in greater detail, with an eye toward understanding why Sabbatianism and Frankism left their mark on Moravia, while Hasidism did not. As will be seen, the relative success or failure of these movements was related in part to the settlement patterns and demographic trends that developed from the eleventh century onward.

Moravia and Its Jews: Eleventh to Fifteenth Century

Moravia takes its name from the Morava River (known in German as the March), which originates in northwest Moravia, near today's Czech-Polish border, and flows southward along the border between the Czech Republic and Slovakia and farther down, between Slovakia and Austria. The river lent its name to the Great Moravian Empire, which flourished in East-Central Europe from the ninth century until it was overrun by Magyar invaders in the tenth. Great Moravia was subsequently divided between the Holy Roman Empire, the kingdoms of Poland and Hungary, and the emerging Czech state. The territory of Moravia, which had once been at the heart of an empire, was subordinated to neighboring Bohemia, which came under the rule of the Přemyslid dynasty.[1]

The Přemyslids ruled the Bohemian Lands (Bohemia and Moravia) from the eleventh century until the dawn of the fourteenth century, with Prague—Bohemia's largest town—serving as the seat of the new Czech state. Under the Přemyslids, the law of primogeniture reflected the relationship between Bohemia and Moravia, with the eldest son inheriting the dynastic seat in Prague and the younger sons inheriting the appanage seats in Moravia's three largest towns: Olmütz, Brünn, and Znaim. In 1182, Holy Roman Emperor Frederick Barbarossa intervened in Přemyslid affairs and raised Moravia to the status of a margravate (border province of the Holy Roman Empire, ruled by a margrave), a status it would retain for the next seven centuries. The Margravate of Moravia was still part of the Přemyslid patrimony, but its new status made it a distinct administrative and political entity within the Bohemian Lands.

The Bohemian Lands became a hereditary kingdom in 1212, when Emperor Frederick II issued the Golden Bull of Sicily, affirming the kingship of Přemysl Otakar I and his successors. The Kingdom of Bohemia acquired a privileged position in relation to the Holy Roman

Empire, and Otakar's grandson, Přemysl Otakar II (1253–1278), was even twice a candidate for the imperial throne. Under Přemyslid rule, Bohemia and Moravia experienced great economic prosperity, with the cultivation of additional agricultural land, the discovery of silver mines, the founding of new villages, and the transformation of existing towns into centers of crafts and commerce. These developments, which proved advantageous to the local Slavic-speaking population, also attracted many German speakers, who migrated to the Bohemian Lands in the twelfth and thirteenth centuries. Many of these German speakers settled in Znaim, Brünn, Olmütz, Mährisch-Neustadt, and Iglau, which were all elevated to the privileged status of "royal town" in the course of the thirteenth century.

Jewish settlement in Bohemia and Moravia also dates back to the period of Přemyslid rule. Although Jews may have come to the region as far back as Roman times, the first documented references to Jewish communities in Bohemia (Prague, Eger, Leitmeritz) and Moravia (Brünn, Olmütz) come from the eleventh and twelfth centuries.[2] The Jews in these communities presumably arrived from other areas of the Holy Roman Empire, bringing Ashkenazic customs and the Yiddish language. In 1254, Přemysl Otakar II granted the Jews of Bohemia and Moravia a legal charter, which elaborated the juridical and economic terms of their residence in the Bohemian Lands. This document, which was based on Duke Frederick II's 1244 charter to the Jews of Austria, suggests that money lending was the basis of Jewish economic life in the Bohemian Lands at the time.[3] In Moravia, this was particularly the case in Brünn and Olmütz, royal towns that were expanding into important commercial centers in Central Europe.

In medieval Hebrew sources, biblical names were often affixed to new areas of Jewish settlement, and the Bohemian Lands were no exception. Just as Germany became known as Ashkenaz (Genesis 10:3), Spain as Sefarad (Obadiah 20), and France as Tsarefat (I Kings 17:9), the Bohemian Lands also acquired a name of biblical origin. As early as the twelfth century, Hebrew sources refer to the Bohemian Lands as the Land of Canaan, a name that, at first glance, seems to conjure up the Promised Land. However, as the thirteenth-century Jewish traveler Benjamin of Tudela explained, this term had an altogether different connotation.

"The Jews who live there call it the Land of Canaan," he wrote, "because the inhabitants of this land sell their sons and daughters to all of the nations."[4] Benjamin was alluding to Noah's postdiluvian curse of Canaan (Genesis 9:25), when Canaan—one of Noah's grandsons—was cursed to be "the lowest of slaves to his brothers." Indeed, the designation of the Bohemian Lands as Canaan may likely be traced to the same folk etymology that derives *Slav* from *slave*.

Medieval Hebrew sources refer to the Slavic language spoken in the Land of Canaan as "the language of Canaan" (*leshon kena'an*), and many Moravian Jews were apparently proficient in this language in the twelfth and thirteenth centuries. Some Jews had Slavic names, such as Benesch, Czierno, and Mardusch,[5] and a number of rabbis from the Bohemian Lands even used Slavic glosses in their scholarly works. The fact that two thirteenth-century rabbis—Abraham ben Azriel, author of the liturgical commentary *Arugat ha-bosem* (Spice garden), and his disciple, Isaac ben Moses, author of the halakhic compendium *Or zaru'a* (Hidden light)—made frequent use of Slavic terms indicates that Jews in the Bohemian Lands had an "active knowledge of the Czech language" in the Přemyslid period.[6]

Přemyslid rule came to an end in 1306, following the murder of the last of the dynastic line. Four years later, the Bohemian crown passed to John of Luxemburg, whose son Charles founded Prague's Charles University in 1348 and went on to become Holy Roman Emperor in 1355. Under the Luxemburgs, the estates system—which had been taking shape since Přemyslid times—became rooted in Bohemia and Moravia, giving the emerging estates (nobility, clergy, burghers) a greater degree of political power and autonomy in relation to the crown. As power shifted and devolved in the Bohemian Lands, many Jews settled in Moravia's noble-owned towns (e.g., Austerlitz, Nikolsburg) or clergy-owned towns, especially those belonging to the bishop of Olmütz (e.g., Kremsier, Trebitsch).[7]

By the fifteenth century the Moravian estates had attained "almost complete autonomy" with respect to the other lands of the Bohemian crown, and as many scholars have pointed out, a distinct Moravian "territorial patriotism" (*Landespatriotismus*) began to emerge, especially among the estates.[8] Moravian territorial patriotism developed under the marked influence of the Hussite Wars that ravaged Bohemia and—to a lesser extent—Moravia between 1420 and 1434. Based on the teachings of the martyred Jan Hus (1369–1415), the Hussite movement first and foremost pursued church reform, pitting religious reformers against the Catholic Church. At the same time, the religious conflict exacerbated social and national tensions, which unfolded differently in Bohemia and Moravia. In Bohemia, Hussitism made its strongest inroads among the Czech-speaking burghers, leading many nineteenth-century Czech historians, such as František Palacký, to portray it as a forerunner of modern Czech nationalism. Anti-Hussite crusaders wreaked tremendous havoc on Bohemia's towns, and the Hussite Wars ended with the secularization of church lands and the elimination of the clergy from Bohemian politics. In Moravia, in contrast, Hussitism found its greatest support among the upper nobility, who tended to have a moderating effect on the movement. The warring factions in Moravia reached an early compromise; church lands were never secularized, and Moravia was spared the wanton destruction that afflicted Bohemia. By the end of the Hussite Wars, the Moravian estates enjoyed a more deeply rooted autonomy than before, and they became the standard-bearers of a territorial patriotism that underscored Moravia's distinctness from neighboring Bohemia.

Moravia's nobility emerged from the Hussite Wars in a stronger position, but the Jews of Moravia (and elsewhere) emerged tainted by their association with the Hussite heresy. Because Hussitism was deeply rooted in the Old Testament, some contemporary rabbis viewed the religious movement with "guarded sympathy" and many Roman Catholics denounced it as a Judaizing sect.[9] Jews were repeatedly accused of supplying arms to the Hussites, and Catholic rulers used this accusation as a pretext for persecuting the Jews in their midst. In 1421, the Jews of Vienna were imprisoned, tortured, forcibly converted, and burned at the stake, in part because of the alleged "confederation between Jews and Hussites."[10] The *Wiener Gesera* (Viennese persecution), as this event has come to be known, was followed by other persecutions, such as the expulsion of Jews from Bavaria in 1422, and—more significant here—the expulsion of Jews from Iglau (in Moravia) in 1426. The Iglau expulsion ushered in a period of expulsions that would completely transform Jewish settlement patterns in Moravia.

Expulsion from Royal Free Towns
in the Fifteenth and Sixteenth Centuries

Iglau was the first royal free town to expel its Jews and the only one to do so during the Hussite Wars. Margrave Albrecht V, who had received Iglau in 1424 as a dowry gift from his father-in-law, Siegmund, was charged with protecting it from the Hussites. In 1426, he acceded to the demands of the Iglau burghers to expel the Jews because of their alleged association with the Taborites, the most radical followers of Jan Hus. The close proximity of Jews and Christians in Iglau, it was argued, constituted a grave danger to the Christian population, which was at risk of being exposed to heretical ideas. The expulsion from Iglau set a precedent that was followed by Albrecht's 15-year-old son and successor, Ladislaus Posthumus, who expelled the Jews of Brünn, Znaim, Olmütz, and Mährisch-Neustadt in 1454, the first year of his reign. The young Ladislaus was heavily influenced by John Capistrano, a vitriolic Franciscan preacher sent to the Slavic lands by Pope Nicholas to shore up the Catholic Church in the wake of the recent scourge of heresy. Capistrano's blistering sermons against the Hussite heresy, which led to his canonization in 1690, were equaled in zeal and vitriol only by his Jew baiting, which gained him the epithet "Flagellator of the Jews." During his sojourns in Moravia in 1451 and 1454, he incited the populace against the Jews and encouraged the local rulers to banish them.[11]

Although often justified in religious terms, the expulsions also testified to the sharp economic tensions between Christians and Jews at the time. All three expulsion decrees from 1454 (the Jews of Olmütz and Mährisch-Neustadt were expelled with one decree) complained of the "depravity and grievance" (*Verterbnuss und beswerung*) that the Jews inflicted—or might inflict—on the Christian burghers through their business practices and general presence.[12] According to the Brünn decree, the local burghers demanded expulsion "because they would suffer great impoverishment and damage were this [expulsion] not to be undertaken."[13] In Brünn, Znaim, Olmütz, and Mährisch-Neustadt, the burghers were released from their debts and given title to Jewish houses, synagogues, and even cemeteries. In exchange, the burghers agreed to cover the taxes that the previous inhabitants paid to the royal treasury.[14] The burghers of Ungarisch-Hradisch, who had been over-looked in 1454, received their reward in 1514 when a much older Ladislaus recycled the expulsion decrees of his youth. The later decree was copied nearly verbatim, with one new addition: "Since they [Jews] are in no [royal] town in our Margravate of Moravia, they should not be here [Ungarisch-Hradisch] among [the Christian burghers]."[15] By 1514, none of Moravia's six royal free towns had a Jewish community within its walls. In Brünn, the Jews' Gate (Figure 1) stood as a reminder of the community's absence.

As the royal free towns banished their Jews in the fifteenth and early sixteenth centuries, the Jewish expellees increasingly came under the protection of Moravia's ascendant nobility. By the end of the Hussite Wars, approximately twenty noble families emerged victorious as the preeminent power in the Margravate of Moravia, dividing the landed property—much of which had previously belonged to the crown and the

Figure 1. View of Jews' Gate, Brünn, 1835. Courtesy of Brno City Archive, XV.b.82.

church—among themselves.[16] This "gentry oligarchy," which included the Pernstein, Dietrichstein, Lichtenstein, and Kaunitz families, came to wield most of the political, economic, and cultural power in Moravia until the seventeenth century. Not only were all political institutions in the hands of these families, but even the bishops of Olmütz and Brünn had to be elected from within their ranks. Like their counterparts in Poland's "gentry paradise," these Moravian noble families recognized the economic utility of the Jews, particularly in their tireless efforts to break the monopolies enjoyed by the royal towns.[17] Indeed, the nobility not only gave Jews refuge in their private towns—granting them privileges in exchange for annual "protection money" (*Schutzgeld*)—but also encouraged them to engage in handicrafts, brewing, and other trades that could undermine the burgher guilds.[18]

In the aftermath of the expulsions, the locus of Jewish settlement in Moravia shifted from the royal free towns to the small and medium-size noble-owned towns. Although some expellees left Moravia,[19] the vast majority remained in the margravate, where they joined the ranks of existing Jewish communities or, in many cases, established communities where none had existed before, often on the outskirts of the royal towns from which they had just been expelled.[20] The Jews of Iglau, for example, established new communities in Puklitz, Pirnitz, and Triesch, all within 15 kilometers of their former place of residence. Jews from Olmütz established the Jewish community of Prossnitz (15 kilometers) and also settled in neighboring Loschitz, Kojetein, Tobitschau, Holleschau, Leipnik, and Prerau. Many Jews from Brünn made their way to nearby Austerlitz (20 kilometers), whose Jewish community dated back to the thirteenth century, whereas others settled in Neu-Rausnitz, Kanitz, Eibenschitz, Pohrlitz, Boskowitz, Gewitsch, and Butschowitz. Jews from Znaim could be found in neighboring communities such as Piesling, Pullitz, Jamnitz, Schaffa, Misslitz, Kromau, Irritz, and Eibenschitz.

The shifting settlement patterns changed the occupational structure of Moravian Jewry as well.[21] Although Moravian Jews continued to be concentrated primarily in petty trade and money lending, their involuntary move to small noble-owned towns opened up new opportunities—particularly in handicrafts. Before the expulsions, there were Jewish butchers and tailors in Moravia, but few Jews engaged in any other handicrafts. In the royal towns, where the burgher guilds fiercely guarded their own privileges, Jews could scarcely dream of engaging in handicrafts; in the smaller towns and villages, the Jewish population was often too small for any occupational differentiation to take place.[22] The expulsions changed all this. Not only did Jews flock to smaller towns, significantly increasing the Jewish population in such places as Prossnitz and Austerlitz,[23] but noble landowners also encouraged the newcomers to learn handicrafts and compete directly with the burgher guilds. Sixteenth- and early seventeenth-century sources attest to the increased involvement of Moravian Jews in handicrafts, especially glassmaking, metalworking, and various branches of the textile industry.[24] In the seventeenth century, Moravia's Jews had a near monopoly on glassmaking and were heavily represented among cutlers, goldsmiths, and sword makers. Jews played a central role in Moravia's textile industry, working as tailors, hatters, stocking makers, and sack makers. A Jewish tailors' collective formed in Prossnitz in 1618.[25] Moravia's Jews were also engaged in a wide range of other handicrafts; there were Jewish butchers, bakers, dairymen, tanners, cobblers, potters, rope makers, bookbinders, and musicians. Kremsier even had a group of Jewish soap boilers.[26]

Moravia's Jews became increasingly involved in handicrafts, but their primary livelihood remained petty trade—in textiles, livestock, and wine.[27] Jews engaged in the textile trade bought up raw materials (wool) and sold finished products (cloth) in Moravia as well as Bohemia, Hungary, Austria, and Poland.[28] Those involved in the livestock trade dealt not only in live cattle, horses, and poultry but also in animal hides, leather, fur pelts, and feathers.[29] Some used their horses and wagons to transport merchandise over long distances, occasionally employing non-Jews to help haul the freight.[30] Moravia's Jews also played an important role in the wine trade, not only as merchants but also as vintners.[31] Poland's kosher wine was supplied, in part, by Moravian Jews, a fact that greatly concerned Poland's rabbis, because Moravia's Jewish wine merchants were known to drink nonkosher wine. Nevertheless, Moses Isserles of Crakow, one of the sixteenth century's most important rabbinic authorities, gave Moravian wine merchants the benefit of the doubt, allowing Poland's Jews to imbibe their intoxicating merchandise.[32]

The Thirty Years War, 1618–1648

The Thirty Years War, "perhaps altogether the major conflict in European history between the Crusades and the Napoleonic Wars,"[33] tore the continent asunder and, in the process, transformed the political, religious, demographic, and economic contours of Europe. What began as a challenge to Habsburg authority in Bohemia by the nobility and the Protestants ended with a formidable reassertion of Catholic and Habsburg imperial supremacy. Initially a "domestic conflict" in Prague, the Thirty Years War left millions of corpses and refugees on a war-ravaged and greatly impoverished continent. Although Europe was immersed in war for most of the seventeenth century, the hostilities in Bohemia and Moravia reached a bloody denouement with the decisive defeat of the estates at the Battle of White Mountain in 1620. In the aftermath, the victorious Emperor Ferdinand II (1619–1637) sought to purge disloyal subjects from these lands. He undertook a process of re-Catholicization, which entailed the execution of rebels, the confiscation of hundreds of noble manors, the expulsion of all Protestant ministers, and the ultimatum that all Christians in the Bohemian Lands choose between Catholicism and exile. His efforts to reassert imperial authority reached a climax in the Renewed Land Ordinances of 1627–28, which, in addition to declaring the Bohemian Lands a hereditary possession of the Habsburgs, also abolished many rights of towns and the nobility.[34] This decree began a period of princely absolutism, characterized by an increased penetration of imperial institutions and centralized government that would reach its culmination in the eighteenth-century reign of Maria Theresa.

Ferdinand II viewed the Jews of the Bohemian Lands first and foremost as a source of revenue for the imperial treasury.[35] He relied on the Jews to finance not only his domestic battles against the Protestants but also his foreign campaigns against the Ottoman Turks. The burden of financing wars was compounded by physical and economic devastation following the Battle of White Mountain and by the death and emigration of many taxpayers. (An estimated 30,000 Protestants chose emigration over Catholicism.) At the same time, attempts to impose greater obligations on the peasant population often resulted in social unrest, such as the peasant rebellions in Bohemia and Moravia in 1624 and those in Upper Austria in 1626.[36] Not surprisingly, Ferdinand II chose to tax the Jews—a population that was unlikely to rebel. In a privilege granted to the Jews of the "hereditary Margravate of Moravia" in 1629, the emperor demanded an annual payment (a so-called contribution) of 12,000 fl. to the imperial treasury. Similar "contributions" were demanded from the Jews of Bohemia and Silesia as well.

The privilege of 1629 has been called the Magna Carta of Moravian Jewry because it established the Jews' rights and duties in relation to the state for the next 125 years.[37] Like similar privileges granted to the Jews of Bohemia (1623, 1627) and Silesia (1627), the primary aim of the 1629 privilege was to ensure that the Jews could meet their new tax obligations.[38] Much to the chagrin of the burghers, the 1629 privilege allowed Jews to attend weekly and annual fairs "just like other Christian merchants and registered traders" in order to "encourage their usefulness [*ihres nuzens*] and the better collection of the above-mentioned annual contribution."[39] It stipulated that occasional tolls and taxes were not to exceed those paid by Christians and also entitled Jews to learn handicrafts—so long as they practiced them within the confines of their own community. (Nonetheless, a special *Leibmaut*, or body tax, was collected from Jews wishing to visit the fairs in Moravia's royal towns.) The opening of new branches of the economy and the emphasis on usefulness may presage some of the ideas expressed in the eighteenth-century debates on Jewish rights, but in 1629 the term *usefulness* had one clear connotation: the ability to provide money for the needs of the monarchy.

Even if the Jews were viewed as financially useful to the empire, the burghers in the royal free towns continued to see them as a threat to their livelihoods. Although the 1629 privilege allowed Jews to attend weekly and annual fairs, the royal towns repeatedly refused to admit them.[40] Already in 1635, a delegation of Jews complained to the Moravian governor, Cardinal Franz Dietrichstein, that Jews were not being admitted into "all places in Moravia, above all the royal towns."[41] Dietrichstein cited the 1629 privilege, but burghers from the royal towns argued that this document violated their own privileges, which had granted them the right *de non tolerandis judaeis* for well over a century. They demanded the immediate repeal of the 1629 privilege and sought protection from the "deceitful and exploitative" trading practices of the Jews, which had allegedly remained unchanged since the fifteenth- and sixteenth-century expulsions. In 1659, after the newly crowned emperor Leopold I (1658–1705) confirmed the Jewish privilege, the royal towns sent a letter to the emperor detailing alleged Jewish abuses—from selling stolen wares to cutting spices with sand and dust.[42] Because the Jews were gnawing away at the already meager earnings of the Christian burghers, argued the letter, it would be best to expel them or—at the very least—severely restrict their rights. The royal towns based their demands on the authority of the 1454 expulsion decrees and used the same line of reasoning. This pattern of conflict between town privilege and Jewish privilege continued unabated until well after the Revolution of 1848.[43]

The 311 Statutes and the Moravian Chief Rabbinate

If the privilege of 1629 was Moravian Jewry's Magna Carta, the 311 Statutes (Shai Takkanot) of 1650 was its constitution. Drafted by representatives of Moravia's Jewish communities, the Shai Takkanot laid the foundations for Jewish self-government on the supracommunal level in the aftermath of the Thirty Years War.[44] The supracommunal organization that came into being was known as the Council of the Land (va'ad ha-medinah) and bore close resemblance—although on a much smaller scale—to the Council of the Four Lands in Poland (and the Council of the Land of Lithuania), which Shmuel Ettinger has described as "the greatest expression of Jewish aspirations towards self-rule" since the Middle Ages.[45] Like its counterparts in the Polish-Lithuanian Commonwealth, the Council of the Land of Moravia derived its authority from above and below: It was recognized by the government as a Jewish representative body and accepted by the local Jewish communities (kehillot) as Moravian Jewry's supreme legislative body. Composed of elected delegates from the Jewish communities, the Council of the Land met once every three years to attend to the myriad fiscal, administrative, religious, and educational affairs of Moravian Jewry as a collectivity.[46] The Council first met in 1650 in Gaya, where the elected delegates drafted the Shai Takkanot (based on earlier statutes from before the Thirty Years War). At subsequent meetings, the delegates enacted additional statutes (sometimes at the behest of the government) and clarified or amended existing ones.

The statutes were enforced by a multitiered bureaucracy, which the Shai Takkanot described in great detail. At the bottom were the *kehillot*, which constituted the bedrock of Jewish communal autonomy in Moravia. The *kehillot* were grouped into three administrative districts (*galilot*), each of which was placed under the supervision of two "heads of the district" (*rashei ha-galilot*).[47] Elected by the Council of the Land for three-year terms, these six district heads were authorized to enforce the statutes by fining—or, in some cases, excommunicating—transgressors in the district under their purview. In each district, the two heads came together twice a year for a "minor council" (*va'ad katan*) at which they addressed such matters.[48] With the participation of a rabbi, the district heads were also authorized to adjudicate civil cases involving two or more Jews (or Jewish communities) within the district. When four or more district heads assembled together, they functioned as "heads of the land" (*rashei ha-medinah*) and constituted a "major council" (*va'ad gadot*). As such, they exercised their authority over Moravian Jewry as a whole. Alongside the district heads were a number of other Jewish functionaries on the supracommunal level. These included tax collectors (*govei medinah*), intercessors (*shtadlanim*), secretaries (*soferim*), and above all, the chief rabbi (*rav ha-medinah*).

The chief rabbi was Moravian Jewry's supreme authority, not only in matters of religion but also with regard to taxation and administering justice. Although his extensive prerogatives were first codified in the Shai Takkanot, the actual position and title can be traced back to at least the middle of the sixteenth century. The precise origins of the Moravian chief rabbinate are still shrouded in mystery, but in all likelihood it came into being after the fifteenth- and sixteenth-century expulsions from Moravia's royal free towns.[49] As Jewish expellees came under the protection of individual noblemen, they formed communities that were often too small to attract a qualified rabbi. As a result, they would elect a rabbi in one of the province's larger communities to serve as their judge. Unsurprisingly, Nikolsburg, Moravia's most populous Jewish community at the time, became the seat of the chief rabbinate. The first chief rabbi for whom there is documentary evidence is Judah Löw ben Betsalel ("the Maharal"), who held this position from 1553 to 1573 before moving to Prague. Subsequently, the post attracted many other illustrious rabbis—including Yomtov Lipmann Heller, Menaḥem Mendel Krochmal, Gershon Ashkenazi, David Oppenheimer, Shmuel Shmelke Horowitz, Mordecai Benet, Nehemias Trebitsch, and Samson Raphael Hirsch—who helped make Nikolsburg one of the most important centers of Jewish learning in Central Europe. Although the chief rabbi resided in Nikolsburg, his authority extended well beyond its borders. As the supreme religious authority in the land, he examined and certified rabbis, religious teachers, and ritual slaughterers before they could serve in Moravia's Jewish communities; he also headed the province's largest yeshiva, which drew students from Moravia and elsewhere in the region.[50] Furthermore, the chief rabbi's presence was mandatory at the triennial Council of the Land, where he personally authorized the supracommunal statutes. His presence was also required at the major council, which served, inter alia, as a court of law.

Growth, Reduction, Separation, and Exclusion, 1650–1780

Absorption of Refugees and Natural Growth

The seventeenth century was a period of tremendous population growth for Moravian Jewry. In the wake of the Chmielnicky massacres (1648–49) in Poland and Ukraine and the subsequent Swedish-Muscovite invasions (1654–1658), a stream of Jewish refugees fled westward, seeking sanctuary from what one Hebrew chronicler called an "abyss of despair."[51] They reached as far as England and the Ottoman Empire, but many stopped their peregrinations when they reached Moravia, which was "a quiet and safe place" in the words of Jacob Emden, whose grandfather was among the refugees.[52] These refugees overwhelmed many of Moravia's Jewish communities, and according to one estimate, immigrants from Poland constituted about 20% of Moravia's total Jewish population around 1675.[53] Among the refugees who settled in Moravia were a number of renowned rabbis, such as Shabbetai Kohen, Ephraim Hakohen, and Gershon Ashkenazi, who helped bring Polish Jewry's celebrated talmudic culture to the yeshivas of Holleschau, Prossnitz, Nikolsburg, and elsewhere.[54] The refugees also brought an element of instability that could be expected from such an uprooted, traumatized, and destitute population.

Before Moravia's Jewish communities could even attempt to absorb refugees from the east, a second wave of Jews arrived from the southwest. In 1670, Emperor Leopold I expelled the Jews from Vienna and Lower Austria for allegedly colluding with the Swedes during the Thirty Years War and with the Turks in subsequent wars. Of the estimated 3,000–4,000 Jews that were dispersed among the neighboring lands, a sizable percentage found refuge in Moravia.[55] Not only did Moravia and Lower Austria share a common border, but also many Jewish families in Vienna traced their ancestral origins back to Moravia. As David Kaufmann explained, "It was mostly the communities in this neighboring province [i.e., Moravia] that had populated the ghetto in Vienna; when the expellees sought out the towns from whence their families had come, it was simply a return to the source."[56] In Moravia, most of the expellees settled near the Lower Austrian border, giving southern Moravia a much larger and denser Jewish population than the rest of the province.[57] Nikolsburg took in the largest number of expellees, but smaller communities—such as Kostel, Eisgrub, Jamnitz, Misslitz, Althart, Pullitz, and Piesling—also took in many of the newcomers.[58] Although most expellees were absorbed into preexisting communities, some went on to establish entirely new ones. For example, the Jewish community in Schaffa, situated on the Moravian-Austrian border, came into being in 1670 when Prince Starhemberg took in expellees from the town of Weitersfeld (in Lower Austria, north of Vienna).[59] Even though some wealthy Jewish families were readmitted to Vienna in 1673 (after payment of 300,000 fl. to the royal treasury), many of the expellees remained in the communities that originally took them in.

The rapid growth of Moravian (and Bohemian) Jewry was particularly noticeable because it occurred during a period of "stagnant or falling population in much or most of continental Europe."[60] In Bohemia and Moravia, the general population declined precipitously in the first half of the seventeenth century, plummeting from 2.5–3 million before the Thirty Years War to a mere 750,000 in its aftermath. Olmütz alone went from 30,000 inhabitants in 1630 to only 1,675 in 1650,[61] and neighboring Prossnitz had become a "deserted settlement" by 1644 because of war and the mass exodus of its Protestant inhabitants.[62] Meanwhile, Moravia's Jewish population, augmented by immigration and natural reproduction, continued to grow. In some communities, such as Prossnitz, the Jewish population even outnumbered the Christian population for a short time.[63] The remarkable growth of Moravia's Jewish communities could be seen in such places as Nikolsburg and Prossnitz, which underwent a three- or fourfold increase by the beginning of the eighteenth century.[64]

Reductio ad Absurdum

After the Thirty Years War, the Bohemian and Moravian estates took steps to halt the massive growth in the Jewish population, initiating a process that would culminate in the "pharaonic" Familiants Laws of 1726–27. In 1650, the provincial diets in both Bohemia and Moravia initiated measures to reduce the Jewish population to prewar numbers—on grounds that the Jews had simply "become too numerous."[65] At the behest of these diets, both of which were dominated by Catholic prelates and the upper nobility,[66] Emperor Ferdinand III (1637–1657) ordered the expulsion of Jews from all locations where they had neither resided in 1618—that is, on the eve of the Thirty Years War—nor received royal permission to settle thereafter. In 1681, Ferdinand's son and successor, Leopold I (1658–1705), moved the end point from 1618 to 1657, effectively granting asylum to the very wartime refugees that the estates had sought to expel. Leopold's measure should not be construed as a sudden act of beneficence toward the Jews of his empire but rather as a response to their expulsion from Vienna and Lower Austria (which he himself had decreed a decade earlier). By moving the terminus ad quem to 1657, Leopold I grudgingly accepted the Polish and Ukrainian Jews who had arrived during his father's reign, but he sought to keep out the new Viennese expellees who had arrived during his own.

The reductions—as these planned expulsions were euphemistically called—were summarily ignored by many noble landowners, whose economic interests continued to be served more by the Jews' annual

Schutzgeld than by the emperor's latest decrees. In 1681, for example, Prince Walter Franz Xaver von Dietrichstein protected the Jews of Nikolsburg, guaranteeing—in accordance with their recently renewed privilege—that "the Jews will not be expelled."[67] Over the next decades, the growth of the Nikolsburg Jewish community, which numbered 146 families in 1657, showed no sign of abatement. The number of families more than doubled by 1690 and reached 620 by 1724.[68] Such population growth, which occurred in many of Moravia's Jewish communities, also corresponded to a sharp rise in the number of houses acquired by Jews. In Kojetein, for example, the number of "Jewish houses" more than doubled during this period, increasing from sixteen in 1657 to twenty-three in 1678 and reaching forty by 1727.[69]

The growth of Moravian Jewry coincided with the reassertion of a triumphant Catholicism in the aftermath of the Thirty Years War. Emboldened by its success in rooting out the Protestant heresies in Bohemia and Moravia, the Catholic Church increasingly turned its attention to the demonstrably visible yet theologically untenable proliferation of Jews in these re-Catholicized lands. In the first decades of the eighteenth century, particularly during the reign of Charles VI (1711–1740), the Jews' growing numerical strength was often portrayed as a threat to the Christian character of Bohemia and Moravia. In 1712, this view found its most salient expression in a report to Charles VI from Johann Eustach Becker, an imperial plenipotentiary in Brünn.[70] Lamenting the massive influx of Jews from Austria and Poland and the heretofore futile attempts to reduce their presence in Moravia, Becker observed that

> new houses are approved . . . even where no Jew has lived previously . . . entire communities are being established, and houses are being taken away from Christians and given to Jews. In many places, the number of synagogues and prayer houses exceeds the number of Christian churches. Furthermore, their domiciles are so close to the Christian churches . . . that they can look inside the church, see the priest on the pulpit and observe the Christian divine service. They watch Christian processions, celebrations, and other ceremonies with great annoyance, just so they can mock them. This leads to tremendous blasphemy.[71]

In Becker's view, the abysmal failure to reduce the Jewish population—and to keep it separate from the Christian one—had enabled Judaism to dwarf Christianity to such an extent that "Christians were even seduced to Judaism."[72]

The religious animosity that poisoned Christian-Jewish relations in this period can be further illustrated by the Aussee affair in 1721–22. A small town in northern Moravia, Aussee was a symbol of Catholicism triumphant. In 1622, after the Protestant owner had been driven into exile, Emperor Ferdinand II presented Aussee to Prince Karl von Lichtenstein on the condition that only Catholics be permitted to reside there.[73] Nonetheless, under the protection of the Lichtensteins, a Jewish community was already flourishing in the second half of the seventeenth century, growing from around thirteen families in 1657 to fifty-nine families by the early 1700s.[74] In 1688, the community received permission to build a synagogue, which would become the locus of the Aussee affair three decades later.[75] On the eve of Yom Kippur (September 30, 1721), a local Catholic priest entered the Aussee synagogue and began preaching a missionary sermon to the assembled worshippers. When he refused to leave the synagogue despite repeated requests, a number of Jews ejected him by force.[76] The Jews subsequently brought charges against the priest for disturbing the peace, but the priest responded with accusations of his own. He claimed that the Jews had not only assaulted his person but also had made disparaging remarks about Christianity.[77] In the ensuing trial, the Moravian governor, Maximilian Ulrich von Kaunitz, dismissed the priest's accusations and fully exonerated the Jews;[78] however, after a successful appeal by the Olmütz Consistory, this verdict was overturned in 1722 by Emperor Charles VI himself.[79] Finding the Jews guilty of blasphemy, the emperor handed down a particularly harsh punishment. Three of the accused were imprisoned, pilloried, branded with a hot iron, and finally exiled; a fourth Jew, who was 74 years old at the time, was sentenced to work on a Catholic church being built in Aussee. Adding insult to injury, Charles VI ordered the demolition of the synagogue and forbade the Jews of Aussee to pray in groups larger than ten.[80] The burghers of Aussee promptly hired day laborers to dismantle the synagogue during the Jewish festival of Shavuot. According to one eyewitness, the laborers urinated on the synagogue as they destroyed it, yelling anti-Jewish curses in the process.[81]

The Aussee affair was a prelude to the anti-Jewish policies that became a hallmark of Charles VI's thirty-year reign. Although he confirmed Moravian Jewry's privilege in 1723 and even reduced the annual "contribution" from 12,000 to 8,000 fl., his most enduring legacy in relation to the Jews of the Bohemian Lands was a series of draconian policies that drastically curtailed their marriage and residence rights. The first of these were the Familiants Laws (Familiantengesetze), promulgated on September 15, 1726. These laws placed strict limits on the number of Jewish families in Bohemia, Moravia, and Silesia and granted marriage rights solely to firstborn sons, and then only upon the death of the father. This policy was followed by the forced segregation of Jewish and Christian populations, resulting in the creation of "closed" Jewish quarters, particularly in Moravia. These laws, which were intended to curb economic competition and social contact between Jews and Christians, wreaked havoc on Jewish community and family life until they were finally repealed during the Revolution of 1848.

Separation and Confinement: Moravia's Jewish Quarters

The so-called separation of the Jews, which I examine first, was implemented under the unmistakable influence of the Catholic Church. Already in 1179, the Third Lateran Council had forbidden Christians to dwell among Jews, but only rarely did European secular authorities translate this prohibition into actual policy. However, under the influence of the Counter-Reformation, secular authorities—first in sixteenth-century Venice and then elsewhere in Europe—began establishing "ghettos," which served to relegate the Jews to their appropriate position in Christian society.[82] In the Bohemian Lands as well, triumphant Catholicism strongly influenced government policy in this respect. Indeed, the stated aim of Charles VI's separation was to allow the "unhampered observance of the divine religion" by ensuring that no Jewish domicile was in view of a church, along a procession route, or in the midst of the Christian population.[83] In Moravia, a special "Jewish commission" was set up in 1727 to identify Jewish domiciles that violated these conditions; they were to be exchanged with Christian domiciles (of equal value) that were located in the midst of the Jewish population.

Understandably, these property transfers faced strong opposition from the Jews and Christians who had been singled out, but the Olmütz Consistory, under the leadership of Cardinal Wolfgang Hannibal von Schrattenbach, persisted. After the Jews of Neu-Rausnitz allegedly mocked a religious procession on Palm Sunday, Cardinal Schrattenbach called for the separations to be carried out posthaste, with the result that Charles VI reissued his decree. Between 1727 and 1731, property and population transfers were carried out in fifty-four Moravian communities, often in a matter of months.[84] (See Figures 2, 3, and 4.) Thus, by the end of 1731, clearly demarcated "Jewish quarters" had been introduced to Moravia.

The Jewish quarters placed tremendous demographic and economic pressures on Moravian Jewry. Because Moravia's Jews were largely confined to "Jewish houses" (i.e., houses that had been owned by Jews for ages or recently transferred to them), the physical space in the Jewish quarters remained relatively fixed even as the Jewish population continued to grow.[85] As a result, Moravia's Jewish quarters became increasingly overcrowded, with several families often crammed into a single house or even room. In Prossnitz, for example, 48 Jewish houses (divided into 120 apartments with a total of 320 rooms) were inhabited by 328 families in 1829.[86] This worked out to an average of almost seven families (thirty-five people) per house, three families (fourteen people) per apartment, and just over one family (five people) per room. Such overcrowding, which can be documented in almost all of Moravia's Jewish communities,[87] attracted the attention of government authorities, who were concerned about the moral and sanitary consequences. "Natural propriety itself abhors such an arrangement," stated a law from 1754. "It will pave the way for sins and fornication, and lead to the spread of contagious diseases."[88] Henceforth, if more than one family were living in a room, the parties were expected to reach an agreement whereby each family would live alone in the room, alternating every year or so. It was not specified, however, where the other families would live while they were waiting their turn. In some cases, Jews could rent or even purchase "Christian houses," but this required special permission from Brünn or Vienna.[89]

Moravian Jewry's already limited economic opportunities were further constricted by conditions in the overcrowded Jewish quarters. As

František Roubík has shown for Bohemia, the forced property transfers of 1727 pushed many Jewish merchants and artisans from the center of town to its periphery, resulting in a corresponding loss of competitiveness.[90] A similar pattern can be detected in Moravia as well.[91] In addition, the spacious workshops required by certain artisans—such as goldsmiths, coopers, stonemasons, and carpenters—were unavailable in many of the cramped Jewish quarters. So were the big outdoor spaces required by weavers, dyers, and metalworkers.[92] Thus, even though as many as 30% of the adult males in some Jewish communities were engaged in artisan crafts in the 1750s, they were almost exclusively tailors, glaziers, or butchers.[93]

With the overwhelming majority of Moravia's Jews engaged in trade of some sort, the creation of Jewish quarters was bound to have a discernible effect on this segment of the Jewish economy as well. Because only a limited number of Jews were permitted to own stores in the Jewish community or lease them in the Christian town, many had to seek economic opportunities on the road. The wealthier ones set up stalls at the large fairs in Olmütz, Brünn, Pilsen, Leipzig, Breslau, and elsewhere, whereas the less affluent visited smaller fairs closer to home.[94] Poorer Jews—known as village goers (*Dorfgeher*), peddlers (*Hausierer*), or bundle Jews (*Pinkeljuden*)—had to eke out a living by selling their wares in the countryside, usually setting out on Sunday morning and returning home on Friday afternoon.[95] They traded in scrap silver, gold, tin, brass, copper, and iron as well as flax, hemp, grain, animal skins, pelts, or whatever they could get their hands on.[96] A fixture of the nineteenth-century literary genre of *Ghettogeschichten* (ghetto tales),[97] these itinerant *Dorfgeher* came to symbolize the economic and moral decay of Jewish life in the Bohemian and Moravian ghettos. Samson Raphael Hirsch drew this link during the Revolution of 1848, stressing the deleterious effect of itinerancy on Jewish family life. In a letter to the Moravian governor, he wrote:

> Only the tiniest number [of Jews] can find their sustenance in the Jewish quarter. . . . The largest number, by far, must seek their bread elsewhere, and for this purpose, they must either get permission to settle in another place or, mostly, move from one fair to another, the husband to this one, the wife to that one, with the result that the husband

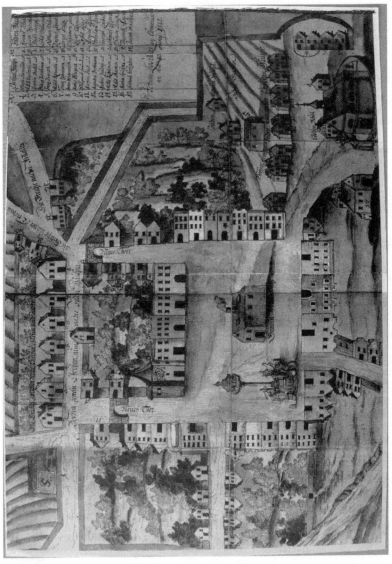

Figure 2. Loschitz separation map, 1727. Jewish houses were located next to the church (bottom right) and moved to the other side of town (top center). Courtesy of Vlastivědné Muzeum v Šumperku. Photo by Luděk Štipl.

Figure 3. Detail from Figure 2 (top center).

Figure 4. Detail from Figure 2 (bottom right).

often goes weeks and months without seeing his children. Mother and father wander all around, while the children stay at home, left in the hands of their nannies. Not even on the High Holy Days are all members of the family together!![98]

By some estimates, up to one-third of all Moravian Jews were *Dorfgeher* in the eighteenth and nineteenth centuries.[99]

Many Moravian Jews tried to escape the economic constraints of the Jewish quarter by leasing distilleries, breweries, potasheries, tanneries, and taverns from the local landowners and by farming various tolls and taxes.[100] Known as *arrendators* or *randars*, these Jewish leaseholders and tax farmers tended to live in rural villages, although they occasionally received permission to reside in Brünn, Olmütz, and other towns that were off-limits to ordinary Jews. After successfully bidding for an *arenda* (lease), the *arrendator* and his family (as well as employees and domestic servants) were permitted to reside in a given village or town, but only for the duration of the lease. Although the *arrendator* was required to pay taxes to the nearest Jewish community, he and his family often lived in splendid isolation from other Jews, interacting primarily with non-Jewish customers and neighbors.[101] This may explain the large number of *arrendators'* children and employees who converted to Catholicism in the course of the eighteenth and nineteenth centuries.[102] Nonetheless, relations with the surrounding Christian population were often quite strained. Peasants resented having to purchase alcohol exclusively from their lord's representatives, that is, the Jewish *arrendators*.[103] Burghers, who had propination rights within the town limits, resented competition from Jewish distillers on the outskirts of the town.[104]

Leaseholding also involved considerable financial risks for the *arrendator*. Because the *arrendator* paid a preset rent, he could turn a profit only if income from brewing, distilling, collecting tolls, and so on exceeded his initial investment. This became increasingly difficult, as bidding wars drove up rents for the limited number of *arendy*.[105] Also, some *arendy* were not very profitable. Ber Schiff, an *arrendator* in Wojetin during the 1820s, complained that he never earned much money because he had "one of the smallest *arendy*, where the number of villagers is tiny."[106] Like most *arrendators*, he sold merchandise on the side to make ends meet, even though this violated the terms of his lease. To make matters worse, geographic isolation made Schiff a frequent target for thieves. After being robbed twice, he decided it was time to return to his native Prossnitz. His decision was not motivated solely by the precariousness of life in Wojetin but also by boredom and loneliness. "I am sick of spending time here with no purpose," he wrote in 1822, "among people without wisdom and intelligence, who do not know me or my qualities."[107]

The Familiants Laws, 1726–27

Far more than the Jewish quarters, the most poignant symbol of Moravian Jewish suffering in the eighteenth and nineteenth centuries was the Familiants Laws of 1726–27. Inspired by Jewish marriage restrictions in neighboring Prussia (1714),[108] the Familiants Laws aimed to prevent any further population increase among the Jews of the Bohemian Lands.[109] Although it could be argued that marriage restrictions were more humane than mass expulsion, the Jews of Bohemia, Moravia, and Silesia did not make such a distinction. Called *gezerat ha-sheniyyot* in Hebrew (in an allusion to talmudic prohibitions on certain kinds of conjugal relations),[110] these laws were invariably described as "pharaonic" because of the severity of the "evil decree" (*gezerah*) and the fixation on firstborn sons.[111]

After a special Jewish census, the number of Jewish families was fixed at 8,451 for Bohemia, 5,106 for Moravia, and 1,245 for Silesia.[112] In each province, individual male Jews—known as "familiants" (*Familianten*)—were assigned separate "familiant numbers" (*Familiantennummern* or *Familiantenstellen*) that entitled them to marry and establish a family. Upon the familiant's death, this familiant number and all the associated rights could be bequeathed—like a precious family heirloom—to the firstborn son. In the event that the firstborn son died before his father, the familiant number could be transferred to a younger son and thus remain in the family. However, if the familiant had no male offspring—or if he converted to Christianity—his familiant number was considered "expired" (*erlöschen*) and his family was deemed "*eo ipso pro extincta*."[113] In such a case, the district office could reassign the highly coveted familiant number to another Jewish male.

Although the Familiants Laws were applied similarly in all the Lands of the Bohemian Crown, one important difference set Moravia apart from both Bohemia and Austrian Silesia. Whereas the familiant numbers in Bohemia and Austrian Silesia were apportioned district by district, the familiant numbers in Moravia were apportioned to individual Jewish communities in direct relation to the size of their Jewish population. For example, Nikolsburg, Moravia's largest Jewish community, was apportioned 600 familiant numbers (later raised to 620), whereas Puklitz, Moravia's smallest Jewish community, was apportioned only 5. This meant that each Moravian familiant was officially bound to a specific community, whereas Bohemian and Silesian familiants were free to reside wherever Jewish residence was permitted. This system not only limited the mobility of Moravia's Jews but also accorded Moravia's Jewish communities significant influence over the apportionment of familiant numbers. Indeed, although the district offices were authorized to reassign "vacated" (*erledigt*) familiant numbers, this was usually done at the recommendation of the Jewish community in question.

The apportionment of a finite supply of familiant numbers naturally lent itself to many abuses. Bribery was rampant, as evidenced by the Moravian Gubernium's repeated decrees forbidding Jewish communal officials from taking payment in exchange for recommending a particular individual.[114] Furthermore, as Adolf Frankel-Grün noted in his study of the Jews in Kremsier, "There was an official trade in the purchase and sale of familiant numbers, to which the communal registers from 1748 to 1848 bear witness."[115] Such "official trade" is clearly documented in the Eisgrub Jewish community, where the apportionment of two "vacated" familiant numbers in 1805 was determined almost exclusively by fiscal considerations.[116] In this case, two wealthy "foreign Moravians" (i.e., individuals from another Moravian Jewish community) were given priority over the impoverished firstborn son of a local Eisgrub familiant. One local official justified this decision by noting that the money contributed to the Jewish community by these two Jews amounted to more than all the capital owned by Eisgrub's other twenty-five familiants combined. Not only did the two pay half of the community's annual taxes of 600 fl., but they also gave a combined gift of 800 fl. for the upkeep of the synagogue, cemetery, and community house.

The Familiants Laws created a fairly rigid social hierarchy within Moravia's Jewish communities—and even within individual families. At the top of the pyramid were familiants and their firstborn sons, followed by an even smaller category of supernumeraries (*überzähligen*). These supernumeraries received special permission to marry but could not transfer this privilege to their offspring.[117] Next came the so-called later-born (*nachgeborenen*) sons, that is, second- and third-born sons of familiants, who were forbidden to marry but could still apply for a familiant number if one became available. Finally, at the bottom of the pyramid were the illegitimate (*unehelichen*) sons, that is, males born out of wedlock or to couples whose marriages were not recognized by the state. Punished for the sins of their fathers, these illegitimate sons were not even eligible to apply for vacant familiant numbers.[118]

Because marriage rights were granted solely to familiants (and to a small number of supernumeraries), a large segment of the population could not legally marry. Thus, if later-born and illegitimate sons wished to avoid a life of celibacy, they were left with four basic options: illegal marriage, illegal cohabitation, conversion to Catholicism, or emigration. Many Jews tried to circumvent the marriage restrictions by having so-called attic weddings (*Bodenhochzeiten*, *Bodenchassines*), which were recognized by Jewish law but not by the government authorities. Held secretly indoors, these weddings tended to be modest affairs, a far cry from the public—and sometimes extravagant—"familiant weddings" held under the starry sky.[119] Not only did these attic weddings highlight the social inequality within Moravia's Jewish communities, but they also took place at great risk to all involved. The couples—considered concubines by law—could be sentenced to public flogging or expulsion from the Lands of the Bohemian Crown, as could the individual who performed the wedding ceremony; in addition, the local authorities could be fined 1,000 fl. for their negligence.[120] Couples who cohabitated without a wedding ceremony were likewise considered concubines and faced similar punishment.[121] To make matters worse, neighbors were given financial incentive to denounce these concubines, and they often did so.[122]

Because the offspring of these illegal relationships were considered illegitimate—and were thus ineligible to apply for familiant numbers—

the number of concubines and secret marriages in a given community inevitably increased with each generation. For example, the Jewish community board in Eiwanowitz estimated in 1845 that 80 of its 340 Jews were offspring of concubines and secret marriages. This number, it noted, included "the grandchildren of those persons who are involved in such forbidden relationships."[123] Evidence from Prossnitz and Nikolsburg suggests that similar conditions existed in many of Moravia's Jewish communities.[124] In an attempt to ameliorate this self-perpetuating problem, Emperor Joseph II slightly raised the number of familiant numbers in 1787, but to little noticeable effect.[125] As a privy counselor in Vienna observed half a century later, "The number of Jewish familiant numbers in Moravia . . . is too small in relation to the current actual Jewish population in this province, and this gives rise to concubines and leads to other adverse legal consequences for their children."[126]

Some illegitimate and later-born sons opted for conversion to Catholicism to circumvent the marriage restrictions. Although many of the conversions between 1726 and 1849 were certainly motivated by sincere belief, anecdotal and statistical evidence suggests that the Familiants Laws also played an important role. For example, Jacob Kohn, whose grandson Theodor went on to become archbishop of Olmütz, allegedly converted in 1826 in order to get married.[127] Furthermore, a sample of 145 male Jewish converts in Moravia between 1786 and 1849 shows that the typical convert was single, 16 to 30 years old, and without a familiant number.[128] In other words, although most of the converts were of marriageable age, few of them had any real prospects of getting married in Moravia—that is, so long as they remained Jews. Most of the converts were born in Moravia, but at least twenty-eight of them had come to Moravia from Bohemia, Silesia, Prussia, and Galicia, perhaps to escape the marriage restrictions in their own native lands.

Emigration—most often to Hungary—constituted one of the only alternatives for nonfamiliants who wished to marry legally without abandoning their faith. Indeed, in a sardonic recognition of this fact, illegitimate and later-born sons were commonly called emigrants (*Emigranten*) by their more fortunate coreligionists.[129] Hungary held particular appeal for Moravia's emigrants because it was the only neighboring land where Jews were not subject to the Familiants Laws or other severe marriage restrictions.[130] In Hungary, which one scholar called the "El Dorado of Bohemian and Moravian Jews,"[131] Jews could obtain permission to marry so long as the lord of the manor allowed it. Emigration, however, entailed some onerous expenses for Moravia's Jews. Not only were they required to pay several years of prospective taxes to their former Jewish community, but from 1796 onward, they also had to pay an emigration tax (*Abfahrtssteuer*)—appraised at 15% of their "money, wares, and effects"—to the Moravian authorities.[132] Furthermore, if these emigrants returned to Moravia after getting married in Hungary—as they frequently did—they were subject to expulsion.[133]

The Familiants Laws slowed down the growth of Moravian Jewry in the eighteenth and nineteenth centuries, but by encouraging emigration, they also contributed to the population increase in and, indeed, formation of Hungarian Jewry.[134] According to the Hungarian Jewish Census (Conscriptio Judeorum) of 1735–1738, an estimated 38% of Hungary's 2,531 Jewish family heads were born in Moravia (compared with only 35% born in Hungary).[135] Of course, not all these Jews arrived in the aftermath of the Familiants Laws. Many had arrived at the end of the seventeenth century as the Turks were driven out of Hungary by the advancing Habsburg armies. In this period, Moravian Jews were drawn to large noble manors, particularly in Western Hungary (today's Burgenland, Austria) and Upper Hungary (today's Slovakia), where the local population had been largely depleted during a century and a half of warfare.[136] In Burgenland, the Eszterházy family granted "letters of protection" (*Schutzbriefe*) to Jews, allowing them to settle in the *shevah kehillot* (seven communities) of Eisenstadt, Mattersdorf, Deutschkreuz, Kobersdorf, Lackenbach, Frauenkirchen, and Kittsee.[137] Many Jews also moved from the Dietrichstein, Kaunitz, and Lichtenstein manors in Moravia to less crowded Hungarian manors belonging to the Pállfy, Batthyány, Zichy, and other noble families.[138] As a result, Moravia's Jewish communities spawned a number of daughter communities in Upper Hungary, such as Vágújhely, Trencsén, and Verbó, which were founded from the 1680s onward by Jewish families from Ungarisch-Brod.[139] Many other communities near the Moravian border, such as Holics, Mijava, Nyitra, and Szenicz, were also founded by Moravian Jews in this period.[140] In addition, a considerable number of Moravian Jews could be found in larger Hungarian cities, such as Pressburg, Pest, Buda, and Óbuda.[141]

Because most Moravian Jews settled close to the Moravian border, their emigration experience did not necessarily involve severing ties with their native communities.[142] In fact, many emigrants (and their descendants) preserved religious and commercial ties with their Moravian families well into the nineteenth century.[143] They sent their children to the celebrated yeshivas in Nikolsburg, Prossnitz, Trebitsch, and Boskowitz, and their Moravian kinfolk, in turn, sent their young ones to the yeshivas in Eisenstadt and Pressburg.[144] Furthermore, they would often turn to Moravia's Jewish communities when looking to fill rabbinic posts. According to Sándor Büchler, most Hungarian rabbis in the eighteenth century were of Moravian origin.[145] Financial ties also bound Moravian emigrants to their places of origin, such as trade with cross-border kinsmen and taxes paid to former communities.[146]

Maria Theresa: Taxation and Regulation

With respect to Jewish policy, Charles VI found a worthy successor in his daughter, Maria Theresa (1740–1780), who ordered the wholesale expulsion of Bohemian and Moravian Jewry in 1744–45. Although much attention has focused on Maria Theresa's almost visceral aversion to the Jews, her edicts of expulsion—and, indeed, most of her subsequent policies toward the Jews—must be understood in terms of the painful loss of most of Silesia, one of the richest Habsburg provinces, at the beginning of her reign. In December 1740, Frederick II of Prussia invaded Silesia, prompting French, Bavarian, and Saxon armies to invade several other Habsburg lands. In what became known as the War of the Austrian Succession (1740–1748), these foreign armies conquered parts of Austria, Bohemia, and Moravia until the Habsburg forces finally regained strength and drove them out. Maria Theresa emerged from the conflict greatly chastened; although her territorial inheritance remained largely intact, she had been forced to cede most of Silesia to Prussia in 1742.[147] She blamed Jewish treachery for some of her setbacks, but she also recognized that Prussia's military victory could be attributed, in large part, to Frederick II's centralized, rationally governed, and well-financed state apparatus. Both of these considerations influenced her subsequent policies toward the Jews.

When Maria Theresa ordered the expulsion of the Jews, first from Prague and then from Bohemia and Moravia, it was commonly understood that she was motivated by persistent rumors of Jewish collaboration with the Prussians. The immediate impetus for the expulsion was the alleged collaboration during the Prussian occupation of Prague in 1744, but similar rumors had circulated in 1742, during Frederick II's military campaign in Moravia. The Jews of Nikolsburg, among others, were accused of spying for the Prussians and "voluntarily" giving them large sums of money.[148] As punishment, the Jews of Moravia were temporarily banned from the fairs in Brünn and Olmütz and forced to pay 50,000 fl. to the state coffers. The expulsion of Prague Jewry was completed by the end of January 1745, but thanks to the diplomatic activities of European Jewry and the intercession of several foreign rulers and governments, the expulsion of Bohemian and Moravian Jewry was averted in May 1745, and the Prague exiles were permitted to return in the summer of 1748.[149] As Barouh Mevorah has shown, it was fear of irreparable damage to the Bohemian and Moravian economy—and not humanitarian concern for the Jews—that finally convinced Maria Theresa to postpone (and, for all intents and purposes, cancel) the expulsion decrees.

This cancellation came at a particularly high price for the Jews of the Bohemian lands. In 1748, Maria Theresa allowed the Jews to remain in exchange for an annual payment of 300,000 fl. in "toleration tax," which was to be paid by the Jews of Bohemia (216,500 fl.), Moravia (82,200 fl.), and the remnant of Austrian Silesia (1,300 fl.).[150] This was part of Maria Theresa's general tax reforms in 1748, which aimed to increase state revenues to cover the costs of the war (including lost taxes from Silesia) and to finance the expansion of the state bureaucracy. As Ruth Kestenberg-Gladstein has shown, these taxes hit the Jews particularly hard: Although the annual taxation for the Christian population was doubled in 1748, it was nearly tripled for the Jewish population.[151] The devastating impact of the toleration tax can be gauged by the fact that seven of the nine ordinances passed by the Moravian Jewish Council of the Land in 1748 dealt with problems stemming from the dramatic increase in taxes.[152] "Now that our [tax] burden has multiplied many times over," explained one ordinance, Jewish communities were allowed to impound the merchandise of Moravian Jewish tax evaders found plying their wares in Moravia. Another ordinance prohibited *arrendators* from entering a synagogue on the High Holy Days without written proof that their taxes had been paid. Two ordinances imposed sumptuary laws on Moravia's Jewish communities, one forbidding women to wear silver, gold, and silk "in these difficult times" and the other placing a ten-guest limit on wedding and circumcision meals, "lest too much [money] be wasted." The members of the Council were particularly concerned about the impact of the onerous taxation on religious life. When a number of communities expressed a desire to fire their rabbis as a way to free up money for the "exorbitant new contribution," the Council reminded them that all Jewish communities numbering thirty families or more were required to employ a rabbi.

Maria Theresa's tax reforms were just one part of her larger program of centralization and bureaucratization in the aftermath of the War of the Austrian Succession. Her administrative reforms, which aimed at increasing royal power and authority along the Prussian model, brought the Jews, along with all other subjects, under "ever-mounting state regulation."[153] In Moravia, administrative affairs were placed under the aegis of the United Court Chancery (Vereinigte Hofkanzlei) in Vienna, which oversaw the activities of the Moravian Gubernium in Brünn. The Gubernium, in turn, oversaw Moravia's six district governments, effectively extending the state bureaucracy to a level just above the manors and towns. This meant that Moravia's Jewish communities, which were located on noble manors or in noble-owned towns, increasingly fell under the authority and jurisdiction of the state bureaucracy.

Maria Theresa's reforms extended to the internal affairs of Moravian Jewry as well. As a rule, the state had refrained from interfering in the religious, educational, and communal affairs of Moravian Jewry insofar as they did not affect the surrounding Christian population. Traditionally, these affairs had been overseen and regulated by Moravian Jewry's institutions of self-government: the *kehilla*, or Jewish community, on the local level, and the va'ad ha-medinah, or Council of the Land, on the supracommunal level. As discussed earlier, the first council, which was convened in Gaya in 1650, drafted statutes, known as the Shai Takkanot, that served as a kind of constitution for Moravian Jewry as a whole. The subsequent councils, which were held more or less triennially until 1748, added amendments to the original *takkanot*, bringing the total number of statutes to 615 by the time Maria Theresa took an interest in the internal affairs of Moravian Jewry. In 1750, as part of her broader efforts to codify the disparate laws of her empire, Maria Theresa ordered the translation of the Shai Takkanot (and the later amendments) into German. (The fact that the *takkanot* had been written in a mixture of Hebrew and Yiddish and thus remained incomprehensible to most government officials underscored just how little the state had encroached on Moravian Jewry's internal autonomy before Maria Theresa's reign.) Based on this translation, which was completed by a Nikolsburg-born convert to Catholicism, Maria Theresa issued the General Regulations for the Administrative, Judicial, and Commercial Affairs of the Jewry in the Margravate of Moravia (General-Polizei-Prozess- und Kommerzial-Ordnung für die Judenschaft des Markgrafthums Mähren) in 1754. The regulations consisted of three separate parts: (1) the Polizei-Ordnung, which regulated details of religious, educational, and communal life; (2) the Prozess-Ordnung, which regulated civil cases between Jews; and (3) the Kommerzial-Ordnung, which regulated lines of credit, types of collateral, and other aspects of Jewish commercial life.

With the promulgation of the General Regulations, most of the statutes enacted by the Council of the Land—including those pertaining to religious and educational matters—became the official law of the land. This meant that certain aspects of Jewish religious and educational life, which had hitherto been the exclusive domain of Moravian Jewry's communal and supracommunal bodies, now fell under the jurisdiction of the United Court Chancery and its ramified bureaucracy in Moravia. For example, Article 1 of the Polizei-Ordnung required all Jewish communities numbering thirty families or more to hire a rabbi and support a yeshiva and required smaller communities to hire a teacher who could "instruct the youth in reading and writing and in the laws of God and Moses."[154] Article 10 regulated the hiring of rabbis, ritual slaughterers, cantors, and other communal officials.[155] These articles, of course, were taken directly from the Shai Takkanot and rendered into German so the state bureaucracy could understand and, if need be, enforce them.

Although the General Regulations left most of the Shai Takkanot intact, they eliminated the highest expression of Jewish supracommunal autonomy in Moravia: the Council of the Land. (The last council met in Butschowitz in 1748, right after the promulgation of the toleration tax.) Indeed, the continued existence of such an autonomous legislative body would have been totally incompatible with Maria Theresa's larger program of centralization. Much of Moravian Jewry's extensive supracommunal bureaucracy, however, remained in place, presumably because of its important role in collecting taxes and administering justice. The heads of the land (rendered into German as *Landesältesten*) retained most of their prerogatives, including the right to elect the chief rabbi.

Moravia, unlike neighboring Bohemia, retained its chief rabbi following Maria Theresa's midcentury reforms. In Bohemia, where the rural Jewish population was larger and more spread out than in Moravia, a system of district rabbis—one for each of Bohemia's twelve administrative districts—had been set up in 1717. Originally created so that the Bohemian chief rabbi in Prague could exercise direct control over the scattered Jewish population in the Bohemian countryside, the district rabbinates eventually made the chief rabbinate superfluous.[156] In 1749, with the death of the last Bohemian chief rabbi, the district rabbis took over all his functions and the Bohemian chief rabbinate ceased to exist. In Moravia, in contrast, where the Jewish population was smaller and much more compact, district rabbis had never been introduced. The Moravian chief rabbi remained the supreme religious authority, also functioning as a mediator between the state and Moravia's Jewish communities.

The election of the chief rabbi took place in Brünn, Moravia's administrative capital, where there had not been a Jewish community since the middle of the fifteenth century.[157] As a traveler to Brünn observed in 1719, "No Jews live in Brünn." Still, he noted, Jews could be found in Brünn "at all times," especially during the annual fairs. They came from the surrounding Jewish communities, such as Pohrlitz, Kanitz, Eibenschitz, Misslitz, Nikolsburg, Holleschau, and Austerlitz, and lived just outside Brünn in crowded dwellings made of "lime, mud, and straw" that often fell victim to fire.[158]

Modern Jewish settlement in Brünn actually dates to the reign of Maria Theresa, which is particularly surprising considering that the Austrian empress temporarily banned Jews from the Brünn (and Olmütz) fairs in 1742, ordered their expulsion from the Bohemian Lands in 1744–45, and expelled 140 Jewish families from Göding (in southeastern Moravia) in 1774.[159] Despite her pronounced antipathy, she tolerated a few wealthy and influential Jews in Brünn, including members of the Bohemian Dobruschka family.[160] Jacob Dobruschka (d. 1763), the paterfamilias, had already settled in Brünn toward the end of Charles VI's reign; in 1734, he purchased the concession for the New World Inn (*Zur neuen Welt*), the only place where Jews were allowed to lodge during Brünn's annual fair. (See Figure 5.) By 1750, he had also leased the tobacco monopoly in Moravia, which was later taken over by his son, Solomon (c. 1715–1774). Solomon, who obtained the lease for collecting the Brünn *Leibmaut* around 1755, also received permission

Figure 5. The New World Inn, Brünn, 1911. Courtesy of Brno City Archive, XIIa-8.

to keep a Torah scroll in his home in 1759, making it the first time since the fifteenth-century expulsion that Jewish worship was officially sanctioned in Brünn. (Brünn's Jewish community, however, was recognized only in 1853; its first synagogue was dedicated two years later, in 1855.) Solomon married Schöndl Hirschl (1735–1791), who not only gave birth to twelve children but also leased the potash monopoly in Moravia and managed the family's growing finances. She is perhaps most famous (or infamous) as the cousin of Jacob Frank, the false messiah who held court in Brünn from 1773 to 1786.

Joseph II and the Politics of Tolerance

Upon her death in 1780, Maria Theresa was succeeded by her son and coregent, Joseph II, whose ten-year reign ushered in a new era for the Jews of the Habsburg monarchy. In contrast to Maria Theresa, who was regarded as an inveterate enemy of the Jews, Joseph II pursued policies that helped earn him the sobriquet "Emperor of the Jews."[161] These policies were embodied in the Edicts of Tolerance issued between 1781 and 1789, which had the twin goals of transforming the Jews into productive citizens and breaking down the social barriers that separated them from the surrounding Christian population. These edicts, which were issued separately for Bohemia (1781), Silesia (1781), Vienna and Lower Austria (1782), Moravia (1782), Hungary (1783), and Galicia (1789), were emblematic of Joseph II's generally enlightened attitude toward the non-Catholic inhabitants of his domain. (He issued an Edict of Tolerance for Protestants and Greek Orthodox in October 1781.)[162] As H. M. Scott has pointed out, Joseph II's policies were motivated by "a mixture of humanitarianism and economic self-interest," drawing on Enlightenment thought (which affirmed the inalienable right to worship according to one's belief) and cameralist teachings (which emphasized the importance of a state's wealth and the prosperity of its subjects).[163]

The Moravian Edict of Tolerance, issued on February 13, 1782, had the stated aim of making the Jews "more useful and of greater service to the state, in particular through better education, instruction of their young people, and through the use of the sciences, arts, and crafts."[164] The emphasis on making Jews "useful"—a leitmotif in all the Edicts of Tolerance—bore the unmistakable influence of contemporary debates regarding the possibility and advisability of reforming the Jews' moral, social, and economic behavior and integrating them into the society at large. Particular emphasis was placed on reducing the Jews' almost castelike concentration in petty trade by encouraging them to engage in more "productive" economic pursuits, such as agriculture, artisan crafts, and manufacturing.[165] To this end, the Moravian Edict of Tolerance not only opened up new branches of trade and commerce to the Jews but also permitted them to lease rural land (for up to twenty years), apprentice themselves to Christian masters, and join artisan guilds (but only where there were Jewish communities). In addition, Jews were encouraged to establish factories, even outside the bounds of the Jewish communities.

Alongside these economic measures, the Edict of Tolerance aimed to bring about a cultural and educational transformation of Moravian Jewry. It encouraged Jewish communities to set up German-Jewish schools (at their own expense) so that students could be instructed in mathematics, geography, German language, and morality—subjects that were absent from the traditional Jewish elementary school (heder). In communities that could not afford their own schools, Jewish children were permitted to attend local Christian schools (with the proviso that they be exempted from religious instruction and not be "compelled or enticed to any action that goes against their religious practice"). Jews were also permitted to enroll in universities and institutions of higher learning, even in places such as Brünn and Znaim, where Jewish residence had been prohibited for centuries. (Jewish students were allowed to reside in these towns—and even lodge with Christian families—but only for the duration of their studies.) With respect to language, the Edict of Tolerance sought to inculcate a knowledge of German in the Jews while relegating Hebrew and Yiddish to the private sphere. After a two-year grace period, only documents written in the "language of the land" (*Landessprache*) would be considered legally valid; those written in Hebrew script would be considered null and void. This measure was viewed as a means for promoting "mutual trust" between Christians and Jews and breaking down the social boundaries that separated them. Significantly, the language of the land was not the language spoken by most of Moravia's inhabitants, that is, Czech (or Moravian), but rather the official administrative language of the Habsburg monarchy, that is, German. (It was not until the second half of the nineteenth century that Czech was recognized, alongside German, as a language of the land in Bohemia and Moravia.)[166] Consequently, the Edict of Tolerance is often seen as the first step in the Germanization of Moravian Jewry—a process that continued unabated until the end of the nineteenth century.

In a flourish of humanitarianism, the Edict of Tolerance also removed many of the special restrictions that had served primarily to stigmatize the Jews. Jews were no longer obliged to wear special clothes, nor were married Jewish men still required to wear beards. The prohibition against leaving one's home before noon on Sundays and Christian holidays was lifted, as was the ban on visiting places of public entertainment. Furthermore, the *Leibmaut*, a tax on livestock that was also imposed on Jews wishing to visit fairs in Moravia's royal towns, was finally abolished.

Despite its generally enlightened spirit, the Edict of Tolerance retained the most onerous of the restrictions that afflicted Moravian Jewry: the Familiants Laws, the Jewish quarters, and the special taxation. Regarding the Familiants Laws, the Edict of Tolerance clearly stated that

> our highest intention is in no way to increase the number of Jewish believers in Our Patrimonial Margravate . . . or to attract foreigners without important reason and special merit. Rather, We expressly wish that they should remain in Our Patrimonial Margravate of Moravia exactly as they are now; their established number is not to be exceeded, nor should Jews settle in the future where no Jews have lived before, except if they wish to build a factory on a piece of ground previously not built on, or if We, ourselves . . . consider this to be beneficial.[167]

Indeed, Joseph II viewed the Edict of Tolerance as a means for making the existing Jews more useful to the state, not as a means for increasing their number. Although he did grant Moravian Jewry an additional 294 familiant numbers in 1787, this gesture had little real impact. The slight increase—from 5,106 to 5,400—merely reinforced the fact that the Familiants Laws would survive Joseph II's politics of tolerance.[168] In 1798, Emperor Franz I reconfirmed the Familiants Laws, keeping the number of Moravian familiants at 5,400—and fixing the number of Moravian Jewish communities at fifty-two.[169] (See Map 2.) In Bohemia, in contrast, the Familiants Laws were slightly relaxed by the Bohemian Judenpatent of 1797. Although the number of Bohemian familiants remained fixed at 8,600, certain "useful" Jews—including farmers, artisans, soldiers, schoolteachers, and communal rabbis—could marry in Bohemia without a familiant number. This was not the case in Moravia.[170]

With regard to taxation, Joseph II was unwilling to forgo the 82,200 fl. that Moravian Jewry paid as its annual "contribution" to the imperial treasury. When he reorganized the system of Jewish taxation in 1787, he did not reduce Moravian Jewry's tax burden at all but merely reapportioned it. Thus, instead of paying a single contribution, Moravian Jewry was required to pay two separate taxes—a family tax (*Familientaxe*) and a consumption tax (*Verzehrungssteuer*)—which together totaled the original amount. The family tax was set at 5 fl. per familiant, for a total of 27,000 fl. (5,400 × 5 fl.) per year. The consumption tax, which was set at 55,200 fl. per year, was collected upon the purchase of various victuals, including kosher meat, goose fat, wine, and vinegar.[171] To make matters worse, in 1788 Joseph II began exacting a special war tax (*Kriegssteuer*) from the Jews of Moravia to cover his costly campaigns against Turkey. Set at 24,660 fl. annually, the war tax increased Moravian Jewry's already onerous tax burden by nearly one-third. (This tax, which was introduced as a temporary measure, remained in place—under various different names—until the special Jewish taxes were abolished in 1848).[172] In addition to all these taxes—for which Moravian Jewry was held collectively responsible—there were many individual taxes, such as the emigration tax (*Abfahrtssteuer*) for Moravian Jews who went abroad and the toleration tax (*Duldungssteuer*) for foreign Jews who settled in Moravia.[173]

As burdensome as these taxes may have been, they served as the basis for one of the most important legacies of the Josephinian period: the Moravian-Jewish Landesmassafond.[174] Created in 1787, the fund was

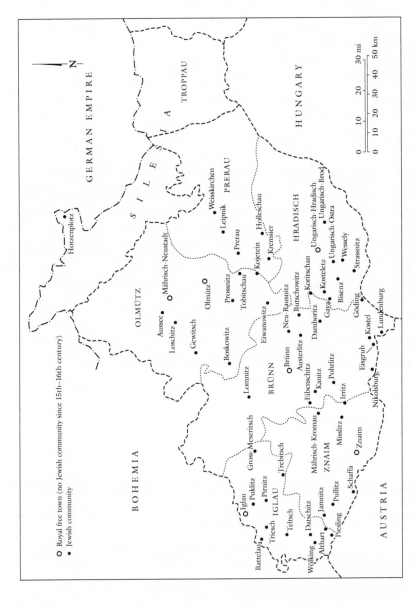

Map 2. Moravia's fifty-two Jewish communities, 1798–1848. Adapted from Hugo Gold, ed., *Die Juden und Judengemeinden Mährens in Vergangeheit und Gegenwart* (Brünn: Jüdischer Buch- und Kunstverlag, 1929).

originally intended to ensure that Moravia's Jewish communities could pay their annual taxes, but it also provided essential support for the religious, educational, and communal needs of Moravian Jewry until well into the twentieth century. The fund's initial capital came out of the lease money paid en masse (hence the name) by the tax farmer who first collected Moravia's family and consumption taxes; it was further augmented by occasional taxes and fines that were specifically earmarked for this purpose. Moravia's impoverished Jewish communities could borrow from the Landesmassafond to meet their tax obligations, but the fund was also put to a wide range of other uses. For example, the salary of the Moravian chief rabbi was taken out of the Landesmassafond, as were the costs associated with his election. In addition, Jewish communities could apply for low-interest loans from the Landesmassafond for the purpose of repairing damaged communal buildings or erecting new ones. (The government officials who administered the fund gave priority to buildings that would be used for "German school instruction.") As the property of "the whole of Moravian Jewry"—as it was officially designated in 1814—the Moravian-Jewish Landesmassafond constituted a financial reserve that would help Moravia's Jewish communities weather some of the most difficult times, especially in the second half of the nineteenth century.

In addition to creating a new institution for Moravian Jewry, Joseph II curtailed the prerogatives of an already existing one: the Moravian chief rabbinate. In 1785, as part of his efforts to introduce a uniform legal code in the Habsburg monarchy, Joseph II eliminated the authority of the chief rabbi—and all other rabbis—to adjudicate civil cases among Jews. (He also eliminated the heads of the land [*rashei ha-medinah* or *Landesältesten*], who had hitherto elected the chief rabbi.) The Prozess-Ordnung of 1754, which had affirmed the chief rabbi as Moravian Jewry's supreme judicial authority, was officially abolished, and Moravia's Jews found themselves under the jurisdiction of regional courts of law.[175] Henceforth the chief rabbi's field of activity was limited primarily to overseeing the educational and religious affairs of Moravian Jewry.[176] He examined and certified rabbis, religious teachers, and ritual slaughterers; bestowed honorary rabbinic titles (*ḥaver*, *morenu*) on Talmud scholars; answered ritual questions; headed the Nikolsburg yeshiva; and announced—in the spring and the fall—which Talmud tractate would be studied in Moravia's yeshivas. The chief rabbi was also authorized to use the ban (*ḥerem*) as a means for enforcing the collection of taxes. Although the chief rabbi's prerogatives were curtailed under Joseph II, his geographic purview was expanded in 1782 to include the remnant of Austrian Silesia.[177] As a result, the 119 families that constituted Austrian Silesian Jewry found themselves under the authority of the Moravian chief rabbi (who was henceforth called the Moravian-Silesian chief rabbi).[178]

Despite the changes introduced under Joseph II, the Moravian-Silesian chief rabbi remained a focal point of Moravian Jewry until the middle of the nineteenth century. In the midst of all the restrictions on residence, occupation, and procreation that had accumulated over the ages, the chief rabbinate had come to serve as a mark of pride for Moravian Jewry. At times, however, the chief rabbinate also served as a source of tension—or a lightning rod for disputes. In the seventeenth and eighteenth centuries, as new ideologies and modes of religious experience spread across Central and Eastern Europe, the chief rabbi was sometimes at the center of controversy, but just as often, this "supreme religious authority" had little real influence over the beliefs and practices of Moravia's Jews.

Moravia: A Sabbatian Nest and a Haven from Hasidism

Moravia's Jews were continuously exposed to religious, educational, and ideological trends, including Sabbatianism and Hasidism, two mass movements that represented "a transformation and watershed" in the history of the Jewish people.[179] Sabbatianism, a messianic movement that emerged in the Ottoman Empire in the seventeenth century, captivated the Jewish world from Adrianople to Amsterdam and from Lemberg to London, until Shabbetai Tsvi, the messianic pretender, apostasized in 1666. Hasidism, a mystical movement that emerged in the Polish-Lithuanian Commonwealth in the eighteenth century, was a more local phenomenon, but it spread to other areas of Eastern Europe, including Galicia and Hungary. In Moravia, the two movements took divergent paths: Sabbatianism—and its late eighteenth-century offshoot, Frankism—found a ready following, whereas Hasidism failed to attract many adherents, even though a key figure in the early Hasidic movement served as Moravia's chief rabbi in the mid-1770s.

Sabbatianism and Frankism in Moravia

Shabbetai Tsvi (1626–1676), a seventeenth-century Ottoman Jew, led the largest messianic movement in Judaism since the time of Jesus. In 1665, he declared himself the messiah, whipping up a messianic frenzy in the Jewish (and non-Jewish) world, which only dissipated after the "Jewish messiah" unexpectedly converted to Islam in the following year. Many of his disenchanted followers simply dismissed Shabbetai Tsvi as a false messiah, but others sought a theological explanation for the paradox of an apostate messiah.[180] Those who belonged to this latter group, known as believers, viewed the apostasy as a mystical necessity and adapted their beliefs and behavior accordingly. The moderate believers openly practiced Judaism, but they surreptitiously violated certain commandments (e.g., eating on Yom Kippur) in an effort to assist Shabbetai Tsvi in his effort to cleanse the world of original sin; the radical believers converted to Islam and viewed their own apostasies—like that of Shabbetai Tsvi—as a descent into the netherworld to redeem the trapped divine sparks and thereby hasten redemption.

Moravia, which Gershom Scholem called "one of the strongholds of Sabbatianism even into the eighteenth century," deserves a special place in the history of European Sabbatianism.[181] From the late seventeenth century onward, Sabbatian preachers and prophets found Moravia particularly hospitable, and during the Emden-Eybeschütz controversy of the mid-eighteenth century, Moravian Jews were quick to come to Jonathan Eybeschütz's defense after Jacob Emden accused him of secret Sabbatian activity. Moreover, in the popular imagination, Prossnitz was associated with Sabbatianism to such an extent that its Jewish inhabitants were called *Schepsen*—a derisive term derived from the Hebrew abbreviation for Shabbetai Tsvi.[182]

Juda Leib ben Jacob (c. 1670–1730) deserves credit for the Prossnitz association with Sabbatianism. This Sabbatian prophet, better known as Leibel Prossnitz (or Prostitz), made Prossnitz his home (and his surname) in the late seventeenth and early eighteenth centuries; there, he found many adherents, including Meir Eisenstadt, who headed the Prossnitz yeshiva at the time. Even though Leibel was excommunicated twice, he retained a strong following in Prossnitz and elsewhere in Moravia.[183]

When Leibel came to Prossnitz, the ground had already been prepared by Judah Ḥasid and Ḥayyim Malakh, two Sabbatian preachers who sojourned in Moravia in 1699 on their way from Poland to the Holy Land. They spent considerable time in both Nikolsburg and Prossnitz, where they may have had an impact on Leibel.

Leibel's adherents may have included Jonathan Eybeschütz, who studied with Meir Eisenstadt in Prossnitz at the beginning of the eighteenth century. In fact, Eybeschütz and Leibel were both excommunicated by the Mannheim rabbinic court in 1725 for alleged Sabbatian activity. During the mid-eighteenth-century Emden-Eybeschütz controversy, which centered around Eybeschütz's suspected Sabbatian activity, Moravia's Jewish communities consistently sided with Eybeschütz, accusing Emden of profaning God's name through his unwarranted attacks on the "Angel of God." In 1751, the Nikolsburg community excommunicated the enemies of Eybeschütz, and the communities of Holleschau, Prossnitz, Neu-Rausnitz, Kremsier, Kromau, and Hotzenplotz quickly followed suit. Emden accused the defenders of Eybeschütz—who were overwhelmingly from Moravia—of being Sabbatians themselves.[184] The Moravian chief rabbi at the time was Issachar Berush Eskeles, who resided in Vienna rather than Nikolsburg. As an absentee chief rabbi, he did not play a significant role in the Emden-Eybeschütz controversy or in the general efforts to uproot Sabbatianism in Moravia.

The jury is still out on Eybeschütz, and it is not known whether his Moravian defenders were motivated by Sabbatian sympathies or by loyalty to an honorary Moravian. (His father, Natan Nata, had been rabbi of Eibenschitz, hence the name; one of his sons was married to the daughter of Gershon Pollitz, rabbi of Nikolsburg.) While Eybeschütz's Sabbatianism is still disputed, there are no doubts about his charismatic son Wolf, who counted a large number of Moravian Jews among his followers, particularly in Holleschau and Prossnitz. Indeed, it was in Prossnitz that he proclaimed himself the messiah in 1762.[185]

Evidence of Sabbatian activity (or at least accusations of Sabbatianism) in Moravia abounds for the last decades of the eighteenth century. This is reflected in the rabbinic responsa, epistles, and sermons of Eleazar Fleckeles, Ezekiel Landau, Mordecai Benet, and Moses Sofer, which point to Sabbatian activity—real or imagined—in Prossnitz, Holleschau, Gaya, Nikolsburg, and Kojetein.[186] In the eyes of Fleckeles, Kojetein—where he served as rabbi from 1779 to 1783—was totally infested with Sabbatians.[187]

This last period coincides with Jacob Frank's sojourn in Brünn (1773–1786). A Podolian-born Jew who fancied himself the reincarnation of Shabbetai Tsvi, Frank has been described by Scholem as "one of the most frightening phenomena in the whole of Jewish history."[188] This "truly corrupt and degenerate individual," in Scholem's words, took the theology of radical Sabbatianism to its nihilistic and orgiastic extreme. Frank not only promoted a culture of ritualized incest but also led his "Frankist" followers to the baptismal font in Lemberg and initiated an anti-Jewish disputation in Kamieniec-Podolski. In 1773, after overstaying his Polish welcome, Frank took his entourage to Brünn, where he set up a lavish court, fit for a nobleman (or a messianic pretender).

Frank chose Brünn because of his family connections (Schöndl Dobruschka), but he must have also assumed that Moravia would provide fertile ground for Frankism, as it had for Sabbatianism. Already in 1769, four years before Frank's arrival in Moravia, two Podolian Frankists had come to Prossnitz, where they were protected by the head of the Jewish community and even allowed to preach in the synagogue.[189] In 1773–74, just after Frank arrived in Moravia, thirty-five Prossnitz Jews converted to Catholicism. These conversions were likely motivated by the same Frankist (or Sabbatian) beliefs that had led Frank's followers in Poland to convert to Catholicism in 1759.[190]

The Limits of Hasidism

Hasidism, like Frankism, had its origins in eighteenth-century Podolia. From there it spread to Congress Poland, Galicia, and Hungary, but it reached an impasse at the Galician-Moravian frontier, which proved to be almost impermeable for this popular mystical movement. Unlike Frankism, which according to one estimate had "adherents in almost every community in Moravia,"[191] Hasidism failed to attract a following in this crown land, despite the fact that Shmuel Shmelke Horowitz, a disciple of Dov Ber of Mezerich ("Maggid of Mezerich"), served as Moravian chief rabbi from 1774 to 1778. Dov Ber (1710–1772) was a direct disciple of Israel ben Eliezer Baal Shem Tov ("the Besht," c. 1700–1760), the founder of Hasidism, and was arguably the main figure behind the dissemination of Hasidic lore and practice in Eastern Europe.

Shmelke arrived in Nikolsburg in 1774, a year after Jacob Frank set up his court in Brünn. During his five years in Moravia, he succeeded in bringing individual Hasids to Nikolsburg but failed to bring the Hasidic movement. Many of his students in Nikolsburg played major roles in disseminating Hasidism in Galicia, Congress Poland, and Hungary, but none of them came from Moravia or even remained there. Shmelke's closest disciple, Moses Leib (1745–1807) of Brody, accompanied him from Sienawa to Nikolsburg but later returned to Galicia, where he became known as the Sasover Rebbe. Jacob Isaac (1745–1815) also accompanied Shmelke to Nikolsburg, but he too sojourned there for only a few years before settling in Lublin, where he rose to prominence as the Seer of Lublin and played a key role in disseminating Hasidism in Congress Poland and Galicia. Israel ben Shabbetai Hopstein (1737–1814), later known as the Maggid of Koznitz (Kozienice), followed a similar path. Like his fellow students, his contribution to the spread of Hasidism was in Congress Poland, not in Moravia. Similarly, Yitshak Isaac Taub (1751–1821), who came to Nikolsburg from Hungary, returned to his native Nagykálló (Kalev in Yiddish), where he became known as the Kalever Rebbe. As the first Hasidic leader to permanently reside in Hungary, he played a crucial role in the development of Hungarian Hasidism.[192]

Why did Shmuel Shmelke Horowitz's disciples succeed in spreading Hasidism in Galicia, Congress Poland, and Hungary but not in the very crown land where they and their master had sojourned for nearly five years? This is part of a general question regarding the limits of Hasidism's western expansion and the more specific reasons for its lack of success in Moravia as well as Bohemia, Silesia, and Prussia.[193] Chone Shmeruk has offered a linguistic explanation, arguing that the differences between Eastern Yiddish (Poland) and Western Yiddish (Bohemia, Moravia, Germany) set up a barrier to the oral transmission of Hasidism in Central and Western Europe.[194] Gershon Hundert has offered a demographic explanation, arguing that rapid Jewish population growth in Eastern Europe—and the concomitant increase in the proportion of young people in the general Jewish population—was particularly significant for a movement that drew its support largely from the young.[195] Hundert's argument has particular bearing on Moravia, because—along with Bohemia—it may be the exception that proves the rule. Indeed, the Jews of Poland were experiencing a population explosion in the eighteenth century, but the Jews of Bohemia and Moravia were reeling under the pressure of the recently promulgated Familiants Laws, which effectively curbed the natural population growth. More important, the young Jewish men who were most affected by the marriage restrictions often chose emigration over celibacy, thereby shrinking the size of the demographic group that was most likely to seek solace, hope, or rebellion in the Hasidic movement.

It is also likely that Hasidism failed to find a foothold in Moravia precisely because Frankism did. These two mystical movements had "a certain historical-terminological-ideological continuity," and Hasidism's opponents were quick to point this out in their efforts to disparage the new movement as just another phase in the Sabbatian heresy.[196] (A disciple of Nahman of Bratslav was alleged to have been a grandson of Leibel Prossnitz!)[197] Even though Hasidic leaders took pains to deflect such accusations, the stigma of Sabbatianism remained so powerful that it may have even affected the spread of Hasidism. As Michael Silber has shown, Polish-Jewish communities with a Sabbatian past proved far less receptive to Hasidism than those without. Their members may have feared that embracing Hasidism would awaken lingering suspicions about the persistence of Sabbatianism (or Frankism) in these communities.[198] In Moravia, where Eleazar Fleckeles's anti-Sabbatian fulminations coincided with Jacob Frank's sojourn in Brünn, there may have been a similar concern.

In Moravia, personal factors also may have contributed to Hasidism's lack of success. Shmelke's disciples described him as a somber, introspective, and reclusive ascetic who undertook frequent fasts and slept little.[199] Shmelke may have possessed a kind of quiet charisma, but he did not exude the joyful exuberance of a Hasidic rebbe (or the diabolical magnetism of Jacob Frank). Moreover, his sojourn in Nikolsburg was marred by an intractable conflict with Abraham Shaye Auspitz, who had been serving as Moravia's provisional chief rabbi before Shmelke's arrival. When Shmelke was elected to this position in 1774, Auspitz's supporters denounced him to the government as unfit for office.[200] Some scholars have wondered whether this denunciation derived from Shmelke's adherence to Hasidism,[201] but it is just as likely that Auspitz and his supporters would have opposed any newcomer who threatened to usurp their authority and influence.[202]

After Shmelke's death in 1778, Moravia developed a reputation as a haven from Hasidism. According to one tradition, Barukh Fränkel-Teomim (1760–1828) came to Leipnik, Moravia, in 1802, precisely because his anti-Hasidism made him persona non grata in Wisznice, Galicia, where he had been serving as rabbi.[203] This tradition is attributed to the Seer of Lublin, one of Shmelke's own students, who had experienced Moravia's unreceptiveness to Hasidism firsthand.

In the end, the chief rabbi had little impact on the spread of Sabbatianism, Frankism, or Hasidism in Moravia, nor could he have been expected to. Although the Shai Takkanot envisioned the chief rabbi as a "supreme religious authority," he sat atop a supracommunal structure that grew out of—and reflected—the complex and intertangled constellation of Jewish communities that were constantly vying with one another for primacy and prestige. Many of these communities boasted rabbis and yeshivas of European renown and laymen of great influence, all of whom could counterbalance and challenge this institution's authority. Had Eskeles not been an absentee chief rabbi or Shmelke not been a reclusive ascetic, it is still not certain whether they could have exerted any real power over the Jews of Holleschau, Prossnitz, Kojetein, or even Nikolsburg.

Only at the end of the eighteenth century did a different kind of chief rabbi emerge. By dint of his profound talmudic erudition, boundless charisma, and legendary humility, Mordecai Benet (1753–1829) was able to earn the respect and support of a broad swath of Moravian Jewry. Know affectionately as Rabbi Reb Mordkhe, this larger-than-life figure used his lengthy tenure as chief rabbi to defend traditional observance in the face of new ideologies that promoted Jewish Enlightenment and religious reform.[204] Subsequent chief rabbis—such as Nehemias Trebitsch of Prague and Samson Raphael Hirsch of Hamburg—endowed the title with great importance, mistakenly assuming that the position itself granted them authority and respect. Benet understood Moravian Jewry much better than his successors; he was familiar with the fiercely independent communities, which had been steeled by the common experience of expulsion, "separation," and "reduction" and celebrated as important centers of Jewish life and learning.

Two

Rabbinic Enlightenment
Mordecai Benet and the Moravian Haskalah, 1789–1829

Mordecai Benet (1753–1829) serves as a perfect lens through which to view the transformations of Moravian Jewish society in the late eighteenth and early nineteenth century (Figure 6). Not only did his forty-year tenure as chief rabbi (1789–1829) span this crucial period, but his position and stature lent him the authority to influence Jewish matters in Moravia and beyond. Born in Csurgó, Hungary, and reared by his mother's family in Nikolsburg, Benet was a product of Central Europe's flourishing yeshivas and a champion of its traditional rabbinic culture. As Moravian chief rabbi, he chose his battles wisely, deeming internal attacks on halakhic tradition by fellow rabbis a far graver threat to traditional Jewish society than efforts by the absolutist state and Jewish enlighteners (*maskilim*) to modernize Jewish education. Benet responded to these internal and external challenges differently, confronting the internal challenges with such vehemence that he has been cast as an ardent defender of Orthodoxy and accommodating the external challenges with such skill that he has been cast as a proponent of the Jewish Enlightenment (Haskalah).

In 1801, Benet gave his rabbinic approbation (*haskama*) to a Hebrew chronicle, titled "Events of the Times" (*Korot ha-ʿIttim*), which was published in Brünn in the same year. The chronicler, Abraham Trebitsch (1759–1837) of Nikolsburg, described selected events from Moravia's recent past, including Benet's election to the Moravian chief rabbinate in 1789. Trebitsch, who also happened to be the chief rabbi's secretary, opened the section on Benet's election with a verse from the book of Psalms: "The righteous man will flourish like the palm tree." To this arboreal metaphor, he juxtaposed another metaphor inspired by the

Figure 6. Mordecai Benet, Moravian-Silesian chief rabbi, 1789–1829. Courtesy of Jewish Museum in Prague, inv. č. 130220.

book of Ecclesiastes: "The sun goes down, and the sun also rises." In all likelihood, a contemporary Moravian Jew would have known that the order of the biblical verse ("The sun also rises, and the sun goes down") had been inverted. He would have also appreciated Trebitsch's artful allusion to the Babylonian Talmud, which compares a "righteous man" to "the sun" and interprets the verse from Ecclesiastes to mean that "a righteous man does not depart from this world until another righteous man is created to replace him."[1]

Trebitsch could have expected his readers to understand *Korot ha-'Ittim*'s ornate Hebrew language and rich talmudic allusions because they—like Trebitsch himself—had likely studied at one or more of Central Europe's celebrated yeshivas. When Trebitsch wrote *Korot ha-'Ittim*, many of these yeshivas were in decline, but Moravia's world of traditional Jewish learning was still flourishing, and Benet's election to the chief rabbinate promised to usher in a new heyday, especially for the Nikolsburg yeshiva. Nevertheless, as Trebitsch's chronicle can readily attest, Moravia's traditional Jewish landscape was already beginning to show cracks and fissures at the end of the eighteenth century. Trebitsch blamed selected Josephinian reforms, such as the removal of internal judicial autonomy (1785), for "diminishing religion and decreasing its glory." He also singled out the introduction of mandatory German instruction (1781–82), which was meant to wean Jewish children from their "stammering tongue" (i.e., Yiddish or Judeo-German).[2]

Yosef Hayim Yerushalmi has shown that Jews often turned to historical writing in times of crisis, and Trebitsch was certainly no exception.[3] Moravia's Jews were not threatened by expulsion or persecution, but active state intervention in internal Jewish affairs, no matter how well intentioned, still represented a dismaying departure from the status quo. So, too, did efforts by contemporary Jews to reform age-old Jewish customs. As a chronicler, Trebitsch was content to describe these dramatic "events of the times"—and occasionally express his disapproval; Mordecai Benet, however, viewed his task in far grander terms. As Moravian chief rabbi, and one of the leading halakhic authorities of the age, Benet saw it as his duty to confront the challenges of the times.

Yeshivas and the Moderate Haskalah

The traditional Jewish landscape in Central Europe experienced a tectonic shift in Benet's own lifetime. At the time of Benet's birth in 1753, there were important yeshivas in Prague, Nikolsburg, Fürth, Altona, Metz, and Frankfurt am Main, all of which attracted students and rabbis from throughout Central and Eastern Europe. Of these six communities, only Nikolsburg still had a yeshiva in 1829, the year that Benet passed away. In the intervening seventy-six years, traditional rabbinic learning suffered a precipitous decline and the yeshiva disappeared from Jewish communities in Western (and parts of Central) Europe. ("The yeshivas have disappeared entirely," wrote Peter Beer, a Bohemian-born Jewish historian, in 1832.)[4] In the same period, the center of gravity shifted eastward to Moravia, where a closely knit constellation of smaller yeshivas still thrived, and southward to Hungary, where newly established yeshivas—most notably in Pressburg—grew in size and prominence.[5]

In Benet's youth, many of these yeshivas were headed by Polish-born rabbinic luminaries such as Jonathan Eybeschütz (Prague, Metz, Altona), Ezekiel Landau (Prague), and Pinḥas Horwitz (Frankfurt)—itself an indication that local talent was in short supply. Only the Fürth yeshiva, which Benet attended around 1770, was headed by a rabbi of Western European origin, Joseph Steinhard.[6] In the last decades of the eighteenth century, Ezekiel Landau emerged as the preeminent talmudic scholar and halakhic decisor (*posek*) in Central Europe. His Prague yeshiva not only attracted students from all over the region but also produced a whole generation of talmudic scholars and community rabbis in Bohemia, Moravia, Galicia, and Hungary.[7] Almost all the Central European rabbinic authorities of Benet's generation—with the exception of Moses Sofer and Akiva Eger—either studied with Landau or received a rabbinic diploma from him. These included Eleazar Fleckeles, Moses Münz, Mordecai Benet, and Landau's oldest son, Samuel.

Like Prague in general, Landau's yeshiva was without peer in Bohemia, but Moravia was an entirely different story. By the end of the eighteenth century, "the majority of [Bohemian] youth who devoted themselves to the study of Torah set their sights on Prague."[8] Kolin and

Jenikau had the only other Bohemian yeshivas of note, but Moravia had at least eight yeshivas that were prestigious enough to attract students from all over Central Europe. Nikolsburg was home to the largest, but Prossnitz, Leipnik, Trebitsch, Triesch, Boskowitz, Holleschau, and Eibenschitz could all boast highly acclaimed yeshivas of their own, not to mention the smaller yeshivas in communities such as Gewitsch, Gross-Meseritsch, Kremsier, Neu-Rausnitz, Mährisch-Weisskirchen, Pohrlitz, and Ungarisch-Brod.[9] Because Moravian Jewry was concentrated in small and medium-size towns—and not in isolated villages, like the majority of Bohemian Jewry outside Prague—Moravia's Jewish communities had the demographic capacity to support their own yeshivas.[10] They also had the financial obligation, because the Shai Takkanot required Nikolsburg to support a yeshiva with twenty-five students, and each community with more than thirty householders was required to support a yeshiva with no less than six students each. As a consequence of the fifteenth-century expulsions, many of these communities were clustered together, so peripatetic students and rabbis could easily move from one yeshiva to another.[11]

Moravia's thriving yeshivas and flourishing rabbinic culture had a moderating effect on the Haskalah, a movement that brought fundamental change to Central European Jewish society at the turn of the nineteenth century. The Jewish Enlightenment, like its general European counterpart, was by no means a monolithic movement. Just as one can speak of multiple enlightenments (French, German, Scottish, English, Swedish, Austrian, Hungarian, Bohemian, and even Moravian), one can speak of multiple haskalahs, each exhibiting its own regional specificity within a shared ideological framework.[12] Nevertheless, these regional haskalahs all drew inspiration from the Berlin Haskalah, which served as a model and template for Jewish enlighteners (*maskilim*) throughout the Habsburg monarchy and Russian Empire. Moses Mendelssohn (1729–1786), the key figure in the Berlin Haskalah, sought to find a balance between modern European culture and traditional Jewish practice, and during his lifetime, the Berlin Haskalah fostered an openness to secular knowledge while maintaining respect for the sanctity of Jewish law and tradition. Mendelssohn's translation of the Hebrew Bible into literary German (1780–1783) was the capstone project of the Berlin Haskalah, and even though this work aroused some opposition in rabbinic circles, it still took a rather conservative approach to Jewish tradition.[13]

Mendelssohn embodied the synthesis between tradition and modernity, but this fragile balance failed to resonate with many of his disciples, who pushed the Haskalah in a more radical direction after their master's death. In its early stages (1770s and 1780s), the Berlin Haskalah aimed to "revive Hebrew" as a language of philosophy, poetry, and prose, but by the end of the eighteenth century, many *maskilim* "despised the tongue of their fathers and cast it behind them."[14] Under Mendelssohn, the Berlin Haskalah was highly critical of rabbinic authority and halakhic inflexibility, but the early *maskilim* still treated their rabbinic opponents—such as the Prague rabbi Ezekiel Landau—with due respect. After Mendelssohn's death in 1786, however, *Ha-me'asef* (The Collector), the main journal of the Berlin Haskalah, became openly hostile toward Jewish law and tradition and even displayed "mocking disrespect" for Landau after he died in 1793.[15] Moreover, some *maskilim* promoted radical religious reforms—such as the abandonment of "shameful, senseless ceremonial law"—which would have made Mendelssohn turn over in his grave.[16]

The antirabbinic militancy that suffused the later phases of the Berlin Haskalah was conspicuously absent in the Habsburg monarchy (except in Galicia, where the *maskilim* viewed "obscurantist" Hasidism as their primary opponent). In Bohemia, Moravia, Hungary, and Vienna, the Haskalah was characterized above all by its moderation, its esteem for the Hebrew language, and its deep respect for rabbinic tradition. Although the absence of Hasidism in the western Habsburg lands may have played a role in moderating the Haskalah, perhaps the most important factor was the thriving rabbinic culture at the turn of the nineteenth century. Noting that "this was the one region where yeshivas still flourished during the crucial transition period," Michael Silber has argued that yeshivas played "the unforeseen role of Haskalah centers *par excellence.*" They offered young Jews an opportunity to "devote their time exclusively to intellectual pursuits" while simultaneously exposing them to "the best traditional rabbinic culture had to offer."[17] In these yeshivas, traditional rabbinic culture was sufficiently rooted and secure to absorb new ideas without feeling threatened.

The bunker mentality that came to characterize Hungarian Orthodoxy in the 1820s and 1830s was foreign to the yeshivas of Bohemia
and Moravia in the late eighteenth and early nineteenth centuries. Far
from shunning extratalmudic learning, many leading rabbis embraced
secular studies and even encouraged their students to broaden their
educational horizons.[18] "In Bohemia and Moravia," wrote Isaac Hirsch
Weiss, "secular studies [*ḥokhmot*] were a daily portion for the Jews,
and the rabbis did not open their mouths in dismay. [On the contrary]
the rabbis themselves would educate their sons in the study of secular
knowledge."[19] Weiss singled out Benet for praise. "Of all the rabbis in
the different lands," he declared, "our great teacher and rabbi . . . Mordecai Benet, rabbi of all of Moravia . . . was an eminent grammarian, an
expert in the science of the Holy Tongue, and his hands perused works
of religious philosophy like [Maimonides'] *Guide to the Perplexed* and
[Joseph Albo's] *Book of Principles*. . . . He knew how to write in German
and he possessed prodigious knowledge of several secular sciences."[20]

In Weiss's portrayal, Benet comes across as a proto-*maskil*, whose love
of Hebrew grammar, affinity for medieval Jewish philosophy, and openness to secular sciences were perfectly in tune with the program of the
moderate Haskalah. Similar sentiments were expressed by Ya'akov Avril
Benet, the chief rabbi's son, and by Judah Jeiteles, a central figure in the
Prague Haskalah, whose rhymed Hebrew eulogy for Mordecai Benet
was published in the maskilic journal *Bikkurei ha-'Ittim* (First fruits of
the times).[21] Still, Benet's openness to secular studies did not make him a
maskil, because he continued to view extratalmudic studies as "embellish-
ments to the Torah" (*parpera'ot la-tora*), which did not possess any inherent value.[22] Benet's authority certainly gave legitimacy to the moderate
Haskalah, but he never espoused the core maskilic ideology that viewed
secular knowledge as an end unto itself. For this reason, Michael Silber
places Benet in the company of Eleazar Fleckeles, Moses Münz, Samuel
Landau, and other Central European rabbinic luminaries who were illus-
trative of a kind of "rabbinic haskalah" (*haskalah rabbanit*) that evinced
sympathy for the moderate Haskalah without fully endorsing it.[23]

For Benet, traditional Jewish practice faced a far greater threat from
internal factors than from "external knowledge." During his first years as
Moravian chief rabbi, he emerged as an outspoken opponent of lenient

halakhic rulings that, in his view, aimed to subvert rabbinic tradition from within. Perhaps the legacy of Sabbatianism made him instinctively wary of any deviation in practice that made claims to a venerable rabbinic pedigree. Or perhaps he simply viewed change in the cloak of tradition as a threat to the integrity of the halakhic process. In either case, his involvement in three controversies at the turn of the nineteenth century helped establish his far-reaching reputation as a steadfast defender of tradition.

The first of these controversies involved *Besamim Rosh* (1793), a book of 392 responsa attributed for the most part to Asher ben Yehiel (c. 1250–1327), one of the greatest rabbinic authorities in the Middle Ages.[24] The responsa were surprisingly lenient; among other things, they permitted eating legumes on Passover, traveling on the Sabbath, shaving with a blade, drinking the coffee and wine of non-Jews, and mourning a person who committed suicide. The lenient nature of these responsa aroused suspicions among many rabbinic authorities, including Benet, who took center stage in an epistolary campaign to expose it as a forgery. There is little doubt that *Besamim Rosh* was forged by Saul Berlin (1740–1794), a Berlin rabbi who aimed to reform certain Jewish practices by "rediscovering" a more lenient halakhic tradition. Significantly, Berlin did not justify these leniencies (or deviations) by appealing to the "spirit of the times" or to an external authority; instead, he invoked "traditional" categories in his duplicitous attempt to effect change from within the rabbinic legal system.[25]

The second controversy involved Aron Chorin (1766–1844), a Moravian-born rabbi in Arad, Hungary, who also invoked traditional categories in his lenient ruling on sturgeon. Unlike Berlin, Chorin did not have to forge "tradition" to declare sturgeon kosher, because he could cite medieval rulings by Rabbenu Tam and Maimonides—as well as a more recent ruling by Ezekiel Landau—that declared this fish (or at least a similarly named one) kosher.[26] Nevertheless, Chorin's ruling conflicted with an age-old custom that had deemed sturgeon nonkosher because of its apparent lack of real scales. Chorin defended his approach in two separate pamphlets that aroused considerable opposition in traditional circles, particularly in Hungary.[27] Benet tried to prevent the publication of the first pamphlet and gave an approbation to another pamphlet that attacked Chorin's position.[28] In his approbation, Benet emphasized that the prohibition against eating sturgeon had been in place "since time immemorial." It did not matter whether the custom was instituted out of doubt (*safka de-dina*) or as a safeguard (*gader*), he insisted, because "even a great rabbinic luminary [*gedol ha-dor*]" could not change it.[29] (In Benet's view, Chorin certainly did not belong to this category.) Custom (*minhag*), he argued, was as sacred and inviolable as biblical law and therefore could not be modified under any circumstances. In this respect, sturgeon served as a kind of litmus test for the sanctity of tradition, leading Benet to invalidate the testimony of anyone who permitted the consumption of this fishy fish.[30] For Benet, the sturgeon controversy placed Chorin beyond the pale. When Chorin published a book in 1803 arguing for the elimination of "irrational" customs, Benet promptly summoned him to appear before a rabbinic court in Hungary and sought to have his book burned.[31]

The third controversy involved Benjamin Wolf Rapoport (1754–1837), a Moravian-born rabbi in Pápa, Hungary, whose lenient halakhic rulings irked Benet and Moses Sofer to such an extent that they tried to have him removed from the Pápa rabbinate. Unlike the *Besamim Rosh* and sturgeon controversies, the Rapoport controversy did not turn into a cause célèbre, but it did underscore the nature of the internal threat perceived by Benet (and Sofer). Rapoport was a talmudic scholar of first rank, and he used his prodigious knowledge to challenge stringent interpretations of Halakha, such as those pertaining to permissible and impermissible marriages.[32] "He permits what his friends forbid," Benet and Sofer reportedly claimed; "he is lenient in matters where the rabbis of the land are stringent."[33] From their perspective, Rapoport was a particularly troublesome figure because he invoked traditional halakhic authority to justify deviations from the legal norm. Benet and Sofer attempted to discredit him because, in their eyes, he was teaching a "new Torah" in the guise of the authentic one.[34]

In all three controversies, Benet sought to safeguard rabbinic tradition by staving off perceived threats from within. In this respect, Berlin, Chorin, and Rapoport were particularly menacing, because their mastery of the rabbinic corpus was used—in Benet's view—to undermine the very integrity of that corpus. Had they totally disregarded the "recognized halakhic channels," their approaches could have been more easily dismissed, but their efforts to subvert rabbinic tradition—*in the name of rabbinic tradition!*—made these rabbis all the more deplorable to Benet and his kindred spirits.[35]

The German-Jewish school system, in contrast, did not constitute the same kind of threat to tradition. Largely because of the influence of Ezekiel Landau, instruction in the German-Jewish schools in Bohemia and Moravia was limited to profane subjects (reading, writing, and arithmetic) that did not impinge on traditional areas of Jewish study (Hebrew Bible, Mishnah, Talmud). When Emperor Joseph II introduced compulsory education for his Jewish subjects in 1781–82, Landau "determined from the beginning to exert his influence on the course of change rather than simply condemn it out of hand."[36] As Hillel Kieval has shown, Landau worked closely with the Bohemian superintendent of schools to ensure that traditional talmudic education was kept out of the new German-Jewish schools and left in the hands of the rabbinic establishment.[37] More important, Landau wanted to keep maskilic teachers out of these schools, because such individuals might blur the lines between sacred and profane by subjecting divine revelation to rational critique. In particular, Landau was alarmed by the educational program of the German *maskil* Naftali Herz Wessely, whose *Words of Peace and Truth* (1782) seemed to invert the traditional epistemological hierarchy by asserting that "human knowledge" was anterior to "divine knowledge." Landau condemned Wessely as "worse than a corpse," observing that a "wicked and arrogant man has arisen from our nation for whom the Torah is not worth anything, for whom profane subjects are better than the study of Torah."[38]

Under Landau's influence, the structure of the German-Jewish schools helped reinforce the primacy of the Torah in Jewish life. Jewish children entered the four-year German-Jewish school only after they had reached the age of 10, thus "providing time for them to receive a grounding in the Torah before they came into contact with secular subjects."[39] Furthermore, instruction in profane subjects was limited to a few hours a day, thereby allowing Jewish boys to devote the rest of their time to the study of Bible, Mishnah, and Talmud in private or community-run heders (religious schools). The Jewish communities helped reinforce the importance of traditional Jewish learning and worship by obligating parents to send their sons to the heder for religious instruction and to the synagogue for morning prayer.[40] In Moravia, the chief rabbi was also in a position to influence the nature of Jewish instruction because he had the exclusive authority to certify *melamedim* (heder teachers) in the entire crown land.

Benet, who was elected chief rabbi almost a decade after compulsory secular education was introduced in Moravia, held no influence over the actual establishment of Moravia's forty-two German-Jewish schools, but as the "supreme religious authority" from 1789 to 1829, he could ensure—like Landau in Prague—that the curriculum steered clear of traditional Jewish subjects.[41] Benet may have been pleased, in fact, that many of the teachers were not even Jewish, because Christian teachers were unlikely (and probably unable) to mix Jewish and secular subjects in the spirit of Wessely's *Words of Peace and Truth*.[42] With respect to private religious teachers, this risk was much greater, and Benet tried to ensure that the *melamedim* he certified were well suited for this task. As Benet explained to Moravian government officials toward the end of his life, religious instruction should be given by rabbis and conducted in Hebrew. He claimed that it would be "uncomfortable, indeed nearly impossible" (*unbequemlich ja fast unmöglich*) for rabbis to give religious instruction "in German fashion" (*in deutschen Style*), by which he presumably meant instruction according to the whims and fancies of the German *maskilim*. Benet also stressed that religious instruction could be given only by certified *melamedim*.[43] Because these *melamedim* had to be certified by the Moravian chief rabbi, Benet was essentially asking for government help in enforcing the separation of religious and secular instruction.

Mordecai Benet and Herz Homberg's *Bne Zion* (1812)

Moral instruction was the one area in which the boundaries between religious and secular instruction remained somewhat blurred. In Christian schools, moral instruction was rooted in Christianity, so their textbooks could not be used in the German-Jewish schools. In 1783, the Christian superintendent of the German-Jewish school in Prague tried to overcome this problem by eliminating everything in the standard moral textbook that was "peculiar to the Christian religion," but this proved to be an unsatisfactory solution.[44] In 1784, Moses Wiener, a Jewish teacher at the Prague school published his own *Primer for Jewish Children* (*Lesebuch für jüdische Kinder*), but this work also contained passages that were "contrary to religion."[45]

To solve the problem of moral instruction in the German-Jewish Schools, the Court Commission on Education in Vienna solicited *Bne Zion* (Sons of Zion), a German-language catechism, or "religious-moral textbook," from Herz Homberg. It was introduced to all the German-Jewish schools in the Habsburg monarchy (replacing Wiener's work). The Court Commission recognized that Homberg's authorship might sully this work in the eyes of many Jews, especially because he had been accused of "immoral and highly unrighteous acts" when he had served as superintendent of the German-Jewish schools in Galicia. Born in Bohemia, Homberg (1749–1841) played a central role in the Berlin Haskalah, first as tutor of Moses Mendelssohn's children and then as a contributor to the *Biur* (1780–1783), Mendelssohn's commentary on the five books of Moses. In 1788, at Mendelssohn's suggestion, the Austrian government appointed him superintendent of the German-Jewish schools in Galicia, a province that had just come under Habsburg rule. Homberg's efforts to reform traditional Jewish education met with considerable resistance in Galicia, and his heavy-handed tactics stirred up tremendous hostility, leading the Austrian authorities to recall him in 1794. In Jewish historiography, Homberg has acquired an exceedingly negative image, and he is usually depicted as a radical enlightener or a corrupt opportunist. Even if this negative image is somewhat exaggerated, it is indisputable that Homberg was a highly controversial figure at the beginning of the nineteenth century.[46]

On January 10, 1810, Benet gave his approbation to *Bne Zion*. Historians of the Jewish Enlightenment have tried to explain (or explain away) this approbation because Homberg has remained one of the most despised figures in traditional Jewish circles.[47] One of Benet's biographers has even gone so far as to omit *Bne Zion* from the list of nearly sixty approbations that he gave in his lifetime.[48] Benet's approbation, however, should not be so confounding because the Court Commission on

Education did its utmost to ensure that Benet would lend his name and authority to Homberg's catechism. The Court Commission wanted to introduce *Bne Zion* to the German-Jewish school system, and it hoped that Benet's approbation would help overcome resistance from traditional Jewish quarters. Benet must have seen the wisdom in accommodating the wishes of the Court Commission.

From later sources, we know that Benet, like many rabbis of his generation, viewed Jewish catechisms with deep suspicion.[49] A catechism, by its nature, aims to distill a religion to its essence, reducing it to a set of core beliefs and principles that can be systematically committed to memory. This was antithetical to traditional approaches to Jewish education, according to which "children . . . acquired the fundamentals of their faith through study of the classic texts."[50] Not surprisingly, *maskilim* were among the main proponents of Jewish catechisms, viewing them as a means to streamline Jewish education and, in the process, free up time for secular studies. The Court Commission on Education viewed catechisms (or "moral-religious textbooks") primarily as a means to instill morality and civility in the subjects of the Habsburg monarchy.

The Court Commission on Education hoped that Benet's approbation, in light of Homberg's ill repute, would smooth the introduction of the new catechism into the monarchy's German-Jewish schools. As the Court Commission observed on August 31, 1810, the "favorable attestation of the Chief Rabbi" offered hope that "this work will also meet with the approval of the Jews."[51] Apparently, the Court Commission did not wish to take any risks with regard to Homberg's authorship, so it recommended including Benet's approbation but omitting the actual author's name.[52] Homberg's name did appear on the title page of the Augsburg edition of *Bne Zion*, which was published (outside the Habsburg monarchy) in 1812, but the Vienna edition, which was published in October of the same year, made no mention of his name.[53] Both editions reproduced Benet's German-language approbation, which pronounced *Bne Zion* to be in complete accord with the Holy Scriptures, the Talmud, and "all of the great teachers of our nation from ancient and modern times."[54]

Bolstered by Benet's approbation, Emperor Franz I decreed on December 14, 1810, first, that the soon to be published *Bne Zion* be used as a textbook in all Jewish schools in the monarchy's hereditary lands and, second, that all Jewish brides and bridegrooms be examined by the district office on its contents before receiving permission to marry. Conceived as a religious-moral textbook, *Bne Zion* was part of the state's efforts to break down barriers between Christians and Jews by emphasizing the universal human ethics that were common to both religious traditions. Consequently, *Bne Zion* did not dwell on Jewish ceremonial laws or distinctly Jewish practices but rather focused on duties toward the state, the divine, one's fellow countrymen, and one's fellow human beings. Homberg rooted these duties in the Jewish tradition by including relevant texts from the Bible and Talmud, but *Bne Zion* was more a work of universal human ethics than a work of Jewish theology. In many respects, it was as an ethics primer *à la juive*.

Although Benet pronounced *Bne Zion* to be in complete accord with Jewish teachings, his endorsement of the book was, at best, lukewarm. On January 13, 1813, only three months after the book was published, Benet asked the Moravian-Silesian Gubernium to modify the court decree from December 14, 1810.[55] According to Benet, the book could not be obtained from the publisher in time, and, to make matters worse, its contents were too unfamiliar and too difficult for most Jews to learn. Jewish children, especially girls, had only a meager education, and the *Bne Zion* examinations required "high intellectual development" (*eine höhere Verstandesbildung*) and a "capacity for remembering" (*Gedächtnissvermögen*) that "undeveloped minds" did not yet possess. Moreover, because Moravia's Jews at best spoke a coarse, vernacular German, "thousands of words in this textbook . . . were unfamiliar to them as words, let alone as actual concepts." For Benet, the situation was even more dismal for Jewish children who attended Czech-language village schools or who lived on isolated, rural leaseholds, where underpaid teachers possessed "a minimal knowledge of spelling and an even shoddier knowledge of German grammar." Indeed, *Bne Zion* was written in such a sophisticated and abstract German that even Jews who had mastered the language might have found it difficult to understand.[56] As Isaac Hirsch Weiss observed, "It was too difficult a work to give to 10-year-olds."[57] It is likely that even the 60-year-old chief rabbi had difficulties understanding the sublime German language of Homberg's book. (His own community of Nikolsburg complained in 1819 that the children at the German-Jewish school were "way behind in their moral-religious instruction" because the chief rabbi had not come there "one single time" to expound on *Bne Zion*.)[58]

Because young couples had to pass an examination demonstrating knowledge of *Bne Zion* before getting a marriage license, the book's inaccessibility often had painful consequences, turning the *Bne Zion* examination into "the first drop of bitterness in the joy of matrimony."[59] Weiss recalled the "distress and embarrassment" felt by many a bride and groom who could not answer the questions and ended up slipping the examiners a bribe instead.[60] Some couples were told the questions in advance, so they could simply memorize the answers (without necessarily understanding them).[61] In 1814, a Jewish schoolteacher in Triesch complained that many Jews went to other towns and provinces where they fraudulently obtained *Bne Zion* certificates (presumably through bribery), which they then submitted to the district office with their marriage applications. This led the Moravian-Silesian Gubernium to decree that the *Bne Zion* examination had to be conducted by teachers, rabbis, or officials of the community where the bride and groom legally resided.[62]

Benet may have seen the generally tepid reception of *Bne Zion* as an opportunity to promote another Jewish textbook that was more to his liking. In 1822, he gave a glowing approbation to a newly written Jewish catechism, *Emunath Israel: A Guide to Instruction in the Mosaic Religion.*[63] This bilingual German-Hebrew catechism was written by Naftali Benet (1789–1857), the chief rabbi's third and youngest son. Mordecai Benet had reviewed it "from beginning to end, to make sure it was free of all iniquity and impediment," so the catechism likely reflected the views of the chief rabbi and was perhaps even written at his behest.[64] Naftali Benet composed *Emunath Israel* while he was employed as a teacher at Nikolsburg's German-Jewish school, where he had been providing instruction in *Bne Zion* since around 1821.[65] In 1824, he submitted the manuscript for *Emunath Israel* to the Court Commission on Education, in the hope that the work would replace *Bne Zion* in the Habsburg monarchy's German-Jewish schools. Naftali Benet's motives may have been entirely pure, but he surely must have realized that writing a compulsory textbook could also be quite lucrative.

Emunath Israel was considerably more conservative than *Bne Zion* and more deeply rooted in rabbinic tradition. Homberg's catechism was entirely in German, whereas Benet's included many Hebrew verses and terms. Homberg's catechism drew primarily on the Hebrew Bible; Benet's placed more emphasis on talmudic and other rabbinic writings. More important, whereas *Bne Zion* expressed universal ethics (or natural religion) in Jewish terms, *Emunath Israel* stressed the importance of Jewish ceremonial law in conjunction with the moral-ethical commandments. In sum, *Bne Zion* imparted "moral-religious" teachings, whereas *Emunath Israel* provided a more substantive introduction to the "faith of Israel."

The Court Commission on Education rejected Naftali Benet's request, noting that *Bne Zion* had already "found entry and obtained authority," thereby making it inadvisable to consider another Jewish catechism, especially one that was "considerably inferior" to *Bne Zion*.[66] The Court Commission found the structure of *Emunath Israel* illogical and the emphasis on rabbinic tradition, ceremonial law, and the Hebrew language particularly troublesome. Turning Mordecai Benet's criticism of *Bne Zion* on its head, the Court Commission noted that *Emunath Israel* contained "many Hebrew verses, most of which are incomprehensible to young and old alike." Naftali Benet's catechism also contained "many talmudic teachings" that were out of place in a government-sanctioned textbook that deals with the moral principles of the Jews.[67] In another report, the Court Commission expressed concern about the strenuous defense of Hebrew prayer as well as the rather positive evaluation of commerce among the Jews.[68] The Court Commission rejected Naftali Benet's catechism as a replacement for *Bne Zion*, but it did recommend *Emunath Israel* as a possible reference work for schoolteachers. In the same report, the Court Commission lavished praise on *Bne Zion*, pointing out that Homberg's work dealt only with religious and moral teachings that conform with Reason and the Holy Scripture, and that it also "omitted mere talmudic teachings."[69]

In writing *Emunath Israel*, Naftali Benet tried to redress the problems that he—and presumably his father—saw with *Bne Zion*. The Court Commission judged his work to be "considerably inferior" to Homberg's catechism, precisely because the Judaism it portrayed involved specific rituals and customs that could not be universalized or reduced to abstract beliefs and concepts. The illogical structure of the work may have stemmed from the fact that this complex mixture of practice and belief did not naturally lend itself to the genre of catechism. Naftali Benet could not simply omit the ceremonial laws and "mere talmudic teachings," which he viewed as the essence of the "Mosaic Religion." Nor could he give up on the Hebrew language, which he—and Mordecai Benet—viewed as the sole language of Jewish prayer.

Mordecai Benet and Hebrew Prayer

The strong defense of Hebrew as the language of prayer in *Emunath Israel* is one indication that the work was written under Mordecai Benet's influence and guidance. When *Bne Zion* was first published in 1812, the question of prayer in the vernacular had scarcely been broached and had not yet become a highly contentious issue in Central European Jewish circles. This changed, however, with the Hamburg temple controversy of 1818–19. A "milestone in the history of the Reform movement," the Hamburg temple controversy turned the question of vernacular prayer into a clear demarcation line between the emerging camps of religious reformers and staunch traditionalists.[70] Benet, who was demonstrably a member of the traditionalist camp, excoriated vernacular prayer and, in the process, adumbrated a defense of the Hebrew language that would have been close to the hearts of many *maskilim*.

The Hamburg temple controversy marked the first time that "the united voice of rabbinical authority" rose up in protest against liturgical reforms and other changes to synagogue worship.[71] After a group of laymen in Hamburg introduced organ music, liturgical reforms, and prayer in the vernacular, the Hamburg rabbinic court gathered twenty-two rabbinic responsa condemning these innovations. These were then published as *Eleh divrei ha-brit* (These are the words of the covenant), a small volume containing responsa from rabbis across Central and Western Europe, including Moses Sofer in Pressburg, Akiva Eger in Posen, and two rabbis in Moravia: Mordecai Benet of Nikolsburg and Eleazar Löw of Triesch.[72] Like the other incensed rabbis, Benet condemned all the innovations in the Hamburg temple, but it was prayer in the vernacular that rankled him most.

Benet's opposition to prayer in the vernacular did not stand on solid halakhic ground. Judeo-German translations of the prayer book had been in use in Central Europe for centuries, particularly among women, who did not have many opportunities to study Hebrew. Moreover, halakhic support for prayer in the vernacular could be found in the Mishnah, Talmud, Maimonides, Nachmanides, Rashi, and other rabbinic authorities.[73] Moral treatises, such as Isaac ben Eliakim's *Lev tov* (Good heart), explicitly stated that "whoever does not understand the Holy Tongue should pray in whatever language he understands well."[74] When two of Moses Mendelssohn's students translated the prayer book into High German in 1786, Eleazar Fleckeles of Prague presented some opposition, but Fleckeles was primarily concerned about the growing neglect of Hebrew, not the permissibility of prayer in the vernacular.[75] Both prayer book translations were originally published in Berlin, and when they were republished in Brünn (1796) and Vienna (1799, 1815), Mordecai Benet did not voice any objection.[76]

In 1818–19, however, the controversy was not about vernacular prayer books per se but rather about prayer in the vernacular. The available German translations were intended for private use, to help elucidate the prayers for women and men who were poorly versed in Hebrew. At the Hamburg temple, however, certain prayers were recited in the vernacular, and a new bilingual prayer book was prepared especially for this purpose.[77] Traditionalist rabbis could object on halakhic grounds to certain liturgical changes in the new prayer book (such as the omission of prayers for a return to Zion), but the question of prayer in the vernacular was less clear-cut. Nevertheless, the fact that religious reformers (including Benet's nemesis, Aron Chorin) advocated reciting some prayers in the vernacular placed the language question at the heart of the ideological struggle between reformers and traditionalists.

Eleh divrei ha-brit contains three responsa by Benet, one of which is devoted almost entirely to the question of prayer in the vernacular. Written on December 31, 1818, this responsum presents a twofold defense of Hebrew prayer, drawing on theological arguments on the one hand and national arguments on the other.[78] According to Benet, when a Jew prays in Hebrew, he must pay fastidious attention to the consonants, vowels, syntax, and grammar, which thereby serves to ensure that his prayers have the proper intention (*kavvana*).[79] When he prays in German (*lashon daytsh*), in contrast, the same level of concentration is not required, so even if his lips are full of praise, "his heart [remains] far from God." Moreover, certain prayers are valid only when recited in Hebrew, and, in any case, the original biblical language is far superior to the German translations. In Hebrew, for example, God's name (*yhvh*) encompasses two divine attributes (Eternal One, Creator), whereas the standard German translation (*Ewiger*) encompasses but one.[80] This difference rendered German totally inadequate in Benet's eyes, because an individual was not really uttering God's name if he failed to keep both divine attributes in mind.

Alongside his theological (or theocentric) defense of Hebrew prayer, Benet offered a national defense, stressing the uniqueness of the Jewish people and their special connection to the holy tongue. "We are God's chosen people (*'am segulato*)," he stressed, "and we can utter the holy name only in the Hebrew language."[81] Having observed the decline in Hebrew knowledge during his lifetime, Benet considered the synagogue a last redoubt for the holy tongue and understandably feared that the introduction of vernacular prayer would lead inexorably to the extinction of Hebrew in the coming generations.

> It is only proper to pray in the holy tongue (*leshon ha-kodesh*) because the Torah will otherwise disappear, God forbid! Young people will stop learning the language of the Hebrews (*mishpatei ha-ivri'im*); the Hebrew language (*s'fat ha-ivri*) will fall into the depths of oblivion; and they will find no use for it at all—not for studying Torah, Gemara, and Poskim, which have been neglected anyway; not for studying the Hebrew Bible, which, in any case, has been fully translated into German. If prayers are now said in another language, then the holy tongue (*leshon ha-kodesh*) will be lost to the people of Israel.[82]

Benet's cri de coeur, like Landau's blanket condemnation of the whole translation project, evinced a palpable fear that the gradual encroachment of German would lead to the total neglect of Hebrew and, by extension, to the abandonment of traditional Jewish learning. Implicitly, Benet's words also expressed a concern that the linguistic bond, which had linked Jews together for centuries, would slowly be torn asunder.[83] As he later wrote to the government authorities, Hebrew should remain the language of prayer because it allows any Jew to take part "no matter what his mother tongue may be."[84]

Mordecai Benet and the German Language

In the first decades of the nineteenth century, German had increasingly become the linguistic bond that linked the Jews of Central Europe, supplanting Judeo-German (not to mention Hebrew) among the younger generations. In Moravia, this linguistic transformation had been brought about, in part, by the extensive network of German-Jewish schools that had been set up under Joseph II in 1782. It should come as no surprise that Naftali Benet (b. 1789) had mastered the German language, but if Naftali's younger brother Ya'akov Avril can be believed, so too had Mordecai Benet (b. 1753). According to Ya'akov Avril, the chief rabbi spoke "mellifluous and pure" German in his meetings with government ministers and noblemen—a claim that Leopold Löw would have had a hard time believing.[85] Mordecai Benet's own level of German notwithstanding, there is ample evidence that the chief rabbi recognized the utility of learning non-Jewish languages. According to Isaac Hirsch Weiss, Benet "did not chastise his sons for learning the language of the people or for reading profane books." On the contrary, he advised them not to avoid such useful knowledge.[86]

Benet's attitude toward the Mendelssohnian Bible translation and commentary (*Biur*) is indicative of the changing times in which he lived. When the *Biur* was first published in Berlin between 1780 and 1783, it was sharply condemned by a number of rabbinic authorities, including Benet's teacher, Ezekiel Landau. In 1785, Landau denounced Mendelssohn's translation because it was written in such a sophisticated German that Jewish children would have to spend "most of the day" learning German grammar—at the expense of Torah—just so they could understand it. As far as Landau was concerned, this not only was a waste of precious time but also constituted a perilous inversion of values: Instead of studying Torah for its own sake, students might end up studying Torah for the sake of learning German. As Landau put it, the Torah was at risk of becoming a mere "handmaiden" for the dissemination of German.[87]

In light of Landau's attitude toward the *Biur*, the following description of Benet may come initially as a surprise: "It is said about him," wrote Isaac Hirsch Weiss, "that he would read the Bible with the German translation of Moses ben Menaḥem [Mendelssohn] and the commentaries of the Biurists, and that he praised Naftali Herz Wessely's commentary on Leviticus in particular."[88] Moreover, wrote Weiss, "he encouraged his students to study . . . the Bible with Rashi and the *Biur*, and acquire other [secular] knowledge that was necessary at that time." Weiss's description echoes Ya'akov Avril Benet's biography of his father,[89] and more important, it is also confirmed by testimony from Mordecai Benet himself. The chief rabbi referred to Mendelssohn as the "wise German translator" (*he-ḥakham ha-metargem ashkenazi*) in his 1818 responsum against the Hamburg temple; in the same year, he also gave an approbation to a Viennese edition of the *Biur* (which also happened to include an additional commentary by Herz Homberg).[90] Benet's approbation was not overflowing with superlatives, nor did it mention Mendelssohn by name, but it lent his considerable rabbinic authority to the Mendelssohnian translation that had so rankled Landau more than thirty years earlier.

Mordecai Benet and Religious Reform in the Habsburg Monarchy

Two decades after Benet established his antireform credentials by helping to expose Saul Berlin's *Besamim Rosh* as a modern forgery and spearheading the effort to discredit Aron Chorin's lenient rulings regarding sturgeon, he vehemently condemned the Hamburg temple, denouncing organ music, liturgical reforms, and vernacular prayer in *Eleh divrei ha-brit*. All these battles were important milestones in the emergence of Orthodoxy, and through them Benet acquired great renown in the Central European rabbinic firmament, but none of these battles involved developments in Moravia or its immediate environs.[91]

It was in the 1820s that Benet confronted the initial stirrings of religious reform in his own bailiwick, first in nearby Vienna and then in the Moravian Jewish communities under his purview.

Religious reform in the Habsburg monarchy first took root in Vienna, home to a small yet wealthy Jewish population. Jews were officially prohibited from settling in Vienna until the Revolution of 1848; those who did live there were primarily large-scale businessmen, bankers, and manufacturers, who were "tolerated" along with their families and servants.[92] Vienna's Jewish community was rather atypical, not only because of the cumulative wealth of its members but also because it did not officially exist. The authorities forbade the Jews of Vienna to organize an official community, levy taxes on members, or hire a rabbi. Permission to hold public worship was only granted in 1811. Although tolerated in the imperial capital, the Jews of Vienna belonged (and paid taxes) to communities in Bohemia, Moravia, Lower Austria, and elsewhere. As Marsha Rozenblit has argued, "The absence of a traditional Jewish community, a *kehillah*, to enforce normative Jewish religious and social behavior certainly facilitated both growing Jewish religious indifference and the adoption of European culture."[93] It also provided an opening for religious reform.

In December 1819, a group of tolerated Jews petitioned the government to allow Hamburg-inspired reforms in Vienna.[94] Prima facie, this petition ought to have found favor in the eyes of Emperor Franz I, who decreed in the following month that all rabbis must be able to demonstrate basic philosophical knowledge and that prayers must be conducted in German or the language of the land. Nevertheless, the authorities did not allow the introduction of the proposed reforms, and even the decree regarding prayer in the vernacular was challenged by a number of leading rabbis—including Mordecai Benet and Samuel Landau—who argued that it was not sanctioned by Jewish tradition. Even though permission to introduce the proposed reforms was refused, in 1826 the authorities allowed Vienna's Jews to hire a rabbi (whose official title was religious teacher) and renovate their small, decrepit house of worship.

The Viennese Jews hired Isak Noa Mannheimer, a Danish-born rabbi and a highly skilled preacher who had trained at the Reform temples in Copenhagen, Berlin, Hamburg, and Leipzig before coming to the Habsburg capital. Although inclined toward more radical reforms, such as organ music, liturgical changes, and prayer in the vernacular, Mannheimer managed to strike a "golden mean" in Vienna, introducing aesthetic changes that raised the dignity of synagogue worship without violating Halakha. In the remodeled neoclassical synagogue on Seitenstettengasse, Mannheimer introduced a number of moderate reforms that came to be known as the Vienna Rite. These included a male choir, rules of decorum, moving the bimah up front, holding weddings indoors, and introducing an inspirational, edifying sermon in pure, refined German. These innovations were clearly inspired by Christian worship, which many Viennese Jews considered more "dignified" than the cacophonous and disorderly worship of the Jews. Unlike the reforms in Hamburg, however, these innovations could all be reconciled with the *Shulḥan Arukh*, the standard code of Jewish law.[95]

Scholars of the Reform movement have tried to explain the moderate character of the Vienna Rite, especially in light of Mannheimer's earlier predilection for more radical reforms.[96] The Catholic environment of the Habsburg monarchy was certainly a factor. Not only was prayer in the vernacular forbidden by Catholicism, but the legacy of the Counter-Reformation also made the Habsburg rulers inherently suspicious of religious reform, be it Christian or Jewish. Another factor was the traditionalism of Habsburg Jewry in the early nineteenth century. Even if the wealthy, acculturated Jews of Vienna increasingly looked to Berlin, Hamburg, and Copenhagen as models to be emulated, these tolerated Jews were still linked to the surrounding Jewish communities, especially in Hungary and Moravia, where talmudic learning was still entrenched and rabbinic authority was still largely intact.

According to tradition, Benet disapproved of the new reforms to such an extent that he went out of his way to avoid Seitenstettengasse (where the remodeled synagogue was located) when he was in Vienna.[97] Nevertheless, Mannheimer's biographer credits the chief rabbi's far-reaching authority for keeping the Vienna Rite relatively moderate. By virtue of the awe and respect that Benet inspired in Vienna and Moravia, Moses Rosenmann argues, "No community or rabbi dared to introduce 'new-fangled' deviations" so long as the chief rabbi was still alive.[98] His influence had limits, however. In 1829, shortly before his death, Benet recommended his son-in-law, Simon Markbreiter, for a rabbinic position in Vienna, perhaps in an effort to counter the reform tendencies of Mannheimer. Despite his intervention, the Jews of Vienna selected Elazar Horwitz (who was recommended by Moses Sofer) instead.[99]

In Vienna, Benet's recommendation was to no avail, but in Moravia he had other tools at his disposal. As Moravian chief rabbi, Benet had the exclusive authority to examine and certify rabbis, and anyone wishing to serve as rabbi in a Moravian Jewish community had to obtain his permission (*hatara*) first. Benet granted *hatarot* rather sparingly, and, reportedly, he even denied one to his own son, Ya'akov Avril.[100] In the 1820s, when one of his former pupils was invited to serve as rabbi (in two different Moravian Jewish communities), Benet did not hesitate to use the prerogatives of his office against him. Löw Schwab had studied in the Nikolsburg yeshiva for six years, but when he was invited to serve as rabbi in Gewitsch in 1824 and Eibenschitz in 1826, Benet grudgingly granted him a *hatara* for the former community and adamantly refused to grant one for the latter. By all accounts, Schwab was a highly skilled talmudist, but his early interest in German literature and profane knowledge made him highly suspect in the eyes of the chief rabbi. Benet had no way of knowing that Schwab would be the first to introduce the Vienna Rite to Moravia (in the 1830s), but his suspicions proved to be highly prescient.

Löw Schwab (1794–1857), who demonstrated prodigious talmudic skill in his native Mährisch-Kromau, studied at many of the leading yeshivas in Moravia and Hungary in the first decade of the nineteenth century.[101] In addition to Nikolsburg, where he studied with Moses Zilz and Mordecai Benet, Schwab studied with Moses Sofer in Pressburg, Joshua Horwitz in Trebitsch, and Chaim Josef Deutschmann in Gewitsch. As a child, Schwab had attended the local German-Jewish school, but he acquired his extensive knowledge of philosophy, mathematics, foreign languages, literature, and history primarily through self-study. Alongside works of medieval Jewish philosophy by Maimonides and Joseph Albo (in which Mordecai Benet himself was well versed), Schwab read Euclid, Mendelssohn, Lessing, and Kant and even tried his hand at poetry.[102] Around 1820, Schwab's modern proclivities aroused some suspicions in Gewitsch, leading a conservative faction to agitate against him. Schwab (and his Gewitsch-born wife) left for Prossnitz in 1821, where he worked as a teacher until the Gewitsch community called him back in 1824, inviting him to be their rabbi.

As was customary in Moravia, the invitation from the Gewitsch community was contingent upon a *hatara* from the chief rabbi. With the strong support of Chaim Deutschmann, Gewitsch's previous rabbi (now in Trebitsch), Schwab probably expected the *hatara* to be a mere formality, but Benet refused to even examine him, let alone grant him a *hatara*. A member of the Gewitsch community had apparently denounced Schwab to the chief rabbi, and Benet agreed to examine him only after Deutschmann's repeated intervention.[103] The eventual examination lasted several weeks, and Schwab's letter to a friend gives an indication of Benet's concerns.

> I was treated so toughly and racked with the most minute details that I wonder myself how I managed to pass. But even now [Benet] could not do away with me, since I managed to answer every one of his questions. Occasionally, after a lively discussion, he would be affectionate and speak so appreciatively and warmly with me that I thought I had emerged victorious. Then he would reflect for a moment, start up again with his suspicions and pounce with his fiery rage on those poor things: the German books. What could I do? Is it in my power to forget everything I have read and learned?[104]

After the examination, Benet allowed Schwab to assume the Gewitsch rabbinate, but he did not give him a written *hatara*. Consequently, when the larger Jewish community of Eibenschitz invited Schwab to be its rabbi in 1826, Schwab had to submit yet another request. This time, Benet flatly refused.

Remarkably, Schwab accepted Benet's decision and made no effort to circumvent his authority—despite prodding from members of the Eibenschitz Jewish community to do so. Although Schwab evinced disappointment in his Hebrew letter to Benet ("Why am I the only one you reject as unqualified?") and expressed deep anguish in his Judeo-German letter to the Eibenschitz Jewish community ("it truly hurts me"), he refused to appeal Benet's decision to a higher authority.[105] He could have petitioned the Gubernium, but he made it clear to the Eibenschitz community that he had no desire to "force his way into the *kehillah* in this manner." Five years later, when he came into a similar conflict with Nehemias Trebitsch, Benet's successor as chief rabbi, Schwab had no qualms about involving the Gubernium, but in 1826, he chose to respect and defend Benet's rabbinic authority. "I wanted to treat the great will of my teacher and master as a symbol of the Supreme Will," he wrote to the Eibenschitz community. It was all the more important to respect his decision, wrote Schwab, "especially in this wanton generation, in which ruiners of our vineyard have increased and multiplied" (*besonders ba-dor ha-paruts ha-ze asher yifru ve-yishratsu bo hamon mehablei karmeynu*).

Ironically, Benet's effort to keep Schwab out of the Eibenschitz rabbinate was only successful because Schwab still had respect for rabbinic authority in general and for his former teacher's authority in particular. Like Benet, Schwab was greatly disturbed by the religious laxity and growing indifference of "this wanton generation," and he feared that disregarding Benet's decision would only exacerbate the crisis of rabbinic authority. In this respect, Schwab was a decidedly conservative rabbinic figure who respected the dictates of Halakha and the importance of time-honored tradition. At this stage in his career, he was not so different from Naftali Benet, the chief rabbi's eldest son, who had written *Emunath Israel* in an effort to make the rabbinic tradition relevant and understandable to a new generation of young Jews.[106] In fact, Schwab even gave an approbation to this book (which appeared alongside Mordecai Benet's approbation in the 1832 edition).[107]

Schwab held Benet in such high esteem that he did not dare to introduce religious reforms during his teacher's lifetime. Only after Benet's death did Schwab emerge as a religious reformer, but even then he remained in the mold of such moderate reformers as Mannheimer, whose largely aesthetic reforms could be reconciled with the *Shulhan Arukh*.[108] As rabbi of Prossnitz (1831–1836), Schwab was the first to introduce decorous worship, German-language sermons, and indoor wedding ceremonies to Moravia. Later, as rabbi of Pest (1836–1857), he promoted similar kinds of reforms, and when the Pest Reform Society (1848–1853) got out of hand, he showed his more conservative colors by doing his utmost to ensure that radical religious reform did not penetrate into Hungary.[109]

The Moravian Haskalah

Ultra-Orthodox historiography tends to conflate Haskalah and Reform, viewing both of them as nihilistic movements seeking to uproot traditional Jewish practice and belief. In keeping with this tendency, a recent publication has praised Mordecai Benet as an inveterate enemy of both movements, even though nineteenth-century writers consistently portrayed him as highly sympathetic to the moderate Haskalah.[110] Benet never espoused the core maskilic ideology that viewed secular knowledge as an end unto itself, but he did share the Haskalah's deep appreciation for certain kinds of extratalmudic knowledge, such as medieval Jewish philosophy, biblical grammar, and refined Hebrew prose. In addition, he cautiously embraced Mendelssohn's writings and even recognized the desirability of learning the German language. Benet was not a *maskil*, but Moravia's rabbinic culture was rooted and secure enough during his tenure as chief rabbi that he could embrace "the winds of knowledge and wisdom [that] blew in from Germany," without dismissing them as a mortal threat to traditional Jewish practice and belief.[111]

The Haskalah flourished in Moravia in the 1820s, 1830s, and 1840s, a full generation after the Berlin Haskalah, never assuming the radical character of its German counterpart. Far from being a poor imitation of the Berlin Haskalah, one could argue that the Moravian Haskalah embodied the true spirit of Mendelssohn, because it managed to strike a balance between Jewish tradition and European rationalism, treating the cross-fertilization as mutually beneficial. Moravia's *maskilim* had little direct contact with Berlin, so their encounters with the Haskalah were mediated by Prague and Vienna, both of which played important roles in the dissemination (and moderation) of maskilic ideas in the Habsburg monarchy.

In Prague, where many Jews had strong ties to Berlin, the Haskalah found fertile ground in the 1780s. The Prague Haskalah, however, never took the radical turn of the Berlin Haskalah, and it remained highly respectful of rabbinic authority. This was best exemplified by Baruch Jeiteles (1762–1813), scion of a prominent Prague Jewish family, who was not only the "undisputed leader" of the Prague Haskalah but also head of one of Prague's yeshivas.[112] When the journal *Ha-me'asef* displayed "mocking disrespect" for Ezekiel Landau (as mentioned earlier), it was Baruch Jeiteles who came to the defense of his former teacher, bitterly attacking the main organ of the Berlin Haskalah for its hostility to Jewish law and tradition. Jeiteles also found a kindred spirit in Landau's youngest son, Israel Landau (1758–1829), who published typical maskilic fare (Hebrew philology, geography) as well as more traditional works on halakhic education.[113]

According to Ruth Kestenberg-Gladstein, the Prague Haskalah had a distinctly "national" character, which was conspicuously absent from its Berlin counterpart. Whereas *maskilim* in Berlin tried to downplay or eliminate Judaism's national components, *maskilim* in Prague—especially those surrounding Baruch Jeiteles—proudly portrayed the Jews as a "nation" (*'am, uma, le'um*) and even referred to the Land of Israel as their "homeland" (*moledet*).[114] Kestenberg-Gladstein speculates that the multinational character of the Habsburg monarchy made it easier for Jews to identify themselves as one nation among many. Like the late eighteenth-century Czech national awakeners, Prague's *maskilim* could celebrate the cultural, historical, and linguistic attributes of Jewish life without making demands that would upset the political status quo.[115] Not surprisingly, Hebrew held a place of pride in the Prague Haskalah, but so too did Yiddish (or Judeo-German), which Israel Landau praised as "my language."[116] (He did not disparage it as a corrupt and useless jargon, unlike many of his Berlin counterparts.)

Prague's *maskilim* published a short-lived Judeo-German journal in 1802, but Vienna was the real center of maskilic publishing in the Habsburg monarchy from 1820 onward. The primary significance of Vienna, which did not have a homegrown Haskalah movement, was its role as a disseminator of maskilic literature. As Bernhard Wachstein has noted, Vienna's first maskilic journal, *Bikkurei ha-'Ittim* (First fruits of the times, 1820–1831), was published in the imperial capital, but it was neither produced nor consumed there.[117] A similar observation could be made about its successor, *Kerem Ḥemed* (Vineyard of delight, 1833–1856), which—despite being published in Vienna—is generally viewed as "the Hebrew annual of the Galician [sic!] Haskalah."[118] Both journals were founded by Galician Jews, and they counted many Galician Jews among their contributors and readers. They also counted a few Bohemian contributors, such as Judah Jeiteles (Baruch's younger brother), Ephraim Wehli, and Wolf Mayer from Prague, and many more Moravian contributors, such as Josef Bergl and Josef Weisse from Prossnitz, Josef Flesch and Heimroth Flesch from Neu-Rausnitz, Mordecai Lichtenstern and Hirschel Duschak from Triesch, and even Naftali Benet from Schaffa.

If *Kerem Ḥemed* was "the Hebrew annual of the Galician Haskalah," then its successor, *Kokhevei Yitsḥak* (Stars of Isaac, 1845–1848, 1850–1873), could just as well be called the Hebrew annual of the Moravian Haskalah. Although its editor, Max Emanuel Stern, came from Pressburg, Hungary, and its contributors hailed from all corners of the Habsburg monarchy, nearly half the articles published between 1845 and 1848 were written by Moravian Jews.[119] These Moravian Jews, who contributed original Hebrew poems, Hebrew translations of German poems, and a wide range of philological, philosophical, historical, and exegetical studies, generally came of age in the 1820s and 1830s. They acquired secular knowledge in Moravia's German-Jewish schools, and most received a traditional Jewish education in the yeshivas of Moravia (Nikolsburg, Prossnitz, Trebitsch, Triesch, Boskowitz, Eibenschitz) or Hungary (Pressburg, Eisenstadt). Nearly all tried their hand at Hebrew poetry, with varying degrees of success. One poem, "Prayer for the Hebrew Language," was certainly no masterpiece, but as a paean to the "mother of all tongues," it expressed a sentiment that ran through the pages of *Kokhevei Yitsḥak* (as well as *Bikkurei ha-ʿIttim* and *Kerem Ḥemed*).[120] This could be seen in the Hebrew correspondence between Gideon Brecher (1797–1873) and Samuel David Luzzatto, in the Hebrew poems written by Eleasar Schnabel (1815–1876), in the talmudic and philological studies by Abraham Schmiedl (1821–1914), and in the Hebrew eulogy for Archduke Carl of Austria (Emperor Franz II's younger brother) composed by Ahron Ehrentheil (1823–1888)—all of which appeared in the pages of *Kokhevei Yitsḥak*.[121]

Gideon Brecher, Eleasar Schnabel, Abraham Schmiedl, and Ahron Ehrentheil were all natives of Prossnitz, which is not surprising, because Prossnitz "served as a center of the Haskalah in Moravia."[122] Prossnitz was *a* center (not *the* center) of the Haskalah because, in contrast to

Bohemia (where the Haskalah was concentrated in Prague), there were several centers of the Haskalah in Moravia—including Neu-Rausnitz, Trebitsch, and Triesch. Prossnitz was the most important center, but Neu-Rausnitz produced Josef Flesch, the "father of the Moravian [Jewish] enlightenment"; Trebitsch was home to Chaim Josef Pollak, *Kokhevei Yitshak*'s most prolific contributor; and Triesch had so many *maskilim* that it was known as Little Berlin.

Josef Flesch (1781–1839) illustrates how the Moravian Haskalah was mediated through Prague and Vienna. Born in Neu-Rausnitz, Moravia's seventh largest Jewish community, Flesch lived in Prague from 1797 to 1801, where he attended yeshiva with his father's childhood friend, Baruch Jeiteles, the central figure in the Prague Haskalah. Upon his return to Moravia in 1801, Flesch spent three years in Leipnik before finally settling down in his native town and becoming a partner in his father's business. In Neu-Rausnitz, he devoted his free time to biblical exegesis, Greek and Latin, classical philosophy, and Hebrew grammar and prose, all the while maintaining links with his fellow *maskilim* in Vienna and Prague. In the 1820s and 1830s, he contributed Hebrew essays and poems to *Bikkurei ha-'Ittim*, and in 1838 he contributed a list of Hebrew exegetes and grammarians to the modern Bible commentary published in Prague by Ezekiel Landau's grandson, Moses Israel Landau.

Flesch's contributions to *Bikkurei ha-'Ittim* included Hebrew riddles and etymologies and a translation of the Kantian philosopher Karl Heinrich Heydenreich into Hebrew, but his most important contribution to the Haskalah was his translation of the writings of Philo Judaeus from Greek into Hebrew.[123] Jewish philosophy held particular appeal for the early *maskilim*, particularly the works of medieval Jewish philosophers such as Maimonides and Judah Halevi. These works, which had been translated from Arabic into Hebrew in the twelfth century, often served as philosophical primers for Jews who were unfamiliar with non-Jewish languages. Philo's works, in contrast, had never been fully translated into Hebrew, even though the sixteenth-century Italian Jewish scholar Azariah de Rossi did translate some sections in his work of critical scholarship, *Me'or 'Enayim* (Light of the eyes). Although Philo's works had been preserved by the church fathers and had been translated into Latin and other European languages, they had remained cut off from the Jewish exegetical and philosophical chain of tradition. Thus, by Hebraicizing Philo, Flesch helped reclaim him for the pantheon of Jewish philosophers and made Greek philosophy—in its Jewish guise—accessible to a new generation of Jews. As Leopold Löw recalled, Flesch's translations had a stimulating effect on yeshiva students in Bohemia and Moravia and even inspired them to engage in serious academic study.[124]

Flesch's translations were certainly read in Prossnitz, which emerged in the 1820s and 1830s as the most important center of the Moravian Haskalah. Gershom Scholem took particular interest in Prossnitz, because, more than any other Jewish community in Europe, it seemed to support his argument for a nexus between Sabbatianism and Haskalah. "It is certainly no accident," he wrote, "that a city like Prossnitz, which served as a center for Haskalah in Moravia . . . was also a bastion of Sabbatianism in that country."[125] According to Scholem, Sabbatianism had "completely destroyed" the world of rabbinic Judaism from within, making former Sabbatian bastions—like Prossnitz—all the more susceptible to the allure of Haskalah. Leopold Löw, who taught in Prossnitz in the 1830s, expressed a similar theory, but the kind of "subterranean" links proposed by Scholem (and Löw) are almost impossible to substantiate.[126] None of the *maskilim* in Prossnitz had a known Sabbatian (or Frankist) lineage, and many of the identifiable Sabbatian families had left Judaism altogether.[127] Furthermore, Scholem's theory does not explain why Holleschau and Kojetein—which were also bastions of Sabbatianism in the eighteenth century—played no significant role in the Moravian Haskalah.

The reasons for Prossnitz's centrality in the Moravian Haskalah are more mundane. Prossnitz—Moravia's second largest Jewish community and a venerable center of rabbinic learning—was also Moravia's wealthiest Jewish community and the hub of Moravia's thriving textile industry in the first half of the nineteenth century. The financial pillar of the community was the Bohemian-born Veit (Feish) Ehrenstamm, an army purveyor who supplied salt, tobacco, wine, grain, carts, horses, and especially uniforms to the Habsburg troops during the Napoleonic Wars. (In 1812, he supplied the army's entire uniform quota.)[128] With his prodigious wealth, Ehrenstamm gave generously to the educational and religious institutions in Prossnitz, donating a new building for the Jewish school (*talmud torah*) in 1820 and endowing a school fund for the religious education of Prossnitz's poorest Jewish children. Ehrenstamm also built himself a private library with well over 200 Hebrew and Aramaic books, comprising more than 500 separate volumes. Perhaps the largest collection of Jewish books in Moravia, Ehrenstamm's library was largely made up of traditional rabbinic literature, but there were also fifteen books on Hebrew grammar, thirteen books on ethics, philosophy, geography, and astronomy, and three volumes of the maskilic journal *Bikkurei ha-'Ittim*.[129] In short, it was a model library of the rabbinic Haskalah.

Alongside Prossnitz's pillar of wealth stood its pillar of learning: Moses Katz Wanefried, a student of Moses Sofer, who headed Prossnitz's celebrated yeshiva from the late 1810s until his death from cholera in 1850.[130] Wanefried was wealthy in his own right, but it was his "glistening brilliance" as a talmudist that attracted students from all over Bohemia, Moravia, Hungary, and Poland.[131] One of these students described Wanefried as "exceeding all other [Prossnitz Jews] in erudition," noting that "students streamed to his lectures from near and far."[132] More important, however, the students who flocked to Wanefried's yeshiva found an environment that was particularly open to secular studies. According to the same student, Wanefried's yeshiva "differed favorably from all other yeshivas" in that "students were allowed to occupy themselves with other disciplines in addition to Talmud."[133]

In addition to Ehrenstamm's library, Prossnitz provided other opportunities for yeshiva students to expose themselves to extratalmudic knowledge. In the 1820s and early 1830s, the home of Jacob Steinschneider (1782–1856), in particular, served as a meeting point for enlightened Jews who wholeheartedly embraced Hebrew language and literature. Steinschneider was a native of Prossnitz, and like Josef Flesch of Neu-Rausnitz, he spent time in Prague around 1800. While there, he studied Talmud (possibly at Baruch Jeiteles's yeshiva) and made an effort to acquire a secular education.[134] Back in Prossnitz, Steinschneider's home attracted like-minded Jews, such as his brother-in-law, Gideon Brecher (1797–1873), a student of Mordecai Benet who had worked as a private teacher in Flesch's Neu-Rausnitz and then studied medicine

in Pest before returning to Prossnitz to work as a medical doctor in the
Jewish community.[135] By the mid-1830s, Brecher's home (which happened to be near Wanefried's yeshiva) took the place of Steinschneider's,
offering yeshiva students and members of the Jewish community a place
to cultivate Hebrew literature, read the newly established German-
Jewish newspapers (such as the *Allgemeine Zeitung des Judenthums*), and
study classical and modern languages.[136]

With Ehrenstamm's prodigious wealth, Wanefried's celebrated yeshiva, and Steinschneider and Brecher's devoted circle of Hebraists,
Prossnitz served as a veritable incubator for Hebrew literature and Jewish scholarship in the 1820s, 1830s, and 1840s. A remarkable number of
Jews who passed through Prossnitz in these decades went on to become
leading figures in the religious, scholarly, and educational firmament of
Central European Jewry (especially in Hungary). Löw Schwab (1794–
1857) taught Veit Ehrenstamm's children in the early 1820s and served as
rabbi of Prossnitz (1831–1836) before being elected rabbi of Pest, Hungary. His son-in-law, Leopold Löw (1811–1875), taught in Prossnitz's
talmud torah (1830–1835) before becoming rabbi in various Hungarian
Jewish communities (Nagykanizsa, Pápa, and Szeged); Löw published
the scholarly journal *Ben Chananja* (Szeged, 1858–1867) and emerged
as the central figure in the Hungarian Wissenschaft des Judentums
(Science of Judaism) movement. Hirsch B. Fassel (1802–1883) served
as rabbi of Prossnitz from 1836 to 1851 before being elected rabbi of
Nagykanizsa, Hungary (where Löw had served before him); a prolific
writer, Fassel published widely on Jewish philosophy and law. While
still in Prossnitz, Fassel ordained Moritz Steinschneider (1816–1907),
Jacob Steinschneider's son and Gideon Brecher's nephew, who went
on to become a leading orientalist in Berlin and the father of modern
Hebrew bibliography. Adolf Jellinek (1821–1893), who attended Wanefried's yeshiva in the 1830s, became a celebrated preacher in Leipzig and
Vienna and a trailblazing scholar of Jewish mysticism. Moritz Eisler
(1823–1902), who attended Wanefried's yeshiva with Jellinek, became
director of the German-Jewish school in Nikolsburg and published a
multivolume work on medieval Jewish philosophy. Josef Weisse (1812–
1897) studied with Steinschneider in Prossnitz and Prague, taught at
Prossnitz's German-Jewish school (1838–1842), and contributed to

Kerem Ḥemed, Kokhevei Yitsḥak, and Moses Israel Landau's modern Bible commentary; as rabbi of Waag-Neustadtl (Vágújhely), Hungary, from 1855 to 1897, he also left his mark as an educational reformer.

Intertwined and often interrelated, this extraordinary constellation of Jewish scholars crystallized around Gideon Brecher, and many of them contributed in some way or another to Brecher's Hebrew commentary on Judah Halevi's *Book of the Kuzari.* Published by Moses Israel Landau in 1838–1840, Brecher's commentary was the apotheosis of the Moravian Haskalah, and as such merits closer examination.[137] The *Kuzari,* a twelfth-century philosophical treatise and apologia for Judaism, was a favorite work of the early *maskilim,* in part because it explored "questions of the relationship between Judaism and philosophical reasoning."[138] Like his maskilic predecessors, Brecher was drawn to the *Kuzari* because it attempted to harmonize Western philosophy and rabbinic Judaism, two traditions that were often considered at odds with one another. The *Kuzari* also harked back to the somewhat idealized golden age of Spanish Jewry, when Jews actively participated in the cultural life of their surroundings without sacrificing their religious faith and observance.[139]

Like the Moravian Haskalah in general, Brecher's work was firmly rooted in Jewish tradition. First of all, he chose the well-established genre of commentary to express his own ideas. By writing glosses to Judah Halevi's text, Brecher placed himself in a Jewish exegetical tradition extending deep into the Middle Ages. Second, he chose to write his commentary in Hebrew, even though German had a richer and more precise philosophical vocabulary. Thus, like many of the early *maskilim,* he attempted to renew Hebrew as a medium for philosophical and scientific inquiry. He even coined numerous neologisms for philosophical concepts that did not yet exist in Hebrew. Furthermore, his choice of Hebrew was especially appropriate for this particular commentary. Although Halevi originally wrote the *Kuzari* in Arabic, his medieval apologia for Judaism was an effusive paean to the Hebrew language.

The *Kuzari* offers a "strongly ethnocentric version of Judaism," so it should come as no surprise that Brecher's commentary has an unmistakably "national" character (in Kestenberg-Gladstein's sense of the term).[140] In the original text, Halevi stresses the sacred nature of Hebrew as the language of revelation, and Brecher takes the opportunity to reflect on the present condition of the Jews, whom he refers to as "the Israelite nation" (*uma ha-yisraelit*).[141] According to Brecher, the moral and intellectual condition of a given nation (*ha-uma*) is reflected in the state of its language (*leshon kol 'am*); as the "achievements and successes" (*gedolot ve-hatslaḥot*) of that nation increase, so too does the state of its language. As Brecher explains, the versatility of the Hebrew language diminished over time because "our thoughts" were unworthy of such a sublime language; "our thoughts demean the purity of the language," he writes, and consequently foreign words had to be imported to "sweeten our thoughts and reveal our secrets." Brecher explains that the language lacks "words for sciences and arts," a point that is indirectly strengthened by his decision to translate this very expression into German (*Kunstrausdrücke*) and Latin (*termini technici*).[142] By coining this expression—and many others—Brecher was doing his part to revive Hebrew as a language of "sciences and arts" and thereby restore "the Israelite nation" to its proper glory. One contemporary was quite pleased with the result, noting that Brecher's commentary was written in an "easily comprehensible, fluent Hebrew."[143]

The "national" character of Brecher's work was determined, in part, by its subject matter. Many *maskilim* were drawn to philosophy because of its universal truths, but the appeal of Judah Halevi's *Kuzari* was often rooted in its distinctly "national" philosophy of religion. An early reviewer of Brecher's *Kuzari* commentary observed that "the philosophical systems of all peoples" (*die philosophischen Systeme aller Völker*) are "the product of national characters" (*das Produkt der National-charaktere*), and he lavished praise on the *Kuzari* as the quintessential expression of the Jews' national character. "Of all . . . Jewish philosophical works," he observed, "none is as truly national [*ächt national*]; none is more suited to the spirit of Judaism [*dem Geiste des Judenthums*] in all of its nuances—political, national, autonomous; none is as fruitful for the scientific development of the Jewish faith" as Judah Halevi's *Kuzari*, which had just been published in a new edition by Gideon Brecher.[144] Similar sentiments were expressed by Rabbi Chaim Josef Pollak of Trebitsch, whose rabbinic approbation extolled the new publication for its ability to show "the youth of our nation" (*tse'irei b'nei ameynu*) that "Israel is not an orphan" in the field of philosophy.[145]

The *Kuzari* commentary was the fruit of Brecher's pen, but it also illustrates the extent to which the Moravian Haskalah was a collaborative and highly intertwined project. In Prossnitz, Brecher could avail himself of Veit Ehrenstamm's copy of the *Kuzari* and could also discuss his own work-in-progress with Rabbi Hirsch Fassel (who contributed an approbation to Volume 2 of the *Kuzari* commentary), Josef Weisse (who contributed a critical essay to Volume 4), and Baruch Schönfeld and Efraim Yisrael Blücher, two young *maskilim* who contributed Hebrew poems to Volume 1. Brecher's nephew, Moritz Steinschneider, was also an important resource. A student at Leipzig University in 1839, Moritz could visit the local libraries on his uncle's behalf and promote Brecher's commentary in the *Allgemeine Zeitung des Judenthums* and *Der Orient*, two German-Jewish weeklies that had recently been founded in Leipzig.[146] Brecher corresponded with Rabbi Löw Schwab, who had left Prossnitz for Pest in 1831, and had an epistolary discussion about the *Kuzari* with Samuel David Luzzatto, an Italian *maskil* in Padua.[147] One of Luzzatto's letters was published in Volume 2 of Brecher's commentary, and part of their correspondence was published in *Kokhevei Yitshak* in 1846.[148] Not surprisingly, even the publication of the Luzzatto-Brecher letters had a strong Moravian connection. Max Emanuel Stern, the editor of *Kokhevei Yitshak*, who had briefly been a teacher in Triesch, thanked "our good friend" Moritz Steinschneider for providing the correspondence.[149] Stern published many exegetical studies by Chaim Josef Pollak, rabbi of Trebitsch (near Triesch), who had written an approbation for Brecher's *Kuzari* commentary. Pollak himself was a Moravian *maskil* par excellence: In addition to leading a celebrated yeshiva, he was also *Kokhevei Yitshak*'s most prolific contributor.

Pollak's approbation for Brecher's commentary captures the essence of the Moravian Haskalah. Composed in sophisticated Hebrew verse and drawing on the rich language and imagery of the Bible, Midrash, and posttalmudic literature, Pollak's approbation affirms the place of scientific inquiry in the Jewish tradition yet emphasizes that "the fear [of God]" and "the true faith" remain the ultimate goal.

> Just as an eagle soars above the other winged creatures,
> [Our sages] rise above their peers,

Placing nothing but the fear [of God] and the true faith as the aim of
   their inquiry,
Casting away foolish views like an affliction,
Distancing them from the inheritance of God,
By means of conclusive proofs and rational syllogisms,
Built upon the foundations of truth and the fundamentals of human
   intellect.[150]

Here, Pollak uses images from the book of Proverbs ("winged crea-
tures") and the book of Isaiah ("casting away . . . like an affliction")
as well as theological terminology from Maimonides' *Guide to the Perplexed* ("the true faith") and philosophical terminology from Judah
Halevi's *Kuzari* ("foolish views").[151] For him, both divine revelation
and medieval Jewish philosophy constituted sources of authority,
woven seamlessly together in a unified Jewish canon. The fact that the
Guide and the *Kuzari* were originally written in Arabic was of little importance. Translated into Hebrew in the twelfth century, these works
had become the core of a Jewish philosophical tradition, providing legitimacy—and Hebrew terminology—for the moderate Haskalah.

Benet—who had given Pollak a *hatara* in 1828—also served as a source
of legitimacy for the moderate Haskalah.[152] During his lifetime, Benet
gave rabbinic approbations to a number of maskilic works, including
Homberg's *Bne Zion* and Mendelssohn's *Biur*, but his eulogizers and
biographers paid special attention to his apparent fondness for medieval Jewish philosophy and his devotion to Hebrew language and grammar.[153] A lengthy footnote to Judah Jeiteles's Hebrew eulogy for Benet
listed the *Guide to the Perplexed* and the *Kuzari* among the works that
the late chief rabbi knew so well that he could recite them by heart (*'ad
she'yada otam l'vate b'sefatam mila be'mila*). After praising Benet's knowledge of Hebrew grammar, Jeiteles's footnote reached a dramatic flourish,
declaring: "What a magnificent vision for our generations: that Torah,
secular knowledge, and Hebrew grammar shall be as one in the hand of
he who serves in holiness."[154] These words, composed on the occasion of
Benet's death, could have served as a slogan for the Moravian Haskalah.

Jeiteles's words were quoted approvingly by Ya'akov Avril Benet
in his Hebrew biography of his father, which appeared in 1832.[155] According to Ya'akov Avril, the chief rabbi considered "practical sciences"

(*ḥokhmot shimushiyot u-madaʾim*) to be the crowning glory of the "polymath" (*ḥakham kolel*), and he consequently devoted "no small amount of time" to the study of philosophy, astronomy, arithmetic, geometry, grammar, and other extratalmudic fields of knowledge (including Kabbalah). Yaʾakov Avril expressed his father's positive attitude toward these fields of knowledge by putting a twist on a familiar biblical verse. In the original (Genesis 2:18), God declares, just before creating woman, that "it is not good for man to be alone; I will make him a helper suited for him." In Yaʾakov Avril's biography, however, the first half of this verse is placed in the mouth of Mordecai Benet, who adds a radically different ending: "It is not good for man to be alone with [nothing but] the wisdom of the Torah." Here, the chief rabbi goes on to praise other founts of knowledge by quoting—and simultaneously subverting—additional verses from the biblical story of Creation:

> I dwelled in the Garden of Eden in primordial times,
> Immersed in Torah [*daʾat torah*] and Knowledge [*daʾat nota*];
> I ate from the Tree of Life, and I lived in the Eternal World
> I also ate from the fruit of the Tree of Knowledge [*ets daʾat neḥmad*]
> To become enlightened [*l'haskil*] and to become better [*l'hiyatev*];
> And my eyes were also illuminated by the rest of the exalted wisdom
>   and knowledge [*ḥokhmot u-yediʾot ramot*].[156]

Mordecai Benet never said these words, but they reflect the late chief rabbi's general attitude toward extratalmudic knowledge, as recalled by his students and contemporaries. During Benet's lifetime, a network of German-Jewish schools and a thriving constellation of yeshivas coexisted in relative harmony, and the Moravian Haskalah drew inspiration from both sources. Like Adam's Eve, secular knowledge was viewed as a "suitable helper," a source of wisdom that would complement the Torah without threatening to uproot or supplant it. This was, in part, because traditional rabbinic culture was still sufficiently rooted and secure in Moravia for secular knowledge to remain a "handmaiden" to the Torah, and not vice versa (as Ezekiel Landau feared after the publication of Mendelssohn's *Biur*).

Mordecai Benet embodied the harmonious coexistence of traditional and secular knowledge, the golden mean that characterized Moravian

Jewry in the late eighteenth and early nineteenth centuries. The chief rabbi passed away on August 12, 1829, while taking a cure in Carlsbad, Bohemia. In the words of Abraham Trebitsch, "The sun set at the end of the summer, and fear and darkness fell on the House of Israel, particularly the people of Nikolsburg." In the (unpublished) second part of *Korot ha-'Ittim*, Trebitsch lamented the passing of Benet, the "faithful shepherd" (*ro'e ne'eman*), who had "erected a [protective] fence [around the Torah] and stood in the breach," the "polymath" (*ḥakham ha-kolel*) whose fame, like that of his biblical namesake, "went forth throughout all the lands" (Esther 9:4).[157]

Trebitsch also described the exhumation of Mordecai Benet from the cemetery in Lichtenstadt (near Carlsbad) and his reburial in the Nikolsburg cemetery on March 7, 1830. The Lichtenstadt Jewish community had been reluctant to give up Benet, insisting that "the tree must remain where it falls," but the Jews of Nikolsburg persisted in their efforts to bring their shepherd back to the community he had served for forty years. Rabbi Moses Sofer of Pressburg wrote a lengthy responsum permitting Benet's exhumation, and Count Dietrichstein of Nikolsburg intervened with the Bohemian Gubernium on the Nikolsburg Jewish community's behalf. Benet's corpse had been buried in the Lichtenstadt cemetery for almost seven months, but when it was finally removed, "there was no stink or stench," according to Trebitsch, "[because] holy flesh does not stink."[158] Trebitsch presumably took these details from Naftali Benet's published eulogy, which also described the great excitement that accompanied the reburial of his late father. According to Naftali, young and old arrived in great numbers from Nikolsburg and the surrounding Jewish communities to bid farewell to "their faithful shepherd, who had left them."[159]

Three

Nehemias Trebitsch and the Decline of the Moravian Chief Rabbinate, 1832–1842

> We are well aware of the respect we owe the dead. We take to heart the teachings of our sages: to treat the name and reputation of the deceased with leniency; therefore, we will only momentarily touch upon the failings, which had a decidedly detrimental impact on the Chief Rabbi's official activity, embroiling many Moravian Jewish communities in objectionable lawsuits and disputes.
>
> *Allgemeine Zeitung des Judenthums*, November 5, 1842

With an almost palpable sigh of relief, the *Allgemeine Zeitung des Judenthums* reported the death of Rabbi Nehemias (Naḥum) Trebitsch in 1842, just ten years after he had succeeded Mordecai Benet as chief rabbi of Moravia and Austrian Silesia. Like Benet, Trebitsch met his death after taking a summer cure in Carlsbad, Bohemia, but the impact of these two deaths could not have been more different. The Nikolsburg Jewish community took painstaking efforts to have Benet disinterred from the Jewish cemetery in Lichtenstadt (near Carlsbad) so that he could be laid to rest in the community he had lovingly served for forty years. No such effort was mounted to bring the deceased Nehemias Trebitsch back to Nikolsburg; instead, the late chief rabbi was buried in his native Prague, far from the province where—in the words of another obituary—"his strict and loveless hostility towards all innovation made him many enemies."[1]

A string of bitter and protracted conflicts during Trebitsch's tenure as chief rabbi (1832–1842) "made him many enemies" among the Jewish population in Moravia. For the most part, these conflicts were initiated by Trebitsch, who sought to use his authority to keep reform-minded rabbis out of the fifty-two Jewish communities under his purview. From the beginning of his tenure as chief rabbi, Trebitsch (Figure 7) continuously tried to shore up his authority over the religious and educational affairs of Moravian Jewry, but his attempts repeatedly backfired. His many "improprieties" riled the Moravian-Silesian Gubernium, especially after his detractors succeeded in portraying him—somewhat disingenuously—as an "enemy of German language and literature." As a result, he was stripped of or denied a number of prerogatives regarding the appointment and certification of communal rabbis and religious teachers. During Trebitsch's ten years in Nikolsburg, these prerogatives devolved—de facto if not de jure—to Moravia's individual Jewish communities. In the case of rabbinic elections, the Gubernium repeatedly resolved disputes so that the "will of the community" took precedence over the will of the chief rabbi. In the case of Jewish education, the chief rabbi was repeatedly denied the exclusive authority to examine and approve religious teachers. When community religious schools were set up in the late 1830s, Trebitsch had little influence beyond the confines of his own community.

Born in Prague on August 14, 1779, Trebitsch spent his first forty-seven years in the Bohemian capital, where he acquired a reputation as a talmudic scholar of first rank. Son of the prayer-leader at Prague's Altneuschul (Old-New Synagogue), Trebitsch received his first instruction in Bible and Talmud at the community-supported *talmud torah* school for indigent children. After his father's death, the young Nehemias was brought up in the house of Rabbi Jacob Günsburg, one of the leading talmudists in Prague. Günsburg sat on Prague's rabbinic court and headed one of Prague's yeshivas for nearly forty years. Trebitsch, one of Günsburg's "most distinguished and beloved students," was ordained by him in 1811 and began conducting Talmud lessons at his yeshiva in the same year.[2] In 1813, Trebitsch was appointed rabbi at Prague's Klausen Synagogue and became a state-approved Talmud teacher in 1823.

Trebitsch's relationship with Mordecai Benet proved decisive for the rest of his rabbinic career. In 1816, Benet bestowed upon Trebitsch the title of *morenu* (our teacher), which allowed him to make halakhic decisions, and described him as "one of the most brilliant, laudable, and learned students of religious jurisprudence."[3] Benet himself admired Trebitsch's "extensive talmudic erudition and extraordinary genius and

RABBI NEHEMIAS TREBITSCH,

k. k. mähr. schles. Oberlandesrabbiner,

geb. am 14. Aug. 1779, gest. am 4. Juli 1842 in Prag.

חכמת אדם תאיר פניו . הי חסיד וחי עניו

צורת הרב הגאון מופת הדור . דישׂכׇּה כמׇהׄרׄרׄ נחום טריביטש זצ׳׳לׄלׄה

מקׇק פראג . רב דׇקׇק נׄשׄ ומדינות מעהרין ושלעזיען . בעהׇלׇמֺה ספֺרֺי שׄלׄוׄם

ירושלים על חירושלמי וקובץ על יד על הרמב׳׳ם .

Figure 7. Nehemias Trebitsch, Moravian-Silesian chief rabbi, 1832–1842.
Courtesy of Jewish Museum in Prague, inv. č. 63124.

sagacity" and expressed a desire to have him close to Nikolsburg.[4] When the Prossnitz community elected a rabbi in September 1825, Benet used his influence to ensure that Trebitsch was their first choice. In March 1826, Trebitsch left Prague, accompanied by "a large crowd of friends and admirers," and was welcomed as the new rabbi in Prossnitz "with particular honor and great distinction."[5]

Trebitsch's rabbinic stature was enhanced by his association with Benet, but his predecessor's specter proved almost impossible to escape after Trebitsch was installed as Moravian chief rabbi in 1832. As Isaac Hirsch Weiss, one of Trebitsch's students in Nikolsburg, observed in his memoirs, "It is no wonder that there were people in the community who could not transfer their love for the deceased rabbi to the living rabbi, for his memory was still alive in their souls." As Weiss recalled, comparisons between the two rabbis were unavoidable, with Trebitsch always on the losing side. One of Benet's former students even disparaged Trebitsch's talmudic knowledge with the following wisecrack: "Our teacher, Rabbi Mordecai received the tablets directly from God, whereas Rabbi Naḥum was nourished merely by their scraps [*nit'asher min ha-pesolet she-ba-luḥot*]."[6] Trebitsch was well aware of the difficulties inherent in succeeding a rabbinic luminary of Benet's stature. In accepting the invitation to become Nikolsburg's communal rabbi, Trebitsch humbled himself before his deceased predecessor, asking, "Who could possibly succeed the king? [Who could possibly] fill his shoes? Who am I that you have placed this authority on my shoulders, elevating me to a higher plane, to the exalted throne sanctified by him?"[7] In subsequent years, these same questions would be asked by Trebitsch's many detractors—with the rhetorical politeness conspicuously absent, however. As a traveler later observed, Trebitsch "possesses the knowledge of his predecessor, but of [Benet's] exquisite character, he does not possess particularly much."[8]

When Trebitsch was elected Moravian chief rabbi in 1830, Benet's specter was already discernible. Trebitsch's only serious challenge came from Isaias Benet, Mordecai Benet's second-born son, and the communal rabbi of Misslitz since 1823.[9] Although the chief rabbinate had never been an inherited office, Isaias asserted a dynastic right to his father's position. Mordecai Benet had made such a deep and lasting impression during his forty-year tenure that the claims of his 38-year-old son found resonance in the ears of the six rabbinic electors. The electors, rabbis from each of Moravia's six administrative districts, convened in Brünn on December 22, 1830, to choose the new chief rabbi.[10] Each elector chose three candidates, ranking them in order of preference. Trebitsch received five *primo* votes and one *secundo* vote, and Isaias Benet received one *primo* vote and five *secundo* votes. As the son of the late chief rabbi, Isaias overshadowed other, more renowned Moravian talmudists, such as Joseph Feilbogen, Bernard Oppenheim, and Abraham Bäck, who received two *tertio* votes each.[11]

Before Trebitsch could be installed as chief rabbi, his election had to be confirmed by the Court Chancery. The Gubernium expected this largely formal procedure to take a few weeks, but Trebitsch had to wait more than sixteen months before his final confirmation came through.[12] A sluggish bureaucracy may have been one factor in this delay, but most of the blame rests with Isaias Benet and his wife, Juditha. In a series of letters to Emperor Franz I, the couple contested Trebitsch's election, arguing that Isaias was rightly entitled to his late father's post. Isaias claimed that from his childhood onward he was "educated and cultivated for the post by his deceased father,"[13] and Juditha presented the chief rabbinate as Isaias's lawful patrimony, arguing that his "deceased father held this post for forty years to the complete and utter satisfaction of the government and could not leave him any other property besides the necessary qualifications for this post."[14] Furthermore, Isaias sought to bolster his own position by underscoring his status as a native-born Moravian. As rabbi of Misslitz, he noted, he was much better acquainted with the conditions of "all the Israelite communities in the province" than the Prague-born Trebitsch. His status as a native son, he argued, made his claim particularly strong, "especially against those who were not born in Moravia." Isaias and Juditha's appeals fell on deaf ears, but they did succeed in delaying Trebitsch's confirmation, leaving Moravia without a chief rabbi until the spring of 1832. The Court Chancery finally confirmed Trebitsch on May 13, 1832, and he was officially installed in Nikolsburg on June 27.[15]

The sixteenth-month delay left Trebitsch powerless to influence the election of his own successor in Prossnitz. Had his election as chief rabbi been confirmed immediately, he could have exercised the chief rabbi's prerogative to approve or disapprove communal rabbis. In the absence of a chief rabbi, however, the Prossnitz Jewish community had considerable latitude in choosing Trebitsch's replacement. The community held elections for a new rabbi while Trebitsch was still in town, and— adding insult to injury—its members elected Löw Schwab (1794–1857), a rabbi known for his reformist tendencies. Although Schwab received his early talmudic education from Mordecai Benet and Moses Sofer, he eventually strayed from both of their paths. As he acquired the reputation of a "German" rabbi, his former teachers turned against him, vehemently opposing his election to one rabbinic post after another. When the Eibenschitz Jewish community elected Schwab in 1824, Benet adamantly refused to approve the election.[16] When he was elected by the Gewitsch Jewish community in the same year, Benet withheld his approval for more than four years. Following Benet's death in 1829, Moses Sofer continued the battle against Schwab, spearheading the opposition after the Prossnitz Jewish community elected him in November 1831.[17] Sofer's efforts notwithstanding, Schwab was confirmed in 1831 as Trebitsch's replacement.

Did Trebitsch play a role in the campaign against Schwab? According to rumors circulating at the time, Trebitsch was working behind the scenes to thwart Schwab's election.[18] Perhaps he even solicited Moses Sofer's help (as he would do later in his drawn-out conflict with Hirsch Fassel, Schwab's successor to the Prossnitz rabbinate). Whatever the case, members of the Prossnitz Jewish community were certainly aware of Trebitsch's enmity toward Schwab,[19] and in all probability they elected Schwab during the interregnum precisely because Trebitsch lacked all power to stop them. Had Trebitsch already been installed as chief rabbi in 1831, he could have simply refused to approve Schwab's election, but as Schwab himself later pointed out, Trebitsch "lacked all authority [*Amtsgewalt*] to act publicly against my nomination as his successor in Prossnitz."[20] Because the confirmation was still tied up by the appeals of Isaias and Juditha Benet, there was nothing Trebitsch could really do.

Powerless to prevent the election of Schwab in 1831, Trebitsch became determined to thwart the election of similarly unacceptable rabbis on his watch. For the next decade, this single-minded determination became the defining feature of Trebitsch's activity as Moravian chief rabbi. Because the Polizei-Ordnung of 1754 required all rabbis to be examined and certified by the chief rabbi before they could assume rabbinic posts, Trebitsch ostensibly had the legal authority to decide who could become a communal rabbi.[21] As the 1833 election in Mährisch-Weisskirchen showed, however, under certain circumstances the chief rabbi's authority could be easily circumvented. When Abraham Placzek was elected to replace David Buchheim as rabbi of Mährisch-Weisskirchen, the Jewish community saw no need to consult the new chief rabbi, because Placzek had already been certified as rabbi of Prerau in 1829. If he was qualified to be rabbi of Prerau, was he not also qualified for Mährisch-Weisskirchen? Trebitsch did not think so. He thought that Placzek's four years of experience in Prerau (44 Jewish families) did not necessarily make him well suited for a much larger community like Mährisch-Weisskirchen (120 Jewish families). He believed that Placzek should have been reexamined before moving from one community to another.[22]

Although Trebitsch's authority was undermined by the election of Placzek, a decree later that year promised to greatly expand it. On September 6, 1833, the Gubernium amended the Polizei-Ordnung of 1754, authorizing the chief rabbi not only to propose candidates for vacant rabbinates but also to fill these rabbinates with his own choice if a Jewish community either failed to publicize its search for a rabbi or rejected the slate of candidates proposed by the chief rabbi.[23] This decree provided the legal basis for Trebitsch's subsequent intervention in Moravian rabbinic elections throughout the 1830s. To contemporaries, the origins of this decree were shrouded in mystery. Trebitsch's "opponents" presumed that the chief rabbi solicited it himself; his "friends" insisted that it took Trebitsch by pleasant surprise.[24] As the archives of the Gubernium reveal, Trebitsch did indeed solicit this decree, but it fell somewhat short of his expectations.

On July 27, 1833, Trebitsch asked the Gubernium to expand the chief rabbi's authority over rabbinic appointments and religious instruction.[25] He offered four suggestions; the first three related to rabbinic appointments, and the last one related to "Hebrew" instruction. First, the chief rabbi's certification of communal rabbis should be valid only for the community in which a rabbi is being installed. Trebitsch cited the

election in Mährisch-Weisskirchen, arguing that a rabbi who is qualified to serve a small community may lack the proper qualifications for
a larger one. Second, the chief rabbi should propose candidates after a
rabbinic post has been vacated. This was presumably meant to prevent
objectionable candidates from ever being considered. Third, in communities without rabbis, only those individuals authorized by the chief
rabbi should perform marriages and keep the communal birth, marriage, and death registers. This was intended to prevent the proliferation
of "corrupted pseudo-scholars" (*bestochenen Scheingelerten*) who often
performed these duties. Trebitsch's fourth suggestion, dealing with religious instruction, will be examined later in this chapter.

The 1833 decree incorporated some of Trebitsch's suggestions but
not all of them. His first suggestion—that the chief rabbi's certification of a communal rabbi should not be transferable from one community to another—was not incorporated into the 1833 decree. This
weakened Trebitsch's position in his opposition to Hirsch Fassel's
election as Prossnitz communal rabbi in 1836. His second suggestion,
however—that the chief rabbi should propose all rabbinic candidates
(*Vorschlagsrecht*)—was incorporated. Endowed with this new prerogative, Trebitsch hoped to keep reform-minded rabbis out of Moravia's
communal rabbinates.

At the time, Löw Schwab was the only Moravian communal rabbi
who exhibited any clear proclivities for religious reform. In 1832,
Schwab ruled that all weddings in Prossnitz would henceforth take
place inside the synagogue—thereby contravening the established tradition of holding Jewish weddings under the open sky. Schwab, like
many German Jewish reformers, considered outdoor weddings unseemly and sought to bring dignity and decorum to Jewish nuptials
by holding the wedding ceremony inside the synagogue.[26] Trebitsch,
however, viewed Schwab's ruling as an "injurious innovation" and an
"insolent profanation" of the Jewish religion. As Schwab later recalled,
Trebitsch "rose up with great zeal and indignation," writing truculent
letters to the Prossnitz Jewish community and even threatening to resort to government intervention.[27]

Schwab is also credited with introducing another hallmark of
German-Jewish reform to Moravia's synagogues: the German-language

sermon.[28] On March 28, 1835, in the Prossnitz synagogue, Schwab departed from the traditional Hebrew or Yiddish *derasha* (homily) when he gave a German eulogy for the recently deceased Emperor Franz I. The eulogy was subsequently published in Vienna, reportedly causing "a great sensation."[29] There is no record of Trebitsch's reaction to Schwab's sermon, but a look at Trebitsch's own eulogy for Emperor Franz I may illuminate the matter. On March 14 in Nikolsburg's Altschul, Trebitsch delivered a traditional Hebrew eulogy for "our master, the pious, mighty, and merciful king, Franz I, Emperor of Austria, may his memory be for a blessing." The full text of the Hebrew eulogy was published in Vienna, together with an abbreviated German translation.[30] Yet, lest anyone think the eulogy itself had been given in German, the title page clearly stated that it was "delivered in the Hebrew language" by Nehemias Trebitsch and translated into German by Joseph Deutsch, a Jewish schoolteacher in Nikolsburg. As became readily apparent, Trebitsch had no tolerance for German sermons or "German preachers" in any of Moravia's synagogues.

Schwab had introduced both the German sermon and the indoor wedding to Moravia's synagogues, and Trebitsch intended to eliminate these practices before they became widespread. With the authority vested in him by the Gubernium, he hoped to weed out "modern" rabbis of Schwab's ilk so that they could not even be considered for communal rabbinates. This hope rested on the supposition that Moravia's Jewish communities would consult him—as required by the 1833 decree—before choosing their rabbis. As Isaac Hirsch Weiss later observed, "Communities began hiring rabbis without first turning to the chief rabbi."[31] In the ensuing six years, three communities ignored Trebitsch's prerogative when choosing their rabbis: Loschitz, Prossnitz (for a second time), and Neu-Rausnitz. Trebitsch contested all three elections with great zeal in an effort not only to rid Moravia of unacceptable rabbis but also to reassert his supreme authority over religious affairs.

In Loschitz and Prossnitz, the contested rabbinic elections brought Trebitsch censure, humiliation, and ignoble defeat. Although situated near one another in the district of Olmütz, the Jewish communities of Loschitz and Prossnitz differed considerably in both size and

stature. The Loschitz Jewish community was medium size by Moravian standards, numbering 71 families (approximately 400 people). It
was large enough to support a rabbi but had never attracted a rabbinic
sage of great renown. Prossnitz, in contrast, boasted the second largest
Jewish community in Moravia, with 328 families (more than 1,700 people). With a celebrated yeshiva and a long tradition of eminent rabbis,
it could vie with Nikolsburg for importance. Within a period of three
months (October 1835–January 1836), Loschitz and Prossnitz elected
new rabbis with intimate ties to Löw Schwab. Loschitz elected Abraham Neuda, Schwab's "personal friend," and Prossnitz elected Hirsch
Fassel, Schwab's protégé.[32]

Abraham Neuda's father, Aron Moses Neuda, had served as communal rabbi in Loschitz for nearly twenty years, until his ailing body
and deteriorating eyesight made it increasingly difficult for him to perform his rabbinic duties. At the time, 22-year-old Abraham had been
studying for four years at the Nikolsburg yeshiva, where he was known
to be one of Trebitsch's favorite pupils.[33] When the Loschitz community asked Trebitsch to appoint him as a substitute rabbi in September
1835, the chief rabbi recommended his student in "the most laudatory
terms." As substitute rabbi, Neuda was authorized by Trebitsch to perform all his ailing father's rabbinic duties and even to decide halakhic
questions. At this stage, as one historian noted, Trebitsch may not have
even suspected that "the good *bachur* [yeshiva student] Neuda secretly
occupied himself with profane studies." This may have first become apparent when, shortly after Neuda's arrival in Loschitz, the young rabbi
delivered a Sabbath sermon "in pure German."[34]

In late September, Aron Neuda's health took a turn for the worse,
and he proposed that his son Abraham replace him "definitively." Even
though Abraham had not yet been examined and certified by Trebitsch,
the Loschitz community asked the Olmütz district office to confirm
him as his father's successor. With this request, the community hoped
to kill two birds with one stone. Not only would the community have
a rabbi to its liking, but the inevitable burden of supporting Aron
Neuda's widow would also be considerably lightened if the rabbinate remained in the family. Along with its request, the Loschitz Jewish
community enclosed letters of recommendation from two Moravian

rabbis, Tsvi Hirsch Toff of Bisenz and Löw Schwab of Prossnitz, but it failed to involve Trebitsch in the process. It is not clear whether the community deliberately circumvented Trebitsch or simply assumed that the chief rabbi had already certified Neuda when he approved him as substitute rabbi a few weeks earlier. Members of the community would later argue that "whoever can occupy a rabbinate as a substitute must also be qualified to serve as an actual rabbi [*wirklicher Rabbiner*]." Working with this assumption, the community leaders prepared a contract for Abraham Neuda on October 11, 1835.

Meanwhile, Löw Schwab accepted an invitation to become rabbi of Pest just four years after his controversial election in Prossnitz. In January 1836, members of the Prossnitz Jewish community met to elect his replacement. Trebitsch, who surely welcomed Schwab's departure with great joy, viewed the election as an opportunity to restore rabbinic glory to the community he had proudly served six years earlier. Yet, much to his chagrin, the Prossnitz community elected Hirsch Fassel—without consulting the chief rabbi first. Born in Boskowitz in 1802, Fassel had studied with Moses Sofer in Pressburg, but like Schwab, he subsequently developed a reputation as a moderate religious reformer.[35] As another strike against him, Fassel had never held a rabbinic post—in contrast to the decidedly more experienced candidate, Chaim Josef Pollak. Pollak, who had been ordained by both Mordecai Benet and Moses Sofer, had served as rabbi and head of the yeshiva in Trebitsch (Moravia's fourth largest Jewish community) since 1828. In the eyes of many, Fassel was unqualified to become the rabbi of Moravia's second largest Jewish community. Ber Schiff, a Prossnitz-born leaseholder living in Wojetin, Bohemia, expressed this opinion in a letter to his nephew, Gideon Brecher. In March 1836, shortly after Fassel was elected, Shiff wrote that the Prossnitz Jewish community had given

> the staff of glory to a man who has not placed his feet on the stones of the rabbinate. They placed the glory on the head of a yeshiva student from Boskowitz who has not yet engaged in instruction, nor delivered sermons [*derashot*]. . . . Who would believe the news that the rabbinical seat in the holy community of Prossnitz . . . will go to a new king, who does not know how to fight a holy war [*milḥemet kodesh*]? I am astounded that they would replace the "land of the

living" [*erets ha-ḥayyim*, i.e., Chaim Pollack] with the "land of the deer" [*erets ha-tsvi*, i.e., Tsvi Hirsch Fassel].[36]

Schiff hid neither his preference for Pollak nor his disdain for Fassel, who had been a failed businessman before applying for the Prossnitz rabbinate.[37] Like Trebitsch, Schiff had no influence over the election's outcome, and Fassel was elected by members of the Prossnitz community who, in the words of Bonaventura Mayer, "had desired a less strict rabbi for a long time, so they could lead a freer life."[38]

Trebitsch contested the elections in both Prossnitz and Loschitz on grounds that neither community had followed proper procedure in electing its rabbi. In both cases the communities had failed to consult the chief rabbi as required by the 1833 decree. The question of certification presented a slightly more complicated problem. In both cases, it could be—and was—argued that Trebitsch had actually approved the rabbinic candidates because he had recommended Neuda in "the most laudatory terms" for the post of substitute rabbi. Although not an actual certification, Trebitsch's recommendation certainly presented Neuda as a qualified rabbinic candidate. Fassel's case was even more problematic. As it later emerged, Trebitsch had certified Fassel at an earlier date, deeming him "suitable" for a rabbinic post.[39] Thus, in contesting Fassel's election, Trebitsch seemed to rescind his earlier certification. As the Gubernium later charged, Trebitsch had "declared [Fassel] suitable as a rabbi, but then dismissed this certificate as inadequate."[40]

Trebitsch did not see any inconsistency because in his view a rabbinic certificate was not transferable from one post to another. Although the Gubernium did not adopt his 1833 suggestion that communal rabbis be certified anew by the chief rabbi whenever they move posts, Trebitsch stood firm in this belief. As he explained in a letter to the Gubernium, Fassel may have been qualified to be the rabbi of a small Jewish community, but he was "inadequate and unsuitable" for the needs of a community the size of Prossnitz because he "had not learned enough to be rabbi of a large town." With this line of reasoning, Trebitsch attempted to explain how he could now oppose Fassel in Prossnitz after having previously certified him. Trebitsch saw no necessary contradiction: Fassel was still qualified to be a rabbi, just not in Moravia's second largest Jewish community. (Trebitsch later used the same argument against Michael Stössel when Neu-Rausnitz, Moravia's sixth largest Jewish community, elected him rabbi in 1839.) In fact, Trebitsch allegedly offered Fassel the communal rabbinate in Boskowitz (Fassel's hometown and a considerably smaller Jewish community) if he would agree to leave Prossnitz.[41]

Throughout 1836 and 1837, Trebitsch pulled out all the stops in his effort to remove Fassel from the Prossnitz rabbinate. Attempting to exercise his authority as chief rabbi, he ordered the Prossnitz Jewish community to dismiss Fassel and appoint a rabbi more to his liking.[42] He proposed five rabbis, all of whom belonged to his own generation—and presumably shared his fierce opposition to German sermons.[43] Like Trebitsch, one of the proposed rabbis (Hirsch Klein of Prossnitz) had vehemently opposed the election of Schwab in 1830. Some Prossnitz Jews may have welcomed Trebitsch's overtures, but the board rebuffed the chief rabbi and stood firmly behind Fassel. Trebitsch directly pressured Fassel to step down. According to Trebitsch's account—related in a letter to Moses Sofer—the chief rabbi repeatedly tried to "make peace" with Fassel, even offering him an opportunity to remain in Prossnitz if certain conditions were met. As he explained to Sofer, "I wrote [to Fassel] that if he took the straight path and listened to my advice . . . then I would love him and do everything for his benefit. In the end, he returned to his former ways and went against my will by performing weddings in the synagogue and the like."[44] If Trebitsch viewed this effort to bring Fassel back in line as an attempt to "make peace," he seems to have been alone in his appraisal. Fassel's friend Gideon Brecher described Trebitsch's missive as nothing more than a "fulminating, threatening letter" (*einen fulminanten Drohbrief*) that admonished Fassel to heed Trebitsch's words, "lest [my] wrath pour out against you."[45] Trebitsch tried to recruit Moses Sofer in his battle, hoping that this preeminent opponent of religious reform would use his connections to remove Fassel—Sofer's wayward student—from the Prossnitz rabbinate. Sofer died shortly thereafter, and Trebitsch was left to fight alone.

Meanwhile, Trebitsch faced similar difficulties in his effort to remove Abraham Neuda from Loschitz. Although the Gubernium had initially

ordered Trebitsch to propose four new candidates for the Loschitz rabbinate, the Loschitz community completely ignored Trebitsch's proposals (four of whom he had earlier proposed for Prossnitz). As members
of the Loschitz community later observed, Trebitsch proposed "four
candidates whose utter uselessness [*gänzliche Unbrauchbarkeit*] was
already evident from their own applications." The Loschitz community found recourse in the Olmütz district office, which investigated
the contested election and then confirmed Abraham Neuda as the rabbi
of Loschitz on August 24, 1837, "in accordance with the will of the
community." Because Neuda had still not been examined by the chief
rabbi, it is not entirely clear how the district office justified this surprising decision. Trebitsch would later claim that Neuda intentionally
misled the district officials, which is one possible explanation.[46] In any
case, Neuda's confirmation—against the will of the chief rabbi—was
commonly seen as a turning point in the Neuda-Trebitsch affair. As the
Gubernium pointed out in 1841, the district office's decision "significantly exacerbated the tensions" between the Loschitz community and
Trebitsch and, of course, between Neuda and Trebitsch.[47] Although the
confirmation was overruled on June 2, 1838, the seeds of mutual mis-
trust had already been sown.

While Trebitsch was contesting the elections in Prossnitz and Loschitz, Fassel and Neuda were not sitting idly by. On the contrary, they
testified against the chief rabbi on July 13, 1836, condemning his arbitrary behavior and accusing him of engaging in criminal acts. A letter
from Moravian governor Ugarte to the Pest magistracy succinctly summarized the numerous grievances that had piled up against Trebitsch
by 1836.

> Many complaints have been raised against the [Moravian] chief rabbi.
> He has been charged primarily with acting arbitrarily: he refuses
> to examine rabbinic candidates he does not desire, he denies them
> certificates of competency, and he imposes rabbis on the Jewish com-
> munities. As a result, a number of communities, e.g., Prossnitz and
> Loschitz, are in conflict with him. This is especially the case with
> Hirsch Fassel, who is desired as a rabbi by the Prossnitz community;
> Löw Schwab, currently rabbi in Pest and formerly in Prossnitz; and
> Abraham Neuda, who the Loschitz community has appointed rabbi.[48]

In addition to these complaints, a more serious charge was made about Trebitsch's attitude toward German language and literature: "The Chief Rabbi has been further charged with persecuting those rabbinical candidates, who possess knowledge outside the talmudic subjects, especially of German literature; and those who wish to obtain a certificate of competency must take an oath not to read any German books nor to give any German speeches."[49] If this charge was true, Trebitsch had contravened two court decrees—one from 1808 forbidding excommunication and the other from 1820 requiring the chief rabbi to disseminate the German language among the Jews. At Governor Ugarte's behest, the Pest magistracy sought to clarify this and other issues by asking Schwab to comment on the litany of charges that had been leveled against Trebitsch. With regard to the chief rabbi's attitude toward extratalmudic knowledge, Schwab declared it an "incontrovertible fact" that Trebitsch was vehemently opposed to all rabbis, rabbinic candidates, and teachers who evinced a predilection for German language and literature; however, Schwab doubted whether Trebitsch's prejudices had actually led to the persecution of rabbinic candidates or the requirement that they take the alleged oath. "Based on my own experience," he wrote, "I am unaware of this; and the rumors that have spread regarding this matter have had no influence on my current remarks, because I do not find them entirely convincing."[50] Regardless of the truth behind these accusations (which will be examined later in this chapter), the Gubernium gave them full credence and took them into consideration when settling the Fassel-Trebitsch dispute.

The Gubernium dealt Trebitsch a double defeat. A gubernial decree from March 23, 1838, confirmed Fassel as Prossnitz's rabbi and removed his right to propose rabbinic candidates.[51] Trebitsch was censured on three counts. First, he had acted "out of order" by giving Fassel a certificate of competency and then declaring this very certificate inadequate. Second, he had violated the law by requiring rabbinic students—under threat of excommunication—to refrain from reading German books and delivering German sermons. Third, in a further abuse of his authority, Trebitsch had improperly taxed private teachers for their certificates of competency. Consequently, at the suggestion of the Nikolsburg police director, the Gubernium ordered Trebitsch's conduct to be "duly watched over" in the future.

In the most serious blow to Trebitsch's authority, the Gubernium eliminated the chief rabbi's prerogative to propose rabbinic candidates to individual communities. This prerogative (*Vorschlagsrecht*), which had been solicited by Trebitsch in 1833, was repealed in 1838 as a result of the chief rabbi's alleged misconduct. Thereafter, Trebitsch's prerogatives in relation to rabbinic elections reverted to those spelled out in the Polizei-Ordnung from 1754, according to which "no Jewish community can confer a rabbinic post by itself, nor can anyone be authorized to take up such a post without first being properly examined and declared suitable by the chief rabbi or his representative."[52] Under the new restrictions, Trebitsch could no longer prevent an examined and certified rabbi like Fassel from being elected to a rabbinic post in Moravia, but he continued to wield significant power over candidates like Neuda, who had still not been properly examined and certified. When the Gubernium decreed on May 19, 1838, that all communal rabbis must have valid certificates of competency from the chief rabbi, the next clash between Trebitsch and Neuda was only a matter of time.

In November 1838, Neuda left for an anticipated two years in Vienna—with the financial backing of the Loschitz community—to conduct "theological research" in the city's world-renowned libraries.[53] The Loschitz community sought a substitute rabbi to fill Neuda's position during his absence. With Trebitsch's consent, the community contracted Moses Rössler of Gewitsch to serve as its rabbi from November 1838 until October 1840. At first glance, the choice of Rössler appears quite odd, because he lacked Neuda's enlightened qualifications. Whereas Neuda was renowned for his edifying German sermons, Rössler was apparently "not entirely conversant in the German language."[54] Whereas Neuda had acquired "a significant degree of literary education" in addition to his rabbinic training, Rössler's formal secular education was limited to two years of *Normalschule*.[55] In light of these contrasts, the Loschitz community presumably selected Rössler as a kind of peace offering, as a means to appease Trebitsch during Neuda's temporary absence. Upon Neuda's premature return in September 1839, however, the conflict between Trebitsch and Neuda resumed with added intensity.

During his ten-month stay in Vienna, Neuda established contact with some of the most prominent religious reformers in the Habsburg monarchy, including Isak Noa Mannheimer and Aron Chorin. As "religious teacher" of the Viennese Jewish community since the 1820s, Mannheimer helped create the Vienna Rite, which eventually served as a model for religious innovation in the rest of the monarchy. Mannheimer was also an orator of great renown, whose preaching style was praised and emulated by "modern" rabbis across Europe.[56] Neuda not only attended Mannheimer's sermons at Vienna's Stadttempel but also received a certificate of competency from the celebrated preacher before returning to Loschitz. While in Vienna, Neuda also received a certificate of competency from Chorin, the septuagenarian rabbi of Arad who had repeatedly come into conflict with Mordecai Benet.[57] These new credentials certainly made Neuda even more suspect in Trebitsch's eyes, but his expanded network of rabbinic contacts also served as additional protection against an arbitrary and vindictive chief rabbi.

Abraham Neuda returned to Loschitz on September 6, 1839, just in time to deliver a German sermon on the first day of Rosh Hashanah.[58] He resumed his rabbinic duties "to the joy of the entire community" but soon confronted two obstacles.[59] First, on September 19, the Gubernium informed Neuda that—in accordance with a decree from May 19, 1838—he still needed to be examined and certified by Trebitsch. Second, Moses Rössler's contract as substitute rabbi was still valid for another year. Although the Loschitz community wished to be rid of him—and not be burdened with salaries for two rabbis—Rössler insisted that the terms of his contract be honored. In a complaint to the Olmütz district office, Rössler noted that Neuda had been hired by the Loschitz Jewish community without the knowledge or approval of the Moravian chief rabbi. On top of that, Rössler argued, Neuda was not even qualified to function as a communal rabbi at this time because he had still not been examined or certified by the chief rabbi.[60] The district office supported the complaint, ruling that Rössler should finish out his contract with the Loschitz Jewish community. Although the Jewish community appealed this decision, it was upheld by the Gubernium. Rössler, it was decided, would remain the substitute rabbi in Loschitz until October 1840. In the meantime, Neuda had to figure out how to obtain proper certification in the face of the perceived "hatefulness that the Chief Rabbi harbors towards him."[61]

Wishing to sidestep Trebitsch entirely, Neuda initially set his sights on the Habsburg provinces of Lombard-Venetia and Bohemia. First, he sought permission to be examined at Padua's Collegio Rabbinico, which had been established in 1829 for the Italian-speaking Jews of Lombard-Venetia. As Europe's first academic institution to combine traditional talmudic learning with general secular studies, the Collegio Rabbinico seemed particularly well suited to Neuda's needs. Because it was the empire's only rabbinical seminary, Neuda hoped he could get a special dispensation to be examined there. In January 1840, the Loschitz community pleaded Neuda's case in a letter to the Court Chancery, requesting that the jurisdiction of the Collegio Rabbinico be extended to all the empire's hereditary lands, because only such a "public and imperial institute" could provide the necessary "impartiality" (*Unpartheylichkeit*). In May 1840, Neuda personally asked the Court Commission on Education for a special dispensation, also arguing that only the Padua institute could guarantee him an impartial examination. In June, however, the Court Commission rejected Neuda's request on several grounds. First, the Collegio Rabbinico was authorized to certify rabbis only in the Italian provinces. Second, according to the Polizei-Ordnung, rabbis were required to obtain certification from the Moravian chief rabbi, "which Neuda has not yet tried to do." Third, if Neuda were granted a dispensation, the authority of the chief rabbi would be greatly undermined. "It is easily conceivable," observed the Court Commission, "that soon no rabbinical candidate will want to be examined by the chief rabbi, and his authoritative influence [*leitender Einfluss*] will be completely paralyzed."[62]

Neuda's efforts in Bohemia proved equally futile. There, he based his case on an 1830 decree regulating the election of the Moravian chief rabbi, which required candidates for this post to have certificates of competency from either two Moravian communal rabbis or two Bohemian district rabbis. Neuda reasoned that the requirements for the highest rabbinic post in the province should be sufficient for communal rabbinates as well. He went to Bohemia, was examined by four district rabbis,[63] and presented his certificates to the Gubernium. His indefatigable efforts notwithstanding, Neuda was still required to obtain certification from Trebitsch.[64]

In their correspondence with the Gubernium, Neuda and the Loschitz community consistently argued that Trebitsch was simply incapable of being an impartial examiner. They did their utmost to portray him as an inveterate enemy of culture and Enlightenment, fully consumed by his own "despotism" and "vindictiveness." As the Loschitz community saw it, Trebitsch was persecuting Neuda "with the bitterest and most unrelenting fury," solely because Neuda "acquired a significant degree of literary education alongside his consummate rabbinical skills" and "respects the purity of linguistic forms in his edifying sermons." In sharp contrast, Trebitsch's knowledge "did not extend beyond the realm of the Talmud," nor was he able to sign "more than his name" in German.[65] Neuda similarly presented his conflict with Trebitsch as a battle between Enlightenment and obscurantism.

> His hatefulness towards me is by no means directed against my personality, but rather, as is generally known, against the manner and method in which I deliver sermons. In the few years since the conflict began, many young rabbinical colleagues have been hounded and persecuted.
>
> My removal from office, which the Chief Rabbi still pursues with great despotism, would give him unbridled authority and influence to stunt the progressive development of talent among my fellow rabbis and to privilege narrow-mindedness over talent. In light of the Chief Rabbi's well-known views, and the manifold complaints against him . . . nothing more could be expected from him than the greatest arbitrariness and despotism.[66]

Neuda explained to the Gubernium that the very nature of a rabbinic examination left him completely defenseless against Trebitsch. Because such examinations are "so all-encompassing, dealing with the smallest details," he wrote, "it is impossible to limit arbitrariness and avoid severity and malevolence." Trebitsch would inevitably become "both judge and jury." The Loschitz community accused Trebitsch of using such examinations—"where the most unbounded arbitrariness reigns"—to keep enlightened candidates out of the rabbinate.

In a letter to the Brünn district office dated November 10, 1840, Trebitsch sought to justify his opposition to Neuda on intellectual, moral, and religious grounds.[67] As Neuda's teacher for "about six years," Trebitsch claimed to be familiar with his erstwhile student's intellectual failings. Neuda was an intellectual lightweight, he maintained, whose "superficial knowledge" made him unqualified to serve as a communal rabbi. This, Trebitsch later claimed, was precisely why Neuda had been trying to avoid an examination for so long.[68] Trebitsch also denounced Neuda as a "reprehensible and immoral" person, accusing him of giving false and malicious testimony. Specifically, he blamed Neuda for testifying that the chief rabbi had required his students to take a pledge (*Handschlag*)—which Neuda allegedly compared to a ban (*Bannfluch*)—not to read German books or deliver German sermons. Trebitsch wrote to the Brünn district office:

> It is doubly punishable, unforgivable, and inconceivable that a student could make a false testimony against his teacher and master, with the result that his [teacher's] reputation is ruined in the eyes of the government, his civil status is threatened, and his religiosity is brought into question. Through this testimony, Abraham Neuda has not only revealed his corrupt soul, but also his ignorance, since a pledge [*Handschlag*] can in no way be compared to a ban [*Bannfluch*].[69]

Neuda's "ignorance" and "corrupt soul" aside, Trebitsch asserted that, as a bachelor, Neuda should have never been considered for a communal rabbinate in the first place. "It is a one-hundred-year practice of the chief rabbinate in Moravia," wrote Trebitsch, "to entrust a rabbinical post, under no condition, to an unmarried candidate. [This] custom is founded on religious principles." In any case, as far as Trebitsch was concerned, the question of the Loschitz rabbinate had already been settled. Moses Rössler, in his view, was Loschitz's legitimate rabbi.

When the Gubernium discussed the Trebitsch-Neuda affair in early January 1841, it gave little credence to Trebitsch's disparaging claims.[70] The Gubernium possessed independent reports from the Brünn district office, the Mährisch-Neustadt magistracy, and the Loschitz mayor, all of which described Neuda as "an intellectually educated, well-behaved young man." Furthermore, the numerous certificates of competency—from several Moravian rabbis (Tsvi Hirsch Toff, Michael Wronik, and Löbel Pollak), three Bohemian district rabbis,[71] the "Viennese Jewish religious teacher" (Mannheimer), and "the rabbi of Pest" (Schwab)—appeared to dispel Trebitsch's claim that Neuda was unqualified to be a rabbi.[72]

At the same time, Neuda's claims against Trebitsch were increasingly confirmed as the chief rabbi became embroiled in at least two more disputed rabbinic elections. These disputes—in Neu-Rausnitz and Misslitz—saw the standard complaints against Trebitsch's "arbitrary" and "despotic" behavior, but they also carried the additional taint of nepotism. In Misslitz, Trebitsch tried to appoint a son-in-law, Simson Kulke, to the rabbinate after Isaias Benet left for Nagykálló, Hungary, in 1840.[73] In Neu-Rausnitz, Trebitsch tried to appoint another son-in-law, Jakob Brüll, even though Michael Stössel had just been elected rabbi. In a by now familiar pattern, the Jewish community failed to consult Trebitsch, who later explained to the Gubernium: "Had the Neu-Rausnitz community followed the good example of other communities and requested approval from me . . . I would have never approved this candidate. Even though he possesses the proper certificates, his reputation . . . has been sullied the world over."[74] Trebitsch, with the support of some Neu-Rausnitz Jews, tried to install Jakob Brüll as rabbi, attracting much criticism in the contemporary German-Jewish press and triggering yet another complaint to the authorities.[75] Because the complaint was anonymous, the Gubernium advised the Court Chancery to ignore it. The Gubernium observed that Trebitsch had not engaged in any disorderly conduct "this time." "Besides," it continued, "his behavior is [already] being strictly watched."[76]

Even if the Gubernium seemed to support Neuda in the six-year-old dispute, there was no getting around the requirement that he be tested by Trebitsch. In a letter to the Court Chancery from January 4, 1841, the Gubernium proposed a solution that would allow Trebitsch to examine Neuda without "any fear of partisanship."[77] A commission was to be set up comprising Trebitsch, two Moravian communal rabbis, and a Catholic commissar. The commissar was to ask questions from Herz Homberg's *Bne Zion*, and the three rabbis were to test Neuda in biblical exegesis and talmudic law.[78] Ferdinand Panschab, Professor of Dogma at the Brünn Theological Seminary, was selected by the Brünn Episcopal Consistory as the Catholic commissar;[79] Trebitsch and Neuda were entitled to select the two additional rabbis. Trebitsch chose Joseph Feilbogen, the 57-year-old rabbi of Holleschau and a celebrated talmudist in his own right. Neuda, in a move surely designed to infuriate and humiliate Trebitsch, chose the 38-year-old Hirsch Fassel of Prossnitz. One can only imagine Trebitsch's silent, simmering rage—and Fassel's irrepressible delight—when the examination took place in Brünn on May 18, 1841.

Even before arriving in Brünn, Neuda could claim an astounding victory over Trebitsch. Neuda not only had forced the chief rabbi to examine him but also had constrained him to do so under extraordinarily favorable conditions. First, the presence of three other examiners meant that Trebitsch's influence would be significantly weakened. Second, the inclusion of a wide range of topics, including biblical exegesis and homiletics, meant that Trebitsch would not always be on familiar terrain. Third, the presence of Professor Panschab meant that the examination would be conducted in German.[80] At the actual examination, each examiner posed three questions, Trebitsch going first. As could be expected, Trebitsch asked difficult and convoluted questions, apparently hoping to stump his former student.[81] Although even Feilbogen reportedly considered the examination "much too difficult,"[82] Abraham Neuda successfully passed, putting an end to his six-year conflict with the chief rabbi. As one historian wrote, Neuda was escorted "in triumph" back to Loschitz.[83]

Neuda's triumph was Trebitsch's final degradation and defeat. Although the chief rabbi's prerogative to test rabbinic candidates was upheld in 1841, the examination in Brünn served to completely undermine any remaining "authoritative influence" that Trebitsch may have possessed. Not only had the Jewish communities of Mährisch-Weisskirchen, Loschitz, Neu-Rausnitz, and Prossnitz ignored, circumvented, or otherwise challenged Trebitsch's authority throughout the 1830s, but the Gubernium had also consistently sided with the chief rabbi's detractors, who had successfully—although perhaps exaggeratedly—portrayed Trebitsch as an obscurantist opponent of Enlightenment who would brazenly disregard the law of the land in his efforts to keep German language and literature from contaminating Moravia's Jews. Largely because of this portrayal, the Gubernium gradually whittled away Trebitsch's rabbinic prerogatives—first through the censure in 1838 (and the concomitant removal of the *Vorschlagsrecht*) and then through the humiliating examination in 1841. When the 63-year-old chief rabbi passed away on July 4, 1842—less than fourteen months after Neuda's examination—it was commonly understood that Trebitsch was not steeled by such adversity but was rather vanquished by it.[84]

An Enemy of the German Language?

The depiction of Trebitsch as "an enemy of all German literature" lay at the root of the chief rabbi's eventual demise, so it is worth examining this characterization in some depth. Although Trebitsch's unbending and undisguised opposition to German sermons is undisputable, his view of German language and literature was not as "medieval" as many of his detractors led the Jewish public and the Gubernium to believe. It must be remembered that Trebitsch, born two years before the promulgation of the Edict of Tolerance, never received a secular education during his youth in Prague. He learned enough German to communicate with the government authorities but apparently failed to fully master the written language. As Isaac Hirsch Weiss recalled, his rabbi and teacher often relied on a certain Bohemian student for help with his German correspondence.[85] Nonetheless, the claim that Trebitsch could not sign "more than his name" in German was a patent lie. In 1838, Nathan Denneberger, a teacher at Nikolsburg's German-Jewish school, came to Trebitsch's defense after Gideon Brecher characterized the chief rabbi as a "coryphaeus of Orthodoxy, engaged in a fruitless struggle with the Genius of the age," and as an "enemy of all German literature."[86] Denneberger, a self-identified reformer, conceded that Trebitsch could not "be celebrated as a learned linguist of modern languages," but he attested to the chief rabbi's general proficiency in the German language. "He was brought up in an age when it was considered a sin for talmudists to touch a German work," Denneberger wrote. "Nevertheless, he reads German works and understands them. Pure German is spoken in his home. His son [Rabbi Seligman Trebitsch] and son-in-law [Rabbi Jakob Brüll] are well-rounded, cultivated men."[87]

If Denneberger could point to Trebitsch's close family circle as evidence of an openness toward the German language, Trebitsch's detractors could draw attention to the chief rabbi's halakhic writings—not to mention the uninterrupted string of conflicts over rabbinic appointments—to reach the opposite conclusion. Much ado was made about a single line in *Shalom Yerushalayim* (1821), a commentary on the Jerusalem Talmud and one of only two halakhic works published by Trebitsch during his lifetime.[88] According to a discussion in Tractate Shabbat of the Jerusalem Talmud, Hillel and Shammai (rabbis from the first century B.C.E.) were in full agreement that "a Jew should not accustom himself or his children to speak in the language of the Gentiles" (*ledaber bi-lshon aku"m*). In his commentary on this discussion, Trebitsch observed that "from this [prohibition, we learn] a wonderful admonition for our generation" (*u-mi-ze tokhaḥa nifla'a le-doreynu*).[89] One of Trebitsch's detractors cited this fleeting observation as a succinct summary of the chief rabbi's rigorously conservative outlook and as solid proof of his intolerant attitude toward the German language as a whole. In the detractor's view, Trebitsch's observation was a clear admonition not only against learning a "proper vernacular language" but also against allowing "preaching rabbis" into the synagogue. As such, he quipped, Trebitsch's opus was inappropriately named. Rather than promoting "the peace of Jerusalem" (*shalom yerushalayim*), it actually instigated conflict and discord.[90]

In light of the accusations leveled against Trebitsch throughout the 1830s, it may come as a surprise that his yeshiva in Nikolsburg was reputed to be quite progressive—at least compared to the yeshivas in nearby Hungary. In fact, after attending a number of Hungarian yeshivas, Isaac Hirsch Weiss came to Nikolsburg largely because Trebitsch's yeshiva was known to be more receptive to secular studies. He had heard that a large number of students not only "had command of important linguistic and other secular knowledge, but were also considered skillful talmudists."[91] Gutmann Klemperer recalled a similar atmosphere at the Prague yeshiva, which Trebitsch had headed before coming to Moravia in 1826.[92] Like Weiss, Klemperer contrasted Trebitsch with the stricter Hungarian rabbis, particularly Moses Sofer. Whereas Sofer had forbidden the reading of Mendelssohn's writings, Trebitsch "had told [Klemperer's] father in 1820 to teach [his son] the Torah with the translation by Moses Dessau [i.e., Mendelssohn]." Whereas Sofer could never admit that his students read books other than those "written in the Hebrew language and in a strictly Orthodox manner," Trebitsch counted among his preeminent students Ahron Rosenbach, who had completed gymnasium and received a doctorate in philosophy.[93] As evidence of Trebitsch's approval of secular studies, Klemperer pointed out that the relationship between rabbi and student "did not change in the slightest" after Rosenbach earned his academic degree. "With doctor's hat on his head, [Rosenbach] came to the rabbi's apartment every Friday evening for prayers—just as before."

Trebitsch was not opposed ipso facto to the study of "German language and literature" so long as such study did not interfere with traditional religious practice. What he resented in Fassel and Neuda were their efforts to introduce changes, such as the German sermon, into the synagogue service. In Trebitsch's eyes, such "innovations" turned the old Jewish value system on its head by using the "spirit of the times" rather than divinely inspired tradition as the yardstick for Jewish ritual practice. In contrast to Rosenbach, Fassel and Neuda did not conduct themselves "just as before" but instead sought to use their newly acquired knowledge to "renew" and "improve" tried and true forms of Jewish worship.

Jewish Schools and Schooling

Just as he tried to keep the German language—and all that it represented—out of the synagogue, Trebitsch also tried to ensure that "German" studies and "Hebrew" studies remained separate and distinct in Moravia's Jewish schools. Ever since the introduction of mandatory schooling under Joseph II, German and Hebrew instruction had been relegated to separate spheres in Moravia and elsewhere in the Habsburg monarchy. Officially, there was a kind of division of labor, with German subjects being taught by state-certified teachers in the German-Jewish *Trivialschulen* (or in Christian *Trivialschulen* if the Jewish community could not afford to establish its own school) and Hebrew subjects being taught by private teachers in individual Jewish homes. Special consideration was taken to ensure that the new German-Jewish *Trivialschulen*—which could be found, by the 1830s, in thirty-four of Moravia's fifty-two Jewish communities—did not interfere with the

Jews' own religious observance. The curriculum focused on technical subjects, such as grammar, penmanship, physical science, and geography, for which "neutral" textbooks already existed. Because there were no neutral German language primers—the existing ones being heavily suffused with Christian moralistic teachings—the Edict of Tolerance allowed the Jews to compile their own moral books ("because of their religious practices"). In places where no German-Jewish schools were established, Jewish parents were ordered to send their children to the local Christian schools; there, Christian and Jewish children learned together, with the proviso that Jewish children be let out of school during religious instruction and not be "compelled or enticed to any action that goes against their religious practice." This meant that Jewish children were excused from school on the Sabbath and festivals and were allowed to keep their heads covered during instruction.[94]

For centuries, Hebrew subjects had been taught in Moravia by private teachers, or *melamedim*. As elsewhere in Eastern and Central Europe, these *melamedim* (also known as *Winkellehrer*, *Stubenlehrer*, or simply *Privatlehrer*) gave primary religious instruction in makeshift private schools called heders or *Winkelschulen*. Although the Shai Takkanot (and later the Polizei-Ordnung of 1754) required each of Moravia's Jewish communities to employ a teacher who could instruct young Jewish boys in the Hebrew language and "Mosaic Law," few regulations were in place stipulating qualifications for *melamedim* or a specific curriculum to be taught in heders. As the memoir literature attests, few *melamedim* had any formal pedagogical training, even as late as the 1820s and 1830s. The *melamed* who taught Ignaz Briess in Prerau in the late 1830s was apparently nothing more than "an old, failed merchant" who taught a motley group of boys "of all different ages and levels" in his cramped living room. In this heder, instruction entailed rote memorization of *ḥumash* (Pentateuch), Mishnah, and Talmud, with little regard for the different abilities of the students.[95] Isaac Hirsch Weiss, who attended a heder in Gross-Meseritsch around 1820, had similar recollections of his early education. He described religious education in Moravia at the time in the following terms:

> In every single community, there were primary teachers, who practiced their vocation without being appointed or sanctioned by any author-

ity; they simply opened up a school. Such a private school was called a *heder*, a very apt name, since the teacher, who was poor as could be, possessed nothing but this single room, where all of his domestic duties were performed, where he and his family slept and took their meals, and where he taught his students. . . . The *melamedim* were mostly men who, in their youth, engaged, more or less, in intensive Torah study, but without great success. Afterward, they pursued a commercial career and ultimately failed in this vocation, too. Teaching was then their last resort. But, even if they were qualified Torah scholars, they generally lacked pedagogical skills and also the first precondition for a primary teacher: perseverance and composure.[96]

Struggling to eke out a meager living, *melamedim* also found themselves in competition with other Jews who, like themselves, came upon teaching as an occupation of last resort. It was not uncommon to find five or six private teachers in one of Moravia's larger Jewish communities, all trying to draw from a finite pool of potential students.[97]

Private teachers did not necessarily limit themselves to instruction in *ḥumash*, Mishnah, and Talmud but could also be found teaching German *Trivialschule* subjects. Many Jewish parents preferred to have their children educated in these subjects by private teachers rather than send them to the German-Jewish *Trivialschule* (or the Christian *Trivialschule*). There were a number of reasons for this. First, because the *Trivialschule* teachers were predominantly Christian (and overseen by a Catholic superintendent), the schools were often viewed as religiously suspect. Only in the 1830s did the schools begin hiring Jewish teachers (who belonged to the new generation of Moravian Jews that had attended *Trivialschule* in their youth). Second, because the German-Jewish *Trivialschule* was often dismissed as a "charity school" for poor or orphaned children, many parents—particularly among the more affluent members of the community—preferred the luxury of a private teacher for their children. Weiss, for example, attended the Gross-Meseritsch *Trivialschule* only on rare occasions. His parents hired a private teacher, who gave daily instruction in German and other profane subjects. Once Weiss had outgrown this teacher, his parents hired Wolf Mühlrad, who later became rabbi of Lundenburg, to teach him religious and profane subjects.[98]

Throughout the first decades of the nineteenth century, private teachers were subject to criticism from all directions. Teachers at Moravia's *Trivialschulen* regularly complained that private teachers were depriving them of much-needed income by keeping Jewish students away from their schools. Because *Trivialschule* teachers were paid by the parents of the students, a reduced number of students meant reduced income for the teachers. The brunt of their criticism was directed at private teachers who taught German subjects without the proper qualifications. *Trivialschule* teachers blamed them not only for taking away students but also for giving these students inadequate instruction. Such complaints found resonance with the government, which continually sought to increase the number of Jewish students attending *Trivialschulen*. The complaints also contributed to the Gubernium's decision to crack down on unauthorized Jewish private teachers in 1826. In that year, the Gubernium decreed that all Jewish private teachers must be certified in the subjects they teach and demonstrate their "irreproachable morality." In addition, the decree stipulated that Jewish private teachers could give only *private* instruction, and only in students' own homes.[99] This was aimed at eliminating larger *Winkelschulen* that functioned, for all intents and purposes, as "public" schools. These schools, which were often held in a private teacher's home, directly competed with the *Trivialschulen*.

Trebitsch also expressed concern about the proliferation of unauthorized private teachers, but for entirely different reasons. Although the Gubernium was troubled by poor attendance at the German-Jewish *Trivialschulen*, the chief rabbi was troubled by the growing threat to traditional Jewish education. As Trebitsch saw it, teachers who combined both Hebrew and German subjects in their private instruction were a corrupting influence on Moravia's Jewish youth and needed to be eliminated before they caused any further harm. As he explained in his letter to the Gubernium (July 27, 1833), the "skulking *Winkellehrer*" who mixed Hebrew and German subjects were usually not qualified to teach either subject.[100] Because they taught an incoherent jumble, Trebitsch claimed, instruction in both Hebrew and German subjects was "either completely distorted or exceedingly deficient." Trebitsch also took private teachers to task for their depraved character, complaining that religious instruction was often given by "persons whose immoral and irreligious behavior precisely contradicts their teachings." As such, he explained, "they serve as a corrupting example for the inexperienced youth." In his letter to the Gubernium, Trebitsch put forth a solution that was intended to restore German and Hebrew instruction to their separate and distinct spheres. With regard to German instruction, he proposed that private teachers be completely eliminated and that Jewish children be sent—"without exception"—to the existing German schools. (This, from a chief rabbi who was repeatedly branded an enemy of German language and literature!) With regard to Hebrew instruction, he proposed that each Jewish community employ several teachers who are "examined directly by the chief rabbi" and recognized by him as qualified to teach Torah, Prophets, Writings, Mishnah, and elementary Talmud. Trebitsch's proposal, like his entire letter to the Gubernium, aimed to reinforce his authority over religious affairs in Moravia. Just as he sought to exert control over rabbinic appointments and thereby keep Moravia's Jewish communities free of German sermons, indoor weddings, and other perceived deviations from Jewish tradition, he also sought to exert control over religious teachers and thereby shield Moravia's Jewish youth from potentially destructive attitudes toward religion.

Trebitsch's proposal was never implemented, but a number of Jewish communities took their own steps—beginning in the late 1830s—to do away with private religious teachers altogether. Inspired in large part by debates on educational reform in the German-Jewish press, lay leaders in Moravia's larger Jewish communities began rallying for a new kind of religious school with properly trained teachers and pedagogically sound curricula. Such schools were designed to take the place of heders and their perfunctory private teachers. They were first established in Prossnitz (1838) and Nikolsburg (1839), but other communities—such as Trebitsch and Gross-Meseritsch—tried to emulate the educational advances of Moravia's two largest Jewish communities. Before examining the Prossnitz and Nikolsburg schools in more detail, it will be helpful to look at a petition from the Gross-Meseritsch Jewish community, which clearly portrays such new schools as an innovative solution to the many and sundry shortcomings of private religious education. The petition, submitted to the Gubernium at the end of 1842, reads as a scathing indictment of private instruction—on pecuniary, pedagogical, religious, and moral grounds.[101] First, it argued, the cost of paying private teachers (including room and board) was so high that private teachers were beyond the means of most families. Second, the Jewish quarter was already so overcrowded that most families did not have a suitable place for instruction in the confines of their own homes. Third, children were taught in private homes, where instruction was subject to all sorts of interruptions and disturbances. Fourth, private teachers were not subject to supervision or control, so students were exposed to arbitrary teaching methods, creating a situation in which a teacher's pecuniary interests took precedence over the needs of his students, leaving parents in the dark about their children's inability to learn and wasting the children's precious time, which could be better spent learning a useful trade. Fifth, private teachers frequently came into conflict with local *Trivialschule* teachers but also with their own professional duties as religious educators. Echoing Trebitsch's observations, the petition claimed that many private teachers "abandoned everything holy and decent" and instilled in their students "disrespect and disdain" for the synagogue. To remedy these problems, the board of the Gross-Meseritsch community sought to set up a community religious school—under the supervision of the local rabbi—just as in Prossnitz and Nikolsburg.

The schools established in Prossnitz and Nikolsburg in the late 1830s represented two different attempts to reform Jewish primary education in Moravia. Although lay leaders took the initiative in both communities, the schools themselves took shape under the discernible influence of the communal rabbis—Hirsch Fassel in Prossnitz and Nehemias Trebitsch in Nikolsburg.[102] Not surprisingly, the ideological split that pitted Fassel and Trebitsch against one another throughout the 1830s also manifested itself in the two rabbis' respective approaches to educational reform. Fassel, who criticized traditional *melamedim* for their inability to make Jewish customs and beliefs relevant to contemporary youth, envisioned a school whose teachers would combine profound talmudic knowledge with a modern critical sensibility. Without such school reform, he feared, the scourge of indifference would continue to grow out of hand.[103] Trebitsch, as we have seen, thought that precisely such an intermingling of religious and secular—whether in a heder or in a full-fledged school—was to be avoided at all costs. Indeed, he had sought the authority to approve religious teachers in all of Moravia's Jewish communities, in large part so that religious teachers with a modern critical sensibility could be kept at bay. Still, with little authority over the affairs of the Prossnitz Jewish community—especially after his censure by the Gubernium in 1838—Trebitsch could exert influence only on his own community. In Prossnitz, much to Trebitsch's chagrin, the new school came into being without his input.

In 1838, substantial changes were introduced to the *talmud torah* school in the Prossnitz Jewish community. This school, which provided religious instruction for Prossnitz's poor and orphaned Jewish children, had been run along the lines of a traditional heder until steps were taken to transform it into a modern "Hebrew school" (*hebräische Lehranstalt*). Gideon Brecher, a driving force behind this transformation, published a series of articles in 1838 arguing that educational reform was essential for battling the religious "indifference" rampant among the younger generation.[104] In his view, traditional religious instruction—which he characterized as "mythical explication of Holy Scripture, obfuscation of the text through aggadic obscurities, and mystification of micrological observances"—was driving the youth away from Jewish observance. His criticism, however, was not limited to the traditional heder alone. He also cautioned against excessive "rationalism," which ignored the fact that religion was, above all, a "matter of the soul" (*Sache des Gemuethes*). Thus, he insisted, any educational reform must strike a happy balance between rationalism and emotion. In this respect, the object of Brecher's scholarly attention, Judah Halevi, also exemplified his educational ideal, as the Spanish-Jewish poet and philosopher employed both rationalism and emotion in his twelfth-century defense of Judaism.

In 1838, the board of the Jewish community—which counted Brecher among its members—hired Josef Weisse (1812–1897), a 26-year-old native of Moravia, to head the school and redesign its curriculum.[105] Born in Plumenau (near Prossnitz), Weisse had spent the previous six years in Prague, where he established lifelong friendships with Moritz

Steinschneider (Brecher's nephew) and Leopold Löw, fellow Moravians who shared an ideological commitment to the critical study of Judaism. While in Prague, Weisse was mentored by Leopold Zunz, a founding member of Berlin's Society for the Culture and Science of the Jews and, for a short time, preacher at Prague's "Association for the Improvement of Jewish Worship."[106] Weisse, whose scholarly interests were clearly influenced by his mentor, wrote rabbinic biographies and exhibited a keen interest in Hebrew literature and poetry.[107] When Prossnitz's Hebrew school opened its doors in 1838, Weisse marked the occasion with an original Hebrew poem.[108]

Weisse's curriculum for the Prossnitz school represented a sharp departure from the traditional course of study in Moravia's heders. Rather than placing emphasis on the rote memorization of rabbinic literature, Weisse's curriculum was designed to ensure that Jewish students learned—and *understood*—the Hebrew Bible as well as the Sabbath, festival, and daily prayers. Special attention was paid to the fundamentals of Hebrew grammar, which was treated as a discrete discipline and deemed essential for understanding Judaism's central texts. With regard to Bible study, the narrative sections were given precedence over strictly halakhic ones. In contrast to traditional heder instruction, which began with the book of Leviticus, Weisse's curriculum started with the books of Genesis, Exodus, Numbers, and Deuteronomy—leaving the dry, ritual-laden book of Leviticus for later. Weisse's curriculum also focused on the Prophets and Writings, which were largely ignored in the traditional heders. In addition, the prayer book was studied—and not just memorized—with the help of a German translation. Daily prayers were learned first, followed by the Sabbath prayers and the occasional festival prayers. This corresponded to the overriding goals of the curriculum, which was designed so that students could learn the basics first and then progress incrementally to the more difficult or less quotidian subjects.

Talmud instruction was not a central feature of the school curriculum. Only students who intended to become rabbis were required to study Talmud—and only after they had completed the basic curriculum in grammar, Bible, and prayer. Beginning in their fourth year, these students received instruction from Hirsch Fassel in Talmud as well as instruction in "practical" and "ceremonial" law. These future rabbis also studied Aramaic grammar and translations (*Targumim*), Jewish history, and biblical geography as part of their professional training. These subjects were considered essential only for those students, like Fassel's son Moritz, who had their sights set on the rabbinate. For others, the basic curriculum—which covered the skills and knowledge necessary for daily religious observance—was deemed sufficient. They could use their additional time to learn "useful" trades—instead of being driven into petty trade or becoming members of what one Moravian Jew later called the "theological proletariat."[109]

To this end, the Prossnitz Jewish community, at the initiative of Hirsch Fassel, set up a Society for the Promotion of Handicrafts Among the Israelites in April 1839, the first such society established in Moravia.[110] Modeled after similar societies in the German states and elsewhere in the Habsburg monarchy, the Prossnitz society had the stated aim of reducing the number of Jews in petty trade by encouraging children "to learn useful trades." The Society for the Promotion of Handicrafts was composed of Prossnitz Jews who helped pay, through weekly donations, for the vocational training of some of the community's poor and orphaned children. By 1843, the Society was supporting twenty-one such individuals: six cobblers, three tailors, three hat makers, three weavers, two cloth makers, one baker, one locksmith, one butcher, and one tanner. Not surprisingly, there was much overlap between the supporters of the Hebrew school and the supporters of the Society for the Promotion of Handicrafts. Although the school and the Society were institutionally separate, they clearly complemented one another. The school was set up to impart the basic knowledge necessary for religious observance, with the expectation that students would devote additional time to training in their chosen vocations. For those who intended to enter the rabbinate or become schoolteachers, the Hebrew school provided specialization in Talmud, Jewish history, and so on. For those who wished to pursue a different path, the Society helped ensure that they had the necessary training.

Although the Society for the Promotion of Handicrafts received government approval almost immediately, the Gubernium did not know what to do with the Hebrew school. In light of the 1826 decree prohibiting Moravia's Jewish communities from running their own public institutions for religious instruction, the Gubernium investigated the legality of the Prossnitz Hebrew school. Fassel testified that the school did not require government approval at all because of its indispensability for the practice of the Jewish religion. He explained that the *Shulḥan Arukh* required every Jewish community to have its own *talmud torah*, without which the children of poor parents would be deprived of instruction in Hebrew and Talmud. In Prossnitz, one of Moravia's largest Jewish communities, the *talmud torah* took the form of a separate institution that employed its own teachers. Housed in a building bequeathed to the community by Veit Ehrenstamm and supported by contributions from community members, the school had already received government approval in 1830.

Simon Bree, the first Jewish teacher at Prossnitz's German-Jewish *Trivialschule*, viewed the Prossnitz Hebrew school as a direct threat to his livelihood and tried to get the Gubernium to shut it down. When Bree was hired in 1830, the superintendent of the Prossnitz school district (Ignaz Kirchner) had hoped that the presence of a Jewish teacher would encourage Jewish parents to send their children to the German-Jewish *Trivialschule* rather than to private teachers.[111] Instead, as Bree's regular complaints to the Gubernium attest, the problem of Jewish truancy continued, allegedly exacerbated by the new Hebrew school.[112] Bree claimed that instruction at the Hebrew school was scheduled for the same time as instruction at the German-Jewish school, thus preventing students who attended the former from also attending the latter. In addition, strenuous instruction at the Hebrew school completely exhausted the students, leaving them with little energy for their studies at the German-Jewish school. (He also asked the Gubernium to determine which of the two teachers—Josef Weisse or Mayer Broll—was responsible for harming the German-Jewish school by "improperly prolonging" instruction time and "overtaxing" the students' abilities.)[113] By framing his complaint in these terms, Bree tried to strike a chord at the Gubernium, which had been trying for years to improve attendance at the province's German-Jewish schools.

Bree also played on the Gubernium's fear of "rationalism" and "indifference" by drawing attention to Josef Weisse's reputed connections to Jewish reformers in northern Germany. "Weisse studied in Prague," Bree pointed out, "where the learned Jews are in contact with the Jews of Berlin, Hamburg, and other places in northern Germany, who pass themselves off as scholars on account of their writings. [These Prague Jews] rejoice at the literary fame [of the northern German Jews], embrace their decisions and proposals, and attempt to introduce the latter here [in Austria]."[114] Josef Weisse, he claimed, fit this mold. Weisse's school curriculum, Bree suggested, was taken directly from the pages of the *Allgemeine Zeitung des Judenthums* ("appearing in Berlin [sic!]"), where the curriculum for Prussia's Jewish *Trivialschulen* had recently been published. Bree's comments were echoed by Ignaz Kirchner, who similarly warned the Gubernium of the dangers emanating from northern Germany. "If one allows all of the writings of the Berlin Jews, without distinction, into the hands of the local inhabitants," he warned, "rationalism and indifference will gradually insinuate themselves among the so-called cultivated Jews of the Austrian Monarchy. As a result, the belief in divine revelation, which provides the sole guaranty for conscientiousness and loyalty towards the government, will disappear among the members of this nation—or at least among its most influential segment."[115] Kirchner considered Weisse's curriculum a paving stone on the path to godlessness and sedition, leading to "the forfeiture and weakening of the spiritual powers of children, but not to their edification, calming, and useful application in life." Kirchner even recommended that Trebitsch propose an alternative school curriculum, based on the rationale that the "strictly Orthodox" chief rabbi would never allow "Berlin Jewish rationalism" into the schools.

In his role as chief rabbi, Trebitsch was asked to comment on the Hebrew school in Prossnitz. As could be expected, he vehemently opposed this educational institution, seeing it as both a deviation from traditional forms of Jewish instruction and a direct challenge to his own rabbinic authority. In his testimony at the district office in Brünn, Trebitsch stressed that the school was not only unprecedented and unnecessary but also illegal.[116] He began by debunking Fassel's claim that a *talmud torah* school, like the one in Prossnitz, could be found in every Jewish community since time immemorial. "It is not true," he testified, "that every Jewish community has an educational institution called a *talmud torah*, where instruction in the Hebrew language and the Old Testament is given publicly." He explained that Fassel had completely misconstrued the *talmud torah*. In fact, the term *talmud torah* did not designate a school at all but rather an endowment—which could be found in every Jewish community—that supports private teachers for the Jewish poor. Such teachers, "who are examined and certified by me, according to the regulations," had always provided instruction in the mentioned subjects ("as well as the Talmud") for rich and poor children alike. Thus a public religious school was unnecessary and redundant. In addition, the 1826 decree had expressly forbidden just this kind of "public educational institution."

Despite the pedagogical, legal, and religious arguments presented by Bree, Kirchner, and Trebitsch, the Gubernium adopted a highly positive stance in relation to the Hebrew school in Prossnitz.[117] Far from viewing the school as a thorn in the side of the German-Jewish school, the Gubernium deemed it "indispensable" for the Jews of Prossnitz. The Gubernium looked especially favorably on Weisse, even though Bree and Kirchner had taken pains to cast aspersions on him. "Josef Weisse enjoys an exceptional reputation among the Jewish people," reported the Gubernium, "not only in the Hebrew language, Bible, and Talmud, but also in Hebrew stylistics and poetry, Aramaic grammar, rabbinic commentaries, biblical geography, and Jewish history." The Gubernium dismissed Kirchner's concerns about Weisse as an ideologically disruptive force. "Rationalism and indifference," it noted, had been endemic (*sehr heimisch*) among the cultivated Jews of Prossnitz, even before Weisse's arrival. The main concern of the Gubernium was the legality of the school in light of the 1826 decree. If the Hebrew school was a public educational institution, then it was clearly interdicted by law. If it was a private educational institution—as Fassel asserted—then a major obstacle could be removed. The Gubernium recommended that this question be investigated further.

Shortly after the establishment of the Hebrew school in Prossnitz, the Nikolsburg Jewish community decided to set up its own religious school (as well as a Society for the Promotion of Handicrafts among the Israelites).[118] In Nikolsburg, as in Prossnitz, the drive for

educational (and occupational) reform originated with the lay leaders, but the actual course of these reforms bore the unmistakable mark
of the respective communal rabbis. It should come as no surprise that
Trebitsch, who shunned the innovations introduced by the Prossnitz
school, took steps to uphold traditional Jewish education, placing a
primary emphasis on the study of Talmud. In October 1838, the board
of the Nikolsburg Jewish community proposed the establishment of a
"combined Hebrew-Talmudic-German educational institution," consisting of two divisions: one focusing on German subjects and the
other on "Hebrew and other moral subjects."[119] Although the proposal envisioned German and Hebrew instruction under one roof,
the two were to be kept separate, with German subjects being overseen by the district superintendent and Hebrew subjects being super-
vised by Trebitsch. Trebitsch gave his assent to this proposal in the
following terms:

> As the supreme religious authority, I must say that I am most pleased
> to see the awakening of the charitable spirit in this community, the
> first and largest [Jewish] community in Moravia, which lends a hand
> to the establishment of this highly important German-Hebrew and
> Talmudic educational institution. As for me, I will immediately put
> together a plan for the public teaching of all Hebrew subjects—and
> especially Talmud—in a well-regulated school.[120]

Trebitsch's curriculum undoubtedly differed substantially from the curriculum of the Prossnitz Hebrew school. Although Weisse and Fassel
had altered the content of Jewish instruction in Prossnitz—placing emphasis on Bible, Hebrew grammar, and the prayer book—Trebitsch repeatedly stressed the centrality of Talmud study. This was presumably
reflected in his curriculum as well.

Trebitsch recognized that the ideological disposition of the religious
teachers would determine whether the school became a transmitter of
religious reform or a tool for strengthening religious knowledge, observance, and piety. As the "supreme religious authority" in Nikolsburg,
he was in a position to weed out the rotten apples and ensure that the
community school hire teachers "to whom Talmud instruction can be
entrusted." In Trebitsch's view, adherence to "true religion" (*wahrer
Religion*) was just as important as talmudic erudition in establishing an

individual teacher's suitability for the job. As he explained to the board of the community:

> With the absolute condition that true religion, and not innovation [*Neuerungssucht*], is the motivating force behind this communal undertaking, it is also necessary to ascertain when hiring teachers, whether they think and act in a religious-moral way, whether they will plant the seed of pure morality and fear of God in the hearts of the youth, so that this institution will become an exemplary institution [*Musteranstalt*] for all of our Moravian coreligionists.[121]

Although his remarks were addressed to the board of the Nikolsburg Jewish community, Trebitsch clearly had the whole of Moravian Jewry in mind. This became apparent in 1839, when he reiterated to the Gubernium his earlier 1833 proposal that the chief rabbi be given exclusive authority to examine and approve all religious teachers in Moravia.[122]

By 1839, there was little hope that Trebitsch's efforts to increase his authority beyond the confines of Nikolsburg would meet with any success. From the very beginning of his tenure as chief rabbi, his attempts to impose his will on Moravia's Jewish communities invariably resulted in a backlash against his rabbinic authority. Although Trebitsch was officially responsible for the educational affairs of Moravian Jewry, his efforts to gain exclusive authority over all the province's religious teachers seemed to many a recipe for disaster. One correspondent warned that such a prerogative would lead to a repeat of the "misunderstandings, frictions, and *hilul ha-shem* [desecration of God's name]" that resulted from Trebitsch's authority over rabbinic candidates. Rather than increase the chief rabbi's prerogatives, the correspondent sought to further diminish them. He proposed a commission—to be elected by Moravia's fifty-two Jewish communities—that would be charged with designing a Hebrew curriculum for Moravia's Jews.[123] Educational policy, he implied, should reflect the collective will of the Jewish communities, not the arbitrary dictates of the chief rabbi.

Throughout the 1830s, the will of the community came to take precedence over the will of the chief rabbi. As it turned out, Nehemias Trebitsch remained in the shadow of his illustrious predecessor and never managed to endear himself to the Jewish population he ostensibly oversaw. Ignored by the Jewish communities in Mährisch-

Weisskirchen, Prossnitz, Loschitz, and Neu-Rausnitz; challenged by rabbis Hirsch Fassel and Abraham Neuda; and censured by the Moravian-Silesian Gubernium, Trebitsch was remembered more than anything else for diminishing the stature of the venerable Moravian chief rabbinate. During his ten years in Nikolsburg, many of the prerogatives associated with this office devolved, for all intents and purposes, to Moravia's Jewish communities.

Four

Locking Antlers

Hirsch Fassel, Samson Raphael Hirsch,
and the Forging of a New Rabbinic Ideal

Following the death of Nehemias Trebitsch in July 1842, the Moravian chief rabbinate remained vacant for nearly five years, leaving Moravian Jewry without a "supreme religious authority" until Samson Raphael Hirsch arrived from Emden, Germany, in the summer of 1847. During this five-year interregnum, one of the longest in the history of the Moravian chief rabbinate, the religious, educational, and legal situation of Moravian Jewry was intensively scrutinized, not only by Moravian Jews themselves but also by the Court Chancery in Vienna and the Moravian-Silesian Gubernium in Brünn. The general consensus was that Moravia's Jews were lagging far behind their coreligionists in the rest of the Habsburg monarchy. As the Gubernium put it in 1847, "There has, indeed, been some progress in recent times for the Israelites in Moravia and Silesia, but not nearly as much as in the neighboring provinces."[1]

Moravia's rabbis—and the chief rabbi in particular—were increasingly viewed as the key to lifting the Jewish population to a higher educational, cultural, and moral level and simultaneously paving the way for the expansion of Moravian Jewry's civic and political rights. As Ismar Schorsch has shown in his study of the "modern" German rabbinate, this represented a sharp departure from the role of the traditional Ashkenazic rabbi, who functioned primarily as an expositor of Jewish civil and religious law.[2] The modern rabbi, unlike his late medieval counterpart, was the central figure in the day-to-day life of the Jewish community. His authority was derived not only from his talmudic erudition but also from his university education and his ability to provide spiritual and religious leadership to his fellow Jews.[3] This new model of rabbinic leadership, which had emerged in the German states in the 1830s, was just appearing in Moravia when Trebitsch passed away. Indeed, in 1842, only a handful of Moravia's rabbis—most of whom had clashed with Trebitsch in the late 1830s and early 1840s—could be considered modern in Schorsch's use of the term. Not even these rabbis, such as Hirsch Fassel, Abraham Neuda, and Michael Stössel, had obtained the hallmark of the modern rabbinate: a university degree. In fact, not until 1846, with the election of Dr. Moritz Duschak to the Aussee rabbinate, could Moravia boast a rabbi with a doctorate.[4]

The closest any Moravian rabbi came to this new rabbinic ideal was Hirsch Fassel, who introduced edifying reforms in the Prossnitz synagogue and stood at the vanguard of Jewish educational and occupational reform in Moravia. Fassel founded Moravia's first modern Hebrew school ("the mother of all similar schools in Moravia") in 1838 and helped establish Moravia's first Society for the Promotion of Handicrafts Among the Israelites a year later.[5] By the time the chief rabbinate became vacant in 1842, no other Moravian rabbi could match Fassel's "modern" credentials. Throughout the 1840s, Fassel's star continued to rise as he took part in the Europe-wide debates on religious reform and fought tirelessly to improve the social and legal situation of Moravian Jewry. To many it seemed that Fassel was poised to become Trebitsch's successor as Moravian chief rabbi.[6]

In the end, however, the native son was passed over in favor of a German import, Samson Raphael Hirsch. Although six years Fassel's junior, the Hamburg-born Hirsch (1808–1888) far outshone his older contemporary in the European Jewish firmament. With the 1836 publication of his path-breaking book, *Nineteen Letters of Ben Uziel*, Hirsch had established himself as the preeminent champion of traditional Judaism in the German-speaking world. In Hirsch, Moravia's Jews saw a celebrity who was worthy of the venerable chief rabbinate and, more important, a charismatic leader whose rabbinic experience in Germany made him particularly well suited to the needs of Moravian Jewry. Hirsch's Germany, beset by religious indifference and split by the increasingly intractable conflict between Orthodoxy and Reform, served as a cautionary example for Moravian Jewry. Many thought that Moravian Jewry, left to its own devices, would inevitably follow the destructive path blazed

by German Jewry. Many hoped that Hirsch, a product of this environment, would be in a unique position to help Moravian Jewry learn from
past mistakes and avoid German Jewry's pitfalls. His eloquent defense
of traditional Judaism, which came in response to the plight of German Jewry, could serve just as well as a blueprint—with the benefit of
hindsight—for the Jews of Moravia. Hirsch's Germany served not only
as a cautionary example but also as a model to be emulated. With respect to social integration, educational advancement, and civic equality, Moravia's Jews could only dream of the opportunities that many
German states provided. Hirsch, who attended the University of Bonn
before becoming chief rabbi in Oldenburg (1830–1841) and Emden
(1841–1847), played an active role in advancing these processes by building bridges between Jews and Christians, establishing modern Jewish
schools under his own purview, and fighting for Jewish emancipation
in East Friesland. As a foreigner in Moravia, Hirsch risked being out
of touch with Moravian Jewry, but his outsider status also provided a
possible advantage: He could hope to transcend the petty quarrels that
had divided Moravia's Jews in the 1830s and 1840s. Unlike Fassel, who
had grown up under the watchful—and often critical—eye of his fellow
Moravian Jews, Hirsch provided an invigorating breath of fresh air.

Emergence of a New Rabbinic Ideal

Even before the final denouement in the Neuda affair, which pitted
Abraham Neuda against Nehemias Trebitsch, the Court Chancery
asked the Gubernium to comment on whether "the post of chief
rabbi—which does not even exist in Bohemia or Galicia—can be completely eliminated in Moravia as well."[7] This issue had been broached
a number of times after Emperor Joseph II reduced the chief rabbi's
scope of activity in the 1780s, but it took on a new urgency after
Trebitsch's "improprieties" reduced the stature of the post even further.[8] The Court Chancery questioned whether Moravian Jewry still
needed a central religious authority and whether a single chief rabbi
was still capable of tending to the "spiritual and moral" needs of more
than 37,000 Jews in fifty-two communities. At the Court Chancery,

Ministers Franz von Pillersdorf and Franz von Stadion viewed the chief rabbi as "a trifle, a historical reminiscence without any real purpose, or at least without the proper means for fulfilling his calling."[9] They cast a glance at the district rabbis in neighboring Bohemia and Galicia and inquired whether such a decentralized system (one district rabbi in each of Moravia's six administrative districts) would be more suitable for the needs of Moravian Jewry.

After consulting with the six Moravian district offices in autumn 1842, the Gubernium took a strong stance on retaining the Moravian chief rabbinate, which it viewed as the religious focal point of Moravian Jewry, a religious authority responsible for maintaining the "uniformity and purity of the Jewish religion."[10] Its report depicted the chief rabbi as a kind of bishop who exercised religious and moral authority over local rabbis, religious teachers, and common Jews. Although one dissenting opinion noted that "Judaism, unlike Christianity, has no secret dogma and no hierarchical organization," the report clearly presented a different view, asserting that a "central point is essential for every religion" and that "the absence of such a leader will lead to schism in doctrine and religious practice and will engender indifference and sectarianism."[11] The report expressed suspicion of any deviation from traditional religious practice, be it religious indifference or religious innovation, viewing "uniformity of doctrine" as a necessary bulwark against the deterioration of traditional Judaism and the encroachment of "new Judaism."[12]

Nonetheless, maintaining the "uniformity and purity of the Jewish religion" did not mean securing strict Orthodoxy at all costs. In fact, several district offices expressed concern over the overwhelmingly Orthodox character of the chief rabbinate. Trebitsch's ten-year tenure certainly contributed to this perception, but the root of the problem lay in the exclusive role of the local rabbis in electing the chief rabbi. All six electors and all six elector substitutes were required to be rabbis, leaving the laity no formal voice in electing the titular head of Moravian Jewry. One district office proposed including laymen in the election process because an "Orthodox conclave" would always prefer a "renowned talmudist" for the post.[13] In a similar vein, a member of the Gubernium lamented that "only narrow-minded talmudists or nationalists are elected" to this post, which does not serve the "general interests" of Moravian Jewry.[14]

While the Gubernium and Court Chancery deliberated on the fate of the Moravian chief rabbinate in 1842–43, individual Moravian Jews submitted suggestions of their own. These suggestions, which ranged from setting up a council of rabbis to involving laymen in the electoral process, sought to reduce the strictly Orthodox character of the chief rabbinate. In October 1842, four Moravian rabbis asked the Gubernium to appoint a "provisional" body to assume the essential tasks of the chief rabbi: the examination of rabbis and religious teachers.[15] The request is significant because three of the four signatories—Hirsch Fassel, Abraham Neuda, and Michael Stössel—had been embroiled in prolonged and vitriolic confrontations with Trebitsch and presumably viewed the provisional appointment as a means of circumventing the conservative electoral process that had brought Trebitsch to Nikolsburg in the first place. In February 1843, the lay leaders of several Jewish communities sought to modify this electoral process by demanding the inclusion of laymen alongside rabbis.[16] Hirsch Kollisch, Aron Karpeles, and Franz Pater of Nikolsburg and Gideon Brecher of Prossnitz were among the ten lay leaders who lobbied for the inclusion of "non-rabbis" as electors so that the election would "represent not only strict Orthodoxy, but also the humanistic principle." At the same time, Max Gomperz, a Jewish businessman in Brünn, requested the inclusion of "private individuals" in the election of the next chief rabbi.[17] A Prossnitz correspondent to the German-Jewish weekly *Der Orient* (possibly Fassel, a regular contributor) praised Gomperz's intervention, viewing the inclusion of laymen as a means for avoiding the "yoke of hierarchy" and the general encroachment on Jewish communal autonomy. The "power of the armored Talmud heroes can only be vitiated," he argued, by involving enlightened laymen in the affairs of Moravian Jewry.[18]

A new ideal chief rabbi emerged in the reports of the Moravian-Silesian Gubernium—a rabbi who could steer Moravian Jewry between the Scylla of Orthodoxy and the Charybdis of Reform, a rabbi who could command respect through talmudic erudition as well as secular enlightenment. The Gubernium sought a moderate, conciliatory figure whose moral and religious authority would not be undermined by factionalism and isolationism. It set its eyes on a candidate who "does not slavishly hang onto the old form" or the "perhaps even more harmful party of religious innovators."[19] Several district offices indicated their preference for "an enlightened man" with "the most thorough religious knowledge," all the while stressing the importance of "nonpartisan[ship]."[20] The new chief rabbi was expected to serve the "general interests" of Moravian Jewry as well as the specifically religious ones. This included, above all, elevating the educational level of Moravian Jewish schools. "Although there are many enlightened men among the Jews of Moravia," claimed the Olmütz district office, "the general educational situation of the ordinary Jewish population makes the continued authoritative influence [of the chief rabbi] indispensable."[21] The new chief rabbi was expected to be a talmudic sage, a secular scholar, an enlightened pedagogue, and a moral beacon.

The Court Chancery's May 1843 decision to retain the post of chief rabbi opened a "new battlefield" for Moravian Jewry's competing factions. The ensuing debate over the election of Trebitsch's successor became a debate over the future character of Moravian Jewry as a whole. Would profound talmudic erudition be the main criterion for the chief rabbi, or would a balance of religious knowledge and academic training be the determining factors? Would the chief rabbi be seen as a "bibliotheca rabbinica" or as a force for the moral, educational, and political betterment of Moravian Jewry?

In February 1843, members of the Nikolsburg board highlighted the changing perceptions of the chief rabbi's "religious" duties. "Religion," they wrote to the Gubernium, "is the ultimate source from which not only all ritual commandments flow, but also all moral notions as well as all facets of practical life."[22] A Moravian correspondent to the *Allgemeine Zeitung des Judenthums* depicted the ideal chief rabbi as a pedagogical innovator, a moderate religious reformer, and a champion of political rights. "We need a man," he wrote, "who . . . not only distributes rabbinic diplomas, but also struggles for us and our rights, who can attend to our youth and their education, who possesses enough courage and determination . . . to pave a spiritually and politically free path."[23] In many respects, this new ideal was formulated as a direct antithesis of the cantankerous and conservative Trebitsch.

Hirsch Fassel Versus Samson Raphael Hirsch

Fassel, one of the few Moravian rabbis who approached this ideal, repeatedly drew attention to himself and his ideas by striking out against prominent rabbis with whom he sharply disagreed. Although the earliest stage of his rabbinic career was defined by his battle with Trebitsch, the next stage was dominated by a very different battle with Samson Raphael Hirsch. Both conflicts were highly personal in nature, but the conflict with Trebitsch focused on "modern" versus "premodern," whereas the argument with Hirsch centered around competing visions of the "modern." For Fassel, the conflict with Hirsch became a full-blown rivalry, bordering on an obsession. By attacking the most prominent and influential proponent of what would later become Neo-Orthodoxy, Fassel hoped to escape obscurity and publicize his own program for reconciling traditional Judaism with the spirit of the times. The rivalry began in 1839, when Fassel wrote a scathing critique of *Ḥorev*, Hirsch's follow-up to the *Nineteen Letters of Ben Uziel*. Hirsch, in turn, responded with an acerbic and highly personal attack on Fassel, questioning his competence as a rabbi and scholar. At the time, the two rabbis were separated geographically, but the ideological divide that separated them was even greater. Fassel, who viewed Hirsch's stress on the legal character of Judaism as stultifying and antiquarian, watched Hirsch's meteoric rise with sheer and apparent envy. While Fassel was trying to publish his own "positive-historical" approach to Judaism in the late 1830s and early 1840s,[24] the younger Hirsch—whom Fassel regarded as a "semi-learned rabbi"—was becoming a household name.[25]

Hirsch's *Nineteen Letters* and *Ḥorev* are generally considered "epoch-making books."[26] *Nineteen Letters*, a defense of traditional Judaism in the modern world, was a landmark in the battle between Orthodoxy and the nascent Reform movement. Hirsch's short treatise was the first work to present a proud and forceful defense of traditional Judaism in clear and lucid German. Written in the form of fictional letters from a rabbi-philosopher (Ben Uziel) to a young Jewish intellectual, *Nineteen Letters* sought to reconcile traditional Jewish practice with the rational spirit of the age. As Ben Uziel, Hirsch imbued seemingly antiquated customs and rituals—which many Reformers wished to discard completely—with new meaning and significance. *Nineteen Letters* had a tremendous impact on many young Jews, including the 19-year-old future historian Heinrich Graetz, who, after reading it, was inspired to move to Oldenburg to become Hirsch's disciple.[27] Hirsch's *Ḥorev: Essays on Israel's Duties in the Dispersion*, published in 1837, has been called "a classical and most original exposition of the rationale and the underlying ideas of Jewish law," which "played an historic and perhaps decisive role in redressing the balance in favor of the conception of authentic Judaism as the Religion of the Law at a time when this conception was seriously challenged."[28] Hirsch's 800-page compendium of Jewish laws not only described the commandments but also gave an interpretation of their spiritual significance. Its publication sparked a heated debate in the German-Jewish world and established Hirsch's reputation as the leading voice of "tradition in the age of Reform."[29]

In 1839, Fassel entered the debate as one of Hirsch's harshest and most unrelenting critics. With the help of Moritz Steinschneider, who was studying in Leipzig at the time, Fassel published a critique of *Ḥorev*, titled *Ḥorev be-tsiyyon* (Desolation in Zion).[30] It was published semi-anonymously, and the author was listed on the title page as a "Jewish scholar and rabbi." Fassel, who revealed himself as the author in the course of the book, systematically demolished *Ḥorev*, accusing Hirsch of unwarranted halakhic stringency and uncritical and—at times—erroneous use of the *Shulḥan Arukh* as the ultimate arbiter of ritual practice. In Fassel's view, halakhic stringency was symptomatic of an antiquarian approach to Judaism—that is, preserving customs for the sake of preserving customs. He criticized *Ḥorev* for such an approach, even accusing Hirsch of being more Orthodox than the Orthodox with regard to certain customs, such as basking one's fingertips in the light of the Havdalah candle at the end of the Sabbath. Fassel also viewed halakhic stringency as evidence of insufficient mastery of rabbinic sources, a crutch for mediocre rabbis who were treading on unfamiliar ground. Echoing the traditionalist critique of Hirsch as a *siddur lamdon* (prayer book scholar), Fassel insisted that a "real *lamdon* [scholar] would certainly not have made the errors" found on the pages of *Ḥorev*.[31] Fassel's tone throughout is highly sarcastic, and his text is sprinkled with ad hominem attacks. As Hirsch observed in his own biting rejoinder to

Ḥorev be-tsiyyon, "Herr Fassel . . . considers the author of *Chaurew* [*sic*] to be a complete idiot."[32]

In 1840, Hirsch responded to *Ḥorev be-tsiyyon* with a highly polemical pamphlet titled *Postscript to the Letters by a Jewish Scholar and Rabbi*. He mercilessly dismantled Fassel's claim to be a "Jewish scholar and rabbi" through a litany of attacks on his talmudic erudition, rabbinic knowledge, and hermeneutical skills. He refuted nearly all of Fassel's sixty-seven criticisms of *Ḥorev*, asserting that "before a 'Jewish scholar and rabbi' wields the critic's sword . . . he must first read and understand the sources."[33] On one occasion, when Hirsch actually conceded that "Herr Fassel is right for the first time," he begged the reader to "take note of this miracle."[34] Hirsch's *Postscript* culminated in a complete censure of Fassel and his entire work. He wrote of *Ḥorev be-tsiyyon*:

> Truly, one does not know which should be more astonishing—the unbounded ignorance and thoughtlessness or the unbounded arrogance. Poor times [are these] when such a clumsy piece of work has the title "Jewish scholar and rabbi" emblazoned on its cover. Even poorer [times are these] when it is necessary to refute such a clumsy piece of work. Truly, if something must startle us out of the indolence with which we look on the dying of Torah knowledge, such "Letters by a Jewish Scholar and Rabbi" must be it.[35]

Leopold Löw encouraged Fassel to respond to Hirsch's defamatory attack, but Fassel temporarily withdrew from the public polemic. Fassel's sudden retreat may have been influenced by other negative responses to his work. Although Isaak Jost praised *Ḥorev be-tsiyyon* as "a product of solid expertise and very respectable conviction,"[36] *Der Orient* cautioned Fassel to avoid the "offensive-mocking" tone in his book that seemed to "invite the public's derision."[37]

In an unpublished letter to Löw, Fassel discussed the futility of responding to Hirsch's *Postscript*, claiming that he never intended to enter into the fray in the first place.

> You asked me why I do not defend myself against the *Postscript* of Herr Hirsch, and I ask you: What for? What is the purpose? . . . What would a defense against a fighter like Hirsch accomplish? . . . Herr Hirsch certainly possesses an inexhaustible supply of invective; he could just fabricate new postscripts. As far as I am concerned, I will

give him no [more] opportunities to populate the world with such monsters. Furthermore, the majority of readers do not take the time to look up passages to determine who is right, and usually give applause to the one who assumes a confident tone and can slander better. In this art, I know with certainty that I will always lag behind Herr Hirsch.[38]

Although Fassel removed himself from the public debate over *Horev*, he pulled out all the stops in his personal letter to Löw. He called Hirsch so "conceited" that he sees himself "as so great and others as completely insignificant."[39] His attack on Hirsch's talmudic proficiency, previously limited to mere jabs, now escalated into heavy blows. "Though he may forever be seen as a coryphaeus of rabbinic Judaism," he wrote, "for me he is nothing more and nothing less than a modern rabbi who has read the Talmud and *Shulḥan Arukh* without understanding the context, and who copied from the *Shulḥan Arukh* without considering its meaning."[40] Fassel saw Hirsch's "gross errors" in *Postscript* as "the clearest proof of how shallow his talmudic knowledge is and how superficial and flat his *Shulḥan Arukh* arguments are."[41] In a final blow, he denigrated Hirsch's personality and his erudition alike. "God could allow [Hirsch] to make such mistakes only if He is punishing him for self-conceit."[42]

That the polemic between Hirsch and Fassel quickly descended to the level of ad hominem attacks and sarcastic quips does not diminish the substantive differences separating the two rabbis, both of whom claimed to be operating in a traditional Jewish framework. Hirsch and Fassel, each in his own way, sought to blaze a path between "nihilistic" Reform and "ossified" Orthodoxy by reconciling tradition with the spirit of the age. Hirsch advocated some purely aesthetic changes (such as trimming the beard or wearing "Western" dress), but he remained resolute in the belief that all commandments—whether biblical or rabbinic—are of divine origin and therefore eternally binding. If certain commandments seemed irrational or otherwise incompatible with the zeitgeist, they were simply misunderstood. (In *Horev*, Hirsch spiritualized many of the commandments to give them contemporary meaning and relevance.)

Fassel, in contrast, believed that certain commandments could be eliminated if specific conditions were met. In an addendum to *Horev*

be-tsiyyon titled "Treatise on the Possibility of an Elimination of Existing Customs in Judaism from an Orthodox Perspective," he laid out
a system of rules that allowed for religious change within the bounds
of Halakha. He later expanded this system in a number of articles and
books. In contradistinction to Hirsch, Fassel regarded the binding nature of certain ceremonial laws as a function of time and place. Drawing
largely on the Talmud, *Mishneh Torah*, and *Shulḥan Arukh* (and their
commentaries), Fassel argued that a custom could be abolished if (1) it
was introduced accidentally, (2) it was never adopted universally, or
(3) the conditions under which it was introduced no longer pertained.
In other words, Fassel argued that scholarly inquiry into the historical
development of a certain custom could have important ramifications for
Jewish ritual observance.

Despite the considerable differences between Hirsch and Fassel in
their approach to religious reform, they shared many of the same views
on educational reform. Fassel's views, interspersed throughout his critique of *Ḥorev*, could easily have been written by Hirsch himself. Fassel
criticized the traditional system of primary education, lamenting the
lack of adequate institutions for instruction in the "moral" and "ceremonial" elements of Judaism.[43] Because Jewish education was relegated
to the home, he argued, children were being reared inadequately. In
some homes, children were taught "no trace of the Jewish life cycle,
except perhaps the simple dogmas of Mosaism"; in other homes, they
were taught "meaningless actions without spirit and life." In both cases,
children lacked schools with trained teachers who could teach them
Bible and religion and imbue Jewish customs with meaning.

Fassel's views on Jewish higher education also shared much in common with Hirsch's writings on the subject. Fassel's criticism of the traditional yeshiva—which he disparaged as "a chaotic bewilderment, a
useless something that is less than nothing"—was twofold.[44] First, he
criticized the unsystematic manner of instruction, which inevitably
forced rabbinic students to become autodidacts. In the yeshiva, there
were no lectures on casuistry or ritual law, he noted, "not to mention
exegesis, hermeneutics, homiletics, and rhetoric." Instead, students
were left on their own to learn "everything that actually belongs to the
rabbinical subjects." Second, Fassel criticized the exclusive focus on Tal-

mud and *Shulḥan Arukh* in an age when the role of the rabbi was undergoing a significant transformation. In addition to being an expositor of talmudic law, the "modern" rabbi was expected to be a beacon of "civilization" and a moral exemplar to the Jewish communities he served. Following an 1842 decree that required Moravia's rabbis to learn Natural Law, Fassel wondered how rabbinic students would acquire all these skills in the framework of a traditional yeshiva. "Where should the poor student find time to navigate a sea as expansive as the *Shulḥan Arukh* all by himself, without a helmsman, without a guide?"[45]

Like Hirsch, Fassel believed that the new times required new institutions of higher learning. To systematize rabbinic instruction, Fassel proposed a rabbinical seminary modeled after the Collegio Rabbinico in Padua. If the "handful of Israelites" in Italy had such an institute, he reasoned, why not the "hundreds of communities" in Bohemia and Moravia?[46] Already in 1837, Fassel had asked the Gubernium to establish a rabbinical seminary, and his determination to achieve this goal had not wavered since.[47] As he wrote in *Ḥorev be-tsiyyon*, "Yes, I confess, the establishment of [a rabbinical seminary] is my greatest wish. I go to sleep with it at night, I wake up with it in the morning."[48] He believed that the seminary's staff (three or four professors) could easily be supported through an annual contribution from the Jewish communities.

When *Ḥorev be-tsiyyon* was published in 1839, Fassel had already composed a compendium of Jewish religious practices for rabbinic students and rabbis alike. Titled *Kaf Moznayyim* (Scale of the Balance)[49] and written in Hebrew, this unpublished work was described by Moritz Steinschneider as "an original adaptation of the [*Shulḥan Arukh*]."[50] Fassel, it seems, viewed it as much more than that. In a letter to Gideon Brecher, Fassel portrayed *Kaf Moznayyim* as the culmination of an ongoing halakhic process dating back to the Talmudic period.[51] Historically, he explained, the halakhic consensus of an earlier generation eventually gives way to misunderstandings and conflicting interpretations. As a result, there is a periodic need for the recodification and reinterpretation of Jewish ritual law. The rabbis of the Talmud, for example, erected *gedarim* (literally "fences," or extra prohibitions) because they had forgotten the original meaning of the text. Afterward, confusion reigned again until Maimonides (1135–1204) tried to "put things back in order" with his *Mishneh Torah*. Because there were misunderstandings about the *Mishneh Torah* as well, Jacob ben Asher (c. 1270–c. 1343) subsequently composed the *Arba'ah Turim* for his generation, and Joseph Karo (1488–1575) composed the *Shulḥan Arukh* for his. Fassel expected his own compendium to become the definitive halakhic guide for Jews in the nineteenth century. He even justified his work in terms strikingly similar to those used by Maimonides and Karo.[52] *Kaf Moznayyim* not only would eliminate conflicting interpretations by conclusively establishing the Halakha in each case but would also avoid rambling discussions by explaining each decision "in the shortest and clearest possible manner."[53]

Kaf Moznayyim was designed for a future rabbinical seminary where the Talmud and *Shulḥan Arukh* would no longer be the exclusive focus of study. As Fassel explained to Brecher, it would serve as a guide for students so they would no longer "have to spend many days [navigating] the sea of the *Shulḥan Arukh* and all of its commentaries."[54] Indeed, if the rabbinic curriculum were expanded to include the Bible, homiletics, and other fields, a more efficient means of teaching Halakha would be nearly indispensable. Fassel expected students to use his compendium not only to prepare for their rabbinic exams but also to make halakhic decisions once they had been ordained. Fassel, it seems, hoped that *Kaf Moznayyim* would become a definitive guide for the new generation of rabbis and rabbinic students, far surpassing Hirsch's *Ḥorev*. Despite Fassel's high expectations—and his indefatigable efforts to find subscribers—*Kaf Moznayyim* was never published.[55]

Although Fassel was undeniably dwarfed by Hirsch, his conflict with the self-styled "coryphaeus of rabbinic Judaism" afforded him the publicity he so craved. As one Prossnitz Jew proudly reported in 1843, Fassel's name was "most gloriously known even in Germany."[56] Indeed, in the course of the 1840s, his rabbinic reputation extended well beyond his native Moravia, reaching Hungary, Germany, and even England. Between 1842 and 1846, at least five Jewish communities—Raab (Győr), Breslau, Kurhessen, Cassel, and London—actively courted him as their rabbi. (Kurhessen and London also courted Hirsch.) In the same period, the Jewish communities in Breslau and Pápa sought his expert opinion on matters relating to scholarly inquiry and religious reform.[57]

As will be seen, Fassel became most closely identified with rabbis from the conservative wing of the Reform movement. These rabbis, including Zacharias Frankel, Leopold Löw, and Adolf Jellinek, believed in the authority of the Oral and Written Torah and repeatedly affirmed the fundamentally legal character of Judaism. At the same time, they did not view Judaism as a static and ossified set of practices but rather as an organically developing religion. They were willing to make certain formal changes so long as they were in full accordance with Jewish law. Zacharias Frankel, one of the leading figures in this group, insisted that any developments had to be guided by "positive-historical" principles, not merely by the spirit and principles of the present. This meant that changes in ritual were permitted only if they did not conflict with the spirit of historical Judaism. Frankel, like Fassel and the others, criticized the more radical reformers (such as Abraham Geiger and Samuel Holdheim) for their often arbitrary and ahistorical approach to Jewish tradition.

In the early 1840s, Fassel was drawn into "the most significant controversy of the early Reform movement"—the Titkin-Geiger conflict in the Prussian city of Breslau.[58] The conflict erupted in 1838 when the Breslau Jewish community board elected Abraham Geiger, a founding father of the Reform movement, to serve alongside Solomon Abraham Titkin, a staunch defender of traditional Judaism. The conflict, which continued beyond Titkin's death in 1843, divided the Breslau Jewish community into two opposing factions and came to symbolize the seemingly unbridgeable chasm between Reform and Orthodoxy. As Michael Meyer has argued, the Titkin-Geiger controversy helped define the theoretical differences between Reform and Orthodoxy, particularly with regard to the question of scholarly inquiry into Jewish practices and beliefs.[59] The Orthodox faction argued that Geiger was not fit for a rabbinic post because his published scholarly articles had brought the authority and validity of rabbinic Judaism into question. As "an official of the existing rabbinic Judaism," a rabbi was expected to uphold traditional Judaism without questioning its fundamental practices and beliefs; otherwise, a person could not rightfully call himself a rabbi. As one of Geiger's detractors remarked, "If he likes, let him call himself a doctor, or scholar, or even preacher. Who can object to that? But with what right rabbi?"[60]

In response to the Orthodox attacks on Geiger's suitability for the rabbinate, the Breslau Jewish community board turned to leading European rabbis—including Fassel—who could be expected to support Geiger in the controversy. In his "Treatise on the Possibility of an Elimination of Existing Customs in Judaism from an Orthodox Perspective," Fassel had shown how a historical understanding of halakhic development could actually justify certain changes to Jewish ceremonial law. Certainly, Fassel could be expected to throw his unequivocal support behind Geiger. In the summer of 1842, the Breslau Jewish community asked Fassel and seventeen other rabbis—including Aron Chorin, Samuel Holdheim, and Ignaz Einhorn—to answer questions relating to the core issues in the prolonged Titkin-Geiger controversy. The rabbis were among the leading reformers in Germany and the Habsburg monarchy, and Fassel was the sole representative from Moravia asked to respond to the following questions: (1) Is progress at all allowed in Judaism? (2) May the many individuals who hold different views from earlier generations regarding the value and validity of talmudic regulations still be called Jews? (3) Can Jewish theology bear scholarly treatment and free inquiry? (4) Is a man who has adopted and disseminated a freer, more scholarly theological conviction entitled to claim the rabbinic office?[61]

At the end of 1842, the Breslau Jewish community published responsa from ten of the rabbis, but not Fassel's.[62] As the board made clear to Fassel, the absence of his responsum was not a mere oversight. The board apologized to Fassel "a thousand times" and explained that a number of passages had to be deleted before it could be published. Apparently Fassel's responsum did not sufficiently support the case for Geiger. As Fassel explained to Moritz Steinschneider, "I see right through them. All ten published responsa explicitly vindicate Herr Geiger. From my responsum one could extract, at most, an indirect vindication, which is not enough for the ministry. Therefore, they ask me to delete many a passage."[63] Fassel's equivocal answer to the board's fourth question—on theological conviction and entitlement to rabbinic office—presented the most difficulty. If an individual's published words gainsay an individual statute of Judaism but not an actual dogma, Fassel explained, then that individual is entitled to claim the rabbinic office. If an individual's published words gainsay one of the dogmas of Judaism, however, he is not entitled to do so. This passage could have been used to dispute Geiger's suitability for the rabbinic post in Breslau.

Instead of deleting the controversial passages, Fassel chose to publish his unexpurgated responsum as a separate brochure. At the urging of Brecher, Fassel turned to Moritz Steinschneider (in Prague), who had arranged for the publication of *Ḥorev be-tsiyyon* three years earlier (while in Leipzig). Fassel was convinced of his own genius and particularly of the utter importance—and originality—of his ideas. As he wrote to Steinschneider, "Call it vanity if you will. Still, I have enough discrimination to see that, in terms of rabbinical scholarship [*Wissenschaft*], none of the published responsa can measure up to mine." Along with his German responsum, Fassel also hoped to publish two Hebrew articles he had written at the behest of Leopold Löw (one arguing for allowing organ music on Sabbath and festivals; the other arguing for permitting Jewish deaf-mutes to study in Christian institutions). As Fassel explained to Steinschneider, the various publications were intended for different audiences. The German responsum was written for "the public," whereas the Hebrew articles were for "learned Jews" (*b'nei torah*).[64]

Fassel's German responsum, "Rabbinic Judaism: A Solicited but Unpublished Opinion for the Israelite Community of Breslau," finally appeared in *Der Orient* in January 1843.[65] In this article, Fassel set forth his conception of Judaism, which he later developed more fully in his first full-length book, *Tsedek ve-mishpat* (Justice and law).[66] According to Fassel, Judaism consists of two sets of divinely commanded laws: principles (*Grundsätzen*) and statutes (*Satzungen*). Principles, exemplified by Maimonides' thirteen principles of faith, pertain to all of humanity ("*eine Sache der Menschheit*"), whereas statutes, or ceremonial laws derived from principles, pertain to Jews alone.[67] Put differently, principles reveal eternal truths to humankind, and statutes instill a particular "sense of belonging" to the Jews. Both sets of laws are equally holy, but there is an essential distinction between them; whereas principles are inalterable and eternal, statutes can be suspended or abrogated under certain conditions.[68]

In making a distinction between statutes and principles, Fassel drew on two sources of authority: Moses Mendelssohn and rabbinic tradition. He cited Mendelssohn's philosophical treatise *Jerusalem* as evidence that one could make such a distinction and still remain true to rabbinic Judaism.[69] Mendelssohn had argued that Judaism comprises "religious dogmas and propositions of immutable truths of God" on the one hand and "laws, judgments, commandments, rules of life, which were peculiar to the nation" on the other. The former were revealed to all rational beings and remained intelligible "at all times and in all places." The latter were revealed to the Jews alone—as a means for bringing them "national" and personal felicity—but inevitably became unintelligible over the course of time.[70]

Mendelssohn constituted a modern authority, but it behooved Fassel to show that the distinction between statutes and principles was firmly rooted in "talmudic tradition" as well. Although he failed to locate a proof text in the Talmud, Fassel found a midrash that appeared to affirm the qualitative difference between statutes and principles. In Bamidbar Rabba, a collection of midrashim on the book of Numbers, a transgressor of "religious law" was treated differently from a transgressor of "moral law."[71] The transgressor of religious law was punished by talmudic law but was not condemned by humanity. The transgressor of moral law, in contrast, was punished by talmudic law and also condemned by humanity. In Fassel's view, this midrash was sufficient proof of a clear and essential dichotomy between Judaism's statutes ("religious laws") and its universal principles ("moral laws"). Although his case would have been stronger had he found a talmudic proof text, Fassel could still assert—as he did at almost every opportunity—that he had remained completely faithful to the "spirit of the Talmud."

As illustrated by his appeal to both Mendelssohn and midrash, Fassel tried to find a middle ground that would unify two competing factions in the Jewish world: one that sought to preserve a petrified Judaism and another that sought to eliminate Judaism's ceremonial aspects. Fassel strove to discard the antiquarianism of the former (exemplified by Hirsch) and the nihilism of the latter (exemplified by Holdheim and Geiger) by supplanting them both with a dynamic Judaism that remained true to both tradition and modernity. In all his works, Fassel affirmed the divinity of the Written *and* Oral Law, claiming to operate "solely in the talmudic sphere with regard to religion." He also believed, however, that the dynamic, flexible, and creative "spirit" of the Talmud had been corrupted and ossified after the Geonic period (sixth–eleventh centuries). He sought to restore this lost dynamism by stripping away post-Geonic laws and customs that were not immanent developments within Judaism but rather external accretions that had accumulated in response to the travails of exile ("the ballast of the later, dismal centuries").[72] He believed that historical Judaism had gone off course, thereby causing certain rituals and customs to develop in a manner that was incompatible with the true spirit of religion. It was time, he insisted, to put Judaism back on course and enable it to attain full perfection (*Vervollkommung*).[73]

By declaring his steadfast belief in the divinity of both the Oral and Written Law, Fassel placed himself in the conservative wing of the nascent Reform movement, most strongly identified with Zacharias Frankel. Others placed him further to the right. Isaak Jost, for example, considered Fassel's responsum to be "from the standpoint of Orthodoxy" because it ascribed equal authority to the Bible and the Talmud.[74] Some members of the Breslau community even considered Fassel Orthodox enough to become Solomon Abraham Titkin's successor. In 1845, when the Breslau community elected Fassel as its second rabbi—alongside Abraham Geiger—it was seen as an effort to appease the Orthodox faction, which had been seething with anger since Geiger's election seven years earlier.[75]

Fassel's election as rabbi in Breslau, Prussia's second largest Jewish community (numbering between 5,000 and 6,000 in 1845), provided further evidence that his rabbinic reputation had spread far and wide. At the same time, the fact that Fassel actually declined the offer—because it would have made him Geiger's subordinate—shed light on his pride and his lofty career ambitions. Fassel was offered the post of "second rabbi," a post that Geiger had occupied from 1838 until Titkin's death in 1843. Upon Titkin's death, Geiger was promoted to "first rabbi," leaving the lesser post of second rabbi to be filled. When Fassel was elected to this post in 1845, he gave the Breslau community a firm ultimatum: Unless he was placed on full parity with Geiger "in every respect," he would decline the offer.[76] When the board refused to accede to his request, he kept his word. Fassel remained in Prossnitz, and Titkin's son Gedaliah became the second rabbi of Breslau.[77]

From Prossnitz, Fassel continued to be involved in debates over religious reform, particularly during the rabbinic assemblies of the mid-
1840s. Held in Braunschweig (1844), Frankfurt-am-Main (1845), and
Breslau (1846), these assemblies were an attempt by reform-minded
rabbis in Germany to institutionalize a variety of religious reforms that
had been introduced by many Central European Jewish communities
during the 1830s and early 1840s.[78] Although intended as powerful dis-
plays of unity, the rabbinic assemblies had the unintended consequence
of mobilizing the conservative opposition, and thus dialectically contributing to the development of Orthodoxy and positive-historical
Judaism. Michael Meyer and Jacob Katz have shown how the Braunschweig Rabbinical Assembly, in particular, played a decisive role in
the reassertion of Orthodoxy.[79] Viewing participants in the assembly as
"usurpers of authority and destroyers of the Jewish faith," Rabbi Jacob
Ettlinger of Altona gathered signatures from 116 like-minded rabbis—
including 17 from Moravia—for a sharply worded letter of protest.[80] In
addition, Tsvi Hirsch Lehrin and Abraham Prins of Holland gathered
forty-two letters of opposition from rabbinic leaders in Europe and
Palestine, including a lengthy epistle from Samson Raphael Hirsch of
Emden.[81] Hirsch, like the other contributors, branded the participants
in the assembly as heretics and rejected their authority to decide basic
issues of ritual law, let alone to abolish customs that had been forbidden
by the Talmud and the rabbis.[82]

Fassel, too, emerged as an outspoken critic of the rabbinic assemblies, becoming one of the driving forces behind the more conservative
"theologians' assembly," which was scheduled to be held in Dresden in
October 1846. The call for a theologians' assembly—issued by Zacharias
Frankel in May 1846—constituted a public act of protest against the
third rabbinic assembly, held in Breslau in the summer of 1846.[83] As
organizer of the Breslau assembly, Abraham Geiger had gone out of
his way to invite moderate reformers such as Zacharias Frankel, Solomon Judah Rapoport, Hirsch Fassel, Adolf Jellinek, Abraham Kohn,
Michael Sachs, and Leopold Löw, but the invitees understood that
this assembly, like the previous two, would be dominated by radical
reformers who recognized neither the legal authority of the Talmud
nor the historical authority of Jewish tradition.[84] Initially, Fassel had

accepted Geiger's invitation, hoping he would be able to stack the assembly with other "like-minded rabbis," but it quickly became apparent that none of them would attend.[85] When he contacted the Moravian-born Adolf Jellinek, who had studied in Prossnitz before moving to Leipzig (and later Vienna), Jellinek informed him that "no rabbi who is not radically destructive [*radical destrüctiv gesinnt*]" would be attending the assembly. If Fassel went to Breslau, Jellinek warned, he would be there "all alone."[86]

Fassel chose not to attend the assembly. He explained his change of heart in a letter that was subsequently published in *Der Orient*, where he criticized the first two rabbinic assemblies for their nihilistic approach to the talmudic tradition and the capricious process by which decisions were reached.[87] "Why storm the fortress," he asked, "when the side gate is open?" In other words, why arbitrarily dismantle the ceremonial laws when the Talmud itself offers means for justifying and implementing certain changes (as he had shown in the addendum to *Ḥorev be-tsiyyon*)? Indeed, Fassel firmly believed that all necessary changes could and should be implemented "on the basis of talmudic tradition . . . and perhaps on this basis alone." Fassel also questioned whether participants in the rabbinic assembly had any authority to make binding decisions for other Jews. On the one hand, Jews who might respect these rabbis were already so far removed from traditional Judaism that they had no use for the assembly's decisions. On the other hand, Jews who might have use for the assembly's decisions had no respect for the participating rabbis. For Fassel, the Breslau rabbinic assembly was an exercise in futility.

In its place, Fassel supported the idea of convening a separate theologians' assembly, with the goal of bringing together "moderate Reformers" (*gemässigte Reformer*) who were firmly rooted in the talmudic tradition.[88] Only then, he believed, could an assembly claim the authority to reform any part of Jewish ceremonial law. In May 1846, at Fassel's instigation, Zacharias Frankel published a call for a theologians' assembly in the pages of *Der Orient*.[89] Frankel's call for participants articulated the underlying principles of what became known as positive-historical Judaism and managed to attract the interest of forty like-minded rabbis and scholars.[90] The assembly was planned for the fall of 1846, but because of strong Orthodox opposition, it was repeatedly postponed. It was rescheduled for July 1848, but with the outbreak of revolution in March 1848, it never took place.[91]

Hirsch Fassel as Political Leader

Before the Revolution of 1848, there was little open discussion of Jewish emancipation in the Habsburg monarchy. Unlike Prussia, Hesse, and other German states, where an "uncensored public discussion" of Jewish emancipation took place in the 1830s and 1840s,[92] the topic was treated gingerly in the Habsburg monarchy, particularly in Austria.[93] This is most clearly illustrated by the 1842 publication of Joseph Wertheimer's *Jews of Austria*, a milestone in the struggle for Jewish emancipation in Austria.[94] In an effort to bring about a complete overhaul of the existing laws in Austria, Wertheimer's book highlighted the disparities between the restrictive Jewish legislation in Bohemia, Moravia, Galicia, and Lower Austria on the one hand and the more progressive legislation in Prussia, Hanover, and Norway on the other. However, because such a book was forbidden under Austria's strict censorship laws, Wertheimer had his manuscript smuggled out of Vienna and published anonymously in Leipzig.[95]

Fassel's tactics were much less controversial, and his goals were far more modest. If his activities in the religious sphere often transcended the borders of the Habsburg monarchy, his activities in the political sphere focused on the specific grievances of Moravian Jewry. Through a series of petitions to Emperor Ferdinand, Fassel tried to redress the most glaring of these concerns.[96] Rather than struggling for the full civic and political emancipation of Habsburg Jewry, Fassel directed his energies toward one particular goal: placing the Jews of Moravia on the same footing as their coreligionists in Bohemia, whose occupational, residential, and marriage rights had been expanded by the Judenpatent of 1797.

Fassel's political activity on behalf of Moravian Jewry began after local officials in Prossnitz took rather drastic steps in their efforts to crack down on Jewish "concubinage." In 1841, the Plumenau Economic Office (Plumenauer Wirtschaftsamt), which had jurisdiction over Prossnitz, implemented a number of measures designed to punish and/or humiliate Prossnitz Jews who were suspected of illegal cohabitation or secret marriage. Women who gave birth to multiple children out of civil wedlock were to be sentenced to "long or short" prison terms as well as "public forced labor" (*öffentliche Zwangsarbeit*) as punishment for "persisting in their immoral behavior." In addition, single Jewish men were to be denied trade licenses (apparently based on the assumption that all single men were illicitly satisfying their natural urges).[97] These excessive measures stirred Fassel to action. A month after they were decreed, Fassel penned a petition to Emperor Ferdinand, decrying the injudicious measures taken against the Jews of Prossnitz and criticizing them for penalizing the guilty and nonguilty in one fell swoop.[98] The punishments, he claimed, were being meted out not only to proven transgressors but also to merely suspected ones. Furthermore, the refusal to grant trade licenses cruelly prevented single men from supporting their natural-born children. Fassel also worried that other Moravian communities would soon follow Prossnitz's example.

In his petition, Fassel transformed a local protest into an appeal on behalf of "the children of affliction, his fellow Jewish brothers in Moravia." Going into "heart-rending details," Fassel highlighted the injustice of Jewish legislation in Moravia, focusing in particular on the Familiants Laws and their deleterious effects.[99]

> For many years the natural increase of Moravian Jewry has been restricted. A Moravian Jew cannot get married legally unless he first obtains a familiant number; he cannot obtain a familiant number unless someone else exits the community—either through death or some other means. This law so severely contravenes nature and all of its most fiery impulses and lusts. Furthermore, it is so injurious to all virtues and morality: as a rule, there are fewer firstborn children than later-born children, and if the latter wish to acquire a familiant number and satisfy their God-given desires by legal means, they are out of luck. They must resort to illegal means, which explains the large number of illegitimate children born in Moravia's Jewish communities—disproportionately high compared to Jewish communities in the empire's other provinces, where the Familiants Laws are not so strict and where it is not so difficult for Jews to get married. As a result, depravity, the breaking of laws, wild cohabitation, secret marriages, etc. are encouraged.[100]

In Fassel's estimate, the number of illegitimate Jews in Moravia was already approaching 5,000, that is, more than 15% of the total Jewish population. As a result, the problem was self-perpetuating and would not disappear by itself; because none of these Jews were entitled to a marriage license, they were all likely to "satisfy the laws of nature" either in secret marriages or outside wedlock, thus exponentially increasing the number of illegitimately born Jews in Moravia. The Jewish communities were already feeling the brunt of this "illegal population growth" because of the insufficient space in Moravia's densely packed Jewish quarters. As Fassel pointed out, this resulted in a shortage of houses and increased competition for the meager employment opportunities. Furthermore, because illegitimately born Jews were forbidden to engage in trade, their chances for eking out a living were so limited that they would place an unbearable financial strain on the Jewish community and its charitable organizations.

In Fassel's view, the discriminatory treatment singled out Moravia's Jews in particular. Nowhere else in the empire, he protested, were the Jews subject to so many biological, occupational, and residential restrictions merely because they act and behave like "human beings and not animals." Fassel appealed to the emperor's sense of justice:

> Why must we, of all the Israelites who live under Austria's mild scepter, be the least favored? Why in Moravia must the Familiants Laws be so strictly enforced? Are we not children of the same kind and merciful father? As subjects, are we not as loyal as the inhabitants of all the other provinces? Don't we pray to our heavenly Father for the well-being of our earthly father just as in the empire's other provinces? What have we done that the law graces us less than our fellow brothers in other provinces?[101]

Fassel called on Austria, "one of the first powers in Europe to alleviate the disgrace, the centuries of darkness and prejudice that had been imposed on [the Jews]," to finally ameliorate the "decrepit plight" of Moravian Jewry through a legislative act. He did not set emancipation as the ultimate goal but rather the extension of more lenient laws—particularly those already in place in Bohemia—to the Jews of Moravia. Fassel's efforts did yield some results but not to the full extent he had hoped. In Prossnitz, forced labor as a punishment for "concubinage" was suspended, but the Familiants Laws and all other restrictions remained in full force. As a contemporary newspaper observed, "The consequence of the Rabbi's petition has been the momentary stop to these barbarous persecutions, but not the attainment of any radical remedy."[102]

The gap between Moravian and Bohemian legislation in relation to the Jews further widened in July 1841, when the Bohemian Judenpatent of 1797 was modified.[103] Although the modification did not relax the Familiants Laws in Bohemia, it did ease the procurement of marriage licenses for Jews in certain occupations, permitting rabbis and school-teachers, for example, to marry, along with Jewish guild members (though without receiving familiant numbers). The modification also lightened restrictions on property ownership, allowing Bohemian Jews who distinguished themselves in "manufacturing, industry and sciences" or through "service to the state" to purchase Christian houses. Some were even permitted to acquire agricultural land so long as they worked it with "their own hands or through other Jews." Certain Jewish taxes were also eliminated, in particular, the emigration tax (which in Bohemia had been set at 20% of one's personal wealth).[104] In addition, the idea of setting up a Padua-style rabbinical seminary was considered.

Like the original Bohemian Judenpatent of 1797, the 1841 modifications were not extended to Moravia. At Fassel's instigation, efforts were made to place Moravian Jewry "at least on the same footing" as Bohemian Jewry.[105] On July 17, 1842, a number of Moravian Jews gathered in Brünn to deliberate on this matter, and a committee of three was charged with writing a petition to the Austrian government. The committee was scheduled to meet again in October, but the deputies apparently never completed their task.[106] Not until three years later did representatives of Moravian Jewry submit another petition—and once again Fassel played a central role.

In the meantime, Fassel devoted his energies to improving relations between Jews and Christians. In the ongoing struggle to ameliorate the plight of Moravia's Jews, Fassel understood the symbolic power of conciliatory gestures toward the surrounding Christian population. On a number of occasions, Fassel implored the Jews of Prossnitz to raise money for their Christian "brethren" in times of need. Had the donations been intended for other Jewish communities, Fassel's appeals would have merely confirmed the widespread impression that Jews were more deeply connected to their distant coreligionists than to their Christian neighbors. Fassel wished to dispel these impressions with acts of munificence toward fellow subjects, irrespective of their religion. In a Passover sermon in April 1843, for example, Fassel called on the Jews of Prossnitz to collect money for victims of a natural disaster in the Erzbirge region of Bohemia.[107] In September 1843, he called on the Jews of his community to raise money for the victims of a devastating fire in the nearby village of Urtschitz (Určice). As *Ost und West* (Prague) reported, "The dignified rabbi of [Prossnitz], Herr H. Fassel, once again put his eloquence [*Kanzelberedsamkeit*] to use in order to guide the charitableness of his listeners to this worthy cause." A "sizable sum" was reportedly collected.[108]

In an unprecedented act, the Catholic priest of Urtschitz, Peter Obderzalek, came to the Prossnitz synagogue to express his gratitude for the generous donation. As reported in *Ost und West*, Obderzalek addressed the Jews "not as a priest of another faith, but rather as a human being, [who came] to pour out his thanks before *his brothers*."[109] Fassel, in his effusive response to the priest's words, further developed this theme of common humanity, raising it to a nearly messianic pitch. The day on which the wolf and lamb shall dwell together, he exclaimed, had already begun to dawn. "The barriers separating brother and brother are loosening ever more," he continued, "and, with God's help, they will soon collapse completely."

The fact that this item appeared in *Ost und West*, the leading German-language paper in Bohemia, should come as no surprise.[110] Fassel, who spared no energy in trying to get his theological essays published, exhibited the same kind of resolve in his efforts to bring this latest accomplishment to the public eye. Right after Obderzalek's visit to Prossnitz, Fassel composed an article about the memorable day and asked Moritz Steinschneider (in Prague) to have it published in *Ost und West*. "It truly deserves widespread publicity," he wrote to Steinschneider. "In Moravia, on the Hana [plain], and in Prossnitz . . . such an occurrence is truly a rarity." *Ost und West* published Fassel's article, bringing this rare occurrence—and Fassel's self-proclaimed eloquence—to the attention of a broader public.[111]

On October 6, 1845, a deputation of Moravian rabbis and community leaders submitted a 24-page petition to Archduke Franz Karl, brother of Emperor Ferdinand (and father of the future emperor Franz Joseph), who was traveling through Moravia at the time.[112] At the head of the deputation stood Fassel, whose advocacy in the 1840s had made him the de facto political leader of Moravian Jewry. The 1845 petition drew heavily on Fassel's 1841 petition, stressing not only the unfulfilled promises and hopes of the Josephinian period but also the ever widening gap between Jewish legislation in Bohemia and Moravia. The similarity between the two petitions reflects the fact that the legal situation of the Jews had remained unchanged in the intervening four years.

The 1845 petition began with an affirmation of loyalty to the House of Habsburg, a paean to the tolerance and munificence of the exalted rulers.

> Since time immemorial, antedating the first historical sources of the [Moravian] Margravate, there have been Israelite coreligionists [*israelitischen Glaubensgenossen*] in this province; and, as far as history informs us, their loyalty to their rulers has been unshakable. Protected by Otakar II, oppressed by Ladislaus, they entered a new era under the most illustrious House of Habsburg. The sovereigns of this noble family have always protected them through rights and privileges. But the laws that have issued forth from the monarchs since Joseph II of blessed memory are of a different quality; they are imbued with the spirit of highest tolerance and true philanthropy; and just as all munificent rulers shine on in the annals of history like stars of the brightest magnitude, so too will they live on in the unforgettable memory of their Israelite subjects.[113]

The petition went on to lament that for Moravia's Jews these laws had remained largely unchanged in the sixty years since the Edict of Tolerance was issued. While the Edict of Tolerance certainly represented a huge step forward, many of its lofty promises were impossible to fulfill. For example, although the edict permitted Jews to engage in handicrafts, the unaltered restrictions on Jewish residence made this permission somewhat illusory. Because Jews were allowed to engage in handicrafts only within the confines of the Jewish quarter, many trades were essentially closed to them. Smiths, coopers, stonemasons, and carpenters, for example, needed large workshops, which were either unavailable or prohibitively expensive in the "narrow streets and circumscribed houses" of Moravia's cramped Jewish quarters. Turners, upholsterers, clock makers, and glove makers required large population centers to market their goods, but Jews were still prohibited from living in Moravia's largest towns. Consequently, a Jew who had learned an artisan trade with all his heart (*mit Lust und Liebe*) often had to return to petty trade. As the petition noted, this was "a deterring example for all his coreligionists who considered devoting themselves to a similar bourgeois [*bürgerlichen*] profession."[114]

Would-be Jewish farmers faced a similar predicament as a result of long-standing restrictions on property ownership. The Edict of Tolerance allowed Moravian Jews to lease agricultural land for twenty years, but it did not permit them to actually buy this land or erect buildings on it. In just twenty years, how could a Jew acquire the "practice and experience of a lifetime" that was required for farming?[115] If he was unable to own the land, how could he bequeath the fruit of his labors to his sons? As the petition explained, the Jews of Moravia would happily "cultivate the natural products of [their] fatherland" if only the state would grant them some security. The petition listed other Habsburg provinces where Jews were allowed to own agricultural land, such as Lombardy-Venice and Bohemia. It even referred to the "Karaite Jews," who were exempt from the general prohibition on Jewish land ownership in Galicia.

With regard to the Familiants Laws, the petition argued that they were not only inconsistent with Jewish legislation in other Habsburg provinces but also morally injurious to the Jews. In the words of the petition, the Moravian Familiants Laws were "an *anomaly* compared to the legislation of the other hereditary provinces" and "an enormous nightmare" (*mächtige Alp*) that burdens the Jews of Moravia, generates strife and litigation in the communities, injures morality, and leads to invalid marriages with unfortunate consequences for parents and children.[116] The petitioners hoped that Moravia would at least be put on parity with Bohemia, where the Judenpatent of 1797 allowed "useful" Jews to get married without a familiant number.

The petition yielded no immediate results, but it did serve as the starting point for deliberations on the Jewish question the following year when the Court Chancery in Vienna asked the Gubernium to describe the prevailing conditions among Moravia's Jewish population. The Gubernium was asked to report on three areas in particular: (1) the religious and moral education of the Jews, (2) Jewish communal and economic life, and (3) Jewish taxation—all of which had been raised in the petition from October 6, 1845. The Gubernium turned to the district offices in Moravia and Austrian Silesia, asking them to propose measures for ameliorating the plight of the Jews in their midst. Based on this input, the Gubernium prepared a report, dated May 8, 1847, "Proposals for the Reform of the Situation of the Jews [*Judenwesen*] in Moravia and Silesia."[117] The report examined many factors that kept the Jews of Moravia physically and socially isolated from the surrounding Christian population. Although the report attributed much of the blame to the Jews and their obstinate predilection for trade ("the core of [their] existence"), it also conceded that the policies of the state, which had been aimed more at protecting the Christian population than at reforming the Jews, were partly responsible for the current situation.[118] The Jewish quarter, for example, which was intended to protect Christians from Jewish competition, had actually strengthened the Jews' clannishness, reinforced their penchant for peddling, and kept them suspended in a perpetual state of moral depravity. If the Jews were to be reformed, all the district officials agreed, such restrictions would have to be relaxed and eventually removed.

The district officials reached a general consensus, but this did not mask the significant differences of opinion between the twelve Moravian officials and their two Silesian counterparts. The Silesian officials advocated full and immediate emancipation of Silesian Jewry—up to and including intermarriage between Jews and Christians.[119] Allowing Jews to purchase arable land, they argued, was the surest way of weaning them from trade and instilling in them a passion for agriculture. Similarly, allowing Jews to acquire real estate outside the Jewish quarter would yield a number of benefits: Not only would complaints of overcrowded Jewish quarters cease "at once," but Jewish "vagabondage" would also become a thing of the past. Moreover, the Silesian officials expected closer physical proximity between Jew and Christian to translate into closer social relations as well. Eventually, it was hoped, the Jews would "merge together" with Christians through marriage and abandon "their old national seclusion [*Abgeschiedenheit*] vis-à-vis all other citizens of the state."

The Moravian officials fully agreed that Jews would benefit from increased interaction with their Christian neighbors, but they pointed out that the relative size of Moravia's Jewish population precluded any discussion of full and immediate emancipation at the time. As one of them declared, "What is possible in Silesia . . . is impossible in Moravia, where the proportion of Jews is too large and the Christian population would be deluged."[120] As the demographic data could easily demonstrate, Jews made up a mere 0.6% of the total population in Silesia and more than 2% of the population in Moravia.[121] This line of reasoning echoed the famous quip by Count István Széchenyi, who explained that Hungary, unlike France and England, could not afford to emancipate its Jews because a bottle of ink would leave no traces if poured into the ocean, but it would spoil a bowl of Hungarian goulash.[122] Like Széchenyi, the Moravian officials recommended steady but cautious reform so that the Christian population would not be overwhelmed by all the Jews in its midst.[123]

The Gubernium drew on the advice of the Moravian district officials and proposed that restrictions be removed only for Jews who "differed from Christians solely with respect to religion."[124] In other words, the Gubernium argued that regeneration should precede rights and not vice versa.[125] In a paragraph that could have been taken straight from the late eighteenth-century debates on Jewish emancipation, the Gubernium insisted that the state's ultimate aim was to place Jew and Christian on equal terms, "but only on condition that [the Jew] proves himself worthy of this award."[126] None of the existing restrictions would be justifiable, it continued, when the Jew finally engages in handicrafts, skilled labor, and industry "just like every other citizen."[127] The report insisted, however, that "the *sudden removal* of restrictions, which the experience of centuries has made necessary, would present the ultimate danger."[128] If the Jews were suddenly "let loose against the Christian population," they would surely nestle themselves in the middle of the Christian town and threaten the livelihood of its inhabitants.[129] For this reason, the Gubernium deemed it unwise to give preferential treatment to both the "worthy" and the "unworthy" with no distinction.[130]

Nonetheless, the Gubernium did recommend relaxing a number of restrictions to create more "worthy" Jews. Echoing the 1845 petition, the Gubernium considered the "restriction on the right to choose a spouse" to be the most severe constraint facing the Jews of Moravia and Silesia.[131] Not only did the Familiants Laws have "an infallibly negative effect" on Jewish morality, but they were also virtually impossible to enforce. As the Gubernium observed, no religious barriers prevented Jews from entering into illegal relationships, particularly because a clergyman was not required to preside at Jewish weddings. "Under an open sky," stated the report, "a Jewish layman [can] pronounce Moses' blessing over a couple, and according to Israelite religious principles, [the couple] is legally married." The effects of these secret weddings could be observed in the demographic data, which attested to the high number of illegitimate children, who, like their parents, were officially prohibited from getting married.[132] According to the report, these data showed that it was impossible to reduce the Jewish population through legislation that was patently "counter to the laws of nature."

The Gubernium did not propose eliminating the Familiants Laws per se, but it did suggest using marriage licenses to entice Jews into more "useful" occupations. Just as the Bohemian Judenpatent of 1797 (and its modifications in 1841) permitted certain Jews to marry without a familiant number (e.g., teachers, rabbis, and manufacturers), the Gubernium believed that similar exceptions should be put into place in Moravia.[133] Above all, the Gubernium believed that marriage laws should be relaxed for Jews who worked the land. Because attempts to attract Jews to agriculture had been "fruitless in every age," it was hoped that such added incentive would finally prove effective.[134] To such an end, the Gubernium suggested permitting marriage for those Jews engaged "exclusively" in tilling the soil.

In a similar vein, the Gubernium viewed expanded property rights as a means for attracting Jews to agriculture and other "useful" occupations. Although the Edict of Tolerance had allowed the Jews of Moravia to lease certain kinds of arable land and rural property for up to twenty years, it never allowed them to actually own it or bequeath it to their children. The Gubernium was convinced that such restrictions on property ownership reinforced the Jewish predilection for itinerant trade;

indeed, when the period of a lease expired, the Jewish leaseholder was often left with no other choice but to uproot himself from the land and embark on a life of "unproductive" trade.[135] If Jews were permitted to own land, however, they would not only become accustomed to a "settled life" (*ein fixes Leben*) but also familiarize themselves with the useful "branches in industry."[136] Indeed, as the Gubernium concluded in its report, the goal of turning the Jews away from trade would more surely be attained by permitting them to own property than by merely allowing them to lease it. Nevertheless, the Gubernium was not prepared to grant the Jews unlimited rural property rights. Instead, it proposed adopting the looser restrictions that had been in place in Bohemia since 1841.[137]

The Gubernium proposed relaxing the restrictions on property ownership in towns as well. As the law stood, Jews were permitted to own only "Jewish houses"; with special permission, they could rent "Christian houses" that abutted the Jewish quarter, but they were not allowed to own them. Here again the Gubernium suggested adopting the Bohemian law, which allowed the purchase of "Christian houses" by Jews engaged in "productive" occupations. For Moravia, this provision was considered especially desirable because it would help alleviate the "wretched conditions in the overcrowded Jewish quarters."[138]

Although most of the Gubernium's proposed reforms could be applied on an individual basis, the issue of Jewish taxation was an entirely different matter. More than any of the occupational, residential, and marriage restrictions, the "Jew tax" treated Jews as a corporate collectivity. As the Gubernium pointed out, this tax differed from all of the empire's other taxes in that it was not levied on individuals or even on individual possessions but rather "on the [Jewish] communities as such."[139] Therefore, if the state's ultimate goal was to integrate Jews into the larger society, then the system of Jewish taxation had to be completely revised. Furthermore, the Jew tax was a frequent source of tension within Moravia's Jewish communities, particularly because the more affluent Jews had to shoulder the tax burden of their indigent coreligionists. This situation was aggravated by the fact that each "familiant number"—and the correlated tax obligations—was linked to a specific Jewish community, even if the individual familiant did not reside there. As a result, the Gubernium received a steady stream of complaints from Jews such as Löbl Kohn, a Nikolsburg familiant residing in Vienna, who resented the excessively high taxes he paid to the Nikolsburg Jewish community, especially since he did not even live there.[140]

The Gubernium viewed the revision of Jewish taxation and the relaxation of certain restrictions as necessary preconditions for Jewish integration and regeneration, but it expected Moravia's communal rabbis to take the lead in this process by setting a moral and educational example for their fellow Jews. For this reason, the Gubernium paid particular attention to the standing of rabbis in their respective communities, expressing concern that eleven of Moravia's fifty-two Jewish communities had no rabbi in 1845 and that those communities that did have rabbis paid them disgracefully low salaries.[141] The Gubernium apparently feared that such salaries were insufficient to attract suitable candidates to Moravia's communal rabbinates or to endow these posts with proper respect. Nonetheless, some promising signs followed an 1842 decree requiring rabbinic candidates to complete pedagogical and philosophical studies before applying for a communal rabbinate.[142] Although the number of new rabbinic candidates with suitable qualifications was still quite small in 1847, the Gubernium proudly reported that some veteran rabbis had gone through the trouble of getting themselves officially certified in pedagogy and philosophy. It singled out Hirsch Fassel for special distinction.[143]

Fassel, whose petition from 1845 served as the basis for deliberations on the Jewish question, was the only rabbi—indeed, the only Jew—who was mentioned by name in the Gubernium's report from May 8, 1847. This honor was a testament to Fassel's indefatigable efforts on behalf of Moravian Jewry throughout the 1840s. Nevertheless, by the spring of 1847, the Gubernium had already turned its attention to a foreign rabbi, who it hoped would guide Moravian Jewry to new moral and educational heights. "If [this rabbi] truly lives up to the favorable description . . . regarding his erudition, moral character, etc., as well as the very keen expectations of Moravian Jewry, which seems to place great faith in this man's outstanding reputation, then we can certainly expect from him practical proposals for the education of rabbis and religious teachers."[144] Although not named, this foreign rabbi was, of course, Samson Raphael Hirsch.

The Election of Samson Raphael Hirsch
as Moravian Chief Rabbi

Although Fassel had emerged as Moravian Jewry's most vocal and visible spokesman during the 1840s, the lay leaders of the Nikolsburg Jewish community—who played a central role in the election of the new Moravian chief rabbi—placed their sights on his archrival, Samson Raphael Hirsch. Because the Moravian chief rabbi and the Nikolsburg local rabbi had traditionally been one and the same person, the Nikolsburg board assumed a decisive role in determining Trebitsch's successor. The two posts were linked primarily for financial reasons; the chief rabbi received one-half of his salary from the Moravian Jewish Landesmassafond (600 fl.) and the other half from the Nikolsburg Jewish community (600 fl.). To attract a suitable candidate to the chief rabbinate, both salaries—and both posts—had to be combined into one, even though the election processes remained separate and distinct. Whereas the chief rabbi was elected by a conclave of six rabbis (and six substitutes), the local rabbi was elected by the lay community board— which counted Hirsch Kollisch, Aron Karpeles, and Franz Pater among its officials in 1843–44. In February 1843, Kollisch, Karpeles, and Pater had not only asked the Gubernium to include "nonrabbis" as electors for the chief rabbi but had also shown their progressive colors by initiating various educational reforms. In 1839, they spearheaded the establishment of the German-Hebrew school in Moravia, where secular and religious subjects were taught under one roof.[145] In 1844, Kollisch, one of the wealthiest members of the community, established and personally funded the first school for Jewish deaf-mutes in the Habsburg monarchy.[146] Their progressive proclivities would clearly affect their choice for Trebitsch's successor; their wealth and influence would add more weight to this choice.

The Nikolsburg board first discussed the election of a new local rabbi in autumn 1843, more than a year after Trebitsch's death. After appointing Hirsch Teltscher, a local talmudic judge, as provisional local rabbi in 1842, the Jewish community took no immediate steps to find a permanent replacement. One observer explained this delay in terms of the factional strife that cleaved Nikolsburg Jewry in the 1840s. On the one hand, Nikolsburg remained the "seat of Orthodoxy and talmudic learning in Moravia"; on the other hand, the close proximity and regular traffic with Vienna had exposed "many wealthy Jews" to the "free ideas" of the imperial residence. The observer noted in May 1843 that no one had "taken any steps towards the election of a local rabbi [in Nikolsburg]." The community was apparently trying to "win time" until the conditions were right.[147] In the summer of 1843, however, the Gubernium ordered the election of a local rabbi within the next six months. The Nikolsburg community board began searching for suitable candidates—setting its initial sights on Dr. Rabbi David Joseph Wahrmann of Wischnitz (Wisnicze), Silesia.[148]

Doctor-rabbis were becoming commonplace in the German lands by the early 1840s, but they were still rare in the Habsburg monarchy. The Nikolsburg community was presumably drawn to Dr. Wahrmann because of his prestigious title, yet they soured on him because of his Reform proclivities. When the Nikolsburg community board sent a delegation to Wischnitz in August 1843, it recoiled at the doctor-rabbi's condition that he be spared the requirement to grow a beard. As one source related, a beard was still considered a *conditio sine qua non* for Moravian rabbis at the time.[149] The community board was looking for a new kind of rabbi, but it still wished to remain within the bounds of tradition. It was ready for a trimmed beard but not a clean-shaven face.

By the winter of 1843, the Nikolsburg board had set its sights on Germany, arguing that it could not find a suitable rabbi in the Habsburg monarchy. In December the board claimed that it was the "unanimous wish of the entire community" to find candidates who possessed not only "superior talmudic knowledge . . . but also a thoroughly grounded academic education . . . along with a truly noble disposition and genuine piety, so that they will be able to comply adequately with the demands of the age and the government officials." According to the board, no domestic candidates possessed the proper balance of these secular and religious qualities. The "old rabbis," it claimed, lacked academic qualifications, and the "new candidates" possessed merely superficial religious knowledge. It passed over "old" talmudic luminaries such as Salomon Quetsch in Leipnik and Joseph Feilbogen in Holleschau as well as "new" rabbis such as Hirsch Fassel and Abraham Neuda. In

December 1843, the Nikolsburg board decided that Samson Raphael Hirsch was the only rabbi who "understands how to draw the proper line [*die richtigste Grenzlinie*] between the prevailing indifference of to-day's rabbis and the old, stringent Orthodoxy [of the older rabbis], and who—through his exemplary, enlightened piety—can raise the devoutness, religion, and piety of the communities under his purview."[150]

The Nikolsburg board understood that the election of the local rabbi had ramifications for all of Moravian Jewry. On March 20, 1844, the boards of various Moravian Jewish communities convened in Brünn—presumably at the initiative of the Nikolsburg board—to discuss inviting Hirsch to Moravia.[151] Although the election would ultimately be conducted by rabbis, the assembly of community boards ensured that the laity would participate in choosing the chief rabbi. The assembly was favorably inclined toward Hirsch, and in April 1844, the Nikolsburg board sent a delegation to Emden to discuss the terms of the invitation, which included a guarantee that Hirsch would be elected chief rabbi (and not just local rabbi) and the promise of an annual salary of 2,100 fl.—well in excess of the 1,200 fl. paid to Trebitsch. In October 1844, Hirsch was unanimously elected to the Nikolsburg local rabbinate; the question of salary was tabled for a later discussion.

Hirsch's qualifications for the chief rabbinate received immediate challenges. As might be expected, the most vociferous opposition to the assembly's decision came from Fassel. In 1844, he labeled the choice of Hirsch a "great mistake" and proposed Dr. Zacharias Frankel, the Bohemian-born rabbi of Dresden, instead.[152] Two years later, in his own application for the chief rabbinate, Fassel questioned the necessity of bringing a foreign rabbi to Moravia in the first place. Waxing patriotic, he refuted the claim made by the Nikolsburg board that no qualified rabbi could be found in Moravia or the other Habsburg lands. Not only were the Moravian-born Löw Schwab and Leopold Löw serving two of the largest Jewish communities in Hungary (Pest and Nagykanizsa), but the Bohemian-born Zacharias Frankel had been elected rabbi of Dresden. Fassel also included himself among the Bohemian and Moravian rabbis who had found acclaim outside the Habsburg monarchy. He noted that both Kurhessen and Cassel ("the second community in the Prussian state, which far exceeds the first community in Moravia in number, wealth, and intelligence") had invited him to be their rabbi. Fassel drew attention to his own Moravian birth and criticized the Nikolsburg community for trying to "fetch the Moravian chief rabbi from the furthest reaches of Germany."[153] It is evident from Fassel's application that he did not expect to be considered for chief rabbi. More than anything else, his application was a formal protest against Hirsch and an attempt to keep his inveterate rival away from Moravia.[154]

The traditionalist opposition to Hirsch cast aspersions on his talmudic erudition and suspicion on his foreign origins. One epigone of Moravian Orthodoxy, Salomon Quetsch in Leipnik, was overlooked by the Nikolsburg board despite having been a candidate for chief rabbi after Benet's death in 1829. As described in a contemporary memoir, "[Quetsch] could not get over the fact that after the death of Trebitsch, not he, who believed he had the most claim to the rabbinate as a child of Nikolsburg, but a foreigner, Rabbi Samson Raphael Hirsch from Emden—whose classical education did not impress him at all, whom he called, pure and simple, an *am ha-aretz* [simpleton]—was elected."[155] Similarly, Benet's eldest son, Naftali, felt entitled to his late father's vacated position. (Isaias, who was in Nagykálló, Hungary, did not stake his claim this time.) In August 1845, Naftali Benet asked the Gubernium to appoint him chief rabbi and thereby put an end to Nikolsburg's illfounded attempts to elect a foreigner. In a patriotic flourish, he deemed the post of chief rabbi suitable solely for a child of Moravia.

> It is certain that patriotic feeling cannot inspire a foreigner like a native, that he is not able to fathom the spirit of a nation foreign to him the way a native son can; that an entirely different process guides his behavior, other principles, a different way of thinking. He possesses different customs and habits, which are to be found by the Jewish nation in foreign states and which cannot be reconciled with the customs and habits of our Moravian Jewish nation.[156]

Benet questioned not only Hirsch's compatibility as a foreigner but also his allegiance to Moravia and Austria. Only a native heart, he wrote, is predisposed to

> the true well-being of his fellow Moravians [*seine Landeskinder*] and [is] capable of making sacrifices for their vitality in the future. This

cannot be expected from a foreigner, since in times of danger and
need, he would rather search for happiness amongst his own. . . .
A foreigner cannot be trusted like a native—especially when one
considers the freethinking of which German foreigners are especially
guilty.[157]

By highlighting Hirsch's German origins, Benet sought to tarnish him
as both an untrustworthy leader and a subversive reformer.

Benet's and Fassel's self-serving patriotism found resonance in the
Gubernium, which also preferred a native son over a foreign import.
As a foreigner, Hirsch needed special dispensation to become Moravian chief rabbi, but the Gubernium at first refused to consent. Soon
after the October 1844 election, the Nikolsburg board requested a dispensation for Hirsch, explaining that there "are no qualified individuals
amongst the domestic [rabbinic] candidates."[158] The Nikolsburg Administrative Office (Oberamt) supported Hirsch, describing him as a
"dignified man, perfectly in tune with the exigencies of the zeitgeist."
His presence in Nikolsburg was especially desirable, because "such a
man, who is so well-versed in literature and also able to teach religion,
hardly exists among [Moravia's] Jews." The Administrative Office assured the Gubernium that a teacher who could foster progress in social life without damaging the "core of religion" was a rare occurrence,
particularly among the Jews.[159] Nevertheless, on April 15, 1845, the Gubernium rejected the board's request for a dispensation, deeming the
grounds "not valid enough." In a letter to the Court Chancery, the Gubernium insisted that "the impossibility of finding a qualified domestic [rabbi] has not been shown."[160] In addition, the Gubernium found
Hirsch's salary demands too high.[161]

The Nikolsburg board still had recourse to the Court Chancery,
which had granted dispensations to "enlightened" foreign rabbis in the
recent past. The Danish preacher Isak Noa Mannheimer had been of-
ficiating at Vienna's Stadttempel since 1824, and the Prussian Michael
Sachs had been installed at Prague's Altschul since 1836. In 1846,
Mannheimer personally intervened on Hirsch's behalf, praising him
to the Court Chancery.[162] Unlike the Gubernium, the Court Chancery
accepted the claim that Hirsch's theological, literary, and pedagogical skills far exceeded those of the local candidates. "It is conceivable,"

it wrote, "that the number of domestic candidates who are perfectly qualified for such a post cannot be very large due to the absence of domestic institutes for the training of rabbis." In fact, Hirsch's German origins were seen by some as an asset, not a liability. "As is known," wrote a dissenting member of the Gubernium, "the Jewish religious teachers in northern Germany distinguish themselves in education and intelligence, while . . . such individuals are hard to find at home, and in the current case even harder, since there are [all sorts of] quarrels among the Moravian Jewish communities." On May 5, 1846, the Court Chancery finally granted Hirsch a dispensation, confirming his appointment as Nikolsburg local rabbi.[163] On May 11, 1846, the *Allgemeine Zeitung des Judenthums* expressed "little doubt" that the rabbinic conclave would elect him chief rabbi as well.[164]

On October 16, 1846, the Gubernium ran an election announcement in the *Brünner Zeitung*, requesting applications from qualified candidates for the chief rabbinate by December 15. Candidacy was limited to Moravian, Silesian, and Bohemian rabbis and rabbinic candidates who had been examined in philosophical and pedagogical studies and exhibited a proficiency in the German language. Although Hirsch's election was a foregone conclusion, seven local rabbis submitted their candidacy: Hirsch Fassel, Abraham Neuda, Jakob Brüll (Nehemias Trebitsch's son-in-law), Dr. Moritz Duschak, Bernard Oppenheim, Moses Nascher, and Simon Lasch. Moses Feilbogen, whose decade-long pursuit of a rabbinic post had yielded no success, decided to try his luck as well. On December 27, the six rabbinic electors—Bernard Oppenheim, Salomon Quetsch, Chaim Pollak, Abraham Placzek, Pinkus Toff, and Abraham Neuda—convened in Brünn to deliberate over the candidates. Neuda, the head of the "Reform faction" among the electors, expressed initial opposition to Hirsch but eventually gave in to the will of the majority.[165] The elections were put off until December 30, apparently to ensure the unanimous election of Hirsch.[166] The six electors gathered in the home of Samson Fränkel, a Jewish banker residing in Brünn, where they each cast three votes—*primo*, *secundo*, and *tertio*. Hirsch was unanimously elected, receiving all six *primo* votes. Bernard Oppenheim, the great-grandson of the early eighteenth-century Moravian chief rabbi David Oppenheimer, came in second place, receiving four *secundo* and two *tertio* votes; Simon Lasch came in third, receiving one *secundo* and two *tertio* votes. The other votes were split up among Fassel, Neuda, and Brüll. On January 27, four and a half years after the death of Nehemias Trebitsch, the Court Chancery confirmed the election of the new Moravian chief rabbi.[167]

The fact that Fassel was not elected chief rabbi came as little surprise. Although he had emerged as Moravia's most prominent "modern" rabbi, he lacked the qualities that made Hirsch the preferred candidate, such as the European renown and near celebrity status that Hirsch had attained after the publication of his two "epoch-making" books in the late 1830s. Furthermore, as a native of Moravia, he was not able to rise above the fray of local politics or fully shed his image as an enfant terrible. In contrast, Hirsch, a foreigner and a charismatic leader, was seen as the rare individual who could rise above petty quarrels and prepare Moravian Jewry for the challenges that lay ahead. Although some considered Hirsch's German origins an asset, his foreign birth was also seen as a potential liability. Many recognized that his success in Moravia demanded the cooperation of his most outspoken critic. "We are anxious to know," wrote a correspondent to *Der Orient*, "how the relationship between Hirsch and Fassel will play out. . . . Will they become rivals or will 'strength in unity' be their motto?"[168] Fassel was dwarfed by Hirsch in the German-speaking Jewish world as a whole, but he was still Moravian Jewry's most visible religious, educational, and political activist. Many harbored hope that Fassel would use his position to facilitate, rather than frustrate, a smooth transition for the new chief rabbi. The correspondent from *Der Orient* hoped that Fassel would accommodate the Hamburg-born Hirsch, who lacked a crucial "knowledge of the terrain."

Five

Conflict and Revolution
Samson Raphael Hirsch and the Politics of Leadership, 1847–1849

> Remove your clothes of mourning, Nikolsburg!
> Wipe away your tears, Moravia!
> The year of redemption is nigh!

Markus (Mordechai) Boss of Prerau composed these lines in Hebrew soon after Samson Raphael Hirsch was elected Moravian chief rabbi at the end of 1846. Published in *Kokhevei Yitshak*, Boss's panegyric cast Hirsch's election in almost messianic terms.[1] In a similar vein, the Leipzig-based *Der Orient* predicted that the new chief rabbi would be "the founder of a new era."[2]

Hirsch (Figure 8) was welcomed to Moravia with all the pomp and circumstance ordinarily reserved for a royal dignitary or head of state. With his wife and five children, he traveled from Emden to Nikolsburg by train, arriving at the Moravian border on June 22, 1847. As his train traveled through Moravia, rabbis and communal leaders stood on station platforms to "joyously greet their religious leader."[3] Hirsch spent his first night in Prerau, where a torch-lit procession escorted him from the train station to his evening's quarters. The following day, on his way to Nikolsburg, he stopped off in Lundenburg, where the local Jewish community—and the youth in particular—received him with great fanfare. In Nikolsburg, Jews of all ages lined the main street in the Jewish quarter, holding "splendiferously decorated banners" to welcome Hirsch to his new home.

A week later, Hirsch was installed in Nikolsburg as chief rabbi of Moravia and Austrian Silesia. At the behest of the Nikolsburg Jewish community, Isak Noa Mannheimer and Cantor Salomon Sulzer came

Figure 8. Samson Raphael Hirsch, Moravian-Silesian chief rabbi, 1847–1851.
Courtesy of Jewish Museum in Prague, inv. č. 7767.

from Vienna to preside at the ceremony. Rabbis and communal leaders arrived from all corners of Moravia, along with a "tremendous crowd of private individuals of both sexes," who wished to participate in this once-in-a-lifetime event. The *Treue-Zions-Wächter*, a Hamburg-based Orthodox newspaper, viewed the sheer numbers as an auspicious sign—a rare expression of unity among a Jewry better known for its unrelenting communal strife. "Never before," wrote the Nikolsburg correspondent, "has Jewish Moravia . . . celebrated such a day. . . . Never before has Moravian Jewry . . . participated as a whole with such joyous unity and affectionate fraternal love as at the installation of Hirsch."[4]

Hirsch's installation did unify Moravian Jewry, in the sense that all eyes were fixed on the new chief rabbi. In the six months between Hirsch's election and his long-awaited arrival, the German-language Jewish press regularly touted his religious and scholarly credentials, depicting him as a panacea for all of Moravian Jewry's religious, social, cultural, and political failings. By the time he finally arrived, he had become the personification of Moravian Jewry's new hopes. "If one wants to signify the epicenter of Jewish Moravian interests in one word," observed *Der Orient* soon after his arrival, "then one [merely] mentions Hirsch. . . . Everyone has focused his attention on our new leader."[5]

Only four years after this initial euphoria, Samson Raphael Hirsch resigned as Moravian chief rabbi, putting an end to "the most frustrating period of his rabbinical life."[6] Hirsch returned to the German lands in the fall of 1851 after accepting an invitation to lead the small Orthodox faction in Frankfurt-am-Main. His subsequent thirty-seven years in Frankfurt—during which he emerged as the nineteenth century's "most uncompromising and militant defender" of German Orthodoxy—have completely eclipsed his brief yet industrious sojourn in Moravia. As a result, his tenure as Moravian chief rabbi—which would have been the apex of most other rabbinic careers—has been relegated to a biographical footnote. Although biographies of Hirsch abound, the scholarly examination of Hirsch's years in Nikolsburg is rather perfunctory—with a marked tendency to focus almost exclusively on the religious nature of Hirsch's difficulties there. It is often assumed that Hirsch's frustrations—culminating in his decision to abandon Moravia in 1851—were rooted in the same intractable conflict between Orthodoxy and Reform that came to define his subsequent career in Frankfurt-am-Main. Religious conflict, however, was only one obstacle that thwarted Hirsch's efforts to reshape and reinvigorate Moravian Jewry. The other obstacles were of his own making.

Hirsch's autocratic and centralizing leadership style brought him into direct and frequent conflict with many of Moravia's Jewish communities. As a newcomer to Moravia, Hirsch underestimated the fierce sense of local communal pride and the concomitant aversion to centralized rabbinic authority. At the same time, he came to Moravia with a "prophetic" self-image combined with an overinflated view of both the Moravian chief rabbinate and his own "mission" in this distant land. He defined and undertook his rabbinic duties in a manner that was perceived as "dictatorial" and "hierarchical," undermining the authority of Moravia's communal rabbis and challenging the autonomy of Moravia's Jewish communities. As a result, Hirsch's efforts to regulate the religious and communal affairs of Moravian Jewry met repeated—and at times vociferous—opposition during his first eight months in office.

It was only with the outbreak of revolution in March 1848 that Hirsch managed to garner wider support. During the revolution, he emerged as a leader the Jews could embrace, not because he changed his leadership style but because he shifted the focus of his activity. Steering relatively clear of the controversial religious sphere, he devoted his energy to a cause that all of Moravian Jewry could rally around: the struggle for civic and political equality. As chief rabbi, he played an important role in this struggle, in his adopted province of Moravia and in the Habsburg monarchy as a whole. By March 1849, when the Jews of the Habsburg Empire were briefly emancipated, Hirsch's fortunes as a leader had undergone a dramatic change. Indeed, the revolution provided him with an opportunity to unify Moravian Jewry, an achievement that had remained elusive in peacetime.

Hirsch set off for Moravia as though on a divine mission. According to one of his many eulogizers, he "went to Nikolsburg, to the Moravian lands, because he thought he could be a savior there. . . . [He thought] he could build a vigorous Judaism there out of the disunited forces that were destroying one another."[7] In an intriguing examination of Hirsch's early writings, Robert Liberles has speculated that

Hirsch viewed his entire rabbinic career in such prophetic terms, drawing inspiration from—and perhaps even identifying with—Elijah the prophet. Like Elijah, Hirsch viewed himself as a solitary defender of God's covenant with Israel, speaking out against those who had foolishly forsaken it.[8] This was even the leitmotif of his inaugural sermon to the Jews of Moravia, which he delivered at his installation on June 30, 1847, a day before the fast of 17 Tammuz.[9] In his sermon, Hirsch promised he would devote all his energy to upholding the integrity of God's Torah, particularly against those who observe the divine commandments according to their own whim and fancy. As a warning, he recalled the string of calamities commemorated by the following day's fast: the breaching of the temple walls, the cessation of temple sacrifice, the profanation of the Holy of Holies, and the smashing of the ten commandments by Moses. Hirsch insinuated that history was repeating itself, pointing out that in Moses' time "everyone picked up a shard [of the smashed tablets] that suited his needs." Hirsch's mission was to restore Israel's loyalty to God's commandments.

Hirsch's divine mission was echoed, and possibly even buttressed, by the contemporary German-language Jewish press. A correspondent from Emden cast Hirsch as a latter-day Abraham setting off on a divinely inspired journey. "Go, you high priest of the eternal faith!" he wrote in a paraphrase of Genesis 12:1–3. "Go unto the land that God shows you, and you shall be a blessing, and all who bless you will be blessed."[10] In drawing an analogy between Hirsch's departure for Moravia and Abraham's departure for Canaan, the correspondent apparently reflected Hirsch's own self-perception. In a sermon to the Jews of Emden, Hirsch reportedly explained that he was unable to resist the "holy zeal (which God plants in the breast of His devout ones) to bring a greater dissemination [of Torah]" to Moravia. Hirsch clearly viewed his new undertaking as a divine mission. "Vast Moravia," he claimed, was fervently awaiting his arrival.[11] The jubilant and euphoric celebrations in June 1847 surely confirmed this impression.

Hirsch considered the Moravian chief rabbinate to be "perhaps the most important field of rabbinical activity" at the time.[12] This perception was shaped to a large extent by the largely defunct Polizei-Ordnung of 1754, which had granted the Moravian chief rabbi "supreme authority" over most aspects of Jewish communal life in the province.[13] According to the Polizei-Ordnung, the chief rabbi not only oversaw religious and juridical matters pertaining to the Jews but also sat atop an extensive hierarchy of elected representatives from Moravia's individual Jewish communities. Although the Polizei-Ordnung described a highly centralized rabbinic hierarchy, most of it had been dismantled by the end of the eighteenth century, leaving the chief rabbi with diminished duties, prerogatives, and authority. A 1785 decree had abolished much of the chief rabbi's juridical authority, and a 1787 decree had eliminated the supracommunal hierarchy over which the chief rabbi had presided. As a result, when Hirsch became chief rabbi in 1847, most of the articles in the Polizei-Ordnung were no longer relevant. Nevertheless, when Hirsch turned to the Moravian-Silesian Gubernium in the summer of 1847 for a precise "job description," the Gubernium simply referred him to the Polizei-Ordnung from 1754.[14]

During his first eight months in Moravia, Hirsch frequently cited the Polizei-Ordnung in his correspondence with the Gubernium. In September 1847, he argued that the Polizei-Ordnung "obliged" the chief rabbi to set up a rabbinical seminary in Nikolsburg.[15] In October 1847, he referred to Article I when he proposed a Jewish religious school system in Moravia.[16] In January 1848, he requested a personal secretary in accordance with Article XXII.[17] In March 1848, he asked for clarification of Article IV's requirement that all newly elected rabbis take an oath of office "in the presence of the chief rabbi in the synagogue in Nikolsburg."[18] Although Hirsch had clearly familiarized himself with the articles of the Polizei-Ordnung, his inquiries to the Gubernium betrayed his general confusion about the duties and prerogatives of the Moravian chief rabbi. As Hirsch would later explain in his letter of resignation to Minister of the Interior Alexander von Bach, the failure of the Gubernium—or anyone else—to clearly define his field of activity in Moravia caused repeated and unnecessary frustrations. Hirsch asked Minister Bach to imagine "how strained the circumstances must have been for [him]" when he arrived in Moravia with no specific instructions, especially after his earlier experience in Oldenburg and Emden had led him to expect a prompt and precise clarification of his duties "from the [very] first moment."[19]

Without a clear job description, Hirsch tended to understand his duties in Moravia in terms of his seventeen years of experience as chief rabbi, first in Oldenburg and then in East Friesland (with his seat in Emden). In these German states, however, the chief rabbinate was a relatively new institution, differing in significant respects from its venerable Moravian counterpart. The Oldenburg chief rabbinate, for example, was created in 1829 as part of the state's efforts to elevate the moral, cultural, and educational level of the Jews. In many respects, the chief rabbi was more a government bureaucrat than a teacher and expositor of Jewish law. He was appointed by the state and charged with overseeing almost every aspect of Jewish life in the duchy's seven Jewish communities. His final word was required not only for hiring religious teachers (as was the case in Moravia) but also for ratifying synagogue regulations and communal statutes, approving school curricula, and apportioning communal funds. (His assent was not required for hiring communal rabbis because the other communities—some of which could not even assemble a prayer quorum [minyan]—were too small and impoverished to hire one.) As the only official rabbi in the Duchy of Oldenburg, the chief rabbi also personally inspected the schools, synagogues, and other institutions of the Jewish communities under his purview. In Oldenburg and later in Emden, Hirsch undertook periodic "inspection tours," dutifully reporting his findings and suggestions to the relevant government authorities.

Hirsch expected to perform similar inspection tours in Moravia, a clear indication that he extrapolated his duties in Moravia from his experiences in Oldenburg and Emden. In a letter to the Gubernium from October 1847, Hirsch insisted that his experience "in both . . . previous positions" had demonstrated that the "supervision and regulation of the inner affairs of the communities" was "indispensable." He proposed "periodic tours," during which he would personally inspect the conditions in each of Moravia's Jewish communities. Hirsch acknowledged, however, that he would have to adapt these inspection tours to the conditions in Moravia. "Due to the size and number of [Moravia's Jewish] communities," Hirsch explained, he "would certainly not be able to visit every community each year." Instead, he would visit one portion of Moravia's Jewish communities annually, thereby reaching every community "in a fixed period of time."[20]

Hirsch viewed the differences between the Moravian chief rabbinate and his previous positions, first and foremost, in quantitative terms. In the late 1840s, Moravia was home to roughly 40,000 Jews spread across fifty-two Jewish communities. In comparison, the Duchy of Oldenburg counted a mere 1,000 Jews among its inhabitants, spread across seven sparsely populated Jewish communities. East Friesland was slightly larger, with just over 2,000 Jews spread across eleven Jewish communities. When Hirsch moved from Emden to Nikolsburg in June 1847, his flock increased nearly twenty-fold. The Jewish community of Nikolsburg alone numbered over 3,670, and was larger than all of Oldenburg and East Friesian Jewry combined. Hirsch became acutely aware of Moravian Jewry's large size when his correspondence with its Jewish communities began to demand excessive amounts of time. In January 1848, he requested a personal secretary, explaining to the Gubernium that "the smallest inquiry [or] instruction must be written and dispatched at least fifty times."[21]

Unlike his predecessors in the chief rabbinate, Hirsch regularly distributed circulars, questionnaires, and pastoral letters to the fifty-two Jewish communities under his purview. Hirsch may have viewed these inquiries and instructions as merely an efficient means for maintaining contact with his new expanded flock, but they actually represented a significant redefinition of the chief rabbi's responsibilities. Hirsch's immediate predecessor, Nehemias Trebitsch, had not corresponded extensively with Moravia's Jewish communities, except perhaps to inform them which talmudic tractate would be studied each year in Moravia's yeshivas. Trebitsch's writing was primarily limited to talmudic commentaries and rabbinic responsa, whereas Hirsch's inquiries and instructions dealt with many of the more quotidian aspects of Jewish communal life, from school attendance to synagogue hygiene. Even the Nikolsburg Administrative Office (Oberamt) recognized that Hirsch's rabbinic responsibilities were far broader than those of his predecessors. In supporting Hirsch's request for a personal secretary, the Administrative Office observed that "S. R. Hirsch has broadened his sphere of activity for the good of [Moravian] Jewry."[22]

Not everyone concurred with the Administrative Office's positive appraisal of Hirsch's expanded sphere of activity. Hirsch's first inquiry created a minor furor, drawing severe criticism for its "hierarchical and dictatorial" tone. In July 1847, immediately after his installation as chief rabbi, Hirsch distributed a questionnaire to all of Moravia's fifty-two Jewish communities in an attempt to acquaint himself with the unfamiliar Jewish population. The questionnaire inquired about the state of the synagogues, schools, ritual baths, burial societies, charitable organizations, and other communal institutions.[23] Hirsch likely viewed the questionnaire as no different from the ones he had distributed as chief rabbi in Oldenburg and Emden. Indeed, the questions were nearly identical.[24] Forty-eight communities responded to the questionnaire without delay, apparently viewing it as perfectly consonant with Hirsch's duties as chief rabbi. Some may have even lauded the effort by this foreign-born rabbi to familiarize himself with their needs. In a transparent challenge to Hirsch's authority, however, four Jewish communities—most notably Prossnitz—did not return the questionnaire. The Prossnitz Jewish community complained that Hirsch had "overstepped his prerogatives" as chief rabbi and asked the Gubernium to clearly define—that is, restrict—Hirsch's administrative capacities, particularly in relation to Moravia's local rabbis and Jewish communities.[25]

Hirsch's questionnaire aroused such indignation because it encroached on the deeply entrenched autonomy of Moravia's Jewish communities.[26] His inquiry into the affairs of individual communities presumed the right to intervene in those affairs as well. In Oldenburg and East Friesland, where the sparsely populated Jewish communities could barely attract a minyan, let alone a learned rabbi, Hirsch had been expected to supervise and regulate communal affairs. In contrast, in Moravia, where many Jewish communities boasted celebrated yeshivas, renowned rabbis, and sizable populations, Hirsch's questionnaire—with its patronizing tone and centralizing tendency—was out of place. One Prossnitz Jew excoriated the "hierarchical and dictatorial language" of the questionnaire, pointing out that Hirsch deigned to refer to himself in the third person. The questionnaire, he declared, was more suitable for the handful of communities in East Friesland, than for Moravia's "large and educated communities such as Prossnitz, Boskowitz, Leipnik, Eibenschitz, etc." He considered the questions to be "ludicrous" because they belittled the qualifications and undermined the authority of Moravia's local rabbis. The Prossnitz Jew cited his own local rabbi, Hirsch Fassel, as a specific example.[27]

It did not take long before Hirsch actually intervened in the affairs of the Prossnitz Jewish community, directly attacking a lenient ruling by Fassel regarding the consumption of rice and legumes on Passover. After the poor grain harvest of 1846, Fassel had delivered two sermons permitting rice and legumes (which are forbidden to Ashkenazic Jews on Passover), arguing in line with many medieval rabbis that this prohibition could be temporarily suspended "in times of emergency."[28] In his ruling, Fassel aligned himself with many German Jewish reformers and created a bit of a stir in his own Moravia. In October 1847, Hirsch explicitly and publicly forbade the Prossnitz Jewish community from adhering to Fassel's ruling.[29] After the fallout from the questionnaire, perhaps Hirsch should have taken a more conciliatory approach toward Fassel—especially with Passover a full six months away. Instead, Hirsch chose to impose his ruling on a recalcitrant community, further alienating one of his most hostile and outspoken critics.

When Hirsch issued a synagogue regulation (Synagogenordnung) in December 1847, his attempt to impose order and decorum was again seen as an encroachment on communal autonomy. Synagogue regulations had played an important role in spreading religious reform in southern and western Germany. Hirsch's regulations, in comparison, were decidedly moderate, leaving the traditional liturgy completely unchanged. They did not suppress the "undignified" folk customs such as noisemaking on Purim and penitential flagellation on the eve of Yom Kippur, which Hirsch had steadfastly defended in *Horev*. In keeping with his aim of dressing traditional Judaism in modern garb, Hirsch's regulations dealt almost exclusively with synagogue decorum. Worshippers were instructed to preserve the sanctity of the synagogue by wearing clean clothes, praying in unison, and behaving in a respectable manner. They were prohibited from wearing dirty or ragged prayer shawls, talking during services, praying too loudly, and bringing children under 5 into the synagogue.[30] One of Hirsch's supporters considered the regulations a long-awaited "breakthrough."[31]

As Armin Schnitzer, a Hungarian Jew studying in Nikolsburg at the time, recalled, Hirsch's attempt to restore dignity to Moravian synagogues was perceived across the religious spectrum as an imperious violation of Jewish communal autonomy. "The synagogue regulation, which was posted at the entrance to all prayer houses in Silesia and Moravia was the 'Gessler hat,' which the communal rabbis had to revere in a silent, helpless rage."[32] In describing the regulations as a Gessler hat, Schnitzer made an unflattering comparison between Hirsch and the haughty governor in Friedrich Schiller's *William Tell*. Gessler, the imperial governor of Schwyz, humiliated the Swiss burghers by commanding them to show as much respect to his hat mounted on a pole as to his own person. In Schnitzer's view, the synagogue regulation was a mark of Hirsch's officiousness, and the fact that the regulation envisioned local rabbis as officials in Hirsch's religious bureaucracy certainly contributed to this impression. Rabbis were instructed not only to enforce Hirsch's rules of decorum but also to submit semiannual reports to him in Nikolsburg.[33]

Other conflicts arose in response to Hirsch's controversial handling of more traditional rabbinic duties. Like Nehemias Trebitsch, Hirsch became embroiled in a disputed rabbinic election in one of Moravia's larger Jewish communities. Unlike his predecessor, whose conflicts with individual Jewish communities were largely of his own making, Hirsch had the misfortune of inheriting a conflict that broke out in Austerlitz shortly before his arrival. In April 1847, the Austerlitz Jewish community overwhelmingly elected Hermann (Hirsch) Duschak as its new rabbi. Moses Feilbogen, one of eight candidates and a perennial applicant for rabbinic posts in Moravia, contested the election, arguing that he was the only qualified candidate and that no one else had been certified in philosophical and pedagogical studies as required by an 1842 decree.[34] Feilbogen was the son of Rabbi Joseph Feilbogen, a talmudic scholar in Holleschau, and Duschak was the younger brother of Dr. Rabbi Moritz Duschak, a moderate reformer in Aussee, but religious controversy did not play a pivotal role in the choice of Duschak over Feilbogen.[35] As members of the Austerlitz Jewish community pointed out to the Gubernium, "Moses Feilbogen has been applying for rabbinic posts for over ten years, but despite all of his certificates he has nowhere been taken into consideration—a proof that he is not suitable for practical life and cannot satisfy the needs of the community."[36] (Although he had never held a rabbinic position, Feilbogen even applied for the Moravian chief rabbinate in 1846.) Nevertheless, the Gubernium called for a second election, which Duschak once again won. The Gubernium accepted Duschak, pending an examination by the new chief rabbi.

In his capacity as Moravian chief rabbi, Hirsch examined Duschak's talmudic knowledge at the end of November 1847 in what should have been a mere formality. Duschak had already received recommendations from three Moravian rabbis (as required in the absence of a chief rabbi), the nearly unanimous support of the Austerlitz Jewish community, and the tentative approval of the Gubernium. Counter to all expectations, however, Duschak failed the Talmud examination. In a letter to the Austerlitz Jewish community, Hirsch expressed his deep regret and harbored hope that the "otherwise qualified" candidate would pass the next time around.[37] In a subsequent letter, Hirsch encouraged the Jews of Austerlitz to "seek peace and restore the fraternal unity" of the community while the Gubernium went about fixing a third election date.[38] Hirsch clearly recognized that his actions might divide the Austerlitz Jewish community, and he tried to remain impartial as the new election and examination dates approached. When Rabbis Joseph Feilbogen and Chaim Josef Pollak sought to intervene on Moses Feilbogen's behalf, Hirsch emphatically rejected their overtures.[39] Despite Hirsch's attempts at damage control, however, his handling of the contested election drew the scorn of at least one Austerlitz Jew. Writing in *Der Orient*, an incensed correspondent from Austerlitz accused the chief rabbi of throwing "a flame of discord . . . into our peaceful community" and criticized his autocratic behavior in the whole Austerlitz affair. If Duschak passed the next exam, he wrote, it would only be "by the divine grace of the papal chief rabbi."[40] Duschak did finally pass, but Hirsch's reputation in Moravia had been further tarnished.

Developments in the Lundenburg Jewish community reflected the shifting attitudes toward Hirsch in his first months as chief rabbi. Wagonloads of Jews had greeted Hirsch with "indescribably immense enthusiasm" when he passed through Lundenburg in June 1847.[41] By March 1848, however, the enthusiasm had soured, at least in the eyes of J. Schuster, who owned a small bakery in Lundenburg. Hirsch, who had promised to ensure "proper observance of the Sabbath," called on the local government officials to shut down Schuster's bakery because his (Christian) employees performed work there on Saturdays. Hirsch evidently suspected Schuster of violating the Sabbath. In a trenchant letter to Hirsch from March 3, 1848, Schuster underscored his bitter disappointment in the new chief rabbi.

> I am surprised the chief rabbi is suspicious of me, the very chief rabbi in which we placed the hope of our youth. At the initiative of this youth, we gave you a welcome fit for a king, because we thought a new era was upon us. We thought the chief rabbi was a sage and a learned philosopher . . . who would do his appointed task of making the dirty, downtrodden, oppressed Jew . . . into a human being.

Schuster continued by characterizing Hirsch's traditionalist approach to Sabbath observance as counterproductive in the struggle for Jewish rights.

> Here, where the Jewish community is so small and my sustenance comes from the *goyim*, am I supposed to tell my Christian customers that there is no bread today because it is the Sabbath!? Will he accept an answer like this? Will he buy bread from me all week long and go to a *goy* baker on the Sabbath? Will he not curse the Jew and his religion . . . ? Should I really abandon my trade (which I am quite proud of) in order to observe the Sabbath . . . and become a peddler from Sunday to Friday, carrying a bundle on my back as I wander around the villages to my shame and to the shame of my people?[42]

Schuster, like many other Moravian Jews, had expected Hirsch to foster the regeneration of Moravian Jewry through malleability in the religious sphere and resolve in the political sphere. Instead, Hirsch's interventionist approach to communal affairs combined with his general neglect of the political struggle had cast a pall of disenchantment over segments of Moravian Jewry by March 1848.

The Revolution of 1848

For Hirsch, the outbreak of revolution in March 1848 came at a propitious moment. He had ruffled many feathers during his first nine months in Moravia, yet the Revolution of 1848 suddenly enabled him to unify Moravian Jewry—albeit temporarily—under his rabbinic aegis. During the revolution, Hirsch emerged as a leader that Moravian Jews could embrace because he focused primarily on the struggle for the Jews' civic and political equality. Hirsch's activities between March 1848 and March 1849 steered relatively clear of the religious sphere, where he had been repeatedly criticized for his dictatorial and hierarchical leadership style. Ironically, these very qualities, which riled much of Moravian Jewry before the revolution, served as a unifying force from March 1848 onward.

From the outbreak of the revolution, Hirsch emerged as the spokesman for Moravian Jewry, expressing words of exhortation and admonishment through a flurry of circulars addressed to Moravia's Jews and Christians alike. In the first week of the revolution, Hirsch published two circulars, the first on March 20 to "our Christian brethren" and the second on March 23 to "the respectable Israelite communities of Moravia." Hirsch envisioned separate and distinct roles for Christians and Jews in the struggle for Jewish emancipation. Christians, motivated by their "sense of justice" and their "enlightened love of fellow man," were expected to make the Jews' struggle their own, to view Jewish emancipation as a necessary and integral part of their own struggle for freedom. Jews, in contrast, were expected to exercise patience and self-restraint, placing faith in their "Christian brethren." Seen in these terms, the "Christian" circular was a call to action and the "Jewish" circular was a call for calm and prudence.

In his appeal to "our Christian brethren," Hirsch stressed the moral necessity of Jewish emancipation in a society built on the principles of "truth" and "justice."[43] The Jews, he maintained, were a "touchstone" by which every nation on earth could test its worth. A nation's behavior toward the Jews demonstrated just how much "the divine had triumphed" and to what extent a nation was animated with "truth and justice, love and sanctity." Conversely, a nation's behavior in relation to its Jews could also expose the "lies and violence, hatred and degeneration" that keep a nation mired in darkness. In Hirsch's view, the German peoples had already proved their worth by "granting untrammeled rights to their Jewish brethren"; however, the people of the Habsburg lands had not yet risen to the occasion. "German princes have already sealed their justice by also granting the Jewish children of their empire equal rights," he observed. "Will Austria's noble sons be the last?"

Hirsch exhorted the "Christians in the common fatherland" to support Jewish emancipation, not only as an expression of "truth" and "justice" but also as an act of expiation for their past sins. In an earlier writing, Hirsch had already expressed the idea that Jewish emancipation was a form of spiritual redemption for Christians. "The Jew will be freed from the shackles of oppression," he wrote in 1843, "but the Christian will attain redemption from his shameful sin."[44] In his circular from March 20, 1848, Hirsch sought to stir his Christian brethren to action with a similar line of argumentation.

> Do not let us go alone to the throne of our common father! Speak with us, for us, and on behalf of us! Show us that justice has become a reality in your bosom. Show that you want to blot out the indignity of centuries. Not just the indignity that you have suffered. No, also the indignity—forgive me—that you have wrought! Show that you recognize us as brethren just as we recognize you as brethren. [Show us] that you are not capable of enjoying your own rights as long as just one of your fellow brethren still has to protest before God's throne that his right to be a human among humans, a citizen among citizens has been denied and trampled on God's earth![45]

Hirsch called attention to the particularity of Jewish suffering (and his Christian brethren's role therein), but he framed his argument for Jewish emancipation in more universalistic terms. Christians should speak out for the Jews, he declared, because they are fellow human beings, fellow citizens, and fellow brethren. In the context of the Habsburg Empire, they were part of an extended family, sharing a common father (the emperor) and a common fatherland. Furthermore, Emperor Ferdinand had long affirmed "the equality of all his children" in his heart and was merely waiting for "the express wish of his people." Perhaps this is why Hirsch addressed the first circular to his Christian brethren, calling on the Christian population to take an active role in the struggle for Jewish emancipation.

Hirsch's second circular admonished the Jews of Moravia to pursue a more quietist path.[46] "Only through self-restraint and calm," he wrote on March 23, "can you be helped." He expressed unqualified faith in

God and "our beloved Emperor," reiterating his conviction that the Christian population would include the Jews in all their demands. "And certainly your Christian brethren will be united with you," he wrote, "and bring your entreaties before the sublime throne of your common sovereign. Their sense of justice and their enlightened love of man will [surely] make them recognize in you equal brothers in a shared fatherland." Hirsch understood Jewish emancipation as a necessary correlate of the dawning constitutional age, so he was confident that the general struggle for individual freedoms would encompass the Jews as well. As he explained, "No special fruit will ripen for us, since we shall find our own welfare in the welfare of the whole." In other words, he was confident that the Jews would be emancipated as citizens, not as Jews.

Despite this optimism, Hirsch recognized that the passions and prejudices of the past were alive and strong. He realized that the individual freedoms promised by the imminent constitutional age would be tempered by the legacies of a fading corporate society, especially with regard to Jewish collective responsibility. In light of this, Hirsch urged Moravian Jewry to be on their best behavior.

> It is possible that the careless ones, first and foremost the youth . . . will be led to words and deeds . . . that will have highly ruinous consequences. You can incite animosity of your land-brethren through impertinent and injudicious remarks, through impudent, cheeky behavior. You can draw the displeasure of the high officials upon yourselves through impropriety and the instigation of disorderly acts (and you know how easily the blameworthiness of one Jew is transferred to all, and how all must atone for the displeasure earned by one).

Hirsch looked toward the future with bounded optimism, understanding full well that the Jews' yearning could be sabotaged by their own indiscretions.

Hirsch's admonitory circular was a response, in part, to the flood of anti-Jewish pamphlets emanating from Vienna in the first weeks of the revolution. Isak Noa Mannheimer viewed the sudden upsurge in anti-Jewish sentiment as a backlash against a petition, circulated in the first days of the Viennese revolution, that called for the immediate emancipation of the Jews. Like Hirsch, Mannheimer firmly believed that the Jews' best interests lay in the struggle for common human rights (as opposed to separate Jewish ones), as he enunciated in his oft-quoted eulogy on March 17 for the first casualties of the revolution. "What is there to do for *us*?" Mannheimer asked. "For *us*: nothing! Everything for the nation and fatherland."[47] Both Hirsch and Mannheimer hoped to deflect discussion of Jewish emancipation per se from the public sphere, preferring to include it in the general struggle for human rights.

Their hopes were dashed, however, when a wave of anti-Jewish violence swept across Hungary, Bohemia, and Moravia in April 1848.[48] As revolution spread from France eastward, it brought anti-Jewish violence in its wake, and the Habsburg monarchy was no exception. In the Kingdom of Hungary, anti-Jewish violence was reported in more than twenty locations, most notably in Pressburg. In Bohemia, Prague became the scene of regular violence. In Moravia, anti-Jewish violence erupted in Olmütz and Gross-Meseritsch in April and along the Hungarian border in early May.[49] Hirsch responded to the violence in Gross-Meseritsch by seeking an audience with Governor Leopold Lažansky, the highest imperial official in Moravia.[50] Lažansky assured Hirsch that any violence against the Jews would be dealt with in the appropriate fashion. "Every right," he promised Hirsch, "will have the strongest protection, and every injustice will receive the most vigorous punishment."[51] In a public letter (written in Czech and German), the governor condemned the "outbreak of fanatical intolerance against the Jewish population" and praised the efforts of the national guard, military, and government officials to "nip the disturbances of the peace in the bud."[52] Because burgher institutions such as the national guard were concerned with maintaining peace and order, Lažansky viewed them as the natural protector of the Jews against the wrath of the populace.

Sharing Lažansky's perception, Hirsch encouraged the Jews of Moravia to turn to the burghers—and not solely to the imperial officials—for protection. It was natural for Hirsch, the highest Jewish authority in Moravia, to look to Lažansky, but he believed that ordinary Jews should forge "horizontal alliances" with ordinary burghers.[53] In his view, the burghers—in contrast to the peasants—were imbued with a "sense of justice" that would eventually prevail over their atavistic animosity toward the Jews. Given this traditional hostility, Hirsch's depiction of the burghers was more wishful thinking than anything else. Hirsch presumably recognized that the Jews, who tended to live among the German-speaking Christian burghers, shared linguistic and cultural affinities that could serve as the basis for a Jewish-Christian rapprochement. In a circular from May 2, in which he conveyed Lažansky's promise of protection to Moravian Jewry, Hirsch counseled his flock to turn to the burghers (and their institutions) should anti-Jewish violence rear its head again.

> Should, God forfend, violence befall you, summon the government and the burghers (who are called upon to protect justice) to protect you. Should they not protect [you], let them know firmly and calmly that you will hold them responsible for all damage and all injury they were called upon to prevent. . . . In such a case where the nearest government does not find itself ready to protect you, turn immediately to their supervisors, and in really urgent cases—but only in such [cases]—turn directly to [Governor Lažansky].[54]

While holding the burghers responsible for upholding justice, Hirsch once again admonished the Jews to exercise calm and self-restraint. Any inappropriate behavior by the Jews might antagonize their Christian neighbors and serve as a pretext for further violence.[55] Several of the pamphlets emanating from Vienna in the early days of the revolution affirmed a causal link between the drive for Jewish emancipation and outbursts of anti-Jewish violence. The most widely circulated of these pamphlets, "Just No Jewish Emancipation!" by Hubert Müller, predicted anti-Jewish violence as a popular reaction to "premature" emancipation and deemed the recent anti-Jewish violence in France and Hungary a "cautionary example" for the Jews of the Habsburg Empire.[56] Müller emphasized the economically immoral and socially reprehensible behavior of the Jews, arguing that this behavior had to be changed *before* full civic and legal emancipation could even be considered. "Jews as they are *now*," he wrote, "are still *not* suited for civic equality and still have not earned it." In Müller's view, the pushy and insolent Jews continued to oppress the Christians through profiteering, currency speculation, and other unconscionable business practices. He explained that his anti-Jewish sentiments should be seen as self-protection, not "fanatical religious hatred." "We do not deny the Jews human rights," he insisted, "but we must protect ourselves so that the Jews do not in the end violate our human rights."

The April violence served as a serious setback in the struggle for Jewish emancipation, as can be seen by the treatment of this matter in two different drafts of the new constitution. An early draft, written before the April violence, guaranteed freedom of religion and full equality under the law to all citizens, irrespective of religion. The final draft, however, which was published by Minister President Franz von Pillersdorf on April 25—a few days after the anti-Jewish violence—temporarily tabled the question of Jewish emancipation.[57] Although the Pillersdorf constitution did grant suffrage to all citizens who met certain property requirements (including Jews), it vouchsafed religious freedom and equality only to the "recognized Christian confessions." Furthermore, the question of rescinding existing interconfessional inequalities was left to the Reichstag, which was to be elected shortly. So, although the Pillersdorf constitution introduced Jewish suffrage and even envisioned the eventual emancipation of the Jews, the long-awaited document was viewed as a double setback for Habsburg Jewry. It not only seemed to affirm the causal link between Jewish emancipation and anti-Jewish violence but also threatened to separate the struggle for Jewish emancipation from the empire-wide struggle for human rights.

In response, Hirsch and the Committee for Moravian Jewry drafted a petition to the Moravian Diet reiterating the wish for "full, undiminished equality of rights" for all citizens (as opposed to a partial amelioration of the Jews' legal status).[58] Hirsch had created the Committee for Moravian Jewry in mid-April after the Moravian Diet solicited information on the wishes and needs of Moravia's diverse population. On April 16, Hirsch called on Moravia's fifty-two Jewish communities to elect delegates for a general assembly to be held in Nikolsburg on April 21–22. With the exception of a few remote communities that failed to receive Hirsch's invitation in time, all other Jewish communities sent delegates to the assembly. As a first order of business, the assembly agreed to send a petition to the Moravian Diet in Brünn, which would present the grievances of Moravian Jewry and implore the members of the Diet to speak out on behalf of their human rights. To draft the petition, the Nikolsburg assembly elected a committee from the "elite of Moravian Jewry," consisting of two representatives from each of Moravia's six administrative districts. As chief rabbi, Hirsch served as chairman of this thirteen-member committee, whose first meeting he set for April 27.[59]

In the five days between the election of the committee and its first meeting, Moravia's political climate changed significantly. The outburst of violence in Gross-Meseritsch (and in nearby Pressburg) on April 23 and the promulgation of the Pillersdorf constitution on April 25 soured the committee's faith in the inexorability of Jewish emancipation. In its petition from April 28, the committee underscored its shattered expectations in light of the recent events, protesting that the Pillersdorf constitution left the Jews' legal status mired in ambiguity.

> The Constitution is now in everyone's hands. All members of the state can lose themselves in merry jubilation over this accomplishment. As an unambiguous citizenry, they can welcome an unclouded future with thankful hearts. We alone, the Jewish sons of the common fatherland, are still told to wait for a further outcome. We alone must defer our ardent wishes, our yearning . . . to additional gentlemen [i.e., the Reichstag].[60]

The committee argued that "half-guaranteed, half-promised rights" actually endangered the Jews, serving to dehumanize them in the popular imagination. The petition claimed that a partial amelioration of the Jews' legal situation would paradoxically worsen the Jews' general plight: "As soon as the state denies the Jew a single right, even a fragment of a right, it renders the Jew in the eyes of the people as a person who does not merit rights, who can be denied his due rights; and it thereby legalizes the very injustice and hostility towards Jews that we want to fight."[61] Using this line of reasoning, the committee asserted that full equality of rights was the only way to prevent a recurrence of anti-Jewish violence on Habsburg soil. The prevention of such violence was in the state's best interest, because anti-Jewish violence was essentially a "means for overthrowing the existing order." In other words, the "simple principle of equality of rights" would "protect the state and [its Jews]."[62]

The Committee for Moravian Jewry may have set its sights beyond the Habsburg state. According to one report, the committee reached a decision not only to draft a petition for the Moravian Diet but also to send a delegation (with Hirsch at its head) to the German parliament in Frankfurt-am-Main. The report noted the "guaranties for liberal disposition and human spirit" at the German parliament, where the "most noble Germans" could be relied on to support full Jewish emancipation.[63] The Committee for Moravian Jewry never sent a delegation to Frankfurt, perhaps to steer clear of the vociferous controversy over Bohemian and Moravian participation in the "German" parliament. (Bohemia, Moravia, and Austrian Silesia were asked to elect delegates to the Frankfurt parliament in April 1848, riling many Czech nationalists, such as František Palacký, who rejected the presumption that these lands were in any way part of "Germany.") Nonetheless, if the committee did consider pleading its case in Frankfurt, this may indicate that the events of April 1848 had worsened the chances that Habsburg Jewry in general and Moravian Jewry in particular would be emancipated any time soon.

With the struggle for emancipation temporarily stalled, Hirsch and Moravia's other "modern rabbis" began receiving sharp criticism for their relative inactivity in the political sphere during the first month of the revolution. As chief rabbi, Hirsch received the brunt of the criticism, but Rabbis Hirsch Fassel, Abraham Schmiedl, Moritz Duschak, and Abraham Neuda were not spared.[64] Criticism of Hirsch peaked after a Sabbath sermon delivered in Nikolsburg in mid-April in which he preached a message that could have been taken out of *Ḥorev*: Only strict observance of religious ritual could save the Jews from the "swelling torrent" of the times.[65] Linking religious laxity to divine punishment, Hirsch called on Jewish women to cover their hair, reprimanded Jewish men for shaving with razors, and warned both sexes against drinking Christian wine. In response to these exhortations, one Moravian Jew sarcastically noted that Hirsch had "more important things" to deal with than Jewish emancipation. He even questioned Hirsch's dedication to the cause. "What does a foreigner," he asked, "who has been with us for only a few months, have to do with our political interests?"

Hirsch reacted to this question with an outpouring of patriotism, calling on Moravia's Jewish households to donate objects of silver to the financially strapped Habsburg government. "The fatherland needs the resources of all its children," he proclaimed in his May 11 appeal for donations. Personal economic hardships notwithstanding, it was time for the Jews—like their non-Jewish compatriots—to help fill the depleted state coffers in these "extraordinary times." He called on Moravia's Jewish households to make donations on the "altar of the fatherland"—"each according to his means, nay, each above and beyond his means."[66] In the course of the next two months, Moravia's Jews donated 243 marks of silver for "patriotic purposes." The silver objects—including rings and other jewelry—were collected by members of the Committee for Moravian Jewry.[67] At the beginning of July, Hirsch personally delivered the silver to the imperial mint in Brünn, where it was turned into coinage.[68]

In late May 1848, Hirsch took a historic, unprecedented, and highly symbolic step when he was elected to the Moravian Diet, becoming one of the first Jews in the Habsburg monarchy to hold public office. His election was made possible after the previous Moravian Diet dissolved itself in early May, preparing the way for new elections—with an expanded electoral base—at the end of May.[69] Called the Peasants' Diet because 103 of the 261 deputies came from rural communities, the new Moravian Diet presented extraordinary political opportunities for Moravia's Jews as well. Because the new electoral law conferred the right to vote on all male adults who were "independent" or paid a direct tax, Jews who fit these criteria could not only vote in the May elections but also be elected to office.[70] Hirsch was elected to the burgher curia as a deputy for Nikolsburg. Two Christian burghers were also elected as deputies for Nikolsburg, but Hirsch stood out unequivocally as the "Jewish deputy" to the Moravian Diet.[71]

Hirsch's election was fraught with symbolism for Jews and Christians alike. A correspondent to *Treue-Zions-Wächter* viewed his election by a "nearly unanimous majority" as evidence that the chief rabbi had found approval among Jews as well as Christians. "He will surely be a nimble protector of the rights of his people," he proclaimed, "and those of his current fatherland—for the welfare and blessing of all."[72] The correspondent's reading of the election appears to have been overly optimistic, because the "nearly unanimous majority" must have been a majority of Jews, not a majority of Christians.[73] Furthermore, although his election may have signaled a tentative reconciliation between Christians and Jews, it simultaneously served as a catalyst for further anti-Jewish sentiment. In June, several burgher deputies tried to eject Hirsch from the Moravian Diet on grounds that he did not enjoy full "citizen's rights."[74] Later in the month, the same burgher deputies tried to exclude him from a committee on Jewish affairs.[75] Their proposal, however, was rejected "by a very large majority" (*mit sehr grossen Majorität*) of the Moravian Diet.[76]

Despite Hirsch's reputation as a polished orator, he delivered no dramatic speeches on the floor of the Diet. In fact, the protocols of the Moravian Diet record only two utterances by the chief rabbi during the body's eight months of deliberation. The *Allgemeine Zeitung des Judenthums* took notice of this, contrasting Hirsch's earlier perorations in the religious sphere with his regrettable silence in the political sphere. "He remains silent when speaking is an obligation," wrote the Leipzig-based paper in its only report from Moravia in 1848, "while on other occasions he should have remained silent."[77]

Although Hirsch's career as an elected deputy was rather lackluster, he proved himself to be a "nimble protector of the rights of his people" in his behind-the-scenes interactions. Over the course of the revolution, he personally interceded on behalf of Moravian Jewry, seeking an audience with Governor Lažansky after the April violence and then again on at least three more occasions. In this respect, the chief rabbi functioned as a kind of *shtadlan* (intercessor)—a communal or supracommunal functionary who represented Jewish interests before secular or other authorities, usually relying on personal contacts and political savvy.[78]

In the summer of 1848, Governor Lažansky asked Hirsch to submit a "brief overview of the onerous grievances that still afflict Moravian Jewry." Hirsch responded with a sixteen-page letter enumerating the manifold restrictions on residence, marriage, emigration, property ownership, and occupation, drawing particular attention to Moravian Jewry's inordinately high tax burden.[79] Hirsch gave a stirring depiction of "our dismal conditions," apologizing to Lažansky for his bold and brazen language. "Words mirror reality," he wrote. "If reality is black, the mirror cannot turn it to rose." Hirsch's blunt—and at times acerbic—language represented a sharp departure from the tone of his earlier circulars, but he still remained true to his emancipation ideology. The Jews' claim to equal rights, he stressed, was based not on the "quantity and pain" (*das Quantum und Quale*) of their suffering but rather on the "imperative of justice."

Nowhere, Hirsch informed Lažansky, had justice "been trampled so gravely and outrageously" as in the "behavior of the state towards the Jews in general, and towards Moravian Jews in particular." Even the occasional easing of Jewish restrictions, he charged, was motivated not by the principles of "justice and humanity" but rather by the state's concern for the "Jews' ability to pay taxes." Hirsch questioned whether such a policy was even economically advantageous to the state ("One must let the lamb graze if one wants to shear it"), but he concerned himself primarily with its deleterious effect on Moravian Jews themselves. Occupational restrictions, he argued, led to a proliferation of itinerant peddlers, who eked out a living in the countryside, leaving their children unattended during the week. "My heart bleeds as I describe these conditions," he wrote. "Ninety-nine percent of Jewish souls in Moravia grow up without the countenance of their father, without the eye of their mother." He blamed the Familiants Laws for putting "the morality of the Jews to a severe and unnatural test" and sowing "discord, hatred and conflict in the bosom of the [Jewish] community, provok[ing] circumvention of the law, bribery, concubinage and scandals of all sorts." The deleterious effects, however, were not limited to the Jews alone. The decay of the Jewish community, Hirsch proclaimed, also robs "the state of . . . an institution founded on the basis of morality."

Like many of his Enlightenment predecessors, Hirsch admitted the Jews' depraved moral state, placing blame for it squarely on the policies of the state. "Hasn't the state done everything," he charged, "to systematically deaden everything sublime and noble in [the Jew] and abandon him irredeemably to immorality and corruption?" Hirsch accused the state of thwarting the Jews' spiritual and moral advancement and called for the state to redress these historic wrongs. Hirsch's letter to Lažansky reached its crescendo with an appeal for full emancipation of the Jews. "With the complete determination of my soul," he wrote, "as man, as deputy, as Jew . . . there is only one answer . . . full emancipation, complete unrestricted equality of rights." Hirsch argued for emancipation on moral, humanistic, and constitutional grounds.

> May one man enslave another? May one man drive his fellow man into the corner in order to guarantee more elbowroom for himself? May

one man use his fellow man as a footstool in order to hold himself up high? May one man deny and rob his fellow man of even one of the holiest inalienable rights and possessions, the very ones that he himself deems his inalienable human rights that are to be respected by all?

After answering these questions with an emphatic "no, no, and evermore no," Hirsch insisted that the "people that still enslaves its Jews is itself not ripe for freedom," thereby rebutting the widespread claim that the Jews were "unripe" for emancipation.

Hirsch's July letter to Lažansky was not published during the revolution and has not been published since. As private correspondence, it is not clear whether it had any immediate impact on the struggle for Jewish emancipation. Nearly seven months later, however, Hirsch reworked this letter—at the behest of Isak Noa Mannheimer—into a memorandum (*Denkschrift*) presenting the case for emancipation to the Reichstag deputies in Kremsier. This memorandum secured Hirsch's reputation as Habsburg Jewry's preeminent spokesman during the revolution, but only after the Moravian chief rabbi had reluctantly—and perhaps even grudgingly—accepted this role.

Hirsch's transformation from the leader of Moravian Jewry to the spokesman for Habsburg Jewry can be understood by examining the relationship—and particularly the correspondence—between Hirsch and Mannheimer in the last months of the revolution. Although the two rabbis had apparently met only once (at Hirsch's installation in June 1847), they regularly corresponded between July 1848 and February 1849, keeping each other apprised of their respective efforts in the struggle for Jewish emancipation. Only the letters from Mannheimer to Hirsch have been preserved, so the content of Hirsch's letters can be reconstructed solely on the basis of these lengthy epistles. The correspondence exhibits a friendly rapport, which may come as a surprise to scholars who imagine Hirsch harboring nothing but contempt for his reform-minded colleague in Vienna. It could be claimed that the struggle for emancipation brought the two rabbis together in a marriage of convenience, but the intimacy of the correspondence reveals a deeper bond. Mannheimer addressed Hirsch as his "esteemed friend," and Hirsch's letters were likely filled with similar expressions of friendship—beyond mere cordiality.

Mannheimer and Hirsch complemented one another in the struggle for emancipation. As Reichstag deputy and vice president of the provisional Reichstag, Mannheimer played a central role in constitutional debates and enjoyed access to the highest echelons of political power in Vienna. Hirsch, as chief rabbi of Moravia, president of the Committee for Moravian Jewry, and a deputy to the Moravian Diet, limited his activities at first to Jewish affairs in his own province. He seemed content to leave the empire-wide political struggle to others. Even when the *Brünner Zeitung* proposed Hirsch in mid-June as a possible candidate for the Reichstag, there is no indication that he entertained the idea.[80] Hirsch was drawn into politics by the exigencies of the time and first sought Mannheimer's help in a matter that affected Moravian Jewry in particular: the elimination of the onerous "Jew tax" (*Judensteuer*).

The Jew tax referred to a number of special taxes that Jews were required to pay *in addition to* the numerous taxes levied on all inhabitants of the Habsburg Empire. Although the Jew tax was collected throughout the empire, the Jews of Moravia suffered under its burden more than Jews in any other province, with the exception of those in Galicia.[81] In Hungary, the Jew tax was gradually phased out, beginning in 1846, yet even beforehand, Hungarian Jewry's tax burden was significantly less than Moravian Jewry's. Furthermore, because the Jew tax in Hungary was commonly perceived as an intrusion into Hungary's internal affairs, refusal to pay was often viewed as an act of solidarity with the Hungarian nation. In Bohemia, a decree from 1846 gradually phased out the Jew tax and held the promise of the imminent elimination of all special taxes. In Moravia, in contrast, several Jewish taxes still burdened the Jews in 1848, namely (1) the familiant tax, (2) the consumption tax on foodstuffs, and (3) the contribution tax (which originated as a war tax during the Napoleonic Wars).

To illustrate the strain these taxes placed on Moravian Jewry, Hirsch described the tax burden of Nikolsburg Jewry in his July 14 letter to Governor Lažansky. Because more than half of the 620 Jewish families were "dirt poor," Hirsch wrote, the remaining 300 families paid the state 14,000 fl. annually "in addition to other general taxes." Furthermore, he added, the Jewish community had to maintain its schools and synagogues, pay its rabbis, ritual slaughterers, and beadles, and support its poor. "How much must the Jew first toil, sweat and wheeze for the state," Hirsch exclaimed, "before he can earn a single kreuzer to buy bread for his wife and child!"[82]

Although the Jews were asked to "sweat and wheeze" for the state, the Jew tax served to reinforce the sojourner status of the Jews in Moravia and the entire empire. Indeed, one Galician Reichstag deputy even derided it as "a foreigner tax."[83] Originating with the "tolerance tax" imposed by Maria Theresa, the Jew tax treated Jews not as a native population but rather as a foreign population enjoying—and paying for—local protection and hospitality. As the burghers of Holleschau reminded members of the Reichstag in September 1848, the "Israelites were welcomed into our states solely through hospitality; therefore, they must take the larger Christian population into consideration."[84] As a result of this perception, the struggle for the elimination of the Jew tax was, in some respects, a struggle for a fatherland. This symbolism was articulated by a Bohemian Jew after the Bohemian Jew tax was provisionally abolished in 1846. "We have been brought one step closer to equality," he rejoiced. "Now we have finally acquired a fatherland, now there is justice for us. With the abolition of this tax a principle has been simultaneously enunciated: that we are no longer simply tolerated foreigners in this land, the land that we have inhabited for over one thousand years . . . that we are citizens and natives." This Jew viewed the elimination of the Jew tax not only as an affirmation of his belonging to the land of his birth but also as a harbinger of emancipation. He optimistically declared that the elimination of the Jew tax would be "crowned with complete equality."[85]

Because the Pillersdorf constitution of April 25, 1848, articulated the principle of equal rights, the total elimination of the Jew tax seemed like a foregone conclusion by the summer of 1848. Hirsch therefore must have been surprised when the Moravian Tax Administration began soliciting bids in July 1848 for the farming of the following year's Jewish consumption tax.[86] In response to this news, Hirsch rushed off a circular to Moravia's Jewish communities, urging the communal leaders to discourage Jews—who were usually the tax farmers—from "giving a hand to our degradation."[87] One Viennese Jewish newspaper expressed hope that the "humiliation taxes" would be abolished by the Reichstag, but Hirsch did not rely on hope alone. Together with the Committee for Moravian Jewry, Hirsch drafted a petition seeking the immediate suspension of bidding in Moravia and sent it to Mannheimer, asking him to distribute it among influential ministers in Vienna.[88]

Hirsch had cultivated relations with government officials in Moravia, but he evidently needed Mannheimer's well-developed connections in Vienna to overturn the July decision by the Moravian Tax Administration. Mannheimer considered Minister of Justice Alexander von Bach "a friend" and enjoyed relatively unobstructed access to Minister of Finance Philipp von Krauss, with whom he frequently discussed the Jew tax. On July 20 Mannheimer submitted Hirsch's petition to the Finance Ministry, appending his own memorandum, which stressed the "highly urgent" nature of the request.[89] Hirsch and Mannheimer's intercession seemed to yield immediate success: Within the next week, bidding for the 1849 Moravian Jew tax was officially suspended by ministerial decree. Soon thereafter, bidding for the Galician Jew tax was discontinued as well.

As his correspondence with Hirsch makes clear, Mannheimer was not merely concerned about the confusion that might ensue if the bidding continued in Moravia. More important, he wanted this issue dealt with swiftly and quietly in the hopes of forestalling an untimely discussion of the Jewish question in the Reichstag. "Any premature deliberations on the Jewish question," he informed Hirsch on July 21, "can only defeat our goals." Mannheimer believed that Jews already played too central a role in the revolution and that any further attention to specifically Jewish issues would be detrimental to the struggle for emancipation. "I, myself, am careful not to mention the word Jew at this time," he stressed. "It is mentioned too often." Mannheimer's desire for Jewish inconspicuousness extended to the floor of the Reichstag as well. He firmly believed that Jewish deputies should remain silent unless their participation was absolutely warranted. "I do not speak in the chamber," he boasted to Hirsch on July 21, "even though I was vice president [of the provisional Reichstag]."

At the beginning of September, the Jew tax once again provided the impetus for behind-the-scenes lobbying; however, this time Hirsch and Mannheimer did not agree on the proper way to proceed. Hirsch sent Mannheimer a petition, apparently intended for Minister Krauss, calling for the definitive elimination of the Jew tax, which had only been suspended in July, not fully eliminated.[90] Mannheimer received Hirsch's petition on September 5, but he was reluctant to convey it to Minister Krauss. Indeed, Mannheimer did not want any special attention focused on the Jew tax; he hoped it would eventually disappear in the context of comprehensive tax reforms. As he explained to Hirsch, he wanted the tax's elimination to be "the result of *essential* reforms in the tax system," not the outcome of an isolated debate on the issue. Furthermore, Mannheimer was disturbed by the possibility that the "Jewish question" (*Judenfrage*) would first be broached in the Reichstag as a "pecuniary question" (*Geldfrage*). Mannheimer raised these concerns in daily discussions with Minister Krauss, but to no avail. Krauss informed him that the sources of state income had to be clarified by early October 1848 so that the 1849 budget could be drafted on time. As a result, Krauss proposed a special law that would officially eliminate the Jew tax beginning on November 1, 1848.[91] Much to Mannheimer's chagrin, the Jewish question would be debated in the Reichstag on September 26 and October 5 as a pecuniary question.

Mannheimer broke his silence in the Reichstag on September 26, making his inaugural speech during the heated debates on the Jew tax. He drew attention to the "exceptional" nature of the tax, stressing constitutional as well as humanitarian grounds for its elimination. Characterizing it as a tax on religion, he questioned whether the taxation of "a belief . . . an idea, a thought" was compatible with the spirit of the constitutional age. The primary focus of his speech was the inordinate suffering of the Jews, who were responsible not only for "taxes that every citizen must pay" but also for "exceptional taxes." To illustrate the devastating burden of these taxes, Mannheimer detailed the tax obligations of a single Jewish community in Moravia. "A small community in Moravia (let us not mention the name)," he told the assembled deputies, "numbers 195 Jewish families; 100 of them are able to pay taxes, the rest are poor and are left to the care of the community. In *addition* to what they pay to support their officials and poor, and in addition to what they pay in municipal taxes as citizens of the state, these 100 families pay an annual, exceptional Jew tax of 3,875 fl."[92] Although Mannheimer withheld the name of this community, the number of

Jewish families indicates that he was referring to Neu-Rausnitz. Like Hirsch, who detailed the tax obligations of Nikolsburg Jewry in his July letter to Lažansky, Mannheimer hoped the dry figures would pull some heartstrings.[93] Indeed, Hirsch may have provided Mannheimer with this specific example—perhaps even knowing that opposition to eliminating the Jew tax would come primarily from Moravian deputies.

Several deputies from Galicia and Bohemia spoke in favor of eliminating the Jew tax, but two Moravian deputies—Joseph Demel and Ferdinand Böse—stridently fought to retain the "exceptional tax." Like Mannheimer, Demel broke his silence in the Reichstag on September 26, launching into what one correspondent called "his inaugural speech of Jew hatred."[94] Earlier in September, Demel had established his anti-Jewish credentials by gathering more than 1,000 signatures in Prossnitz for a petition against Jewish emancipation.[95] He may have also been involved in excluding Prossnitz Jews from the May elections to the Moravian Diet.[96] In his speech to the Reichstag, Demel engaged in some not too subtle sophistry, arguing that the Jew tax was an injustice for Christians, not for Jews. Attempts to show that the Jews were taxed higher than Christians, he claimed, were completely false. "I will demonstrate that it is not the Jews who suffer from inequality, but rather the Christians," he insisted. "Jews are taxed less than other citizens, and they also benefit from other privileges." Demel argued that the Jewish merchant (*Handelsmann*) was actually taxed less than the Christian merchant because the Jews were registered in the lower paying tax category of shopkeeper (*Krämer*). Because merchants paid an annual tax of 30 fl. and shopkeepers only 6–8 fl., Demel concluded that Jews saved much more money than they actually paid in special Jewish taxes.[97] In addition, Demel alleged that Jews benefited from two other "privileges." First, Jews were exempt from many taxes because they engaged in activities that were not fully taxed, such as money changing and trading shares. Second, Jews were exempt from the costly obligation of quartering soldiers. "Sirs," he asked the assembled deputies, "if the Jew tax has really oppressed the Jews so much, how did it become possible for precisely this sector of the citizenry to become the wealthiest, and for all the capital [*Geldkraft*] to be concentrated in its hands?" When the debate on the Jew tax resumed nine days later, Böse echoed

Demel's argumentation, describing Christians as "far more oppressed than the Jews."[98]

Demel's and Böse's vociferous opposition aside, the vast majority of Reichstag deputies supported the elimination of the Jew tax when the vote took place on October 5, 1848. For the Jews of the monarchy, the vote seemed a harbinger of emancipation, especially when a number of Reichstag deputies portrayed the elimination of all special taxes as a constitutional necessity. "The Jew tax must be eliminated soon," declared one deputy right before the vote, "if we want to interpret the constitutional principles faithfully."[99] Hirsch, in his first circular since May, exulted in this step along the seemingly inexorable path toward full equality of rights. "Dear brothers!" he began his circular to the Jews of Moravia on October 8.

> The first chain link in our centuries-long humiliation is broken. Thank the Father in heaven who brought us to such a time. The newly awakened sense of justice in the breast of the nations has brought us the first fruits of redemption. With a nearly unanimous vote, the deputies of the people in the constitutional Reichstag have declared the elimination of the Jew tax, and we can happily entertain the hope that the same sense of justice will soon break all other shackles and restrictions. . . . We can hope that the time is no longer far when, in our beautiful fatherland, too, the Jew will be granted full and equal rights and duties; and we will be able to devote ourselves with equal rights to all good and honest struggles—as human beings among human beings, as citizens among citizens.[100]

Hirsch, it appears, perceived the elimination of the Jew tax as a vindication of his belief, proclaimed at the outset of the revolution, that "our Christian brethren . . . will happily prove their sense of justice and their enlightened love of fellow man by recognizing in [the Jews] brethren with equal rights in a common fatherland."[101] Hirsch's optimism, however, was a little premature.

In the first weeks of October, Moravian officials continued to collect the Jew tax, propelling Hirsch and the Committee for Moravian Jewry to intercede once again. On October 18, Hirsch and Franz Note, a Nikolsburg member of the committee, complained to the Gubernium that the Jew tax for 1849 was being collected in Gewitsch and Kojetein.

Furthermore, the Prossnitz synagogue was threatened with closure if taxes were not paid by October 16. Hirsch asked the Gubernium to instruct the district offices to cease collecting the Jew tax, but the Gubernium responded by merely explaining the source of confusion: The Jew tax had not been eliminated "in a constitutional manner," nor had any ministerial decree been received to that effect.[102]

The elimination of the Jew tax generated confusion not only among local government officials but also among Moravia's Jewish population. The vote on October 5 removed a heavy financial burden from the Jews, but it threatened to cut off the most important source of income for Moravia's Jewish communities. Indeed, the salaries of rabbis, teachers, ritual slaughterers, and other Jewish communal officials had been previously covered by certain special Jewish taxes. Hirsch recognized the looming threat of communal insolvency—experienced by Prussian Jewry only a few years before—and appealed to the Jews of Moravia to continue paying these specific taxes. In his circular from October 8, he distinguished between the "shameful burden of exceptional taxes" and the "fair, just burden of communal taxes," criticizing those Jews who viewed the repeal of the former as grounds to stop paying the latter. By October 8, a number of Jewish communities had already complained to the Committee for Moravian Jewry about such recalcitrant members.[103]

With many Jews exhibiting a readiness to shirk their communal responsibilities as soon as the Jew tax was lifted, Hirsch was aware that full emancipation could loosen the ties that bound individual Jews to Judaism and their Jewish communities. More than a decade earlier, Hirsch had grappled with a similar issue in his *Nineteen Letters of Ben Uziel*, where he recognized the possibility that "freedom from unjust oppression" could lead to "capricious curtailment of the Torah, capricious abandonment of the chief element of our vitality."[104] Nonetheless, Hirsch strongly supported emancipation, viewing it first and foremost as a means to elevate Judaism, to remove the bonds that had constrained its natural development for centuries. So long as emancipation was not an end in and of itself, he argued, it would create "a new condition of [Israel's] mission." "For Israel, I only bless [emancipation]," he declared, "if at the same time there awakes in Israel the true spirit, which, independent of emancipation or non-emancipation, strives to fulfill the

Israel-mission; to elevate and ennoble ourselves, to implant the spirit of Judaism in our souls, in order that it may produce a life in which that spirit shall be reflected and realized."[105] Hirsch worried, however, that some Jews would perceive emancipation as an opportunity for material enrichment rather than spiritual ennoblement. "If Israel regards this glorious concession merely as a means of securing a greater degree of comfort in life, and greater opportunities for the acquisition of wealth and enjoyments," he wrote in *Ben Uziel*, "it would show that Israel had not comprehended the spirit of its own Law, nor learnt from the Galuth [exile]." In Hirsch's view, Judaism should "gladly welcome emancipation" only insofar as it enabled Jews to become Jews "in the true sense of the word."[106]

Hirsch's circular from October 8, 1848 (one day after Yom Kippur), reiterated this fear of Jewish self-abnegation, stressing that emancipation was worthwhile only if, in the end, Jews remained Jews. Hirsch portrayed the approaching emancipation as a "victory of truth over lies, of justice over violence, of pure knowledge of God over prejudice and delusion," but only if "we enjoy the fruits of this victory *as Jews*." "For truly, my brethren," Hirsch asked with great pathos, "what would we have accomplished if now that, if it please God, we will soon be free Jews, we were to cease being Jews?"[107] Like many Yom Kippur sermons, Hirsch's circular emphasized the urgent need to support communal institutions financially, lest the bedrock of Jewish communal life, which had survived the "yoke" and "whip," should crumble with the first ray of freedom.[108]

Hirsch's Yom Kippur circular focused on internal Jewish affairs, devoting little space to the ongoing empire-wide struggle for equal civic and political rights. In fact, Hirsch seemed to have removed himself from the political arena at this stage, preferring to leave the general struggle for Jewish emancipation to Mannheimer and other (Jewish and non-Jewish) Reichstag deputies. In the first eight months of the revolution, Hirsch never really aspired to be a spokesman for the interests of Habsburg Jewry as a whole. Rather, Hirsch focused primarily on the plight of Moravian Jewry, only interceding in the affairs of the Reichstag when Moravian interests—such as the elimination of the Jew tax—were directly at stake. His circulars from March 1848 were addressed to Moravia's Christians and Jews; his petition from May 1848 was addressed to the Moravian Diet; his letter from July 1848 was intended for Moravian governor Lažansky.

Hirsch may have preferred to devote his skills and energy to Moravian Jewish affairs, but the October Uprising in Vienna—during which Emperor Ferdinand found refuge in Olmütz and the Reichstag reconvened in Kremsier—suddenly elevated the political importance of Moravia and, by extension, the Moravian chief rabbi. As periphery became center, Hirsch found himself in close proximity to the emperor and the popularly elected Reichstag. As Salo W. Baron has noted, the debates on Jewish emancipation were to take place in "Hirsch's own bailiwick."[109] Even so, Hirsch was still reluctant to assume a higher profile in Habsburg Jewish affairs. During the Reichstag's first three months in Kremsier, there is no evidence that the Moravian chief rabbi visited the deputies or perceived it as his duty to do so. Nor did he seek an audience with the emperor in nearby Olmütz. Between early October 1848 and early February 1849—when a flurry of anti-emancipation petitions were sent to the Reichstag by Bohemian, and especially Moravian, towns and villages—Hirsch preferred to lie low. In this four-month period he published only one circular, compared with four circulars in the preceding seven months. This one circular, dated December 26, 1848, appeared a few weeks after the 18-year-old Franz Joseph was crowned emperor in Olmütz on December 2.[110] Hirsch began with words of praise for the new emperor, but this was not his main purpose. Rather, Hirsch set out to explain why—contrary to the express wishes of several Jewish communities—he refused to lead a separate Jewish delegation to Olmütz to congratulate Franz Joseph in person.[111]

Hirsch's circular can also be seen as an attempt to explain—or perhaps justify—his reduced visibility in the winter of 1848–49. Hirsch had tried to draw as little attention as possible to separate "Jewish" causes or any actions that would reinforce a perception of the Jews as a separate corporation—particularly as the empire was in the process of being reconstituted on the basis of individual rights and freedoms. With emancipation on the horizon, Hirsch viewed a separate Jewish delegation as "unseemly," because it could easily be misinterpreted by "our non-Jewish brethren" (*nichtjüdischen Staatsbrüdern*) as a willful separation from other citizens of the state. "Dear brothers," he wrote, "we want no special [status] in the state; we want to be absorbed into the collectivity [*Gesammtheit*] of members of the state, and as such, [we] require no separate representation."[112] Hirsch defined the Jews in solely confessional terms, denying them any corporate character that might be inconsistent with the emerging constitutional state. He explained that the Jews constitute a separate association (*Genossenschaft*) but should by no means be viewed as a separate corporation (*Körperschaft*) in relation to the state. "Only where the other different confessions of the fatherland act as distinct religious associations," he declared, "can we also appear as such, but we may never and shall never separate ourselves from citizens of the state, from sons of the province."[113]

In Hirsch's view, a separate Jewish delegation was not only inimical to the spirit of the age but also superfluous. As he pointed out, the Moravian Diet—which was elected by Jews and non-Jews alike—had already paid its respects to the new emperor immediately after his coronation. Because "Jewish Moravians" were represented "just like any other sons of the province," the Jews had already paid their respects. "How unseemly it would be," Hirsch observed, "if we did not want to be included in this common act and appeared once again as a separate group before the steps of the throne."[114]

If Hirsch preferred to take what Mannheimer termed a "wait and see" (*shev v'al t'aseh*) approach to emancipation,[115] why does the scholarship on Hirsch—with few exceptions—portray him as a preeminent champion of emancipation in the Habsburg monarchy? Hirsch did eventually rise to the occasion, becoming a visible and charismatic presence in Kremsier, where he tirelessly lobbied Reichstag deputies in February 1849 as deliberations on Jewish emancipation rapidly approached. In this new, expanded role, Hirsch penned a memorandum (*Denkschrift*), in which he fervently "[stood] up for the Jews with heart and soul."[116] Filled with fiery rhetoric and heart-wrenching emotion, Hirsch's memorandum was intended for the Reichstag deputies who were still wavering with respect to Jewish emancipation. It also reached the public at large, particularly after being published in a number of Jewish and non-Jewish newspapers in the Habsburg Empire and abroad. One scholar viewed Hirsch's impassioned plea as the key to securing Jewish emancipation.[117] Although this claim is certainly exaggerated, it attests to the perceived impact of Hirsch's memorandum on the Jews' struggle for civic and political rights in the Habsburg Empire.

The memorandum, however, was not Hirsch's own idea. Nor, it seems, were the lobbying efforts. In the course of the Mannheimer-Hirsch correspondence, it becomes clear that Hirsch wrote the memorandum and distributed it at Kremsier only after persistent prodding by Mannheimer in the last months of 1848. Mannheimer, who had been "careful not to mention Jews" in July, recognized by late autumn that a concerted "Jewish" effort was necessary to ensure Jewish emancipation. At some point in November, Mannheimer made a special trip to Nikolsburg—presumably while en route from Vienna to Kremsier—to solicit Hirsch's help.[118] During their November meeting, Mannheimer asked Hirsch to draft a memorandum describing the decrepit state of Moravian Jewry, apparently in the hopes that Hirsch's lachrymose depiction would sway some of the wavering deputies. Hirsch may have been roused to the cause, but his memorandum was, oddly enough, not forthcoming.

On December 8, a number of weeks after the meeting in Nikolsburg, Mannheimer penned a vehement and blunt letter to Hirsch, who had still not risen to the occasion. Mannheimer's letter reads as a cri de coeur, filled with indignation and disappointment at Hirsch's failure to keep his word. Mannheimer, who had been anticipating Hirsch's memorandum "week in and week out," also expressed bewilderment at Hirsch's failure to visit Kremsier after the Reichstag was moved there at the end of October. "It would have only been customary," Mannheimer wrote, for the Moravian chief rabbi to visit the Reichstag. Mannheimer hoped that Hirsch would use his unique standing in Moravia to help secure support for Jewish emancipation among the Reichstag deputies.[119] Mannheimer, himself a deputy, regretted not being able to undertake such lobbying activity because of a possible conflict of interest. Hirsch, however, was in an ideal position to intercede. As Mannheimer explained:

> *Your* intercession is all the more desirable, precisely because it is occasional, entirely by chance, without any intentions or relation to the looming [Reichstag] deliberations. . . . Nothing but your presence [at Kremsier] and a discussion of the conditions [of Moravian Jewry] from

a general standpoint are needed in order to deepen the interest of the relevant deputies [*Rath-Excellenzen*] and to bring Moravian affairs to the fore.[120]

For symbolic reasons, Mannheimer considered Hirsch's mere presence at Kremsier to be just as important as the memorandum on Moravian Jewry. He believed that Hirsch's persona (*Persönlichkeit*) alone would be enough to dispel the doubts harbored by the increasingly vocal opponents of Jewish emancipation. The university-educated, silver-tongued chief rabbi could serve as a testament to the Jews' potential for full integration in European society. "The figure [*Gestaltung*] of the Chief Rabbi, as it is represented in you will be taken *eo ipso* as a guaranty of the rising cultural and educational level among Moravian Jews and of their willingness to make concessions." Through a mixture of flattery and reproach, Mannheimer made Hirsch aware of his political capital and begged him not to squander it. "I am attuned—even more than you yourself may be—to the authority and respect of your personal position [*Stellung*]," wrote Mannheimer. "If it stood at my disposal, I would happily use it to secure every possible advantage [*Ansehe*] and all possible support [*Förderung*] and publicity [*Verbreitung*] [for our cause]."[121]

Despite some early reluctance, Hirsch eventually heeded Mannheimer's call, becoming a towering presence at Kremsier in February 1849. There, he not only distributed his memorandum but also engaged in last-minute lobbying just before the anticipated debates on Jewish emancipation. Hirsch was late in rising to the occasion, but the resources he required had long been at his disposal: the Committee for Moravian Jewry, organized in April 1848, and his letter to Governor Lažansky from July 1848.

By early February, Hirsch had transformed the Committee for Moravian Jewry into the United Committee for the Jewish Communities of Individual Provinces of the Austrian Empire for the Protection of Their Civic and Political Rights, a lobbying organization for Austrian Jewry as a whole. Mendel Hirsch, the chief rabbi's eldest son, described the United Committee as an amalgamation of the individual Jewish committees that had arisen in other parts of the empire (particularly Bohemia and Vienna), but the preeminent role of the Moravian committee—and Hirsch in particular—is unmistakable.[122] Of the United Committee's twenty-five members, well over half had been on the Committee for Moravian Jewry.[123] Furthermore, Hirsch emerged as the United Committee's undisputed leader, despite the presence of a number of imposing Viennese and Bohemian Jews, such as Ludwig August Frankl, editor of *Sonntagsblätter*, member of the Academic Legion, and secretary of the Viennese Jewish community; Joseph Wertheimer, an early champion of Jewish emancipation; Heinrich Schirowski, general secretary of the Northern Railroad; and Dr. Wolfgang Wessely, professor of law at Prague University.

In February, the United Committee met in the home of Raphael Kohn, a wealthy member of the Kremsier Jewish community, to devise a strategy for influencing the upcoming vote on Paragraph 16 of the constitution.[124] Paragraph 16, as formulated in the draft of the Fundamental Laws that was completed at the end of December 1848, promised to grant civic and political rights to all citizens *regardless of religious confession*. Just as Hirsch and Mannheimer had initially hoped, the draft law placed Jewish emancipation in universal terms; the Jews seemed poised to attain equal rights as equal citizens and not as Jews per se. Nonetheless, Paragraph 16 was commonly equated with Jewish emancipation. With the emancipation of the peasants in September 1848, most of the Christian population had already been granted civic and political rights, leaving the impression that Paragraph 16 pertained first and foremost to the Jews.

The United Committee sought to shore up support for Jewish emancipation, particularly among the Czech, Tyrolean, and Styrian deputies. In Tyrol and Styria, where Jewish residence had been prohibited for centuries, the deputies sought to retain the privilege *de non tolerandis judaeis* to prevent an influx of Jews. The Czech deputies, and above all František Palacký, viewed constitutional matters through the lens of the nationality question; in this respect, confessional equality was ancillary to fostering Czech linguistic, educational, and political aspirations. Mendel Hirsch recalled a nerve-wracking meeting between the United Committee and Palacký that centered on Czech opposition to Jewish emancipation. After a spokesman for the United Committee (possibly Hirsch) insisted that Czechs could not demand national and confessional equality for themselves without at the same time supporting these rights for the Jews, Palacký reportedly responded, "We are consistent only when it is to our benefit. We evaluate each [constitutional] article from the standpoint of our party."[125]

In early February 1849, the United Committee distributed a lengthy memorandum to individual deputies along with an attached note: "Do not reject this memorandum; it is handed to you with the brotherly sentiments of a Jew." This was the memorandum that Hirsch had promised to Mannheimer three months earlier, and its four densely printed folio pages bore Hirsch's unmistakable mark.[126] The chief rabbi's name appeared in boldface at the bottom of the memorandum, above a list of the twenty-four other members of the United Committee. *Der Orient* correctly identified the document as "Hirsch's memorandum," but few could have known that this was virtually the same memorandum he had submitted to Governor Lažansky seven months earlier. Previous scholars have assumed that this memorandum dates from 1849, when the outcome of the Reichstag debates on Jewish emancipation was mired in uncertainty. However, the bulk of this memorandum dates from July 1848, when emancipation still seemed a foregone conclusion. In early 1849, Hirsch simply made slight emendations to his earlier letter and added new introductory and concluding paragraphs.

Hirsch's new introduction expressed profound disappointment, detailing a litany of shattered hopes since "dawn broke in our fatherland" in March 1848.

> The time arrived when all enslaved people should have again breathed freely, when all inveterate injustice should have been atoned for; and a state should have been erected with Truth alone as the foundation, with Justice alone as the standard and with the welfare of all as the crown of perfection.
>
> The Jewish members of the state turned as well, their countenances radiating hope, towards the dawn of the peoples. They had been the most enslaved people in the land; no one felt the scourge of madness and injustice as they did; no one was robbed of the holiest, inalienable rights as they were. If atonement is to be performed, *here* is where it should be carried out.
>
> Nevertheless, we, their representatives, have kept silent until now. Calmly we awaited the ever-advancing sense of justice, the triumphal

divinity in the breast of the people, and we confidently believed that justice for all would mean justice for Jews as well. Any doubt seemed to us an offense against the enlightenment of the people, against the justness and wisdom of the new leader of the state. It seemed an impossibility that our hopes would be unfulfilled, our rights denied. We kept silent, for keeping silent seemed our duty, even more so after the ministry's program and his majesty's manifesto solemnly proclaimed equality of rights for all members of the state as the first principle of the new state.

However, the preliminary deliberations on the Fundamental Laws, as reported in the newspapers, have painfully shaken our confidence. Nonetheless, our faith in the enlightened views and unprejudiced convictions of the Reichstag remains completely unshaken; a faith that—the preliminary deliberations aside—will be strengthened during the forthcoming deliberations on the Fundamental Laws. We only fear that if, here and there, even a tiny portion of the people's representatives can make allowances for existing prejudices, exclude the Jews from the general legal basis, sow the ground for the new constitutional state with old injustice . . . and claim justice and freedom for themselves alone, they are obliterating justice and freedom for themselves and everyone else.

Against this we can no longer remain silent; for the sake of the many hundreds of thousands who have elected us as representatives; for the sake of our sons and grandsons, whose most sacred possessions—their felicity as humans and citizens, their honor as humans and citizens—could be withheld indefinitely; for the sake of our very fatherland, which until now has treated us like stepchildren. Our hearts, however, beat with all the fervor of true, equally born sons; and [our fatherland] cannot and will not find welfare and peace as long as a single human soul still protests before God about the injustice, violence, and theft of his most sacred possessions, as long as there is no atonement in the new age for the centuries of oppression and misery.[127]

It is impossible to know whether Hirsch's memorandum—or his personal intervention—would have eventually yielded the necessary votes in favor of Jewish emancipation; Franz Joseph dissolved the Kremsier Reichstag right before the scheduled deliberations on Paragraph 16. On March 7, 1849, the emperor promulgated his own constitution (drafted by Interior Minister Franz Stadion), which granted equal civic and political rights to all citizens, regardless of religious confession. As a result, the Jews were emancipated by imperial fiat, not by the popularly elected Reichstag, leading some scholars to downplay Hirsch's role in the entire struggle for emancipation.[128]

Many contemporaries, however, came to see the Moravian chief rabbi as the central figure in the Jews' struggle for civic and political rights. The Christian inhabitants of Prerau viewed him as the linchpin in the Jews' efforts to attain full emancipation. The Prerau petition to the Reichstag from February 16, 1849, clearly reveals the concern with which they viewed Hirsch and his memorandum (which had been published a week earlier): "Thirty-two rabbis sit in the Reichstag, among whom the Nikolsburg Chief Rabbi is the most significant. With his rhetorical skills, he could soften the hearts of all the non-Jewish deputies and attain this undesired *Jewish emancipation*, thereby filling the common people with anger."[129] The petition's wild exaggeration of the number of rabbis in the Reichstag (there were only two: Mannheimer and Meisels) reflects the general tendency of anti-Jewish petitions to characterize the Revolution of 1848 as a "Jewish revolution," but the inclusion of the "Nikolsburg Chief Rabbi" further indicates a dramatic shift in the popular perception of Hirsch after his memorandum was published. Before February 1849, Hirsch received little attention in the non-Jewish press—and absolutely no mention in the numerous anti-Jewish petitions that arrived at the Reichstag between August 1848 and January 1849. By February 1849, however, the inhabitants of Prerau viewed Hirsch as such a formidable political force that they mistook him for a full-fledged Reichstag deputy. This mistake, repeated by a number of Hirsch's biographers,[130] can be understood in light of the attention showered on Hirsch's memorandum. The *Deutsche Allgemeine Zeitung*, for example, expressed pleasant surprise at finding none of the "meek and melancholy tone" that so often characterized Jewish petitions. It quoted extensively from the memorandum, marveling at "such a language [which] has never been heard from Jews of Austria."[131]

Among Moravian Jews, the memorandum transformed some of Hirsch's most ardent critics into his most fervent supporters. Moritz Jellinek of Ungarisch-Brod is a case in point. An unyielding critic of Hirsch throughout the revolution, Jellinek rarely had flattering words for the chief rabbi. He deemed Hirsch's circular from October 8 "just as inconsequential and meaningless as all the previous instructions from this deer without horns [i.e., Hirsch]" and offered it as proof of the "political incompetence of theologians."[132] After the publication of Hirsch's memorandum, Jellinek made an abrupt about-face, lauding Hirsch's indefatigable work at Kremsier. "[Hirsch] has made a good impression on me," Jellinek reported from Kremsier on February 12, 1849. "He is a man full of energy and vigor, and stands up for the Jews with heart and soul. His memorandum has caused such a sensation here that the narrow-minded Tyroleans are somewhat startled by the manly words a Jew is capable of uttering."[133] *Der Orient* reported that such about-faces were fairly widespread, stating that many Moravian Jews who opposed Hirsch's religious orientation "made their peace" with him once the memorandum showed him to be a "man of energy, strength, and dignity." "Moravian Jews were accustomed to whimpering, moaning, and begging," wrote *Der Orient*. "Hirsch taught them, by virtue of their worth as human beings, to demand their rights with a manly and energetic tongue."[134]

These words were a far cry from the angry disappointment expressed by J. Schuster, the Jewish baker in Lundenburg, on the eve of the revolution. Schuster had sharply criticized Hirsch in March 1848 for enforcing outdated ritual observances instead of performing his "appointed task of making the dirty, downtrodden, oppressed Jew . . . into a human being." So long as Hirsch devoted his energy to regulating Moravian Jewry's religious affairs, his actions riled vocal segments of the Jewish population, particularly in Hirsch Fassel's community of Prossnitz. Only when Hirsch steered clear of religious affairs, devoting his energy to the struggle for civic and political rights, did he manage to avoid the conflicts that had plagued him during his first eight months in office. From this perspective, the Revolution of 1848 came at a particularly propitious time. It provided Hirsch with an opportunity born of crisis, a chance to unify Moravian Jewry under his aegis. But now that the common goal had been accomplished and the Jews had been emancipated, would this unity prove to be ephemeral? Would Hirsch be able to sustain this unity in religious and communal affairs as well?

Six

On the Altar of Freedom

Moravian Jewry and the Revolution of 1848

"The drive for freedom was more intensely developed in [the Jews of Moravia]," wrote Adolf Frankel-Grün, "because they experienced the pre-March oppression more than their coreligionists in the other lands."[1] Frankel-Grün penned these words two generations after the Revolution of 1848, long after the Jew tax, the occupational and residential restrictions, and the Familiants Laws had been repealed, yet the Jews of Moravia had retained their reputation for having "most enthusiastically participated" in the revolution. Samson Raphael Hirsch's prominent role in the struggle for emancipation certainly contributed to this reputation, but not as much as the visible and celebrated "martyrdom" of two Moravian Jews in the first eight months of the revolution: Carl Heinrich Spitzer of Bisenz and Hermann Jellinek of Drslawitz (near Ungarisch-Brod). Spitzer, the "first victim" of the revolution, was killed when Austrian troops shot into a crowd of students on March 13, 1848. Jellinek, a radical democratic journalist, was executed as a revolutionary on November 23, 1848. Each met his death in Vienna, but contemporaries did not view their Moravian birth as mere happenstance. In light of the pathos-filled image of a Moravian Jewry "patiently bearing wounded hearts," it was perhaps fitting that Moravian Jewry's earliest contribution to the Revolution of 1848 took the form of martyrdom, or in Hirsch Fassel's words, "sacrifice on the altar of freedom."[2]

In death, Spitzer and Jellinek became symbols of two contradictory trends in relation to the Jews. As Jacob Toury has demonstrated, the Revolution of 1848 saw not only the ephemeral triumph of liberalism, which framed the struggle for Jewish emancipation in universal humanistic terms, but also the early stirrings of modern secular antisemitism, which cast the Jews as conspirators, political agitators, and subverters of the Christian state.[3] Spitzer, who met his death as an anonymous face in the mass of humanity, came to symbolize the former trend, whereas Jellinek, who was singled out in large part because of his Jewish origins, came to symbolize the latter. During the revolution, both trends were represented in Moravia as well. On some occasions, Jews were welcomed as "fellow citizens" struggling for a common goal alongside their "Christian brethren"; on other occasions, they were shunned as "foreigners" pursuing selfish interests to the great detriment of the indigenous, that is, Christian, population. One measure of these conflicting trends was the question of Jewish membership in the national guards, which had been set up by the burghers in the early days of the revolution. In some towns, such as Boskowitz, Jews were accepted as full members as a matter of course; in other towns, such as Prossnitz, even the establishment of a separate Jewish national guard was not enough to prevent rumblings of anti-Jewish violence in September 1848. From the beginning of the revolution, efforts to place the Jews on equal terms with their Christian neighbors were repeatedly and invariably met with threats of anti-Jewish violence. In Moravia, such violence erupted only sporadically, but the repeated threats served as a constant reminder that the prospect of Jewish emancipation—although supported by some of Moravia's non-Jewish population—instilled fear in many others, who predicted that "Jewish equality" would inevitably lead to "Jewish subjugation" of Christians, particularly in the economic sphere.

On March 13, 1848, as Viennese students thronged toward the Lower Austrian Diet to submit their revolutionary demands, imperial troops fired into the crowd, turning a 17-year-old Moravian Jew into the first martyr of the revolution. Carl Heinrich Spitzer (Figure 9), a student at the Vienna Polytechnic, found his final resting place in a common grave in Vienna. By the time he was buried on March 17, the revolution had already yielded its first fruits as Emperor Ferdinand acceded to the students' demands for a national guard, a free press, and the promise of a constitution. Spitzer and four other fallen students were extolled

Figure 9. Carl Heinrich Spitzer, first victim of the Revolution of 1848 in Vienna. *Österreichisches Central Organ für Glaubensfreiheit, Cultur und Literatur der Juden* (Vienna), March 23, 1848, 6.

as "heroes of freedom," transformed through their deaths into sacrifices for "the fatherland, for justice and freedom."

Spitzer's funeral embodied the tolerant spirit reigning in Vienna in the early days of the revolution. At the behest of Father Anton Füster, the priest of the Academic Legion, not only were Jew and Christian buried together in a common grave (at the Schmelzer Cemetery) but also rabbi and priest delivered funeral orations side by side.[4] Isak Noa Mannheimer delivered a eulogy for the fallen students, viewing the common burial as an expression of common humanity: "Let the miracle of our time, that the noble fallen ones are resting in one *common* grave despite their different confessions, be a sign that brotherly harmony will also prevail amongst the living." Mannheimer continued the metaphor in an appeal to his "Christian brethren" for Jewish emancipation. "You wanted the dead Jews to rest with you in your earth," he said. "They fought for you, they bled for you! They are resting in your earth! Allow those who fought the same battle and the more difficult one, to live with you on one earth, to live like you, free and unconstrained."[5] The obvious symbolism of a common burial—at a time when Jews and Christians were still living separately in most of the empire—was echoed in the numerous eulogies delivered in memory of the fallen students.[6] In Hirsch Fassel's eulogy, delivered in the Prossnitz synagogue a week later, he called the martyrdom of Spitzer and the others "the very first act of emancipation of the Jews of Austria, but a truly heart-wrenching emancipation."[7]

In a manifestation of "provincial patriotism," Jews and non-Jews drew attention to Spitzer's Moravian origins. Amid the confusion of the revolution, a second casualty from March 13, Bernhard Herschmann, was also identified as a Moravian Jew, leaving the impression that two of the five fallen students had come from Moravia's Jewish communities. Fassel highlighted the Moravian Jewish contribution to the revolution in his eulogy: "Brave Israelites have also fought in this freedom fight and two of them have shed their blood—two young Israelites, full of hope. Both from Moravia, they lie united with the other Christian freedom heroes in the silent grave in Vienna."[8] Moritz Jellinek (whose younger brother, Hermann, was executed eight months later) transformed Spitzer into a revolutionary leader. "What an honor," he wrote from Ungarisch-Brod, "that a Jewish youth, a *Moravian*, from Butschowitz [*sic*], stood at the head [*Spitz*] of the famous Viennese students."[9] Moravian pride also came from non-Jewish corners. The Bisenz Youth published a broadside to commemorate the "glorious death of our deceased *Landsmann*." "We are proud of you!" it proclaimed. "We are allowed to be, since our little father-town was worthily represented in the battle for freedom."[10]

In the first months of the revolution, Spitzer underwent a process of near beatification. As portraits, poems, and biographies appeared, his martyrdom was increasingly depicted in religious terms, both Jewish and Christian. In an apostrophe to Spitzer, Mannheimer secularized the traditional notion of Jewish martyrdom: "You have sanctified the name of God." The Christian language of martyrdom was most pronounced in the "hagiography" published by Karl Streng of the Danube Steamship Travel Bureau.[11] "The man, born of woman," he wrote, "lived for only a short time." The *Sonntagsblätter* also highlighted the redemptive quality of Spitzer's death: "Since he helped free the fatherland, since his death has given millions of new life, God bless him!" Spitzer's image as a sacrifice for freedom was further nourished when the *Central-Organ* published letters found in his briefcase. In a letter from February 1847 to his "friend and *Landsmann*" Heinrich Eisler, Spitzer lamented the wretched social conditions in Vienna. "The hunger is terrible. The poverty is extremely oppressive, the number of beggars is so great that I can scarcely walk five steps without bumping into one." In a letter from the autumn of 1847, Spitzer uttered his surprise that such hunger and poverty had not yet led to unrest ("Still no revolution in Vienna?!").[12] These letters, discovered posthumously, helped turn Spitzer—whose death was sometimes dismissed as a "pure coincidence"[13]—into a symbol of the Jews' readiness to perform acts of self-sacrifice for the good of society. His funeral, more than any other event of the revolution, came to symbolize the hope of Christian-Jewish reconciliation.

If Spitzer's death in March 1848 was by "pure coincidence," Hermann Jellinek's execution in November 1848 was most surely by design. As editor of the *Radikale*, a Viennese daily, Jellinek stood accused of "open incitement to armed insurrection" after calling on his readers to fight the imperial troops who were suppressing the October Uprising in Vienna.[14] As punishment for his crime, Jellinek was shot to death, together with his non-Jewish publisher, A. J. Becher, on November 23. This ushered in the counterrevolution, and the joint death of a Christian and a Jew took on a completely different meaning than it did during the early heady days of the revolution. If Spitzer's death showed that both Christians and Jews were prepared to make sacrifices in pursuit of freedom, Jellinek's death showed that Christians, but especially Jews, were to blame for the seditious radicalization of the revolution in the summer and autumn of 1848. Indeed, it was clear to many contemporaries that Jellinek was executed not merely for his complicity as an individual but primarily for his complicity as a Jew. As the poet Eduard Bauernfeld quipped, Jellinek was put to death because "they needed a Jew and there was no one else at hand!"[15]

Although Jellinek was extolled as a martyr by many of his like-minded contemporaries, he also served as a potent symbol for opponents of Jewish emancipation, who reviled the "disgraceful shamelessness of [the Jewish] literati and journalists" that he epitomized.[16] The Revolution of 1848 was commonly portrayed as a "Jewish revolution" (*Judenrevolution*) because of the high visibility of Jews among the leaders of the revolution in general and among Vienna's radical journalists and publicists in particular. Although most of the revolution's Jewish leaders came from the ranks of Hungarian and Bohemian Jewry (Dr. Adolf Fischhof, Dr. Joseph Goldmark, Ludwig August Frankl, Moritz Hartmann), many of its Jewish journalists—particularly those in the "democratic" or "republican" camps—came from Moravia. These included Sigmund Engländer, Adolf Buchheim, Siegmund Kolisch, Simon Deutsch, and of course, Hermann Jellinek.[17] Engländer, "an enthusiastic disciple of Moses Hess," edited the *Wiener Katzenmusik* during the revolution, in which he fervently espoused democracy and Jewish emancipation; during the October Uprising he called for popular resistance against the imperial troops.[18] The burghers of Trebitsch excoriated him in particular for "disseminating disobedience and subversive speeches" and for bringing about general misery.[19] Engländer was condemned to death by military tribunal, but he managed to escape Jellinek's fate by fleeing to France. Adolf Buchheim, a grandson of Gerson Buchheim, rabbi of Austerlitz, edited Vienna's *Politischer Studenten-Courier* during the revolution and penned the "Song of the Barricades," a revolutionary anthem, before fleeing to Brussels in autumn 1848.[20] Siegmund Kolisch joined the staff of the *Radikale* and fled to Paris in the autumn of 1848 after standing trial for incitement.[21] Simon Deutsch also wrote for the *Radikale* and similarly found refuge in Paris after the October Uprising in Vienna. (He later moved to the Ottoman Empire, where he was among the founders of the Young Turk movement.)[22]

Even though precise data are lacking, a significant percentage of the estimated 4,000 Jews living in Vienna at the outbreak of the revolution were born in Moravia or to Moravian parents.[23] Indeed, southwestern Moravia—which encompassed Nikolsburg, Bisenz, Drslawitz, and most of the other locations from which the mentioned martyrs and journalists hailed—could almost be considered a distant suburb of Vienna. Many Moravian Jews had family and business connections in Vienna; others moved there for study or trade. In the two and a half decades before the revolution, Vienna was home to individuals from most of Moravia's fifty-two Jewish communities, with as much as 25% of the Nikolsburg Jewish community residing there—legally or illegally—at the time of the revolution.[24]

Many Moravian Jews found themselves in other centers of the revolution in 1848, both inside and outside the borders of the Habsburg Empire. Hermann Jellinek's eldest brother, Adolf Jellinek, who later became a celebrated preacher at Vienna's Stadttempel on Seitenstettengasse, was in Leipzig throughout the revolution. Moritz Steinschneider, who later rose to prominence as the father of Hebrew bibliography, spent the revolution in Prague. Löw Schwab and his son-in-law, Leopold Löw, both of whom had accepted rabbinic posts in Hungary in the 1830s, not only participated in the Hungarian revolution but were also briefly imprisoned for their role in opposing Habsburg rule. Throughout the revolution, these Moravian Jews—as well as many others—sent letters to their families in Prossnitz, Ungarisch-Brod, and elsewhere, keeping them apprised of significant events throughout the "year of freedom."

The daily and weekly newspapers that proliferated after the censorship laws were lifted on March 15, 1848, supplied Moravia's Jewish and Christian inhabitants with their most regular source of news throughout the revolution. The number of political newspapers in

Austria increased nearly fivefold between March and October 1848; there were only 79 papers on the eve of the revolution, but 388 newspapers were published in the first seven months of the revolution. (Censorship was reintroduced after the October Uprising in Vienna had been suppressed at the end of October 1848.) Although sixteen of them appeared in Moravia, the vast majority were published in Vienna and circulated throughout the empire. Writing from Prossnitz in October 1848, Adolf Brecher (son of the Moravian *maskil* Gideon Brecher) described his voracious appetite for the latest news from Vienna in the following words:

> In light of the latest happenings, the crisis in which our recent freedom now finds itself, I have turned all of my attention to politics, and this currently absorbs all of my time. I am in the coffee house already at 6:30 a.m. and I study the newspapers until approximately 10 a.m. At 10 a.m. I visit my friends and we discuss—newspapers. In the afternoon, newspapers; in the evening, newspapers; at night I dream about newspapers.[25]

Brecher also read the German-language Jewish papers, which reported on the strides and pitfalls in the struggle for Jewish emancipation throughout Europe. Although the *Allgemeine Zeitung des Judenthums*, published in Leipzig, barely reported on Moravia, it provided extensive coverage of the revolution in the German states and elsewhere. *Der Orient*, also published in Leipzig, provided extensive coverage of events in the Habsburg Empire, thanks in particular to regular contributions from Moritz Jellinek, the middle Jellinek brother, who reported from Ungarisch-Brod, Vienna, and Kremsier. Adolf Jellinek, who was studying in Leipzig at the time, may have put his brother Moritz in touch with the editor and publisher of *Der Orient*, Julius Fürst. *Treue-Zions-Wächter*, an Orthodox organ published in Altona-Hamburg, also had a Moravian correspondent, who paid special attention to the activities of Moravia's Hamburg-born chief rabbi. Whereas the *Allgemeine Zeitung des Judenthums*, *Der Orient*, and *Treue-Zions-Wächter* were all published before the Revolution of 1848, the Habsburg monarchy's sole Jewish newspaper in 1848—the *Österreichisches Central-Organ für Glaubensfreiheit, Kultur, Geschichte und Literatur der Juden* (Austrian Central Organ for Religious Freedom, Culture and History and Literature of the Jews)—was itself a product of the revolution.[26] Founded by Isidor Busch, a Prague-born Jew, the *Central-Organ* was published in Vienna between March and October 1848. During its eight months of publication, the *Central-Organ* not only kept its readers abreast of the ongoing struggle for equal rights but also published essays on Jewish culture and history as well as short works of Jewish fiction (such as Leopold Kompert's "Ghetto tales"). Many of Hirsch's circulars were also reproduced in the *Central-Organ*, thereby exposing the Jews of the entire Habsburg monarchy—and not just Moravia—to the chief rabbi's words of exhortation and admonishment. The *Central-Organ* had a unifying function during the revolution, serving as a central forum for the Jews of Bohemia, Moravia, Hungary, Galicia, and Vienna.

Although the *Central-Organ* brought the disparate Habsburg Jewish communities together, each experienced the revolution quite differently—particularly with regard to the emerging national movements. Salo W. Baron claims that "the new national struggles in Hungary, Galicia, [and] Bohemia-Moravia placed the Jewish communities before the menacing alternatives of either provoking the deep hostility of the parties they failed to support or antagonizing them all by futilely proclaiming neutrality."[27] Baron's appraisal is particularly true for Bohemia, where Czech-German tensions reached a crescendo during the Revolution of 1848, but the situation was rather different in Moravia (and Austrian Silesia). Indeed, the nationalist passions that enveloped Bohemia during the revolution found but a faint echo in Moravia.

In Moravia, a regional and *supra*national "Moravian" identity was still widespread in 1848. As one historian observed, "A supranational Moravian sense of community—parallel to the 'Bohemianism' of the pre-revolutionary period—preserved itself and largely determined the atmosphere" during the revolution.[28] In Moravia, the shared geographic, historic, and cultural milieu continued to unite Slavic- and German-speaking inhabitants, even as the nearby "Bohemians" were increasingly recast as "Czechs" and "Germans." Some inhabitants of Moravia expressed support for the national demands of the St. Václav Committee in Prague at the beginning of the revolution, but the national consciousness was relatively muted among Moravians in general, whatever language(s) they spoke.[29] The May 1848 elections for the German National Assembly illustrate the stark contrast between

Bohemia and Moravia with regard to Czech and German nationalism. The elections presupposed that the Bohemian Lands were an integral part of the German body politic, and Czech leaders in Prague, with František Palacký at the helm, decried the elections as a mortal threat to Czech national existence and called on Czechs to boycott the elections throughout Bohemia, Moravia, and Austrian Silesia. In Bohemia, the boycott proved especially successful; out of sixty-eight voting districts, only twenty (in predominantly German-speaking areas) held elections. In Moravia, in contrast, the boycott fell rather flat; elections were held in twenty-three out of twenty-eight voting districts, including several with predominantly Slavic-speaking populations. Some scholars view this as a "clear success for the nationally oriented German political elite," but it should rather be considered evidence of a more peaceful rapport among the Slavic- and German-speaking inhabitants of Moravia.[30]

This relatively peaceful rapport caught the attention of a Moravian correspondent, who was likely accustomed to the continual barrage of reports on the Czech-German conflict in Bohemia. "Here," he wrote from Brünn in March 1849, "the open discord between nationalities is not yet noticeable, and in this regard, we believe there will be nothing to fear for some time. With the exception of a few dreamers [Phantasten], the Slavic party is content with the guaranteed equality of rights."[31] The only sign of Slavic political activity, he noted, was the recently established branch of Slovanská Lipa (Slavic Linden)—one of only six in Moravia at that point, compared to sixty-six in Bohemia.[32] Slovanská Lipa, the first Czech political organization, actively pursued Czech political, educational, economic, and cultural interests. Although a branch had been established in Brünn, the correspondent perceived "no sign of its existence" in March 1849.

Similarly, there were few stirrings of German nationalism in Moravia during the revolution. In fact, the League of Germans from Bohemia, Moravia, and Silesia for the Preservation of Their Nationality (Verein der Deutschen aus Böhmen, Mähren und Schlesien zur Aufrechthaltung ihrer Nationalität) was founded in Vienna, not in the Czech lands. Although the League disseminated propaganda in Bohemia, Moravia, and Silesia—particularly before the Frankfurt parliament elections— it was more of a factor in Bohemia than in Moravia or Silesia. At its

August 1848 congress in Teplitz (Teplice), all sixty-nine delegates came from Bohemia. Not a single Moravian or Silesian attended.[33]

The relatively subdued national tensions in Moravia at this time are usually explained in largely sociological terms. As an economically independent and nationally conscious bourgeoisie emerged in Bohemia (and Prague, in particular) in the decades before the revolution, it increasingly came into economic competition—and sometimes violent conflict—with the German-speaking bourgeoisie. In Moravia, where embourgeoisement was intimately tied to Germanization, this volatile development was delayed. In general, the upwardly mobile segments of the Moravian population—some Jews included—either already spoke German or adopted German as part of their embourgeoisement. Consequently, language was much more a function of class than of nationality, with German the language of the middle and upper classes and Czech (or Bohemian, as it was often called) the language of the peasants and the proletariat.[34]

Furthermore, anti-German sentiment was not an integral part of the regional "Moravian" identity. Unlike the Bohemian Czech identity, which was constructed in opposition to the "Germans," the "Moravian" identity was constructed largely in opposition to the "Bohemians." Even though a distinct "Moravian" identity can be traced back to the Middle Ages, the "Moravian sense of community" in 1848 can be seen as a reaction to Bohemian Czech drives for hegemony in Moravia and Silesia.[35] Czech leaders in Prague, such as František Ladislav Rieger, called for the union of the Lands of the Bohemian Crown and the establishment of a single unified diet for Bohemia, Moravia, and Austrian Silesia, but the Moravian Diet overwhelmingly rejected these demands.[36] In fact, when the Moravian Diet drafted a constitution in August 1848, it envisioned Moravia as an "independent province, bound only and organically, to the constitutional empire of Austria."[37] Stanley Z. Pech, a scholar of the Revolution of 1848, considers the Diet's actions to be an accurate reflection of public opinion in Moravia. "Czech national consciousness in that province," he writes, "was still only in its incipient stage; besides, there was a strong sentiment of provincial Moravian patriotism which was shared by Moravian Czechs and Germans alike and which would be at odds with any strengthening of constitutional ties with Bohemia."[38]

The failure of the Czech-German conflict to make serious inroads into Moravia before 1848 had important ramifications for Moravian Jewry as a whole. The Jews of Bohemia were constantly caught in the maelstrom of Czech-German tensions. They were increasingly labeled Germans (or German sympathizers), and, as such, they often felt the brunt of Czech anti-German violence.[39] The Jews of Moravia, in contrast, lived through the revolution in relative peace and quiet. Although Moravia did experience some anti-Jewish violence in the spring and summer of 1848, these minor incidents had nothing to do with the nationality conflict. Even the Moravian-born Adolf Jellinek, who expressed great disdain for Slavs in general (and Czechs in particular), did not resort to "national" explanations for the anti-Jewish violence in Moravia.[40] Jellinek, like most of his contemporaries, framed the anti-Jewish sentiment in Moravia almost entirely in socioeconomic terms—with occasional religious overtones. The unfolding of events in Moravia was influenced much more by the mood in Vienna than in Bohemia. This became especially apparent at the beginning of the revolution, when the movement against Jewish emancipation spread from Vienna to the surrounding provinces.

"Just No Jewish Emancipation!"

A flurry of vehemently anti-emancipation pamphlets emanated from Vienna in the first weeks of the revolution. These pamphlets, most notably Hubert Müller's "Just No Jewish Emancipation," quickly found their way to Bohemia and Moravia, where they had an unmistakable impact on the general emancipation discourse. Müller's pamphlet sold more than 25,000 copies, with a separate print run of 4,000 copies in Prague alone. Furthermore, it was extensively quoted in Moravia's petitions to the Reichstag (August 1848–February 1849), a testament to its wide circulation in this province as well.[41]

Müller's pamphlet set the tone and provided the basic repertoire of arguments for much of the anti-emancipation propaganda during the Revolution of 1848. Müller steered clear of the standard religious arguments against Jewish emancipation, insisting that "fanatical religious hatred does not animate us." Instead, it was the Jews' "most disreputable behavior" in relation to the Christian population that made Jewish emancipation ill-advised at this stage. The pamphlet did not deny the possibility—and perhaps even the desirability—of Jewish emancipation at a later stage, but it emphatically and unequivocally declared that "the Jews *as they are now* are still not suited for civic equality. They have still not *earned* it." According to Müller, the Jews were expected to shed their manifold antisocial traits *before* full emancipation could even be considered. In other words, the Jews were not entitled a priori to equal civic and political rights but rather had to prove—through a process of moral regeneration—that they were worthy of them. "Until they succeed in winning the love and respect of the world around them," Müller insisted, the Jews should be given only "partial rights."

In Müller's view, the Jews had done nothing to ingratiate themselves with the majority population. Quite to the contrary, they had done everything to antagonize their Christian neighbors, especially in the economic sphere. In a litany of charges, Müller described the kinds of "Jewish" behavior (and the ramifications) that had prevented the Christian population from embracing the Jews in their midst: (1) the impudent, immodest pushiness of the Jews; (2) the bold arrogance of their rich and dignified ones; (3) the disgraceful shamelessness of their literati and journalists; (4) their dirty speculation, leading to the destruction of public credit; (5) their corrupt intrigues in trade and on the stock market; (6) their machinations, leading to exorbitant inflation in the cost of foodstuffs; (7) the resulting oppression of the poorer classes; and (8) the Jews' unconscionable oppression of "our" traders and businessmen. To Müller, such behavior served as clear confirmation not only that the Jews wallowed in moral turpitude but also that they considered themselves separate from—and superior to—the surrounding Christian population. In such circumstances, could Christians really be expected to embrace the Jews as equal citizens? "We will support equal rights," Müller wrote, "when the Jews prove to us that they are truly capable of embracing us, when they make modesty [*Bescheidenheit*] their first virtue." In the meantime, the Christians had to protect themselves "so that the Jews do not in the end violate our human rights."

Müller conjured up the specter of anti-Jewish popular violence in the event of a "premature" Jewish emancipation, citing "the [anti-]Jewish persecutions in Alsace, in Hungary, etc." as a "cautionary example." By the time Müller's pamphlet appeared in late March, anti-Jewish violence had become an almost predictable by-product of the revolutions in Europe. As Jacob Toury observed, "In the 'year of freedom,' pogroms threatened Jews from Amsterdam to Rome, from Lombardy to Galicia, from France to Serbia."[42] The first anti-Jewish violence erupted in Alsace. When news of the revolution in Paris reached this French-German border area on February 26, local peasants plundered Jewish houses and laid waste to synagogues until order was restored by the army two days later.[43] In the Habsburg Empire, anti-Jewish violence erupted just days after the outbreak of the revolution. On March 17, the Jews of Pressburg, Hungary, were excluded from a celebratory torch-lit procession, allegedly for their own safety. On the following day, an unruly crowd assembled in front of Pressburg's Jewish quarter, preparing to storm the gates. After being dispersed by the military, the crowd poured out its wrath on Jewish residents of the Christian town, stoning their houses and causing much physical damage.

Throughout the next six weeks, anti-Jewish violence was reported elsewhere in the Habsburg Empire, particularly in Hungary and Bohemia. In the Kingdom of Hungary, more than twenty towns experienced anti-Jewish violence in April and May, with a "raw looting frenzy" erupting in Pressburg's Jewish quarter (for the second time) on Easter Sunday (April 23). In Bohemia, there were reports of anti-Jewish violence at the beginning of April, but the worst came in early May, when Prague's Jewish quarter was hit by several days of rioting.[44]

Like Hubert Müller's pamphlet, contemporary news reports tended to explain the springtime violence—particularly in Hungary—in socioeconomic terms, dismissing religious motives entirely. Whereas all agreed that the perpetrators stemmed from the volatile and "degenerate" masses, there was no consensus about the immediate causes of the unrest. Müller saw the violence as a reflexive response to the Jews' "most disreputable behavior," but many newspapers preferred to place the blame elsewhere. The *Brünner Zeitung*, for example, viewed the Easter riots in Pressburg as a simple expression of the masses' moral depravity. "Was it Jew-hatred that robbed these unfortunate [Jews] of their paltry possessions?" asked a lead article in early May. "No, that was not Jew-hatred. It was the raw looting frenzy of a degenerate swarm of rabble."[45] The *Central-Organ* presented a more sophisticated analysis of the Easter riots, presenting them as a form of social protest.[46]

> The persecutions against the Jews in our day have no religious, but rather a social, basis. . . . The persecutions against the Jews are entirely a consequence of the property question. . . . The Jews personify capital [*Geldbesitz*] in the public opinion, because proportionally they have most of the money trade in their hands. While others engage in agriculture, industry, animal husbandry, and state administration, the Jews have no other trade besides the acquisition of money [*Reichwerden*]. . . . The hatred and the abhorrence is far from all religious considerations. It is natural that the first attacks of the proletariat, which sought the practical settlement of the property question, should have been against the Jews, whom [the proletariat] saw and envied as property owners who do not work, wealthy ones who do not exert any effort, happy ones who have no needs.[47]

It could be argued that similar conditions existed in Moravia, but in sharp contrast to Bohemia and Hungary, this province remained relatively unaffected by anti-Jewish violence in the spring of 1848. The few incidents in Moravia—especially in Olmütz (April 12) and Gross-Meseritsch (April 23)—paled in comparison to the violence that swept the neighboring provinces. This is evident in a letter that Ber Schiff, a Jewish leaseholder in Moravia, wrote to his nephew three months *after* these two episodes. "We, the inhabitants of Moravia, have had peace," he wrote on July 16, "and God has had mercy on us and saved us until now." Schiff was grateful for the relative peace and quiet in Moravia, but he was rather perplexed at the same time. Like many others, he expected the anti-Jewish violence to cross over from Hungary and take root in Moravia. "In honesty," he wrote several months later, "when I heard about the persecutions in Hungary . . . I felt in my heart that such ill-fortune would also occur to the Jewry residing in the district of Hana.[48] . . . Hatred for the Jews is second nature [among the local Christians]; they imbibe it with their mother's milk."[49] A cantor from Boskowitz expressed similar fears. "We are anxious about the unrest that has recently erupted in the nearby Hungarian comitats," he wrote to his son, Rabbi Joseph Weisse in Gaya. "The disturbances in Hungary are causing great apprehension about the future. O, may our peaceful Moravia be spared!"[50]

Moravia was spared the brunt of the anti-Jewish violence in the spring of 1848, not because its Jews and Christians lived in perfect harmony but rather because of the relative tranquility reigning in Moravia at the time. Bohemia was deeply riven by the Czech-German conflict, and Hungary was engaged in a protracted war of independence; in contrast, Moravia seemed a veritable island of calm during the tumultuous revolution (as illustrated by Emperor Ferdinand's decision to relocate both his court and the Reichstag to Moravia when Vienna was besieged in October 1848). Because the centralized civil administration in Moravia was not disrupted by the revolution and because the local military troops were not distracted by national insurgencies, both could work together to ensure that the "Hungarian" violence did not destabilize Moravia. In addition, the national guard battalions, which came into being at the outbreak of the revolution, helped maintain peace and order. As Governor Leopold Lažansky explained in a proclamation from May 8, "In those places where Judeo-phobic sentiment has led to [Judeo-phobic] acts, the actions of the government officials—supported by the national guard and the military—have thus far succeeded in nipping criminal disturbances of this sort in the bud."[51]

Although threats to Jewish property were reported in Ungarisch-Brod (near the Hungarian border) at the beginning of May, anti-Jewish violence in Moravia was limited to "lynch justice" in Olmütz and the "monstrance affair" in Gross-Meseritsch.[52] What is most striking about these incidents is how they differed from the patterns set in Hungary and Bohemia. In Olmütz, 250 burghers unabashedly took credit for expelling a number of Jews from the weekly market, and in Gross-Meseritsch, the anti-Jewish violence conformed to traditional forms of religiously motivated Jew hatred.

"Lynch Justice" in Olmütz

Amid the general disorder and mayhem in the first month of the revolution, the burghers of Olmütz took the law in their own hands, performing an act of "lynch justice" against a Jewish family they had been trying to expel for several years.[53] Although there had been no Jewish community in Olmütz since the 1454 expulsion, Jews had been permitted to attend weekly markets since the seventeenth century and, in exceptional cases, even establish temporary residence within the town limits. In 1848, at least twenty-six Jewish concession holders resided in Olmütz, leasing breweries, laundries, and street-lighting concessions; some even leased kosher eating houses for the large number of Jews who engaged in petty trade of textiles, grains, and other wares at the weekly markets.[54] Concession holders could apply for three-year renewable residence permits, but their contracts explicitly forbade them from engaging in trade. In the years preceding the Revolution of 1848, the burghers of Olmütz had unrelentingly sought the expulsion of one individual, Moses Hamburger, who had ignored this restriction with impunity. On April 12, 1848, the Olmütz burghers forcibly expelled Hamburger and his family along with other Jews who had allegedly engaged in profiteering and speculation to the great detriment of the town's Christian inhabitants.

Hamburger, like most of the Jews trading or residing in Olmütz, came from the neighboring Jewish community of Prossnitz. Having leased the military laundry concession since 1838, he was entitled to live with his family in Olmütz. However, when he tried to renew his residence permit in 1847, the Olmütz magistracy leveled a litany of charges against him, accusing him of engaging in deleterious economic pursuits alongside his laundry concession. The magistracy claimed that Hamburger did not even work in the laundry business but used it as a pretext to get a residence permit so he could pursue "his own business, consisting of money and grain speculation." According to the magistracy, Hamburger's "grain profiteering" and "manipulation of grain prices" had agitated the local population to such an extent that violent excesses at the grain market had been prevented so far "only through painstaking intervention of the police." Arguing that Hamburger's continued residence would only lead to further disturbances, the magistracy demanded that his residence permit be denied.[55]

By 1848, the magistracy's attempt at a lawful expulsion had failed, and the burghers selected the fourth weekly market of the revolution for their act of "lynch justice." Because of the inveterate competition between local Christian and visiting Jewish merchants, the Olmütz market had become a traditional venue for Christian-Jewish hostility. Throughout the early nineteenth century, Christian merchants repeatedly tried to schedule markets on Jewish festivals and holy days to prevent Jewish attendance.[56] Until 1828 Jewish merchants had to store their wares 2 miles outside Olmütz, hauling them to the market on their backs.[57] In light of such tensions, it is not surprising that the expulsion of the Hamburger family "with the rawest expressions of intolerant brutality" was accompanied by "a demonstration against several *Handelsjuden* from Prossnitz,"[58] including two Jewish cattle merchants who were "soundly beaten up."[59] The Olmütz national guard helped to restore order but did not prevent the expulsion of the Hamburger family and one other resident Jew. The following day, the Prossnitz Jewish community publicly thanked the Olmütz national guard for their role,[60] but many Jews avoided the next market on April 19 out of fear,[61] and all Jews were excluded from the market on May 3 following a rumor that the Jews in Prague had killed a number of Christians.[62]

The incident reverberated in the pages of an Olmütz daily, *Die Neue Zeit*, for the next three weeks. An April 22 letter signed Pfefferkorn decried the "most iniquitous and unjust intolerance" against the Jews in Olmütz and sought to muster some compassion for them by detailing the oppressive legal restrictions that drove the Jews almost exclusively into petty trade. Without demanding emancipation, Pfefferkorn called on the reader to "go into the houses of the poor Jews, look at their lodgings, their highly taxed paltry meal, get to know their other necessaries of life, and say—whether they are too deplorable; go to them, and your Jew hatred will disappear; you, yourselves, will wish that their condition improve, that they be made more capable of living, that they be able to lead a better existence."[63]

On May 6, 250 Olmütz burghers took Pfefferkorn's letter as an opportunity not to renounce their Jew hatred but rather to justify their expulsion of Hamburger and to underscore the malicious character of Jews in general.[64] In a manifesto inserted into *Die Neue Zeit*, they denounced Hamburger not only for his many years of grain trading "to the detriment of the public" but also for the "artifices and far-fetched pretexts" he used to "usurp domicile in the town of Olmütz." They were not acting "against him *solely* as an Israelite" (emphasis mine) but also as "someone who does not belong to Olmütz." Still, their grievances against the Jews were abundant. The 250 burghers accused the Jews of deceit and intrigue not only in their grain, cattle, and textile trade but also in their ability to avoid prosecution for transgressing the laws of the land. In a final jab at Pfefferkorn, the burghers informed this "warm defender of the Jews" that "our town has no small number of destitute of the Christian faith, who are not capable of enjoying better conditions, because so many trades have been taken from them and secured for the Jews." Pfefferkorn did not need to go "first into the houses of the poor Prossnitz Jews" to observe such hardship.

Although Hamburger explained his expulsion to the Olmütz district office as a manifestation of anti-Jewish sentiment, the district office saw this as an attempt by Hamburger to deflect the responsibility from himself. The district office deemed Hamburger's character and behavior to be the decisive factors in incurring the wrath of the burghers. "Although Hamburger tries to explain the injustice directed at him as the animosity of the public against his coreligionists in general," the district office wrote to the Moravian-Silesian Gubernium, "this claim contradicts itself . . . [because even] after the catastrophe happened to him, hundreds of his coreligionists have continued their trade undisturbed by the local inhabitants." The expulsion, it concluded, was carried out "not because of his confession, but rather because of his conduct." Still, when the district office advised against renewing Hamburger's residence permit in Olmütz in December 1848, it acknowledged "prejudices against the Jewish nation" in addition to the "public disposition" against Hamburger.[65]

The Gross-Meseritsch "Monstrance Affair"

In contrast to the expulsion of the Hamburger family from Olmütz, the anti-Jewish disturbances that occurred in Gross-Meseritsch conformed prima facie to traditional forms of religiously motivated Jew hatred. These disturbances fell on Easter Sunday (and the seventh day of Passover), after the Jews were accused of stealing a religious object—a jewel-encrusted gold and silver monstrance valued at 2,000 fl. Furthermore, whereas the Olmütz burghers assigned guilt to individual Jews for their profiteering and speculating, the Gross-Meseritsch priest, Father Kuczura, blamed the Jews as a collectivity for the disappearance of the monstrance. Nevertheless, even though the events in Gross-Meseritsch were covered in a religious veneer, social tensions appeared to be at the root of these disturbances as well.

On April 23, as the Catholic church was opened at noon for Easter Sunday worship, the monstrance was discovered to be missing from its place in the tabernacle.[66] Father Kuczura deemed it a theft and placed the blame on "the entire Jewry" of Gross-Meseritsch. As one Jewish correspondent observed sardonically, "We know well the collective responsibility of the Jews for all misdeeds." In the afternoon, the "fanatical masses" assembled on the street, blaming the Jews and threatening violence. Father Kuczura initiated house searches in the Jewish town "in which there was naturally no lack of brutality." When the monstrance was not found, the masses stormed into the Jewish town and violence followed "à la Pressburg."

At this stage, Christian Fiala, a local administrator (*Ober- und Justizamtmann*), arrived with some fellow burghers to calm the crowd, but their words were of no use. The frenzied masses began throwing stones at Fiala, chased him home, and smashed his windows with heavy rocks. One of the rocks hit his 7-year-old daughter on the head with a nearly fatal impact. Several burghers whisked Fiala and his family away, and the masses returned to the Jewish town, arming themselves with garden stakes and clubs. Beginning at 5 p.m., the masses broke windows, stalls, and lanterns, robbed money and wares, and emptied out barrels of spirits. At 8 p.m., several burghers took it upon themselves to drive the "seditious rabble" out of the Jewish town by force. Although Gross-Meseritsch did not yet have a national guard, the burghers set up watch posts throughout Gross-Meseritsch and its suburbs, and a strict curfew was imposed on the town after 9 p.m. At Fiala's behest, District Officer (*Hauptmann*) Leopold Ritter von Gersch and an infantry regiment arrived from Iglau the next day to restore order. District Officer von Gersch called for the formation of a national guard.

The next day, Easter Monday, the monstrance had still not been found. After a 17-year-old Christian girl claimed to have seen a red-bearded Jew leaving the church two days earlier, all the male Jews of Gross-Meseritsch were assembled in the synagogue for identification. The girl failed to identify the thief, and Rabbi Jacob Pollack was forced to stand before the open ark and swear on a Torah scroll that he knew nothing about the theft. Still, the masses were not appeased, and they threatened continued violence if the monstrance was not found within twelve hours. On the next day, April 25, the magistracy received an anonymous letter in Czech, indicating the exact location in the church where the monstrance was hidden. The monstrance was found in the indicated hiding place, but the anti-Jewish agitation did not cease. Two silver screws and seven precious gems were missing from the monstrance, and the fanatically excited masses issued new threats. Finally, on May 6, the "Adventure of the Gross-Meseritsch Monstrance" came to an end when the silver screws and gemstones were found in the attic of a Christian tailor named Tutschek. As son of a Gross-Meseritsch church beadle, Tutschek had unrestricted access to the church and was suspected of committing four other church thefts in the previous twenty years.

One Jewish paper presented the incident as an aberration, in which justice was eventually served and the Jews rightly exonerated. "No one believed [the rumor]," wrote the correspondent. "Since few of the [Gross-Meseritsch] Jews are engaged in trade, most of them being poor artisans, largely in debt to the Christians burghers, they live on the best of terms with the inhabitants and enjoy an irreproachable, honorable reputation." In sharp contrast to the situation in Olmütz, relations between burghers and Jews were not seen as a cause of tension. In fact, the high concentration of Jews in artisan trades was credited for the amicable relations until the sudden outburst on April 23. Reporting on the outburst, both the *Central-Organ* and the *Brünner Zeitung* emphasized the role of the upstanding burghers in quelling the violence of the fanatically excited masses. Nonetheless, the formation of separate Jewish and Christian national guard battalions on April 24 and the submission of a highly anti-Jewish petition to the Moravian Diet in July belie this idyllic depiction of relations between Christian burgher and Jew.[67]

Although the religious aspect of the affair was not given prominence, neither the *Brünner Zeitung* nor the *Central-Organ* totally ignored it. The *Brünner Zeitung* explained the continued rioting even after the culprit was identified as a refusal by the masses "to admit that the perpetrator was a Christian." The *Central-Organ* compared Tutschek's crime to a previous blood libel in Gross-Meseritsch, when a Christian girl was intentionally hidden to incite the populace against the Jews. However, the Jewish correspondent did not see any deep-rooted religious animosity in the monstrance affair. "The mob, itself," he wrote, "expressed shame and regret; every good-minded person expressed heartfelt sympathy as well as admiration of our composure." Looking forward to "a trusting bond between Christian and Jew" in Gross-Meseritsch, he wrote, "no one is more forgiving than we [Jews]."

Petitions to the Moravian Diet (April–August 1848)

The inhabitants of Olmütz and Gross-Meseritsch chose to vent their anti-Jewish sentiments through "lynch justice" in April 1848, but they were also given an opportunity to express their grievances in a less disruptive manner—through petitions to the Moravian Diet. Between April and August hundreds of Moravian towns, villages, and guilds submitted petitions to the Diet, expressing their fears, desires, and expectations to the provincial legislative body. Although most of the nearly 300 petitions make no mention of the Jews, 22 of them include the Jews in their manifold grievances. These petitions reflect some of the general themes—such as fear of economic domination—that pervaded the Viennese pamphlets in March 1848, but they also reveal—often in great detail—the specific cases affecting Moravia's villagers and burghers.[68]

Anti-Jewish themes were most pronounced in towns and villages where Jewish residence had been prohibited for centuries. The overwhelming majority of petitions (sixteen of twenty-two) came from places with scarcely a Jewish resident, where Jews were encountered primarily as itinerant peddlers, cereal traders, and leaseholders. The other six petitions came from towns with large Jewish communities: Prossnitz,

Trebitsch, Eibenschitz, Ungarisch-Brod, Gross-Meseritsch, and Krem-sier. By and large, the petitioners sought to preserve, reinstate, or tighten various restrictions on the "injurious" economic activity of the Jews. There were many calls to prohibit Jews from leasing breweries and distilleries[69] and, above all, from trading in cereals, reflecting the wide-spread belief that Jewish grain speculation was responsible for the famine and economic hardship of 1846 and 1847. As the Sternberg magistracy explained, "The price of victuals has risen in the past two years, thereby destroying families and swelling the ranks of the poor. This is not the re-sult of natural causes, but rather due to excessive grain profiteering [*über-triebenden Getreidewucher*] . . . especially by the Israelites." To rectify this situation, the Sternberg magistracy proposed the wholesale exclusion of Jews from the cereal trade "for the good of the entire land."

In a similar vein, many petitioners sought to exclude Jews from leaseholding and itinerant peddling (*Hausierung*) to protect Chris-tian artisans, merchants, and peasants from Jewish competition. This tendency is again most evident in the Sternberg petition, which blamed a single Jewish leaseholder for jeopardizing the livelihoods of the town's entire population. In Sternberg, the propination right be-longed exclusively to the town (according to a fifteenth-century privi-lege), and revenues from the sale of spirits provided the main source of income for Sternberg's public welfare institutions. The Sternberg magistracy complained, however, that this right was being impinged by a Jewish leaseholder in the nearby village of Knibitz. Because Knibitz was a noble-owned village—and, as such, not subject to the magistracy—this Jew could operate his distillery in close proximity to Sternberg without requiring the magistracy's approval. The mag-istracy protested that the resulting loss of revenue would spell eco-nomic ruin for the local population. "An entire community of more than 8,000 souls," it exclaimed, "cannot be sacrificed for the sake of a single foreign Jew."

A number of petitions sought to change weekly markets to Satur-days to keep away Jewish competitors. The petitioners from Freiberg, for example, explained that their weekly markets had been held since time immemorial on Saturdays—in accordance with their privilege. A few years earlier, however, neighboring Jews, who allegedly engaged in the "usurious trade of victuals" (*wücherischen Händel der Viktualien*), succeeded in getting the market day changed since "their Sabbath falls on Saturday." As a result, the petitioners complained, prices rose to such a degree that local inhabitants could no longer afford their houses. It was high time, they insisted, for the privilege to be honored and for the weekly market to be returned to Saturday. In one of the most vituperative petitions, two tanners from Prossnitz sought to exclude Jews from the weekly market, arguing that Jews were under the jurisdiction of the Plumenau estate and were therefore "foreigners" in Prossnitz. They blamed the Jews for ruining three of the four tanners in Prossnitz and for bringing general ill to all. "Through the artifice that the Jewish nation absorbs with the mother's milk," they wrote, "through underhanded dealings and deceit, they know how to turn black into white, to offer bad wares as the best, to lure all the peasants to them as customers, and to depress the prices to such an extent that the skillfully trained master cannot compete with him." As a result, the Prossnitz tanners sought to exclude Jews from the weekly market "as is the case in the other towns of the province."

Like the Prossnitz tanners and the Sternberg magistracy, the petitioners tended to justify their demands in terms of age-old corporate privileges. A society based on individual rights, they feared, would render Christians defenseless against Jewish cunning and deceit. Corporate privilege, in contrast, would continue to serve as a bulwark against Jewish economic domination. Villagers from Borovnice, Javorek, and Krasn, for example, demanded that Jews be denied equal rights lest "all the shops, leases, custom-posts, inns, breweries and distilleries end up in their hands," thereby leaving the villagers "completely deceived and cheated by the Jews." In a similar vein, villagers from Bohumilice, Borkovany, Kasnice, Klobouky, and Sitborice opposed equal civic rights for Jews, buttressing their demands with economic—not religious—arguments.

By framing their demands in economic terms, the petitioners sought to draw a distinction between legitimate anti-Jewish grievances on the one hand and "intolerant" or "unenlightened" Jew hatred on the other. This was most striking in Gross-Meseritsch, whose magistracy opposed equal rights for Jews "not out of religious hatred, but rather because the Jews do not recognize our fatherland as their own." Although it repudiated "religious hatred," the Gross-Meseritsch petition simultaneously recapitulated traditional anti-Jewish canards, most noticeably the allegation that the Jews' "religion and foreign customs" have set the Jews apart for centuries as "strangers in the land." The same petition also imputed general immorality and sexual depravity to the Jews, demanding a ban not only on Jewish employment of Christian servants ("in order to prevent disorder and fornication") but also on the playing of music in Jewish taverns ("lest it corrupt the Christians").

Many of the petitions to the Moravian Diet singled out particular grievances against the Jews, but none of the petitions can be viewed as a coherent ideological treatise against Jewish emancipation per se. This can be explained by a number of factors. First, the petitions gave voice to a whole spectrum of grievances, not just those against the Jews. Second, well over half the petitions were written before the Pillersdorf constitution (April 25, 1848) had even articulated the principle of civic and political equality for all citizens. Third, because the question of Jewish emancipation was not to be decided by the provincial diets but rather by the Reichstag, a number of groups sent separate anti-emancipation petitions directly to Vienna (and later to Kremsier). On April 18, for example, the Sternberg magistracy described the local burghers' intention to send a separate petition against the "still untimely Jewish emancipation and its injurious impact on the local situation." The Reichstag received this petition just six months later, along with at least sixteen similar petitions—primarily from Moravia.

Petitions to the Reichstag (August 1848–February 1849)

Between August 1848 and February 1849, the Reichstag received at least seventeen petitions against Jewish emancipation—one from Vienna, three from Bohemia, and thirteen from Moravia.[70] The reason that the overwhelming majority came from Moravia is quite mundane. In October 1848, the Reichstag was transferred from Vienna to Kremsier, where it met until being disbanded by Emperor

Franz Joseph in February 1849. Most of the anti-Jewish petitions to the Reichstag date from this period, when Austria's political center was temporarily located in Moravia. Just as Hirsch's intensified political activism can be partly explained by his fortuitous proximity to Kremsier, so too can the sudden spate of Moravian petitions against Jewish emancipation. Nonetheless, the petitions contained very real concerns.

Like the petitions to the Moravian Diet, the vast majority of these petitions came from royal towns (e.g., Znaim, Iglau, Sternberg, Mährisch-Schönberg) and rural villages (e.g., Lanitz, Bezmierow, Loganowski, Hradiska), which had no Jewish communities whatsoever. In fact, only four of the thirteen Moravian petitions came from places with Jewish communities (Trebitsch, Holleschau, Prerau, Pohrlitz).[71] The burgher petitions were usually written in German and the rural petitions in Czech, but there were no discernibly "German" or "Czech" arguments against Jewish emancipation. Instead, the arguments reflected the fears and grievances shared by two strata that felt particularly threatened by the prospect of Jewish emancipation: the villagers and especially the burghers.

In their petitions to the Reichstag, Moravia's burghers and villagers perceived the Jewish question first and foremost as a property question. As the law stood in Moravia in 1848, Jews were forbidden to purchase any real estate other than the specially designated Jewish houses located in Moravia's fifty-two Jewish communities. Only with special permission from the Gubernium could Jews acquire short-term leases on agricultural land or burgher houses, but they could not actually own "Christian" property. Moravia's Jews perceived such property restrictions as a grave injustice, but the petitioners viewed them as a necessary safeguard against the dispossession and impoverishment of Moravia's Christian inhabitants. If the Jews were suddenly granted civic and political equality, the petitions warned, all of Moravia's real estate would end up in Jewish hands. As the Prerau petition put it, "Emancipation would enable the Jews to buy up burgher houses or [parcels of] agricultural land—three or four per person. . . . The emancipated Jews would strip the Christians naked, and then let themselves be served by humiliated Christian slaves."[72] Similar sentiments—including the recurring motif of "Christian enslavement to the Jews"—were expressed in almost all the petitions.

As evidence, the petitions cited recent cases in which Jewish merchants had brought economic ruin to the Christian population—despite the residential and occupational restrictions that were still in place. If the Jews had already wreaked such havoc on the surrounding population, ran the argument, "how will it be if the Jews attain full freedom?"[73] In one of the most vitriolic petitions, the burghers of Trebitsch described how the Jews, by means of "intrigues," "schemes," and "deceitful practices," had already robbed the Christian artisans "not only of their hard-earned profits [*bürgerlichen sauber erwerbenen Gewinn*] but also of their property." It was thanks solely to the existing restrictive laws, they insisted, "that the burgher could still work, that he could still live." In the event of Jewish emancipation, they argued, things would only get worse. The Trebitsch burghers went on to predict even more dire repercussions.

> If the Jews are given rights under the existing conditions, it is certain that [their] cheating, oppression, and deceitfulness will develop even more freely, that the poor artisans will become the private slaves of the Jews, that they will relentlessly sue for their unlawfully and cunningly acquired debts, that they will make others sell real estate under its value and then acquire it themselves. Then, where there was once an industrious Christian town [*gewerbsthätige Christenstadt*], Jews will appear as the only house owners and burghers and be up to their same old mischief. In a similar fashion, they will force the cottagers from the [agricultural] land, but they will not work this land themselves; instead, they will use Christians for this, graciously tossing them a paltry day wage. Soon the Jew will rule: all commerce and wealth will be in his hands alone, and he alone will decide whether his Christian fellow man [*seinen christlichen Mitmenschen*] will exist alongside him. These consequences of emancipation are certain, and cannot be disputed away.[74]

The perceived inevitability of this scenario was rooted in the assumption that the Jew, by his very nature, could conceive of his Christian neighbor solely as an exploitable source of income, never as a "fellow man."

According to many of the petitions, the Jews possessed certain "inborn" traits—such as laziness and lust for wealth—that would not disappear with emancipation but actually become more insidious. A number of petitions brought empirical evidence to prove that the Jews, no matter where they lived, had remained unchanged—and unchangeable—throughout the centuries. As the burghers of Iglau wrote:

> The history of remote antiquity, the Middle Ages and recent times, indeed, the history of all peoples, furnishes the most compelling evidence that the Jews always covet wealth and allow themselves any means to obtain it. Whoever is versed in history knows that the Jews, in all ages and in all lands where they are found, use cunning, deceit, seduction, and—where they are the stronger ones—violence in order to acquire the property of gentiles [*Andersglaubigen*].[75]

In sharp contrast to proponents of emancipation who adduced historical evidence to show that externally imposed restrictions and pressures had debased the Jews and driven them almost exclusively into commerce, the burghers of Iglau used the historical record to argue the opposite: Because the Jew exhibits moral depravity and material covetousness wherever he is found, these traits could not possibly be a product of his environment but rather were the very essence of his being. As the burghers of Trebitsch put it:

> The Jew will remain just as he has been from time immemorial, and if he were emancipated today, he would not condescend to any other work but commerce—due to his customary and inborn laziness; and he would take advantage of the other inhabitants in a more unconstrained and more all-embracing manner. His principles, his inborn customs, his lifestyle do not allow him to pursue any other path.[76]

These "inborn" customs also raised questions about the Jew's loyalty to the state. Indeed, if his material interests took precedence over all else, if the pursuit of profit preempted duties to the state and duties to one's fellow man, how could the Jew possibly become a loyal citizen? The petitions framed the question of loyalty in secular terms, steering clear of the religious arguments found throughout the large corpus of anti-emancipation literature published in the first half of the nineteenth century. Rather than emphasizing the messianic belief or the belief in a return to Zion, the petitions portrayed the Jew's single-minded quest for material gain as the clearest evidence of his suspect loyalty. As 531 signatories from ten villages explained in their joint petition:

> As Christians, we are familiar with the commandment, "Love thy neighbor as thyself"! The noble Jew comes here, and we press him to our bosom, we give him a brotherly kiss! But he must act like a noble man! He must show us that the welfare of the fatherland, the security of the state, the welfare of its citizens is more important than private interest. However, from daily experience we observe the excessively preponderate number of Jews that are ruled by such a drive for profit, such a predilection for money, that they readily sacrifice not only the sense of self-respect but also the principles of honesty; that the words "usury" and "speculation" can excite them until they forget their natural human duties. Among members of Christendom, [such traits] are either entirely absent or extraordinarily rare.[77]

In accusing the Jews of subordinating morality and loyalty to material self-interest, these petitioners drew an essential distinction between Christian and Jew: Christians were prepared to make personal sacrifices for the common good; Jews were poised to sacrifice the common good for their own personal gain. One could look, for example, at the English Jew who loaned money to the French government while his own country was at war with France. Or, as the Trebitsch burghers pointed out, one needed to look no farther than Hungary, where the Jewish population—"out of avarice" (*aus Gewinnsucht*)—was secretly provisioning the rebels in their revolt against Habsburg rule.

While condemning the Jews' alleged disloyalty to the state, the petitions simultaneously denied the Jews the possibility of having an organic connection to the lands in which they lived or to the people among whom they dwelled. The Christian majority was considered the native population, and the Jewish minority was assigned a sojourner status. As the Holleschau burghers put it, "The Israelites have been welcomed into our states solely as guests; they have to take the larger, Christian population into consideration."[78] The 531 villagers maintained that the Jews were not "intrinsic members of the nation" (*eigentlichen Angehörigen der Nation*) but rather a "nation unto themselves, dwelling among strangers; cosmopolitans [*Weltbürger*] who neither can nor will ever assimilate with the institutions of a land." As such, the Jews could not lay claim to equality of rights—especially with regard to the acquisition of real estate. A number of burgher petitions further underscored the Jews' sojourner status in Moravia by using a narrow and exclusionary definition of the "people" (*Volk*). Six hundred forty-one burghers from Sternberg, for example, justified their opposition to Jewish emancipation by insisting that "emancipation is not grounded in the will of the people."[79] Similarly, the burghers of Mährisch-Schönberg claimed to represent the "true conviction of the people of Moravia" (*wahre Volksgessinung der Provinz Mähren*) in their petition to the Reichstag.[80] It was self-evident that the "people of Moravia" did not include the Jews of Moravia.

In addition to excluding the Jews from the general body politic, such appeals to the "will of the people" played on the government's perpetual fear of social unrest from the unruly and discontented masses. A number of burgher petitions subjected the question of Jewish emancipation to a class analysis, concluding that a hasty emancipation would not only devastate the peaceful middle classes but also increase the ranks (and rage) of the volatile proletariat. No one made this linkage clearer than the burghers of Sternberg, who predicted that Jewish emancipation would inevitably bring about "the ruin of . . . the entire industrial middle class," resulting in the "proliferation of the proletariat." Pointing out that the welfare of a constitutional state is rooted in a sizable middle class, the burghers of Sternberg argued that Jewish emancipation actually ran counter to the state's own interests. The state had to defend middle class interests "in order to satisfy the laws of humanity and the constitutional principle." In particular, the state had to restrain the Jews' "excessive competitiveness," which "preys on the life-work of the middle-class traders, turns them into a proletariat," and then further impoverishes them.

Like Hubert Müller's pamphlet from the early days of the revolution, the Sternberg petition, among others, warned that a "premature" or "hasty" emancipation would further enrage the people, inevitably leading to anti-Jewish violence à la Alsace and Pressburg. Holleschau burghers warned of "disturbances of the peace" in the event of Jewish emancipation, and the Iglau burghers insisted that they would be "unable to prevent the blood of Jews from flowing here in streams." Burgher petitions from Znaim, Trebitsch, and Mährisch-Schönberg expressed similar predictions and threats, all to be outdone by the burghers of Sternberg. "[The Jews] themselves should stop thinking about emancipation," they warned, "if they do not want to become victims of the people's vengeance. Should the Reichstag emancipate [the Jews], entire provinces will be startled and brandish weapons for [the Jews'] expulsion—perhaps even their extermination [*Vernichtung*]."

Although the threat of anti-Jewish violence was implicit in all the petitions, it was articulated—often quite graphically—solely in the burgher petitions. Perhaps this theme was avoided in the rural petitions out of fear that the signatories, who came mostly from the peasant masses, would be held directly accountable for any disturbances of the peace. The burghers, in contrast, were seen by the government as a stabilizing force, capable of restoring order should the unruly masses get out of hand. Indeed, from the outset of the revolution, the burghers had been permitted to organize national guard battalions for this specific purpose. It was these battalions, the burghers suggested, that would be incapable of quelling the tremendous—and inevitable—social unrest in the event of Jewish emancipation. Thus they could argue that their opposition to Jewish emancipation was not out of self-interest alone but also out of concern for societal stability and the welfare of the state. This concern was extended, with questionable sincerity, to the Jews' welfare as well. "Civil equality is out of the question," declared the burghers of Mährisch-Schönberg, "out of consideration for the Jews, themselves!"

Voices in Favor of Jewish Emancipation

Not a single Moravian petition to the Reichstag actually advocated Jewish emancipation,[81] but the cause did find substantial support on the pages of Moravia's liberal German-language newspapers, especially *Die Neue Zeit*, Olmütz's first daily, and the *Brünner Zeitung*, Moravia's official daily newspaper.[82] In the winter of 1848–49, these papers made consistent and principled arguments for the civic and political equality of all citizens, serving as a kind of counterbalance to the flurry of anti-emancipation petitions that were being submitted to the Reichstag at the same time. The editors of these papers, both of Jewish origin, had their own vested interests in the matter at hand. Dr. Alois Jeitteles, one of the few Jews officially residing in Brünn before the revolution, edited the *Brünner Zeitung* from October 1, 1848, until his death ten years later.[83] His younger cousin, Dr. Andreas Ludwig Joseph Heinrich Jeitteles, who converted from Judaism to Catholicism before becoming professor of medicine at the Olmütz university, edited *Die Neue Zeit* during the revolution (and served as a delegate to the Frankfurt Parliament in 1848).[84] Despite the Jewishness of the Jeitteles cousins, there was nothing distinctly "Jewish" about the approach to emancipation taken by their respective newspapers. Like Moravia's smaller German newspapers, including the *Brünner Tags-Courier* (which was edited by Rudolf Kolisch, a Jew from Koritschan, Moravia)[85] and the *Österreichischer constitutioneller Bote*, both *Die Neue Zeit* and the *Brünner Zeitung* argued that Jewish emancipation was, first and foremost, a necessity of the constitutional state.[86]

Moravia's German newspapers countered the arguments found in the anti-emancipation petitions with appeals to constitutional rights and "Christian" compassion. "Jewish emancipation," declared an article in *Die Neue Zeit*, "is the natural outcome of a free constitution. There are no moral grounds for denying the Jews equal rights." It conceded that "there may be some political grounds, but they are not so sublime that they cannot be silenced through true Christian feeling."[87] Similarly, an article in the *Österreichischer constitutioneller Bote* (published in Brünn) called on the Reichstag to grant the Jews full emancipation as their "human" and "Christian" duty. "Heed the Redeemer's words," it admonished them. "In my Father's house there are many dwelling places" (John 14:2).[88]

Several articles argued that Jewish emancipation could not be disentangled from the more urgent issue of reorganizing the state on a liberal constitutional basis. A lead article in the *Brünner Zeitung* expressed the expectation that the Jews would be emancipated as individuals, not as a separate nationality or religious group. "The emancipation of Jews and

Christians *as such* are mutually dependent," it proclaimed, because the "unique quintessence of the individual" must be respected in the newly organized state.⁸⁹ Similarly, an article in the *Brünner Tags-Courier* criticized the anti-emancipation petitions for seeking to undermine the very principles on which the new constitutional state was to be founded. It took issue, in particular, with the recurrent demand—expressed in all the Moravian petitions—to keep Jewish residential restrictions in place. If such a demand were upheld, observed the *Brünner Tags-Courier*, it would "belie the universally recognized principle of equality of rights and duties for all Christians and Jews."⁹⁰

In presenting ideological arguments in favor of emancipation, the articles remained relatively consistent. With regard to the oft-threatened specter of anti-Jewish violence, however, the responses diverged. An article in the *Österreichischer constitutioneller Bote* dismissed the possibility of such violence outright. By finally destigmatizing the Jews, it argued, Jewish emancipation would actually reduce anti-Jewish sentiment among the broader population. "It is only the stigmatizing exceptional laws," it explained, "that have made the Jews free game in the eyes of the ruffian masses [*rohe Pöbelhorden*]!" In the "enlightened present," it continued, the Jew would no longer be despised, plundered, and slaughtered as he was in the "dark Middle Ages." On the contrary, as contemporary events "in both hemispheres" had already illustrated, "his Christian fellow citizens welcome his emancipation with joy. So it must be, for love and respect are reserved for the free man, the whip and the hatchet for the slave."⁹¹ The *Brünner Zeitung* did not dismiss the possibility of violence in the event of Jewish emancipation but actually considered it an inevitable—though ephemeral—response to such a dramatic societal transformation. It conceded that Jewish emancipation would engender confusion and require "sacrifice," but far less than in the event of its delay. "The longer the blessings of the future are withheld from us," it warned, "the more imperative will be the sacrifices of the present. [These sacrifices] are evidence that the people [*Volk*] are still not fully aware of their own interests, that the state [*Staatsgesellschaft*] must first get over the worst before organizing itself anew."⁹² In other words, the birth pangs of the new constitutional era were bound to be painful (perhaps even violent) but would be less painful than eliminating atavistic corporate privileges at a later date.

The struggle for Jewish emancipation was not limited to the pages of Moravia's German papers but found expression in its theaters as well. Salomon Hermann Mosenthal's drama, *Deborah the Jewess*, had its Habsburg premier in Brünn on February 10, 1849, just two weeks before the anticipated Reichstag debate on Jewish emancipation in nearby Kremsier.[93] The play received favorable reviews in Moravia's local newspapers, which praised its emancipationist message far more than its artistic qualities. Several papers drew attention to the "manifestation of humanity" and the "prejudice-free" reaction of the audience, particularly during the "lines relating to 'the emancipation of the Jews.'"[94] Like Gotthold Ephraim Lessing's *Nathan the Wise* of the previous century, Mosenthal's *Deborah* came to symbolize the possibility of full Jewish integration into the surrounding society.

In essence, the debate over Jewish emancipation was a debate over the social and legal boundaries separating Christians and Jews. The petitioners, journalists, and theater directors who participated in this debate hoped to influence public opinion, with the ultimate goal of convincing their elected deputies to either reinforce or remove the existing boundaries. For this reason, the public debate reached its greatest intensity in late 1848 and early 1849, as the Kremsier Reichstag was preparing for deliberations on Paragraph 16 of the constitution. However, the debate over Jewish emancipation also took place "on the ground," particularly when criteria for membership in traditionally burgher institutions was at issue. This became apparent after the establishment of the national guard, a burgher institution par excellence, in the first days of the revolution.

Jews in the National Guard?

Although Emperor Ferdinand ceded the right to form national guards in the first days of the revolution, the newly established national guards were not necessarily revolutionary in character. In many respects, they were an outgrowth of the old corporate system rather than a complete break from it. The right to form a national guard was a "burgher right," not a universal and inalienable right for all inhabitants of the empire. As such, membership was fraught with symbolism. In the words of one historian of 1848, the national guard was a "symbol of free citizenry—of the political emancipation of the third [i.e., burgher] estate."[95] Consequently, Jewish membership in the national guard was viewed by some as a step toward emancipation and, not surprisingly, served as a frequent flash point in Christian-Jewish relations during the first months of the revolution.

When national guards came into being in Moravia and elsewhere in March 1848, they served as a litmus test for Christian-Jewish coexistence. According to the Statutes for the Organization of the National Guard (§2), any town with a population larger than 1,000 was entitled to form a national guard of its own.[96] In Moravia, where most of the fifty-two Jewish communities were situated in medium-size towns, the question of Jewish membership was a recurring theme in the spring and fall of 1848. Some Christian guards welcomed the Jews into their ranks, whereas others followed the inimical patterns set in Pressburg and Prague. In the April riots in Pressburg, the burghers demanded the complete exclusion of Jews from the national guard. In Prague, where anti-Jewish riots had erupted already in 1845, the Jews were advised to form their own separate national guard in 1848 to keep Christian-Jewish tensions at bay.[97]

Samson Raphael Hirsch looked positively on Jewish participation in common national guards, but he viewed the formation of separate Jewish national guards as reckless provocation. "If you are asked," he wrote on May 2, 1848, "be willing and ready for national guard service, but only under one condition—that you join the guard with the other inhabitants of your town. You are neither capable of establishing a separate national guard for yourselves, nor is it advisable. . . . In these agitated times it is hazardous."[98] Hirsch's exhortation was consistent with his general emancipation ideology that Jews and Christians must fight side by side for universal rights. Separate national guards were tantamount to separate struggles for emancipation.

In Aussee, Boskowitz, Misslitz, and Jamnitz the Jews were welcomed into the local national guards with no distinction between Jew and Christian. E. Ehrenhaft, a Jewish member of the Aussee national guard, praised the humanity of the Christian burghers, who even elected two Jews as corporals. In a letter to an Olmütz daily, he quoted the Christian commandant E. Zipfl, who viewed the Aussee national guard as the embodiment of brotherly love. "In my heart," said Zipfl, "all subjects, all people—without regard to faith or religion—[are] dear and worthy. . . . All of you are my brothers. . . . The unmerited hatred, which has weighed us down like a nightmare for centuries, has dissolved here in fraternal unification and Christian love of fellow man."[99] Similar sentiments were expressed by a Jewish correspondent from Boskowitz, where a Jew served as drill sergeant of the local national guard.[100] "We Jews," he wrote, "live here in peace and harmony with our Christian brethren, who even accepted us most amicably into the honorable ranks of the local national guard."[101] In Aussee, Boskowitz, Misslitz, and Jamnitz, where Jews and Christians lived in relative harmony, the national guard fortified these fraternal bonds. In other towns, where Christian-Jewish tension was legion, the national guard brought the conflict into sharper relief.

In Ungarisch-Brod, Eibenschitz, Mährisch-Kromau, Kremsier, Trebitsch, Gross-Meseritsch, and Prossnitz, the Christian burghers excluded Jews from their local national guards, often before any Jews requested to join their ranks.[102] Not surprisingly, burghers from four of these towns had also sent anti-Jewish petitions to the Moravian Diet. The burghers from Gross-Meseritsch, for example, protested Jewish emancipation, labeling the Jews disloyal "strangers in the land." In Gross-Meseritsch, more than 100 Jews joined the "fully uniformed Israelite National Guard" after the Christian guard refused to admit them. E. Berger, a Gross-Meseritsch Jew, lamented the situation, expressing his wish that the "Christian guard come to us with brotherly love—for unity gives strength, and the national guard requires strength if it wants to fulfill its lofty goals in times of danger." Berger understood the Jews and the Christian burghers to be threatened by the very same masses—a fact that became clear when the Gross-Meseritsch mayor was attacked by the mob during the monstrance affair in late April. However, although a common threat required common defense, it did not mandate equal membership in a burgher institution.

In Ungarisch-Brod and Prossnitz the Christian burghers expected military assistance from the Jews, but they did not want this to assume the trappings of emancipation. When Ungarisch-Brod was threatened by plunderers in early May, the Christian national guard ensured that the Jews were supplied with arms.[103] Likewise, the burghers of Prossnitz had insisted in early April that the Jews set up a night guard to patrol the town walls.[104] In neither case were the Jews accepted into the ranks of the national guard; nor were they outfitted with the standard cap and sword of the newly established burgher institution. Consequently, when the Jewish national guards in Ungarisch-Brod and Prossnitz adopted the same accoutrements, Hirsch's exhortation became a self-fulfilling prophecy. Christian burghers and masses alike viewed the Jewish national guards as a provocation, often harassing their members and knocking off their caps. In July 1848, a delegation of Ungarisch-Brod Jews headed by Moritz Jellinek went to Vienna to complain about the "brutality and wrath of the masses." "Since Christian intolerance did not include us in their ranks," the delegation's letter stated, "we formed a separate company with approval from the commander-in-chief and outfitted ourselves with weapons and uniforms at our own cost. But, for several days, the attitude toward us has become more infuriating; they insulted many members of our community because they were wearing the national guard insignia. We implored the officials in vain; they afforded us no protection." The Jews of Ungarisch-Brod appealed to Vienna, because they viewed the conflict over the national guard as the first skirmish in a prolonged battle for emancipation. "If we give up one right today," they feared, "we will be robbed of others tomorrow."[105]

Only in Prossnitz, where Jew hatred had been described as proverbial, did the conflict over the Jewish national guard escalate into full-fledged violence.[106] In April 1848, Michael Scheef, a Prossnitz Jew who had spent March in the Viennese Academic Legion, attempted to join the newly formed Prossnitz national guard.[107] Scheef believed he could impose the inclusiveness of the Viennese National Guard and Academic Legion on his Moravian hometown, but his attempt met immediate and impassioned resistance. The Prossnitz national guard vehemently rejected his application, enumerating six reasons why Jewish participation was "inadmissible," among them the separate jurisdiction of the

Jewish town, the general lack of interest from other Prossnitz Jews, and the already sufficiently large Christian membership. It also justified the exclusion on legal grounds, noting that the Jews did not have the coveted "burgher right." The strongest argument, however, was rooted in the social tensions between Prossnitz Jews and Christians. Citing the great damage inflicted on the local population through the "meddling of the Jews in the Christian trades," the national guard commandants issued an oblique threat. "In light of the current disposition of the local inhabitants against the Jews, as a result of their enlistment [in the Christian national guard], it is not advisable to promote it officially, because the [national guard] . . . will not be able to quell an eventual uprising against the Jews."[108] The Olmütz district office, acknowledging the risk of unrest, prepared the way for a separate Jewish national guard in Prossnitz.

Because the Prossnitz Jewish community counted over 1,000 inhabitants and was under separate jurisdiction from the Christian town, the Olmütz district office decided in July 1848 that the Jews were not only permitted but also required to form their own national guard. In a gesture of misplaced optimism, the district office even approved the amalgamation of the Jewish and Christian national guards—"should the Prossnitz burghers so desire."[109] After 200 Prossnitz Jews organized their own national guard under the leadership of Leopold Hamburger, the tensions between Jews and Christians began to rise. On the night of August 28, the Jewish national guard fought back a "mass of plebeians" who stormed the Jewish town. Throughout August and September "street urchins" repeatedly assaulted Jews wearing the national guard insignia, often at the instigation of Christian national guard members. In early September, the Prossnitz magistracy warned the head of the Jewish national guard that "if Jews are seen with the insignia of the national guard, it will lead to a bloodbath."[110] After the Prossnitz burgher Karl Wagner attacked the insignia-wearing Joseph Pollak on September 26, the Prossnitz Administrative Office (Oberamt) announced its intentions to investigate Wagner to "set an example for others . . . so that this fanatical rage, which has gotten out of hand in the towns in recent times, can be suppressed before it comes to regrettable incidents." These incidents coincided with an attack on the factory of a Prossnitz

Jew, Bernard Beck, and the indefatigable efforts by Prossnitz's deputy Joseph Demel to gather signatures for his petition against Jewish emancipation.[111] By the end of September, a fleeting spark was enough to ignite the Prossnitz powder keg.

On September 28, 1848, the spark arrived when forty or so Jewish soldiers came from Olmütz to celebrate Shabbat Shuvah, the Sabbath between Rosh Hashanah and Yom Kippur, with the Prossnitz Jewish community. On the morning of September 30, several Jewish national guardists were attacked; in a separate incident, a fight broke out between a handful of Jewish soldiers, a Christian shoemaker, and a number of Christian day laborers. As the soldiers retreated into the Jewish town, the "plebeian masses" prepared to storm in after them.[112] Members of the Jewish national guard began to assemble, but the magistracy entreated them not to fight and sent the Jewish soldiers back to Olmütz. Nonetheless, the "plebeian masses" stormed the Jewish town, and the Christian national guard arrived to "restore order," meaning to remove the irritant—that is, disarm the Jewish national guard. When the Christian national guard officers demanded disarmament "to appease the masses," the commandant of the Jewish national guard, Leopold Hamburger, duly obliged. Nonetheless, the masses, dissatisfied with the meager quantity of weapons, continued their rampage for another few hours until the Christian national guard finally quelled the riot. Order was restored, but in the words of one observer, "Burning hatred between Jews and Christians [was still] smoldering under the ashes."[113]

While the ashes were still cooling, the Prossnitz magistracy instated an 8 p.m. curfew and began investigating the anti-Jewish incident, seeking to identify the perpetrators as well as the basic causes of the unrest. The leaders of the Christian and Jewish national guards agreed that the national guard insignia was the immediate cause of violence. At the behest of the Christian national guard, Leopold Hamburger ordered Jewish guardists not to enter the Christian town with the national guard insignia "so that the immediate cause for future unrest is eliminated." Although the insignia served as the catalyst of violence, members of both national guards understood that the tensions ran much deeper. Hamburger viewed the conflict in terms of the "jealousy between the Christian and the Jewish guard," which had been exacerbated by attempts to bring about reconciliation "in a political manner." Two Prossnitz burghers, Fortunat Hofmann and Johan Barak, blamed the unrest on the "impudent" behavior of the Jews in the national guard but identified the Jews' economic activity as a contributing factor. They both cited the "Jews' encroachment on trade."[114]

For Hofmann, Barak, and other Prossnitz burghers, the "encroachment on trade" and the establishment of a Jewish national guard were intimately linked. In both cases, the Jews had succeeded in arrogating to themselves the privileges of the burgher estate without actually becoming part of it. As both the Prossnitz tanners and the administrative council of the Christian national guard had pointed out, the Jews of Prossnitz did not possess the "burgher right," but they acted as though they did. Karl Wagner, a Prossnitz burgher and national guardist, drew attention to this perceived infraction in his testimony before the magistracy. Wagner, a gingerbread maker (*Lebzelter*) and Christian national guardist, had attacked the Jewish national guardist Joseph Pollak on September 24 and was one of the instigators of the unrest on September 30. In justifying his violence to the magistracy, he explained:

> In my opinion, [membership in] the national guard is based on intelligence and property, and it follows that only cultured [*gebildete*] and well-to-do men with untarnished reputations should be appointed to this institution. At present, in the Jewish town, a national guard has been formed, and Jews who live from detestable peddling have joined it. It is general knowledge that the Jews go to the villages to hawk their goods, wearing the insignia of the [national] guard; when they arrive in the village, they put on different clothes and change their dress as their interests demand. As a result, antipathy toward the Jewish national guard has come about in Prossnitz.[115]

Wagner's antagonism toward the Prossnitz Jews was twofold. Not only had the Jews joined an institution of the burgher estate, but they were also allegedly using its privileges for their own economic gain. Wagner's testimony reflected the fears articulated in the manifold petitions against Jewish emancipation. Jewish emancipation, it was argued, would result in "enslavement to the Jews." According to the Prossnitz deputy Joseph Demel, the Jews had already become the richest segment of society despite the existence of the Jew tax and other special Jewish taxes and restrictions. Under such circumstances, he argued, weren't the Jews the oppressors and the Christians the oppressed?[116] Demel's view resonated among Prossnitz's Christian population, which vehemently opposed the emancipation of the Jews. The liberal newspaper from neighboring Olmütz lamented the fact that "people in our neighboring town [Prossnitz] want to extinguish the sunshine of constitutional freedom and fraternization."[117] The conflict over the Prossnitz national guard was an attempt to keep the barriers between Jew and Christian intact, to demarcate the legal as well as social boundaries between the emancipated burgher and the unemancipated Jew.

As the struggle for emancipation dragged on throughout 1848, some Moravian Jews began to fear that they would be left in the shadows as their Christian neighbors basked in the sunshine of freedom. The many pro-emancipation voices notwithstanding, there were 2,593 signatures on the anti-emancipation petitions from Moravia alone. Even though the Aussee national guard exhibited "Christian love" by welcoming Jews into its ranks, the Prossnitz national guard would not even consent to the existence of a separate Jewish national guard—lest it be seen as a prelude to emancipation. Furthermore, the storming of the Prossnitz Jewish town on September 30—more than five months after the "lynching" in Olmütz and the monstrance affair in Gross-Meseritsch—served as an ominous reminder that popular sentiment against Jewish emancipation had not subsided. According to one rumor circulating in Kremsier in February 1849, the Jews themselves did not want full emancipation "since they fear the consequences."[118] The fact that this rumor could be found credible sheds light on the uncertainty of Jewish emancipation just as the Reichstag was preparing to deliberate on this topic.

This uncertainty found poetic expression in the pages of *Der Orient*. In a lament titled "The Emancipation of Moravian Jews," Salomon Wolf of Prerau gave voice to the despondency that had taken root in his fellow Moravian Jews by the fall of 1848.[119] His six-stanza poem went as follows:

O, how sadly veiled
Lies the golden shimmer of hope!
O, how sad is the rejoicing
On Israel's mossy ruins!

And over the districts of Austria
Does Moravia want to behold
A mild springtime sky?
Life: a room for weaving and creating
But not for Jews!

Even the terrible demons
Of the ghastly Orcus
Bewail and bemoan the children of Jehovah.
More heavenly is hell than dwelling with Israel
Such is the prophecy of doom, no lark's happy song.

So, should a burgher fight for Israel,
He also brings freedom to Pawlo and Janko.
And if the former allowed freedom to shine
The latter would reply: "not for Jews."

So, only hope can inspire you, Israel
For Israel there is nothing but "hope."
And should all the worlds fall apart
Should the whole universe shout "republic"
The Old Father, who chose Israel,
Is ensured "eternal loyalty" from his people.

To bear her wounds with patience
And march to your end with a smile
Israel, it is no alchemy!
The Good Master's chains
Make you slaves of the highest spirit.
Israel, this is noble slavery!

With the emancipation of the peasants in September 1848 (shortly before Wolf's poem was published), the struggle for Jewish emancipation had effectively been severed from the struggle for universal human rights. As Wolf lamented, even if enlightened burghers viewed the "fight for Israel" as part and parcel of the universal struggle, "Pawlo and Janko" had failed to understand that the two struggles were intimately intertwined. As a result, while part of the population could exult in the Pillersdorf constitution (which deferred the question of Jewish emancipation to the Reichstag) or the emancipation of the peasants, the Jews remained excluded. As Wolf put it, "O, how sad is the

rejoicing / On Israel's mossy ruins." Even if a republic were to be established, Israel seemed destined to remain in bondage, "to bear her
wounds with patience."

Another measure of the despondency articulated by Wolf's poem was
the emergence of an emigration movement in the Habsburg Empire in
May 1848. Called "On, to America!" (*Auf, nach Amerika!*), this movement was promoted on the pages of the *Central-Organ* after the anti-
Jewish violence in the spring of 1848.[120] Leopold Kompert, better known
for his tales of the Bohemian ghettos, published the first appeal for mass
emigration on May 6, introducing it with a verse from Jeremiah (8:20):
"The harvest is past, the summer is ended, and we are not saved!" Because the Jews were still being treated differently from the "sovereign
peoples" of Austria, Kompert admonished his fellow Jews to take their
future in their own hands. "We have received no succor [here in Aus-
tria]," he wrote. "Seek it out in distant America!"[121] The editorial board
of the *Central-Organ* threw its full support behind Kompert's article,
calling on readers to send donations for prospective immigrants.[122] It
also published the names of twenty-seven Jews—thirteen from Hungary,
eight from Bohemia, four from Galicia, and two from Moravia—who
had joined the newly established "emigration society" (*Auswanderungs-
Gesellschaft*) in preparation for their departure to America.[123]

For Moravia, one could argue that such a call for mass emigration
was not particularly novel or noteworthy. Ever since the promulgation
of the Familiants Laws in 1726, emigration had become such a fixture of
the Moravian Jewish landscape that second- and third-born sons were
derisively called emigrants—in recognition of the fact that emigration
was perhaps the only legal remedy to the myriad restrictions they faced
in the land of their birth. In the eighteenth and early nineteenth centuries, many of these Jews moved to Hungary to pursue a livelihood
with greater ease. In the 1840s, as Europe suffered mediocre harvests,
some began to set their sights much farther away.[124] As *Der Orient* reported in 1846, "Many Moravian [Jewish] families want to emigrate to
America."[125]

What distinguished "On, to America!" from these earlier waves of
emigration was its unabashedly political character—at the very moment
when the Jews' loyalty to the state was being questioned. Whereas much

of the earlier emigration could be explained in economic terms, the current emigration to America was rooted in "the fear that the Reichstag will not declare the emancipation of the Jews."[126] In December 1848, a correspondent from *Jewish Intelligence*, the organ of an English missionary society that was active in the region, explained the diverse motives for emigration in the following terms: "I asked [the lay head of the Prague community] if it were true that so many Jews were emigrating from Prague to America, and with what object? He said many were doing so, hoping to better themselves, others because they had no faith in the love and good will of modern free-thinking Christians, others because they expected a stormy future for Europe."[127] Similar considerations may have also been in the minds of Moravian Jews who chose to emigrate in 1848. As Ignaz Briess of Prerau recalled in his memoirs, both an uncle and a great-uncle emigrated to America in 1848, the former becoming mayor of Niagara Falls. In jest, Briess speculated that an "atavistic emigration instinct" must have existed in his family.[128]

One Moravian Jew, however, found little to joke about with regard to "On, to America!" Abraham Schmiedl, the Prossnitz-born rabbi of Hotzenplotz (and brother-in-law of Abraham Neuda), penned an impassioned article—titled "Remain in the Land!"—in which he stridently opposed all politically motivated emigration because of its potentially deleterious effect on the struggle for emancipation.[129] As Schmiedl saw it, the emigration movement played into the hands of the opponents of emancipation, because it seemed to underscore the Jews' tenuous attachment to the land of their birth. Now, with emancipation in reach, the Jews needed to rise to the occasion and fight the final battle for their rightful patrimony. "Remain in the land," wrote Schmiedl, "since for more than half a millennium your people has prayed on this land and endured a more difficult battle than the soldier on the [battle]field. . . . History knows of no greater fame than when an army fights until the last man. . . . We've been decried as cowards for long enough—we want to show that we are heroes."

As can be seen, "national" pride was a driving force behind Schmiedl's opposition to politically motivated emigration in general and "On, to America!" in particular. Schmiedl had no problem with the Jew who opted for emigration out of economic interests. It was the Jew who emigrated solely "because he is a Jew" that riled Schmiedl most. He believed it was incumbent upon Jews to fight—like members of other oppressed nations—for full emancipation. He criticized Jewish leaders such as Hirsch and Mannheimer—though not by name—who actively discouraged Jews from speaking out for their own interests "lest the hatred and fury" of the people be awakened. Instead, Schmiedl believed that Jews should emulate other nations that "have fought and still fight for their oppressed right." He called on his fellow Jews to fight "our war for emancipation," not with "sword and fist" but rather with "the word and the quill." "We will knock and pound on the fortress of freedom until the door finally opens, blow trumpets and horns until the fences crumble and grant us free entrance. And so it will be." Unlike Leopold Kompert and the other supporters of "On, to America!" Abraham Schmiedl did not view continued Jewish suffering as a cause for despair but rather as an added incentive to fight. In his view, "more than half a millennium" of suffering had not only strengthened the Jews' claims for justice but also intensified their drive for freedom. To Schmiedl, this was nowhere more apparent than in "the middle of the Moravian ghetto," from where he wrote his article.

✳

It is no surprise that "Remain in the Land!" was penned by a Moravian Jew. In repudiating the defeatism of "On, to America!" Schmiedl's article evinced a stubborn faith in the redemptive quality of sacrifice, an unwavering belief that Moravian Jewry's past and present suffering would not be in vain. From this perspective, the fact that two of the revolution's most visible "sacrifices on the altar of freedom" (Carl Heinrich Spitzer and Hermann Jellinek) were Moravian Jews seemed self-evident, not only to contemporaries such as Hirsch Fassel and Moritz Jellinek but also to later historians, such as Adolf Frankel-Grün. Indeed, if Moravian Jewry had "experienced the pre-March oppression more than their coreligionists in the other lands," it seemed only logical that the "martyrs" of the revolution would come from its midst.

Nonetheless, Moravian Jewry as a whole fared quite well during the Revolution of 1848, experiencing little of the anti-Jewish violence that swept neighboring Hungary and Bohemia at the time. This can be explained, in part, by the relative tranquility reigning in Moravia during the Revolution of 1848, but the regional and *supra*national nature of Moravian identity also played an important role. Indeed, it was not just the inordinate suffering of Moravian Jewry before the revolution that made Schmiedl highlight his Moravian origins; even more so, it was his deep identification with a province in which he and his coreligionists harbored hopes of becoming—in Hirsch's term—"Jewish Moravians."

Seven

Emancipation and Its Aftershocks
The Reorganization of Moravian Jewry

"The Jews should be denied everything as a nation, but granted everything as individuals."[1] Speaking before the French National Assembly in 1789, Count Stanislas de Clermont-Tonnere famously articulated the essential tension between collective and individual rights that would characterize all subsequent debates on Jewish emancipation. This offer of emancipation was not one-sided but required something from the Jews in return: the abnegation of any "national" characteristics and the dissolution of all institutions—particularly the autonomous Jewish community—that perpetuated or reinforced a separate corporate existence. "The existence of a nation within a nation is unacceptable to our country," de Clermont-Tonnere declared. "Every Jew must individually become a citizen. If they do not want this, they must inform us and we shall then be compelled to expel them."[2]

Like the Jews of France in 1789, the Jews of the Habsburg monarchy formed a separate corporation at the outbreak of the Revolution of 1848. The hallmark of this corporate status was the autonomous Jewish community, which not only encompassed religious, educational, and charitable institutions but also constituted a self-governing political body with the authority to impose taxes and even regulate the behavior of its members. In Moravia, the Jewish community was a kind of town within a town, usually nestled within the larger Christian town or situated alongside it. Its inhabitants were subject to different sets of laws and fell under different jurisdictions. In the eyes of many, the Jews' separate existence merely reinforced their "national seclusion vis-à-vis all other citizens of the state."[3]

The fate of Moravia's autonomous Jewish communities assumed

paramount importance following the promulgation of the constitution in March 1849. The planned dissolution of these communities, which proponents of emancipation viewed as an absolute necessity, brought new challenges to Christian-Jewish relations and placed new strains on the institutions of Jewish communal life. Although the amalgamation of Jewish and Christian communities conjured up images of ecumenical harmony, large segments of the Christian population continued to view the existence of separate Jewish communities—and the corresponding residential and occupational restrictions—as an indispensable bulwark against "Jewish domination" in the economic and social spheres. These sentiments gathered wider currency as individual Jews began "harvesting the fruits of emancipation too soon." On another level, the imminent dissolution of the Jewish communities threatened to wreak havoc on Moravia's Jewish schools, synagogues, and charitable organizations. In light of this looming institutional crisis, Samson Raphael Hirsch tried to reorganize Moravia's Jewish affairs lest the "sacred and holy . . . be buried in the sunlight of freedom."[4]

Cautious Exuberance in the Constitutional Age

In many Moravian towns and villages, celebrations of the new constitution assumed an ecumenical character, bringing Jews and Christians together in parades, ceremonies, and merrymaking. The constitution was read aloud, the national hymn was sung, national guardsmen fired celebratory salvos, and festive prayer services were held in churches and synagogues. Jews and Christians joined together not only in the outdoor festivities but also, more notably, in their respective houses of worship. The festivities in Boskowitz, for example, were conducted "*jointly* by the Christian and Jewish populations, and, indeed, in the church . . . and the synagogue."[5] The festive character of these prayer services, together with the generally secular nature of the celebrations, made the church and synagogue more welcoming to adherents of other faiths.

The attendance of Christian dignitaries in Moravia's synagogues presented a rare opportunity to showcase the oratory skills of the rabbis, the musical talent of the choirs, the decorum of the children, and above all, the firm patriotism of Moravian Jewry. Because the celebrations were held on weekdays, the Jews could embellish the performances with instrumental accompaniment, which was strictly forbidden on the Sabbath. The festive prayer service in the Leipnik synagogue contained all these elements, as described by the *Brünner Tags-Courier*.

> In the presence of Christian dignitaries, the festivities in Leipnik (March 17) were celebrated by the Israelite community in the resplendently illuminated synagogue in the following manner: The school-children led the procession into the temple, where the "Hallelujah Psalm 150" was sung to choral accompaniment, the newly composed prayer for the emperor was recited before a raised Torah scroll, and, after the rabbi [Salomon Quetsch] gave a suitable speech, the *Volkslied* [imperial anthem] was sung by all present with *vivat* [and] to musical accompaniment.[6]

With the exception of the raised Torah scroll, nothing in this prayer service would have been unfamiliar to the Christian visitors. Instead, the recitation of the prayer for the emperor, the performance of Psalm 150, and the singing of the *Volkslied* all served to emphasize a common heritage and fate shared by equal citizens of the constitutional Habsburg monarchy. In Holleschau, the Jewish community symbolically expressed this common bond by distributing alms to the local poor "without differentiation by religion."[7]

Although Jews and Christians celebrated the constitution together, it was generally recognized—by Jew and non-Jew alike—that the Jews had much more to celebrate. The official *Brünner Zeitung* highlighted the effusive jubilation among the Jews of the monarchy. "It is natural that the Israelites *in particular* are reveling in this great act of justice and humanity, that they are celebrating it heartily," read an article from March 17, 1849. "Through the unequivocal word of the monarch, they have been turned from brutish [*vertierten*] taxpayers into human beings, from slaves into free citizens of the state."[8] Indeed, because the peasants had already been emancipated in September 1848, it was the legal status of the Jews that was most thoroughly transformed by the March 1849 constitution.

Even Hirsch, who had refused to head a special Jewish delegation to the emperor four months earlier, now deemed it appropriate to convey thanks on behalf of the "Jewish Moravians." On March 28, he headed a

Jewish delegation to Olmütz and delivered an address to Franz Joseph in person.[9] If all "sons of the fatherland" welcome the constitution, how much more so, reasoned Hirsch, do the "Jewish sons of the fatherland." Although both Jews and Christians had attained equal rights, the Jews in particular had reached a special milestone: the end of their "centuries-long suffering."

> With the most fervent thanks, this imperial word was welcomed by all
> sons of the fatherland as a holy foundation for your felicitous future,
> built on justice and wisdom. With what joyful emotion, then, must the
> Jewish sons of the fatherland behold this herald of salvation. For them,
> this word was a guaranty of the ultimate fulfillment of their hopes,
> of the ultimate atonement for their lachrymose past, of the ultimate
> end of their centuries-long suffering. For them, this word was a guar-
> anty that the ruler and fatherland finally recognize them as equal sons,
> and that [these Jewish sons], as equal brothers among brothers, will let
> their strengths develop toward the common weal of the fatherland.[10]

Through a semantic shift from "Moravian Jews" to "Jewish Moravians," Hirsch emphasized an essential change in the Jews' relationship to the state. Once viewed as sojourners, the Jewish Moravians had acquired a homeland with the proclamation of the constitution. Nonetheless, the semantic shift was not used by the proclaimer of this constitution himself. In his brief reply to Hirsch's address, Franz Joseph continued to refer to the Jews of Moravia as "Moravian Israelites."[11]

The good tidings of the constitution were tempered by initial re-ports—later proved false—of anti-Jewish violence in several Moravian towns. One newspaper reportedly welcomed the alleged violence,[12] but others blamed the rumors on "malicious and besotted" rabble-rousers.[13] Although the rumors were false, they articulated a growing fear that Jewish emancipation would be met with popular violence. Had not the burghers of Iglau warned the Reichstag that they would be unable to stop "the blood of Jews from flowing here in streams after the procla-mation of [Jewish] emancipation"? Had not the burghers of Sternberg warned that "entire provinces" would brandish weapons against their Jews, calling for their expulsion, and even extermination?

The fear of popular anti-Jewish violence also pervaded Hirsch's first postemancipation circular to the Jews of Moravia. "The non-Jewish population," he wrote on March 16, 1849, "is filled with fear—albeit a groundless fear—of the overzealous ambitions of the Jews; and our enemies will do their utmost to exploit this fear, and, when possible, call for excesses [against the Jews]."[14] These "overzealous ambitions" had been carefully detailed in Hubert Müller's anti-Jewish broadside and then rehashed in the anti-Jewish petitions. Hirsch admonished the Jews of Moravia to avoid antagonizing their Christian neighbors. "More than ever," he declared, the Jews had to exercise self-restraint and behave prudently.

Hirsch Fassel delivered a similar admonishment during the March 17, 1849, celebration in the Prossnitz synagogue. In a sermon titled "The Constitution and Solomon's Temple," Fassel adjured the Jews of Moravia not to claim their new rights prematurely.[15] Solomon's Temple, Fassel explained, had been dedicated eleven months after its completion so that all the inner furnishings could be assembled before the Temple was "opened for the service of the Lord." Likewise, Fassel stressed, although the "house of the constitution" had been recently completed, the "inner furnishings" had to be constructed before it could be inhabited. These inner furnishings were the "organic laws" that would regulate schools, religious affairs, towns, and taxation—all of which had important bearing on the Jews. Fassel echoed Hirsch's call for calm and prudence, calling on the Jews to avoid "provocations, defiant and arrogant words" and to be "judicious and mindful" in their acts. Above all, Fassel called for patience. "We were not able to use our human rights for so many centuries," he observed, "so let us refrain from using them for a little while longer." He insisted it would be foolhardy to "interfere prematurely in the clockwork of legislation."

Fassel's remarks underscored one of the ambiguities of the constitution: Although the Jews had been legally emancipated, the details of their integration into general society had yet to be worked out. True, Paragraph 1 of the Fundamental Laws clearly declared "civil and political rights independent of religious creed"; however, three subsequent paragraphs complicated matters. Paragraph 13 stipulated that separate "organic laws"—which would translate constitutional principles into practice—be legislated by the Reichstag. More significantly, Paragraphs 120 and 121 declared that old laws and ordinances would remain in effect until the new laws were approved. This ambiguous state of affairs led one contemporary to question whether the Jews of the Habsburg monarchy were indeed emancipated. "According to the provisions of emancipation articulated by the Constitution," he asked in April 1849, "are the Jews emancipated *at this moment?*"[16] He also noted that the Reichstag's authority to amend the constitution could jeopardize certain principles, such as equal rights for members of all religious confessions. In October 1849, Moritz Jellinek echoed these sentiments, deeming Jewish emancipation "precarious and uncertain."[17]

Despite the ambiguities, Jellinek's skepticism was not universally shared, and Hirsch and Fassel's exhortations met many a deaf ear. Many Moravian Jews believed they had experienced enough oppression before the revolution to justify the immediate exercise of new freedoms. In the words of one Moravian Jew, "When the doors of the prison are opened, must one remain inside?" Jellinek considered such individuals "too surprised, too overawed and too lazy" to read the constitution with open eyes. They looked at Paragraph 1 of the Fundamental Laws "not as it is, but rather as it should have been."[18] In other words, many Jews assumed that the constitution had immediately lifted all restrictions distinguishing Jews from their Christian neighbors.

The optimism shared by many Jews was met with consternation by government officials. Because of the uncertain timeline for implementing the constitution, mild confusion reigned in several Moravian district offices. The Prerau district office, for example, asked Governor Lažansky on April 20, 1849, to clarify the "future status of members of the Israelite confession as citizens of the state."[19] The district office was of the opinion that, in accordance with Paragraphs 120 and 121 of the constitution, all existing restrictions—including the familiant numbers, special marriage licenses, and tolerance permits—should remain in effect until the appropriate provisional laws appeared. At the same time, however, it was aware of doubts being raised by many officials and "especially by the Jewish communities." For example, when the Jews of Weisskirchen were asked to announce candidacy for the available familiant numbers, "not a single candidate registered, because the [Jewish] community is of the view that the distribution of familiant numbers has been eliminated by the Fundamental Laws."

Some Moravian district offices, however, held a different opinion. As a result, Jewish marriages were subject to the whims of local government officials for nearly half a year after the proclamation of the constitution. Although one Jew from Prerau recalled in his memoirs that all single Jews were permitted to marry after March 4, 1849, the evidence of the Moravian-Silesian Gubernium attests otherwise.[20] Attitudes of local officials varied from district to district, with the Brünn officials assuming a rather lenient position and the Prerau and Hradisch officials a rather inflexible one. The first legal wedding of a nonfamiliant was performed in Lundenburg in March 1849 after the Brünn district office instructed local officials to treat Jewish weddings like Christian ones.[21] In contrast, the Hradisch district office informed marriage candidates in Ungarisch-Brod, Gaya, Bisenz, Strassnitz, Holleschau, and elsewhere that Jews were still required to obtain a familiant number before getting married.

Governor Lažansky overruled the decisions of the Hradisch district office, thereby highlighting a discrepancy between the official policy of the Gubernium and the arbitrary behavior of the district and local offices. A contemporary Jewish observer, aware of this discrepancy, noted a tendency among Moravian Jews to circumvent the local officials by appealing directly to the Gubernium. "Many couples who are no longer willing to wait for the death of an old familiant," he wrote, "have brought their marriage requests to the higher authorities, because they were sent away from the lower authorities."[22] The attitudes of the local officials, however, may have been motivated by ignorance rather than malice. As a report from May 1849 noted, a Jew still had to obtain a familiant number "by the sweat of his brow" and "with all the money in his pocket," because the district offices had been given no other instructions.[23]

In the summer of 1849 Hirsch Fassel and Moritz Jellinek sought to bring clarity to this question once and for all. On May 3 Fassel asked the Gubernium to distribute instructions regarding Jewish marriages to all the district offices in Moravia.[24] In June, the Gubernium informed some district offices that special approval was no longer necessary for Jews to marry. It is "self-evident," wrote the Gubernium, "that all restrictions that previously obtained regarding Jewish marriages no longer apply."[25] Nevertheless, the Hradisch district office still insisted in

August that Jewish marriages involving nonfamiliants remained illegal according to Paragraph 121 of the constitution.[26] Only after the personal intervention of Moritz Jellinek from Ungarisch-Brod (in the Hradisch district) did Lažansky instruct the Hradisch district office that familiant numbers were no longer necessary.

The officially recognized repeal of the Familiants Laws precipitated a wave of "constitutional weddings," which legalized many of the secretive "attic weddings" in the prerevolutionary period. "The Jews marry in masses," wrote one contemporary, noting that these marriages were actually "remarriages" between "so-called emigrants" who had married without official permission or recognition. Official statistics testify to this wave of Jewish nuptials. There were 600 Jewish weddings in 1849, compared with 150 in 1848 and an average of 189 per year over the previous two decades.[27] The "constitutional weddings" performed a highly symbolic function, not only eradicating "family errors" but also marking the entry of Moravian Jews into civil society. As such, these weddings often became occasions for communal—rather than merely familial—jubilation. For example, when a fourth-born Prossnitz Jew married in August 1849, the entire Prossnitz Jewish community attended his wedding.[28] Six months earlier the legal marriage of a fourth-born son would have been a near impossibility, but in August it symbolized the new possibilities of the constitutional era. The Jews of Prossnitz viewed the wedding as an opportunity to express their gratitude toward Franz Joseph. During the ceremony, they sang his praises along with the imperial hymn.

In some Jewish communities, the euphoria over constitutional weddings was tempered by complaints against individual rabbis who were allegedly profiting unfairly from the increased demand for their services. In Moravia, local rabbis charged fees for two documents required for marriage license applications: birth certificates and religion certificates (based on a test from Herz Homberg's catechism, *Bne Zion*). Dr. Moritz Duschak, the Aussee local rabbi, complained that rabbis unauthorized to issue such documents were exploiting the "anarchy of the times" for their own financial gain.[29] Duschak accused Leopold Singer, the Aussee substitute rabbi (who had "no authorization from the chief rabbi") of testing twenty-nine prospective brides and grooms in a five-day period. Singer's income from these twenty-nine individuals presumably represented a financial loss for Duschak. Moritz Jellinek alleged that certain rabbis, including Ungarisch-Brod rabbi Moshe Nascher, were issuing marriage-related documents at inflated prices. Nascher, he maintained, was charging 10 fl. instead of the usual 6 fl. 20 kr. for birth and religion certificates. Although excoriating Nascher, Jellinek cited other rabbis whose exemplary behavior deserved special mention.[30]

The rush to get married (or remarried) brought some intra-Jewish tensions into sharper relief, but it did not have a noticeable effect on Jewish-Christian relations in Moravia. The perceived Jewish "rush" to acquire real estate, in contrast, threatened to expose the ephemerality of the Jewish-Christian harmony exhibited at the joint celebrations of the constitution in mid-March. As Jellinek quipped in the early autumn of 1849, "As long as the Jews lay claim to those rights that do not injure their Christian brother *materially*, e.g. marriage, [the Christian brother] will offer no resistance and place no obstacles in the way." However, as soon as the Jews lay claim to property rights, local government officials offered the "most prodigious" resistance.[31] Events in the Prerau district serve as a case in point. In April 1849, after several Jews had begun negotiations for the purchase of Christian houses and applied for permission to trade in Christian towns, the Prerau district office sought to undermine, or at least delay, these efforts. In its letter to the Gubernium, the Prerau district office invoked the specter of anti-Jewish violence to support its position. "These overly hasty steps by the Israelites," it wrote, "create tension in the Christian communities that could easily lead to unrest."[32] It did not take long for this warning to turn into a self-fulfilling prophecy. When a Jew moved into Leipnik's Christian town (in the district of Prerau) a few months later, Christian burghers smeared his house with their own excrement.[33]

The scatological vandalism was an isolated incident in the summer of 1849, but it expressed a recurrent belief that Jewish "acquisitiveness" had to be restrained and the terms of Jewish emancipation reevaluated. In an article from the end of May, *Morawské Noviny*, a Czech daily published in Brünn, reported growing dissatisfaction with Jewish emancipation. "People are angry with the Jews," it declared, "and not without reason." The article went on to accuse Jews of encroaching on "Christian livelihoods" by buying up burgher houses and speculating on local crops.[34] The most strident opposition to Jewish emancipation came from the Nikolsburg Administrative Office (Oberamt), which hoped the old legal and occupational restrictions would be reinstated. In a letter to the Gubernium from August 1849, the Nikolsburg Administrative Office insisted that

> the equality of rights recently granted to [the Jews] makes them, with few exceptions, exceedingly impudent, and the inhabitants of the [Christian] community greatly regret that the Jews were made equal with other members of the state. The consequences will probably teach [us] that the Jew is hazardous not only to the citizen but also to the state. It is therefore desirable that his rights be curtailed.[35]

In this effort to restrict the Jews' newly granted rights, the Nikolsburg Administrative Office understood Jewish emancipation to be, in the words of Jellinek, "precarious and uncertain." It hoped to modify the terms of emancipation before these rights became irrevocable. In particular, it sought to curtail the property and occupation rights, which threatened to infringe on the material interests of the Christian population. Recycling a motif common in the anti-Jewish petitions, the Nikolsburg Administrative Office warned that the Jews would use their new rights to "oppress the other nations." The Jews were depicted as a deviously acquisitive nation whose "inborn propensity for usury and deceit of all sorts" necessitated restrictive laws to protect the otherwise defenseless Christian tradesman and peasant. However, contrary to the express wishes of both the Nikolsburg Administrative Office and the Prerau district office, the Gubernium unambiguously declared its position in April 1849: "All restrictions [on the Jews] must be recognized as fully abolished."[36]

The Provisional Township Law and Moravia's Jewish Communities

The conflict between the will of the imperial government and the desires of the local Christian population came into sharpest relief after the promulgation on March 17, 1849, of the Provisional Township Law.[37] As the first of the "organic laws" intended to flesh out the details of the new constitution, the Provisional Township Law required Moravia's interlocking Jewish and Christian communities to amalgamate into single townships. With this law, Minister Franz Stadion sought to restructure the political administration of the monarchy from the bottom up, assigning a foundational role to the autonomous local township. Stadion envisioned a centralized administrative pyramid in which the local township would constitute the basic political unit, serving as "the bedrock of the free state."[38] The new local township would replace the mess of interlocking towns, thereby unifying the separate institutions, officials, and systems of taxation into a single administrative body. However, not every town was granted the status of an autonomous local township (*Ortsgemeinde*). Paragraph 1 of the new law defined a local township as a community that (1) kept a separate cadastre and (2) had not been amalgamated with other similar towns. Paragraph 2 required certain geographically contiguous communities to amalgamate into a single local township. It stipulated that a town and its suburbs (*Vorstädte*) would henceforth constitute a single local township. For example, the Ungarisch-Brod *Vorstadt* and the Ungarisch-Brod *Christenstadt* would be amalgamated into a single local township called Ungarisch-Brod. What, however, would happen to the Ungarisch-Brod *Judenstadt* according to the new law?

The Provisional Township Law, like the constitution (which was also drafted by Stadion), made no specific mention of Jews or Jewish townships. This was consistent with an ideology that replaced corporate rights with individual rights, treating Jews as equal individuals in the emerging civil state. Just as Stadion viewed individuals as building blocks of the new state, he viewed local townships as the building blocks of the new political system.[39] Although his Provisional Township Law failed to mention Jews, it seemed a logical assumption that Jewish townships would be absorbed by neighboring Christian townships, just as Jewish individuals would be absorbed by the larger civil society. Indeed, Paragraphs 1 and 2 seemed to require the amalgamation of Jewish and Christian towns, because in most cases they shared common cadastres and common names. However, a Moravian correspondent to *Der Orient* pointed out that these same paragraphs could be used to reach the opposite conclusion. Because Jewish townships were not mentioned in the Provisional Township Law, couldn't a case be made for their complete exclusion from the autonomous local townships that were coming into being?[40]

A number of deputies to the Moravian Diet had foreseen this problem when they debated a proposed Moravian Township Law in December 1848. Like the Provisional Township Law of March 1849, a draft of the Moravian Township Law declared that in towns where "two or more townships previously existed in one locale, they should [henceforth] constitute a single township."[41] Deputy Ferdinand Heidler feared that this paragraph would create confusion because it failed to mention Jewish townships per se. He proposed an additional clause ("The same applies to Jewish townships as well") to avoid future misunderstandings. Heidler's effort to include the Jews in the new legislation, however, did not stem from a humanistic impulse. He was concerned that Jews would use the ambiguity of the Township Law to exclude themselves from the autonomous local townships in general and from the incumbent communal taxes in particular. In fact, the debate in the Moravian Diet was framed in largely economic terms. Joseph Quasnitschka, a rural deputy from Wzdaunky, underscored that amalgamation of Jewish and Christian townships would be difficult because Jewish townships "rarely possess communal capital."[42] Similarly, Mathias Blaha, a rural deputy from Teltsch, vociferously objected to amalgamation because of the notorious poverty of Jewish townships. "Christian townships possess real estate; Jewish townships merely familiant numbers," he quipped.[43]

Although some deputies viewed amalgamation in primarily economic terms, others emphasized the moral and social benefits of bringing Jews and Christians together in one body politic. Ferdinand Koller, the mayor of Uncova and a deputy for the large landowners, understood the Jews' depraved and downtrodden state as a function of their social isolation. He believed that interaction with the more cultivated Christians would help rectify this unfortunate situation. "It is highly desirable," he declared, "that the Jewish township be amalgamated with the Christian township. . . . The plight of the Jews will improve markedly, their moral education will be fostered, and many a grievance will be removed."[44] Joseph Czibulka, a burgher deputy from Boskowitz, similarly viewed the amalgamation of Christian and Jewish townships in a positive light, believing it would "pave the way for Jewish emancipation."[45] Not surprisingly, Hirsch also hoped that amalgamation would facilitate the social integration of Christian and Jewish Moravians, welcoming it exuberantly in one of his few utterances on the floor of the Moravian Diet. To great applause, he proclaimed the Jews' readiness to sacrifice their communal autonomy for a higher cause. Even though Jews would constitute a minority in the amalgamated townships, he argued, they would welcome amalgamation with joy.[46]

When the Provisional Township Law went into effect in March 1849, the same themes that occupied the deputies of the Moravian Diet reappeared. To dispel any confusion, Governor Lažansky made it clear that Paragraph 2 (regarding the incorporation of suburbs) applied to Jewish townships as well. In a letter to Stadion on April 23, 1849, he noted that Jewish townships were usually "built into" the Christian townships and therefore were territorially contiguous.[47] However, Lažansky expressed concern that the full amalgamation of Jewish and Christian townships would present insurmountable difficulties because of the "inveterate prejudices and belligerence of the Christian townships." He especially feared that the distribution of communal revenue would constitute a flash point in Christian-Jewish relations. In a subsequent letter to Stadion on June 19, 1849, Lažansky proposed a "mitigating" solution based on Paragraph 5 of the Provisional Township Law, which allowed an autonomous local community (*Ortsgemeinde*) with a sizable population to divide into smaller *Fraktionen*.[48] Each *Fraktion* could be assigned a "certain sphere of activity" while remaining an integral part of the autonomous local community. Lažansky proposed that Jewish townships (as *Fraktionen*) be ceded the "widest possible" sphere of activity in general and a completely separate sphere of activity with regard to the financial administration of Jewish educational, religious, and charitable institutions.

Lažansky viewed the *Fraktion* as a way to retain Jewish cultural and religious autonomy within the framework of the autonomous local township. He considered it "inadvisable" to dissolve "the Jewish townships as moral bodies [*moralische Körper*]" because the situation and needs of the Jews were "completely different" from those of the neighboring Christians. He advocated keeping educational, religious, and charitable institutions completely separate, especially because these Jewish institutions "involved special costs." So long as social barriers between Jews and Christians remained firmly in place, Lažansky feared that the disbursement of common funds for exclusively Jewish institutions would only exacerbate the palpable tension between the two populations. Indeed, as Deputies Quasnitschka and Blaha proclaimed in December 1848, the Christian population was loath to assume financial responsibility for its destitute Jewish neighbors.

The *Brünner Zeitung* echoed these financial concerns and implored Moravia's Jews to take responsibility for their own communal institutions, especially those serving the poor. A front-page article from July 13, 1849, expressed grave concern that the existing Jewish welfare network would be undermined by the "disintegration of the current Jewish community life."[49] Before describing the inauspicious consequences of communal disintegration, the article presented a somewhat glorified depiction of the "well-organized" Jewish communal life, which had been achieved "through great sacrifices" on the part of Moravia's Jews.

> Schools, religious instruction, prayer, and the community leadership were maintained through communal contributions. Support of the [Jewish] poor, whose numbers cannot be dismissed as small, was and is highly honorable for the Moravian communities. A Jewish beggar is a rarity, since every poor person can find assistance in his home community.

The article expressed concern that the functioning of these communal institutions would be disrupted during the "period of transition." It feared, in particular, that Jewish communal institutions would become financially untenable as affluent Jews left their homes and began paying taxes elsewhere. The potential impoverishment of the Jewish communities, however, was not viewed as a uniquely Jewish problem. On the contrary, because Moravia's Christian and Jewish townships were slated for amalgamation, the Jewish poor were potentially a burden to all. "This is no longer their concern alone," the article proclaimed. "It concerns the entire province. It affects everyone, especially [in] those places with Jewish communities."

With a decree from November 18, 1849, Minister of Justice Anton von Schmerling seemingly put to rest any doubts about the amalgamation of Jewish and Christian townships. Based on Paragraph 1 of the Fundamental Laws (which made the "enjoyment of civic and political rights independent of religious confession"), the November decree stipulated that confessional differences be entirely ignored when creating new townships. Schmerling considered the continued existence of Jewish townships—as separate and discrete *political* corporations—to be not only a violation of the constitution but also a hindrance to full Jewish emancipation.[50]

In January 1850, Boskowitz became the first Moravian town to amalgamate its Christian and Jewish townships. In Boskowitz and elsewhere, amalgamation came to be seen as a sign of Christian-Jewish reconciliation. In many respects, Boskowitz had already become a symbol of Christian-Jewish harmony in the course of the revolution. The Boskowitz national guard had accepted Jews into its ranks with no apparent resistance, and Joseph Czibulka had already advocated the unification of Christian and Jewish towns in December 1848. The *Brünner Courier*'s characterization of the Boskowitz amalgamation as "the clearest evidence of the true constitutional convictions of the local burghers" seemed right on the mark—especially after two Boskowitz Jews were elected to the local council.[51] The year 1850 got off to an auspicious start, but the "constitutional convictions" of the Boskowitz burghers had begun to sour by summer's end. In August, the Boskowitz Christian township reversed its earlier decision to amalgamate with the Boskowitz Jewish township, giving "no explanation" whatsoever.[52] Indeed, by the summer, relations between Christians and Jews had deteriorated so drastically in Moravia that no explanation was really needed.

In May 1850, a wave of anti-Jewish violence swept Moravia—a delayed fulfillment of the threats contained in Müller's "Just No Jewish Emancipation" pamphlet from March 1848 and the Prerau district office's warning from April 1849. Violence struck those places in particular where Jews had acquired shops and houses in the Christian parts of town. Anti-Jewish violence erupted in Trebitsch on May 1, spreading to Strassnitz and then Prerau, where more than 2,500 inhabitants took part in anti-Jewish excesses on May 28 and 29. As similar incidents were reported all over Moravia, such excesses seemed to be the "order of the day" throughout the month of May.[53] The *Allgemeine Zeitung des Judenthums* perceived this wave of violence as a delayed reaction to Jewish emancipation. "In Moravia," read one report, "the maltreatment of Jews . . . was kept in store. What was threatened often enough by the opponents of emancipation—i.e., that the people [*Volk*] would rise up and persecute the Jews . . . if any state proclaimed [the Jews'] equality—did not materialize anywhere . . . except in Moravia."[54] In May 1850, however, it was not merely the *Volk* who rose up against the Jews. Moravian burghers appear to have instigated and supported much of the springtime violence.

In Trebitsch, violence broke out after Franz Neumann, a Jewish cloth merchant, moved into a house in the Trebitsch Christian township on April 24, 1850. The windows of Neumann's new house were smashed that evening, and the walls were smeared with feces the following day. These incidents, along with some caterwauling on April 28, were reported to the Iglau district office, which decided against immediate intervention. Perhaps emboldened by the lack of official response, "several hundred individuals" attacked Neumann's house with axes and cleavers on the evening of May 1. They broke down doors and windows, demolished furniture, strewed bed feathers, and looted the storeroom. During the ransacking, Neumann and his family sought temporary refuge at a neighbor's house but were turned away. They reportedly spent the night in a rowboat on the Iglawa River "in order to save their lives."[55] Meanwhile, the local burgher guard performed its duties rather perfunctorily, failing to contain the outbreak of violence.[56] The Trebitsch Jewish community notified the Iglau district officer (*Bezirkshauptmann*), apparently bypassing the local Trebitsch authorities entirely. When District Officer Hübner came to Trebitsch, however, he was greeted with further anti-Jewish violence. Only with the May 4 arrival of an imperial army regiment stationed nearby was peace and order temporarily restored. Hübner began an official investigation and promised to bring the perpetrators to justice.

The disturbances in Trebitsch set off the first of two waves of anti-Jewish violence in Moravia. As Hübner was restoring the peace in Trebitsch, his own Iglau became the scene of anti-Jewish furor,[57] followed soon thereafter by similar incidents in Strassnitz,[58] Pirnitz,[59] and Nikolsburg[60]—all in early May. After a brief respite, a second wave of violence erupted in late May and early June, enveloping Wollein, Dolfos, Prerau,[61] Olmütz,[62] and Holleschau.[63] Most of the incidents occurred after individual Jews purchased or leased property that had traditionally been in Christian hands. Military battalions were often called in to quell the violence, usually after local burgher guards failed to perform their duties. At the scenes of the worst violence—Trebitsch, Strassnitz, and Prerau—official investigations were undertaken.

Contemporary reports, especially in Jewish and German liberal papers, underscored the complicity of the Christian burghers in the anti-Jewish violence. Whereas the "proletarian" or "plebeian" masses had been vilified for the sporadic anti-Jewish violence in Moravia in 1848, the burghers received the brunt of the blame in the spring of 1850. After the unrest in Trebitsch, for example, the *Allgemeine Zeitung des Judenthums* declared that "the proletariat alone cannot be blamed. Someone must have incited them."[64] The *Brünner Zeitung* went further and identified the inciters as those "who saw their material interests threatened by the Israelites"—a clear reference to the burgher population.[65] Similarly, the *Neue Zeit* emphasized that "Jew hatred, or rather Jew envy" did not reside solely in society's lowest strata.[66]

The complicity of the burghers was frequently documented through the activity—or rather inactivity—of burgher institutions, such as the community councils and burgher guards. One paper quipped that the pillaging in Trebitsch "seems to have caused our so-called *Honorationen* [i.e., educated burghers] much pleasure, since they stood by and watched as Neumann's clothing storeroom was robbed."[67] The burgher guards were also criticized for being remiss in their civic duties. In a fairly typical report, the *Neue Zeit* observed that the burgher guards in both Trebitsch and Iglau had "scarcely mobilized" during the turbulence of early May.[68] It was the imperial army, in fact, that was largely credited with restoring order to Moravia's towns.

The prompt response of the imperial institutions was frequently contrasted with the lethargic or perfunctory response of the burgher institutions. One newspaper observed that the "scenes had occurred primarily in towns and villages without imperial representation, where authority was vested "solely in the hands of the township."[69] In district capitals, on the other hand, "disorder was subdued as soon as it began."[70] Another paper blamed the "negligence of the lower officials" for the "proliferation of mischief" and praised the "higher officials, especially in Olmütz and Brünn," for responding properly.[71] In light of this, it is not surprising that the Jews of Trebitsch chose to send a delegation to the Gubernium in Brünn after suffering attacks in early May. The Jews of Moravia had a tradition of seeking imperial intervention after being disappointed by local officials, as they did the previous year when local officials refused to grant them marriage licenses.

Although there was a marked tendency to blame the burghers for the anti-Jewish violence in 1850, the Jews were by no means exculpated. The Jewish victims were often accused—even by liberal German papers—of inviting the burghers' wrath upon themselves. The *Brünner Zeitung*, for example, explained the Trebitsch unrest as a reaction to Franz Neumann's "unauthorized sale of cloth."[72] It also apportioned part of the blame for the Strassnitz unrest to a Jewish tanner who allegedly aired out infected hides in the Christian township.[73] In an article from June 1850, the *Allgemeine Zeitung des Judenthums* took note of this tendency to blame the Jews for their recent misfortunes: "Clever people are saying: the Jews in Moravia bear the guilt. They should not have drawn attention to themselves. They should have not yet asserted their rights."[74] The Trebitsch burghers adopted a similar line of reasoning in defense of their own anti-Jewish actions in early May. In an open letter to the *Allgemeine Zeitung des Judenthums*, the Trebitsch community council accused Franz Neumann of instigating the violence by throwing stones at the crowd that had assembled below his window on the evening of May 1.[75] The council asserted that the "regrettable" incident could have been prevented if the Jews of Trebitsch had behaved differently in three respects: (1) if Neumann and a second Jew had not "overstepped their trade licenses," (2) if the Jews had not sent a delegation to Brünn, and (3) if the Jews had not priced the poor merchants out of house and home by paying excessive rents in the Christian township. Because the Jews were portrayed as perpetrators, it is hardly surprising that the criminal investigation—which led to the arrest of seventeen Trebitsch burghers—did little to ease Christian-Jewish tensions. In fact, when these burghers were brought to trial in the district capital (Iglau), they were perceived by many as "martyrs of the people."[76] According to one paper, the perceived injustice of this trial had led to the renewal of anti-Jewish violence at the end of May. The attacks in Wollein, Prerau, and Holleschau were reportedly initiated by relatives and associates of the Trebitsch "martyrs" who sought to avenge a grave injustice.[77]

Nearly all the attempts to explain or justify the anti-Jewish violence were framed in economic rather than religious terms. Nevertheless, religious animosity seems to have played an important role in some towns, especially Prerau, where a Jew leased a building in which an altar had been erected for a recent Corpus Christi celebration. The local priest demanded that the Jew be evicted, and soon thereafter the worst anti-Jewish violence of 1850 enveloped the town. One Prerau resident recognized the role of religious intolerance but assigned the blame, once again, to the Jews. "It is difficult for the common people to befriend the Jews," he wrote, because Jews "consider Christians unclean." He called for an "enlightened rabbi" to dispel Christian fears by teaching the Jews to behave prudently.[78]

There were also calls for the Catholic clergy to bring the Christian population into line. The *Allgemeine Zeitung des Judenthums* accused the lower clergy in particular of being remiss in their moral duties. "How easily these persecutions could have been prevented," it lamented, "had the sublime word of the emperor been conveyed to the people by the lower clergy."[79] The archbishop of Olmütz, one of the highest ranking Catholic clergymen in the Habsburg Empire, had also failed to exercise his moral authority during the worst of the violence, according to the paper. Only in August 1850, at the behest of the Gubernium, did the archbishop publish a pastoral letter adjuring the Catholic clergy to maintain peace between Jews and Christians. In his letter, he reminded his flock that the commandment to love thy neighbor applies to "every person, regardless of birth, station, or creed," but he failed to offer an unequivocal defense of Jewish rights per se. Instead, quoting Luke 20:25 ("Render unto Caesar what is Caesar's and unto God what is God's"), he deemed the question of civic and political rights as the state's concern, not the church's. He instructed his fellow clergymen to preach obedience to the constitution, which had recently granted equal rights to all citizens. The archbishop did not hide his displeasure with the constitution (which had also "removed clerical influence" from the political sphere) or with the emancipation of the Jews. However, he did condemn violence as a means for effecting change. "The desired modification of the laws [granting equal civic and political rights]," he wrote, "cannot be attained through rioting and violence, but rather through legal means."[80]

Even though the archbishop of Olmütz counseled peaceful and legal means for overturning Jewish emancipation, rioting and violence had already proved themselves effective tools in fighting the amalgamation of Moravia's Jewish and Christian townships. After the anti-Jewish disturbances in May 1850, Governor Lažansky and Minister of the Interior Alexander von Bach recognized the need to reduce the mounting tensions in Moravia. The two met in Vienna on June 24, 1850, issuing a decree the following day that effectively reversed Schmerling's decree from seven months earlier. In contrast to Schmerling's decree, which required the dissolution of all autonomous Jewish townships, the new decree allowed for certain exceptions, stipulating that autonomous Jewish townships could be created in locales where Jewish and Christian townships already had separate administrative structures and where there was strong opposition to unification. Lažansky and Bach deemed these new measures a necessary response to the "protests from many towns in Moravia."[81]

As the "protests" of May 1850 had illustrated, opposition to amalgamation came overwhelmingly from the Christian side. Some Moravian Jews did view the retention of Jewish communal autonomy in a positive light (one newspaper even accused Jews of instigating the May violence to achieve this goal);[82] however, a majority appeared to see it as a grievous setback in the struggle for civic and legal equality. In an article titled "Ghetto redivivus," one Moravian Jew expressed his shattered expectations after the ministerial decree from June 25.

> We jubilantly anticipated the tearing down of the ghetto gates. Everywhere, the merging of communities, the incorporation of the Jewish communities (with the exception of religious matters) into the collective majority, was welcomed. Bright light and fresh air were to flow into the dark, narrow streets; and serene harmony and healthy sense

were to be the consequences thereof. Only in the temple, before the sacred Torah scroll, would the Israelite have a special status.[83]

However, the ministerial decree came across as a repudiation of everything the constitution represented. One individual argued that it violated Paragraph 1 of the Fundamental Laws, because the Jew would henceforth be "crowded into the narrow confines of a completely segregated *Extraterritorium* and prohibited from participating in the affairs of the township, which have great bearing on him."[84] In other words, his political rights would be restricted because of his religion. The author of "Ghetto redivivus" predicted that "bricks would again be brought in to erect a ghetto gate."

The ministerial decree effectively transferred the question of amalgamation and separation from the imperial government to the local Christian townships. As a result, unified opposition from the Christian townships (or their representative bodies) was sufficient to scuttle amalgamation, even in places where steps had already been taken to implement it. This was most evident in Ungarisch-Brod (where the burghers had refused to admit Jews into the national guard two years earlier). Already in early 1850, representatives of the Ungarisch-Brod Christian township had protested against amalgamation with the Jewish township but to no avail. On April 2, 1850, the local district officer ordered the amalgamation of the Ungarisch-Brod Christian township, the Ungarisch-Brod Jewish township, and the Ungarisch-Brod suburbs — in accordance with the Provisional Township Law of March 17, 1849. However, just two weeks after the ministerial decree from June 25, 1850, the decision was annulled. "If it is really the wish of the majority of the Christian burghers," wrote the district officer, "the amalgamation of the Ungarisch-Brod Christian township with the Jewish township can be abandoned." As a result of this decision, the Christian township amalgamated with its Christian suburbs, and the Ungarisch-Brod Jewish township remained politically separate.

The writer of "Ghetto redivivus" feared that the decision regarding Ungarisch-Brod would set a legal precedent not only in Moravia but also in all Habsburg provinces. If the "wish of the majority of Christian burghers" became the only criterion, he argued, autonomous Jewish townships would undoubtedly be reestablished in Galicia, Bohemia, and Hungary—"against the explicit word of the law and against the overall tendency of the constitutional state." Nevertheless, despite protests from Christian burghers in both Lemberg and Prague, the Ungarisch-Brod precedent did not extend beyond Moravia (with one notable exception: Hohenems in Voralberg). Only in Moravia did Jewish townships continue to exist as separate political entities. In fact, between August and September 1850, twenty-five of Moravia's fifty-two Jewish townships were constituted as autonomous Jewish townships. The remaining twenty-seven Jewish townships were amalgamated with the neighboring Christian ones.

The amalgamation of nearly half of Moravia's Jewish townships was not a sign of sudden reconciliation between Moravia's Christians and Jews. Of the twenty-seven newly amalgamated townships, only two of them—Gross-Meseritsch and Butschowitz—did so voluntarily. The others were forced to amalgamate by the Gubernium because they were too small to have separate administrative structures (as the June 25 decree required). Thus, of the Christian townships that were allowed to determine the fate of the Jewish townships in their midst, all but two rejected amalgamation. Even the Christian township in Boskowitz, which had amalgamated with the Jewish township in January, chose to reject it in August. In Prossnitz, where anti-Jewish sentiment had run high throughout the revolution, the exclusion of the Jewish township was marked by a festive celebration in the Catholic church.[85]

In those townships that did amalgamate, the joining together of Jews and Christians was frequently touted as a sign of long-awaited reconciliation. The *Brünner Zeitung* and the *Wiener Zeitung* both drew attention to the fact that Jews had been elected to local councils in a number of amalgamated townships, including Butschowitz, Misslitz, and Gross-Meseritsch. These elections signified the equal participation of Jews and Christians in civic and political life and were welcomed as an antidote to the rampant Jew hatred that had swept Moravia just a few months earlier. According to the *Brünner Zeitung*, the elections showed that "the sad specter of Jew hatred has not, as despondent ones began to fear, found a home in the beautiful marches [Marken] of our fatherland."[86] The *Wiener Zeitung* saw the amalgamations and the subsequent election of Jews as the crowning achievement of the constitution: "That in so many places, the Jewish and Christian townships have linked themselves with one another speaks in great measure for the wise, loyal spirit of the townships and the proper understanding of constitutional equality of rights, which knows no religious difference. And in such townships . . . there are also Israelite community members who stand in unanimous respect and who have been elected and accepted into the local council."[87]

Efforts to translate constitutional principles into practice faced repeated obstacles, particularly in places where segments of the Christian population thought that their material interests were at risk. Although social and religious factors cannot be dismissed entirely, the violent reaction to Jewish acquisition of "Christian" property and the vehement rejection of Jewish-Christian amalgamation were unmistakably triggered by economic fears on the part of the Christian population. However, the economic fears were of two different sorts. On the one hand there was a pronounced fear that the Jews would dispossess and "subjugate" the Christian population if all restrictions on their "inborn" acquisitiveness were removed. On the other hand there was a fear that the Jews would become a financial burden to the Christians if both populations were put on equal footing in one body politic. These financial considerations had serious repercussions for Moravia's Jewish communal life as well.

Jewish Communal Crisis

"The effects of the revolution on Jewish communal life seemed to be at first quite disastrous," wrote Salo W. Baron. "Many communities . . . suffered a decline in membership and revenue, which disrupted most of their activity."[88] Moravia was certainly no exception. Between 1848 and 1850, Moravia's fifty-two Jewish communities faced an unprecedented crisis as Jews (sometimes en masse) stopped paying the taxes that supported their religious, educational, and charitable institutions. The crisis was compounded by the fact that many Jews took advantage of their newly obtained freedom of movement and migrated to larger cities such as Brünn and Vienna. As a result, some Jewish communities not only were deprived of important taxpayers but also lost large segments of their population.

Moravia's Jewish communities were perennially short of funds, but the financial crisis of 1848–1850 can be linked to the abolition of the Jew tax on October 5, 1848. The long-awaited abolition of the Jew tax turned out to be a double-edged sword, not only freeing Jews from all special taxes but also eliminating a major source of income for Jewish communal institutions. Although the decision of the Reichstag abolished only "special Jewish taxes," many Moravian Jews assumed it abolished all taxes payable to the Jewish community—including the *Domestikal* taxes covering communal expenses. Rampant refusal to pay this tax threatened many Moravian Jewish communities with bankruptcy.

Already before the abolition of the Jew tax, the Committee for Moravian Jewry received complaints from a number of communities about the refusal of Jewish residents to pay *Domestikal* taxes. In an impassioned circular from October 8, 1848, Hirsch reminded the Jews of Moravia of their responsibility to pay these taxes. "Our equality has not yet become a reality," he wrote. "The tax problem has scarcely been resolved, yet here and there communities are [already] having difficulty raising *Domestikal* taxes for our own, inner affairs. . . . Because the humiliating burden of exceptional taxes has been lifted, some wish to discard the honorable, equitable burden of communal taxes as well." Hirsch implored the Jews to put their communal finances in order without resorting to government intervention.[89] Nevertheless, the Gubernium received complaints over the next months from a number of Jewish communities—including Mährisch-Kromau and Gewitsch— about nonpayment of taxes.[90] In March 1849, the Znaim district office reported that "the majority of Israelites in Schaffa have refused to pay their *Domestikal* taxes."[91]

As tax revenue diminished, particular blame was placed on Jews residing outside their official communities. Before the revolution, these "external" members frequently complained to the Gubernium about inflated tax assessment by the Jewish community. Whether leasing a brewery in a rural village, residing in a far-off town, or conducting trade in one of the empire's metropolises, these external members were often taxed at a higher rate because of their absence from the official community. In one case, a Trebitsch familiant living in Trübau, Bohemia, for thirty-six years insisted that he had been overtaxed as a result of his absence from Trebitsch.[92] The Göding Jewish community testified that external members were usually taxed more than other members, often serving as "scapegoats for the entire community."[93] As a result, external members paid disproportionately higher taxes to support institutions they rarely used. It is no surprise that these Jews in particular were among the first to withhold their communal taxes.

As external members stopped paying taxes, the financial burden on the local Jews grew. According to a November 1849 report from the Znaim district office, local Jews had been left with a "much larger share" of the tax burden in the absence of their coreligionists.[94] First, although communal taxes remained the same, the number of taxpayers had, in many cases, decreased. Second, and more important, the external members had often shouldered a larger share of the tax burden in the first place. Some, like the Trebitsch familiant in Bohemia, may have been scapegoats. Others, such as the Moravian Jewish merchants residing in Vienna, Prague, and Brünn, were often the financial mainstays of their communities. As the *Brünner Zeitung* pointed out in July 1849, "Large amounts [of taxes] are already leaving the Jewish communities in Moravia . . . because the most affluent members—merchants or those pursuing more lucrative vocations—live outside the community."[95] Because they were no longer bound to their ancestral Jewish communities, these Jews could sever all financial ties as well. Therefore, if a Moravian Jew were accepted as a burgher in Vienna, "he could no longer be forced to pay communal taxes to Nikolsburg or Bisenz, when he has absolutely no relationship to this or that place."[96]

Jewish communal institutions felt the brunt of the tax crisis, many seeming to totter on the edge of dissolution. With depleted funds, some communities could not muster enough money to pay communal officials.[97] As a result, the employment prospects of Moravian Jewry's rabbis, teachers, cantors, and ritual slaughterers remained uncertain. In June 1849, a report in *Der Orient* described the plight of many communities as follows:

> Ever since the emancipation of the Jews, many Moravian communities have entered a real state of disorganization. Many people believe

that the obligation to contribute to communal expenses has ended
along with [state] oppression. As a result, the religious officials such as
rabbis, teachers, cantors, and slaughterers are often mired in hardship
and uncertainty.[98]

Rabbis implored their communities to pay taxes but often to no avail.[99]
Three teachers appealed to the Ministry of Education to avert their increasingly bleak fate. Their jobs were threatened not only by reduced
tax revenue but also by the decreased Jewish populations in their respective communities. "As a result of the constitutionally guaranteed
freedom of movement," they wrote on June 29, 1849, "individual communities will diminish so significantly that, even if they do not entirely
dissolve, the current members will be unable to pay the current communal expenses and properly fund the school." The teachers envisioned
two inauspicious scenarios. If Christian and Jewish schools are brought
together, the Jewish teachers will be eliminated and "so many families
will be left breadless and in the direst of need." If the Jewish schools remain, the already meager salaries will be further reduced. As a solution,
the teachers proposed a "religious fund for Israelite-German teachers"
to be created out of the Moravian Jewish Landesmassafond.[100] The
Israelite-German teachers were not the only ones who set their hopes
on the Landesmassafond as a panacea for the Jewish communal crisis.

Reorganization of Jewish Communal Life

As freedom of movement and dwindling revenue threatened Moravian
Jewry's religious, educational, and charitable institutions, Hirsch set
out to reorganize and reinvigorate Jewish communal life, lest the "sacred and holy . . . be buried in the sunlight of freedom." Having successfully unified Moravian Jewry in the pursuit of civic and political rights,
Hirsch hoped he could now use this fragile consensus to overhaul
Jewish communal affairs. To this end, he called for a new ad hoc body
to replace the Committee for Moravian Jewry, which had been elected
the previous year. On March 13, 1849, Hirsch circulated a broadside to
the Moravian Jewish communities, outlining the steps to be taken.[101]
"With the attainment of equal rights in the spring of this year," he wrote

a week after the publication of the new constitution, "the elected Committee [for Moravian Jewry] accomplished its mission. It seems desirable that representatives, elected and authorized by each community in our province, convene again as soon as possible in order to achieve our next great and sacred goal." Hirsch invited Moravia's fifty-two Jewish communities to send delegates to Nikolsburg on April 23, 1849, to elect a new representative body: the Committee for the Reorganization of Jewish Moravian Religious Affairs. The committee would be charged with the task of restructuring and reorganizing Moravian Jewry's religious, educational, and charitable institutions.[102] Hirsch hoped that a common sacred goal could prevent a reversion to the querulous and confrontational atmosphere that characterized Moravian Jewish affairs on the eve of the revolution. Under the motto "Unity above all," he urged Moravia's Jews to subordinate their personal and local needs to the needs of Moravian Jewry as a whole. Only then, Hirsch declared, can "our prodigious task be accomplished with dignity."

As it turned out, Hirsch convened the representative assembly without first obtaining official permission from the government authorities. He assumed that the second paragraph of the Fundamental Laws—which granted each "recognized religious association" the right to organize and manage its own affairs—provided the necessary legal basis for such an assembly. Governor Lažansky was of a different opinion, but he was prepared to disregard Hirsch's oversight in light of the recent and precipitous deterioration of Jewish religious institutions in Moravia. As Lažansky wrote to Leo von Thun, Minister of Religion and Education, Hirsch

> was in no way authorized to convene a formal representative assembly of the fifty-two Jewish communities without previously obtaining an official permit, even less so since the stated goals in his invitation deal not only with religious affairs, but also with communal interests and educational affairs. However, since the unsanctioned incident was based on a misunderstanding of the constitutional Fundamental Laws, I believed I could overlook it, since the need for an agreement among the Jewish communities regarding the necessary reform of their religious affairs is unmistakable.[103]

Because of the urgency of the matter, Lažansky excused Hirsch's breach of protocol and allowed the general assembly to take place.

On April 23, 1849, representatives from most of Moravia's Jewish communities convened in Nikolsburg for a two-day general assembly. Hirsch had already set the agenda in his broadside from March 13, 1849, in which he called for institutional solutions to two problems confronting Moravian Jewry at the time: the perennial problem of occupational stratification and the suddenly spiraling problem of communal disintegration. The general assembly in Nikolsburg occupied itself primarily with these issues. Its first order of business was the establishment of the Franz Joseph Fund for the Promotion of Agriculture and Handicrafts. Afterward, it elected a thirteen-member committee to frame a new organizational structure for Moravian Jewry.

By setting the establishment of the supracommunal Franz Joseph Fund as the first item on his agenda, Hirsch managed to commence the assembly on a note of unity. The fund, bearing the name of the Jews' emancipator, served as a "monument of thanks" for the recently acquired civic and political rights. As such, it demonstrated the Jews' patriotic desire to create "institutions through which a prudent and judicious use of the newly acquired occupational freedom could be encouraged."[104] A product of the pre-1848 discourse on the Jewish question, the fund was meant to show that Jews too could become "productive" members of society. It replicated institutions that had emerged in the 1830s and 1840s as part of the struggle for emancipation—with one major difference: Whereas the earlier funds served individual communities (such as Prossnitz and Nikolsburg), the new Franz Joseph Fund was to serve Moravian Jewry as a whole. As an expression of this unity, Hirsch asked Moravia's Jewish communities to display their "sense of community" (*Gemeinsinn*) through donations to the newly established fund.

Although intended to underscore a sense of community, Hirsch's request for donations simultaneously exposed the financial and organizational problems that threatened to further fragment Moravian Jewry in the spring of 1849. First, because Jewish communal taxation was still in a state of disarray, the Franz Joseph Fund had to be financed exclusively through voluntary contributions. Second, because Moravian Jews were no longer bound to the fifty-two Jewish communities, the request for donations had to take recent population movements—particularly to Vienna and Brünn—into consideration. Indeed, the archive of the

Viennese Jewish community preserves a broadside—addressed to the "honorable Israelite communities of Moravia"—that tried to accommodate the new demographic changes. "For our Moravian brethren residing in Vienna and Brünn," reads its last paragraph, "a special subscription for the [Franz Joseph] Fund will be set up; and we therefore request that the individual communities not make demands on them."[105]

Following the establishment of the fund, the general assembly in Nikolsburg elected thirteen members—including Hirsch—to the Committee for the Reorganization of Jewish Moravian Religious Affairs. Four members had served with Hirsch on the earlier committee: Hirsch Fassel of Prossnitz, Josef Weisse of Gaya, Franz Flesch of Brünn, and Isaac Ledner of Triesch. The eight additional elected members were, like Flesch and Ledner, prominent businessmen or Jewish community leaders in their respective towns (Brünn, Nikolsburg, Kremsier, Jamnitz, Göding). Under the chairmanship of Hirsch, these rabbis and laymen met periodically between April and July 1849 to put together new supracommunal statutes, which were intended to stimulate "a new efflorescence of . . . spiritual, religious life" in Moravia.[106]

The new supracommunal statutes were necessitated by what Hirsch termed the "bifurcated communal life" in constitutional Austria.[107] With the anticipated dissolution of the autonomous Jewish communities, the Jews of Moravia would henceforth belong simultaneously to two separate communities—one defined in civic terms, the other in religious. As Hirsch explained on March 14, 1849:

> The Jew will be integrated into the larger society [*Gemeindebürgerverband*] with respect to all civic matters. However, our special religious affairs—maintenance of our devotional, educational, and charitable institutions and foundations, responsibility for hiring and supporting our rabbis and teachers—will continue to constitute the essence of our special religious community.[108]

In other words, the Jews' duties toward the fatherland would be performed in the civic community, and their duties toward God would be performed in the religious community. Of course, this bifurcation was predicated on the assumption that the first organic law, that is, the Provisional Township Law, would fully transform Moravia's politico-religious Jewish communities into exclusively religious Jewish communities. However, as one skeptical contemporary presciently pointed out, this was by no means guaranteed. He questioned the wisdom of crafting supracommunal statutes before all provisions of the new constitution had been fully implemented.[109] Indeed, in light of the eventual modification of the Provisional Township Law in June 1850, this skepticism appears to have been well founded.

Despite the occasional voice of skepticism or dissent, the committee of thirteen approached its new task with vigor and optimism. Between April and July 1849, the committee members drafted a new organizational structure—and corresponding statutes—for Moravian Jewry. They based their deliberations on declarations submitted by thirty-six communities and on the questionnaires that Hirsch had circulated back in 1847. In addition, the Shai Takkanot served as a model. Hirsch dominated the deliberations, facing little resistance or dissent from the other members, perhaps because of the absence of his only real rival among the committee members. Fassel had fallen ill in May and could not contribute to the debate from Carlsbad, where he was convalescing throughout the summer. (A handwritten draft was sent to him on July 29, 1849, and he authorized Josef Weisse to sign it as his proxy.)[110] On July 31, the committee—minus Fassel—met in Nikolsburg to finalize the draft. It was printed in Brünn in August under the title *Proposal for a Synagogue Constitution for Followers of the Jewish Faith in Moravia*.[111] The document was sent to Moravia's fifty-two Jewish communities, which were asked to send their comments to the committee by October 15. The communities were also asked to send delegates to a general assembly—to be held in Nikolsburg on November 6–7—to discuss the proposed *Synagogue Constitution*.

The title of the draft emphasized the confessional character of Judaism. Jews were referred to as "followers of the Jewish faith," and each individual Jewish religious community was now called a *Synagoge* instead of a *Gemeinde*. As the drafters explained, the term *Gemeinde* referred to a religious *and* political corporate body, which would soon cease to exist. As the Jewish community would soon encompass "only the religious and moral affairs of the Jewish Moravians," a new, less ambiguous term was required. To "avoid misunderstanding," the drafters selected the central religious institution—the synagogue—as a metonym for the entire religious community. This new nomenclature entailed a sometimes confusing redefinition of the most basic terms in Jewish communal life. An individual "Jewish community" was now an *Ortssynagoge*, or town synagogue; an assemblage of *Ortssynagogen* in a single district now constituted a *Synagogenbezirk*, or synagogue district; and "Moravian Jewry" as a whole was now the *Landessynagoge*, or the provincial synagogue. Since the term *synagogue* was now being used in the original Greek sense of assembly or community, the drafters of the *Synagogue Constitution* relied on another, simpler term for the physical structure in which religious services are held: *Bethaus*, or house of prayer.

In 224 paragraphs, the *Synagogue Constitution* grappled with two challenges of the constitutional age: (1) how to administer and tax a Jewry that was no longer confined to fifty-two closed communities and (2) how to create and finance new institutions for the promotion of Jewish religious life in a manner suitable to the new age. The preamble conjured up a Moravian Jewry "shaken to its deepest innards" and in urgent need of reorganization and reinvigoration and called for the "unification of all views and energies" for the common, lofty goal of building a "new edifice on the ruins of the old." While emphasizing unity, it also tried to consider the particular needs of Moravia's Jewish communities. Indeed, the preamble made special mention of two paragraphs (§8 and §83) that were intended to dispel any fear that the new organizational structure would erode—or in any way encroach on—Jewish communal autonomy. These paragraphs promised to allow for the "free inner movement of the 'synagogues' with respect to local conditions," even though town synagogue affairs were to be standardized and regulated according to "uniform general principles." This was a clear attempt to reconcile the inherent tension between supracommunal unity and local communal autonomy, the very tension that had plagued Hirsch during his first months as chief rabbi. Little did Hirsch realize that the question of communal autonomy would become the bone of contention that would eventually doom the entire endeavor.[112]

The *Synagogue Constitution* envisioned a multitiered centralized hierarchy, roughly modeled after the supracommunal organization of the Shai Takkanot (which had been dissolved in the late eighteenth century). At the bottom of the hierarchy were the town synagogues, that is, the successors of Moravia's fifty-two Jewish communities, scattered over Moravia's six administrative districts. All the town synagogues within a single administrative district were to elect a "district delegation" (*Bezirksdelegation*). Each delegation, consisting of a paid district rabbi (*Bezirksrabbiner*) and two counselors, was to meet four times a year to oversee the religious, educational, and charitable institutions of the individual town synagogues under its purview. In total, six district rabbis (one per district) and twelve counselors (two per district) were to serve on the district delegations.

Above the district delegation stood the Provincial Synagogue Council (Landessynagogenrath), which had far-reaching authority over nearly every aspect of Moravian Jewish communal life. Although subordinate to a popularly elected triennial general assembly (*Landessynagogenversammlung*), the Provincial Synagogue Council was actually the most powerful tier in the proposed hierarchy. According to §131 of the *Synagogue Constitution*, the Provincial Synagogue Council was to

> exercise supervision and authority over all communal [*synagogale*] institutions and employees; make final decisions in all communal matters; execute all resolutions passed by the *Landessynagoge* [i.e., Moravian Jewry] and all related regulations, decrees, and instructions; determine the curricula for all teaching institutions and introduce appropriate textbooks; examine rabbis, religious instructors, teachers, and other communal officials; and generally execute everything that appears beneficial for the moral-religious aims of the communal institutions.

The Provincial Synagogue Council comprised two bodies: the Lesser Council (Engere Rath) and the Greater Council (Grössere Rath). These councils, which harked back to the *va'ad katan* and *va'ad gadol* of the Shai Takkanot, are best conceived as two concentric circles. At the center was the five-member Lesser Council, which was composed of the chief rabbi (chairman), a paid secretary, a teacher from the proposed rabbinical seminary, and two elected counselors. The Lesser Council was to attend to the quotidian affairs of Moravian Jewry and would be authorized to call the Greater Council into session "in especially important cases." The Greater Council was composed of the five-member Lesser Council and an outer circle of the twelve counselors who served on the district delegation. However, because the Greater Council was to be convened only on an ad hoc basis, the vast authority of the Provincial Synagogue Council would be concentrated in the Lesser Council. Thus it could be argued that five men—with the chief rabbi at the helm—were slated to preside over all of Moravian Jewry. In the eyes of one critic of the *Synagogue Constitution*, this made the Provincial Synagogue Council tantamount to *gouvernement personel*.[113]

Each tier of the administrative hierarchy was to have a corresponding set of educational institutions. At the town synagogue level, a network of Jewish elementary schools (*jüdische Volksschule*) was to be established with classes in religious and civil (*bürgerlich*) subjects. At the district level, six talmudic preparatory classes (*talmudische Vorbereitungsclasse*) were to be added, one in each district. These classes were to be taught by the district rabbis, financed by the provincial synagogue (i.e., Moravian Jewry), and attended by Moravia's future rabbis, religious teachers, and cantors. After finishing the preparatory class, these students would continue their studies at the one educational institution intended to serve all of Moravian Jewry: a three-year rabbinical seminary (*jüdisch-akademische Lehranstalt*) to be established in the Moravian town with "the most and best institutions of higher learning." Moravia's "future theologians" were to receive religious instruction from the chief rabbi (and a number of hired teachers) while receiving secular instruction at both the rabbinical seminary and the local gymnasium. Once again, all costs were to be covered by Moravian Jewry.

What were the sources of funding for the multitiered administrative hierarchy and its corresponding institutions? Who would pay for the new officials (counselors, district rabbis, secretary, seminary teachers) and new institutions (talmudic preparatory classes, rabbinic seminary)? Who would pay travel and other expenses for the triennial general assembly, the quarterly district delegation gatherings, the periodic meetings of the Provincial Synagogue Council? The *Synagogue Constitution* envisioned the creation of a centralized *Landessynagogencasse*, administered by the secretary of the Provincial Synagogue Council and deriving its income from two sources: the Jewish Moravian Landesmassafond and the obligatory taxes to be levied on individual members of the town synagogues (and *not* on the town synagogue as a collectivity).

These individual tax obligations were to be appraised by the triennial general assembly.

A general assembly (*Landessynagogenversammlung*) was to be convened every three years, in the tradition of the triennial Council of the Land that had met in Moravia from the sixteenth through the eighteenth century. Like its venerable antecedent, the general assembly was to include elected delegates from all of Moravia's Jewish communities and thereby constitute a representative body for Moravian Jewry as a whole. In August 1849, Moravia's fifty-two Jewish communities were asked to send delegates to the first general assembly, scheduled to take place in Nikolsburg on November 6–7. The larger communities could send up to three delegates, the smaller ones up to two. This assembly, at which the *Synagogue Constitution* was to be the only order of business, had a dual function. First, it was intended to underscore the unity of Moravian Jewry at this important yet precarious juncture. Second, as Moravian Jewry's representative body, the general assembly was expected to sanction the *Synagogue Constitution* and thereby endow it with popular legitimacy. As the preamble to the *Synagogue Constitution* put it, "The authority to make suitable amendments always rests with the general assembly; therefore the interests of the honorable [Jewish] communities will in no way be compromised by the adoption of this constitution."

Had the November assembly been a referendum on the *Synagogue Constitution*, it would have suffered an immediate and resounding defeat. Of the eighty invited delegates, only eighteen attended—representing less than one-fourth of the Moravian Jewish communities. Fassel presided over the preassembly on November 5, later justifying his presence as "repent[ance] for my hasty signing of the *Synagogue Constitution* [in July]."[114] He attended as an ardent opponent, speaking out against the *Synagogue Constitution* and abstaining from the second day of deliberations. On his watch as chairman of the preassembly, a lengthy list of complaints was drafted, challenging not only the "hierarchical" and "despotic" elements of the document but also the authority of a minority assembly to make binding decisions for Moravian Jewry as a whole. When Hirsch took over the presidium during the actual assembly, these complaints were never discussed, but the Nikolsburg delegates had been instructed by their constituents to attack all paragraphs that threatened communal autonomy or reeked of hierarchy.

Hirsch dominated the two-day assembly, ignoring parliamentary procedure and preventing many participants from getting a word in edgewise. "Seldom was someone other than [Hirsch] heard," observed one polemicist.[115] Fassel claimed that the meeting on November 6 had been fruitless because of Hirsch's domineering and arbitrary leadership style. "Parliamentary procedure," he noted ironically, "dictates that the president cannot participate in the debate and that he cannot preside over the vote on his own proposal."[116] According to one source, many deputies who wished to speak were not given the opportunity.[117] It appears that Hirsch sought to defeat the opposition largely by filibustering them. Although "Israelite men of all colors" spoke out against the *Synagogue Constitution*, Hirsch scheduled another assembly for December 31, 1849, in the hopes of obtaining majority support. In the meantime, the barrage of opposition grew.

In a private letter to Hirsch in early November, Fassel adumbrated the basic criticisms of the *Synagogue Constitution* that would resurface over the ensuing months with increasing vitriol and to wider audiences.[118] He criticized the "deadening spirit" and the "spirit of despotism" that pervaded the entire *Synagogue Constitution*, taking particular aim at the centralized hierarchy that was completely foreign to rabbinic Judaism. The *Synagogue Constitution*, he argued, constricted natural development and progress and threatened the autonomy of individual communities guaranteed in the *Shulḥan Arukh*. Centralization, he wrote, limits the independence of individual communities and turns young officials into "spineless machines or hypocrites." He characterized the Landessynagogenrath as an autocratic and arbitrary body that overshadowed and overpowered the supposedly democratic representative bodies such as the *Landessynagogenversammlung*. Fassel, unlike subsequent critics, particularly emphasized the deleterious and stultifying effect that the rigid *Synagogue Constitution* would have on the religious life of Moravia's Jews, warning that it would bring about "destructive Reform movements," because the imposed religious yoke would be impossible to bear.

Fassel's own community of Prossnitz sent an impassioned letter to the chief rabbi on November 22, 1849, insisting that the *Synagogue*

Constitution would lead "to disorder, dissension, discord, and despotism" in the Jewish communities of Moravia.[119] Their criticism of the *Synagogue Constitution* focused on four aspects in particular: (1) It "cripples and destroys all autonomy" through a despotism that will engender interminable strife; (2) it eliminates the independence of local rabbis, who will become "spineless tools" and ruthlessly compete for the newly created titles such as "district rabbi"; (3) the pyramid-shaped hierarchy will be an "oppressive force," making the new officials and dignitaries "lords of the intellectual, moral, and material possessions of the community"; and (4) the new institutions will create unnecessary taxes. The Prossnitz community specifically attacked the Landessynagogenrath as a source of strife and dissent, the central control of religious affairs as "religious coercion," and the proposed Jewish theological seminary as unsuitable for the small province of Moravia. It rejected the *Synagogue Constitution* outright, extolling communal autonomy as an inviolable principle. In many respects, this letter expressed the same criticism that had been leveled at Hirsch two years before.

On December 3, 1849, the Prossnitz Jewish community made its criticism public through a circular to the larger Jewish communities in Moravia.[120] It also sent a letter to Hirsch, criticizing the new political role he envisioned for himself and other rabbis: "We strongly believe that the rabbi's duties should be limited to instruction, exhortation, and the fostering of religious life through the written and spoken word and that governing lies outside of his orbit."[121]

With the December 31 assembly approaching, Hirsch feared that the vociferous opposition from Moravia's second largest Jewish community would sabotage his plans for reorganizing Moravian Jewry. In a letter to the Prossnitz community, he claimed that the public criticism of the *Synagogue Constitution* was threatening "the only possible arrangement [to remedy] that which imperils us."[122] "The health of our future," he insisted, "depends on the realization of this particular *Synagogue Constitution*." He called on the Prossnitz community to recognize the urgency of the matter, but his letter did not have the desired effect. Four of the six largest Jewish communities sent neither representatives nor written support to the general assembly. Prossnitz, Boskowitz, Trebitsch, and

Neu-Rausnitz—encompassing approximately one-fourth of Moravia's total Jewish population—boycotted the assembly. Fourteen smaller communities followed suit.

The general assembly took place in Nikolsburg from December 31, 1849, to January 5, 1850. Hirsch managed to gather twenty-seven delegates from twenty-four communities along with written declarations of support from eleven others.[123] In total, thirty-five of the fifty-two Jewish communities were represented at the assembly—just over two-thirds of Moravian Jewry. The rules of procedure, established on the first day, mandated that only a simple majority of the twenty-seven delegates was necessary to reach a decision. Thus fourteen delegates could conceivably decide for all of Moravian Jewry. Furthermore, the rules of procedure gave Hirsch, as chairman of the assembly, a unique privilege: "When the chairman believes that the speaker has exhausted a topic, he rings a bell."[124]

During the six days of deliberations, most of the *Synagogue Constitution* was ratified by members of the assembly. Of the 224 paragraphs, 13 were amended and 19 expunged.[125] The changes reflected the criticisms that had been leveled at the document throughout the previous year: the appearance of hierarchy, constricted communal autonomy, and increased taxation. The Landessynagogenrath (§§133–36), dubbed *gouvernment personel* by one of the *Synagogue Constitution*'s sharpest critics, was eliminated; so were the district rabbis (§§138–39), who were seen as a drain on communal funds and an interference in local communal affairs. On January 5, 1850, the delegates elected a six-member committee to prepare the *Synagogue Constitution* for official approval by the Gubernium. Rabbis Josef Weisse of Gaya and Abraham Placzek of Boskowitz as well as Samson Fränkel of Brünn, Hermann Kohn of Kremsier, Franz Pater of Nikolsburg, and Friedrich Karplus of Göding were elected to the committee.[126] On April 28, they submitted the revised *Synagogue Constitution* to the Gubernium, which scheduled a deliberation in Brünn between June 12 and 19. Nonetheless, opposition to the *Synagogue Constitution* showed no sign of abating. In the first half of 1850, for example, Nathan Deneberg fulminated against the "fiasco" in his vituperative and ad hominem pamphlet *Critique of the Proposal for a Synagogue Constitution for the Followers of the Jewish Faith in Moravia.*[127]

Governor Lažansky recognized the pressing need for reorganizing Jewish communal affairs in Moravia. He had condoned Hirsch's unauthorized assembly in Nikolsburg in April 1849 because of the matter's urgency. Furthermore, he hosted the deliberations in the governor's mansion in Brünn in the summer of 1850, presiding personally at the closing session on June 19. He understood that membership in a Jewish religious community could not be voluntary because "a large portion of Jewish coreligionists" would place their material interests first, pay the minimum possible religious contribution, and thereby bring about the "complete disintegration of Jewish religious institutions."[128] He viewed a centralized hierarchy as suitable for Moravian Jewry but acknowledged the aversion of many Moravian Jews to "the appearance of a hierarchical authority." In a lengthy letter to Leo von Thun, Minister of Religion and Education, he proposed minor amendments "in part for the public interest of the government, in part for the efficient regulation of Jewish religious affairs" and concluded with overwhelming support for the *Synagogue Constitution*. On June 19, the deliberations in Brünn yielded three decisions: (1) The amended *Synagogue Constitution* was accepted "definitively as the norm for Jewish religious affairs in Moravia"; (2) the registration of births, marriages, and deaths would be conducted according to the same guidelines for Jews and Christians; and (3) one portion of the Moravian Jewish Landesmassafond would go toward the establishment of a theological seminary in Moravia.[129]

Even after the Gubernium sanctioned the *Synagogue Constitution*, opposition continued, especially with regard to its most costly aspect—the proposed Jewish theological seminary in Brünn or Nikolsburg. Since as early as the late 1830s, many Moravian rabbis and laymen—with Fassel as their lead—had identified such a seminary for the academic and theological education of rabbis and teachers as a desideratum in Moravia. A seminary had been established in Padua in 1829, but the hereditary lands of the Habsburg Empire lacked such an institution. When Hirsch was elected chief rabbi in 1847, hopes ran high that he would establish a seminary in Nikolsburg, the center of rabbinic learning in Moravia. "All Moravian communities would happily contribute," reported *Der Orient* in February 1847, "and so Moravia, with Hirsch at its helm, could serve as a beautiful example in the establishment of a seminary. . . . This institution alone would make Hirsch unforgettable."[130] In his first months as chief rabbi, Hirsch had already called for the establishment of a "Padua-like institution" in Nikolsburg, even inviting his former student Heinrich Graetz as a prospective teacher in 1849.[131] However, by the summer of 1850, communities such as Prossnitz came to see the proposed seminary as the institute "that will most oppress the Jews of Moravia."[132]

Critics of the seminary did not oppose the institution per se but rather its establishment in Moravia at the expense of Moravian Jewry. All the early critiques of the *Synagogue Constitution* denigrated the proposed Moravian seminary, but the opposition reached a new pitch after the June 19 decision to allocate funds from the Moravian Jewish Landesmassafond for this purpose. On June 26, 1850, the Prossnitz Jewish community sent a missive to Lažansky excoriating the recently sanctioned *Synagogue Constitution* in general and the proposed seminary in particular.[133] Moravia, it insisted, was not suitable for such an institution because of its peripheral location and meager Jewish population. It proposed a seminary instead in a "focal point of the Monarchy," such as Prague or Vienna, where there were universities, voluminous libraries, and larger Jewish populations. "Moravia," it stressed, "[has] the smallest Jewish population of all the provinces inhabited by Jews." It questioned the necessity of a seminary where "maybe one candidate will be employed as a rabbi or a teacher every ten years." A Nikolsburg correspondent noted that two or three years had passed since a single Moravian rabbinate had been filled, despite the forty or fifty qualified local candidates. He predicted an "inundat[ion] by theologians" and the creation of a "theological proletariat" if a seminary were to be established exclusively for Moravia.[134]

More deplorable than a seminary serving exclusively Moravian Jewry was a seminary funded exclusively by Moravian Jewry. In the eyes of the Prossnitz Jewish community, a portion of the Landesmassafond had been earmarked for an institution that did not serve Moravian Jewry's most pressing interests at this time of dire financial crisis. Many communities were financially insolvent and could not afford to pay their rabbis, teachers, and other officials because of confusion after the abolition of the Jew tax. "The only hope for the Moravian communities," wrote the Prossnitz Jewish community, "is that the capital of the

Landesmassafond—assembled from the contributions by their grand-parents, parents, and themselves under the paternal supervision of the government"—be used to support rabbis and teachers. The Prossnitz community viewed it as "unjust" that Moravian Jewry's patrimony should fund such an inessential and costly institution as a seminary. "Moravian Jewry will happily contribute" to a seminary, it declared, but not "for Moravia alone, and at Moravia's sole expense."[135] The Jewish community of Trebitsch echoed these sentiments and proposed a novel solution: dividing the Landesmassafond among Moravia's Jewish com-munities to cover religious and educational needs and to distribute the costs of the seminary "among all the Israelite inhabitants of Austria."[136] The Prossnitz view fell on deaf ears at the Gubernium, and the Trebitsch plan arrived too late. On August 4, 1850, Lažansky informed Minister Thun that allocations from the Landesmassafond were well grounded, because the seminary was "clearly in the interest of all of Moravian Jewry." The existence of a rabbinic academy in Padua was proof enough that the small size of Moravia's Jewish population was immaterial. On October 10, the Gubernium turned to Thun, requesting a portion of the Landesmassafond for "purposes of the *Landessynagoge*."[137] However, nei-ther the seminary nor the *Synagogue Constitution* ever became a reality.

Why was the *Synagogue Constitution* never implemented? It had been designed with the Provisional Township Law in mind, but, as already mentioned, this law—the "foundation" of the *Synagogue Constitution*—was significantly modified. Indeed, in response to the anti-Jewish vio-lence that swept Moravia in May 1850, Minister Bach permitted certain Jewish communities to continue their separate autonomous existence despite an earlier decree requiring their amalgamation with neighbor-ing (and often interlocking) Christian communities. The reversal—on June 25, 1850—occurred just six days after the deliberations in Brünn, at which Governor Lažansky not only sanctioned the *Synagogue Constitu-tion* but also allocated funds from the Landesmassafond for the estab-lishment of a Jewish theological seminary. As a result of the reversal, uniform conditions did not prevail in Moravian Jewish communal life. Although all fifty-two Jewish communities were supposed to shed their political character and be transformed into exclusively religious com-munities (i.e., town synagogues), twenty-five of them were (re)constituted as politically autonomous communities by the fall of 1850. How could the *Synagogue Constitution*, which sought to provide uniform regulations for Jewish religious life in Moravia, be implemented if some Jewish communities retained their political *and* religious character?

Hirsch believed that the *Synagogue Constitution* could—and should—be implemented regardless, arguing in a letter to Lažansky that this was the only way to ensure the financial well-being of Moravia's Jewish communal institutions.[138] Implementation was "urgent," he insisted, because the collection of *Domestikal* taxes was essential for covering the Jews' religious and educational needs for the following year. Even if the Gubernium chose to implement only those sections of the *Synagogue Constitution* that dealt with tax collection, this would still be a step in the right direction. Indeed, because the mechanism it outlined for tax collection was predicated on the establishment of a network of town synagogues, its introduction would have meant that the full implementation of the *Synagogue Constitution*—and the concomitant reorganization of Jewish communal life—was on course.

However, the Gubernium opted for another, simpler solution to Moravian Jewry's financial crisis. Instead of introducing a new organizational structure solely for the sake of tax collection, the Gubernium found it easier to work directly with Moravia's fifty-two Jewish communities. On September 13, 1850, at the behest of the Ministry of Religion and Education and in consultation with the Committee for the Reorganization of Jewish Moravian Religious Affairs, Lažansky promulgated the Provisional Regulations for the Coverage and Distribution of *Domestikal* Taxes for the Jewish Religious Communities in Moravia.[139] These regulations stipulated that Moravia's fifty-two Jewish communities (*Judengemeinden*) would henceforth be considered Jewish *religious* communities (*jüdische Religionsgemeinden*) and that each "follower of the Jewish faith" would pay taxes for the support of religious and educational institutions in his particular religious community. Because many Moravian Jews had changed their place of residence since the outbreak of the revolution, the new regulations set an arbitrary criterion for determining to which religious community an individual Jew was legally bound: Unless a Jew was officially accepted into another community before September 13, 1850—the date the regulations went into effect—he was to be considered a member of whichever community he had previously been bound to. This effort to maintain the status quo particularly benefited Jewish communities that had lost (or were at risk of losing) their members; indeed, these communities were temporarily guaranteed a stable base of taxpayers. The new regulations were conceived as a stopgap measure, intended to remain in effect only "until the *Synagogue Constitution* for the Jews of Moravia receives official sanction." However, like many "provisional" or "temporary" laws, they remained in effect for a number of decades, determining matters of taxation and religious community membership until 1890–1892.[140]

In sharp contrast to Hirsch's *Synagogue Constitution*, the new "provisional" regulations were highly decentralized, relegating matters of taxation and community membership almost entirely to the individual Jewish religious communities. Just as all Moravian Jews had been required to pay taxes to one of Moravia's fifty-two Jewish communities (*Judengemeinden*) before the revolution, so too were all "followers of the Jewish faith" required to pay taxes to one of Moravia's fifty-two Jewish religious communities (*jüdische Religionsgemeinden*) after the revolution. There were, however, three major differences. First, the quantity and quality of the taxes were substantially different. Whereas Moravia's Jews had previously paid a constellation of "special"—and particularly onerous—Jewish taxes (e.g., family tax, consumption tax), the only "Jewish" tax they were now required to pay was the *Domestikal* tax, which directly supported their own religious and educational institutions. As far as other taxes were concerned, the Jews were placed on par with their fellow Christian citizens. Second, the new regulations sought to eliminate many of the abuses that were widespread under the previous system, particularly the "scapegoating" of external community members, who had often paid disproportionately higher taxes to support institutions they rarely used. To remedy this situation, the new regulations introduced a progressive tax scale, which considered not only a taxpayer's income but also the extent to which he could avail himself of a community's religious and educational institutions. For example, individuals who lived more than a Sabbath's journey from the religious community had a lower tax burden than those who resided in its center. Furthermore, Jews who belonged to one religious community but used the services of another paid prorated taxes to both. The third and perhaps most important difference between the old and new regulations centered around the question of collective responsibility. In accordance with the new constitution, which replaced corporate rights with individual rights, Moravia's Jewish taxpayers were now responsible solely for their own taxes, not for those of their coreligionists.

The shift from corporate to individual rights brought the continued existence of Moravian Jewry's most important financial resource—the Landesmassafond—into question. On February 8, 1851, the Finance Ministry sought to absorb this fund "for purposes of state," arguing that its collective owner had ceased to exist. According to the Finance Ministry, the political rights vouchsafed to every citizen by the constitution had effectively eliminated the "corporate special status of Jewry in the political respect" and thus obviated the need for a special Moravian Jewish fund.[141] Furthermore, it argued, because the purpose of the fund was to help heavily indebted Jewish communities pay the Jew tax, the fund had become irrelevant after the tax's abolition. In light of this reasoning, the Finance Ministry queried the Moravian-Silesian Gubernium, the Ministry of the Interior, and the Ministry of Religion and Education to determine "whether the Moravian Landesmassafond [was] still warranted under the current circumstances, or whether, as the capital belonging to an abolished corporation, it should be absorbed for purposes of state." On February 25, 1851, the Committee for the Reorganization of Jewish Moravian Religious Affairs submitted a letter, now lost, to the Ministry of the Interior that may have influenced the positions of the Ministry of the Interior, the Ministry of Religion and Education, and the Gubernium.

The Gubernium emphatically defended the Landesmassafond as the property of Moravian Jewry, stressing the continued existence of "political" Jewish communities two years after the promulgation of the constitution.[142] "Even if the Constitution permits Jewish communities to dissolve as such in the political respect," the Gubernium wrote, "it does not follow that they *must* dissolve as such. . . . They still exist in those places where they have not until now come to an agreement with the Christian population regarding amalgamation." Even in those places where Jewish communities had amalgamated with their Christian counterparts, the Gubernium noted, Jewish communities continued to exist as "religious and school communities." The Gubernium maintained that the fund remained relevant after the abolition of the Jew tax because the Jews remained taxpaying citizens. "The abolition of the special Jew tax," it noted, "in no way makes the Jews tax-exempt, since they have to carry an equal tax burden with the non-Jewish population as far as public taxes and communal expenses are concerned." Because the fund "originated from surplus in the special Jew tax," it continued, the fund must remain the "indisputable property" of Moravia's Jewish taxpayers. In this respect, the Ministry of Interior and the Ministry of Religion and Education fully sided with the Gubernium.

The Ministry of Religion and Education viewed the Landesmassafond as essential for maintaining the religious, educational, and charitable institutions of Moravian Jewry.[143] The Jewish communities received no state funding for the maintenance of their religious and educational institutions, and they kept separate charitable institutions—even in the amalgamated communities—because of "their dietary laws." The Landesmassafond was also important for the establishment of a theological seminary but most important as a means to prevent the further deterioration of Jewish communal life at this crucial transitional phase. "The elimination of the Landesmassafond from Moravian Jewry at this moment . . . would be the most grievous deviation from their most important interests. This is even more critical, because the ubiquitous strivings of the Reform party in Judaism . . . which aims for the complete destruction of all positive faith, can only be effectively countered if we charitably accommodate the religious needs of the Jews, thereby elevating and strengthening the religious feeling within them."

✳

The confusion over the Landesmassafond highlights the essential tension between individual and corporate rights that emerged after the promulgation of the constitution in March 1849. Although the Jews of Moravia were granted rights as individuals, a number of factors perpetuated and reinforced their separate corporate existence. By far, the most important factor was the autonomous Jewish community, which had encompassed the Jews' religious, educational, and charitable institutions and served as a self-governing body with the authority to impose taxes and regulate the behavior of its members. The Jewish taxes, from which the Landesmassafond was originally created, served as a constant reminder of the collective responsibility of Moravian Jewry. So did the anti-Jewish violence in the spring of 1850, which punished Moravian Jewry for the misdeeds of a handful of Jews who "harvested the fruits of emancipation too soon."

Eight

Drifting Rabbis, Shifting Centers, and the Burgeoning Czech-German Conflict

During the Habsburg monarchy's last six decades of existence, few events occupied as central a place in the Jews' collective memory as the Revolution of 1848. Although many of their newly acquired rights were rescinded during the two decades following the revolution, it remained an important milestone on the road to emancipation. Indeed, the eventual reemancipation of Habsburg Jewry in 1867 was commonly seen as the culmination of a process that started with the outbreak of revolution in Vienna on March 13, 1848.[1] Similarly, many of the developments that shaped Moravian Jewry in the second half of the nineteenth century can be traced back to the momentous events of 1848–49. The revolution put the Moravian chief rabbinate in the political spotlight, but Samson Raphael Hirsch's frustrated efforts at reorganizing Moravian Jewry's religious, educational, and communal affairs—and his subsequent decision to leave Moravia—brought the further existence of this institution into permanent question. Debates about the future of the chief rabbinate went on for decades, particularly as demographic changes—another product of the revolution—threatened the continued existence of Moravia's traditional Jewish communities. These communities, once the centers of Moravian Jewish life, came into increasing conflict with the new parvenu communities—most notably Brünn—which experienced tremendous population growth after the revolution. The revolution also revealed new fissures in the often tense relations between Moravia's Jewish and non-Jewish inhabitants. Before the revolution, anti-Jewish sentiment was primarily a function of the economic tensions between Christians and Jews. These tensions predominated during the revolution as well, but it became increasingly clear that Moravia's Jews would soon be caught in the middle of the inchoate Czech-German conflict. Indeed, Moravian Jewry's preference for German language and culture proved to be a dangerous liability as Czech national consciousness rose among Moravia's Slavic majority in the second half of the nineteenth century.

From Emancipation Rescinded
to Emancipation Regained, 1851–1867

The gradual rollback of Jewish emancipation began with the Sylvester Patent of December 31, 1851, which annulled many of the achievements of the revolution and ushered in a period of "personal absolutism" that lasted until the end of the decade.[2] Issued by Franz Joseph on New Year's Eve, the Sylvester Patent canceled most of the constitution, retaining only those provisions that freed peasants from servile dues and granted citizens equality before the law. It also canceled the Fundamental Laws, except for the provision guaranteeing freedom of worship to all "recognized" churches and religious communities. Karl von Kübeck, the chief author of the Sylvester Patent, sought to explicitly affirm civic equality for the Jews, but Franz Joseph personally rejected this, calling instead for the reinstatement of special restrictions that had been in place before the revolution.[3] On July 25, 1853, marriage restrictions were reintroduced for the Jews of the monarchy. Although they were less onerous than the Familiants Laws, their obvious purpose—"to control the too rapid increase of the Israelite population"—was all too familiar to the Jews of Moravia.[4] To make matters worse, restrictions on Jewish ownership of real estate were reintroduced a few months later.

Restrictions on ownership of real estate were "provisionally" reintroduced by an imperial decree from October 2, 1853.[5] The decree, which came in response to repeated—and apparently exaggerated—protests against Jewish land acquisition,[6] permitted Jews to hold on to real estate that they had legally purchased before that date, but it forbade them to acquire any new real estate (except under pre-1848 conditions). The reinstatement came as a complete shock to Moravia's Jews, who just months before could marvel at the fact that Jewish ownership of "burgher houses" and "inns" had become commonplace. "No one takes offense at this anymore," remarked a correspondent from Moravia. "Wherever the sun shines, the darkness [of the past] vanishes into thin air."[7] The October decree, however, furnished clear evidence that there was still a partial eclipse in the Habsburg monarchy. Not long after it was issued, a delegation of Moravian Jews—who were all too familiar with the meaning of "provisional"—submitted a petition to Franz Joseph in the hope that his majesty would rescind the decree.[8]

The decree was rescinded in 1860, but during the seven years that it remained in effect, many towns and villages—in Moravia and elsewhere in the Habsburg monarchy—viewed it as an effective instrument in their effort to maintain the pre-1848 status quo.[9] In Moravia, the town of Znaim stood out in this respect. In 1856–57, the town council tried to have Znaim's right *de non tolerandis judaeis* reinstated, claiming that the 1853 decree had put all the pre-1848 residence restrictions back into effect.[10] The Znaim councilmen further rehashed many of the arguments that had appeared in the anti-emancipation petitions of 1848–49, warning that the Jews would irreparably injure the "religion, morality, [and] family happiness [*Familienglück*] of the town's Christian inhabitants."[11] "The Jews will stream into Znaim in the hundreds," they predicted, "drive up the rents, and monopolize all business and trade with their money and deception. They will turn the Catholic town of Znaim into a Jewish town [*Judenstadt*]; the inhabitants will sink into poverty and be forced to hire themselves out as day-laborers to the Jews."[12] These arguments, however, failed to persuade the members of the emperor's advisory council, who had final say in the matter. They pointed out that the October decree restricted the Jews' right to acquire real estate but did not forbid them to live in Znaim and Moravia's other towns. They also dismissed the councilmen's fears as totally unfounded, as "not one single Jew" had acquired property in Znaim between 1848 and 1853, despite the fact that many Jews lived nearby.[13] In addition, even in towns where Jews had moved in large numbers since 1848—such as Brünn, Olmütz, and Iglau—the dreadful scenario envisioned by the inhabitants of Znaim had not materialized.

The incident in Znaim turned out to be a vestige of the past, not a harbinger of the future. Indeed, the years to come saw the gradual restoration of the Jews' civic and political rights, a process that was set in motion by a series of Habsburg military defeats, first in 1859 at the hands of France and Piedmont and then in 1866 at the hands of Prussia. These defeats forced Franz Joseph to recognize that absolutism could not guarantee the long-term survival of his empire and prompted him to make certain concessions at home. Although the Jews were not his primary concern, they were among the first to benefit from the concessions. In November 1859, special restrictions on Jewish marriage were lifted, making Jews and Christians equal in this respect. Restrictions on the ownership of real estate were finally lifted in February 1860, allowing Jews to purchase property in most of the monarchy.[14] Furthermore, the February Patent of 1861 reenfranchised men who paid at least 10 fl. in direct taxes — regardless of their religion — and allowed them to be elected to the newly reconvened provincial diets.[15] Max Gomperz, a Jewish banker in Brünn, was elected to the Moravian Diet in the same year.[16] For the Jews of the monarchy as a whole, full emancipation arrived six years later with the Austro-Hungarian Compromise (Ausgleich) of 1867. Imbued with the spirit of Liberalism, the constitutional laws of that year abolished all civic inequalities, including those that had set the Jews apart from their fellow citizens.[17] This brought full closure to one of the most important issues to emerge during the Revolution of 1848, but many internal issues that emerged at the same time still remained unresolved.

The Departure of Samson Raphael Hirsch and the Beginning of the Provisional Chief Rabbinate

Moravian Jewry suffered a major setback in 1851 when Hirsch Fassel and Samson Raphael Hirsch both accepted rabbinic posts outside Moravia, effectively orphaning the province's two largest Jewish communities and leaving Moravian Jewry without a chief rabbi. At the end of March, Fassel left Prossnitz for Nagykanizsa, Hungary, taking on a post that had previously been occupied by his friend and fellow Moravian Leopold Löw.[18] Five months later, Hirsch left Nikolsburg for Frankfurt-am-Main, becoming rabbi of the Israelitische Religionsgesellschaft (IRG), a small but wealthy Orthodox congregation that had split off from Frankfurt's larger Jewish community. Fassel's exit could have been anticipated, given that he had been applying for other rabbinic posts for nearly a decade. Hirsch's departure, however, occurred just four years after his triumphant arrival in Nikolsburg, and its suddenness left Moravian Jewry crestfallen and confused. Few could have known that he was already in the midst of negotiations for a rabbinic post in his native Hamburg when the IRG approached him in 1851.[19] Still, many must have wondered why Hirsch would abandon Moravia's 40,000 Jews and relinquish the "most important field of rabbinical activity" to become the rabbi of a small splinter group in Frankfurt.

In his study of the IRG, Robert Liberles provides a number of answers to this perplexing question.[20] While acknowledging that Hirsch's difficulties in Nikolsburg contributed to his decision to leave Moravia, Liberles pays considerably more attention to the allure of the position offered to him by the IRG. Founded in Frankfurt in 1850, the IRG was organized as an independent Orthodox congregation, separate from the official Jewish community (which had been dominated by reformers for nearly a decade). Granted permission to appoint its own rabbi, the IRG set its initial sights on Michael Sachs in Berlin, but negotiations fell through at the last minute. The IRG's attention was then directed to Hirsch by Rabbi Gerson Josaphat, Hirsch's roommate during his yeshiva days in Mannheim. In a letter to Hirsch, dated February 5, 1851, Josaphat explained that a new Orthodox community had been formed in Frankfurt, "consisting of the most honorable and wealthiest people and with the Rothschild family at their head." "The position of rabbi here is a distinguished one," he added. "The genuinely religious rabbi will find fertile ground."[21] Josaphat believed that the position was a perfect fit for Hirsch, and Hirsch was apparently in full agreement.

As Liberles points out, the position in Frankfurt appealed to Hirsch for a number of reasons. First, it meant a return to Germany, where he was more familiar with the lay of the land. Second, it meant a return to the religious struggles of the day. Moravian Jewry was riven by the tensions between Orthodoxy and Reform, but it remained on the periphery of the conflict. Frankfurt, in contrast, "threw Hirsch into the very midst of the battle and revived those inner emotions that had so moved him in his formative years."[22] Third, the IRG was a relatively cohesive and unified group of "true adherents of traditional Judaism."[23] In contrast to Moravia, where the fragmented nature of the Jewish population required Hirsch to constantly compromise and make accommodations, the monolithic IRG provided a more suitable venue for Hirsch's uncompromising temperament. A fourth reason, which Liberles does not mention, was the financial incentive. With the backing of the Rothschild family and other well-heeled Frankfurt Jews, the IRG could offer Hirsch a considerably larger salary than he received in Moravia. With a wife, five children, and an enormous ego to support, this must have made Frankfurt all the more appealing. Hirsch accepted the position without even consulting the board of the Nikolsburg Jewish community.

On May 4, Hirsch addressed a letter to the Committee for the Reorganization of Moravian Jewish Religious Affairs, announcing (and explaining) his decision to leave Moravia.[24] In words aimed more at easing his own conscience than at persuading the members of the committee, he insisted that his intentions had always been sincere: When he moved to Moravia in 1847, he had planned on staying until his "dying breath," but "the heavens" had ordained otherwise. The invitation from the IRG, he explained, was an offer he could not refuse because it was in such "perfect harmony with the holy mission" to which he had consecrated his life. Hirsch had once described Moravia in similar terms, but after his brief tenure in Nikolsburg, he changed his tune. As he explained to the members of the committee: "When I look back on the past four years, in which I was blessed with the fortune of working together with you, honorable sirs, I say with great sorrow that so few of the things that we set out to accomplish for the benefit of our brethren were ever carried out. Hardly any of them were even started, all of them have been postponed to the future." With a palpable sense of frustration, Hirsch told the committee that he had submitted his resignation to the Moravian-Silesian Governorship (Statthalterei, as the Gubernium was renamed in 1850) and planned to leave Nikolsburg by the end of July.[25]

Upon receiving Hirsch's letter, the committee wasted no time in trying to convince him to stay. On May 5, the committee sent a circular to Moravia's Jewish communities, calling on them to send representatives to Brünn on May 11–12 to discuss the matter.[26] Most of the communities—including Prossnitz—were represented by their lay leaders, who were determined to figure out the exact reasons for Hirsch's sudden resignation. Rather than second-guess the chief rabbi, the entire assembly set off for Nikolsburg on May 13 to ask him in person.[27] In the name of Moravian Jewry, the members of the assembly begged Hirsch to reconsider, drawing attention to the "great sorrow and immeasurable misfortune" that his departure would bring upon the Jews of Moravia.[28] Visibly moved, Hirsch elaborated on his decision to accept the IRG's invitation. In Frankfurt, he explained, he had been offered a field of activity that was in complete harmony with his convictions and his lifework, in contrast to Moravia, where no such field of activity existed under the current conditions. Members of the assembly interpreted this explanation to mean that Hirsch was abandoning his flock solely because he had insufficient authority over Moravian Jewry's religious and educational affairs.

In a last effort to change Hirsch's mind, the members of the assembly offered him almost everything he had ever requested during his four years in Moravia. Pending government approval, they offered to appoint him superintendent of Moravia's Jewish schools, to establish a seminary for rabbis and teachers (under his supervision), to raise his annual salary, and to transfer the seat of the chief rabbinate from Nikolsburg to Brünn (where he would be closer to Moravia's seat of government).[29] The Ministry of Religion and Education was amazed at the "extraordinary efforts" taken by Moravia's Jewish communities to retain their chief rabbi, but perhaps no one was more astonished than Hirsch himself.[30] As Liberles has pointed out, "the sudden rapprochement on the side of the communities" took Hirsch by complete surprise, even tempting him to remain in Moravia.[31] After receiving the offer, Hirsch asked the board of the IRG in Frankfurt to release him from his prior commitment, agreeing to accept their decision—be it yes or no—as binding.[32] The board rejected his request, despite repeated pleas from the Committee for the Reorganization of Moravian Jewish Religious Affairs, and Hirsch's four-year tenure in Moravia rapidly approached its end.[33] On August 12, he bid a final farewell to Moravian Jewry and set off for his new position.[34]

Shortly before leaving for Frankfurt, Hirsch made a number of suggestions regarding the post he was about to vacate.[35] He believed that a successor should eventually be elected, but only after a waiting period. Because of the religious cleavages at the time, he thought it would be impossible to find one rabbi who combined religious moderation with a thorough mastery of Jewish and general knowledge. At this juncture, he proposed that the responsibilities of the chief rabbinate be assumed not by a single individual but rather by a "collegium" consisting of three rabbis and three or four laymen. Such a collegium, he believed, would not only protect Moravia's Jewish communities from religious extremism but also prevent unqualified rabbis from obtaining posts in Moravia during the absence of a chief rabbi. He proposed that the Committee for the Reorganization of Moravian Jewish Religious Affairs—which already consisted of a mixture of rabbis and laymen—be used for this purpose.

Hirsch's departure ignited a heated debate about the future of the Moravian chief rabbinate as an institution. The debate split Moravia's Jewish communities into two opposing camps, one seeking to retain and strengthen the chief rabbinate, the other pushing for its immediate—and, to their mind, long overdue—abolition. Geographically, the two camps roughly corresponded to the two administrative districts—Brünn and Olmütz—that had replaced Moravia's six smaller administrative districts. In the Brünn district, which was dominated by Nikolsburg, most of the Jewish communities considered the chief rabbinate "absolutely necessary and beneficial" for the well-being of Moravian Jewry, especially at this crucial time of transition.[36] Now more than ever, they argued, a strong central religious authority was needed to guide Moravia's Jews into the new era. In the Olmütz district, which was dominated by Prossnitz, most of the Jewish communities strongly favored abolishing the chief rabbinate once and for all. In a petition to the Governorship, they emphatically declared that the election of a new chief rabbi was "against the loyal wishes of Moravian Jewry."[37] They insisted that a "quick look at the history of the Moravian chief rabbinate" provided ample evidence that this "wretched institution" had caused more harm than good to Moravian Jewry, particularly in its social and spiritual development. Had it not been for this institution, they claimed, Moravia's schools and synagogues would not be in such a "state of neglect," nor would sermons and decorous prayer services be such "rare occurrences" in the province. Moreover, the chief rabbinate had disrupted the traditional parity among rabbis by creating an artificial rabbinic hierarchy "with no historical basis in Judaism." This made the chief rabbinate a perennial source of controversy, which became increasingly apparent as the enmity between Reform and Orthodoxy grew in intensity. Even if a new chief rabbi were desirable, argued the Olmütz petition, it would be difficult to find someone who could bridge this chasm, win the trust of the government, *and* establish his authority in the eyes of Moravian Jewry. As the petition noted, this was particularly true at a time when Moravia's two largest Jewish communities—Nikolsburg and Prossnitz—did not even have rabbis of their own.

To a large extent, the debate over the future of the chief rabbinate was an epilogue to the ongoing conflict between Prossnitz and Nikolsburg. Nikolsburg had always prided itself on being Moravia's most important Jewish community, with its stature as a "city and mother in Israel" (*'ir v'em b'yisrael*) rooted not only in its considerable Jewish population and renowned yeshiva but also in the fact that it was the official seat of the Moravian chief rabbinate. Nikolsburg had more to lose than any other community if the chief rabbinate were to be abolished, which may explain why its board spearheaded the effort to retain—and even fortify—this institution as it came under attack by other Jewish communities.[38] Prossnitz, the largest Jewish community in the Olmütz district, had a history of challenging the supremacy of Nikolsburg and "its" chief rabbi. Indeed, Löw Schwab and Hirsch Fassel, both of whom were elected to the Prossnitz rabbinate despite strong opposition from Nehemias Trebitsch, repeatedly stood up against the chief rabbinate in Nikolsburg. Fassel, in particular, rallied his community against the "despotic" and "hierarchical" ways of both Trebitsch and Hirsch. When the debate over the future of the Moravian chief rabbinate erupted in the summer of 1851, Fassel had already freed himself from the "yoke of the chief rabbinate," but this did not prevent him from sharing his opinion on the matter. As he wrote from Nagykanizsa, "Moravia [ought to] come to its senses and petition *in unison* for the abolition of the chief rabbinate."[39]

Ultimately, the chief rabbinate was not abolished, but its stature and importance suffered irreversibly after Hirsch's resignation. This was due primarily to the Governorship's decision to fill the position of chief rabbi on a strictly provisional basis, rather than seeking a permanent replacement for Hirsch. Such a provisional position, which offered no job security, could hardly attract a rabbi of great renown, especially because the official salary was set at a mere 600 fl. per year. (By comparison, Hirsch could expect to be paid 3,500 fl. per year in Frankfurt.)[40] At the behest of Moravia's Jewish communities, the Governorship appointed Abraham Placzek, the 52-year-old rabbi of Boskowitz, to the provisional position, entrusting him with the principal duties of the chief rabbi: the examination of rabbis and religious teachers in Moravia. Placzek was a highly respected talmudist, but his other credentials left much to be desired, particularly compared with his illustrious predecessor. His shortcomings—and strengths—were detailed by a government official in Boskowitz. "Placzek is not an outstanding preacher," he wrote. "He is not a philosopher, nor does he possess higher scientific knowledge. He is, however, a talmudist without equal in Moravia. He is strictly religious and is respected *by all* rabbis in the province, because he is honest and upright and none of his deeds are tainted by self-interest."[41] After four fractious years of Hirsch the Jews of Moravia recognized that the virtues of a conciliatory figure ("respected *by all* rabbis in the province") and the promise of peace and tranquility would compensate for lack of charisma, oratory skill, and "modern" credentials.

The appointment of Abraham Placzek as chief rabbi and the ensuing transfer of the chief rabbinate to Boskowitz marked the end of an era for Nikolsburg. With the Nikolsburg local rabbinate no longer linked to the Moravian chief rabbinate, Nikolsburg could hardly attract—or afford—a rabbi with the stature it had grown so accustomed to over the preceding centuries. After Hirsch's departure, the duties of the local rabbi temporarily devolved onto four rabbinic judges until a new rabbi could be elected. The community set its sights on Simeon Sofer ("Mikhtav Sofer"), rabbi of Mattersdorf, Hungary, at the time, but this distinguished son of Moses Sofer ("Hatam Sofer") politely declined the invitation.[42] In 1855, the community finally settled on Salomon Quetsch, rabbi of Leipnik and one of Moravia's leading talmudists. A student of

Mordecai Benet, Quetsch provided a direct link to Nikolsburg's glorious past, but his brief tenure there as rabbi did not bode well for the future of the community. Only nine months into his new position, the 57-year-old rabbi suddenly passed away. Following his death, Nikolsburg's once famous yeshiva closed its doors and the Jewish community gradually declined in importance. As one contemporary observed a few years later, "Nikolsburg seems to have relinquished its centuries-long claim to primacy [among Moravia's Jewish communities]."[43]

Shifting Centers of Moravian Jewry: Brünn and Vienna

The decline of Nikolsburg was symptomatic of a larger demographic transformation in Moravia: the migration of Moravia's Jews from rural communities to the larger metropolises, both inside (Brünn) and outside (Vienna) Moravia. Jews eagerly migrated to Brünn in particular, where economic conditions were far more favorable than in Moravia's cramped Jewish quarters. Brünn was not only the administrative capital of the province but also an important center of textile production. With the mechanization of the spinning process in the first decades of the nineteenth century, Brünn's wool industry became one of the largest in Europe, employing thousands of workers and producing more than one-fourth of the monarchy's entire output of woolens in 1840.[44] The completion of the Vienna-Brünn rail connection in 1839 considerably expanded the market for these manufactured goods. Moravia's Jews played a major role in Brünn's wool industry, even though only a handful of them were officially permitted to live in the provincial capital before 1848. These "tolerated" Jews had been permitted to set up textile factories in Brünn and even live there with family members, domestic servants, and employees.[45] Alongside these individuals—who accounted for only 135 of Brünn's 17,262 inhabitants in 1834—hundreds of Moravian Jews came to Brünn every week to visit the fairs or buy goods directly from the factories.[46] Although forbidden to live in Brünn, many of these merchants stayed in its suburbs from Monday to Friday, renting rooms in Christian houses or finding lodging in the New World Inn.[47] Jews were forbidden to remain in town over the weekend, so many of them spent the Sabbath in Brünn's suburbs. The Jewish population of Brünn surged as soon as the residence restrictions were lifted, increasing more than fivefold in the first decade after the revolution, from 445 in 1848 to 2,230 by 1857.[48] Thereafter, it continued to grow, albeit at a slower pace. In 1869, Brünn's 4,505 Jews made it Moravia's single largest Jewish population center (11% of Moravia's Jewish inhabitants). In 1900, its 8,238 Jews constituted 19% of Moravia's total Jewish population.

Other Moravian towns, where Jewish settlement had been off-limits since the fifteenth and sixteenth centuries, also experienced significant Jewish population growth. Iglau, Olmütz, Mährisch-Ostrau, Ungarisch-Hradisch, and Znaim attracted Jews from nearby communities and quite often from neighboring provinces. Mährisch-Ostrau, in particular, experienced tremendous growth, thanks to the Witkowitz Ironworks (owned by Salomon von Rothschild and the Gutmann brothers in Vienna), which transformed this sleepy backwater into an important center of industry and commerce. Situated on Moravia's northeastern border, just 100 kilometers from Crakow, Mährisch-Ostrau attracted Jews (and non-Jews) from the surrounding communities and increasingly from Galicia and Hungary. The Jewish population rose from 50 or so in the 1850s to more than 4,500 in 1900, turning Mährisch-Ostrau into an important center of Jewish life in Moravia (and later in Czechoslovakia).[49]

After the revolution, Moravia's Jews also migrated in large numbers to Vienna, the center of wealth, culture, and political power in the Habsburg monarchy. Many of Moravia's Jews could trace their origins back to the Viennese expulsion in 1670, so this migration was, in some respects, a return to their roots. The Jews of Nikolsburg, in particular, had strong familial and commercial ties to Vienna, and many of them had moved there even before the revolution.[50] When Jewish residential restrictions were finally lifted in 1848, Moravian Jews flocked to Vienna with the same enthusiasm as their coreligionists from Bohemia, Galicia, and Hungary, rapidly transforming the city into the largest Jewish population center in the Habsburg monarchy.[51] Jacob and Amelie Freud made this move in 1860, leaving the village of Freiberg and taking their 2-year-old Anna and 4-year-old Sigmund to the imperial capital. By 1869, there were 7,929 Moravian Jews in Vienna, constituting almost 20% of Vienna's total Jewish population. (Their number was surpassed only by Hungarian Jews—primarily from the area of today's Slovakia—who constituted almost 44% of Vienna's Jewish population.)[52] Many of them, like the Gutmann brothers and the Mandl family, were quite prosperous.[53]

The explosive population growth in Brünn and Vienna came at the expense of Moravia's original fifty-two Jewish communities, many of which had suffered massive overcrowding before the revolution but now faced a noticeable decline in population. For example, the Jewish population in Trebitsch fell from 1,612 in 1848 to 1,528 in 1859, and Holleschau saw a decline from 1,694 to 1,600 over the same period.[54] The population decrease was even more precipitous in some of the smaller communities, such as Mährisch-Kromau (348 ➤ 276), Strassnitz (569 ➤ 396), and Kosteletz (43 ➤ 24), which lost 20%, 30%, and 45%, respectively, of their pre-1848 Jewish population in the same time period. The fate of these communities was linked to their declining economic situation—often a result of being bypassed by Moravia's expanding railway network. Koritschan was "one of Moravia's poorest Jewish communities," in the words of its board members, precisely because it was cut off from the province's railroads and other major commercial arteries.[55] By the same logic, it would stand to reason that Jewish communities situated on the rail lines would have a more positive fate. Many of these communities experienced moderate population growth in the decade after the revolution, including Lundenburg (434 ➤ 457), Bisenz (910 ➤ 965), Prerau (342 ➤ 406), and Göding (109 ➤ 205), which were all located on the Emperor Ferdinand Northern Railway.[56]

Rural Jewish Communities in Decline

As Moravia's Jews flocked to larger towns and cities, both inside and outside the province, the future of Moravia's rural Jewish communities looked increasingly grim. The communal crisis that erupted in the wake of the revolution never fully subsided, and in the 1850s and 1860s many of Moravia's communities were still tottering on the edge of insolvency and dissolution. The Provisional Regulations of September 13,

1850, were intended to prevent—or at least postpone—this seemingly inevitable fate by requiring all of Moravia's Jews, regardless of their current residence, to pay religious taxes to the Jewish religious community (*jüdische Cultusgemeinde*) to which they officially belonged in 1850. These regulations, however, proved particularly difficult to enforce because many "external" members—that is, Jews who no longer resided in a particular Jewish community but were considered members for purposes of religious taxation—simply refused to pay their taxes. This was the case with Markus Ernst Pollak, a Jew from Ungarisch-Brod who had spent most of his life in Prerau. Only after four years of appeals and counterappeals did the Ungarisch-Brod Jewish community finally succeed in collecting Pollak's overdue taxes from 1850.[57] The Loschitz Jewish community took similar pains to collect taxes from Dr. Leopold Jellinek, an external member who had relocated to Rechnitz (Rohoncz), Hungary, in 1851. Loath to pay religious taxes in two places at once, Jellinek petitioned the Governorship to officially release him from his membership in the Loschitz Jewish community.[58] When the Governorship acceded to his request in 1857, the Loschitz community appealed the decision, conjuring up a gloom-and-doom scenario in the process.[59] Not only would the loss of Jellinek's annual taxes harm the "already poor community," but the Governorship's decision would also set a precedent for other external members, who amounted to 50 of Loschitz's 120 taxpayers in 1857 and accounted for "well over a third" of the community's annual religious taxes. If these members followed Jellinek's lead, the board warned, the Loschitz community would have no choice but to dissolve itself. Equally dire sentiments were expressed by other Jewish communities, such as Koritschan, where the upkeep of religious and educational institutions was "wholly dependent on taxes paid by *external* members."[60]

Many of these external members had moved to Brünn, which was becoming the largest Jewish population center in Moravia. Although its Jewish population had reached 2,230 by 1857, none of these Jews actually belonged to the Brünn Jewish community. This was for the simple reason that Brünn had no Jewish community until 1859. Because Brünn was not one of Moravia's original fifty-two Jewish communities, it had not been designated a "Jewish religious community" by the Provisional

Regulations of September 13, 1850. As a result, the Jews of Brünn were obligated to pay for the upkeep of religious, educational, and charitable institutions in their former communities but not in their current place of residence. In an attempt to rectify this situation, in 1851 eighteen of Brünn's most prominent Jews sought permission to establish a religious community (*Cultusgemeinde*), but much to their disappointment, the Governorship granted permission to form only a religious society (*Cultusverein*). This difference was not merely semantic but had practical implications. Whereas membership in a *Cultusgemeinde* would have been compulsory for all Jews in Brünn, membership in the newly established *Cultusverein* was purely voluntary. Thus the *Cultusverein* was allowed to build a synagogue, ritual bath, and cemetery as well as hire a rabbi, religious teacher, and ritual slaughterer, but the considerable costs had to be covered by voluntary donations rather than through obligatory dues.[61]

Governor Lažansky's opposition to the establishment of a *Cultusgemeinde* in Brünn reflected a deep concern for the well-being of Moravia's fifty-two Jewish communities, whose tax revenues were dwindling as the wealthiest members moved away. Because the Jews of Brünn were the main lifeline for many of these communities, Lažansky feared that the establishment of a compulsory *Cultusgemeinde* would simply hasten their disintegration. As he explained to Minister of Religion and Education Leo von Thun in 1851, "Should a formal Jewish *Cultusgemeinde* be constituted in Brünn, the taxes that the Israelites in Brünn currently pay to their original religious communities will completely dry up. The damage to these communities will be all the more grievous, because the Israelites living here [in Brünn] are quite well-off and therefore pay the highest taxes to their former religious communities."[62] Lažansky's main concern was for the Jews in Moravia's original fifty-two communities; he did not seem to think that the outflow of taxes would impede the development of Brünn's religious, educational, and charitable institutions. Indeed, with the establishment of a voluntary *Cultusverein*, the Jews of Brünn could raise funds for their own institutional needs.

Officially constituted in 1852, the Israelite Religious Society of Brünn (Brünner Israelitischer Cultusverein) successfully laid the groundwork for Jewish religious life in the provincial capital. In its first year, the Society purchased land for a Jewish cemetery and established a *ḥevrah kadisha* (burial society).[63] In the following year, it received permission from the government to build a synagogue, the first one in Brünn since the fifteenth century. Designed by the celebrated Viennese architects Schwendenwein and Romano and dedicated by Isak Noa Mannheimer in 1855, this magnificent Neo-Romanesque edifice was a striking symbol of Brünn Jewry's towering ambitions (Figure 10).[64] The enormous cost of the synagogue, however, also served as a reminder of the Israelite Religious Society's unfortunate financial situation.[65] Lacking any mechanism or authority to collect taxes from the Jews of Brünn, the Society had to rely for the most part on the largesse of its members—who numbered only fifty-eight at the end of 1858. To make matters worse, the Society's "all too precarious existence"—in the words of one contemporary—made it nearly impossible to attract a rabbi of any stature.[66] In the face of these obstacles, in 1858 the members of the Society submitted a

Figure 10. Synagogue in Brünn, 1863. Courtesy of Brno City Archive, II.b.12.

request to be recognized once and for all as a *Cultusgemeinde*. This time their efforts met with greater success. On February 7, 1859, the Ministry of Religion and Education finally granted their request despite Governor Lažansky's continued opposition.[67]

The establishment of a *Cultusgemeinde* was a victory for Brünn Jewry, but it also exacerbated tensions between Brünn and the original fifty-two Jewish communities. After the Jews of Brünn were officially released from paying taxes to their former communities on March 15, 1860, the boards of four Moravian Jewish communities issued a formal protest against the government's decision to allow the establishment of a new *Cultusgemeinde*.[68] Significantly, the protest came not from the smaller communities, such as Loschitz and Koritschan, but from the largest and most distinguished ones: Nikolsburg, Prossnitz, Boskowitz, and Kremsier. More than any other communities, they stood to lose not only their wealthiest taxpayers but also their centuries-old stature as Moravia's most important centers of Jewish life and learning. Indeed, with the rise of Brünn, the parvenu among Moravia's venerable Jewish communities, Moravian Jewry underwent a profound and lasting change.[69] For the first time in its history, Moravian Jewry could be conceived of in terms of center and periphery. This dichotomy found expression in a Viennese Jewish weekly, which increasingly distinguished between Brünn on the one hand and the "rural communities" (*Landgemeinden*) on the other. Among these rural communities were not only the diminutive Pohrlitz, Battelau, and Bisenz but also Nikolsburg, former seat of the Moravian chief rabbinate.[70]

Despite the gloom-and-doom predictions, the establishment of a *Cultusgemeinde* in Brünn did not send Moravia's fifty-two Jewish communities into an uncontrollable downward spiral, nor did the subsequent establishment of new *Cultusgemeinden* in Iglau (1862), Znaim (1870), Mährisch-Ostrau (1875), Olmütz (1892), Ungarisch-Hradisch (1892), and Wallachisch-Meseritsch (1892), all of which, like Brünn, had initially been constituted as *Cultusvereine* in the 1850s and 1860s. The Jewish communities remained solvent in large part because of the foresight of the Ministry of the Interior, which, on October 21, 1857, decreed that subsidies for Moravia's rabbis, religious teachers, cantors, and ritual slaughterers (and pensions for their wives) could be taken out of the Moravian Jewish Landesmassafond. Thus Moravia's religious functionaries could still be paid, even if individual communities lacked the financial resources to cover their salaries.

The Moravian Jewish Landesmassafond:
Symbol and Savior

The Landesmassafond played a central role in averting the almost certain dissolution of Moravia's rural Jewish communities, and it also emerged as an important symbol of Moravian Jewish solidarity at a crucial moment in time. At the end of the 1850s, the future of the Landesmassafond came into question, just as it had in the immediate aftermath of the revolution. Predictably, the Finance Ministry proposed that the fund be channeled into the state coffers (and dedicated to Emperor Franz Joseph), but most state officials—in both Vienna and Brünn—believed that it should remain the collective property of Moravian Jewry.[71] The ensuing debate did not concern ownership of the fund per se but rather who should be entrusted with administering its sizable capital. Ever since the creation of the Landesmassafond in 1787, the Gubernium (and from 1850, the Governorship) had administered it on behalf of Moravian Jewry. After the Moravian Diet was elected in March 1861 (for the first time since the revolution), some of its members argued that the Landesmassafond should be placed in their trusteeship. Although Moravia's Jews were not always content with the way in which the Governorship administered the fund, the prospect of the Diet taking control prompted some of them to action.[72] On April 27, 1862, representatives from forty-five Jewish communities assembled in Brünn's recently built synagogue to discuss the future of the Landesmassafond.[73] They proposed that the fund be administered by elected representatives of Moravian Jewry and be used exclusively for religious and educational purposes.[74] Despite opposition from members of the Diet, the Governorship supported this position, noting in 1863 that the Landesmassafond was the "legal expression of the will of Moravian Jewry."[75]

Determining the collective will of Moravian Jewry, however, was no simple matter. When the Governorship asked Moravia's fifty-three

Jewish religious communities (i.e., the original fifty-two plus Brünn) to express their wishes regarding the future uses of the Landesmassafond, their responses varied widely. Some responses focused on the particular needs of individual communities, whereas others were more concerned about the well-being of Moravian Jewry as a whole. For example, one proposal recommended dividing the fund proportionally among the original fifty-two Jewish communities based on their population size before the revolution. Other proposals suggested establishing new institutions that would serve the collective needs of Moravia's Jewish communities, such as a teachers' seminary, an orphanage, or a scholarship fund for rabbinical students.[76] The contemporary Jewish press, which featured extensive discussions on the future of the Landesmassafond, was highly critical of the "separatist" or "crassly egoistic" proposals that placed the financial interests of individual communities above the "moral-religious" interests of Moravian Jewry.[77] Contributors to *Die Neuzeit*, in particular, hoped that the Landesmassafond—and its elected board of Jewish trustees—would emerge as the expression and guarantor of a cohesive and unifying Moravian Jewish identity.[78]

At the behest of the Ministry of the Interior, Moravia's religious Jewish communities elected delegates to an assembly in Brünn that was invested with the authority to determine the future of the Landesmassafond. When the assembly met on November 17, 1868, it was the first time that such a representative body had been convened since Hirsch had invited delegates to deliberate on the common affairs of Moravian Jewry in 1849–50. The new assembly, however, differed from its predecessor because it marked the establishment of a formal institutional framework for the expression of Moravian Jewry's collective will. Indeed, the fifty-two delegates unanimously decided not only to keep the fund's capital intact (rather than divide it up among the individual religious communities) but also to establish two permanent bodies—a general assembly and a board of trustees—to manage its use.[79] The general assembly, consisting of elected delegates from each of Moravia's religious communities, would meet every three years in Brünn to discuss general fund-related issues and to elect an eleven-member board of trustees that would have direct responsibility for the administration of the fund as well as the allocation of its annual revenues. The board would meet in Brünn three times a year to decide which individuals, institutions, and communities were entitled to financial assistance from the "indivisible and inalienable patrimony of Moravian Jewry."[80]

Although established for the singular task of administering the Landesmassafond, the general assembly also played an important role in unifying Moravia's increasingly fragmented Jewish population. Elected every three years, it provided a regular forum for the disparate religious communities to come together as one and discuss their common interests and concerns. More important, it allowed all the communities, regardless of their size, to meet on equal terms. The centrality of Brünn was self-evident—both the general assembly and the board of trustees met there—but the Brünn Jewish community wielded no more influence than Moravia's smaller and less prominent communities. In fact, each religious community, from tiny Koritschan to the more sizable Nikolsburg, had but one delegate—and one vote—in the general assembly.[81] Furthermore, because the general assembly did not sit atop a highly ramified bureaucracy—as would have been the case with Hirsch's proposed Landessynagogenrath—it was perceived as neither "dictatorial" nor "hierarchical." Because it had no legislative, executive, or judicial powers and—most important—no authority to levy taxes, it did not constitute a threat to communal autonomy. To a large extent, the general assembly's most important function was as a symbol of unity and cohesion. In the words of one observer, this new representative body helped instill in Moravian Jewry a "spirit of community" and a "sense of solidarity" that had been waning ever since the revolution.[82]

The triennial assembly meeting provided a forum to discuss the collective affairs of Moravian Jewry, with the agenda usually set by the eleven-member board of trustees. After the revolution, Moravian Jewry's communal affairs had fallen into disarray, and although the Landesmassafond provided a modicum of relief, the situation had become increasingly untenable as old rural communities steadily declined and new urban communities rose to greater prominence. In the early 1870s, trustees of the Landesmassafond called for the adoption of new uniform communal statutes that would reorganize inter- and intracommunal affairs in light of this shifting demographic balance.[83]

In 1876, the board drafted and circulated model statutes (*Muster-statut*), which were discussed in the contemporary press and at the Landesmassafond general assembly in Brünn.[84] The statutes envisioned the division of Moravian Jewry into geographically demarcated "community districts" (*Gemeinde-Gebiete*), which would encompass Moravia's entire territory, not just the traditional sites of Jewish settlement. Jews would belong to the community district in which they resided; for purposes of membership and taxation, each community district would constitute a single religious community, with the hope that this new arrangement would finally put an end to the confusion that had been such a disruptive feature of Moravian Jewish life since the revolution.

The statutes, however, did not garner widespread support, and another sixteen years passed before Moravian Jewry's communal affairs were finally reorganized. In 1892 (on the basis of an 1890 law), the state officially recognized fifty religious communities (thirty-nine historical ones and eleven that had been created since 1859) and dissolved twelve communities—including Irritz, Kosteletz, and Puklitz—where Jews could hardly be found by that point.[85] (Hotzenplotz was assigned to Austrian Silesia, where ten religious communities were recognized.)[86] In the spirit of the proposed statutes from 1876, the dissolved communities were merged with the nearby religious communities, creating community districts that could adapt to the shifting demographics of Moravian Jewry.

Various groups, however, criticized the 1876 statutes. Some criticized them for inadequately addressing the concerns of Moravia's small Jewish communities in decline. Others criticized them for placing too much power in the hands of the lay community boards, thereby turning rabbis into "marionettes" and creating a "hierarchy of the incompetent and half-educated."[87] This second criticism was reminiscent of reactions to Hirsch's *Synagogue Constitution*, except that in 1849–50, the chief rabbi stood at the top of the hierarchy, whereas in 1876 it was the eleven "businessmen" (*Kaufleute*) on the board of the Landesmassafond.[88] This was a fitting metaphor for the changes that had occurred in the quarter-century since the revolution.

Non-Jews also took an interest in the proposed statutes because the reorganization of Jewish communal life had potential reverberations for

Moravia as a whole. "No politician can remain indifferent," observed Vienna's *Neue Freie Presse*, reminding its readers that Moravia's idiosyncratic Jewish community regulations had inadvertently turned Moravia's Jews into political "kingmakers."[89] The Viennese newspaper was referring to Moravia's political Jewish communities, which had become a perennial source of contention in the political sphere but were unaddressed by the proposed statutes, which dealt with only "religious" communities, not "political" ones.

Political Jewish Communities

The political Jewish communities (*politische Judengemeinden*; PJCs) were separate and distinct from the Jewish religious communities (*jüdische Cultusgemeinden*) even though both derived from the autonomous Jewish community (*kehillah*) that had been the locus of Jewish life from medieval times until the Age of Emancipation. These communities should have been dissolved in 1849 and incorporated into the neighboring (and often interlocking) Christian towns, as a necessary step toward fully integrating Jews into the surrounding society. With the outbreak of anti-Jewish violence in 1850, however, the Gubernium permitted twenty-five of the fifty-two Jewish communities to remain as separate municipalities. (Two more communities were reconstituted as PJCs in 1867, bringing the total number to twenty-seven.) These communities remained administratively separate entities, with their own elected officials (including mayor), police departments, and, in Boskowitz, even a volunteer fire brigade.[90] These "Jewish townships," as Jacob Toury called them, remained a locus of Jewish political activity until they were dissolved between 1919 and 1924 by the newly established Czechoslovak Republic.[91]

Many viewed the PJCs as a retrograde outcome of the anti-Jewish hostilities that swept Moravia in 1850. In the mid-1880s, nearly forty years after the Revolution of 1848 and nearly twenty years after the emancipation of Habsburg Jewry, a Prague-based Jewish almanac lamented their seemingly atavistic survival, decrying them as an unfortunate reminder of the "ghetto period." From the almanac's perspective, the PJC constituted a "community within a community" or even a "state within a state," thereby perpetuating the "exceptional status" (*Sonderstellung*) of the Jews that was supposed to have disappeared with emancipation.[92] Two decades later, the almanac's criticism remained just as sharp. "In Moravia," it observed, "the Jews are still unable to part from their ghettos, which live on under the banner of 'Jewish political communities'; giving up their own mayor's office and all of the other honorary offices causes [them] such pain."[93]

Moravian Jewry and the Czech-German Conflict

By the end of the nineteenth century, the Czech-German conflict had become the defining feature of Moravia's economic, political, and cultural life, and the Czech national movement despised the PJCs as an obstacle to Czech national ambitions in Moravia. Czech national consciousness developed later in Moravia than in Bohemia, and the German minority retained political and economic power much longer, creating a delicate balance that sometimes gave the PJCs a decisive role in elections and other flash points between Moravia's increasingly aggressive Czech and German movements.

As late as the Revolution of 1848, national consciousness had been rather muted among the inhabitants of Moravia, especially in comparison to neighboring Bohemia. At the time, a regional and *supra*national "Moravian" identity still proved stronger than both the "Czech" national identity promoted by the St. Václav Committee in Prague and the "German" identity promoted by the Vienna-based League of Germans from Bohemia, Moravia, and Silesia for the Preservation of Their Nationality. By the 1860s, however, the all-encompassing "Moravian" regional identity gradually gave way to two mutually exclusive national identities—"Czech" and "German"—each supported by its own schools, theaters, social clubs, professional organizations, and so on. Czech-German distinctions came to dominate public life in Moravia to such an extent that seemingly personal decisions—such as school choice, theater attendance, and club membership—assumed paramount importance in the increasingly volatile nationality conflict.[94] Elections frequently served as flash points in the conflicts as Czechs and Germans vied for influence not only in the Austrian Parliament and Moravian Diet but also in the municipal councils, local school boards, and chambers of commerce in Brünn and Olmütz.

Although Czech speakers constituted approximately 70% of Moravia's population in the second half of the nineteenth century, Moravia's Jews consistently sided with—and cast their lot with—the German-speaking minority.[95] This trend can be explained in part by the general linguistic, cultural, and political predilections of Habsburg Jewry as a whole. Like their coreligionists in Bohemia and Lower Austria (and to some extent Hungary and Galicia), Moravia's Jews underwent a process of linguistic and cultural Germanization in the first half of the nineteenth century, fostered in part by the German-Jewish schools that had been set up under Joseph II. As the language of government, large-scale commerce, and higher education, German enjoyed a prestige that was unrivaled by any other language of the Habsburg monarchy, making it all the more attractive to Jewish inhabitants. Czech, in contrast, was often seen as a provincial language with little or no practical use. A Jewish parent from Pirnitz, for example, wondered why Jewish school-children should "waste their time with the useless Bohemian language," arguing that German was much more useful for a people of trade and commerce like the Jews.[96] As a Moravian German paper noted in 1872, Jewish communities were "morally obligated" (*moralisch gezwungen*) to maintain their own German schools; otherwise they would have to send their German-speaking children to "Bohemian schools."[97] German had become the lingua franca of Central Europe's Jews, who tended to view it as a supranational language of culture, enlightenment, and commerce, not as a "national" idiom. Moreover, Jews often associated German with the spirit of Josephinism (which had brought the Edicts of Tolerance in the 1780s) and with the forces of Liberalism (which had brought emancipation in 1849 and again in 1867).[98]

The Jews of Moravia retained their allegiance to German language, culture, and politics much longer than their coreligionists in neighboring Bohemia, primarily because Moravia's Germans—in contrast to their counterparts in Bohemia—held on to economic and political power until the beginning of the twentieth century. Unlike the Bohemian Diet, which passed into Czech hands in 1865, the Moravian Diet retained its German majority until the Moravian Compromise of 1905. The situation was similar on the municipal level. In Bohemia, Czechs gained a majority in the Prague and Pilsen municipal councils in the 1860s, whereas in Moravia, Germans retained control of the Brünn, Olmütz, and Mährisch-Ostrau municipal councils until the end of World War I.[99] Moravia's Germans—who constituted only 30% of the total population—owed their political dominance to an 1861 electoral law that was specifically designed "to create an artificial German majority" in provinces with mixed German-Slavic populations.[100] This law placed Moravia's PJCs on the front line of the Czech-German conflict.

The electoral law of 1861 gave the PJCs disproportionate influence in elections to the Moravian Diet, often enabling Jewish voters to cast the deciding ballot in closely contested races between Czech and German candidates. Drafted by Minister of State Anton von Schmerling, the law aimed to secure German dominance in the provincial diets, which was particularly challenging in such places as Moravia, where there were twice as many Czechs as Germans. Schmerling managed to accomplish his goal only through a kind of gerrymandering that was frequently derided as "electoral geometry" (*Wahlgeometrie*). His electoral law set up a rural curia, an urban curia, a curia for great landowners, and later, a curia for the chambers of commerce. In his efforts to ensure a German majority, Schmerling manipulated the urban curia in particular, factoring the PJCs into his equation.[101]

Because of their relatively small size, the PJCs could have belonged to the rural curia, but Schmerling placed twenty-two of them in the urban curia, where they could have more of an electoral impact. If Jews had been placed in the Czech-dominated rural curia, their votes would have made little difference. In the highly contested urban curia, however, their votes could—and in certain cases did—tip the scales in favor of German candidates. The Jewish vote was decisive in a number of close elections, leading Czech nationalists to view the PJCs as "rotten, backward bastions of German domination" in an increasingly turbulent Czech sea.[102]

To make matters worse, Jews eventually came to constitute a minority in many of the PJCs. As Jews moved out of the rural communities, they often rented their former homes to "Czech lower middle-class elements and working class people," making Czech-speaking Christians the majority population in many of the PJCs.[103] In 1900, only thirteen of the twenty-seven PJCs still had a Jewish majority.[104] Nevertheless, Jews retained political power in these communities because property owners and taxpayers in the PJCs retained the right to vote there, generating resentment on the part of the Czech inhabitants, whose interests were not always represented by their Germanized Jewish landlords.

From the 1870s onward, Czech leaders repeatedly tried to have the PJCs dissolved or assigned to the rural curia, where the Jewish vote would lose its weight amid the overwhelmingly large Czech population. In 1876, the town of Gaya tried to strike inhabitants of the Gaya PJC from its voting rosters, and in 1879, eleven Moravian towns—including Gaya—contested the results of the Austrian parliamentary elections, arguing that seven PJCs had "illegally" voted in the urban curia.[105] The catalyst for this protest was the election of Rudolf Auspitz, a Jewish deputy from the Nikolsburg voting district and a member of the German Liberal Party.[106] A decade later, when a Czech leader again sought to dissolve Moravia's PJCs, a contemporary newspaper explained that Czechs saw it as the only way they could win in a voting district that favored German candidates.[107]

The Czech-Jewish movement, which emerged in Bohemia in the mid-1870s, viewed the PJCs as an impediment to the full integration of Jews into the majority population and repeatedly called for the dissolution of this "Moravian curiosity." In general, leaders of the Czech-Jewish movement in Bohemia were frustrated by the pronounced German proclivities of their coreligionists in Moravia, and despite attempts to attract adherents, they failed to establish a foothold in Moravia until the eve of World War I. (Moravia's first Czech-Jewish organization was established in 1913.)[108] At the turn of the century, Bohemian-based Czech-Jewish newspapers, such as *Českožidovské listy* (Czech-Jewish Press), *Rozvoj* (Development), and *Kalendář česko-židovský* (Czech-Jewish Almanac), regularly complained about Moravian Jewry's indifference to the Czech national cause and relentlessly criticized their allegiance to German language, culture, and politics.[109] A 1910 article in *Kalendář česko-židovský*, titled the "Czech-Jewish movement in

Moravia," concluded that Moravia did not have a Czech-Jewish movement at all. Comparing Bohemia and Moravia, the article made the following observation.

> Admittedly, in Bohemia we also have Budweis, where the Czech majority is dominated by the German minority, but what is that compared to Mährisch-Ostrau, Leipnik, Místek, Lundenburg, and other Moravian towns! The Jews of Moravia deserve credit for the sad fact that the Czech land of Moravia, which is in reality more Czech than Bohemia [čestější než Čechy], has had a strong German color until now. The Moravian Jew is viewed as a Jew who is not a German, as something abnormal. The Jewish political communities, where official business is conducted in German, are another Moravian curiosity. The Czech majority in the Moravian Diet should be able to dissolve these communities, which constitute an artificial barrier between the Jewish and non-Jewish inhabitants and make it easier for the Jews to stubbornly persist in their ancestral vices, in particular, Germanization.[110]

In addition to attacking the PJCs, the Czech-Jewish movement relentlessly criticized Moravia's German-Jewish schools, which offered instruction in German. (Only in Trebitsch was there a Jewish school that offered instruction in Czech as well.)[111] Czech nationalists, who expended considerable energy and vitriol in their effort to promote Czech schooling, viewed German-Jewish schools as "a dangerous lever in the Germanization of Czech cities and communities" and sought to convince parents to send their children to Czech schools instead.[112] A Prague-based Czech-Jewish association echoed this sentiment, accusing Jews who sent their offspring to German schools of "educat[ing] their children to be enemies of the Czech nation."[113] Similar sentiments were expressed regarding Moravia's network of German-Jewish schools, especially because they attracted non-Jewish students in the last two decades of the nineteenth century. As Czech speakers moved into formerly German-speaking towns and as German speakers became an ever more embattled minority, Jewish schools were often the only German-language schools that remained. At the school in Nikolsburg, for example, only 104 of 325 students were Jews in 1897, and in the same year, this formally "Jewish" school hired a Christian head teacher.[114] The Viennese Jewish *Österreichische Wochenschrift* recalled

Nikolsburg's glorious past as a "secure fortress of Judaism in Moravia" and lamented that "the majority of the children at this *Jewish* school belong to the Christian confession."[115] On a symbolic level, the German-Jewish schools remained a Jewish territory, even as they attracted an increasingly Christian student body and even as Jews increasingly attended non-Jewish schools. As such, they remained a perennial target for Czech nationalists of all confessions. When the Jewish school in Ungarish-Brod began offering Czech as an elective course in 1894, *Českožidovské listy* noted that "we should not underestimate this. It is a sign of progress that students can study Czech at all."[116]

As patrons of German schools and kingmakers in close elections, Moravia's Jews incurred the wrath of Czech nationalists who viewed them as "victorious troopers of the German minority" in Moravia.[117] In the last decade of the nineteenth century, Moravia's Jews paid dearly for their perceived allegiance to German language, culture, and politics, suffering economically from anti-German boycotts and falling victim to anti-German violence wherever it occurred. In the fall of 1899, for example, the repeal of the Badeni language ordinance set off a wave of anti-German (and anti-Jewish) violence in the Bohemian Lands. Promulgated in 1897, the Badeni language ordinance had been perceived as a victory for the Czechs because it required all civil servants in the Bohemian Lands to be proficient in both German and Czech, thereby privileging Czech speakers, who were more likely to be bilingual. Following its repeal two years later, Czechs vented their anger at the German-speaking population, targeting Jews in particular. Between October and December 1899, 265 incidents were reported in the Bohemian Lands, 200 of them in Moravia.[118] The majority of the incidents were overtly anti-Jewish, particularly in Holleschau, Wsetin, and Prerau, where the worst violence occurred. (The anti-Jewish sentiment was also fueled by a ritual murder accusation in nearby Polná, which had led to the conviction of Leopold Hilsner, a Jew, in September 1899.)[119]

Ironically, Moravia's Jews were attacked as "Germans" just as Moravia's German Liberal Party began to abandon its most loyal supporters. The German Liberals died a slower death in Moravia than elsewhere in the Habsburg monarchy, thanks in part to the Jewish vote. In the mid-1890s, however, they began to form political alliances with other German parties, such as the avowedly antisemitic German National Party, leading many Jews to question their own knee-jerk support for a party that was now working against them. Although many Jews continued to support the German Liberals, others voted for Czech candidates or simply abstained from voting altogether. In 1895, the general assembly of the Landesmassafond attempted to devise a common strategy for dealing with the deteriorating situation: sending "threatening letters" to German deputies from districts where Jews were a potential swing vote. If the German deputies refused to take a "different stance" toward antisemitism, the letter warned, Jews would abstain from the upcoming election and thereby guarantee a Czech victory.[120]

By the end of the nineteenth century, Moravia's Jews had become "reluctant kingmakers." They were often able to tip the electoral scales, but it was not always in their interests to do so.[121] At first, the Moravian Compromise of 1905, which introduced *national* voting curiae (and voting lists), seemed to promise some relief. According to Paragraph 30, "eligible voters who belong neither to the Czech nor the German nationality" were to be placed on the voting list of the majority of voters in a given town, meaning that Jews would be registered as Czechs where there was a Czech majority and as Germans where there was a German one. Like other Moravian voters, Jews could also switch lists if they could demonstrate that they had been registered on the wrong one. With individual Jews now forced to choose between the two camps, a German Liberal deputy from Brünn hoped that individual Jews would finally be recognized as a "constituent element of the German or Czech people [*Volkstum*]." As such, he reasoned, they would no longer occupy the ambiguous—and increasingly precarious—middle ground between two belligerent nationalities.[122]

Others were less optimistic, pointing out that the Moravian Compromise treated the Jews as "nonexistent" and would actually worsen their plight. "It would be a fatal mistake to believe that the national battle-ax is finally buried and the Jews are henceforth removed . . . from the nationality conflict," wrote a Moravian Zionist who feared that the national voting lists could be used as "blacklists" in the economic boycotts.[123] From his perspective, the Moravian Compromise "jerked" Moravia's

Jews into "nationally foreign" voting lists and "neutralized" them in the political sphere. Now that they had lost their kingmaker status, they were caught between two warring camps with no political capital at all.

For some Jews, Zionism presented an escape from the Czech-German conflict, and the Moravian Compromise offered a potential framework for recognizing a separate Jewish nationality—with its own voting list and cultural institutions. Zionists and other Jewish nationalists viewed Moravia's PJCs as a convenient basis for a Jewish national curia and began to embrace them as a rare expression of Jewish political autonomy in the Diaspora. Although Czech Jews often decried the PJCs as atavistic reminders of the "ghetto period," some Zionists saw them as instrumental in preserving and reinforcing a distinctly "national" identity and tried in vain to transform them into a Jewish national curia. The historian Ruth Kestenberg-Gladstein has argued that the PJCs helped "imbue the Jews with a strong sense of self-respect," explaining why "Jewish students from Moravia were among the first followers of Theodor Herzl."[124] One of these students, the Brünn-born Robert Stricker (1879–1944), may have had Moravia's Czech-German conflict in mind when he insisted that a Zionist cannot under any circumstances be a member of a non-Jewish national movement.[125]

As the Czech-German conflict rose to a feverish pitch in the last decades of the nineteenth century, Moravia's Jews increasingly sought an escape from the economic boycotts and anti-German violence that befell them. Stricker was one of many Jews who left Moravia at the turn of the century, contributing to the steady decline in Moravia's Jewish population. From a peak of 45,324, or 2% of Moravia's total inhabitants, in 1890, Moravia's Jewish population declined to 44,225 (1.82%) in 1900 and to 41,255 (1.57%) in 1910.[126] For Stricker and others who left, the most popular destination was Vienna.

Moravian Jews in Vienna

At the turn of the century, Vienna was home to more Moravian Jews than either Brünn or Mährisch-Ostrau. Thanks to short distances and easy rail access, the move to Vienna did not entail severing ties with native communities, and Jews could visit friends and family on a regular basis, celebrating Jewish festivals and special occasions with them. They could also be buried in their ancestral communities rather than in Vienna's Jewish cemeteries.

Like other Jewish immigrants to Vienna, Jews from Moravia established *Landsmannschaften* (hometown societies) to provide sickness and death benefits for members and humanitarian aid to the communities from whence they came.[127] Such organizations not only reinforced the immigrants' ties to their places of origin but also helped to create a social network that bound them together as a discrete community in Vienna. Moravian Jews in Vienna tended to live in close proximity to one another, not only gravitating to the same districts but also to the same neighborhoods.[128] As Tina Walzer has demonstrated, this tendency was even more pronounced among Jewish immigrants from Moravia than among their counterparts from Bohemia.[129] This difference, she has speculated, can be explained by the different experiences they had before moving to Vienna. Unlike the Bohemian Jews, who came mostly from Prague and were more familiar with urban life, the Moravian Jews tried to preserve the "social proximity" of their small, compact communities of origin. This allowed them to uphold cultural traditions and maintain social contacts that would have otherwise been lost in the hustle and bustle of the Viennese metropolis.[130]

Although Vienna's proximity to Moravia allowed these transplanted Jews to retain a link to their ancestral communities, these very communities ceased to be recognizable as the ones they had left behind. The palpable passing of an era prompted a number of Moravian Jews to commit the recent past to writing, preserving it for posterity before it slipped irretrievably away. Already in the 1860s, Eduard Kulke (Nikolsburg 1831–Vienna 1897), a grandson of Chief Rabbi Nehemias Trebitsch, chose the medium of fiction to conjure up images of Moravian Jewish life in the first half of the nineteenth century.[131] Modeled after Leopold Kompert's *Ghettogeschichten* (Ghetto tales), many of Kulke's stories centered around the *arrendator* and the *Hausierer*, two of Moravian Jewry's most representative figures before the Revolution of 1848. Toward the end of his life, Isaac Hirsch Weiss (Gross-Meseritsch 1815–Vienna 1905), a student of Nehemias Trebitsch and a leading scholar of rabbinic Judaism, wrote an autobiography that constitutes one of the most important sources for the history of Moravian Jewry in the first half of the nineteenth century. Published in 1895, long after Moravia's last yeshivas had shut down, Weiss's autobiography is an elegy to the dynamic rabbinic culture that characterized the Moravia of his youth.[132] Works of historiography written in this period served a similarly elegiac function, glorifying the social and spiritual life of Moravian Jewry on the one hand while bidding it a solemn farewell on the other. Many of these works took the form of communal histories, a particularly apt genre when one considers that throughout much of the eighteenth and nineteenth centuries, residential, occupational, and matrimonial rights had been inextricably linked to membership in one of Moravia's fifty-two Jewish communities.[133] This historiographic trend reached its culmination with the publication in 1929 of *The Jews and Jewish Communities of Moravia in the Past and Present*, a 623-page collection of communal profiles written by Moravian Jews residing in both Moravia and Vienna. As the editor noted in the preface, the publication of this book was motivated by "the consideration that, in a short time, our rural communities will disappear entirely as a result of depopulation and dissolution." "At this last moment," he continued, "we must do our utmost so that we can at least save the Jewish national heritage [*Volksgut*] through image and word and preserve it for posterity."[134]

Conclusion

A year before the publication of *The Jews and Jewish Communities of Moravia*, Louis Ginzberg published a short biography of Isaac Hirsch Weiss (1815–1905), who had spent the last forty years of his long life at Vienna's Beth ha-Midrash, a rabbinic academy founded by his fellow Moravian Adolf Jellinek. Like Adolf Jellinek, Moritz Steinschneider, Leopold Löw, and many of their childhood friends, Weiss had spent his formative years in Moravia's (and Hungary's) celebrated yeshivas but rose to prominence only after leaving the land of his birth. In Weiss's youth, Moravia's Jews were beset by myriad restrictions that led many of them to seek their livelihoods—and spouses—outside Moravia's borders. The

restrictions were lifted during the Revolution of 1848 and then again in
the 1860s, but other factors—such as the irresistible allure of Vienna or
the insurmountable pressure of the Czech-German conflict—contributed to the continued outward migration. Nevertheless, Moravia's Jews
retained close ties to their native communities, and, as Ginzberg has
argued, unmistakable elements of their Moravian upbringing.

> The life of Isaac Hirsch Weiss reflects the Jewish history of his native
> land, Moravia. Only Moravia could produce the historian of Jewish
> tradition. Germany had no men who possessed the requisite talmudic-
> rabbinic knowledge, and Poles, as a result of their one-sided talmudic
> education, lacked system and clearness. The life history of this great
> scholar assumes even greater importance if one recalls that it is the his-
> tory of a man who has lived ninety years. He is not only the greatest
> Jew of Moravia, but the last representative of "geographical Judaism."[135]

Fittingly, the term *geographical Judaism* was coined in a review of
Weiss's scholarly masterpiece *Dor Dor ve'Dorshav* (known by its English
title *The History of Jewish Tradition*) to indicate that each Jewish community developed "an individuality and character of its own, reflecting
the thought and habits of the country which it represents."[136] In Ginzberg's flowery portrait of Weiss, one can identify what he considers the
"individuality and character" of Moravian Jewry: a perfect synthesis of
East and West—a balancing act between "the requisite talmudic knowledge" on the one hand and a "system of clearness" on the other. In
other words, Moravian Jewry's salient feature in the nineteenth century
was its characteristic moderation in an age of religious, ideological, and
political ferment.

   This balancing act was sustained to a large extent by the illiberal
politics of the absolutist state. The manifold restrictions on residence,
livelihood, movement, and marriage may have placed undue pressures
on Moravia's Jews, but these same measures also enabled "small country towns" such as Holleschau, Prossnitz, Triesch, and Ungarisch-Brod
to flourish as important centers of Jewish life and learning in Central
Europe's ramified network of Jewish communities. The repeal of these
restrictions marked the dawning of a new age for Moravia's Jews, opening up new occupational and residential opportunities and paving the
way for fuller participation in public life. Emancipation, however, came

at a price, and the post-1848 Jewish communal crisis was only one indication that the "sacred and holy" were suddenly at risk of being "buried in the sunlight of freedom." Repeated efforts to reorganize Moravia's Jewish communal life—and thereby avert the collapse of its venerable religious institutions—inevitably raised profound questions about the nature of Moravian Jewry as a whole. These questions were further complicated by the anomalous coexistence of religious and political Jewish communities, each semantically underscoring a different—and conflicting—understanding of the Moravian Jewish collectivity.

In theory, emancipation had transformed Moravia's Jews into Jewish Moravians, but ironically, this occurred just as the regional and *supra*national Moravian identity began to give way to mutually exclusive Czech and German national identities. Jewish Moravians, who suddenly found themselves in a bind, often took sides in the Czech-German conflict, but they just as often tried to escape from it. Some affirmed a Jewish "national" identity, which may have been preserved and reinforced by Moravia's Jewish schools and political Jewish communities. Others left Moravia entirely, becoming the *Emigranten* of the late nineteenth century. Unlike their forebears who moved to Hungary to escape hardships that were later eased by emancipation, these *Emigranten* moved to Vienna to escape hardships that stemmed from emancipation. They did not set up daughter communities, but they did establish *Landsmannschaften* (hometown societies) in Vienna, which reinforced ties to the small country towns that had been the locus of Moravian Jewish life since the sixteenth century. By the beginning of the twentieth century, all that remained of the compact and cohesive constellation of Jewish communities that had characterized Moravia for centuries were the bittersweet and nostalgic memories of these *Emigranten* and their counterparts who stayed in Moravia, predominantly in Brünn, Mährisch-Ostrau, and other cities that had once been forbidden to Jews. Their offspring, such as Stefan Zweig, often romanticized this "world of yesterday," allowing the conflicts and hardships that permeated Moravian Jewish life in the preceding centuries to fade into distant memory.

Reference Matter

Appendix 1
Moravia's Fifty-Two Jewish Communities, 1798–1848

German	Czech	Hebrew/ Yiddish	Number of familiants
Brünn district (Brünner Kreis)			
Nikolsburg	Mikulov	ניקולסבורג	620
Boskowitz	Boskovice	באסקוויץ	326
Neu-Rausnitz	Rousínov	רויסטיץ	195
Kanitz	Dolní Kounice	קוניץ	111
Pohrlitz	Pohrelice	פארליץ	105
Kostel	Podivín	קאסטל	81
Butschowitz	Bučovice	בודשפיץ	78
Austerlitz	Slavkov u Brna	אויסטרליץ	72
Lundenburg	Břeclav	לונדנברג	66
Damboritz	Dambořice	דאמברשיץ	57
Lomnitz	Lomnice	לאמניץ	56
Eiwanowitz	Ivanovice na Hané	אייבניץ	47
Eisgrub	Lednice	אייזגרוב	27
Göding	Hodonín	גידונג	13
Olmütz district (Olmützer Kreis)			
Prossnitz	Prostějov	פרוסטיץ	328
Gewitsch	Jevíčko	געביטש	138
Aussee	Úsov	אויסע	110
Kojetein	Kojetín	גויטיין	76
Loschitz	Loštice	לאשיץ	71
Tobitschau	Tovačov	דאבאטשוייא	25
Iglau district (Iglauer Kreis)			
Trebitsch	Třebíč	טריביטש	260
Gross-Meseritsch	Velké Meziříčí	מעזריטש	151
Triesch	Třešť	טריטש	102
Pirnitz	Brtnice	בארטניץ	61

German	Czech	Hebrew/ Yiddish	Number of familiants
Datschitz	Dačice	דאטשיץ	30
Battelau	Batelov	באטלויא	26
Wölking	Bolikov		25
Teltsch	Telč	טעלטש	7
Puklitz	Puklice	פוקליץ	5

Znaim district (Znaimer Kreis)

Eibenschitz	Ivančice	אייבשיץ	144
Misslitz	Miroslav	מישליפ	119
Schaffa	Šafov	שאפי	119
Jamnitz	Jemnice	יעמניץ	58
Piesling	Písečné	פיזלינג	52
Mährisch-Kromau	Moravský Krumlov	קרומניא	49
Pullitz	Police u Jemnice	פוליץ	22
Irritz	Jiřice	איריץ	17
Althart	Staré Hobzí		14

Hradisch district (Hradischer Kreis)

Holleschau	Holešov	העלישויא	265
Ungarisch-Brod	Uherský Brod	ברודא	160
Bisenz	Bzenec	פיזענץ	130
Ungarisch-Ostra	Uherský Ostroh	שטייניץ	89
Strassnitz	Štrážnice	דרעזניץ	84
Gaya	Kyjov	גאיי	74
Koritschan	Koričany	קארטשוין	36
Kosteletz	Kostelec	קאסטליץ	20
Wessely	Veselí nad Moravou	וועסעלי	19

Prerau district (Prerauer Kreis)

Leipnik	Lipník nad Bečvou	לייפניק	255
Kremsier	Kroměříž	קרעמזיר	106
Weisskirchen	Hranice	הרייניץ	120
Prerau	Přerov	פרעררויא	44

Troppau district (Troppauer Kreis)*

Hotzenplotz	Osoblaha	האציפלאץ	135

* The Troppau district was in Austrian Silesia, but the Hotzenplotz Jewish community was counted as one of Moravia's fifty-two Jewish communities.

Appendix 2
Moravian Jewish Communities Established After 1848

German	Czech	Hebrew/ Yiddish	Year established
Brünn	Brno	ברין	1859
Iglau	Jihlava	איגלא	1862
Znaim	Znojmo	זנאים	1870
Mährisch-Ostrau	Ostrava		1875
Auspitz	Hustopeče	אוספיץ	1892
Neutitschein	Nový Jicín		1892
Olmütz	Olomouc	אולמיץ	1892
Ungarisch-Hradisch	Uherské Hradiště	הראדיש	1892
Wallachisch-Meseritsch	Valašské Meziříčí,		1892
Wischau	Vyškov	ווישוי	1892
Zwittau	Svitavy	צוויטוי	1892

Appendix 3

Jewish Population in Moravia and Austrian Silesia, 1754–1921

Year	Moravia	Austrian Silesia
1754	19,752	575
1775	23,382[a]	
1785	26,665[a]	
1801	27,822[a]	
1830	29,462[b]	1,038[c]
1848	37,548[c]	2,165[f]
1857	41,529[d]	3,280
1869	42,899[d]	6,142
1880	44,175	8,580
1890	45,324	10,042
1900	44,255	11,988
1910	41,158	13,422
1921	37,989	7,317

SOURCES: Leo Goldhammer, "Die Juden Mährens. Eine kurze Darstellung in Zahlen," in Hugo Gold, ed., *Die Juden und Judengemeinden Mährens in Vergangenheit und Gegenwart: ein Sammelwerk* (Brünn: Jüdischer Buch- und Kunstverlag, 1929), 598–602; Theodor Haas, *Die Juden in Mähren: Darstellung der Rechtsgeschichte und Statistik unter besonderer Berücksichtigung des 19. Jahrhunderts* (Brünn: Jüdischer Buch- und Kunstverlag, 1908), 17, 64; Tomáš Pěkný, *Historie Židů v Čechách a na Moravě* (Prague: Sefer, 1993), 634–38; Janusz Spyra, *Żydzi na Śląsku Austriackim (1742–1918)* (Katowice: Muzeum Śląskie, 2005), 316–18.

[a] Totals for 1775, 1785, and 1801 include Austrian Silesia.
[b] Total for 1830 includes Hotzenplotz; Pěkný places the total for Moravia and Austrian Silesia at 32,244.
[c] Pěkný places the total for Moravia and Austrian Silesia at 40,064 in 1846, and 40,681 in 1849.
[d] Haas's totals differ slightly for 1857 (42,611) and 1869 (42,644).
[e] Total for 1831.
[f] Total for 1846.

Abbreviations Used Only in Notes and Bibliography

AHY	*Austrian History Yearbook*
AMO	Archiv města Olomouce
AMP	Archiv města Prostějova
AVA	Allgemeines Verwaltungsarchiv, Vienna
AZJ	*Allgemeine Zeitung des Judenthums*
BCh	*Ben-Chananja*
BZ	*Brünner Zeitung*
CAHJP	Central Archive for the History of the Jewish People, Jerusalem
CB aus Böhmen	*Constitutionelle Bote aus Böhmen*
HHStA	Haus, Hof- und Staatsarchiv, Vienna
INJ	*Israelit des 19. Jahrhunderts*
JB	*Judaica Bohemiae*
JGGJČR	*Jahrbuch der Gesellschaft für Geschichte der Juden in der Čechoslovakischen Republik*
JJLG	*Jahrbuch der Jüdisch-Literarischen Gesellschaft*
JNUL	Jewish National and University Library, Jerusalem
JQR	*Jewish Quarterly Review*
JSS	*Jewish Social Studies*
JTSA	Jewish Theological Seminary of America, New York
KI	*Kokheve Yitzhak*
LBI	Leo Baeck Institute, New York
LBIYB	*Yearbook of the Leo Baeck Institute*
MGWJ	*Monatschrift für Geschichte und Wissenschaft des Judentums*

Müller	Willibald Müller, *Urkundliche Beiträge zur Geschichte der mähr. Judenschaft*
MZA	Moravský zemský archiv, Brno
MZA Kunštat	Moravský zemský archiv, Kunštat
MZsL	Peter Újvári, *Magyar zsidó lexikon*
MZsSz	*Magyar zsidó szemle*
NZ	*Die Neue Zeit*
ÖCO	*Österreichisches Central-Organ für Glaubenfreiheit, Cultur und Literatur der Juden*
ÖW	*Dr. Bloch's Österreichische Wochenschrift*
PAAJR	*Proceedings of the American Academy of Jewish Research*
PAJHS	*Proceedings of the American Jewish Historical Society*
RSHCJ	*Review of the Society for the History of Czechoslovak Jews*
TZW	*Treue-Zions-Wächter*
VJ	*Voice of Jacob*
WB	*Wiener Blätter*
WZfJT	*Wissenschaftliche Zeitschrift für jüdische Theologie*
ZGJT	*Zeitschrift für die Geschichte der Juden in Tschechoslovakei*

Notes

Introduction

1. Zweig, *World of Yesterday*, 6. In the original translation, "in kleinen ländlichen Orten" is rendered as "in small country villages," but I have chosen to translate *Ort* as town, not village.

2. Ignatz Krampflicek, "Notizen über Austerlitz," *Mittheilungen zur Jüdischen Volkskunde* 32(4) (1909): 122.

3. Max Grunwald, "Wiener jüdische Familien aus Mähren," in Gold, *Die Juden*, 83.

4. Grunwald, "Wiener jüdische Familien," 83.

5. Grunwald, "Wiener jüdische Familien," 83.

6. Moritz Duschak, "Zur Geschichte der Juden in Mähren," *BCh* 4(34) (August 23, 1861): 295.

7. Kieval, *Languages of Community*, 40; Gerson Wolf, "Statistik der Juden in Böhmen, Mähren und Schlesien im Jahre 1754," *BCh* 7(41) (1864): 819–21; Kestenberg-Gladstein, "Mifked yehudei Beim sh'mehutz le-Prag be-shnat 1724." In 1754, there were 28,894 Jews in Bohemia, composing 1.5% of the total population.

8. Richarz, "Ländliches Judentum," 1–8; Kaplan, *Jewish Daily Life*, 95–97. Alsatian Jewry was in a comparable situation, Schwarzfuchs, "Alsace and Southern Germany," 15.

9. Kieval, *Languages of Community*, 40.

10. Wolf, "Statistik der Juden," 820. In 1754, there were 19,792 Jews in Moravia, composing 2.3% of the total population.

11. Stampfer, "1764 Census," 126–28. There were 20,107 Jews in the Lublin region.

12. Hundert, *Jews in Poland-Lithuania*, 21–23.

13. Hundert, *Jews in Poland-Lithuania*, 22.

14. Baer, *Das Protokollbuch*, 82; Cohen, *Die Landjudenschaften in Deutschland*, v. I, xiii–xix.

15. Halpern, *Takkanot medinat Mehrin*, 19–20. Two consecutive assemblies

were held in Kanitz in 1665 and 1774, but perhaps the nine-year interval between the assemblies made this acceptable.

16. It met in Gaya, Holleschau, Kanitz (six times), Strassnitz, Austerlitz (twice), Ungarisch-Brod (three times), Kremsier (twice), Göding (twice), Lundenburg, Butschowitz (three times), and Neu-Rausnitz.

17. Duschak, "Zur Geschichte der Juden," 295–96.

18. Wolf, *Die alten Statuten der jüdischen Gemeinden*.

19. Elvert, *Zur Geschichte der Juden*.

20. Weiss, *Zikhronotai*.

21. Broda, *Megillat Sedarim*; Fränkl, *Sefer yeshu'ot yisrael*.

22. Frankel-Grün, *Geschichte der Juden in Kremsier*; Frankel-Grün, *Geschichte der Juden in Ungarisch-Brod*.

23. Bondy and Dworsky, *Zur Geschichte der Juden*.

24. Bondy and Dworsky, *Zur Geschichte der Juden*, 1.

25. Bretholz, *Quellen zur Geschichte der Juden in Mähren*.

26. Gold, *Die Juden und Judengemeinden Mährens*.

27. Hugo Gold, "Gleitwort," *ZGJT* 1(1) (1930): 1.

28. Kahane, "Nikolsburg"; Halpern, *Takkanot medinat Mehrin*; Roth, *Takkanot Nikolsburg*.

29. Society for the History of Czechoslovak Jews, *Jews of Czechoslovakia*, v. 1, 1.

30. Gold, *Gedenkbuch*.

31. "Éditorial," *JB* 1 (1965): 3.

32. Kestenberg-Gladstein, "Hussitentum und Judentum"; Kestenberg-Gladstein, "Wirtschaftsgeschichte der böhmischen Landjuden"; Kestenberg-Gladstein, "Čechen und Juden." Guido Kisch also wrote for the *Jahrbuch* and *Judaica Bohemiae*.

33. Kestenberg-Gladstein, *Neuere Geschichte der Juden*. A second volume was published posthumously, but it pales in comparison to the first. Kestenberg-Gladstein, *Heraus aus der "Gasse."*

34. Kieval, *Making of Czech Jewry*. Kieval also published a number of articles on Bohemian Jewry, which are collected in his *Languages of Community*.

35. The proceedings of these conferences have been published by the Kroměříž regional museum as *Židé a Morava*. The 26th Nikolsburg Symposium (2000) was also devoted to this topic. Kordiovský et al., *Moravští Židé v rakousko-uherské monarchii*.

36. Bránský, *Židé v Boskovicích*; Nezhodová, *Židovský Mikulov*.

Chapter 1

1. For a general overview of Moravia's early history, see Agnew, *Czechs*, 3–67.

2. Bondy and Dworsky, *Zur Geschichte der Juden*; Bretholz, *Quellen*; and Bretholz, *Geschichte der Juden in Mähren im Mittelalter*. As all three books point out, Jewish traders are mentioned in the *Raffelstetten* toll regulations (903–906) and in

a travelogue by Ibrahim Ibn-Jakub (c. 965), but these do not constitute evidence of Jewish settlement in Bohemia and Moravia. Bondy and Dworsky, *Zur Geschichte der Juden*, 1–2; Bretholz, *Quellen*, vii–xii; Bretholz, *Geschichte*, 31–55, 66–68. On the Crusader massacre of Jews in Prague (1096), see Steinherz, "Kreuzfahrer und Juden in Prag."

3. For the charter, see Bondy and Dworsky, *Zur Geschichte der Juden*, 17–28; and Bretholz, *Quellen*, 3–8.

4. Krauss, "Der hebräischen Benennungen der modernen Völker," 397–400; and Tykocinski, "Lebenszeit und Heimat des Isaak Or Sarua."

5. Štěpán, "Die gesellschaftliche und rechtliche Stellung"; Bretholz, *Quellen*, 267–75.

6. Šedinová, "Alttschechische Glossen in mittelalterlichen hebräischen Schriften."

7. Štěpán, "Die gesellschaftliche und rechtliche Stellung," 3–21.

8. Válka, "Moravia and the Crisis of the Estate's System," 149–50; Bahlcke, *Regionalismus und Staatsintegration in Widerstreit*, 32–34.

9. Ruth Kestenberg-Gladstein, "Hussites," in *Encyclopedia Judaica*, v. 8, 1136.

10. Kestenberg-Gladstein, "Hussitentum und Judentum," 18–19. They were also accused of desecrating the Host.

11. Hofer, *Johannes von Capistrano*, 356.

12. Müller, *Urkundliche Beiträge*, 14–17.

13. Müller, *Urkundliche Beiträge*, 14.

14. Müller, *Urkundliche Beiträge*, 14–17.

15. Hugo Gold, "Geschichte der Juden in Ungarisch-Hradisch," in Gold, *Die Juden*, 561–62.

16. Válka, "Moravia and the Crisis of the Estate's System," 150.

17. On the efforts of the nobility to break the monopolies of the royal towns, see Válka, "Die Stellung Mährens," 300. For examples of a similar dynamic in eighteenth-century Poland, see Hundert, *Jews in a Polish Private Town*; and Rosman, *The Lords' Jews*.

18. Engel, "Die Ausweisung der Juden," 71.

19. Among the Jews who left Moravia after the expulsions were Isaac Zarfati, who emigrated to the Ottoman Empire, and Rabbi Israel Bruna, who settled in Regensburg, Germany. Nehemias Brüll, "Zur Geschichte der Juden in Mähren," *Wiener Jahrbuch der Israeliten* (1867–1868), 187–88. On Moravian Jewish emigration to Poland (e.g., Oświęcim, Kazimierz), see Engel, "Die Ausweisung der Juden," 63, 79.

20. Heinrich Flesch, "Die Einwanderung der Juden in Mähren," in Gold, *Die Juden*, 1–7; Müller, *Urkundliche Beiträge*, 11. Helmut Teufel speculates that the Jews settled in close proximity to the royal towns because they were hoping that the expulsion decrees would be rescinded and they would be allowed to return. Teufel, "Zur politischen und sozialen Geschichte," 116.

21. Engel, "Die Ausweisung der Juden," 71–76.

22. Heilig, "Die Vorläufer der mährischen Konfektionsindustrie," 326.

23. Heilig, "Die Vorläufer der mährischen Konfektionsindustrie," 322–23; Heinrich Flesch, "Geschichte der Juden in Austerlitz," in Gold, *Die Juden*, 111.

24. Flesch, "Urkundliches"; Wischnitzer, "Origins of the Jewish Artisan Class," 335–50; Teufel, "Zur politischen und sozialen Geschichte," 166–92; Brilling, "Zur Geschichte des jüdischen Goldschmiedegewerbes," 137–46; Israel Weinstock, "Versuch eines Grundrisses der Sozial- und Wirtschaftsgeschichte der Juden in Mähren," Ph.D. dissertation, University of Vienna, 1934.

25. Heilig, "Die Vorläufer der mährischen Konfektionsindustrie," 324–26.

26. Engel, "Die Ausweisung der Juden," 71–75.

27. Teufel, "Zur politischen und sozialen Geschichte," 207–83.

28. An early nineteenth-century French traveler to Moravia observed the following: "Le commerce des laines, et surtout celui des laines de Znaim, se trouve, comme nous l'avons déjà observé, presque tout entier dans les mains des juifs" [As we have already observed, the trade in wool, and above all the wool of Znaim, is almost entirely in the hands of the Jews]. Marcel de-Serres, *Voyage en Autriche* (Paris, 1814), v. 2, 522.

29. de-Serres, *Voyage en Autriche*, v. 2, 223.

30. A responsum by Menaḥem Mendel Krochmal, chief rabbi of Nikolsburg in the mid-seventeenth century, mentions this issue. Katz, *"Shabbes Goy,"* 92–93.

31. On Jewish vintners in southwestern Moravia, particularly in Bisenz and Nikolsburg, see Teufel, "Zur politischen und sozialen Geschichte," 202–6, 239.

32. Fram, *Ideals Face Reality*, 96–98.

33. Kann, *History of the Habsburg Empire*, 45.

34. Limm, *Thirty Years War*, 17.

35. Wolf, *Ferdinand II*.

36. Because of the prewar prosperity of Bohemia and Moravia, the Bohemian Lands had been more heavily taxed than the rest of the hereditary lands. Despite the devastation wrought by the war, the higher taxation was retained as a kind of punishment. As a result, greater demands were made on the peasant population, which entered a period of "second serfdom." There were numerous peasant revolts throughout the seventeenth century. Bosl, *Handbuch*, v. 2, 323.

37. The 1629 privilege is reproduced in Müller, *Urkundliche Beiträge*, 19–22. At the Jews' behest, it was renewed by Ferdinand III (1657), Leopold I (1659), and Charles VI (1723). In 1754, Maria Theresa issued the General-Polizei-Prozess- und Kommerzialordnung für die Judenschaft des Markgrafthums Mähren, which codified many of the rights and obligations contained in the earlier privileges.

38. Drabek, "Die Juden in den böhmischen Ländern," 123–25.

39. Müller, *Urkundliche Beiträge*, 19–20.

40. Müller, *Urkundliche Beiträge*, 22–23.

41. Müller, *Urkundliche Beiträge*, 22.

42. Müller, *Urkundliche Beiträge*, 26–28.

43. As late as 1857, the town of Znaim harked back to the 1454 expulsion decrees in an effort to exclude Jews from the town, lest the "inhabitants sink into poverty." HHStA, Ministerrat, Reichsrat, Box 187, no. 1857/1739, November 25, 1857.

44. All Hebrew letters have a numerical value. *Shin* = 300, *yod* = 10, and *alef* = 1, so *Shai* = 311.

45. Ettinger, "Council of the Four Lands," 94.

46. At the last council (Butschowitz, 1748), there were sixty-one delegates from forty-one Jewish communities. (Jewish communities that paid 1% or more of Moravian Jewry's total "contribution" were entitled to send two delegates each; in 1748, twenty communities met this criterion.)

47. These were the upper district (*galil elyon*), the middle district (*galil emtsa*), and the lower district (*galil ha-tahton*). The upper district comprised seventeen communities in northern Moravia, near the Bohemian and Silesian borders; the middle district comprised nineteen communities in southwest Moravia, near the Austrian border; the lower district comprised nine communities in southeast Moravia, near the Hungarian border.

48. It was called the minor council to distinguish it from the major council (*va'ad gadol*), as the Council of the Land was sometimes known.

49. On the origins and history of the Moravian chief rabbinate, see Löw, "Das mährische Landesrabbinat," 165–218; Alfred Willmann, "Die mährischen Landesrabbiner," in Gold, *Die Juden*, 45–49; and Friedländer, *Kore Haddoroth*, 14–61.

50. Abraham Levie, a Dutch Jewish traveler, visited Moravia in 1719 and reported in his Yiddish travelogue that many foreign Jews were studying in Nikolsburg. Levie, *Travels Among Jews and Gentiles*, 71.

51. Hanover, *Abyss of Despair*.

52. Emden, *Megilat Sefer*, 24–25.

53. "In the Hapsburg monarchy," writes Moses Shulvass, "Moravia was the main province into which Polish Jews moved during the years 1648–1657. Between 1657 and 1677 we find Polish immigrants in at least 16 towns and cities there. It seems that the number who immigrated to Bohemia was much smaller. . . . They preferred Moravia, both because it was closer to the Polish border and because it offered better economic opportunities." Shulvass, *From East to West*, 39–40, 46.

54. Already in 1636, Menaḥem Mendel Krochmal had left his native Cracow for Moravia, where he served as rabbi in Kremsier and Prossnitz before settling in Nikolsburg as the chief rabbi of Moravia. In 1648, one of his sisters joined him in Nikolsburg after fleeing from Chelm with her three children (Shulvass, *From East to West*, 25). Shabbetai Kohen (ShaKh), author of *Sifte Kohen*, fled Vilna in 1648 and became rabbi of Holleschau. Ephraim Hakohen, author of *Sha'ar Efrayim*, also fled Vilna in 1648 and became rabbi of Trebitsch (and then Buda). Gershon Ashkenazi, a native of Cracow and son-in-law of Krochmal, served as rabbi of Prossnitz from 1649 to 1659 and as rabbi of Nikolsburg from 1661 to 1664.

55. Kaufmann, *Die letzte Vertreibung*.

56. Kaufmann, *Die letzte Vertreibung*, 166.

57. This remained the case well into the twentieth century. Moses, *Die Juden in Südmähren*, 2.

58. In 1670, Prince Dietrichstein, the owner of Nikolsburg, took in eighty Jewish families in exchange for a hefty payment (*Schutzgeld*). Kaufmann, *Die letzte Vertreibung*, 167–77. The Viennese *Memorbuch*, which recorded death dates for members of the Viennese Jewish community, was brought to Misslitz by expellees and remained there until the 1930s. Moses, *Die Juden in Sudmähren*, 4.

59. Moses, *Die Juden in Sudmähren*, 177. See also D. Alt, "Geschichte der Juden in Schaffa," in Gold, *Die Juden*, 513.

60. Israel, *European Jewry*, 134.

61. Figures, taken from Seton-Watson, *History of the Czechs and Slovaks*, 130, are based on estimates by Antonin Gindely, *Geschichte des dreissigjährigen Kriegs* (Prague: F. Tempsky, 1869–1880); and Alfons Huber, *Geschichte Österreichs* (Gotha: Perthes, 1885).

62. Heilig, "Die Vorläufer der mährischen Konfektionsindustrie," 331.

63. Heilig, *Eine mährische Stadt*, 10.

64. Israel, *European Jewry*, 138.

65. Theodor Haas, "Statistische Betrachtungen über die jüdische Bevölkerung Mährens in Vergangenheit und Gegenwart," in Gold, *Die Juden*, 592.

66. On the composition of the diets in this period, see Kann and David, *Peoples of the Eastern Habsburg Lands*, 110–12.

67. Kahane, "Nikolsburg," 215; Elvert, *Zur Geschichte der Juden*, 176.

68. Bruno Mauritz Trapp, "Geschichte der Juden in Nikolsburg," in Gold, *Die Juden*, 422–23.

69. Müller, *Urkundliche Beiträge*, 47.

70. The full report is reproduced in Müller, *Urkundliche Beiträge*, 34–38.

71. Müller, *Urkundliche Beiträge*, 35.

72. Müller, *Urkundliche Beiträge*, 36.

73. Wolny, *Die Markgrafschaft Mähren*, v. 5, "Aussee."

74. Oskar Kwasnik-Rabinowicz, "Geschichte der Juden in Mähr: Aussee," in Gold, *Die Juden*, 332.

75. Details on the Aussee affair are taken from *Megillat Sedarim*, a Hebrew chronicle written soon after the events described. Broda, *Megillat Sedarim*; and Baumgarten, "Zur Mährisch Ausseer Affaire," 506–37. Abraham Broda Leipnik (1690–1774) was a *dayyan* (rabbinical judge) in Aussee.

76. Broda, *Megillat Sedarim*, 17.

77. Broda, *Megillat Sedarim*, 18–19.

78. Broda, *Megillat Sedarim*, 21. Abraham Broda called Kaunitz a "lover of the Jews" (*ohev yisrael*), noting that three Moravian Jewish communities (Ungarisch-Brod, Austerlitz, and Neu-Rausnitz) were under his protection.

79. Broda, *Megillat Sedarim*, 22–25.

80. Broda, *Megillat Sedarim*, 25. The Jews were not permitted to rebuild their synagogue until 1783. HHStA, Staatrat, 1783/4321.

81. Broda, *Megillat Sedarim*, 30–31.

82. On the symbolic geography of the ghetto and its role in reestablishing church authority, see Benjamin Ravid, "Excursus 1: The Venetian Ghetto in Historical Perspective," in Modena, *Autobiography of a Seventeenth-Century Venetian Rabbi*, 280–83.

83. The decree, dated December 8, 1826, is reproduced in Müller, *Urkundliche Beiträge*, 47–48.

84. Müller, *Urkundliche Beiträge*, 50–63. The details of these property transfers are well documented. Klenovský, "Plány separace židovského osídlení," 54–56; Klenovský, *Židovské Město v Prostějově*, 14–17; Lapáček, "Pokusy o seperaci," 23–29; and Lapáček, "Poznámky separaci Židů v Lipníku," 27–30.

85. Kestenberg-Gladstein, *Neuere Geschichte der Juden*, 11; Scari, *Systematische Darstellung*, 108–9.

86. "Prossnitz," MZA Brno, B14, M617, 1829.

87. MZA Brno, B14, M617, 1829. See Gewitsch (three families/house), Holleschau (five families/house), Kremsier (three families/house), and Loschitz (three families per house) in particular. See also Rosenbusch, "Zur Statistik der Wohnungsfrage," 176–78.

88. General-Polizei-Prozess- und Kommerzialordnung, art. 17. Quoted from Müller, *Urkundliche Beiträge*, 97. See Scari, *Systematische Darstellung*, 169.

89. For example, see HHStA, Staatrat, 1838/686, 1838/5383, 1839/86, 1839/1994.

90. Roubík, "Die Judensiedlungen in Böhmen," 287. See also Kestenberg-Gladstein, *Neuere Geschichte der Juden*, 11–12.

91. See note 84 for literature on forced property transfers in Moravia.

92. These artisans are mentioned specifically in a petition submitted by "the truly devoted Israelite communities of Moravia" to Emperor Ferdinand in 1845. *AZJ*, December 22, 1845, 758.

93. Of the twenty-two artisans in Kanitz in 1751 (30.7% of the adult male population), there were thirteen tailors, two glaziers, five butchers, one baker, and one needle maker. Of the eleven artisans in Aussee in 1753 (18.6%), there were six tailors, two glaziers, two butchers, and one button maker. Of the sixteen artisans in Misslitz in 1753 (26.7%), there were twelve tailors, three butchers, and one barber. See Gold, *Die Juden*, 275, 338, 389–90. In Nikolsburg, the artisans were primarily tailors, butchers, and cobblers (the last two had their own synagogues). See Kahane, "Nikolsburg," 242.

94. Between 1675 and 1764, Jews from twenty-five Moravian Jewish communities could be found at the Leipzig fairs, including 130 from Nikolsburg, 79 from Kremsier, 23 from Prossnitz, and 12 from Trebitsch. Freudenthal, *Leipziger Messegäste*. On Moravian Jews at the Breslau fair, see Brilling, "Die Handelsbeziehungen," 1–20.

95. This occupational structure is described by Briess in *Schilderung*, 29, 66. It is described in almost identical terms by Eduard Kulke (1831–1897), a Moravian-Jewish author and the grandson of Rabbi Nehemias Trebitsch. See Kulke, *Geschichten*, 14–15.

96. Müller, *Urkundliche Beiträge*, 177.

97. Leopold Kompert, "Der Dorfgeher," in his *Böhmische Juden*, 3–82; Eduard Kulke, "Er hat Fisch gegessen," in his *Geschichten*, 1–128. See Wittemann, *Drauss en vor dem Ghetto*.

98. S. R. Hirsch to Leopold Lažansky, July 14, 1848, MZA, B14, M618, no. 750/79.

99. In 1781, a representative of the Moravian Gubernium estimated that one-third of Moravia's Jews were "Hausierer, sogenannte Pinkler und ihre Handlanger." Müller, *Urkundliche Beiträge*, 177. In 1829, 21% of the Jews in the Olmütz, Iglau, Hradisch, Znaim, and Prerau districts were *Hausierer*; in some Jewish communities, such as Aussee, Eibenschitz, Pullitz, and Koritschan, *Hausierer* constituted more than 50% of the Jewish population. MZA, B14, M617, 1829 (no data are available for the Brünn district).

100. For the laws regulating Moravian Jewish leaseholders, see Scari, *Systematische Darstellung*, 115–21. On leaseholders (*arrendators*) in the Polish-Lithuanian Commonwealth, see Rosman, *The Lords' Jews*, 106–42.

101. In 1696, the Council of the Land decreed that *arrendators* had to pay taxes to the closest Jewish community. The fact that this decree was repeated again in 1671 and 1720 indicates that it was largely ignored. In 1728, it was decreed that *arrendators* who did not pay their taxes could be excluded from the synagogue on High Holidays. Halpern, *Takkanot medinat Mehrin*, 162, 172, 201, 233.

102. In a sample of Moravian Jewish converts to Catholicism between 1786 and 1849, the number of children of *arrendators* is striking. For example, Joseph Bokas, an 18-year-old in Stittkowitz, converted in 1797 because, "due to the absence of other Jews, he received the large part of his schooling among Christians." A year later, Abraham, who worked for a Jewish distiller in Oslaw, converted to Catholicism "because he was attracted to Christian ceremonies, which he observed during his frequent contact with Christian children." In the same year, Jakob Ruberl, an *arrendator* in Daleschitz, explained his daughter's conversion by pointing out that she had "a tendency to hang around with Christian boys." MZA, B14, M718, 1797/1210, 1798/7265, and 1798/6636.

103. Radimský and Wurmová, *Petice moravského lidu*, 136.

104. Radimský and Wurmová, *Petice moravského lidu*, 62.

105. The Council of the Land tried to prevent this by forbidding a Jew to negotiate with the lessor during the term of another Jew's lease. This was decreed in 1650 and again in 1694. Halpern, *Takkanot medinat Mehrin*, 63, 150. For similar ordinances in Poland, see Rosman, *The Lords' Jews*, 120–21.

106. Ber Schiff to Jehoshua Schreiber, Koppl Deutsch, Michael Leb Stein-

schneider, and David Fuchs, 28 Sivan 5582 (June 17, 1822), Gideon Brecher Correspondence, JTSA, AR 22. This letter was addressed to the board of the Prossnitz Jewish community.

107. Ber Schiff to Jehoshua Schreiber, Koppl Deutsch, Michael Leb Steinschneider, and David Fuchs.

108. In Prussia, only one son was allowed to inherit his father's residence rights (which entitled him to marry). However, in contrast to the Bohemian Lands, additional sons could get married in Prussia if they possessed enough capital and paid a special fee. With the Austrian annexation of Galicia between 1772 and 1795, Maria Theresa imposed marriage restrictions on the Jewish population that came under her rule. For these restrictions, which were largely ignored, see Grodziski, "Jewish Question in Galicia," 63–64; and Goldberg, "Jewish Marriage," 16–18. On marriage restrictions in Bavaria, see Lowenstein, "Limitation of Fertility," 94–111.

109. For the Moravian Familiants Laws, see Elvert, *Zur Geschichte der Juden*, 176–77; and Scari, *Systematische Darstellung*, 3–34. See also Emden, *Megilat Sefer*, 120.

110. Kahane, "Gezerat ha-sheniyyot," 203–6. The allusion is to BT Yevamot 20a.

111. For example, Gerson Wolf refers to the "pharaonische Gesetz" in his *Joseph Wertheimer*, 61.

112. After most of Silesia was ceded to Prussia fifteen years later, the number of Jewish families in Austrian Silesia was lowered to 119. In 1787, Joseph II raised the numbers for Bohemia and Moravia to 8,600 and 5,400, respectively; the number for Silesia remained 119.

113. Flesch, "Urkundliches," 270.

114. Scari, *Systematische Darstellung*, 9, 11, 29–30; Weiss, *Zikhronotai*, 14–15.

115. Frankel-Grün, *Geschichte der Juden in Kremsier*, v. 2, 172.

116. Details taken from Herrisch, "Die Judengemeinde," 292–94.

117. The number of supernumeraries gradually decreased. For example, alongside the 102 familiants in Triesch in 1787, there were twenty supernumeraries; in 1829, Triesch had none. For 1787, see Hugo Gold, "Geschichte der Juden in Triesch," in Gold, *Die Juden*, 541. For 1829, see "Triesch," MZA, B14, M617, 1829. In Kojetein, there were thirty-six supernumeraries in 1798 and only four in 1829; see "Kojetein," MZA, B14, M617, 1829.

118. After rejecting an illegitimate son's request for a familiant number in 1838, the Moravian Gubernium noted that "the legal consequences of illegitimate birth are much harder on the illegitimate children of the Jews than of the Christians. The illegitimate child of a Jew . . . loses all prospect of obtaining a familiant number, since the requirements for a familiant number explicitly mention legitimate birth." MZA, B14, M593, no. 49308, January 5, 1838.

119. For descriptions, see Briess, *Schilderung*, 21–23.

120. Flesch, "Urkundliches," 270–71.

121. To mislead the authorities, the female partner in such relationships was

sometimes registered as the male partner's "domestic servant." For a fictional treatment of such an arrangement in Bohemia, see Leopold Kompert, "Ohne Bewilligung," in his *Aus dem Ghetto*, 293–350.

122. In 1833, it was decreed that one-third of the fine go to the denouncer; see Scari, *Systematische Darstellung*, 29–30. Sometimes the denouncer was motivated more by malice than by financial gain. In 1840, for example, Bernard Kreisky, a familiant in Kanitz, asked the Moravian Gubernium to expel Max Grünfeld, a Jew from Mährisch-Kromau, who was "secretly married to a certain Anna Spitzer." MZA, B14, M601, no. 22513, May 21, 1841. Bernard Kreisky was presumably an ancestor of Austrian chancellor Bruno Kreisky (1911–1990), whose paternal line came from Kanitz. On Kreisky's Moravian-Jewish origins, see Meysels, "Brunos 'Roots,'" 17.

123. Eiwanowitz Jewish community to Moravian-Silesian Gubernium, August 28, 1845, MZA, B14, M609, no. 36753.

124. *INJ* 10 (1845): 142–44.

125. In Bohemia, the number was raised from 8,451 to 8,600; in Moravia, from 5,106 to 5,400; in Silesia, it remained at 119. The moderate increase in familiant numbers did not keep up with the Jewish population growth. In 1754, there were 3.8 Jews for every familiant number in Moravia and Silesia (3.4 in Bohemia); in 1800, there were 5.0 Jews per familiant number (5.6 in Bohemia); by 1840, the number of Jews per familiant number had risen to 6.8 (7.5 in Bohemia). Calculations are based on data in Haas, *Die Juden in Mähren*, 58–64.

126. HHStA, Staatrat, 1846, 5692/5460.

127. Frankel-Grün, *Jüdische Zeitgeschichte und Zeitgenossen*, 2; Miller, "Rise and Fall of Archbishop Kohn," 446–74.

128. MZA, B14, M717–18, 1786 and 1849. Of the eighty converts for whom an age is indicated, sixty-two of them were between 16 and 30. Only nine of them had familiant numbers.

129. Briess, *Schilderung*, 23.

130. These "illegitimate" and "later-born" sons were also called "Hungarians." Adolf Schmiedl played with this appellation as follows: "We also call them by the more distinctive name, 'Hungarians.' O, you 'Hungarians' [*Ungarischen*], you should not emigrate so reluctantly [*ungern*] to prosperous Hungary [*Ungarn*]." *Der Orient*, November 19, 1847, 373. For identification of the author as Adolf Schmiedl, see *Der Orient*, June 10, 1848, 189.

131. Wolf, *Joseph Wertheimer*, 62.

132. Scari, *Systematische Darstellung*, 76–77.

133. Scari, *Systematische Darstellung*, 41. When Adolf Schulhof, a later-born son of a Pirnitz familiant, tried to return to Pirnitz from Hungary in 1842, his father drew attention to the fact that Adolf had not gotten married during his time away: "Nearly six years ago, my son Adolf Schulhof received permission to emigrate to Hungary, because as a later-born son he had no prospect of acquiring a familiant

number in Pirnitz. Since he was not able to subsist in Hungary, he returned home *without having gotten married*" (original emphasis). MZA, B14, M602, no. 7568, February 12, 1842.

134. According to Jan Heřman, "Between 1754 and 1850, the number of Jews in Bohemia increased from 29,091 (1.48% of the total population) to 75,459 (1.72%). In Moravia the number of Jews rose from 20,327 in 1754 (2.29%) to 40,681 (1.81%) in 1850. During this period the growth of the Jewish population in Bohemia was more rapid than for the population as a whole, while it was slower in Moravia." Heřman, "Evolution of the Jewish Population," 2.

135. Marton, *A magyar zsidóság családfája*, 50. Eleven percent were born in Poland, 3% in Bohemia, 5.2% in other Habsburg territories, and 1.2% in Germany; the place of birth for 6.6% of the Jewish family heads is unknown.

136. In 1735–38, 62% of the Jews in the Hungarian counties along the Moravian border (Nyitra, Pozsony, and Trencsén) were born in Moravia. Marton, *A magyar zsidóság családfája*, 52.

137. Gates-Coon, *Landed Estates*, 115–16; Markbreiter, *Beiträge zur Geschichte*, 20–25; Wachstein, *Urkunden und Akten*, 48–50, 59, 65, 68, 81.

138. Mislovics, "Demographic and Socio-Economic History," 47–52, 102–7.

139. Fülöp Grünwald and Sandor Scheiber called Ungarish-Brod "the true mothertown of Hungarian Jewry" because of the large number of Jews who came to Hungary from this Kaunitz-owned town. Grünwald and Scheiber, "Adalékok a magyar zsidóság településtörténetéhez," 15; K. Nürnberger, "Geschichte der Juden in Ung. Brod," in Gold, *Die Juden*, 551; Frankel-Grün, *Geschichte der Juden in Ungarisch-Brod*, 18.

140. B. Mandl, "Zur Geschichte der jüdischen Gemeinde in Holitsch," *ZGJT* 1 (1930–31): 180–83.

141. According to the Conscriptio Judeorum of 1735–38, there were nine Moravian Jewish family heads in Pressburg, six in Buda, and eighteen in Óbuda. Most of them came from manors belonging to Dietrichstein, Kaunitz, and Lichtenstein. *Monumenta Hungariae Judaica* 3 (1937): 700–707, 712–17, 720–27, 756–59.

142. Holics, for example, was right across the border from Göding; Szenicz and Mijava were less than 25 kilometers from Strassnitz.

143. Lányi and Propperné, *Szlovenszkói zsidó hitközségek története*, 185–87, 225, 274, 279, 282. In the early eighteenth century, the Jews of Liptószentmiklós (Liptovský-Sväty-Mikuláš) went to Holleschau to celebrate important festivals (see p. 185).

144. For example, see Schnitzer, *Jüdische Kulturbilder*, 35–75; and Weiss, *Zikhronotai*, 28. Weiss, a native of Gross-Meseritsch, studied for a few years in Eisenstadt, where his paternal uncle was a rabbi. As Elias Österreicher noted in *Der Jude in Ungarn* (Pest, 1842), "For the Jew in Hungary, Prague was his Göttingen and Nikolsburg was his Halle." Quoted from Marton, *A magyar zsidóság családfája*, 64.

145. Büchler, "Zsidó letelepedések Magyarországon," 384.

146. For example, see *Monumenta Hungariae Judaica* 3 (1937): 254.

147. Browning, *War of the Austrian Succession*.

148. Fränkl, *Sefer yeshu'ot yisrael*, 10–11.

149. Mevorah, "Ma'asei hishtadlut b'Europa"; Bergl, "Das Exil der Prager Judenschaft."

150. Dickson, *Finance and Government*, v. 2, 221.

151. Kestenberg-Gladstein, *Neuere Geschichte der Juden*, 79.

152. These ordinances can be found in Halpern, *Takkanot medinat Mehrin*, 233–34.

153. Kann and David, *Peoples of the Eastern Habsburg Lands*, 186–91.

154. Müller, *Urkundliche Beiträge*, 87–88.

155. Müller, *Urkundliche Beiträge*, 94.

156. Jakobovits, "Das Prager und Böhmische Landesrabbinat," 115.

157. Moritz Brunner, "Geschichte der Juden in Brünn," in Gold, *Die Juden*, 137–72; Grünfeld, *Zur Geschichte der Judengemeinde in Brünn*; Welzl, "Zur Geschichte der Juden in Brünn," 296–357.

158. Roest, "Het verhaal," 162–63.

159. On the expulsion from Göding, see A. Trebitsch, *Korot ha-Ittim*, f. 24a; and Gustav Treixler, "Geschichte der Juden in Göding," in Gold, *Die Juden*, 220. Many of the Göding Jews settled in nearby Kosteletz. In 1787, Emperor Joseph II allowed thirteen Jewish families to return to Göding.

160. Růžička, "Die österreichischen Dichter," 282–90; Krauss, "Schöndl Dobruschka," 143–48.

161. This sobriquet is attributed to Joseph II's detractors, who viewed his reforms as too far-reaching. Scott, "Reform in the Habsburg Monarchy," 171.

162. On Joseph II's "politics of tolerance," see Karniel, *Die Toleranzpolitik Kaiser Josephs II*; and Beales, *Joseph II: Against the World*, 168–213.

163. Scott, "Reform in the Habsburg Monarchy," 168–69. The influence of cameralism on Joseph II is evident in the following remark to Maria Theresa (1777): "For me toleration means only that in purely temporal matters, I would, without taking account of religion, employ and allow to own lands, enter trades and become citizens those who are competent and who would bring advantage and industry to the [monarchy]." Quoted in Beales, *Joseph II: In the Shadow of Maria Theresa*, 469.

164. The full text of the Moravian Edict of Tolerance can be found in Müller, *Urkundliche Beiträge*, 185–90. An English translation can be found in Iggers, *Jews of Bohemia and Moravia*, 48–52. On the origins of the Moravian Edict of Tolerance, see "Wie das Toleranzpatent für Mähren entstand," in Müller, *Urkundliche Beiträge*, 167–90; and Singer, "Zur Geschichte der Toleranzpatente," 231–311.

165. Sorkin, *Transformation of German Jewry*; Robertson, *Jewish Question*; Katz, *Out of the Ghetto*.

166. Kestenberg-Gladstein, *Neuere Geschichte der Juden*, 40–41.

167. Iggers, *Jews of Bohemia and Moravia*, 48–49.

168. *Zur Geschichte der Juden in Mähren*, 7.

169. A full list of the fifty-two Jewish communities (with the number of familiant numbers assigned to each one) can be found in Scari, *Systematische Darstellung*, 4–8. The number of Jewish communities and familiant numbers remained static until the Revolution of 1848.

170. Adler, "Das Judenpatent von 1797," 202–3, 212–16.

171. A patent from November 17, 1787, specified the taxes for each item. Some examples: slaughtered beef, veal, and lamb—2 kr. per pound; duck—3 kr. apiece; turkey—10 kr. apiece; goose fat—3 kr. per pound; kosher wine (and wine vinegar)—2 kr. per bottle. *Zur Geschichte der Juden in Mähren*, 8–18; Scari, *Systematische Darstellung*, 179–80.

172. The *Kriegssteuer* was transformed into the *Klassensteuer* in 1799 and the *Contributions-Drittel-Zuschlag* in 1811. Scari, *Systematische Darstellung*, 204–6.

173. Scari, *Systematische Darstellung*, 206–9.

174. Hugo Meissner, "Der mährisch-jüdische Landesmassafond," in Gold, *Die Juden*, 67–71; Scari, *Systematische Darstellung*, 209–13; Emanuel Baumgarten, "Ursprung und Bestimmung des mähr.-jüd. Landes-Massafondes," *WB* (August 7–17, 1851), 329, 332–33, 340–41.

175. Scari, *Systematische Darstellung*, 160–63.

176. Scari, *Systematische Darstellung*, 82–84.

177. This took place after an administrative reorganization placed Austrian Silesia under the authority of the Moravian Gubernium in Brünn (which was thereafter called the Moravian-Silesian Gubernium).

178. Singer, "Zur Geschichte der Toleranzpatente," 297–301. On the Jews of Austrian Silesia from 1742 to 1918, see Spyra, "Židé v rakouském Sleszku," 7–47.

179. Katz, "Suggested Relationship," 504.

180. Scholem, *Sabbatai Sevi*.

181. Scholem, *Sabbatai Sevi*, 564.

182. Max Grunwald, "Wiener jüdische Familien aus Mähren," in Gold, *Die Juden*, 83.

183. On Leibel Prossnitz, see Schudt, *Jüdischer Merckwürdigkeiten*, 334; Neubauer, "Der Wahnwitz und die Schwindeleien der Sabbatianer," 207–12; Leib ben Ozer, *Sipur ma'ase Shabbetai Tsvi*, 166–88; and Liebes, "Author of the Book *Tsaddik Yesod Olam*."

184. Moritz Duschak, "Die Herschel-Eibenschitz'sche Fehde in Mähren," *Die Neuzeit* (1864): 23, 34–35, 46–47.

185. Kwasnik-Rabinowicz, "Wolf Eibenschitz," 269–70; Maciejko, "Sabbatian Charlatans."

186. On Sabbatian activity in Gaya, see M. Benet, *Parshat Mordekhai*, Yoreh De'ah, no. 6.

187. Žáček, "Zwei Beiträge zur Geschichte," 370–72; Brüll, "Geschichte der

jüdischen Gemeinde," 318–20; and Leopold Löw, "Eherechtliche Studien," *BCh* 5 (1862): 399. On the affair of Lazi Kohen, a Sabbatian in Kojetein c. 1785, see Fleckeles, *Teshuvah me'ahava*, pt. 1, no. 69. (This affair involved Rabbis Fleckeles, Ezekiel Landau, and Mordecai Benet.) See also Fleckeles, *Ahavat David*, [f. 1a].

188. Scholem, "Redemption Through Sin," 126; on Frankism, see Maciejko, *Mixed Multitude*.

189. Emden, *Sefer Hitabkut*, 83b.

190. On these conversions, see Wolf, *Judentaufen in Oesterreich*, 78–79; Duschak, "Geschichte der israelitischen Gemeinde," 522; and Duschak, "Die Herschel-Eibenschitz'sche Fehde in Mähren," 46.

191. Beer, *Geschichte, Lehren und Meinungen*, v. 2, 324.

192. On Shmelke's students, see Rabinowicz, *Beyn Peshisha le-Lublin*, 26–27. On Horowitz's period in Moravia, see Nosek, "Shemuel Shmelke," 75–94.

193. For the geographic boundaries of the early Hasidic movement, see "Hasidism: Beginnings and Expansion" and "The Hasidic Movement: Nineteenth Century," in Friesel, *Atlas of Modern Jewish History*, 47, 57.

194. Bartal, *Jews of Eastern Europe*, 48.

195. Hundert, *Jews in Poland-Lithuania*, 179–81.

196. Liebes, *Studies in Jewish Myth*, 134; Wilensky, "Hasidic-Mitnaggedic Polemics," 244–71.

197. Liebes, *Studies in Jewish Myth*, 195n56.

198. Silber, "Relationship Between Hasidism and Sabbateanism," World Congress of Jewish Studies, Jerusalem, 1981; Hasidism Reappraised, ed. Ada Rapoport-Albert (London: Valentine Mitchell, 1996).

199. Rabinowicz, *Beyn Peshisha le-Lublin*, 35.

200. Müller, *Urkundliche Beiträge*, 160.

201. Dynner, *Men of Silk*, 52.

202. Michelsohn, *Sefer Ohel Elimelekh*, 137–38.

203. Kammelhar, *Dor De'ah*, 223. I thank Maoz Kahane for bringing this tradition to my attention.

204. Feuchtwang, "Markus Benedikt," 549. For other, largely hagiographic biographies, see Benet, *Toldot . . . ha-Rav . . . Mordekhai Benet*; Faerber, *Pe'er Mordekhai*; and Rosenwasser, *Rabbi Mordechai Benet*.

Chapter 2

1. A. Trebitsch, *Korot ha-Ittim*, 35b. Benet's approbation is on pp. 2a–2b. Trebitsch inverted the original verse (Ecclesiastes 1:5): "The sun also rises, and the sun goes down." BT Kiddushin 72b understands this verse to mean that "a righteous man does not die until a new one is created to take his place." On *Korot ha-Ittim*, see Šedinová, "Hebrew Historiography"; Cermanová, "Events of the Times"; Cermanová, "Censorship of Hebrew Manuscripts"; and Cermanová, "Second Part."

2. A. Trebitsch, *Korot ha-Ittim*, 29b.

3. Yerushalmi, *Zakhor*, 60.

4. Beer, *Skizze einer Geschichte*, 81. In 1715, Zelig Margoliot wrote, "Because of our many sins, the yeshivot have become extinct in the Land of Poland"; quoted in Silber, "Historical Experience," 147. On the decline of yeshivas from the seventeenth century onward, see Katz, *Tradition and Crisis*, 198–99.

5. Breuer, *Ohalei tora*, 41–44.

6. Jonathan Eybeschütz (Crakow, 1690–Altona, 1794); Ezekiel Landau (Opatow, 1713–Prague, 1793); Pinḥas Horwitz (Czortkow, 1731–Frankfurt am Main, 1805); Joseph Steinhard (Schwabach, c. 1720–Fürth, 1776).

7. Richtmann, *Landau Ezekiel*.

8. Weiss, *Zikhronotai*, 73.

9. Weiss, *Zikhronotai*, 77–79.

10. The Nikolsburg ordinances (*takkanot*) required the Jewish community to support a yeshiva. Roth, *Takkanot Nikolsburg*, 71.

11. In the 1780s and 1790s, for example, the Frankfurt-born Moses Sofer spent time in Boskowitz, Prossnitz, and Strassnitz before finally moving to Hungary. In the 1810s and 1820s, the Bohemian-born and Prague-educated Joachim (Chaim) Deutschmann served as rabbi in Gewitsch and Trebitsch before assuming a post in Kolin.

12. Porter and Teich, *Enlightenment*; Sorkin, *Moses Mendelssohn*.

13. E. Breuer, *Limits of Enlightenment*.

14. Shavit, "A Duty Too Heavy," 113. The quote is attributed to Isaac Euchel.

15. Kieval, *Languages of Community*, 46.

16. Bendavid, *Etwas zur Charackteristick der Juden*, 54–55. Quoted in Robertson, *Jewish Question*, 71. See also Abramsky, "Crisis of Authority," 24–25.

17. Silber, "Historical Experience," 114.

18. Silber, "Historical Experience," 113–14.

19. Weiss, *Zikhronotai*, 36.

20. Weiss, *Zikhronotai*, 36.

21. Benet, *Toldot*, 22; Judah Jeiteles, "Kina tahat shir," *Bikkurei ha-'Ittim* 12 (1830–31): 187.

22. Weiss, *Zikhronotai*, 37.

23. Silber, "Historical Experience," 114.

24. Samet, "Besamim Rosh," 509–23; Feiner, *Jewish Enlightenment*, 337–40.

25. Fishman, "Forging Jewish Memory," 81.

26. On the sturgeon controversy, see Löw, *Aron Chorin*, 10–19; Faerber, *Pe'er Mordekhai*, 114–17.

27. Chorin, *Imre No'am*; and Chorin, *Shiryon kaskasim*.

28. Grieshaber, *Makkel Noam*.

29. Grieshaber, *Makkel Noam*, [2].

30. See Löw, *Aron Chorin*, 15.

31. Chorin, *Sefer Emek ha-Shaveh*.

32. On Sofer's criticism of Rapoport's leniency, see M. Sofer, *Sefer Ḥatam Sofer*, Even Ha-Ezer, pt. 2, responsum 134, 66b. This responsum is from 1805.

33. Carmoly, *Ha-orevim u'vnei yonah*, 21. Rapoport's alleged response: "It is true that I am lenient in areas where R. Moses Sofer and R. Mordecai Benet are stringent, but this is because I have studied more than them, and I know what they will never know and never understand."

34. Carmoly, *Ha-orevim u'vnei yonah*, 21.

35. The expression "recognized halakhic channels" is taken from Fishman, "Forging Jewish Memory," 81.

36. Kieval, *Languages of Community*, 47.

37. Kieval, *Languages of Community*, 47–62, esp. 55–56.

38. E. Landau, *Derushei ha-Tselaḥ*, f. 53a. Translation taken from Kieval, *Languages of Community*, 48. See also Yisrael Natan Heschel, "De'atam shel gedolei ha-dor," 163.

39. Kieval, *Languages of Community*, 56.

40. This obligation can be found in the statutes of the Prossnitz Jewish community from 1782. Kaufmann, "Mi'pinkasa shel k.k. Prostitz," 19–20. For similar statutes predating the Josephinian period, see Roth, *Takkanot Nikolsburg*, 75; and Halpern, *Takkanot medinat Mehrin*, 6.

41. By 1784, German-Jewish schools had been established in forty-two of Moravia's fifty-two Jewish communities. By 1807, fifty-one German-Jewish schools had been established, but the number decreased to thirty-four in the subsequent decades. Hecht, "Gib dem Knaben Unterricht nach seiner Weise."

42. For a list of Jewish and Christian teachers, see MZA, B14, 1959, no. 15462, June 28, 1785.

43. Letter from Markus Benedikt [Mordecai Benet] to Nikolsburg Wirtschaftsamt, January 16, 1825, Jewish Museum Archive (Prague), no. 47455. Also available on microfilm at CAHJP, HM2/7809.

44. Kieval, *Languages of Community*, 54–57.

45. Kieval, *Languages of Community*, 57.

46. Manekin, "Herz Homberg," 153–202.

47. Walk, "Benei Ziyyon le-Herz Homberg," 218.

48. Farber, *Pe'er Mordekhai*, 85–110. On the negative portrayal of Homberg, see Manekin, "Herz Homberg," 153–202.

49. Letter from M. Benet to Samuel Landau, 3 Tishrei 5584 (September 8, 1823), published in Heschel, "Igrot ha-geonim," 154–55.

50. Katz, *Tradition and Crisis*, 162; Petuchowski, "Manuals and Catechisms," 47–64.

51. Přibam, *Urkunden und Akten*, v. 2, 165–66.

52. Přibam, *Urkunden und Akten*, v. 2, 171.

53. Homberg, *Bne-Zion: Ein religiös-moralisches Lehrbuch für die Jugend israeli-*

tischer Religion (Augsburg, 1812); [Homberg], *Bne-Zion: Ein religiös-moralisches Lehrbuch für die Jugend israelitischer Nation* (Vienna, 1812).

54. Homberg, *Bne-Zion* (both editions), [vi].

55. Letter from Markus Benedikt [Mordecai Benet] to the Moravian-Silesian Gubernium, January 13, 1813, MZA, B4, M565, Normalien, Bne Zion, 1811–1830.

56. Wenzel, "Judentum," 335–58; Hecht, *Ein jüdischer Aufklärer in Böhmen*, 160–61.

57. Weiss, *Zikhronotai*, 34–35.

58. Letter from the Nikolsburg Jewish community to the district officer Chiody, February 19, 1819, Jewish Museum Archive (Prague), no. 45896.

59. Briess, *Schilderung*, 16.

60. Weiss, *Zikhronotai*, 34–35.

61. For amusing tales about *Bne Zion* examinations in the Pilsen district of Bohemia, see Ehrmann, *Die Tante*, 132–36. For an English translation, see Iggers, *Jews of Bohemia and Moravia*, 113–15.

62. Letter from Joseph Schlesinger, German-Jewish teacher in Triesch, to the Moravian-Silesian Gubernium, October 30, 1814, MZA, B14, M565, Normalien, no. 26635.

63. Benedict [Naftali Benet], *Emunath Israel* (Vienna edition). Mordecai Benet's approbation (August 1822) appears in German and Hebrew. An abridged, fully bilingual edition, with German and Hebrew on facing pages, was published in Prague by M. I. Landau in 1832.

64. Letter from M. Benet to Samuel Landau, 3 Tishrei 5584 (September 8, 1823). Heschel, "Igrot ha-geonim," 154. In a letter to the government authorities, Mordecai Benet noted that *Emunath Israel* was written under his "guidance" (*Anleitung*). Benet, *Toldot*, 38. This letter notes that Naftali Benet's catechism is still in manuscript form, so the letter can be dated to about 1823, the same year as Benet's letter to Samuel Landau.

65. "Gutachten d. Stud. Hofkomm. bzgl. Rel. Buch von Naptali Benedict," January 29, 1826, AVA, Studienhofkommission 24F, Karton 890. According to this document, Naftali Benet completed "catechistic and pedagogical studies" at the Viennese *Normalschule* five years earlier and was currently teaching at the German-Jewish school in Nikolsburg.

66. "Gutachten d. Stud. Hofkomm. bzgl. Rel. Buch von Naptali Benedict."

67. "Gutachten d. Stud. Hofkomm. bzgl. Rel. Buch von Naptali Benedict."

68. "Fortsetzung von Emunath Israel (Benedict)," Report from Court Commission on Education to Emperor Franz I, October 16, 1827, AVA, Studienhofkommission 24F, Karton 890.

69. "Gutachten d. Stud. Hofkomm. bzgl. Rel. Buch von Naptali Benedict."

70. Samet, "Beginnings of Orthodoxy," 249–69.

71. Meyer, *Response to Modernity*, 59.

72. *Eleh divrei ha-brit*. Mordecai Benet's responsa appear in Hebrew on pp. 11–15

and 18–21 and in Judeo-German on pp. 107–9 and 110–11. On Eleazar Löw, see Münz, *Rabbi Eleasar*, 79–84.

73. Washofsky, "Halakhah in Translation," 146–48; [Auerbach], *Sind die Israeliten verpflichtet*; [Bresselau], *Ueber die Gebete der Israeliten in der Landessprache.* Bresselau was one of the editors of the Hamburg temple prayer book, and this 32-page volume was prepared in response to the controversy that surrounded it.

74. Quoted in Meyer, *Response to Modernity*, 8. *Lev Tov* was first published in Prague in 1620.

75. Gottschalk, "Die Anfänge der deutschen Gebetübersetzungen," 62–63. Fleckeles's remarks were originally published in Fleckeles, *'Olat Hodesh*, v. 2, a collection of his sermons.

76. Friedländer, *Gebete der Juden auf das ganze Jahr*; Euchel, *Gebet der hochdeutschen und polnischen Juden.* R. Samuel Landau, son of Ezekiel Landau of Prague, recommended using these German translations to help teach Hebrew prayers to 6- and 7-year-old boys. See his *Ahavat Tsiyyon*, 27b.

77. Fränkel and Bresselau, *Ordnung der öffentlichen Andacht.*

78. *Eleh divrei ha-brit*, 11–16.

79. *Eleh divrei ha-brit*, 13.

80. *Eleh divrei ha-brit*, 14. Moses Mendelssohn, who coined the term "Ewiger," was well aware of its inadequacy. Sandler, *Mendelssohn's Edition of the Pentateuch*, 63–64.

81. Sandler, *Mendelssohn's Edition of the Pentateuch*, 63–64.

82. Sandler, *Mendelssohn's Edition of the Pentateuch*, 15.

83. This idea is expressed explicitly in a letter from R. Samuel Levi Eger of Braunschweig to Israel Jacobson, from 1810, in which he wrote the following: "If we now pray in German here and the Jews of France in French, those in Italy in Italian—the bundle will come apart." Quoted in Meyer, *Response to Modernity*, 39.

84. "Können beim Bethen in der hebräischen Sprache auch jeder Israelit wessen Landes—oder Muttersprache er immer sei Theil nehmen." Quoted (in Judeo-German) in Benet, *Toldot*, 41. This letter was written c. 1823.

85. Benet, *Toldot*, 22. On Löw's doubts about Mordecai Benet's knowledge of German, see Löw, "Das mährische Landesrabbinat," 192.

86. Weiss, *Zikhronotai*, 36; Benet, *Toldot*, 22.

87. This is taken from Ezekiel Landau's approbation (*haskama*) for *Hamisha humshei torah* (Prague, 1785); this work was published with a rough, nonliterary German translation of the Torah, which was more to Landau's liking. See also Sandler, *Mendelssohn's Edition of the Pentateuch*, 203–4; Viner, *R. Yehezkel Landau*, 118; and Weiss, *Zikhronotai*, 73.

88. Weiss, *Zikhronotai*, 36–37.

89. According to Ya'akov Avril, Mordecai Benet "knew the books of RM"D [Rabbi Moshe of Dessau, i.e., Mendelssohn] very well." Y. A. Benet, *Toldot*, 22. Interestingly, this line appears in the first publication of this work (Ofen, 1832), but

it was removed from all subsequent reprints. See, for example, *Toldot Mordekhai Benet* (Tarnow: Piment, 1929), 19.

90. *Eleh divrei ha-brit*, 14; *Sefer Netivot ha-Shalom* (Vienna: Anton Schmid, 1818). In *Pe'er Mordekhai*, Farber lists Benet's approbation of this work, but he adds the following comment: "The nature of this book and approbation are not known to us, because our eyes did not view either of them" (p. 100). It is more than likely that Farber simply did not want to acknowledge Benet's approbation of Mendelssohn's *Biur*.

91. Even Arad, which was part of the Habsburg monarchy, was about 600 kilometers from Nikolsburg, roughly the same distance as Berlin.

92. Rozenblit, "Jewish Assimilation," 227.

93. Rozenblit, "Jewish Assimilation," 227.

94. Husserl, *Gründungsgeschichte des Stadt-Tempels der Israel*, 81–90.

95. Silber, "Historical Experience," 122.

96. Meyer, *Response to Modernity*, 143–51.

97. Wachstein, "Shnei mikhtavim," 94. However, in a responsum from 1859 dealing with synagogue choirs, R. Azriel Hildesheimer expresses his surprise that neither Mordecai Benet nor Moses Sofer fought against the reformers (*kat ha-mithadshim*) in Vienna, Prague, or Pest. "There is no doubt that they saw what was coming," he wrote, "but since they could not fight against them [the reformers] in this matter, they kept their distance and did not issue a prohibition or a permission." Hildesheimer, *She'elot u'teshuvot*, v. 2, no. 246, 427–28.

98. Rosenmann, *Dr. Adolf Jellinek*, 12. Rosenmann also wrote a biography of Mannheimer: *Isak Noa Mannheimer*.

99. Wachstein, "Shnei mikhtavim," 94–97.

100. Farber, *Pe'er Mordekhai*, 111–13; Walden, *Yekhabed av*, 33.

101. On Schwab, see Ehrentheil, *Jüdische Charakterbilder*, 42–57.

102. Ehrentheil, *Jüdische Charakterbilder*, 46–48.

103. Josef Tomler, "R. Joachim Deutschmann," *BCh* 5(12) (March 21, 1862): 105.

104. Ehrentheil, *Jüdische Charakterbilder*, 50–51.

105. Draft letter from Löw Schwab to Mordecai Benet (in Hebrew), Löw Schwab Archive, ARC, 4° 1619/3, JNUL, Jerusalem; draft letter from Löw Schwab to Eibenschitz Jewish community (in Judeo-German), ARC, 4° 1619/4.

106. As indicated by a letter from Naftali Benet to Löw Schwab (1833), the two rabbis were also close friends. Löw Schwab Archive, ARC, 4° 1619/8, JNUL, Jerusalem.

107. Interestingly, Schwab's approbation (1824) appears only in Hebrew, whereas Mordecai Benet's approbation appears in both Hebrew and German. Benedict [Naftali Benet], *Emunath Yisrael* (Prague edition).

108. According to the *Zsidó Lexikon*, Schwab "strictly adhered to tradition" and "only allowed ceremonial changes that were unavoidably necessary." Nevertheless, he was demonized in ultra-Orthodox literature, such as *Yekhabed av*, 33, which

asserts the following about him: "If Hell did not already exist, they would have to build a new Hell [just] to burn Rabbi Schwab."

109. Michael K. Silber, "Social Composition," 99–128. Among other radical reforms, the Pest Reform Society proposed abolishing circumcision and moving the Sabbath to Sunday. On Schwab's parameters for religious reform, see *Zulässigkeit und Dringlichkeit der Synagogen-Reformen*, 82–85.

110. Wachstein, "Shnei mikhtavim," 94.

111. This turn of phrase is taken from Weiss, *Zikhronotai*, 37.

112. Silber, "Historical Experience," 115.

113. Kieval, *Languages of Community*, 49.

114. Kestenberg-Gladstein, "Ofiyah ha-le'umi," 221–33; Kestenberg-Gladstein, *Neuere Geschichte der Juden*, 200, 207–9, 225.

115. With regard to the Czechs, I am referring to the first of Miroslav Hroch's three phases in the creation of a national identity, which focuses on cultural and linguistic revival, "without pressing specifically national demands to remedy deficits." Hroch, "From National Movement," 81.

116. Kestenberg-Gladstein, *Neuere Geschichte der Juden*, 162–63.

117. Wachstein, *Die hebräische Publizistik*, xxxix; on *Bikkurei ha-'Ittim*, see Zinberg, *History of Jewish Literature*, v. 10, 27–43, 80.

118. Wistrich, "Modernization of Viennese Jewry," 67; on *Kerem Ḥemed*, see Zinberg, *History of Jewish Literature*, v. 10, 80–83.

119. In the twelve issues published between 1845 and 1848, 49% of the pages contained articles and other contributions by thirty-four different Moravian Jews.

120. H. Wassertrilling, "Tefilah le-safa ha-ivriya," *KI* 6 (1846): 66–68. Hirsch (Hermann) Wassertrilling was from Boskowitz.

121. For Gideon Brecher's correspondence with S. D. Luzzatto (Shadal), see *KI* 5 (1845): 28–36; *KI* 6 (1846): 95–100; and *KI* 7 (1846): 77–78. For poems by Eleasar Schnabel, see *KI* 3 (1846): 65–66; *KI* 5 (1846): 67–68; and *KI* 11 (1847): 38–48. For studies by Abraham Schmiedl, see *KI* 1 (1845): 64–67; *KI* 2 (1845): 81–85; and *KI* 3 (1846): 20–22. The eulogy by Ahron Erentheil is in *KI* 10 (1847): 57.

122. Scholem, "Redemption Through Sin," 141.

123. Flesch, *Ha-yoresh divrei elohim*; Flesch, *Ḥayyei moshe*.

124. Leopold Löw, "Abraham und Josef Flesch und ihre Zeit," *BCh* 1 (1858): 549.

125. Scholem, "Redemption Through Sin," 141; Scholem, "Review," 332.

126. Löw, *Gesammelte Schriften*, v. 2, 172. Translation adapted from Katz, "Suggested Relationship," 510.

127. In 1773–74, six Prossnitz families (thirty-five individuals) converted to Catholicism. According to local tradition, these families were followers of Jacob Frank, who had recently arrived in Moravia. Duschak, "Geschichte der israelitischen Gemeinde," 522; Wolf, *Judentaufen in Oesterreich*, 78–79.

128. Heilig, "Aufstieg und Verfall," 101–22; Heilig, "Aktuelles aus der Geschichte," 9–28.

129. A handwritten list of the books in Ehrenstamm's library can be found at the Jewish Museum in Prague, ms. 86. The manuscript has been dated to 1818, but it contains many works from the 1820s, such as *Bikkurei ha-ʿIttim*. The following works are of note: Joseph Albo's *Book of Principles* (Frankfurt), Bahya ibn Pakuda's *Duties of the Heart* (Amsterdam), Maimonides' *Guide to the Perplexed* (Berlin), Judah Halevi's *Kuzari*, and Naftali Benet's *Emunath Yisrael* (Vienna, 1824).

130. Brocke and Carlebach, *Biographisches Handbuch der Rabbiner*, v. 2, 878; Eisler, "R. Moses Katz Wanefried," 205–7; Kayserling, "Die jüdische Literatur von Moses Mendelssohn," v. 2, 760; M. Stein, "Was man alles vom Deckel eines Buches herunterliest," *Judisches Archiv* 1(11–12) (August–October 1928), 22; Weiss, *Zikhronotai*. One of his students, Aharon Halevi from Zlíč, Bohemia, wrote down some of Wanefried's talmudic novellas from 1819; JNUL, Manuscript collection, 8° 3051 (MF B782).

131. "Briefe aus Mähren," *MGWJ* 2 (1853): 386. Weiss did not share this high appraisal of Wanefried's talmudic skills. See Weiss, *Zikhronotai*, 79.

132. Eisler, "R. Moses Katz Wanefried," 206. Wanefried's grandfather, Samuel, was married to a granddaughter of the court Jew, Samson Wertheimer.

133. Eisler, "R. Moses Katz Wanefried," 206.

134. Marx, *Essays in Jewish Biography*, 113.

135. Duschak, "Dr. Gideon Brecher," 9–11.

136. Eisler, "R. Moses Katz Wanefried," 206.

137. J. Halevi, *Ha-kuzari*, with Hebrew commentary by G. Brecher (Prague: M. I. Landau, 1838–1840).

138. Shear, "Judah Halevi's *Kuzari*," 74.

139. Ismar Schorsch, "Myth of Sephardic Supremacy," *LBIYB* 34 (1989): 47–66.

140. Shear, "Judah Halevi's *Kuzari*," 72.

141. Halevi, *Ha-kuzari*, v. 1, 78a–78b.

142. Among other terms that Brecher coined or employed are *yeshut kafula* = *eine zweifache Realität* (32a); *yesod ḥok ha-musari* = *Moralprinzip* (53b); *eyn mikre muḥletet nimtset* = *es gibt keinen reinen Zufall* (63b); and *ḥibbur kokhevei shamayim* = *Sternbilder* (72a).

143. "Das Buch Kuzari mit einem Commentar herausgegeben von G. Brecher," *Literaturblatt des Orients* (January 25, 1840), 57.

144. "Das Buch Kuzari," 54–55. The publication of Brecher's commentary was greatly anticipated in the pages of the *AZJ*. See *AZJ* (March 15, 1838), 125.

145. Chaim Josef Pollak, "Mikhtav," in Halevi, *Ha-kuzari*, 2b.

146. Letter from G. Brecher to Samuel David Luzzatto, 3 Av 5601 (July 21, 1841), Gideon Brecher Correspondence, JTSA, AR 22. Brecher mentions the assistance he received from Steinschneider, who was also trying to find a publisher for Brecher's work in Leipzig.

147. Letter from G. Brecher to Löw Schwab, August 5, 1840, Löw Schwab Collection, JNUL, 4° 1619/12.

148. "Schreiben von Prof. S. L. Luzzatto in Padua, mitgeteilt von Dr. Gideon Brecher in Prossnitz," *KI* 5 (1846): 28–34; "Antwort des Dr. Gideon Brecher in Prossnitz," *KI* 5 (1846): 35–36; *KI* 6 (1846): 95–100; and *KI* 7 (1846): 77–78. Some letters can also be found in the Gideon Brecher Correspondence, JTSA, AR 22.

149. *KI* 5 (1846): 28; on Stern's sojourn in Triesch in 1838, see Deutsch and Gräffer, *Jüdischer Plutarch*, v. 1, 246–52.

150. Pollak, "Mikhtav," 2b.

151. Proverbs 1:17; Isaiah 30:22; Maimonides, *Guide to the Perplexed* 1:33; Halevi, *Ha-kuzari* 5:1.

152. Pollak's *hatara* is reproduced in Jakob Kořatek, "Geschichte der Juden in Trebitsch," in Gold, *Die Juden*, 529. Kořatek erroneously dates this *hatara* to 1816.

153. Benet also gave approbations to the following geographic, historical, and theological works: Yedadya ben Abraham Bedersi, *Behinat Olam* (Brünn: J. K. Neumann, 1797); Trebitsch, *Korot ha-Ittim*; Herz Homberg, *Imre Shefer* (Vienna: Josef Hraschansky, 1808); and Shimshon Bloch, *Shvilei Olam* (1825).

154. Jeiteles, "Kina tahat shir," 188.

155. Benet, *Toldot*, 22.

156. Benet, *Toldot*, 22.

157. Cermanová, "Druhý díl kroniky," 276.

158. Cermanová, "Druhý díl kroniky," 280.

159. Benet, *Misped gadol*, 33.

Chapter 3

The first half of this chapter was originally published as "Crisis of Rabbinical Authority" in *Judaica Bohemiae* 44 (2008): 65–91, published by the Jewish Museum of Prague. Reprinted with permission.

1. "Nekrologe," *Kalendar und Jahrbuch für Israeliten* 2 (1843–44), 233.

2. Schlesinger, *Biographische Skizze*, 10.

3. Benet's certificate is quoted in a letter from Karl Fischer, Hebrew censor in Prague, July 8, 1823, Národní Archiv (Prague), ČG-Publicum 97/12, Karton 7334 (1825). I thank Louise Hecht for bringing this document to my attention.

4. Letter from Karl Fischer.

5. Letter from Karl Fischer.

6. Weiss, *Zikhronotai*, 44.

7. Kahan, "Drei unveröffentlichte Briefe," 71.

8. Mayer, *Die Juden unserer Zeit*, 43.

9. Early on, the Nikolsburg Jewish community favored Eleazar Landau of Prague, grandson of Ezekiel Landau. Koppel Deutsch of Prossnitz vehemently opposed Landau, arguing that it was not customary to elect a chief rabbi whose character was unknown. Löw, "Das mährische Landesrabbinat," 198. Akiva Eger (1761–1837), rabbi of Posen, was also approached by the Nikolsburg Jewish com-

munity. See letter (1830) to his son-in-law, Moses Sofer, in Sofer, *Igrot Sofrim*, v. 1, 20–31.

10. The six electors were Moses Karpeles (1765–1837) in Boskowitz, Joseph Feilbogen (1784–1869) in Gross-Meseritsch, Bernard Oppenheim (1791–1859) in Eibenschitz, Bernard Kramer in Hotzenplotz, Aron Stössel (1796/7–1849) in Gaya, and Aron Neuda (d. 1835) in Loschitz. Feilbogen and Oppenheim were candidates as well as electors. Löw, "Das mährische Landesrabbinat," 201.

11. Löw, "Das mährische Landesrabbinat," 201.

12. The Moravian-Silesian Gubernium expected approval from the Court Chancery within a "suitable period, in any event by the end of January [1831]." Letter from the Moravian-Silesian Gubernium to the Court Chancery, December 28, 1830, AVA, Alter Kultus–Israelitischer Kultus, Rabbiner: Mähren-Schlesien, Karton 3 (IV T 5).

13. Letter from Jesayes Benedikt [Isaias Benet] to Emperor Franz I, June 29, 1831, AVA, Alter Kultus–Israelitischer Kultus, Rabbiner: Mähren-Schlesien, Karton 3 (IV T 5).

14. Letter from Juditha Benedikt [Benet] to Emperor Franz I, February 6, 1832, AVA, Alter Kultus–Israelitischer Kultus, Rabbiner: Mähren-Schlesien, Karton 3 (IV T 5).

15. The letter of confirmation is reprinted in Schlesinger, *Biographisches Skizze*, 11. Trebitsch's installation ceremony is described by Abraham Trebitsch in *Korot ha-Ittim* (quoted in Buxbaum, "Introduction," 11).

16. A number of letters regarding Schwab's election to the Eibenschitz rabbinate and Benet's subsequent refusal to approve him can be found in the Löw Schwab Archive, JNUL, 4°, 1619/2.

17. In Prossnitz, there was some opposition from the more conservative elements. As Gideon Brecher observed, "While N. Trebitsch was still amongst us, all the people gathered together . . . and elected Löw Schwab—with the exception of M[oses] Katz Wan[e]fried and H[irsch] Klein and their party," who opposed his election. G. Brecher to Ber Schiff (1830), Gideon Brecher Correspondence, JTSA, AR 22.

18. Letter from L. Schwab to the Pest Magistracy, 1837. Quoted in Löw, "Das mährische Landesrabbinat," 207.

19. Weiss, *Zikhronotai*, 45.

20. Letter from L. Schwab to Pest Magistracy, 1837. Quoted in Löw, "Das mährische Landesrabbinat," 207.

21. General-Polizei-Ordnung, Art. I, §6. Scari, *Systematische Darstellung*, §47.

22. Trebitsch to the Moravian-Silesian Gubernium, July 27, 1833, MZA, B14, M565, no. 28709.

23. Scari, *Systematische Darstellung*, 88–89; Löw, "Das mährische Landesrabbinat," 202.

24. Löw, "Das mährische Landesrabbinat," 202.

25. Trebitsch to the Moravian-Silesian Gubernium, July 27, 1833, MZA, B14, M565, no. 28709.

26. On the debate over weddings in synagogues, see Guttmann, *Struggle over Reform*, 58–64.

27. Letter from L. Schwab to Pest Magistracy, 1837. Quoted in Löw, "Das mährische Landesrabbinat," 202.

28. For a discussion of the German sermon, see Altmann, "New Style of Preaching," 65–116.

29. Schwab, *Das Gedächtniss*; Löw, "Das mährische Landesrabbinat," 212–13.

30. Trebitsch, *Trauerrede*.

31. Weiss, *Zikhronotai*, 45.

32. *Israelitische Annalen*, March 20, 1840, 110.

33. Friedlaender, *Kore Haddoroth*, 53.

34. Friedlaender, *Kore Haddoroth*, 53. According to Friedlaender, Neuda's study companions included Majer Zipser, A. Ehrlich, and Michael Lazar Kohn. On Neuda's friendship with Zipser, see Reich, *Beth-El*, v. 2, 11–13.

35. *Die Neuzeit*, January 4, 1884, 3; *AZJ*, January 15, 1884, 45.

36. Ber Schiff to G. Brecher, 1836, Gideon Brecher Correspondence, JTSA, AR 22.

37. Újvári, *Magyar zsidó Lexikon*, 202; *AZJ*, January 15, 1884, 45.

38. Mayer, *Die Juden unserer Zeit*, 44. Mayer's observation is borne out by a letter from Mordecai Benet's eldest son, Naftali, to Isaac Brill of Prossnitz from 13 Heshvan 5596 (November 5, 1835). Naftali inquired about the post in Prossnitz, expressing his willingness to give sermons in both German (*pa'am bi-sfat le'umim*) and Hebrew (*u-fa'am bi-l'shonenu ha-kadosha ve-ha-yekara*). He also promised to distinguish himself as a moderate (*anokhi elekh ba-derekh ha-memutsa*). Gideon Brecher Correspondence, JTSA, AR 22.

39. This certification must have taken place at some point between 1832 and 1835, but it is not clear which Jewish community Fassel had been considered for.

40. AVA, Alter Kultus–Israelitischer Kultus, Rabbiner: Mähren-Schlesien, Karton 3 (IV T 5), no. 3856/646, 1838.

41. This offer may have been made after Moses Karpeles, the rabbi of Boskowitz, died in 1837.

42. A section of this letter, dated March 30, 1837, is quoted by Fassel in a letter to Leopold Löw, April 15, 1853. Löw, *Gesammelten Schriften*, v. 5, 147–48.

43. The five rabbis were Salomon Haas (d. 1847) of Strassnitz, Heschel Gläser (d. 1854) of Kremsier, Lowy Hahn (d. 1847) of Tobitschau, Aron Schüller (d. 1846) of Jamnitz, and Hirsch Klein of Prossnitz. Heschel Gläser adamantly refused to give a German sermon in Kremsier in 1843, despite pressure from members of the Jewish community; see *AZJ*, September 18, 1843, 573.

44. N. Trebitsch to Moses Sofer, in Sofer, *Igrot Sofrim*, v. 2, 68–70.

45. G. Brecher to L. Löw, June 26, 1851; Löw, *Gesammelte Schriften*, v. 5, 145–47.

46. Trebitsch to Brünn District Office, November 30, 1840, MZA, B14, M602, no. 53210.

47. Moravian-Silesian Gubernium to Court Chancery, January 4, 1841, AVA, Alter Kultus–Israelitischer Kultus, Rabbiner: Mähren-Schlesien, Karton 3 (IV T 5), no. 53210.

48. Löw, "Das mährische Landesrabbinat," 203–4.

49. Löw, "Das mährische Landesrabbinat," 204.

50. Löw, "Das mährische Landesrabbinat," 205–6.

51. AVA, Alter Kultus–Israelitischer Kultus, Rabbiner: Mähren-Schlesien, Karton 3 (IV T 5), no. 3856/646, 1838.

52. AVA, Alter Kultus–Israelitischer Kultus, Rabbiner: Mähren-Schlesien, Karton 3 (IV T 5), no. 3856/646, 1838.

53. Loschitz Jewish community to Court Chancery, February 1, 1840, MZA, B14, M602, no. 10435.

54. Loschitz Jewish community to Court Chancery.

55. Loschitz Jewish community to Court Chancery.

56. Rozenblit, "Struggle over Religious Reform."

57. Löw, "Aron Chorin," 251–420.

58. Abraham Neuda, "Das Jahrhundert nach seinen Licht- und Schattenseiten, gehalten am Neujahrstage (Rosch Haschana) 5600," in his *Mase davar adonai*, 8–26.

59. Loschitz Jewish community to Court Chancery, February 1, 1840, MZA, B14, M602, no. 10435.

60. Olmütz District Office to the Moravian-Silesian Gubernium, July 24, 1840, MZA, B14, M602, no. 29274.

61. Moravian-Silesian Gubernium to Court Chancery, January 4, 1841, AVA, Alter Kultus–Israelitischer Kultus, Rabbiner: Mähren-Schlesien, Karton 3 (IV T 5), no. 53210.

62. Pillersdorf to the Moravian-Silesian Gubernium, June 10, 1840, MZA, B14, M602, no. 25942; Moravian-Silesian Gubernium to Court Chancery, January 4, 1841, AVA, Alter Kultus–Israelitischer Kultus, Rabbiner: Mähren-Schlesien, Karton 3 (IV T 5), no. 53210.

63. District rabbis from Beraun, Leitmeritz, Saatz, and Ellenbogen.

64. Abraham Neuda to Court Chancery, September 30, 1840, MZA, B14, M602, no. 44035.

65. Loschitz Jewish community to Court Chancery, February 1, 1840, MZA, B14, M602, no. 10435.

66. Abr. Neuda to Court Chancery, September 30, 1840, MZA, B14, M602, no. 44035.

67. Trebitsch to Brünn District Office, November 30, 1840, MZA, B14, M602, no. 53210.

68. Trebitsch to Brünn District Office, December 10, 1840. Quoted in a letter from the Moravian-Silesian Gubernium to the Court Chancery, January 4, 1841,

AVA, Alter Kultus–Israelitischer Kultus, Rabbiner: Mähren-Schlesien, Karton 3 (IV T 5), no. 53210.

69. Trebitsch to Brünn District Office, December 10, 1840.

70. Moravian-Silesian Gubernium to Court Chancery, January 4, 1841, AVA, Alter Kultus–Israelitischer Kultus, Rabbiner: Mähren-Schlesien, Karton 3 (IV T 5), no. 53210.

71. Although Neuda had been examined by four Bohemian district rabbis, the Moravian-Silesian Gubernium was apparently in possession of only three certificates of competency.

72. In fact, only one of Trebitsch's claims—that Neuda's bachelor status made him unqualified for a rabbinic post—seemed to trouble any of the discussants. Perhaps they were wary of interfering with a custom that Trebitsch claimed was "founded on religious principles."

73. Mitterauer, *Gelobt sei*, 84.

74. Trebitsch to the Moravian-Silesian Gubernium, September 17, 1840, MZA, B14, M605.

75. *AZJ*, November 9, 1839, 576; *Israelitische Annalen*, April 10, 1840, 133–34.

76. Moravian-Silesian Gubernium to Court Chancery, December 20, 1841, MZA, B14, M605, no. 3021.

77. Moravian-Silesian Gubernium to Court Chancery, January 4, 1841, AVA, Alter Kultus–Israelitischer Kultus, Rabbiner: Mähren-Schlesien, Karton 3 (IV T 5), no. 53210.

78. Pillersdorf to the Moravian-Silesian Gubernium, March 11, 1841, AVA, Alter Kultus–Israelitischer Kultus, Rabbiner: Mähren-Schlesien, Karton 3 (IV T 5). See also Löw, "Das mährische Landesrabbinat," 208–9.

79. Brünn Episcopal Consistory to the Moravian-Silesian Gubernium, April 23, 1841, MZA, B14, M602, no. 17758.

80. Löw, "Das mährische Landesrabbinat," 211.

81. Weiss, *Zikhronotai*, 48. The questions are reproduced in Weiss, *Zikhronotai*, 48n; and Löw, "Das mährische Landesrabbinat," 210n. For English translation, see Miller, "Crisis of Rabbinical Authority," 90.

82. Friedlaender, *Kore Haddoroth*, 54.

83. Friedlaender, *Kore Haddoroth*, 54.

84. Schlesinger, *Biographische Skizze*, 14. "Doch es konnte in einer Zeit, wo so viele religiöse Spaltungen in Israel nicht fremd sind, auch nicht fehlen, dass ein solcher Mann, hat schwer die Bürde seines Amtes fühlen musste [und manche lieblose Beurtheilung sein Herz verwundete]" (In a time when the many religious divisions are no stranger to Israel, it was unavoidable that such a man had difficulties fulfilling the burdens of his office and that some unloving judgment wounded his heart).

85. Weiss, *Zikhronotai*, 41n.

86. G. B[recher], "Zwei allgemeine und ein specieller Brief," *AZJ*, April 17,

1838, 183–84; "Dritter Brief," April 24, 1838, 195–96. See also letter from G. Brecher to Löw, June 26, 1851, in Löw, *Gesammelte Schriften*, v. 5, 145–47.

87. Nathan Denneberger, "Rabbiner," *AZJ*, July 28, 1838, 365–66. According to *Israelitische Annalen* (March 13, 1840, 100), Trebitsch examined his Talmud students in Prague in "pure German" and allowed his son Seligmann to study ancient and modern languages.

88. The other work was Trebitsch's *Kovets 'al Yad ha-ḥazakah*, a volume of commentary on Maimonides' *Mishne Torah*. Recently, a number of Trebitsch's manuscripts (in the private collection of Macḥon Yerushalayim) have been published, for example, *Sefer Shalom Yerushalayim: ḥidushim u-ferushim, hagahot ve-tikunim 'al Talmud Yerushalmi, Seder Zera'im* and *Sefer Shalom Yerushalayim: ḥidushim 'al ha-Mishnah, Masekhet Zevaḥim*. A collection of his rabbinic responsa was published as *She'elot u-teshuvot Rabi Naḥum Trebitsch*.

89. Trebitsch, *Sefer Shalom yerushalayim* (Vienna, 1821), commentary on paragraph 463.

90. "Aus Mähren," *AZJ*, November 5, 1842, 663–66. See also Löw, "Das mährische Landesrabbinat," 204n1.

91. Weiss, *Meine Lehrjahre*, 76. Among these students were Abraham Neuda, Michael Lazar Kohn, Majer Zipser, and A. Ehrlich.

92. Klemperer, "Remeniszenzen," 25–37.

93. Dr. Ahron (Adolf) Rosenbach (1799–1870), head of the firm Bloch & Sohn in Prague, owned a significant Jewish library and gave occasional lectures in philosophy. Although Klemperer recalled that Rosenbach received his doctorate in Prague, Rosenmann states that he received it at the university in Vienna. Rosenmann, *Dr. Adolf Jellinek*, 23n41.

94. Translations of the Moravian Edict of Toleration are adapted from Iggers, *Jews of Bohemia and Moravia*, 48–52. For the original German, see Müller, *Urkundliche Beiträge*, 185–90. See Kieval, "Caution's Progress," 71–105.

95. Briess, *Schilderung*, 57.

96. Weiss, *Meine Lehrjahre*, 16–18.

97. In *Schulgesetzgebung und Methodik der alten Israeliten*, Moritz Duschak described the situation of private teachers as follows: "There was no shortage of teachers; when one left, another would come who legitimized himself through his overflowing knowledge and his skill. . . . Since the permanence of the job was not guaranteed, and since [the teacher] could be easily dismissed if his knowledge, actions, and [way of] life were found to be unsatisfactory, the loss of a bad teacher was not a big deal. The teaching methods and educational level of the teacher were not inquired about, no certificate of maturity or good standing was required, and it was considered a happy coincidence if the teacher happened to be endowed with a *ḥaver* or *morenu* title. The term of the contract was usually one semester, from Passover until Sukkot, and then from Sukkot until Passover" (p. 45).

98. Duschak, *Schulgesetzgebung*, 22. According to one obituary, not only was

Wolf Mühlrad (1807–1862) an "astute talmudist, well-read in every branch of rabbinic and Jewish literature," but he also wrote a "correct and graceful" German even though he was a complete autodidact in this language. *BCh* 5(3) (1862), 21–22.

99. Scari, *Systematische Darstellung*, 102.

100. Trebitsch to the Moravian-Silesian Gubernium, July 27, 1833, MZA, B14, M565, no. 28709.

101. Gross-Meseritsch Jewish community to the Moravian-Silesian Gubernium, December 28, 1842, MZA, B14, M613, no. 13993.

102. Trebitsch, like his predecessors in the Moravian chief rabbinate, was also communal rabbi of Nikolsburg.

103. For Fassel's criticism of traditional heder education, see *Ḥorev be-tsiyyon*, 24–26.

104. *AZJ*, April 17–23, 1838, 183–84, 195–96.

105. *Wurzbach* 54 (1856): 159–60; *Die Neuzeit*, December 10, 1897, 503–5; *AZJ*, November 29, 1912, 570–72.

106. Meyer, *Response to Modernity*, 153–54; Sadek, "La synagogue réformée," 119–23.

107. Joseph Weisse, "Biographische Einleitung" to Jedaja Penini Bedarschi in *Bechinat Olam* (Vienna: F. Edler von Schmid and S. S. Busch, 1847).

108. The poem was published in *KI* 2 (1845): 75–76.

109. *WB*, August 11, 1850.

110. *AZJ*, May 29, 1843, 324. The Society was set up in April 1839 and given government approval three months later. MZA, M599, no. 12869, April 3, 1840.

111. Ignaz Kirchner, Prossnitz Schuldistriktsaufseher und Land-Pfarrer in Moskowitz to Plumenau district office, March 17, 1839, MZA Kunštat, F 264, ev. č. 257, sign. M XXVI, Fasz. 39.

112. MZA Kunštat, F 264, ev. č. 257, sign. M XXVI, Fasz. 33.

113. MZA, B14, M597, no. 25248, December 29, 1838.

114. MZA, B14, M597, no. 25248, December 29, 1838.

115. MZA, B14, M597, no. 25248, December 29, 1838.

116. MZA, B14, M597, August 8, 1838.

117. MZA, B14, M565, no. 44444, October 19, 1841.

118. The school was officially established on April 19, 1839. For a history of Jewish education in Nikolsburg, see Anton Altrichter, "Das jüdische Schulwesen in Nikolsburg," CAHJP HM 2/8202.

119. Jewish Museum in Prague, Sitzungsprotokolle des Gemeinde-Vorstands (Mikulov), October 7, 1838.

120. Jewish Museum in Prague, Sitzungsprotokolle des Gemeinde-Vorstands (Mikulov).

121. Jewish Museum in Prague, Sitzungsprotokolle des Gemeinde-Vorstands (Mikulov).

122. *AZJ*, November 2, 1839, 565–66.

123. *AZJ*, November 2, 1839, 565–66.

Chapter 4

1. "Bericht über die Anträge zur Reform des Judenwesen in Mähren und Schlesien," July 7, 1847, MZA, B14 (starsí), M618, no. 23390/1156, f. 15.

2. Schorsch, "Emancipation," 10.

3. Schorsch, "Emancipation," 10.

4. In the German states, there were sixty-seven rabbis with doctorates by 1848. This number includes Zacharias Frankel, Michael Sachs, Simeon Schwabacher, and Saul Isaac Kämpf, who served as rabbis in Bohemia during the 1840s. See Schorsch, "Emancipation," 39–41. In October 1842, the Court Chancery established new educational and pastoral requirements for Moravia's communal rabbis. Drawing on edicts issued for Galicia and Bohemia in 1841, the Chancery decreed that in ten years' time, all rabbis would be required to complete courses in philosophy and pedagogy before assuming a post in one of Moravia's Jewish communities. Because of the current "shortage of such candidates," however, the Chancery allowed uncertified candidates to be elected until 1852 so long as they could exhibit some proficiency in these areas. The rabbis were also expected to help spread German and exert a morally edifying influence on their individual communities. With this in mind, the 1842 decree required rabbis to deliver "dogmatic-moral lectures" (*dogmatisch-moralische Vorträge*) in German at the end of each prayer service. MZA, B14, M565, no. 53018. The decree for Moravia is dated October 26, 1842. The decrees for Galicia and Bohemia are dated April 5, 1841, and July 15, 1841, respectively.

5. "Berichte über Synagoge und Schule," *Zeitschrift für die religiösen Interessen des Judenthums* 1(2) (May 1844), 79–82, 1(9) (December 1844), 339–43.

6. In February 1847, a Jew from Prossnitz reported the following: "We can say with pride that our rabbi has been the most vigorous in fostering Jewish-Moravian interests, and until now, he has outmatched his fellow rabbis in Nikolsburg—the largest community in Moravia—in expertise and insight." *Der Orient*, February 26, 1847, 68.

7. With a decree from March 11, 1841, the Court Chancery asked the Moravian-Silesian Gubernium to comment on the future of the Moravian chief rabbinate. This decree, dated August 3, 1842, is referred to in MZA, B14, M611, no. 34839.

8. MZA, B14, M611, no. 53896, November 10, 1842.

9. MZA, B14, M611, no. 53896, November 10, 1842.

10. This is how the responsibilities of the Moravian chief rabbi are defined in §142 of the Polizei-Ordnung.

11. MZA, B14, M611, no. 53896, November 10, 1842.

12. MZA, B14, M611, no. 53896, November 10, 1842.

13. MZA, B14, M611, no. 53896, November 10, 1842.

14. MZA, B14, M611, no. 53896, November 10, 1842.

15. MZA, B14, M611, no. 43756, October 15, 1842.

16. This undated letter was received by the Moravian-Silesian Gubernium on February 24, 1843. MZA, B14, M611, no. 24760, July 14, 1843.

17. *Der Orient*, February 21, 1843, 60–61.

18. *Der Orient*, February 21, 1843, 60–61.

19. MZA, B14, M611, no. 53896, November 10, 1842.

20. MZA, B14, M611, no. 53896, November 10, 1842.

21. MZA, B14, M611, no. 49308, October 26, 1842.

22. Jewish Museum in Prague, Sitzungsprotokolle des Gemeinde-Vorstands (Mikulov), February 1843.

23. *AZJ*, May 29, 1843, 324.

24. The term *positive-historical* was central to Zacharias Frankel's thought, but it also characterizes Fassel's approach to Jewish tradition, which, in the words of one contemporary, was "in accordance with the Frankelian principle (*Frankel'schen Princip*)." *Der Orient*, March 15, 1846, 82. For a discussion of this term, see Ismar Schorsch, "Zacharias Frankel and the European Origins of Conservative Judaism," in his *From Text to Context*, 255–65.

25. Fassel, *Ḥorev be-tsiyyon*, 29.

26. Grunfeld, "Introduction" to S. R. Hirsch's *Judaism Eternal*, xix. S. R. Hirsch, *Neunzehn Briefe über Judenthum* (Altona: J. F. Hammerich, 1836); S. R. Hirsch, *Ḥorev: Versuche über Jissroels Pflichten in der Zerstreuung für Jissroel's denkende Junglinge und Jungfrauen* (Altona: J. F. Hammerich, 1837).

27. Graetz, *Tagebuch und Briefe*, 15.

28. I. Grunfeld, "Introduction" to Hirsch's *Horeb: A Philosophy of Jewish Laws and Observances*, xix.

29. Rosenbloom, *Tradition in the Age of Reform*. On the reception of *Nineteen Letters* and *Ḥorev*, see Grunfeld, "Introduction" to Hirsch's *Horeb*, xxxiv–xl.

30. Fassel, *Ḥorev be-tsiyyon*. The title is an allusion to Isaiah 25:5 ("You shall bring down the noise of strangers, as the heat in a dry place [*ke-ḥorev be-tsayon*]." I have vocalized the title as *Ḥorev be-tsiyyon* (Desolation in Zion) as opposed to *Ḥorev be-tsayon* (Heat in a dry place), because it better reflects the spirit of Fassel's book. Fassel received his copy of *Ḥorev* from Steinschneider; by Purim 1839, he had read Hirsch's work, subjected it to thorough analysis, and sent a critique of it—written as seven separate epistles—back to Steinschneider. Steinschneider published these epistles as *Ḥorev be-tsiyyon* and appended an introduction of his own. Steinschneider wrote under the pen name M. S. Charbonah, an allusion to the book of Esther 1:10. See Tal, *Samson Raphael Hirsch*, 11, for the identification of M. S. Charbonah as Moritz Steinschneider.

31. Fassel, *Ḥorev be-tsiyyon*, 15.

32. Hirsch, *Postscripta*, 27.

33. Hirsch, *Postscripta*, 17.

34. Hirsch, *Postscripta*, 16.

35. Hirsch, *Postscripta*, 30–31.

36. Jost, *Culturgeschichte der Israeliten*, 46.

37. *Der Orient*, June 13, 1840, 186.

38. Fassel to Löw, n.d., Leopold Löw Archive, JNUL, 4 794/2, f. 20.

39. Fassel to Löw, n.d., Leopold Löw Archive, JNUL, 4 794/2, f. 13.

40. Fassel to Löw, n.d., Leopold Löw Archive, JNUL, 4 794/2, f. 1.

41. Fassel to Löw, n.d., Leopold Löw Archive, JNUL, 4 794/2, f. 1.

42. Fassel to Löw, n.d., Leopold Löw Archive, JNUL, 4 794/2, f. 19.

43. Fassel, *Horev be-tsiyyon*, 25–26.

44. Fassel, *Horev be-tsiyyon*, 26.

45. Fassel, *Horev be-tsiyyon*, 27.

46. Fassel, *Horev be-tsiyyon*, 29.

47. Wolf, "Die Versuche zur Errichtung," 45.

48. Fassel, *Horev be-tsiyyon*, 29.

49. The title indicates the balanced, reasoned nature of this work. As Fassel explained in the introduction to Part 3 of *Kaf Moznayyim*, "I proceed in the order of the *Shulhan Arukh*, and for each law (*din*) and *halakha* that I learned in the *Shulhan Arukh*, I asked the earlier and later authorities (*rishonim* and *ahronim*), and I weighed their opinions on the balance of my wisdom and knowledge (*moznei sikhli v'ha-dea*) that God granted." *Sefer Moznei Tsedek*, HUC, ms. 197, f. 2a.

50. Fassel, *Horev be-tsiyyon*, 30n. This footnote was written by Steinschneider, who "eagerly await[ed]" the publication of *Kaf Moznayyim*. The first part of the unpublished work, which was called *Moznei Tsedek* (Scales of justice), can be found in manuscript at the Hebrew Union College in Cincinnati, Ohio (HUC mss. 196–97) and at the Jewish Theological Seminary of America (JTSA) in New York (ms. 9570). The HUC manuscript was donated by Salomon H. Sonneschein (1839–1908), Fassel's son-in-law, who served a Reform temple in St. Louis, Missouri. The JTSA manuscript is part of the Moritz Steinschneider Collection. The page layout of *Moznei Tsedek* resembles the standard printed *Shulhan Arukh*, with the Halakha in the middle of the page and the commentaries on the side.

51. Fassel to G. Brecher, 14 Heshvan 5605 (October 27, 1844), Gideon Brecher Papers, JTSA, AR 22. Fassel describes the halakhic process in almost identical terms in the introduction to *Sefer Moznei Tsedek*, HUC ms. 196, f. 3a.

52. Twersky, "The Shulhan 'Aruk."

53. Fassel, *Horev be-tsiyyon*, 30n. To establish the Halakha conclusively, Fassel deferred to "majority opinion."

54. Fassel to G. Brecher, 14 Heshvan 5605 (October 27, 1844), Gideon Brecher Papers, JTSA, AR 22.

55. While visiting Breslau in 1844, Fassel tried to gather subscriptions (*INJ*, December 22, 1844, 414). Fassel also mentions his failure to gather enough subscriptions in his application for the Moravian chief rabbinate (MZA, B14, M614, December 13, 1846). The manuscript received an imprimatur from the Viennese censor on May 28, 1845; *Sefer Moznei Tsedek*, HUC ms. 196, last folio.

56. *Der Orient*, January 24, 1843, 30.

57. *Zulässigkeit und Dringlichkeit der Synagogen-Reformen.* In 1844, the Jewish

community in Pápa, Hungary, sought opinions of prominent rabbis regarding a number of religious reforms, including moving the bimah to the front of the synagogue, conducting weddings in the synagogue, and introducing choral prayer. Among the twenty-one respondents were I. N. Mannheimer, Abraham Neuda, L. Schwab, L. Löw, Zacharias Frankel, and Majer Zipser. Fassel's response appears on pp. 56–58.

58. Meyer, *Response to Modernity*, 109.

59. Meyer, *Response to Modernity*, 112.

60. Quoted in Meyer, *Response to Modernity*, 112.

61. The questions are reprinted in Löw, *Gesammelte Schriften*, v. 5, 210; and *Literaturblatt des Orients* 8 (1843): 114. My translations are based on Meyer, *Response to Modernity*, 113.

62. *Rabbinische Gutachten.* A second volume of seven responsa was published in 1843.

63. Fassel to M. Steinschneider, November 14, 1842, Moritz Steinschneider Correspondence, JTSA, AR 108, Box 13.

64. Fassel to M. Steinschneider, November 14, 1842. Fassel's attempt to reach a wider audience fell somewhat short of his expectations. He had hoped that his German responsum to the Breslau community would be published as a separate brochure (so it would have "more of an effect"), but he had to settle for publication in *Der Orient* instead. (See letter from Fassel to Steinschneider, November 29, 1842, Moritz Steinschneider Correspondence, JTSA, AR 108, Box 13.) His articles on organ playing and deaf-mutes were rejected by Moses Landau, editor of the scholarly publication *Kerem Ḥemed* and by Zacharias Frankel, editor of the short-lived *Zeitschrift für die religiösen Interessen des Judenthums.* Although Landau's reasons for rejecting the articles are unknown, Frankel believed that Fassel's positions were much too lenient (*makil*). (See letter from Fassel to Steinschneider, December 27, 1844, Moritz Steinschneider Correspondence, JTSA, AR 108, Box 13.)

65. Hirsch B. Fassel, "Das rabbinische Judenthum: Ein abverlangtes, aber ungedrucktes Votum an das Israel—Obervorsteher-Collegium zu Breslau," *Literaturblatt des Orients* 5–8 (1843): 65–71, 81–85, 97–103, 113–20.

66. Fassel, *Tsedek ve-mishpat.*

67. Fassel further divided principles (*Satzungen*) into doctrines of justice (*Rechtlehre*) and doctrines of virtue (*Tugendlehre*), which were the foundations of "absolute humanity" for all humankind.

68. Put another way, statutes are "those laws that God revealed" and principles are "those laws that God still reveals."

69. Fassel, *Tsedek ve-mishpat*, viii.

70. Mendelssohn, *Jerusalem*, 90–92.

71. Fassel, *Tsedek ve-mishpat*, viii.

72. Fassel, "Das rabbinische Judenthum," 100.

73. Fassel, *Tsedek ve-mishpat*, ix.

74. Jost, *Culturgeschichte der Israeliten*, 179. Fassel's responsum was heavily criticized in *INJ*, December 22, 1844, 414.

75. Geiger, *Abraham Geiger's Leben*, 113.

76. Fassel to M. Steinschneider, January 28, 1845, Moritz Steinschneider Correspondence, JTSA, AR 108.

77. Geiger, *Abraham Geiger's Leben*, 113; Meyer, *Response to Modernity*, 111.

78. For a detailed discussion of the rabbinic assemblies, see Meyer, *Response to Modernity*, 132–42.

79. Meyer, *Response to Modernity*, 134–36; Jacob Katz, "The Controversy over the Temple in Hamburg and the Rabbinical Assembly in Braunschweig: Milestones in the Development of Orthodoxy," in his *Divine Law in Human Hands*, 230–54.

80. Meyer, *Response to Modernity*, 135. The seventeen Moravian rabbis were Gerson Buchheim (Austerlitz), Joseph Feilbogen (Holleschau), Juda Freund (Pohrlitz), Herschel Gläser (Kremsier), Leopold Gläser (Pirnitz), Salomon Haas (Strassnitz), Salomon Kulke (Kostel), Moses Müller (Ungarisch-Ostra), Bernard Oppenheim (Eibenschitz), Abraham Placzek (Boskowitz), Joachim (Chaim Josef) Pollak (Trebitsch), Salomon Quetsch (Leipnik), and Esaias Reiniger (Weisskirchen), as well as four rabbis from Nikolsburg (Herschl Felsner, Moises Paschkes, Samuel Cohn, and Isaac Weinberger).

81. These letters were published as *Torat ha-ken'aot Kin'at tsiyyon*. Hirsch's letter appears on pp. 3–5 of *Torat ha-ken'aot*.

82. Katz, *Divine Law in Human Hands*, 242.

83. Zacharias Frankel, "Aufruf zu einer Versammlung jüdischer Theologen," *Der Orient*, May 16, 1846, 149–51.

84. For Geiger's letter of invitation to Löw, see Löw, *Gesammelte Schriften*, v. 5, 135–36.

85. See Fassel's letter to Löw from March 1, 1846, in Löw, *Gesammelte Schriften*, v. 5, 135.

86. Hirsch B. Fassel, "Die Versammlung der jüdischen Theologen," *Der Orient*, June 25, 1846, 212. Fassel also mentions Jellinek's observations in a letter to Leopold Löw from June 8, 1846, found in Löw, *Gesammelte Schriften*, v. 5, 136–37.

87. Fassel, "Die Versammlung der jüdischen Theologen," 212.

88. See Fassel's letter to Löw, June 8, 1846.

89. Fassel describes his role in a letter to Löw and in the pages of *Der Orient*. See his letter to Löw from June 8, 1846, and his article, "Die Versammlung der jüdischen Theologen," 212.

90. Frankel, "Aufruf zu einer Versammlung jüdischer Theologen," 149–51. Frankel declared that Judaism, as a dynamic and evolving religion, was open to innovation, but only if historical developments were taken into consideration. "Judaism must be developed on a historical basis," he wrote. "Our goal is not the destruction of the faith, but rather its preservation. Its foundational pillars, rooted

deep in the past, must not be destroyed; they must be the linchpin of its further evolution."

91. Horwitz, *Zacharias Frankel*, 32–34; Brämer, *Rabbiner Zacharias Frankel*, 225–54.

92. Sorkin, *Transformation of German Jewry*, 145.

93. Here, I use Austria to refer to all Habsburg lands outside the Kingdom of Hungary.

94. [Wertheimer], *Die Juden in Österreich*.

95. [Wertheimer], *Die Juden in Österreich*, xv; Wolf, *Joseph Wertheimer*, 45.

96. As Wolf has pointed out, "In Austria, where the press was muzzled and the parliament was nonexistent, the only [political] means available to the Jews was submitting petitions." Wolf, *Joseph Wertheimer*, 47–48.

97. Plumenauer Wirtschaftsamt to the Moravian-Silesian Gubernium, May 12, 1842, MZA, B14, M604, no. 22509. This is not the original 1841 decree but rather a letter to the Moravian-Silesian Gubernium providing details of the new policy that was implemented. See also *AZJ*, June 12, 1843, 356–58; and *VJ*, August 4, 1843, 213.

98. The petition is published in full in *AZJ*, June 12, 1843, 356–58. No date is listed, but based on internal evidence, it is clear that the petition was submitted at some point in 1841. The petition is summarized in English in *VJ*, August 4, 1843, 213.

99. *VJ*, August 4, 1843, 213.

100. *AZJ*, June 12, 1843, 356–58.

101. *AZJ*, June 12, 1843, 356–58.

102. *VJ*, August 4, 1843, 213.

103. *Der Orient*, August 21–28, 1841, 232, 239–40.

104. In Moravia and Silesia, the emigration tax was set at 15%. Scari, *Systematische Darstellung*, 76–77.

105. *VJ*, September 2, 1842, 198.

106. *AZJ*, June 12, 1843, 356–58; *Der Orient*, January 31, 1843, 37–38; *Der Orient*, April 4, 1843, 109–10.

107. *Der Orient*, June 13, 1843, 191.

108. Originally published in *Ost und West: Blätter für Kunst, Literatur und geselliges Leben*, the article was reprinted in *AZJ*, December 4, 1843, 728–29; and in *INJ*, December 24, 1843, 209.

109. Quoted in *AZJ*, December 4, 1843, 728–29 (emphasis in original).

110. Hofman, *Die Prager Zeitschrift "Ost und West."*

111. At Fassel's request, the *Allgemeine Zeitung des Judenthums* and *Der Orient* helped publicize Obderzalek's visit to Prossnitz among their Jewish readership. Fassel to M. Steinschneider, October 3, 1843, Steinschneider Collection, JTSA, AR 108, Box 13.

112. *AZJ*, December 22, 1845, 757–62; *AZJ*, May 11, 1846, 293. For the original petition, see MZA, B14 (starsí), M618, no. 43666/2509.

113. *AZJ*, December 22, 1845, 757.

114. *AZJ*, December 22, 1845, 758.

115. *AZJ*, December 22, 1845, 761.

116. *AZJ*, December 22, 1845, 759.

117. "Bericht über die Anträge zur Reform des Judenwesens in Mähren und Schlesien."

118. "Bericht über die Anträge," ff. 34–35.

119. "Bericht über die Anträge," ff. 7–8.

120. "Bericht über die Anträge," f. 70.

121. *Tafeln zur Statistik der oesterreichischen Monarchie*, v. 1, Table 2, p. 4. These figures are from 1851, when the *Tafeln* started keeping separate statistics for Moravia and Silesia. In Silesia, there were 2,456 Jews out of a total population of 438,586; in Moravia, there were 38,225 Jews out of a total population of 1,799,838.

122. Barany, *Stephen Széchenyi*, 90–93.

123. On Széchenyi's attitudes toward the Jews, see Katz, *From Prejudice to Destruction*, 230–35.

124. "Bericht über die Anträge," 40.

125. This is what David Sorkin has called "the notion of a quid pro quo in which regeneration would precede rights." Sorkin, *Transformation of German Jewry*, 5.

126. "Bericht über die Anträge," f. 39.

127. "Bericht über die Anträge."

128. "Bericht über die Anträge," f. 39.

129. "Bericht über die Anträge," f. 69.

130. "Bericht über die Anträge," f. 39.

131. "Bericht über die Anträge," f. 52.

132. "Bericht über die Anträge," f. 53.

133. "Bericht über die Anträge," ff. 56–58.

134. "Bericht über die Anträge," f. 59.

135. "Bericht über die Anträge," f. 57.

136. "Bericht über die Anträge."

137. "Bericht über die Anträge," f. 98. Jews in Bohemia were permitted to own certain kinds of agricultural land, on condition that it was worked by Jews themselves and not by hired hands. (An exception was made during planting and harvest season, when Christian laborers were allowed to be hired.) The Gubernium looked favorably on the Bohemian example, considering it "the surest means of instilling love of agriculture" in the Jews of Moravia.

138. "Bericht über die Anträge," ff. 97–98.

139. "Bericht über die Anträge," f. 107.

140. "Bericht über die Anträge," ff. 24–26. The archives of the Moravian Gubernium are full of similar cases. For example, see MZA, B14, M594–96.

141. "Bericht über die Anträge," f. 31. The rabbis in Nikolsburg and Prossnitz were paid a respectable 600 fl. In Moravia's other communities, the salaries ranged

from 100 fl. to 500 fl. per year. Outside Nikolsburg and Prossnitz, the average salary was 208 fl.

142. On the 1842 decree, see note 4.

143. "Bericht über die Anträge," f. 43. For details on Fassel's certification exam, see AVA, Studienhofkommission, Karton 552, no. 9013/1381, December 30, 1843.

144. "Bericht über die Anträge," f. 112.

145. *AZJ*, September 7, 1839, 448.

146. *AZJ*, December 23, 1844, 759.

147. *AZJ*, July 3, 1843, 398.

148. *AZJ*, September 18, 1843, 572. Dr. Wahrmann was the son of Israel Wahrmann, the late rabbi of Pest. In 1829, three years after the elder Wahrmann died, David Joseph Wahrmann was elected to succeed him. Because he delayed his arrival, however, Löw Schwab of Prossnitz was elected instead. Wahrmann went on to become the rabbi of Grosswardein (Nagyvárad). *MZsL*, 956; and *Jewish Encyclopedia*, v. 3, 419.

149. *AZJ*, September 18, 1843, 573.

150. Jewish Museum in Prague, Sitzungsprotokolle des Gemeinde-Vorstands (Mikulov), December 26, 1843.

151. *AZJ*, April 8, 1844, 213.

152. *AZJ*, April 8, 1844, 213.

153. MZA, B14, M614, December 13, 1846.

154. The *Israelit des 19. Jahrhunderts*, a German-Jewish weekly aligned with the Reform movement, entered the fray with a shrill attack on Hirsch (*INJ*, December 15, 1844, 405–6). An anonymous correspondent "from the Moravian frontier" derided Hirsch's "maniacal wrongheadedness and gaping ignorance" (*die tollhäuslerische Verschobenheit und die gespreizte Ignoranz*), exposing him to the public as a "refined Jesuit" with "clerical hands" (*Pfaffenhände*). According to the same correspondent, the Nikolsburg Jewish community selected Hirsch in order to humiliate Fassel ("against whom they harbor a deep-seated hatred"). Fassel dismissed this as a baseless rumor (*Der Orient*, February 5, 1845, 46–47).

155. Schnitzer, *Jüdische Kulturbilder*, 46. When Quetsch visited his native Nikolsburg after Hirsch's arrival, he refused to pay a visit to the chief rabbi.

156. MZA, B14, M609, February 24, 1845.

157. MZA, B14, M609, February 24, 1845.

158. HHStA, Staatsrat Vorträge, 1846, 1668/1598.

159. MZA, B14, M614, no. 13764, January 27, 1845.

160. HHStA, Staatsrat Vorträge, 1846, 1668/1598.

161. AVA, Alter Kultus, Karton 3, May 5, 1846.

162. *AZJ*, August 31, 1846, 523; *Der Orient*, December 10, 1846, 390; HHStA, Staatsrat Vorträge, 1846, 1668/1598.

163. HHStA, Staatsrat Vorträge, 1846, 1668/1598.

164. *AZJ*, May 11, 1846, 293.

165. *AZJ*, January 18, 1847, 63.

166. In fact, one of the reasons that the Court Chancery gave a dispensation to Hirsch was that, "because of the differences of opinion [*Zefwürfnisse*], it is difficult to find among the Moravian applicants a man that all voices support." AVA, Alter Kultus, Karton 3, May 5, 1846.

167. MZA, B14, M614, no. 3929, January 21, 1847.

168. *Der Orient*, February 26, 1847, 68.

Chapter 5

1. Markus Boss, "Kol rina ve-yeshuah," *KI* 4 (1847): 70–71. Markus Boss (Prerau 1815/1818–Leipnik 1861), a private teacher in Leipnik, published numerous Hebrew poems in *Kokhevei Yitshak*. Wachstein, *Die Hebräische Publizistik*, 20–24. Boss also wrote a Hebrew eulogy for Hermann Jellinek (*Literaturblatt des Orients*, January 20, 1849, 40–41), which is not cited by Wachstein.

2. *Der Orient*, February 26, 1847, 68.

3. Bing, *'Ateret tsevi!* 5–6.

4. *TZW*, January 26, 1847, 31.

5. *Der Orient*, August 27, 1847, 279.

6. Hirschler, "Rabbi and Statesman," 121–49.

7. Tal, *Samson Raphael Hirsch*, 13.

8. Liberles, "Champion of Orthodoxy," 43–60.

9. Hirsch's sermon was summarized in *TZW*, July 20, 1847, 239–40.

10. *Der Orient*, January 29, 1847, 34–35.

11. *Der Orient*, January 29, 1847, 34–35.

12. Asaria, "Hirsch's Wirken," 12–18.

13. Halpern, "Introduction" to his *Takanot medinat mehrin*, xiii.

14. "Concept einer Eingabe des Oberlandesrabbiners Samson Raphael Hirsch an den Oesterreichischen Kultusminister in Betreff seiner Amtsniederlegung," in Feuchtwang, *Samson Raphael Hirsch*, 27.

15. MZA, B14, M618, no. 4279/453.

16. MZA, B14, M618, no. 750/79.

17. MZA, B14, M619, no. 14296/1463.

18. MZA, B14, M618, no. 8537/881.

19. "Concept einer Eingabe," 27.

20. Hirsch to the Moravian-Silesian Gubernium, October 27, 1847, MZA, B14, M618, no. 750/79.

21. Hirsch to the Moravian-Silesian Gubernium, January 12, 1848, MZA, B14, M619, no. 14296/1463.

22. Nikolsburg Oberamt to Brünn district office, February 2, 1848, MZA, B14, M619, no. 14296/1463.

23. *TZW*, August 3, 1847, 253–54.

24. For Hirsch's questions in the Duchy of Oldenburg, see Trepp, *Die Oldenburger Judenschaft*, 167–85. For Hirsch's questions in Emden (East Friesland), see Asaria, "Hirsch's Wirken," 12–18.

25. Prossnitz Jewish Community to Moravian-Silesian Gubernium, February 24, 1848, MZA, B14, M618, no. 7268/739.

26. David Feuchtwang makes a similar point in his *Samson Raphael Hirsch*, 21.

27. *AZJ*, November 8, 1847, 680.

28. Fassel, *Reis und Hülsenfrüchte*.

29. *Der Orient*, October 22, 1847, 340–41.

30. Hirsch's Synagogenordnung was published in *Der Orient*, March 4, 1848, 76–78. An autographed copy, written in Judeo-German, can be found in the Moritz Güdemann Collection at LBI, AR 7067, 3/6, Box 3. On Synagogenordnungen in Germany, see Lowenstein, "The 1840s," 261–63; and Petuchowski, *Prayerbook Reform*, 105–27.

31. *Der Orient*, March 4, 1848, 76.

32. Schnitzer, *Jüdische Kulturbilder*, 60.

33. *Der Orient*, March 4, 1848, 78.

34. MZA, B14, M613, no. 39947, September 28, 1847. In 1842, all communal rabbis were required to be certified in philosophical and pedagogical studies within ten years. Ten years had not yet passed, so Duschak could still be considered for the Austerlitz position even though he lacked the certificates. The Jewish communities in Gaya and Lomnitz had recently elected rabbis who did not meet the criteria of the court decree.

35. Duschak's trial sermon was even published in the Orthodox *Treue-Zions-Wächter*, May 11, 1847, 150.

36. Brünn district office to the Moravian-Silesian Gubernium, September 28, 1847, MZA, B14, M614, no. 39947.

37. *TZW*, April 4, 1848, 110. The letter is dated November 24, 1847.

38. *TZW*, April 11, 1848, 117–18. The letter is dated December 2, 1847.

39. Hirsch, *Sefer shemesh marpeh*, 220–21. Letters 20 and 21 contain Hirsch's responses to Feilbogen and Pollak, respectively. The names are expunged from the published letters but are clearly visible in the originals. For original letters, see the Sänger Collection at the Institute for the Research of Diaspora Jewry, Bar-Ilan University.

40. *Der Orient*, January 22, 1848, 29–30.

41. *TZW*, July 6, 1847, 223–24; Bing, *'Ateret tsevi!* 5–6.

42. Hirsch, *Sefer shemesh marpeh*, 221–23 (Letter 22); Sänger Collection (Hebrew, Aleph 3).

43. S. R. Hirsch, "Ein Wort zur Zeit an unsere christlichen Brüder," *ÖCO*, March 23, 1848, 17.

44. S. R. Hirsch, *Protest eines Juden gegen das Votum eines Christen fuer die Emanzipation der Juden* (1843). Quoted in Breuer, "Emancipation," 48.

45. Hirsch, "Ein Wort zur Zeit," 17.

46. This circular is reprinted in Frankel-Grün, *Geschichte der Juden in Kremsier,* v. 2, 122–24.

47. I. N. Mannheimer, "Erklärung bezüglich der Judenfrage," *ÖCO,* March 23, 1848, 1.

48. Toury, *Turmoil and Confusion.*

49. *ÖCO,* April 22, 1848, 59; *TZW,* June 6, 1848, 181; *Der Orient,* June 17, 1848, 195–96.

50. Wieser, *Chronik,* 97–150.

51. Frankel-Grün, *Geschichte der Juden in Kremsier,* v. 2, 125–28.

52. *BZ,* May 12, 1848.

53. The term *horizontal alliance* is taken from Yerushalmi, *Lisbon Massacre,* xi.

54. Quoted in Frankel-Grün, *Geschichte der Juden in Kremsier,* v. 2, 125–28.

55. Frankel-Grün, *Geschichte der Juden in Kremsier,* v. 2, 125–28.

56. Tietze, *Die Juden Wiens,* 187. Müller sold more than 25,000 copies of his pamphlet, "Nur keine Juden-Emancipation." Four thousand copies were reprinted in Prague for distribution in Bohemia. Segments of this pamphlet were quoted verbatim in three Moravian petitions against Jewish emancipation (Mährisch-Schönberg, Znaim, Trebitsch) and paraphrased in several others. HHStA, Oesterr. Reichstag 1848/1849, Fasz. 125.IX, nos. 3821, 4724, 4960.

57. Macartney, *Habsburg Empire,* 356.

58. Radimský and Wurmová, *Petice moravského lidu,* no. 42, 79. The petition was signed by S. R. Hirsch, Hirsch Fassel (Prossnitz), Johann Ernst (Brünn), Dr. Grünfeld (Brünn), Franz Pater (Nikolsburg), I. S. Kunewalder (Leipnik), Sigmund Wolf (Mähr-Weisskirchen), Josef Weisse (Gaya), Dr. Alois Jeitteles (Brünn), Ezechiel Lazar (Jamnitz), Emanuel Lendermann (Pullitz), Isaac Ledner (Triesch), and Markus Schürmann (Gross-Meseritsch). With the exception of Ezechiel Lazar, all of them also signed Hirsch's memorandum to the Reichstag in February 1849.

59. *TZW,* May 16, 1848, 158–59.

60. Radimský and Wurmová, *Petice moravského lidu,* 79.

61. Radimský and Wurmová, *Petice moravského lidu,* 79.

62. Radimský and Wurmová, *Petice moravského lidu,* 79.

63. *TZW,* June 6, 1848, 181.

64. The following criticism was published in *Der Orient,* May 6, 1848, 149, by a Moravian contributor who identified himself as "Familiant": "Neuda is ill, Schmiedl is weak—Duschak is in poor health and Fassel avenges himself by staying silent, although we expected so much from him. . . . It is truly disgraceful that such an intelligent man remains idle at a time of such helplessness and confusion. Is freedom not worth any sacrifice?"

65. *Der Orient,* June 6, 1848, 149.

66. S. R. Hirsch, "Aufruf zu patriotischen Gaben," in Frankel-Grün, *Geschichte der Juden in Kremsier,* v. 2, 125.

67. Briess, *Schilderung*, 30.

68. *Brünner Tags-Courier*, July 14, 1848, 72.

69. Bosl, *Handbuch*, v. 3, 38; Urban, *Die tschechische Gesellschaft*, 90; Pech, *Czech Revolution*, 105–17.

70. Krejčí, *History of Elections*, 74.

71. *Národní Nowiny*, 1848, 347–48. Hirsch is referred to as "Jiří Hirsch, rabín."

72. *TZW*, June 20, 1848, 199.

73. In 1846, Jews made up just under 40% of Nikolsburg's total population; there were 5,683 Christians and 3,730 Jews. Jews presumably accounted for approximately 40% of the electorate as well. If so, then Hirsch's election may have resulted from the support of "a nearly unanimous majority" of Jews. For election results, see MZA, A5, 1 a 2 N–P, Karton 8, no. 439, May 31, 1848. According to this document, "S. R. Hirsch Dr. der Philosophie und Oberlandrabiner in Mähren" was elected "by an absolute majority" (*durch absolute Stimmenmehrheit*).

74. *Der Orient*, August 12, 1848, 624; *ÖCO*, July 11, 1848, 209.

75. *Mährisches Landtagsblatt*, no. 28, August 18, 1848, 124.

76. J. Travníček et al. to Präsidium, June 26, 1848, MZA, A5, 20, VI/2, no. 808/848.

77. *AZJ*, August 7, 1848, 476.

78. On the *shtadlan*, see Katz, *Tradition and Crisis*, 71–72.

79. S. R. Hirsch to Lažansky, July 14, 1848, MZA, B14, M618, no. 750/79.

80. *BZ*, June 17, 1848, 1321–22. Hirsch is listed as "Salomon [*sic*] Hirsch, Oberlandesrabbiner in Brünn [*sic*]."

81. For figures, see Silber, "Shorshei ha-pilug," 98–100.

82. S. R. Hirsch to Lažansky, July 14, 1848, MZA, B14, M618, no. 750/79.

83. The Galician deputy was Alois Borrosch. See *Verhandlungen des oesterreichischen Reichstages nach der stenographischen Aufnahme*, October 5, 1848, 791.

84. HHStA, fasz. 125.IX.24, no. 34/1.

85. *Der Orient*, September 24, 1846, 307.

86. *ÖCO*, July 22, 1848, 228.

87. *ÖCO*, August 4, 1848, 252.

88. *ÖCO*, July 22, 1848, 228; letter from Mannheimer to Hirsch, July 21, 1848, Sänger Collection (German, no. 58).

89. Letter from Mannheimer to Hirsch, July 21, 1848.

90. The details of Hirsch's petition have been culled from Mannheimer's letter to Hirsch, September 5, 1848, Sänger Collection (German, no. 59).

91. *ÖCO*, September 13, 1848, 340–41.

92. *Verhandlungen*, September 26, 1848, 617.

93. According to the numbers cited by Hirsch and Mannheimer, the Jewish taxes placed a heavier burden on Nikolsburg Jewry. Nikolsburg's 300 taxpayers paid an average of 47 fl. in Jewish taxes; Neu-Rausnitz's 100 taxpayers paid an average of 39 fl.

94. *Der Orient*, November 4, 1848, 357. Demel's speech can be found in *Verhandlungen*, September 26, 1848, 615; Böse's speech can be found in *Verhandlungen*, October 5, 1848, 800.

95. *ÖCO*, September 17, 1848, 353.

96. *ÖCO*, October 19, 1848, 408–9. Because the Jewish voters were excluded, the Moravian-Silesian Gubernium invalidated the elections and called for new ones. MZA, A5, 1 a 2 N–P, Karton 8, no. 1510, October 4, 1848. The original complaint by the Prossnitz Jewish community was submitted on June 1, 1848.

97. *Verhandlungen*, September 26, 1848, 615. Demel estimated that the approximately 100,000 Jewish merchants (*handeltreibenden Juden*) in Bohemia, Moravia, and Galicia paid the lower tax, thereby saving 22–24 fl. annually. Based on this calculation, the Jews saved between 2,200,000 and 2,400,000 fl. annually, considerably more than the 972,500 fl. they paid in Jewish taxes. For figures, see Silber, "Shorshei ha-pilug," 98.

98. *Verhandlungen*, October 5, 1848, 800.

99. The deputy was Franz Placek. See *Verhandlungen*, October 5, 1848, 620.

100. Frankel-Grün, *Geschichte der Juden in Kremsier*, v. 2, 128–31. The argument bears striking resemblance to Ber Isaac Berr's speech before the French National Assembly in 1789. Hertzberg, *French Enlightenment*, 345–46.

101. Circular from March 23, 1848, in Frankel-Grün, *Geschichte der Juden in Kremsier*, v. 2, 122–24.

102. MZA, B14, M619, no. 40903/3373, November 2, 1848.

103. Frankel-Grün, *Geschichte der Juden in Kremsier*, v. 2, 129.

104. Hirsch, *Nineteen Letters*, 167–68.

105. Hirsch, *Nineteen Letters*, 167–68.

106. Hirsch, *Nineteen Letters*, 166–68.

107. Frankel-Grün, *Geschichte der Juden in Kremsier*, v. 2, 128.

108. Frankel-Grün, *Geschichte der Juden in Kremsier*, v. 2, 128.

109. Baron, "Revolution of 1848," 1–66.

110. Frankel-Grün, *Geschichte der Juden in Kremsier*, v. 2, 131–32.

111. Frankel-Grün, *Geschichte der Juden in Kremsier*, v. 2, 131–32.

112. Frankel-Grün, *Geschichte der Juden in Kremsier*, v. 2, 131–32.

113. Frankel-Grün, *Geschichte der Juden in Kremsier*, v. 2, 131–32; *Das Vaterland*, January 1, 1849, 7.

114. *Das Vaterland*, January 1, 1849, 7.

115. Letter from Mannheimer to Hirsch, December. 8, 1848, Sänger Collection (German no. 55).

116. M[oritz] J[ellinek], "Kremsier," *Der Orient*, March 3, 1849, 43.

117. Grunfeld, "Introduction" to Hirsch's *Judaism Eternal*, xl.

118. This trip is mentioned in a letter from Mannheimer to Hirsch, December 8, 1848, Sänger Collection (German no. 55).

119. Mannheimer to Hirsch, December 8, 1848.

120. Mannheimer to Hirsch, December 8, 1848.

121. Mannheimer to Hirsch, December 8, 1848.

122. M[endel] Hirsch, "Villafranca und Kremsier," 598.

123. The twenty-five members of the United Committee are listed at the end of Hirsch's memorandum. There were fourteen members from Moravia (Rabbi Samson Raphael Hirsch, Johann Ernst, Franz Flesch, Dr. Grünfeld, Rabbi Hirsch Fassel, Elias Kohn, J. Kunewader, E. Landesmann, I. Ledner, J. Löwi, Franz Pater, M. Schnürmann, Rabbi Josef Weisse, Sigmund Wolf), seven members from Vienna (A. B. Bacher, Dr. M. Cusin, Leopold Epstein, Dr. Jeitelles, Ludwig August Frankel, Heinrich Schirowski, Joseph Wertheimer), and four members from Bohemia (three of whom were Moses J. Landau, Rabbi Salomon Sachs, and Dr. Wolfgang Wessely).

124. Frankel-Grün, *Geschichte der Juden in Kremsier*, v. 2, 3–4.

125. Hirsch, "Villafranca und Kremsier," 598–99. It is not clear who served as spokesman for the United Committee. A Czech-speaking member may have addressed Palacký to help dispel the perception that Moravian—and especially Bohemian—Jews identified both linguistically and culturally with the Germans. On Palacký's opposition to Jewish emancipation, see Baron, "Impact of the Revolution," 242–43.

126. A copy of the original memorandum can be found in the CAHJP, Archiv der Israelitischen Kultusgemeinde, Wien, A/W 207. It was reprinted in *Jeschurun* 5 (1858–59): 606–22.

127. *Jeschurun* 5 (1858–59): 606–22.

128. Rosenbloom, *Tradition in an Age of Reform*, 86.

129. HHStA, Oesterreichischer Reichstag 1848/49, Fasz. 125.IX.24, no. 34/13, February 16, 1849.

130. Tal, *Samson Raphael Hirsch*, 15; Grunfeld, "Introduction" to Hirsch's *Judaism Eternal*, xxxix. Of course, the fact that Hirsch served as a deputy in the Moravian Diet may have contributed to the confusion.

131. Quoted in *Der Orient*, February 24, 1849, 39–40.

132. M[oritz] J[ellinek], "Ungarischbrod," *Der Orient*, November 11, 1848, 364.

133. Jellinek, "Kremsier," 43.

134. *Der Orient*, March 3, 1849, 43.

Chapter 6

1. Frankel-Grün, *Jüdische Zeitgeschichte und Zeitgenossen*, vii.

2. Fassel, *Warum freuet sich unser Land?*

3. Toury, *Turmoil and Confusion*.

4. Sauer, "Anton Füster," 249–56.

5. I. N. Mannheimer, "Erklärung bezüglich der Judenfrage," *ÖCO*, March 24, 1848, 1.

6. For example, see Kämpf, *Řeč*.

7. Fassel, *Warum freuet sich unser Land?* 13.

8. Fassel, *Warum freuet sich unser Land?* 13.

9. *Der Orient*, April 1, 1848, 110.

10. Die Bisenzer Jugend, *Von den Jugendgenossen Carl Heinrich Spitzer's, des Erstgefallenen* (Bisenz, 1848), Nationalbibliothek (Vienna), Flugblätter-Sammlung, Kronl. 1848/14/19a.

11. Streng, *Ausführliche Biographie*, 14–15.

12. "Geschichte der glorreichen Tage vom 13. Bis 18. März, eingeleitet durch eine Biographie Carl Heinr. Spitzer's," *ÖCO*, March 23, 1848, 6–11.

13. *Schild und Schwert*, November 30, 1848, 71.

14. Klaus Kempter, *Die Jellineks*, 88–98; Wolfgang Häusler, "Hermann Jellinek," 125–75; *Jüdisches Athenäum*, 112–17.

15. Quoted in Walter Grab, "Das Wiener Judentum," 203.

16. Quoted from petition submitted by the burghers of Trebitsch to the Reichstag on February 26, 1849, HHStA, Oesterreichischer Reichstag 1848/49, Fasz. 125. IX.24, no. 34/19 (4960).

17. Helfert, *Die Wiener Journalistik*, index.

18. Grab, "Das Wiener Judentum," 203.

19. See petition submitted by burghers of Trebitsch, HHStA, Oesterreichischer Reichstag 1848/49, Fasz. 125.IX.24, no. 4960.

20. Gold, *Geschichte der Juden in Wien*, 32; see also letter from Adolf Buchheim to Ludwig August Frankel, May 6, 1850, Wiener Stadt- und Landesbibliothek, Handschriftensammlung, no. 101261.

21. Donath, "Siegmund Kolischs"; Marada, "Zapomenutý žurnalista Sigmund Kolisch."

22. Johann Nordmann, "Von einem Achtundvierziger," *AZJ*, May 1, 1883, 293–96; Miller, "From Liberal Nationalism to Cosmopolitan Patriotism."

23. Estimates of the number of Jews in Vienna (and its suburbs) on the eve of the revolution range from 3,000 to 12,000. According to Marsha Rozenblit, the most accurate estimate is 4,000. Rozenblit, *Jews of Vienna*, 17.

24. Max Grünwald, "Wiener jüdische Familien aus Mähren," in Gold, *Die Juden*, 83–98. Leopold Moses estimated that Moravian Jews constituted 12–13% of the Jewish population of Vienna in the 1850s. Moses, "Woher stammen die Juden Wiens?" in his *Spaziergänge*, 48.

25. Adolf Brecher to Auguste Auerbach, October 16, 1848, published in Steinschneider, *Briefwechsel*, 322.

26. Kisch, *In Search of Freedom*, 43; Friesel, "The *Oesterreichisches Central-Organ*," 118–49; Abrams, "Austro-Czech Intelligentsia," 1–20.

27. Baron, "Revolution of 1848," 1.

28. Bosl, *Handbuch*, v. 3, 38.

29. Kořalka, *Tschechen im Habsburgerreich*, 92–93; Trapl, *České národní obrozene na Moravě*; Řepa, *Moravané nebo Češi?*

30. Havránek, "Böhmen im Fruhjahr 1848," 192–93.

31. *Der Lloyd*, March 8, 1849.

32. Havránek, "Böhmen im Fruhjahr 1848," 191. On the Slovanská Lípa, see Pech, *Czech Revolution*, 344–45.

33. Polišenský, *Aristocrats*, 178–79.

34. Bosl, *Handbuch*, v. 3, 38–39.

35. On Moravian regional identity, see Bahlcke, *Regionalismus und Staatsintegration im Widerstreit*, 32–39; and Drabek, "Concept of the Nation," 305–11.

36. Novotný, *Letáky z roku 1848*, 135–54. For Rieger's "Slovo k moravanům," see 140–54.

37. Pech, *Czech Revolution*, 107; Schopf, *Die Revolution*.

38. Schopf, *Die Revolution*, 74.

39. Czech nationalists increasingly identified Jews as Germans because of their perceived proclivity for German language and culture. This is best illustrated by a remark made by Karl Havlíček, a leading figure in the Czech national awakening. "If [the Jews] wish to forsake their national language and literature," he wrote in 1844, "let them attach themselves to the Germans and their literature; for the German tongue has already in the course of time become the second mother tongue of Jewry." Quoted in Goldstücker, "Jews Between Czechs and Germans," 68. Pavel Joseph Šafařik, another leading figure in the Czech national awakening, wanted even converted Jews banned from the Slavic Congress of 1848, out of fear that they could be informers sent by the Germans; see Jacob Shatzky, "Jewish Ideologies in Austria During the Revolution of 1848," in Baron et al., *Freedom and Reason*, 418.

40. Adolf Jellinek, "Die Juden in Oesterreich," *Der Orient*, June 17, 1848, 193–94.

41. Tietze, *Die Juden Wiens*, 187. According to Tietze, Müller sold more than 25,000 copies of his pamphlet, "Nur keine Juden-Emanzipation," which also appeared under the title "Ein ruhiges Wort gegen Juden-Emancipation: Von einem Freunde der guten Sache." (These pamphlets can be found in HHStA, Oestrr. Reichstag 1848/49, Fasz. 153, nos. 23 and 217.) A preface to the version printed in Prague indicates that "4,000 copies of the original Viennese pamphlet" were reprinted. Sections of this pamphlet were quoted verbatim in three of the Moravian petitions against Jewish emancipation (Mährisch-Schönberg, Znaim, Trebitsch) and paraphrased in others. For these petitions, see HHStA, Oesterreichischer Reichstag 1848/49, Fasz. 125.IX.24, nos. 3821, 4724, and 4960. On these petitions, see Hörhan, "Die Petitionen," 233–49.

42. Toury, *Turmoil and Confusion*, 24.

43. On anti-Jewish violence in Alsace, see Rohrbacher, *Gewalt im Biedermeier*, 181–85.

44. Toury, *Turmoil and Confusion*; see index for Warasdin, Temesvár, Pest, Stein am Anger, Nadasch, Tyrnau, Modern, St. Georgen, Bösing, Neutra Comi-

tat, Comorn, Waag-Neustadtl, Ledetsch, and Presburg. On Prague, see Roubík, *Český rok 1848*, 221–23.

45. "Pressburgs blutige Ostern," *BZ*, May 1, 1848.

46. For an analysis of anti-Jewish violence as a form of social protest, see Rohrbacher, *Gewalt im Biedermeier*, 11–34.

47. "Die Judenverfolgung und die Judensache," *ÖCO*, April 22, 1848, 79.

48. Olmütz and Prossnitz are both located on the Hana plain.

49. Ber Schiff to G. Brecher, March 25, 1849, Gideon Brecher Correspondence, JTSA, AR 22.

50. Cantor Weisse to Josef Weisse, Elul 5608 (August–September 1848), LBI, AR4032.

51. *BZ*, May 12, 1848.

52. *Der Orient*, June 17, 1848, 195–96, reported on a number of incidents in the vicinity of Ungarisch-Brod at the beginning of May. When an "enormous mass of peasants" tried to plunder Ungarisch-Brod's Jewish quarter on May 3, *Oberamtmann* Flemmich prevented the plundering with "vigilance and judiciousness." When Jews in the nearby villages of Suchalosa, Bistritz, and Schumnitz were threatened with violence, Flemmich also intervened on their behalf. Soon thereafter, Flemmich sent an infantry company to the Hungarian border to prevent further incidents.

53. Ohm-Januschowsky, *Chronik*, 52. "Lynch justice" is Ohm-Januschowsky's term.

54. AMO, M1-1, inv. č. 582, J6.

55. MZA, B14, M620, no. 6699, February 15, 1849.

56. AMO, M1-1, inv. č. 339.

57. AMO, M1-1, inv. č. 582, J6.

58. "Die Juden in Olmütz am 12. April 1848," *NZ*, April 22, 1848.

59. *ÖCO*, April 22, 1848, 59.

60. *BZ*, April 13, 1848.

61. "Die Juden in Olmütz am 12. April 1848," *NZ*, April 22, 1848.

62. *ÖCO*, May 7–13, 1848, 103.

63. "Die Juden in Olmütz am 12. April 1848," *NZ*, April 22, 1848.

64. "Entgegnung von 250 Olmützer Bürgern, die Ausweisung der Juden am 12. April d. J. betreffend," *NZ*, May 6, 1848. After stating that "there is no injustice committed against Jews that cannot be defended as just by Christians," a report in *ÖCO*, May 9–27, 1848, 129, stated that Fassel "is supposed to have written a public letter against [the 250 burghers]."

65. MZA, B14, M620, no. 6699, December 19, 1848.

66. For details on the events in Gross-Meseritsch, see *BZ*, May 2, 1848, and May 10, 1848; *ÖCO*, May 8–20, 1848; and Steiner, "Das Bilbul von Gross-Meseritsch," 93–96.

67. *ÖCO*, September 13, 1848, 341.

68. Radimský and Wurmová, *Petice moravského lidu.*

69. See petitions from Zlabings, Liebau, and Bystritz.

70. "Petitionen von Juden um Emancipation, dann Petitionen dagegen," HH-StA, Oesterreichischer Reichstag 1848/49, Fasz. 125.IX.24. On February 26, 1849, the *Brünner Tags-Courier* noted the intention of "many Moravian and Bohemian towns" to submit a protest against Jewish emancipation to the Kremsier Reichstag (p. 227).

71. According to the *ÖCO*, September 17, 1848, 353, Prossnitz burghers also submitted a petition to the Reichstag with more than 1,000 signatures. This petition is not with the other anti-emancipation petitions in the HHStA.

72. Inhabitants of Prerau and its environs to the Reichstag, February 16, 1849, HHStA, Fasz. 125.IX.24, no. 34/13 (4665), 274 signatures, in Czech.

73. Burghers of Trebitsch to the Reichstag, February 26, 1849, HHStA, Fasz. 125.IX.24, no. 34/19 (4960), 331 signatures, in German.

74. Burghers of Trebitsch to the Reichstag, February 26, 1849.

75. Burghers of Iglau to the Reichstag, October 21, 1848, HHStA, Fasz. 125.IX.24, no. 34/4 (2874), 271 signatures, in German.

76. Burghers of Trebitsch to the Reichstag, February 26, 1849.

77. Ten communities in Moravia to the Reichstag, August 1848, HHStA, Fasz. 125.IX.24, no. 2 (303), 531 signatures, in Czech.

78. Burghers of Holleschau to the Reichstag, September 29, 1848, HHStA, Fasz. 125.IX.24, no. 34/1 (1969), 127 signatures, in German.

79. Burghers of Sternberg to the Reichstag, October 4, 1848, HHStA, Fasz. 125.IX.24, no. 34/5 (3199), 641 signatures, in German.

80. Burghers of Mährisch-Schönberg to Reichstag, November 10, 1848, HH-StA, Fasz. 125.IX.24, no. 34/9 (3821), 181 signatures, in German.

81. The only pro-emancipation petitions came from Galicia, where thirty-four Jewish communities submitted identical petitions to the Reichstag.

82. The *Brünner Zeitung* was published in German and Czech beginning on January 1, 1849. In Czech, it was published as *Brnenský Noviny.*

83. On Alois Jeitteles, see *BCh* (1858), 240; and Wurzbach, *Biographisches Lexikon*, v. 10, 117–18.

84. On Andreas Jeitteles, see Wurzbach, *Biographisches Lexikon*, v. 10, 119–20.

85. Rudolf Kolisch was the brother of Siegmund Kolisch, who wrote for the Viennese newspaper *Die Radikale* and was tried for incitement in October 1848. Rudolf Kolisch was also suspected of fomenting revolutionary activity in one of Brünn's coffeehouses in October 1848. On this incident, see MZA, B95, 1/22, 364, no. 479/49, January 3, 1849.

86. Unfortunately, Moravia's Czech-language press cannot be used for comparison with regard to the question of Jewish emancipation. Although three of the sixteen periodicals that appeared in Moravia in 1848–49 were published in Czech, two of them ceased publication within weeks of their first issue. Only *Týdenník*, a Brünn weekly established in January 1848, continued to appear throughout the revolution.

However, even its political supplement, *Morawské Noviny*, failed to address the question of Jewish emancipation until *after* the promulgation of the Stadion constitution on March 4, 1849. Wurmová, *Soupis*; Hatschek, *Die periodische Presse Mährens*.

87. *NZ*, December 14, 1848.

88. "Zur Frage der Juden-Emancipation," *Österreichischer constitutioneller Bote*, December 27–28, 1848, 562–63, 567–68.

89. *BZ*, February 20, 1849.

90. *Brünner Tags-Courier*, February 26, 1849, 227.

91. "Zur Frage der Juden-Emancipation," *Österreichischer constitutioneller Bote*, December 27–28, 1848, 562–63, 567–68.

92. *BZ*, February 20, 1849.

93. S. H. Mosenthal, *Deborah: Volksschauspiel in 4 Acten* (Berlin: Sittenfeld, 1849). Published in English as *Deborah, or, The Jewish Maiden's Wrong: A Drama in Three Acts* (London: T. H. Lacy, 1864) and *Deborah: A Drama in Four Acts* (New York: Baker & Godwin, 1866). The *Jewish Encyclopedia* (v. 9, 42) erroneously states that *Deborah* premiered in Berlin in 1850.

94. *Brünner Tags-Courier*, February 11, 1849; *Österreichischer constitutioneller Bote*, February 1849, 133.

95. Pech, *Czech Revolution*, 70.

96. Rath, *Viennese Revolution*, 122–24.

97. *ÖCO*, 114, 168, 240; *Brünner Tags-Courier*, June 30, 1848, 258.

98. Frankel-Grün, *Geschichte der Juden in Kremsier*, v. 2, Beilage 3.

99. *NZ*, June 7, 1848.

100. Bránský, *Židé v Boskovicich*, 103.

101. *ÖCO*, July 14, 1848, 217.

102. On Trebitsch, see Sameš, "K historii revolučního," 60.

103. *Der Orient*, June 17, 1848, 195–96.

104. MZA Kunštat, F 264, ev. číslo 570, sig. M XIV, Fasz. 84; Plumenau—Nachtwache Verstärkung in der Prossnitzer Judenstadt, April 16, 1848.

105. *Der Orient*, August 26, 1848, 274–75.

106. *ÖCO*, September 17, 1848, 353.

107. Olmütz district office to Magistracy, April 23, 1848, AMP, inv. č. 902, sig. 232/32.

108. Administrative council of the Prossnitz national guard to the Olmütz district office, June 28, 1848, AMP, inv. č. 902, sig. 232/32.

109. Olmütz district office to magistracy, July 4, 1848, AMP, inv. č. 902, sig. 232/32.

110. *ÖCO*, September 17, 1848, 353.

111. *ÖCO*, September 17, 1848, 353.

112. Protokoll von Thomas Tychy, October 25, 1848, AMP, inv. č. 902, sig. 44, no. 17.

113. *ÖCO*, October 19, 1848, 408–9; quoted from *Prager Zeitung*.

114. Protokolle von Fortunat Hofmann, October 28, 1848, and Protokolle von Johan Barak, October 30, 1848, AMP, inv. č. 902, sig. 44, nos. 36 and 43.

115. Protokolle von Karl Wagner, October 26, 1848, AMP, inv. č. 902, sig. 44, no. 23.

116. *Verhandlungen des oesterreichischen Reichstages*, September 26, 1848, 615.

117. NZ, October 3, 1848.

118. *Der Orient*, March 3, 1849, 43.

119. Salomon Wolf, "Die Emancipation der mährischen Juden," *Der Orient*, September 23, 1848, 312. According to Wachstein, Salomon Wolf was the son of Abraham Wolf, a prayer leader in Prerau, and the grandson of Benjamin Wolf ben Salomo Prerau, author of *Ben Yemini* (Vienna: Anton Strauss, 1823). Wachstein, *Die Hebräische Publizistik*, 247.

120. Kisch, "Revolution of 1848," 185–234; Kisch, *In Search of Freedom*, 45–57, 215–29; Goldhammer, "Jewish Emigration," 5–38.

121. *ÖCO*, May 6, 1848, 77–78; Kisch, *In Search of Freedom*, 45–47, 215–19.

122. Isidor Busch, the editor and publisher of the *ÖCO*, emigrated to the United States by the end of 1848. Kisch, *In Search of Freedom*, 47.

123. *ÖCO*, May 6, 1848, facing p. 77; Kisch, *In Search of Freedom*, 221.

124. Beginning in the early 1840s, Europe suffered from mediocre harvests, leading to broader crop failure in 1845–47. Prices of basic foodstuffs more than doubled in the years before the revolution, and much of Europe seemed to be on the verge of a catastrophic famine. Although famine was averted, the economic crisis did precipitate a wave of emigration to the United States, particularly from Germany. It is estimated that nearly half a million Jews and non-Jews left Germany for America in the 1840s alone. Sperber, *European Revolutions*, 105–7; Nugent, "Migration," 103–8.

125. *Der Orient*, November 5, 1846, 351.

126. *Österreichischer constitutioneller Bote*, January 2, 1849.

127. *Jewish Intelligence*, December 1848, 380.

128. Briess, *Schilderung*, 31.

129. *ÖCO*, June 10, 1848, 147–49; Kisch, *In Search of Freedom*, 51–52.

Chapter 7

1. Quoted in Mendes-Flohr and Reinharz, *The Jew in the Modern World*, 115.

2. Mendes-Flohr and Reinharz, *The Jew in the Modern World*, 115.

3. "Bericht über die Anträge zur Reform des Judenwesen in Mähren und Schlesien," July 7, 1847, MZA, B14 (starsí), M618, no. 23390/1156, ff. 7–8.

4. Frankel-Grün, *Geschichte der Juden in Kremsier*, v. 2, 132–34.

5. *Brünner Tags-Courier*, April 2, 1849, 366.

6. *Brünner Tags-Courier*, April 2, 1849, 366.

7. *Brünner Tags-Courier*, April 2, 1849, 366.

8. BZ, March 17, 1849 (emphasis mine).

9. Hirsch was accompanied by four members of the Committee for Moravian Jewry: Isaac Ledner of Triesch and Jakob Lowi, Hirsch Fassel, and Rabbi Josef Weisse of Gaya. *Der Orient*, April 28, 1849, 88.

10. Hirsch's address appeared in the *BZ*, April 24, 1849.

11. *BZ*, April 24, 1849.

12. The *Brünner Tags-Courier*, March 17, 1849, cites a "provincial journal" that welcomed the alleged anti-Jewish violence.

13. *BZ*, March 17, 1849.

14. Frankel-Grün, *Geschichte der Juden in Kremsier*, v. 2, 132–34.

15. Fassel, *Die Verfassungsurkunde und der Tempel Salomos: Rede, bei dem in der Prossnitzer Synagoge am 17. März 1849 gefeierten Dankfeste für die verliehene Verfassung* (Prossnitz, 1849).

16. *Der Orient*, April 14, 1849, 75–76.

17. *Der Orient*, October 13, 1849, 181–83.

18. *Der Orient*, October 13, 1849, 181–83.

19. MZA, B14, M620, no. 15906, April 20, 1849.

20. Briess, *Schilderung*, 20.

21. *Der Orient*, October 20, 1849, 186–87. According to Frankel-Grün, the last wedding of a familiant was performed in Nikolsburg on November 23, 1848. Frankel-Grün, *Geschichte der Juden in Kremsier*, v. 2, 10.

22. *Der Orient*, April 28, 1849, 88.

23. *Der Orient*, July 14, 1849, 130.

24. MZA, B14, M620, no. 17263, May 3, 1849.

25. MZA, B14, M621, no. 22655, June 13, 1849.

26. MZA, B14, M621, no. 26792, August 6, 1849.

27. *Tafeln zur Statistik der oesterreichischen Monarchie*. There were 601 Jewish weddings in 1850 and 516 in 1851. Afterward, the number of weddings leveled out at an average of 284 per year between 1852 and 1865.

28. *Der Orient*, August 25, 1849, 153.

29. *Der Orient*, September 8, 1849, 163.

30. These were Hirsch Fassel of Prossnitz, Josef Weisse of Gaya, Dr. Moritz Duschak of Aussee, Abraham Neuda of Loschitz, Samuel Feilbogen of Strassnitz, Hermann Pollach of Damboritz, and Wolf Mühlrad of Lundenburg.

31. *Der Orient*, October 27, 1849, 189.

32. MZA, B14, M620, no. 15906, April 20, 1849.

33. *Der Orient*, October 27, 1849, 189.

34. "Z Gemnice w Znogemstku 28 kwetna," *Morawské Noviny*, May 31, 1849.

35. "Komitét na organisaci zidovskych zalezitosti," August 30, 1849, MZA, B13 2/20, 1016.

36. "Komitét na organisaci židovskych žalezitosti."

37. Following Toury, I have translated *Provisorisches Gemeindegesetz* as "Provisional Township Law." Because of the confusion that may result from the multiple

uses and definitions of the term *Gemeinde*, I use "township" to refer to the territorially defined political entity that was intended by this law. Toury, "Townships," 55–72.

38. Urban, *Die tschechische Gesellschaft*, v. 1, 137.

39. Urban, *Die tschechische Gesellschaft*, v. 1, 137.

40. *Der Orient*, July 14, 1849.

41. *Mährisches Landtagsblatt*, December 19, 1848, 558.

42. *Mährisches Landtagsblatt*, December 19, 1848, 559.

43. *Mährisches Landtagsblatt*, December 19, 1848, 560.

44. *Mährisches Landtagsblatt*, December 19, 1848, 558.

45. *Mährisches Landtagsblatt*, December 19, 1848, 559.

46. *Mährisches Landtagsblatt*, December 19, 1848, 559.

47. AVA, Ministerium des Innern, Präsidiale 11 (Mähren), Box 432, April 23, 1849. I thank Peter Urbanitsch for bringing this document to my attention.

48. AVA, Ministerium des Innern, Präsidiale 11 (Mähren), Box 432, June 29, 1849.

49. *BZ*, July 13, 1849.

50. Toury, "Townships," 65–66; Frankel-Grün, *Geschichte der Juden in Kremsier*, v. 2, 10.

51. *Brünner Tags-Courier*, January 12, 1850, 47.

52. *Der Orient*, August 10, 1850, 126–27.

53. *AZJ*, June 24, 1850, 360.

54. "Die Judenverfolgungen in Mähren," *AZJ*, June 3, 1850, 306.

55. *Der Orient*, May 25, 1850, 126–27.

56. *CB aus Böhmen*, May 16, 1850.

57. *CB aus Böhmen*, May 16, 1850; Sameš, "Protižidovské hnutí v Třebíči," 112–15.

58. *NZ*, May 23, 1850.

59. *NZ*, May 23, 1850.

60. *NZ*, May 19, 1850.

61. *NZ*, June 6, 1850; *BZ*, June 8, 1850.

62. *NZ*, June 2, 1850.

63. *NZ*, June 6, 1850.

64. *AZJ*, May 27, 1850, 296–97.

65. *BZ*, May 18, 1850.

66. *NZ*, May 23, 1850.

67. *AZJ*, May 20, 1850, 287.

68. *NZ*, May 23, 1850.

69. *CB aus Böhmen*, June 7, 1850.

70. *CB aus Böhmen*, June 7, 1850.

71. Quoted in *NZ*, June 6, 1850.

72. *BZ*, May 18, 1850.

73. *BZ*, May 30, 1850.

74. "Die Judenverfolgungen in Mähren," *AZJ*, June 3, 1850, 306.

75. *AZJ*, June 17, 1850, 339–40.

76. *NZ*, June 9, 1850.

77. *CB aus Böhmen*, June 7, 1850.

78. *Morawské noviny*, June 27, 1850.

79. *AZJ*, May 27, 1850, 296–97.

80. *BZ*, August 4, 1850; "Fürsterzbischofliche Verordnung für den mähr. schles. Diöcesanclerus," *WB, Beiblatt zu Nr. 4*, August 4, 1850, 34.

81. Protocoll des Ministerrathes, HHStA, Box 10, 2549/1850.

82. *AZJ*, June 24, 1850, 360.

83. "Ghetto redivivus," *WB, Beiblatt zu Nr. 3*, July 27, 1850, 21–22; *WB*, August 1, 1850, 28.

84. *WB*, August 8, 1850.

85. *NZ*, September 3, 1850.

86. Quoted in *AZJ*, August 12, 1850, 457; and *Wiener Zeitung*, July 30, 1850.

87. *Wiener Zeitung*, September 3, 1850.

88. Baron, "Jewish Communal Crisis," 99.

89. Frankel-Grün, *Geschichte der Juden in Kremsier*, v. 2, 128–31.

90. Mährisch-Kromau Jewish community to the Moravian-Silesian Gubernium, January 23, 1849, MZA, B14, M620, no. 2806; Gewitsch Jewish community to the Moravian-Silesian Gubernium, June 29, 1849, MZA, B14, M621, no. 24766.

91. Znaim district office to the Moravian-Silesian Gubernium, March 6, 1849, MZA, B14, M620, no. 9479.

92. Veit Frid. Jamnitz to the Moravian-Silesian Gubernium, March 10, 1849, MZA, B14, M620, no. 6840.

93. Göding Jewish community to Presidium of the Moravian-Silesian Gubernium, May 10, 1850, MZA, B13, 2/20, 1016, no. 3412.

94. Znaim district office to the Moravian-Silesian Gubernium, November 19, 1849, MZA, B14, M621, no. 42049.

95. *BZ*, July 13, 1849.

96. *BZ*, July 13, 1849.

97. Znaim district office to the Moravian-Silesian Gubernium, March 6, 1849, MZA, B14, M620, no. 9479.

98. *Der Orient*, June 30, 1849, 123.

99. *Der Orient*, June 23, 1849, 118.

100. Simon Bree, Michael Goldshmied, and Emanuel Georg to Unterrichts-Ministerium, June 29, 1849, MZA Kunštat, Plumenau, fond 264, inv. č. 593, sig. M XXVI, fasc. 40.

101. Frankel-Grün, *Geschichte der Juden in Kremsier*, v. 2, 132–34.

102. In Bohemia, a committee met with similar goals between November 1850 and February 1851. Kohn, *Die Notablenversammlung*.

103. Lažansky to Thun, June 29, 1850, AVA, Neuer Kultus, D1, Box 507, no. 2042/50.

104. Frankel-Grün, *Geschichte der Juden in Kremsier*, v. 2, 132–34.

105. CAHJP, Archiv der Israelitischen Kultusgemeinde Wien, A/W 207.

106. Frankel-Grün, *Geschichte der Juden in Kremsier*, v. 2, 128–31.

107. Frankel-Grün, *Geschichte der Juden in Kremsier*, v. 2, 132–34.

108. Frankel-Grün, *Geschichte der Juden in Kremsier*, v. 2, 132–34.

109. *Der Orient*, August 4, 1849, 141.

110. Fassel, "An meine Glaubensbrüder in Böhmen," *WB*, December 26, 1850, 231–32.

111. Das Comité für die Reorganisation der jüdisch. mähr. Religionsangelegenheiten, *Entwurf einer Synagogal-Verfassung der Bekenner des jüdischen Glaubens in Mähren* (Brünn: Franz Gastl, 1849).

112. Wolf, *Joseph Wertheimer*, 191. "For Moravia, Chief Rabbi Hirsch drafted statutes that were, however, met with great hostility. They were too bureaucratic and hierarchical."

113. Lažansky to Thun, June 29, 1850, AVA, Neuer Kultus, D1, Box 507, no. 2042/50.

114. Fassel, "An meine Glaubensbrüder in Böhmen," 231–32. Fassel quotes from his letter to Hirsch, written in December 1849.

115. Deneberg, *Kritik*, 10. Although published anonymously, the *Kritik* was identified as the work of Nathan Deneberg as soon as it appeared. *WB, Beiblatt zu Nr. 1*, July 14, 1850, 8.

116. Fassel, "An meine Glaubensbrüder in Böhmen," 231–32.

117. Deneberg, *Kritik*, 10.

118. Fassel, "An meine Glaubensbrüder in Böhmen."

119. Prossnitz Jewish community to Hirsch, November 22, 1849, Sänger Collection (German, bet 67).

120. I have not been able to locate this circular.

121. Prossnitz Jewish community to Hirsch, December 3, 1849, Sänger Collection (German, bet 66).

122. Prossnitz Jewish community to Hirsch, November 22, 1849, Sänger Collection (German, bet 67).

123. "Protocol" from assembly in Nikolsburg, December 31, 1849–January 5, 1850, AVA, Neuer Kultus, D3, Box 515a.

124. "Protocol" from assembly in Nikolsburg.

125. "Protocol" from assembly in Nikolsburg.

126. "Protocol" from assembly in Nikolsburg.

127. Deneberg, *Kritik*.

128. Lažansky to Thun, June 29, 1850, AVA, Neuer Kultus, D1, Box 507.

129. *Brünner Tags-Courier*, June 20–21, 1850; *NZ*, June 21, 1850; *AZJ*, August 8, 1850; *Morawské Noviny*, June 25, 1850.

130. *Der Orient*, February 19, 1847, 60–61.

131. Graetz, *Tagebuch und Briefe*, 191. At Hirsch's behest, Graetz was invited to teach at the Jewish school in Lundenburg. He taught there until 1852, when he accepted an invitation to teach at the newly established Jewish Theological Seminary in Breslau. Schwenger, "Die jüdische Schule in Lundenburg," 171–73. For

Hirsch's request to set up a "Padua-like institution" in Nikolsburg, see his letter to the Moravian-Silesian Gubernium, February 3, 1848, MZA, B14, M618, no. 4279/453. Hirsch argued that Moravia was uniquely suited for a rabbinic seminary, because—unlike Bohemia—it still had a chief rabbi.

132. Prossnitz Jewish community to Lažansky, June 26, 1850, AVA, Neuer Kultus, D4, Box 342 (red), no. 2246/32.

133. Prossnitz Jewish community to Lažansky, June 26, 1850.

134. *WB*, August 11, 1850.

135. Prossnitz Jewish community to Lažansky, June 26, 1850.

136. Trebitsch Jewish community to the Moravian-Silesian Gubernium, August 5, 1850, MZA, B13, 2/20, 1016, no. 15592.

137. Bach to Thun, October 10, 1850, AVA, Neuer Kultus, D12, no. 2034/26.

138. Hirsch's letter is mentioned in a letter from the Moravian-Silesian Gubernium to Minister Thun, August 24, 1850, AVA, Neuer Kultus, D5, Box 517, no. 2435/35.

139. *"Kundmachung der provisorischen Bestimmungen wegen Bedeckung und Auftheilung der Domesticalbedürfnisse bei den jüdischen Religionsgemeinden in Mähren"* (Brünn, 1850), *AZJ*, October 21, 1850.

140. The Law Regulating the State of Israelite Jewish Communities (March 21, 1890) regulated Jewish community membership in the Austrian half of the Austro-Hungarian monarchy. It stipulated that every Jew must be a member of a religious community in the district where he resides and gave the religious communities the right to tax their members. In Moravia, the law went into effect on January 1, 1892. See *Die Neuzeit*, September 18, 1891, 364.

141. Finance Minister Krauss's argument (submitted on February 8, 1851) is summarized in Bach's letter to Thun, February 25, 1851, AVA, Neuer Kultus, D12, no. 672.

142. Bach's letter to Thun, February 25, 1851.

143. Draft of letter from Thun to Finance Minister Krauss, 1851, AVA, Neuer Kultus, D12, no. 672.

Chapter 8

A small portion of this chapter was originally published as "Voice and Vulnerability: Vagaries of Jewish National Identity in Turn-of-the-Century Moravia," *Simon Dubnow Institute Yearbook* 5 (2006): 159–71. © Vandenhoeck & Ruprecht GmbH & Co. KG.

1. Arnold Ascher, "Der 13. März 1848," *B'nai B'rith Mitteilungen für Österreich* 28(3) (March 1928): 81–94; Baron, "Impact of the Revolution," 195–248.

2. Macartney, *Habsburg Empire*, 454–55.

3. Macartney, *Habsburg Empire*, 454n2.

4. *AZJ*, January 11, 1858, 36. This article, written by Dr. Moritz Duschak, rabbi of Gaya, complained about the marriage restrictions from July 25, 1853. To receive a marriage license, the couple had to meet the following conditions: (1) the bride

and groom had to demonstrate financial security; (2) the bride had to be at least 18 years old and the groom at least 24; and (3) the bride and groom had to each obtain two certificates attesting to their moral integrity, one from a rabbi and one from the head of his or her community (*Ortsgemeinde*).

5. *AZJ*, October 17, 1853, 543; *NZ*, November 1, 1853.

6. "It would not be uninteresting," observed a correspondent to the *AZJ* (November 21, 1853, 611), "if one could organize a *precise survey* of [all the places] where the Jews have purchased property in Austria since 1848. This number would show, at most, the *invalidity of all these denunciations*." A survey was, in fact, conducted in Moravia at the end of January 1854. According to the survey data for the juridical district (*Landesgerichtssprengel*) of Olmütz, the number of "Christian houses" in Jewish hands rose from seventy-one in 1848 to seventy-six in 1853. For the juridical district of Neutitschein, the number rose from sixty to ninety-three in the same period (many of them purchased by one individual, Baron Salomon von Rothschild). The data regarding the acquisition of "peasant property" (*Bauerngründe*) in this period indicate that parcels of land were purchased in the district of Datschitz but nowhere else. Reportedly, Jews acquired these parcels of land in Datschitz through foreclosure after the peasants could not pay back their loans. "Were it not for the Constitution [of March 4, 1849]," one peasant from Datschitz complained, "these lands would not have been given to the Jews; the people of the land [*Landesbevölkerung*] are grateful for the [decree from October 2, 1853]. Without it, the Jews would have acquired lots of peasant property in a very short time . . . and exploited the labor of the population for their own advantage." According to the same report, there were no complaints in the district of Auspitz because the inhabitants "belong to the more affluent and enlightened denizens of Moravia [and] are not so easily deceived by the Jews." For survey data and related reports, see MZA, B13 2/20, Karton 1016, nos. 1040 (*Landesgerichtssprengel* Neutitschein), 1298 (*Landesgerichtssprengel* Olmütz), 962 (Neustadt), 1090 (Olmütz), 1100 (Auspitz), 1102 (Datschitz), 1277 (Brünn), 1317 (Hohenstadt), 1347 (Neutitschein), 1368 (Mistek), 1394 (Znaim), 1399 (Mährish-Trübau), 1415 (Kremsier), and 1666 (Ungarisch-Hradisch).

7. "Briefe aus Mähren," *Wiener Vierteljahrschrift* (1853), 60–64.

8. The petition was submitted on November 3, 1853. Frankel-Grün, *Jüdische Zeitgeschichte und Zeitgenossen*, 35.

9. For example, in the mid-1850s, the town councils in Saatz (Zatec), Bohemia, and Marburg (Maribor), Styria, tried to expel newly arrived Jews on grounds that no Jews had been permitted to live in these towns before 1848. *AZJ*, March 22, 1858, 176. In Moravia, similar incidents were reported in Wischau and Raitz. The incident in Raitz occurred in 1861, after the Jews' right to acquire real estate was restored. *AZJ*, March 22, 1848, 176; and *AZJ*, September 10, 1861, 535.

10. HHStA, Ministerrat, Reichsrat Protokolle 1857/1739 (Karton 187), November 25, 1857.

11. In fact, the burghers of Znaim had made similar points in their petition

to the Reichstag from February 24, 1849. HHStA, Österreichischer Reichstag 1848/1849, Fasz. 125.IX.24, 34/14, no. 4724.

12. HHStA, Ministerrat, Reichsrat Protokolle 1857/1739 (Karton 187), November 25, 1857.

13. The emperor's advisers noted that in Znaim's immediate surroundings, there were 600 Jews in Schaffa, 700 Jews in Misslitz, and 350 Jews in Mährisch-Kromau.

14. The restrictions were fully lifted in Lower Austria, Bohemia, Moravia, Silesia, the Hungarian Lands, the Littoral, and Dalmatia. In Galicia and Bukovina, certain restrictions were left in place. No mention was made of the Alpine Lands, which had almost no Jews at the time. Macartney, *Habsburg Empire*, 502n3.

15. Franchise was granted to men over 24 years of age; the right to be elected was granted to men over 30. Krejčí, *History of Elections*, 63–64.

16. *AZJ*, April 30, 1861, 250. Gomperz was elected as a deputy for the Brünn Chamber of Commerce.

17. Bihl, "Die Juden," 894; Duschak, *Geschichte der Verfassung*.

18. *WB*, April 3, 1851, 182. Nagykanizsa (Gross-Kanischa) was one of the most progressive Jewish communities in Hungary, thanks in part to the efforts of Leopold Löw, who served as rabbi there in 1840–46.

19. Letters from Hirsch to members of Hamburg's German-Jewish community, December 30, 1850, and January 30, 1851, CAHJP, AHW 543b, fasc. 2, ff. 95–100. The Hamburg rabbinate was vacant after the death of Isaac Bernays (1792–1849), Hirsch's rabbi and teacher. I thank Carsten Wilke for bringing this to my attention.

20. Liberles, *Religious Conflict*, 133–35.

21. The letter can be found in *Samson Raphael Hirsch: Jubilaeums-Nummer der Israelit* (Frankfurt, 1908), 36. The translation is taken from Liberles, *Religious Conflict*, 111–12.

22. Liberles, *Religious Conflict*, 134.

23. Liberles, *Religious Conflict*, 134.

24. This letter can be found in Friedlaender, *Kore Haddoroth*, 57–59.

25. Hirsch's letter of resignation can be found in MZA, B13, Fasz. 2/20, no. 1884, May 4, 1851.

26. The circular was reprinted in *WB*, May 18, 1851, 228–29.

27. *WB*, May 22, 1851, 237; *WB*, May 25, 1851, 239–40.

28. "Die neuesten Vorgänge in Mähren," *WB*, May 25, 1851, 239–40.

29. "Die neuesten Vorgänge in Mähren."

30. AVA, Neuer Kultus, Israelitischer Kultus, D3, no. 2354/45, July 13, 1851.

31. Liberles, *Religious Conflict*, 112.

32. Hirsch's letter was printed in *Nachalath Z'wi* 6 (1936): 252–56.

33. "Aus Mähren," *WB*, August 14, 1851, 35. This article contains a circular from the Moravian Jewish Committee (dated July 31, 1851) that describes the failed efforts to convince the board of the Israelitische Religionsgesellschaft to release Hirsch from his prior commitment to come to Frankfurt.

34. "Hirsch's Abschied aus Mähren," *WB*, August 21, 1851, 343.

35. MZA, B13, Fasz. 2/20, no. 3635, August 11, 1851.

36. "Brünn," *WB*, September 21, 1851, 379. Twenty-eight of the thirty-six Jewish communities in the Brünn district supported this position.

37. Representatives from twelve of the sixteen Jewish communities in the Olmütz district signed a petition against retaining the chief rabbinate. For the petition, see MZA, B13, Fasz. 2/20, no. 4169, September 3, 1851. Similar arguments were expressed in *WB*, August 17, 1851, 339–40; *WB*, August 21, 1851, 345; *WB*, August 28, 1851, 351; and *WB*, August 31, 1851, 355–56.

38. In a letter to the Governorship (Statthalterei), the board of the Nikolsburg Jewish community stressed that the election of the chief rabbi was "always such a holy occasion *for our community*" [italics mine]. MZA, B13, Fasz. 2/20, August 26, 1851.

39. "Stimmen über das mährische Landesrabbinat," *WB*, August 31, 1851, 355–56.

40. Liberles, *Religious Conflict*, 110.

41. MZA, B13, Fasz. 2/20, no. 3946, August 27, 1851. Emphasis in original.

42. Simeon Sofer (Schreiber) (1820–1883) turned down the invitation in a letter to Hirsch Kollisch, dated 18 Shevat 5614 (February 16, 1854). The letter appears in Sofer, *Igrot Soferim*, v. 2, 18–19. In 1861, Sofer accepted an invitation to Cracow, where he served as rabbi until his death in 1883.

43. "Das Mährische Landesrabbinat," *BCh*, January 18, 1861, 19. In the 1860s, Rabbi Dr. Meir Feuchtwang (1814–1888) ran a small yeshiva in Nikolsburg. "Ein Beitrag zur Jeschiba-Angelegenheiten," *Der Israelit*, May 16, 1866, 349–50.

44. Arnošt Klíma, "Industrial Growth and Entrepreneurship in the Early Stages of Industrialization in the Czech Lands," in his *Economy, Industry, and Society*, 142–43. On the textile industry in Brünn, see Janák, "Vlnařská velkovýroby," 184–229; František, *Vlnařství a bavlnářství*; and Freudenberger, *Industrialization*.

45. Janák, "Počátky židovského vlnařského podnikáni," 47–62.

46. In 1844, Salloman Pollak, a Nikolsburg familiant, had been buying goods from one of Brünn's wool factories for more than twenty-five years. MZA, B14, M607, no. 11378, March 8, 1844.

47. These Jews, many of whom came from the nearby Jewish communities of Neu-Rausnitz and Butschowitz, were concentrated in Kröma (Křenová), a suburb of Brünn. In 1847, two Christian inhabitants of Brünn complained to the local police that "every week there are 250 Jews here, in addition to the tolerated Israelites. All of them take lodgings in the suburbs, primarily in Kröma, and return to their homes on Friday." According to the complaint, one-fifth of the Jews were from Neu-Rausnitz. MZA, B14, M614, no. 24443, May 31, 1847.

48. Moritz Brünner, "Geschichte der Juden in Brünn," in Gold, *Die Juden*, 158; Haas, *Die Juden in Mähren*, 58. (Much of this growth presumably took place before October 2, 1853, when the pre-1848 restrictions on real estate ownership were reinstated.)

49. Štěpán, "Vznik židovské obce," 227–37.

50. Moses Leopold, "Herkunft und Berufe der Wiener Juden vor 1848," in his *Spaziergänge*, 51–59; Till, "Zur Herkunft," 30–35.

51. Rozenblit, *Jews of Vienna*, 5.

52. Jeiteles, *Die Kultusgemeinde der Israeliten*, 54–55.

53. Rozenblit, *Jews of Vienna*, 35; Arnbom, *Friedmann*.

54. All population figures are taken from Haas, *Die Juden in Mähren*, 58–64.

55. MZA, B14, M624, August 28, 1861, no. 17344. Koritschan's Jewish population fell from 168 in 1848 to 151 in 1859.

56. Lundenburg, Bisenz, Prerau, and Göding experienced a population increase of 5%, 6%, 19%, and 88%, respectively. The *AZJ*, October 3, 1853, 516–17, credits the railroads for bringing Lundenburg "out of its oblivion."

57. The appeals and counterappeals can be found in AVA, Neuer Kultus, D5 (517), 16407/1854. The archives of the Moravian-Silesian Governorship are full of similar cases in the 1850s and 1860s. MZA, B14, M622–25.

58. MZA, B14, M623, no. 17596, June 25, 1858.

59. AVA, Neuer Kultus, D3 (515a), 2007/45. The petition was submitted on January 25, 1858.

60. MZA, B14, M624, no. 17344, August 28, 1861. Emphasis in the original. See also *Die Neuzeit*, June 6, 1862, 267.

61. Jacob Toury missed this important distinction between *Cultusgemeinde* and *Cultusverein* in his "Townships," 68.

62. AVA, Neuer Kultus, D3 (515a), 3961/94, no. 5030. Lažanksy's letter is dated November 27, 1851.

63. *AZJ*, March 14, 1853, 149–50.

64. Brünner, "Geschichte der Juden in Brünn," 156; Klenovský, *Jewish Monuments in Brno*, 24–28.

65. For a detailed overview of the construction costs, which totaled 101,108 fl., see Brünner, "Geschichte der Juden in Brünn," 157.

66. *AZJ*, March 21, 1859, 192. Efforts to lure Leopold Löw away from Szeged, Hungary, proved fruitless. *AZJ*, September 22, 1856, 530; and *AZJ*, September 29, 1856, 543.

67. In a letter to the Ministry of Religion and Education dated December 7, 1858, Lažansky opposed the establishment of a *Cultusgemeinde* with the same arguments he used in 1851. AVA, Neuer Kultus, D3 (515a), 21920, no. 8397.

68. Grünfeld, *Zur Geschichte der Juden*, 11.

69. *Die Neuzeit*, July 17, 1868, 345. Here, Brünn is referred to as a "Parvenü-Gemeinde."

70. *Die Neuzeit*, January 24, 1868, 43; and *Die Neuzeit*, April 3, 1868, 168.

71. Hugo Meissner, "Der mährisch-jüdische Landesmassafond," in Gold, *Die Juden*, 68.

72. For an expression of dissatisfaction at the way the Landesmassafond was being administered, see *Die Neuzeit*, May 2, 1862, 209.

73. *Die Neuzeit*, May 2, 1862, 209; *AZJ*, July 8, 1862, 380.

74. *Die Neuzeit*, May 16, 1862, 233.

75. MZA, B13 2/20, 1016, no. 21553/1723, March 12, 1863; *Beschlüsse des Landtages der Markgrafschaft Mähren in den Sessionen der Jahre 1861–1868* (Brünn, 1869), 148.

76. Meissner, "Der mährisch-jüdische Landesmassafond," 69–70; "Zur Verwendung des mährisch-jüd. Landesmassafond," *Die Neuzeit*, July 3–17, 1863, 317–18, 339–40.

77. *Die Neuzeit*, June 6, 1862, 267; *Die Neuzeit*, July 24, 1863, 351; *Die Neuzeit*, July 17, 1868, 346.

78. "Von dem mährisch-jüdischen Landesmassafonde," *Die Neuzeit*, June 10, 1868, 336–37; *Die Neuzeit*, July 17, 1868, 345–46.

79. *Das Abendland*, December 1, 1868, 181.

80. *Statut für den mährisch-jüdischen Landesmassa-Fond* (Brünn, 1869), 3.

81. This was also reflected in the makeup of the eleven-member board of trustees. The members of the first board (elected on November 17, 1868) belonged to the following eleven communities: Althart, Jamnitz, Piesling, Brünn, Mährisch-Kromau, Kojetein, Göding, Prossnitz, Kremsier, Butschowitz, and Mährisch-Weisskirchen. *Das Abendland*, December 1, 1868, 181.

82. *Die Neuzeit*, July 17, 1868, 346.

83. *Die Neuzeit*, July 18, 1873, 289.

84. The "Musterstatut für die israelitischen Cultusgemeinden in Mähren" can be found in *Die Neuzeit*, June 30–July 28, 1876, 206, 214–15, 223–24, 232–33, 239–40.

85. *Die Neuzeit*, September 18, 1891, 364.

86. Theodor Haas, "Die Juden in Oesterreichisch-Schlesien," *Jüdische Zeitung*, August 7, 1908, 3.

87. Article from *Tagesbote aus Mähren und Schlesien*, quoted in *Die Neuzeit*, August 4, 1876, 245.

88. *Die Neuzeit*, August 4, 1876, 245.

89. "Das Musterstatut für die mährische Judenschaft," *Neue Freie Presse*, July 30, 1876, 4.

90. Klimeš and Tausch, "Hasičský sbor židovské obce v boskovicích," 83–92.

91. The first and most comprehensive study of Moravia's political Jewish communities was published in 1898 while these communities were still in existence: Emil Goldmann, "Die politische Judengemeinden in Mähren," 557–95. Theodor Haas devoted some pages to them in his *Juden in Mähren*, 31–34. Toury also examined the political Jewish communities, but his work suffers from his failure to consult Goldmann's seminal article. Toury, "Townships," 55–72. Aharon M. K. Rabinowicz wrote the entry on "Politische Judengemeinden" in the *Encyclopedia Judaica*, which he later expanded into "Jewish Political Community," 136–51 (English section). Unfortunately, this article is full of factual errors. For a recent article on this topic, see Urbanitsch, "Die politischen Judengemeinde," 39–53.

92. "Jahresrevue 1884," *Brandeis Illustrierter Volkskalendar*, v. 5 (1885–86).

93. "Jarhresrevue 1904," *Brandeis Illustrierter Volkskalendar*, v. 25 (1905–6).

94. On these developments in Bohemia, see King, *Budweisers*. On schooling, see Zahra, *Kidnapped Souls*.

95. For population statistics, see Kořalka, *Tschechen im Habsburgerreich*, 129.

96. MZA, F 13, inv. č. 534, Karton 756, sign. 49/14, Velkostatek Brtnice.

97. "Zur Reorganisation der isr. deutschen Privatschulen Mährens," *Mährisches Schul-Blatt* (1872), 59–60.

98. For further analysis of Bohemian and Moravian Jewry's identification with German language, culture, and politics, see Cohen, *Politics of Ethnic Survival*, 78–82; Kestenberg-Gladstein, "Identifikation der Prager Juden," 171; and Kořalka, *Tschechen im Habsburgerreich*, 133.

99. Kořalka, *Tschechen im Habsburgerreich*, 138.

100. Louis Eisenmann, *Le compromis austro-hongrois de 1867: Étude sur la dualisme* (Paris: Société nouvelle de librairie et d'édition, 1904), 282. Quoted in Wiskemann, *Czechs and Germans*, 29.

101. Kann and David, *Peoples of the Eastern Habsburg Lands*, 297–99; Wiskemann, *Czechs and Germans*, 29–30.

102. "Die mährische Landtagswahlreform und die Juden," *Die Welt*, December 3, 1905, 12–13.

103. Kestenberg-Gladstein, "Jews Between Czechs and Germans," 47.

104. Urbanitsch, "Die politischen Judengemeinde," 45–46.

105. Toury, "Townships," 69–70.

106. "Bericht des Legitimationsauschusses über die am 3. Juli 1879 vorgenommene Wahl des Reichsrathsabgeordneten Rudolf Auspitz für die Städtegruppe Nikolsburg, Auspitz, Göding, Austerlitz, Kanitz, Butschowitz, Gaya, Wischau, Strassnitz, Lundenburg, Pohrlitz," in *Stenographische Protokolle über die Sitzung des Hauses der Abgeordneten des österreichischen Reichsrates*, IX. Sess., no. 151 der Beilagen, February 27, 1880.

107. "Lundenburg," *Die Neuzeit*, September 19, 1890, 371.

108. Čapková, *Češi, Němci, Židé?* 141.

109. On the Czech-Jewish movement, see Krejčová, "Nástin spolové činnosti českožidovského asimilacního hnutí," 85–109; Iveta Vondrášková, "The Czech-Jewish Assimilation Movement and Its Reflection of Czech National Traditions," *JB* 36 (2000): 143–59; and Kieval, *Making of Czech Jewry*.

110. J. Rosenzweig-Moir, "Česko-židovské hnutí na Moravě," *Kalendař českožidovský* (1911–12), 7–13. Quoted in Nezhodová, *Židovský Mikulov*, 196.

111. Haas, *Die Juden in Mähren*, 53.

112. Karel Adámek, *Z naší doby*, v. 2 (Velké Meziříčí, 1886–1890). Quoted and translated in Kieval, *Making of Czech Jewry*, 47.

113. Quoted in Zahra, *Kidnapped Souls*, 21.

114. "Die jüdische Schulen in Mähren," *Dr. Bloch's Österreichische Wochenschrift*, October 1, 1897, 808.

115. "Nikolsburg," *Dr. Bloch's Österreichische Wochenschrift*, September 3, 1897, 727. Emphasis in the original.

116. "Z Moravy," *Českožidovské listy*, September 15, 1894, 10.

117. M. Nacher, "Mährisch-Ostrauer Brief," *Jüdische Volksblatt*, January 13, 1905.

118. Krejčová and Míšková, "Anmerkungen zur Frage des Antisemitismus," 57.

119. Frankl, "Background of the Hilsner Case," 34–118; and Frankl, *"Emancipace od židů."*

120. "Die Juden in Mähren und die liberale Partei," *ÖW*, May 24, 1895, 382–83.

121. Miller, "Reluctant Kingmakers," 111–24.

122. Originally published in *Der Weg* (Vienna). Quoted in *Monatschrift der Österreichisch-Israelitischen Union* 17(12) (December 1905): 1.

123. "Die mährische Landtagswahlreform und die Juden," *Die Welt*, December 1, 1905, 12–13.

124. Kestenberg-Gladstein, "Jews Between Czechs and Germans," 47. These students included Berthold Feiwel, an organizer of the First Zionist Congress, an editor of *Die Welt*, and a founder of the *Jüdischer Verlag*; and Robert Stricker, a Zionist writer, editor, and politician.

125. P. Kantor, "Stricker as Member of 'Veritas,'" in Fraenkel, *Robert Stricker*, 50.

126. Leo Goldhammer, "Die Juden Mährens: Eine kurze Darstellung in Zahlen," in Gold, *Die Juden*, 598.

127. Marsha Rozenblit lists *Landsmannschaften* from Austerlitz, Ungarisch-Brod, Holleschau, Pohrlitz, Triesch, Gross-Meseritsch, and Trebitsch. Rozenblit, *Jews of Vienna*, 202–3, 237n15. On the "Verein der Mährisch-Ausseer in Wien," see *ÖW*, April 10, 1896. On the "Verein der Nikolsburger in Wien," see Nezhodová, *Židovský Mikulov*, 187–90. On the "Humanitärer Verein der Gross-Meseritscher in Wien," see Jewish Museum in Prague, Velké Meziříčí, sig. 53.397 and 41.845.

128. Rozenblit, *Jews of Vienna*, 94–98; Walzer, "Mährische Juden," 27–34.

129. Walzer, "Mährische Juden," 27–34.

130. Walzer, "Mährische Juden," 27–34.

131. See Kulke's *Geschichten* (Leipzig: Oskar Leiner, 1869), *Geschichten aus dem jüdischen Volksleben: Ein Festgeschenk für die israelitische Jugend* (Hamburg, 1871), and *Die schöne Hausiererin* (Prague: J. B. Brandeis, 1895).

132. Weiss, *Zikhronotai*.

133. Adolf Frankel-Grün wrote histories of the Jews of Kremsier and Ungarisch-Brod. See his *Geschichte der Juden in Kremsier* and *Geschichte der Juden in Ungarisch-Brod*.

134. Gold, *Die Juden*, [v].

135. Ginzberg, *Students, Scholars, and Saints*, 220.

136. Solomon Schechter, "Review of I. H. Weiss, *The History of Jewish Tradition*," *JQR* 4(15) (April 1892): 468.

Bibliography

Archival and Manuscript Sources

Brno, Czech Republic

Moravský zemský archiv (MZA)
Moravské mistodržitelství—presidium, Fond B13 2/20, Box 1016
Moravské mistodržitelství, Fond B14, Boxes M564–627 (1789–1867)
Moravské mistodržitelství, Fond B14, Boxes M717–18 (1786–1878)
Moravskoslezské gubernium—presidium, Fond B95, Boxes 363–64
Sněmovní akta 1628–1848, Fond A4, Boxes 8 and 20
Velkostatek Brtnice, F13
Velkostatek Plumlov, F264 (at MZA Kunštat branch office)

Cincinnati, Ohio

Hebrew Union College (HUC)
Hirsch B. Fassel, *Sefer Moznei Tsedek*, Mss. 196–97

Jerusalem, Israel

Central Archives for the History of the Jewish People (CAHJP)
Anton Altrichter, "Das jüdische Schulwesen in Nikolsburg," HM 2/8202
Archiv der Israelitischen Kultusgemeinde (IKG), Wien (A/W)
Archive of Jewish Communities in Altona, Hamburg, Wandsbek (AHW)

Jewish National and University Library (JNUL)
Leopold Löw Archive, JNUL, 4° 794
Löw Schwab Archive, JNUL, 4° 1619

New York, New York

Leo Baeck Institute (LBI)
Moritz Güdeman Collection, AR 7067, 3/6, Box 3
Josef Weisse Collection, AR 4032

Jewish Theological Seminary of America (JTSA)
Gideon Brecher Correspondence, AR 22
Hirsch B. Fassel, *Moznei Tsedek*, ms. 9570
Moritz Steinschneider Correspondence, AR 108

Olomouc, Czech Republic

Archiv města Olomouce (AMO)
Boxes 339, 484, and 582

Prague, Czech Republic

Národní archiv Praha
České gubernium—publicum 97/12, Box 7734 (1825)

Židovské muzeum Praha
Sitzungsprotokolle des Gemeinde-Vorstands, Mikulov, 1833–1859 (also available
    on microfilm at CAHJP, Jerusalem, HM 7806–7)
List of books in Veith Ehrenstamm's library, Prossnitz, ms. 86
Humanitärer Verein der Gross-Meseritscher in Wien, Velké Meziříčí, sig. 53.397,
    41.845

Prostějov, Czech Republic

Archiv města Prostějova (AMP), located in Okresní archiv v Prostějova
Narodní garda, inv. čislo 902, sig. 44, 232–33

Ramat Gan, Israel

Institute for the Research of Diaspora Jewry, Bar-Ilan University
Sänger Collection (Papers of Samson Raphael Hirsch)

Vienna, Austria

Allgemeines Verwaltungsarchiv (AVA)
Alter Kultus–Israelitischer Kultus, Boxes 3–8 (IV T 5–15)
Ministerium des Innerns, Präsidiale 11 (Mähren), 1848–99, Box 432
Neuer Kultus–Israelitischer Kultus: D1 (Mähren), Box 501; D3 (Mähren–
    Kultusgemeinden), Box 515a; D4 (Mähren–Gottesdienst, Synagogen),
    Box 342 (rot); D5 (Mähren–Kultusbeiträge), Box 517; D12 (Mähr. jüd.
    Landesmassafond)

Haus-, Hof- und Staatsarchiv, Österreichisches Staatsarchiv (HHStA)
Österreichischer Reichstag 1848/49, Fasz. 125.IX.24, "Petitionen von Juden um
    Emancipation, dann Petitionen dagegen"
Protokolle des Ministerrathes, 1850–1860. Staatsrat Vorträge, 1840–1848

Österreichische Nationalbibliothek
Flugblätter-Sammlung, Kronländer 1848/14/19a

Newspapers and Periodicals

Das Abendland, Prague, 1864–1868

Allgemeine Zeitung des Judenthums, Leipzig, 1837–1867

Ben-Chananja, Szeged, 1859–1864

Brünner Anzeiger und Tageblatt, Brno, 1855–1856

Brünner Tags-Courier, Brno, 1848–1851

Brünner Zeitung, Brno, 1847–1851

Českožidovské listy, Prague, 1894–1904

Constitutionelle Bote aus Böhmen, Prague, 1850

Dr. Bloch's Österreichische Wochenschrift: Centralorgan für gesammten Interessen des Judenthums, Vienna, 1884–1905

Hickl's Jüdische Volkskalendar, Brno, 1903–1939

Der Israelit, Mainz, 1860–1870

Israelitische Annalen, Frankfurt am Main, 1839–1841

The Jewish Intelligence, London, 1840–1850

Kalendář česko-židovský, Prague, 1881–1914

Kalendar und Jahrbuch für Israeliten, Vienna, 1842–1851

Kokheve Yitshak, Vienna, 1845–1873

Der Lloyd, Vienna, 1848–1850

Mährisches Landtagsblatt, Brno, 1849

Mährisches Schul-Blatt: Organ des allgemeinen mährischen Landes-Lehrervereines, Brno, 1872–1885

Morawské noviny, Brno, 1848–1850

Národní noviny, Prague, 1848

Die Neue Zeit: Blätter für nationale Interessen, Olomouc, 1848–1854

Neuigkeiten, zugleich Fremdblatt für Brünn, Brno, 1851

Die Neuzeit, Vienna, 1861–1903

Der Orient: Berichte, Studien und Kritik für jüdische Geschichte und Literatur, Leipzig, 1840–1851

Der österreichische constitutionelle Bote für Stadt und Land, Brno, 1848–1851

Österreichisches Central Organ für Glaubensfreiheit, Cultur und Literature der Juden, Vienna, 1848

Schild und Schwert, Vienna, 1848

Telegraph für Stadt und Land, Brno, 1848

Treue-Zions-Wächter, Hamburg-Altona, 1845–1854

Das Vaterland, Brno, 1848–1849

Voice of Jacob, London, 1841–1848

Wiener Blätter, Vienna, 1850–1851

Wiener Zeitung, Vienna, 1848–1851

Wissenschaftliche Zeitschrift für jüdische Theologie, Frankfurt am Main, 1835–1847

Zeitschrift für die religiösen Interessen des Judenthums, Berlin-Leipzig, 1844–1846

Die Zeitstimme, Prague, 1863–1864

Books and Articles

Aberbach, Moshe, ed. *Aharon M. K. Rabinowicz Jubilee Volume*. Jerusalem: Bialik Institute, 1996.

Abrams, Bradley. "The Austro-Czech Intelligentsia of 1848 and the Österreichisches Central-Organ für Glaubensfreiheit, Cultur und Literatur der Juden." *Bohemia* 31 (1990): 1–20.

Abramsky, Chimen. "The Crisis of Authority Within European Jewry in the Eighteenth Century." In Siegfried Stein and Raphael Loewe, eds., *Studies in Jewish Religious and Intellectual History*. Tuscaloosa: University of Alabama Press, 1979.

Adler, Simon. "Das Judenpatent von 1797." *JGGJČR* 5 (1933): 199–229.

Agnew, Hugh. *The Czechs and the Lands of the Bohemian Crown*. Stanford, Calif.: Hoover Institution Press, 2004.

Altmann, Alexander. "The New Style of Preaching in Nineteenth-Century German Jewry." In Alexander Altmann, ed., *Studies in Nineteenth-Century Jewish Intellectual History*. Cambridge, Mass.: Harvard University Press, 1964.

Arnbom, Marie-Theres. *Friedmann, Gutmann, Lieben, Mandl, Strakosch: Fünf Familienporträts aus Wien vor 1938*. Vienna: Böhlau, 2002.

Asaria, Zwi. "Samson Raphael Hirsch's Wirken in Lande Niedersachsen." *Udim* 1 (5731/1970): 12–18.

[Auerbach, Isaak Levin]. *Sind die Israeliten verpflichtet ihre Gebete durchaus in der hebräischen Sprache zu verrichten?* Berlin: Zürngibl, 1818.

Baer, Fritz. *Das Protokollbuch der Landjudenschaft des Herzogtums Kleve*. Berlin: C. A. Schwetschke, 1922.

Bahlcke, Joachim. *Regionalismus und Staatsintegration im Widerstreit: Die Länder der böhmischen Krone im ersten Jahrhundert der Habsburgerherrschaft (1526–1619)*. Munich: R. Oldenbourg, 1994.

Barany, George. *Stephen Széchenyi and the Awakening of Hungarian Nationalism*. Princeton, N.J.: Princeton University Press, 1968.

Baron, Salo. "Aspects of the Jewish Communal Crisis in 1848." *JSS* 14 (1952): 99–144.

———. "The Impact of the Revolution of 1848 on Jewish Emancipation." *JSS* 12 (1949): 195–248.

———. "The Revolution of 1848 and Jewish Scholarship." *PAAJR* 18 (1948–49): 1–66; 20 (1951): 1–100.

———, Ernest Nagel, and Koppel S. Pinson, eds. *Freedom and Reason: Studies in Philosophy and Jewish Culture in Memory of Morris Raphael Cohen*. Glencoe, Ill.: Free Press, 1951.

Bartal, Israel. *The Jews of Eastern Europe, 1772–1881*, Chaya Naor, trans. Philadelphia: University of Pennsylvania Press, 2005.

———. "The *Pinkas* of the Council of the Four Lands." In Antony Polansky,

Jakub Basista, and Andrzej Link-Lenczowski, eds., *The Jews in Old Poland, 1000–1795.* London: I. B. Tauris, 1993.

Baumgarten, Emanuel. "Zur Mährisch Ausseer Affaire." In Marcus Brann and F. Rosenthal, eds., *Gedenkbuch zur Errinerung an David Kaufmann.* Breslau: S. Schottländer, 1900.

Beales, Derek. *Joseph II: Against the World, 1780–1790.* Cambridge, U.K.: Cambridge University Press, 2009.

———. *Joseph II: In the Shadow of Maria Theresa, 1740–1781.* Cambridge, U.K.: Cambridge University Press, 1987.

Beer, Peter. *Geschichte, Lehren und Meinungen aller bestandenen und noch bestehenden religiösen Sekten der Juden un der Geheimlehre oder Cabbalah,* 2 vols. Brünn: J. G. Trassler, 1822–1823.

———. *Skizze einer Geschichte der Erziehung und Unterrichts bei den Israeliten, von der frühesten Zeit bis auf die Gegenwart.* Prague: M. I. Landau, 1832.

Bendavid, Lazarus. *Etwas zur Charackteristick der Juden.* Leipzig: J. Stahel, 1793.

Benedict, Naphtaly [Naftali Benet]. *Emunath Israel: Ein Hülfsbuch zum Unterrichte in der Mosaischen Religion.* Vienna: A. Strauss, 1824; Prague: M. I. Landau, 1832.

Benet, Mordecai. *Parshat Mordekhai.* M.-Sziget: Mendel Vider, 1899.

Benet, Naftali. *Misped gadol ve-khaved me'od 'al mot adoni, avi, mori, ve-rabi . . . Mordekhai Benet.* Vienna: Anton Edlem von Schmid, 1830.

Benet, Ya'akov Abril. *Toldot . . . ha-Rav . . . Mordekhai Benet.* Ofen, 1832.

Bergl, Josef. "Das Exil der Prager Judenschaft von 1745 bis 1748." *JGGJČR* I (1929): 263–331.

Bernard, Paul. "Joseph II and the Jews: The Origins of the Toleration Patent of 1782." *AHY* 4–5 (1968): 101–19.

Beschlüsse des Landtages der Markgrafschaft Mähren in den Sessionen der Jahre 1861–1868. Brünn: Břeža, Winiker, 1869.

Bihl, Wolfdieter. "Die Juden." In Adam Wandruszka and Peter Urbanitsch, eds., *Die Habsburgermonarchie, 1848–1918,* v. 3, *Völker des Reichs.* Vienna: Österreichische Akademie der Wissenschaften, 1980.

Bing, Hermann. *'Ateret tsevi! Umständliche Schilderung des feierlichen Enzuges und der feierlichen Installation Sr. Ehrwürden des Herrn Samson Raphael Hirsch als Ober-Landes-Rabbiner von Mähren und Schlesien am 23. und 30. Juni 1847 in Nikolsburg.* Vienna: Franz Edlen von Schmid & J. J. Busch, 1847.

Bondy, Gottlieb, and Franz Dworsky. *Zur Geschichte der Juden in Böhmen, Mähren und Schlesien von 906 bis 1620,* 2 vols. Prague: G. Bondy, 1906.

Bosl, Karl. *Handbuch der Geschichte der böhmischen Länder,* 4 vols. Stuttgart: Anton Hiersemann, 1974.

Brämer, Andreas. *Rabbiner Zacharias Frankel: Wissenschaft des Judentums und konservative Reform im 19. Jahrhundert.* Hildesheim: Olms, 2000.

Brann, Marcus, and F. Rosenthal, eds. *Gedenkbuch zur Errinerung an David Kaufmann.* Breslau: S. Schottländer, 1900.

Bránský, Jaroslav. *Židé v Boskovicích.* Boskovice: Klub přátel Boskovic & nakladatelství Albert, 1999.

Brecher, Gideon. *Die Beschneidung der Israeliten, von der historischen, praktisch-operativen und ritualen Seite, zunächst für den Selbstunterricht . . . Mit einem Approbationsschreiben von Hrn. Rab. H. B. Fassel und einem Anhange über Beschneidung der Muhamedaner von M. Steinschneider.* Vienna: Franz Edl. v. Schmid & J. J. Busch, 1845.

———. "Commentary" on J. Halevi, *Ha-kuzari.* Prague: M. I. Landau, 1838–1840 (in Hebrew).

[Bresselau, Meir Israel]. *Ueber die Gebete der Israeliten in der Landessprache: Aus den Quellen des Talmuds und der spätern Gesetzlehrer erörtert.* Hamburg, 1819.

Bretholz, Bertold. *Geschichte der Juden in Mähren im Mittelalter.* Brünn: R. M. Rohrer, 1934.

———. *Quellen zur Geschichte der Juden in Mähren vom XI. bis zum XV. Jahrhundert (1067–1411).* Prague: Taussig & Taussig, 1935.

Breuer, Edward. *The Limits of Enlightenment: Jews, Germans, and the Eighteenth-Century Study of Scripture.* Cambridge, Mass.: Harvard University Press, 1996.

Breuer, Mordechai. "Emancipation and the Rabbis." *Niv Hamidrashin* 13–14 (5738–39/1978–79): 27–51.

———. *Ohalei tora: ha-yeshiva tavnita ve-toldoteha.* Jerusalem: Merkaz Shazar, 2003.

Briess, Ignaz. *Schilderung aus dem ehemaligen Ghettoleben vom Jahre 1838–1848.* Brünn: M. Hickl, 1922.

Brilling, Bernhard. "Die Handelsbeziehungen der mährischen Judenschaft zu Breslau im 16. und 17. Jhrh." *ZGJT* 2(1) (1931): 1–20.

———. "Zur Geschichte des jüdischen Goldschmiedegewerbes in Mähren (1550–1800)." *Zeitschrift für Geschichte der Juden* 6 (1969): 137–46.

Brocke, Michael, and Julius Carlebach, eds. *Biographisches Handbuch der Rabbiner*, 2 vols. Munich: K. G. Saur, 2004.

Broda, Abraham. *Megillat Sedarim*, Emanuel Baumgarten, ed. Berlin: Ḥevrat mezikei nirdamim, 1895.

Browning, Reed. *The War of the Austrian Succession.* Phoenix Mill, U.K.: Sutton, 1994.

Brüll, Nehemiah. "Geschichte der jüdischen Gemeinde zu Kojetein in Mähren." *BCh* 5 (1862): 318–20.

Büchler, Sándor. "Zsidó letelepedések magyarországon a mohácsi vész után." *MZsSz* 10 (1893): 313–29, 370–87.

Buxbaum, Yosef. "Introduction." In N. Trebitsch, *Shalom Yerushalayim: ḥidushim u-ferushim, hagahot ve-tikunim 'al Talmud Yerushalmi, Seder Zera'im.* Jerusalem: Machon Yerushalayim, 1980.

Čapková, Kateřina. *Češi, Němci, Židé? Národní identita Židů v Čechách, 1918–1938.* Prague: Paseka, 2005.

Carmoly, E. *Ha-orevim u'vnei yonah.* Rödelheim: Lehrberger, 1861.

Cermanová (Vondrášková), Iveta. "The Censorship of Hebrew Manuscripts in Vienna in the Early 19th Century: The Case of Abraham Trebitsch." *JB* 39 (2003): 93–103.

———. "The Czech-Jewish Assimilation Movement and Its Reflection of Czech National Traditions." *JB* 36 (2000): 143–59.

———. "Druhý díl kroniky 'Děje časů' od Abrahama Trebitsche z Mikulova: Příspěvek k výzkumu židovské historiografie 19. století." Ph.D. dissertation, Charles University, Prague, 2005.

———. "'The Events of the Times' by Abraham Trebitsch of Mikulov (Nikolsburg): The Chronicle and Its Relationship to the Development of Modern Historiography." *JB* 37 (2001): 92–144.

———. "The Second Part of the Chronicle 'The Events of the Times' ('Qorot ha-Ittim') by Abraham Trebitsch of Mikulov (Nikolsburg)." *JB* 40 (2004): 22–64.

Chorin, Aron. *Imre No'am.* Prague, 1798.

———. *Sefer Emek ha-Shaveh.* Prague: Elsenwanger, 1803.

———. *Shiryon kaskasim.* Prague, 1799.

Cohen, Daniel, ed. *Die Landjudenschaften in Deutschland als Organe jüdischer Selbstverwaltung von der frühen Neuzeit bis ins neunzehnte Jahrhundert,* 3 vols. Jerusalem: Israelische Akademie der Wissenschaften, 1996.

Cohen, Gary. *The Politics of Ethnic Survival: Germans in Prague, 1861–1914.* Princeton, N.J.: Princeton University Press, 1981.

Das Comité für die Reorganisation der jüdisch. mähr. Religionsangelegenheiten. *Entwurf einer Synagogal-Verfassung der Bekenner des jüdischen Glaubens in Mähren.* Brünn: Franz Gastl, 1849.

[Deneberg, Nathan]. *Kritik des Entwurfes einer Synagogal-Verfassung der Bekenner des jüdischen Glaubens in Mähren nebst den momentan nöthigen Verbesserungs-Vorschlägen.* Brünn: Winiker, 1850.

Deutsch, Simon, and Franz Gräffer. *Jüdischer Plutarch.* Vienna: Ulrich Klopf, 1848.

Dickson, P. G. M. *Finance and Government Under Maria Theresia, 1740–1780,* 2 vols. Oxford: Clarendon Press, 1987.

Donath, Oskar. "Siegmund Kolischs Leben und Wirken." *Jahresbericht der Deutschen Landes-Oberrealschule in Göding* 14 (1912): 1–72.

Dotyky: Židé v dějinách Jihlavska. Jihlava: Státní okresní archiv, 1998.

Drabek, Anna M. "The Concept of the 'Nation' in Bohemia and Moravia at the Turn of the Century." *History of European Ideas* 15(1–3) (1992): 305–11.

———. "Die Juden in den böhmischen Ländern zur Zeit des landesfürstlichen Absolutismus." In Ferdinand Seibt, ed., *Die Juden in den böhmischen Ländern.* Munich & Vienna: Oldenbourg, 1983.

———. "Das Judentum der böhmischen Ländern vor der Emanzipation." *Studia Judaica Austriaca* 10 (1984): 5–30.

Dubnow, Simon. *History of the Jews in Russia and Poland*, 3 vols. Philadelphia: Jewish Publication Society, 1916.

Duschak, Moritz. "Dr. Gideon Brecher: Biografische Skizze." In *Die Jubiläums-Feier des Dr. Gideon Brecher in Prossnitz am 14. Jänner 1865*. Prossnitz: Ignaz Rottberger, 1865.

———. "Geschichte der israelitischen Gemeinde zu Prossnitz." *BCh* 6 (1863): 520–22.

———. *Geschichte der Verfassung mit besonderer Beziehung auf die österreichisch-ungarischen Israeliten*. Vienna, 1888.

———. *Schulgesetzgebung und Methodik der alten Israeliten, nebst einem geschichtlichen Anhange und einer Beilage über höhere israelitische Lehranstalten*. Vienna: Wilhelm Braumüller, 1872.

———. *Die Theilnahme an dem Schicksale unserer Brüder: Rede, gehalten am Passah-Fest im Jahre 5607 (1847)*. Prague, 1847.

Dynner, Glenn. *Men of Silk: The Hasidic Conquest of Polish Jewry*. New York: Oxford University Press, 2006.

Ehrentheil, M. *Jüdische Charakterbilder*. Pest: Robert Lampel, 1867.

Ehrmann, Daniel. *Die Tante: Ein Sittenbild aus dem jüdischen Familienleben*. Vienna: A. Hölder, 1881.

Eisler, Moritz. "R. Moses Katz Wanefried: Eine Reminisenz aus dem Leben des Herrn Dr. Adolf Jellinek." *Die Neuzeit* (1891): 205–7.

Eleh divrei ha-brit. Altona, 1819.

Eliáš, Bohuslav. "Zur Geschichte der Israelitengemeinde von Prostějov (Prossnitz)." *Husserl Studies* 10 (1994): 237–48.

Elvert, Christian d'. *Zur Geschichte der Juden in Maehren und Oesterr. Schlesien, mit Ruecksicht auf Oesterreich-Ungarn ueberhaupt und die Nachbarlaender*. Brünn: C. Winiker, 1895.

Emden, Jacob. *Megilat Sefer*. New York: Y. Gelbman, 1955.

———. *Sefer Hitabkut*. Lvov: M. Wolf, 1877.

Encyclopedia Judaica, 17 vols. Jerusalem: Keter, 1996.

Engel, Alfred. "Die Ausweisung der Juden aus den königlichen Städten und ihre Folgen." *JGGJČR* 2 (1930): 50–96.

———, ed. *Sefer zikaron li-ftiḥat ha-muze'on ha-yehudi be-k"k N[ikol]s[burg] = Památník židovského ústředního musea pro Moravsko-Slezsko = Gedenkbuch im Auftrage des Kuratoriums*. Mikulov: Nekudah, 1936.

Ettinger, Shmuel. "The Council of the Four Lands." In Antony Polonsky, Jakub Basista, and Andrzej Link-Lenczowski, eds., *The Jews in Old Poland, 1000–1795*. London: Institute for Polish-Jewish Studies, 1993.

Euchel, Isaac. *Gebet der hochdeutschen und polnischen Juden*. Vienna: Anton Pichler, 1799; Vienna: Anton Schmid, 1815.

Evans, R. J. W., ed. *Crown, Church, and Estates: Central European Politics in the Sixteenth and Seventeenth Centuries*. New York: St. Martin's Press, 1991.

Faerber, R. *Pe'er Mordekhai: toldot Rabi Mordekhai Benet mi-Nikolsburg*. Tel Aviv: Hotsa'at Ataza, 1951.

Farkas, David. *Guide for Manuscripts and Printed Matter from the Legacy of Rabbi Samson Raphael Hirsch: The Sänger Collection*. Ramat Gan: Institute for Research on Jews of the Diaspora, Bar-Ilan University, 1982.

Fassel, Hirsch B. *Ḥorev be-tsiyyon oder Briefe eines jüdischen Gelehrten und Rabbinen-über das Werk: "Ḥorev Versuche über Jissroels Pflichten in der Zerstreuung von S.R. Hirsch—Nebst einer Abhandlung über die Möglichkeit einer Abschaffung bestehender Gebräuche im Judenthum vom orthodoxen Standpunkte.*" Leipzig: C. L. Fritzsche, 1839.

―――. *Reis und Hülsenfrüchte am Pesach erlaubte Speisen: Ausgesprochen am 4. und 11. April 1846 in der grossen Synagoge zu Prossnitz*. Prague: M. I. Landau, 1846.

―――. *Tsedek ve-mishpat: Tugend und Rechtslehre nach den Principien des Talmuds und nach der Form der Philosophie*. Vienna: Ullrich Klopf, 1848.

―――. "Ueber Trauungen in der Synagoge." *WZfJT* (1839): 36–39.

―――. *Die Verfassungsurkunde und der Tempel Salomos: Rede, bei dem in der Prossnitzer Synagoge am 17. März 1849 gefeierten Dankfeste fur die verliehene Verfassung*. Prossnitz: Der Vorstand der israelitischen Gemeinde, 1849.

―――. *Warum freuet sich unser Land? und warum freuen sich die Israeliten unseres Landes? Ein Wort zur Zeit*. Olmütz: A. Skarnitzl, 1848.

―――. *Zwei gottesdienstliche Vorträge, gehalten in der Synagoge zu Prossnitz*. Olmütz, 1838.

Feiner, Shmuel. *The Jewish Enlightenment*, Chaya Naor, trans. Philadelphia: University of Pennsylvania Press, 2003.

Feuchtwang, David. "Markus Benedikt (Rabbi Mordechai Benet)." In Samuel Krauss, ed., *Festschrift Adolf Schwarz zum siebzigsten Geburtstag*. Berlin & Vienna: R. Loweit, 1917.

―――. "Samson Raphael Hirsch als Oberlandesrabbiner von Mähren." In *Samson Raphael Hirsch Jubiläumsnummer des "Israelit."* Frankfurt am Main, 1908, 19–25.

Fiedler, Jiři. *Jewish Sights in Bohemia and Moravia*. Prague: Sefer, 1991.

Fishman, Talya. "Forging Jewish Memory: Besamim Rosh and the Invention of Pre-Emancipation Jewish Culture." In Elisheva Carlebach, John M. Efron, and David N. Myers, eds., *Jewish History and Jewish Memory: Essays in Honor of Yosef Hayim Yerushalmi*. Hanover, N.H.: University Press of New England, 1998.

Fleckeles, Eleazar. *Ahavat David*. Prague, 1800.

―――. *'Olat Ḥodesh*, v. 2. Prague, 1787.

―――. *Teshuvah me'ahava*. Prague, 1809.

Flesch, Heinrich. "Urkundliches über die mährischen Familienstellen." *MGWJ* 71 (1927): 267–74.

―――. "Urkundliches über jüdische Handwerker in Mähren." *MGWJ* 74(3) (1930): 197–217.

Flesch, Josef. *Ha-yoresh divrei elohim.* Prague: M. I. Landau, 1830.

―――. *Ḥayyei moshe.* Prague: M. I. Landau, 1838.

Fraenkel, Josef. *Robert Stricker.* London: Ararat, 1950.

Fram, Edward. *Ideals Face Reality: Jewish Law and Life in Poland 1550–1655.* Cincinnati: HUC Press, 1997.

Fränkel, S. J., and M. J. Bresselau, eds. *Ordnung der öffentlichen Andacht für die Sabbath- und Festtage des ganzen Jahres: Nach dem Gebrauche des Neuen-Tempel-Vereins in Hamburg.* Hamburg, 1819.

Frankel-Grün, Adolf. *Geschichte der Juden in Kremsier mit Ruecksicht auf die Nachbargemeinden,* 3 vols. Breslau: S. Schottländer, 1896–1901.

―――. *Geschichte der Juden in Ungarisch-Brod: Nebst Biographien von R. Moses Perls, P. Singer, Ad. Jellinek, P. F. Frankl, etc. nach Archivalien dargestellt.* Vienna: M. Waizner, 1905.

―――. *Jüdische Zeitgeschichte und Zeitgenossen.* Vienna: M. Waizner, 1903.

―――. *Zur Geschichte der Judenemanzipation in Oesterreich 1848–1908.* Vienna: M. Waizner, 1908.

Fränkl, Beniamen Israel. *Sefer yeshu'ot yisrael,* Emanuel Baumgarten, ed. Berlin, [1898].

Frankl, Michal. "The Background of the Hilsner Case: Political Allegations and Accusations of Ritual Murder, 1896–1900." *JB* 36 (2000): 34–118.

―――. *"Emancipace od židů": Český antisemitismus na konci 19. století.* Prague: Paseka, 2007.

František, Mainuš. *Vlnařství a bavlnářství na Moravě a ve Slezku v XVIII. stoleti.* Prague: Státní pedagogické nakladatelství, 1960.

Freimann, J. "Geschichte der Juden in Prossnitz." *JJLG* 15 (1923): 26–58.

Freudenberger, Herman. *The Industrialization of a Central European City: Brno and the Fine Woolen Industry in the 18th Century.* Edington, U.K.: Pasold Research Fund, 1977.

Freudenthal, Max. *Leipziger Messegäste: Die jüdischen Besucher der Leipziger Messen in den Jahren 1675 bis 1764.* Frankfurt am Main: J. Kauffmann, 1928.

Friedlaender, Markus Hirsch. *Kore Haddoroth: Beiträge zur Geschichte der Juden in Mähren.* Brünn: R. M. Rohrer, 1876.

―――. *Das Talmudstudium in der ersten Haelfte des 19. Jahrhunderts in den Jeschibot zu Nikolsburg, Posen und Pressburg.* Vienna: M. Waizner, 1901.

―――. *Tiferet Jisrael: Schilderungen aus dem inneren Leben der Juden in Maehren in vormaerzlichen Zeiten—ein Beitrag zur Cultur- und Sittengeschichte.* Brünn: R. M. Rohrer, 1878.

Friedländer, David. *Gebete der Juden auf das ganze Jahr.* Brünn: Karl Neumann, 1796.

Friesel, Evyatar. *Atlas of Modern Jewish History.* Jerusalem: Carta, 1990.

———. "The *Österreichisches Central-Organ*, Vienna 1848: A Radical Jewish Periodical." *LBIYB* 47 (2002): 118–49.

Gates-Coon, Rebecca. *The Landed Estates of the Esterházy Princes: Hungary During the Reforms of Maria Theresia and Joseph II.* Baltimore: Johns Hopkins University Press, 1994.

Geiger, Ludwig. *Abraham Geiger's Leben in Briefen.* Breslau: Wilh. Jacobsohn, 1885.

Ginzberg, Louis. *Students, Scholars, and Saints.* Philadelphia: Jewish Publication Society, 1928.

Glinert, Lewis, ed. *Hebrew in Ashkenaz.* New York: Oxford University Press, 1993.

Gold, Hugo, ed. *Gedenkbuch der untergegangenen Judengemeinden Mährens.* Tel Aviv: Olamenu, 1974.

———. *Geschichte der Juden in Wien.* Tel Aviv: Olamenu, 1966.

———, ed. *Die Juden und Judengemeinden Mährens in Vergangenheit und Gegenwart: Ein Sammelwerk.* Brünn: Jüdischer Buch- und Kunstverlag, 1929.

Goldberg, Jacob. "Jewish Marriage in Eighteenth-Century Poland." *Polin* 10 (1997): 3–39.

Goldhammer, Leo. "Jewish Emigration from Austria-Hungary in 1848–1849." *YIVO Bletter* 38 (1954): 5–38.

Goldmann, Emil. "Die politische Judengemeinden in Mähren." *Zeitschrift für Volkswirtschaft, Socialpolitik und Verwaltung* 17 (1898): 557–95.

Goldstücker, Eduard. "Jews Between Czechs and Germans Around 1848." *LBIYB* 17 (1972): 61–71.

Gottschalk, Benno. "Die Anfänge der deutschen Gebetübersetzungen." In *Festgabe für Claude G. Montefiore.* Berlin: Philo, 1928.

Grab, Walter. "Das Wiener Judentum: Eine historische Überblick." In his *Zwei Seiten einer Medaille: Demokratische Revolution und Judenemanzipation.* Köln: PapyRossa, 2000.

Graetz, Heinrich. *Tagebuch und Briefe*, Reuven Michael, ed. Tübingen: Mohr, 1977.

Grieshaber, Isaac. *Makkel Noam.* Vienna: Josef Hraschansky, 1799.

Grodziski, Stanisław. "The Jewish Question in Galicia: The Reforms of Maria Theresa and Joseph II." *Polin* 12 (1999): 61–72.

Grunfeld, Isidor. "Introduction." In Samson Raphael Hirsch, *Judaism Eternal.* London: Soncino Press, 1956.

Grünfeld, Max. *Zur Geschichte der Judengemeinde in Brünn.* Brünn: Jüdischer Buch- und Kunstverlag, 1922.

Grünwald, Fülöp, and Sandor Scheiber. "Adalékok a magyar zsidóság településtörténetéhez a XVIII. század első felében." *Magyar-zsidó oklevéltár* 7 (1963): 5–48.

Guttmann, Alexander. *The Struggle over Reform in Rabbinic Literature.* Jerusalem & New York: World Union for Progressive Judaism, 1977.

Haas, Theodor. *Die Juden in Mähren: Darstellung der Rechtsgeschichte und Statistik unter besonderer Berücksichtigung des 19. Jahrhunderts.* Brünn: Jüdischer Buch- und Kunstverlag, 1908.

Hahn, Fred. "Jews from the Bohemian Lands in the United States, 1848–1938." In Eva Schmidt-Hartmann and Stanley B. Winters, eds., *Grossbritannien, die USA und die böhmischen Länder 1848–1938.* Munich: R. Oldenbourg, 1991.

Halpern, Israel, "Nisuei bahala b'mizraḥ europa." *Zion* 27 (1962): 36–58.

———, ed. *Pinkas va'ad arba' aratsot / Actus Congressus generalis Judaeorum regni Poloniae, 1580–1764,* 2nd ed. Jerusalem: Mosad Bialik, 1989.

———. *Takkanot medinat Mehrin (410–505) / Constitutiones congressus Generalis Judaeorum Moraviensium (1650–1748).* Jerusalem: Hevrat mezikei nirdamim, 1951.

Hammer, Käthe. "Die Judenfrage in den westlichen Kronländern Österreichs im Jahre 1848." Ph.D. dissertation, Universität Wien, Vienna, 1948.

Hanover, Nathan. *Abyss of Despair.* New York: Bloch, 1950.

Hatschek, Oskar. *Die periodische Presse Mährens von ihren Anfänge bis zum Jahre 1862.* Prossnitz, 1904.

Häusler, Wolfgang. "Hermann Jellinek (1823–1848), ein Demokrat in der Wiener Revolution." *Jahrbuch des Instituts für deutsche Geschichte* 5 (1976): 125–75.

———. "Toleranz, Emanzipation und Antisemitismus: Das österreichische Judentum des bürgerlichen Zeitalters." In Nikolaus Vielmetti, ed., *Das österreichische Judentum: Voraussetzungen und Geschichte.* Vienna & Munich: Jugend und Volk, 1974.

Havránek, Jan. "Böhmen im Fruhjahr 1848: Vorbild der nationalen Problematik in Europa für das folgende Jahrhundert." In Heiner Timmermann, ed., *1848—Revolution in Europa: Verlauf, politische Programme, Folgen und Wirken.* Berlin: Duncker & Humblot, 1999.

Hecht, Louise. "'Gib dem Knaben Unterricht nach seiner Weise' (Spr. 22, 6): Theorie und Praxis des modernen jüdischen Schulsystems in der Habsburger Monarchie." *Jahrbuch der Österreichischen Gesellschaft zur Erforschung des 18. Jahrhunderts* 18–19 (2004): 117–34.

———. *Ein jüdischer Aufklärer in Böhmen: Der Pädagoge und Reformer Peter Beer (1758–1838).* Cologne: Böhlau, 2008.

Heilig, Bernhard. *Actuelles aus der Geschichte des Hauses Ehrenstamm, 1752–1852.* Brünn: J. Wesnitzky, 1934.

———. "Aufstieg und Verfall des Hauses Ehrenstamm." *Bulletin für die Mitglieder der Gesellschaft der Freunde des Leo Baeck Instituts* 10 (1960): 101–22.

———. *Eine mährische Stadt und ihr Ghetto.* Brünn: J. Wesnitzky, 1932.

———. *Der sozialökonomische Rückschritt in der modernen Heimarbeit. Auf Grund von Erhebungen im Konfektionszentrum Prossnitz.* Prague, 1936.

———. "Die Vorläufer der mährischen Konfektionsindustrie in ihrem Kampf mit den Zünften." *JGGJČR* 3 (1931): 307–448.

Helfert, Joseph Alexander. *Die Wiener Journalistik im Jahre 1848.* Vienna: Manz, 1877.

Heřman, Jan. "The Evolution of the Jewish Population of Bohemia and Moravia, 1754–1953." In U. O. Schmelz, P. Glikson, and Sergio DellaPergola, eds., *Papers in Jewish Demography, 1973*. Jerusalem: Institute of Contemporary Jewry, 1977.

Herrisch, Isidor. "Die Judengemeinde zu Eisgrub in Mähren." *ZGJT* 2(4) (1934): 292–94.

Hertzberg, Arthur. *The French Enlightenment and the Jews*. New York: Columbia University Press, 1968.

Heschel, Yisrael Natan. "De'atam shel gedolei ha-dor b'milḥematam neged ha-maskil Naftali Herz Weisl." *Kovets bet aharon ve-yisrael* 8(1) (Tishrei-Heshvan 5753 [1992]): 139–67.

———. "Igrot ha-geonim R. Mordekhai Benet ve-R. Shmuel Landau zts"l odot bakshat hamalkhut leshanot nusaḥ ha-tefilah ve-sidrei ha-limud bi-shnat 5523." *Kovets bet aharon ve-yisrael* 11(3) (Shvat-Adar 5756 [1996]): 154–55.

Hildesheimer, Ezriel. *She'elot u'teshuvot*. Tel Aviv: L. Friedman, 1986.

Hillel, F. *Die Rabbiner und die verdienstvollen Familien der Leipniker Judengemeinde im 17., 18. und 19. Jahrhundert: Ein Beitrag zur Geschichte der mährischen Judenheit*. Mährisch-Ostrau: R. Färber, 1929.

Hirsch, Mendel. "Villafranca und Kremsier: Ein Beitrag zur jüdischen Zeitgeschichte." *Jeschurun* 5 (1858–59): 593–622.

Hirsch, Samson Raphael. *Horeb: A Philosophy of Jewish Laws and Observances*, translated from the German with introduction and annotations by I. Grunfeld. London: Soncino Press, 1962.

———. *Judaism Eternal: Selected Essays from the Writings of Samson Raphael Hirsch*, 2 vols. London: Soncino Press, 1956.

———. *The Nineteen Letters of Ben Uziel*, Bernard Drachman, trans. New York & London: Funk & Wagnalls, 1899.

———. *Postscripta zu den unter dem Titel Ḥorev be-tsiyyon erschienenen Briefen eines jüdischen Gelehrten und Rabbinen über das Werk: "Ḥoreb" von dem Verfasser des Ḥorev*. Altona: J. F. Hammerich, 1840.

———. *Sefer Shemesh Marpeh: she'elot u-teshuvot, ḥidushe ha-Shas, igrot u-mikhtavim*. New York: Mesorah, 1992.

Hirschler, Gertrude. "Rabbi and Statesman: Samson Raphael Hirsch, Landesrabbiner in Moravia (1847–1851)." *RSHCJ* 1 (1987): 121–49.

Hlošek, J. *Židé na Moravě*. Brno: České hospodářské společností pro markrabství moravské, 1925.

Hoensch, Jörg K., Stanislav Biman, and L'ubomír Lipták, eds. *Judenemanzipation—Antisemitismus—Verfolgung in Deutschland, Österreich-Ungarn, den Böhmischen Ländern und in der Slovakei*. Essen: Klartext, 1999.

Hofer, Johannes. *Johannes Capistrano: Ein Leben im Kampf um die Reform der Kirche*. Innsbruck: Tyrolia, 1936.

Hofman, Alois. *Die Prager Zeitschrift "Ost und West": Ein Beitrag zur Geschichte der deutsch-slawischen Verständigung im Vormärz*. Berlin: Akademie, 1957.

Homberg, Herz. *Bne-Zion: Ein religiös-moralisches Lehrbuch für die Jugend israelitischer Nation*. Vienna: Im Verlagsgewölbe des K. K. Schulbücher-Verschleisses, 1812.

————. *Bne-Zion: Ein religiös-moralisches Lehrbuch für die Jugend israelitischer Religion*. Augsburg: Mathais Rieger, 1812.

Hörhan, Otto. "Die Petitionen an den Kremsierer Reichstag 1848/49." Ph.D. dissertation, Universität Wien, Vienna, 1966.

Horwitz, Rivka. *Zacharias Frankel ve-reshit ha-yehadut ha-positivit historit*. Jerusalem: Merkaz Shazar, 1984.

Hroch, Miroslav. "From National Movement to the Fully-Formed Nation: The Nation-Building Process in Europe." In Gopal Balakrishnan, ed., *Mapping the Nation*. London & New York: Verso, 1996.

Hundert, Gershon D. *The Jews in a Polish Private Town: The Case of Opataw in the Eighteenth Century*. Baltimore: Johns Hopkins University Press, 1992.

————. *Jews in Poland-Lithuania in the Eighteenth Century: A Genealogy of Modernity*. Berkeley: University of California Press, 2004.

Husserl, Sigmund. *Gründungsgeschichte des Stadt-Tempels der Israel: Kultusgemeinde Wien*. Vienna & Leipzig: Wilhelm Braumüller, 1906.

Iggers, Wilma, ed. *The Jews of Bohemia and Moravia: A Historical Reader*. Detroit: Wayne State University Press, 1992.

Israel, Jonathan I. *European Jewry in the Age of Mercantilism 1550–1750*. London & Portland: Littman Library of Jewish Civilization, 1998.

Jakobovits, Tobias. "Das Prager und Böhmische Landesrabbinat, Ende des 17. und Anfang des 18. Jahrhunderts." *JGGJČR* 5 (1933): 79–136.

Janák, Jan. "Počátky židovského vlnařského podnikáni na Moravě a ve Slezsku." In *Židé a Morava (Sborník příspěků z konference konané v říjnu 1994 v Kroměříži)*. Kroměříž: Muzeum Kroměřížska, 1995.

————. "Vlnařská velkovýroba na Moravě a ve Slezsku v letech 1740–1848." *Moravský historický sborník* 1 (1986): 184–229.

Jeiteles, Israel. *Die Kultusgemeinde der Israeliten in Wien mit Benützung des statistischen Volkszählungsoperates v. J. 1869*. Vienna: Rosner, 1873.

The Jewish Encyclopedia, 12 vols. New York & London: Funk & Wagnalls, 1901–6.

Jost, I. M. *Culturgeschichte der Israeliten der ersten Hälfte des 19. Jahrhunderts*. Breslau: Wilh. Jacobsohn, 1846.

Jüdisches Athenäum: Galerie berühmter Männer jüdischer Abstammung und jüdischen Glaubens, von der letzten Hälfte des achtzehnten, bis zum Schluss der ersten Hälfte des neunzehnten Jahrhunderts. Grimma & Leipzig: Verlags-Comptoirs, 1851.

Kahan, Isak. "Drei unveröffentlichte Briefe des Nikolsburger Lokalrabbiners Nachum Trebitsch." In Alfred Engel, ed., *Sefer Zikharon l'petihat ha-muzeon ha-yehudi be-k"k N[ikol]s[burg]*. Mikulov: Nekudah, 1936.

Kahane, Y. Z. "'Gezerat ha-sheniyyot' be-Moravia." *Zion* 8 (1943): 203–6.

———. "Nikolsburg." In Judah Leib Fishman-Maimon, ed., *'Arim ve-'imahot be-yisrael*, v. 4. Jerusalem: Mosad Ha-Rav Kook, 1950.

Kammelhar, Yekutiel Aryeh. *Dor De'ah*. New York: Naftali Braunfeld, 1952.

Kämpf, Saul Isaac. *Řeč, držená při slavnosti, jenž se odbývala dne 23. Března 1848 v židovské nové modlitebnici v Praze na památku padlých za svobodu studujících dne 13. t.m. ve. Vídni / Rede gehalten bei der am 23. März 1848 im israelitischen Tempel zu Prag stattgefundenen Todtenfeier für die am 13. d.M. in Wien als Freiheitsopfer gefallenen Studirenden*. Prague: M. I. Landau, 1848.

Kann, Robert A. *A History of the Habsburg Empire, 1526–1918*. Berkeley: University of California Press, 1974.

———, and Zdeněk V. David. *A History of East Central Europe*, v. 6, *The Peoples of the Eastern Habsburg Lands, 1526–1918*. Seattle: University of Washington Press, 1984.

Kaplan, Marion A., ed. *Jewish Daily Life in Germany, 1615–1945*. Oxford: Oxford University Press, 2005.

Karniel, Josef. *Die Toleranzpolitik Kaiser Josephs II*. Gerlingen: Bleicher, 1986.

Kárník, Zdeněk, ed. *Sborník k problematice multietnicity: České země jako multietnická společnost—Češi, Němci a Žide ve společenském životě českých zemí 1848–1918*. Prague: Filozofická fakulta Univerzity Karlovy, 1996.

Katz, Jacob. *Divine Law in Human Hands: Case Studies in Halakhic Flexibility*. Jerusalem: Magness Press, 1998.

———. *From Prejudice to Destruction*. Cambridge, Mass.: Harvard University Press, 1980.

———. *Halakhah va-meitsar*. Jerusalem: Magness Press, 1992.

———. *Out of the Ghetto: The Social Background of Jewish Emancipation, 1770–1870*. Cambridge, Mass.: Harvard University Press, 1973.

———. "Rabbi Shimson Raphael Hirsch, ha-meimin u-masmil." In his *Halakhah va-meitsar*. Jerusalem: Magness Press, 1992.

———. *The "Shabbes Goy."* Philadelphia: Jewish Publication Society, 1989.

———. "The Suggested Relationship Between Sabbatianism, Haskalah, and Reform." In his *Divine Law in Human Hands*. Jerusalem: Magness Press, 1998.

———, ed. *Toward Modernity: The European Jewish Model*. New Brunswick, N.J.: Transaction, 1987.

———. *Tradition and Crisis: Jewish Society at the End of the Middle Ages*. New York: New York University Press, 1993.

Kaufmann, David. *Die letzte Vertreibung der Juden aus Wien und Niederösterreich: Ihre Vorgeschichte (1625–1670) und ihre Opfer*. Budapest: Országos rabbiképző intézet, 1888.

———. "Mi'pinkasa shel K. K. Prostitz." *Otsar ha-Sifrut* 3 (1889–90): 19–20.

Kayserling, Meyer. "Die jüdische Literatur von Moses Mendelssohn bis auf die Gegenwart." In Jacob Winter and August Wünsche, eds., *Die Jüdische Literatur seit Abschluss des Kanons*. Trier: S. Mayer, 1896.

Kempter, Klaus. *Die Jellineks 1820–1955: Eine familienbiographische Studie zum deutschjüdischen Bildingsbürgertum*. Düsseldorf: Droste, 1998.

Kestenberg-Gladstein, Ruth. "Čechen und Juden in altväterlichen Zeit." *JB* 4(1) (1968): 64–72.

———. *Heraus aus der "Gasse,"* Dorothea Kuhrau-Neumärker, ed. Münster: LIT, 2002.

———. "Hussitentum und Judentum." *JGGJČR* 8 (1936): 1–24.

———. "Identifikation der Prager Juden vor und während der Assimilation." In Ferdinand Seibt, ed., *Die Juden in den böhmischen Ländern*. Munich: R. Oldenbourg, 1983.

———. "The Jews Between Czechs and Germans in the Historic Lands, 1848–1918." In Society for the History of Czechoslovak Jews, *The Jews of Czechoslovakia: Historical Studies and Surveys*, v. 1. Philadelphia: Jewish Publication Society, 1968.

———. "Mifked yehudei Beim she-meḥuts le-Prag be-shnat 172." *Zion* 9 (1944): 1–26.

———. *Neuere Geschichte der Juden in den böhmischen Ländern. Erster Teil: Die Zeit der Aufklärung*. Tübingen: J. C. B. Mohr, 1969.

———. "Ofiyah ha-le'umi shel haskalat Prag." *Molad* 23 (1965): 221–33.

———. "Wirtschaftsgeschichte der böhmischen Landjuden des 18. Jahrhunderts." *JB* 3(2) (1967): 101–34.

Kieval, Hillel J. "Caution's Progress: Enlightenment and Tradition in Jewish Prague." In Jacob Katz, ed., *Toward Modernity: The European Jewish Model*. New Brunswick, N.J.: Transaction, 1987.

———. *Languages of Community: The Jewish Experience in the Czech Lands*. Berkeley: University of California Press, 2000.

———. *The Making of Czech Jewry: National Conflict and Jewish Society in Bohemia, 1870–1918*. New York: Oxford University Press, 1988.

Kin'at tsiyyon. Amsterdam: Props, 1846.

King, Jeremy. *Budweisers into Czechs and Germans: A Local History of Bohemian Politics, 1848–1948*. Princeton, N.J.: Princeton University Press, 2002.

Kisch, Guido. *In Search of Freedom: A History of American Jews from Czechoslovakia*. London: E. Goldston, 1949.

———. "The Revolution of 1848 and the Jewish 'On to America' Movement." *PAJHS* 38 (1948–49): 185–234.

Klemperer, Gutmann. "Remeniszenzen aus meiner frühen Jugendzeit." *ZGJT* 6 (1936): 25–37.

Klenovský, Jaroslav. *Jewish Monuments in Brno*. Brno: Moravian Museum, 1995.

———. "Plány separace židovského osídlení na Moravě z let 1727–8." In *Židé a*

Morava (Sborník příspěků z konference konané v listopadu 1995 v Kroměříži). Kroměříž: Muzeum Kroměřížska, 1996.

———. *Židovské Město v Prostějově*. Brno: Prostějov, 1997.

Klíma, Arnošt. *Economy, Industry, and Society in Bohemia in the 17th–19th Centuries*. Prague: Charles University, 1991.

Klimeš, Jan, and Jaromír Tausch. "Hasičský sbor židovské obce v boskovicích." In *Židé a Morava (Sborník z konference konané v listopadu 1998 v Kroměříži)*. Kroměříž: Muzeum Kroměřížska, 1999.

Klugman, Eliyahu Meir. *Rabbi Samson Raphael Hirsch: Architect of Torah Judaism for the Modern World*. New York: Mesorah, 1996.

Kohn, Albert, ed. *Die Notablenversammlung der Israeliten Böhmens in Prag: Ihre Berathungen und Beschlüsse (Mit statistischen Tabellen über die israelitischen Gemeinden, Synagogen, Schulen und Rabbinate in Böhmen)*. Vienna: Leopold Sommer, 1852.

Kohut, Adolf. *Berühmte israelitische Männer und Frauen in der Kulturgeschichte der Menschheit: Lebens- und Charakterbilder aus Vergangenheit und Gegenwart*, 2 vols. Leipzig-Reudnitz: A. H. Payne, 1900–1901.

Kompert, Leopold. *Aus dem Ghetto*. Leipzig: Friedrich Wilhelm Grunow, 1848.

———. *Böhmische Juden: Geschichten*. Vienna: Jasper, Hügel & Manz, 1851.

Kořalka, Jiří. *Tschechen im Habsburgerreich und in Europa 1815–1914*. Vienna: Verlag für Geschichte und Politik, 1991.

Kordiovský, Emil, Helmut Teufel, and Jana Starek, eds. *Moravští Židé v rakousko-uherské monarchii, 1780–1918: Mikulovské sympozium, 24.–25. října, 2000* [Mährische Juden in der österreichisch-ungarischen Monarchie, 1780–1918: Nikolsburger Symposium, 24.–25. Oktober, 2000]. 26th Mikulovské Sympozium. Mikulov: Státní okresní archiv Břeclav, 2003.

Krauss, Samuel. "Der hebräischen Benennungen der modernen Völker." In Salo W. Baron and Alexander Marx, eds., *Jewish Studies in Memory of George A. Kohut*. New York: Alexander Kohut Memorial Foundation, 1935.

———. "Schöndl Dobruschka." In *Festschrift Armand Kaminka zum siebzigsten Geburtstage*. Vienna: Maimonides-Institut, 1937.

Krejčí, Oskar. *History of Elections in Bohemia and Moravia*. Boulder, Colo.: East European Monographs, 1995.

Krejčová, Helena. "Nástin spolkové činnosti českožidovského asimilačního hnutí." In Zdeněk Kárník, ed., *Sborník k problematice multietnicity: České země jako multietnická společnost—Češi, Němci a Žide ve společenském životě českých zemí 1848–1918*. Prague: Filozofická fakulta Univerzity Karlovy, 1996.

———, and Alena Míšková. "Anmerkungen zur Frage des Antisemitismus in den Böhmischen Ländern Ende des 19. Jahrhunderts." In Jörg K. Hoensch, Stanislav Biman, and Lubomír Lipták, eds., *Judenemanzipation—Antisemitismus—Verfolgung in Deutschland, Österreich-Ungarn, den Böhmischen Ländern und in der Slowakei*. Essen: Klartext, 1999.

Křen, Jan. *Die Konfliktgemeinschaft: Tschechen und Deutschen 1780–1918*, Peter Heumos, trans. Munich: R. Oldenbourg, 1996.

Kühndel, Jan. "Edmund Husserls Heimat und Herkunft." *Archiv für Geschichte der Philosophie* 51(3) (1969): 286–90.

Kulke, Eduard. *Geschichten*. Leipzig: Oskar Leiner, 1869.

Kwasnik-Rabinowicz, Oskar. "Wolf Eibenschitz," *ZGJT* 1(4) (June 1931).

Landau, Ezekiel. *Derushei ha-Tselaḥ*. Warsaw: Alafin, 1886.

Landau, Samuel. *Ahavat Tsiyyon*. Prague, 1829.

Lányi, Menyhért, and Békefi Hermin Propperné. *Szlovenszkói Zsidó Hitközségek Története*. Kassa: Athenaeum, 1933.

Lapáček, Jiří. "Pokusy o seperaci, translokaci a permutaci Židů na Přerovsku v letech 1726–1730." In *Židé a Morava (Sborník příspěků z konference konané v říjnu 1994 v Kroměříži)*. Kroměříž: Muzeum Kroměřížska, 1995.

———. "Poznámky separaci Židů v Lipníku nad Bečvou." In *Židé a Morava (Sborník příspěků z konference konané v listopadu 1996 v Kroměříži)*. Kroměříž: Muzeum Kroměřížska, 1997.

Leib ben Ozer. *Sipur ma'ase Shabbetai Tsvi: Bashraybung fun Shabse Tsvi*. Jerusalem: Merkaz Shazar, 1978.

Leopold, Moses. *Spaziergänge: Studien und Skizzen zur Geschichte der Juden in Österreich*. Vienna: Löcker, 1994.

Levie, Abraham. *Travels Among Jews and Gentiles: Abraham Levie's Travelogue, Amsterdam 1764*, Shlomo Berger, ed. Leiden: Brill, 2002.

Levin, M. *Gedenkrede bei der Enthüllung eines neuen Grabsteines für den Ober-Landesrabbiner von Mähren und Schlesien Rabbi Mordechai Benet s.A.* Vienna: Israelitische Kultusgemeinde Nikolsburg, 1908.

Liberles, Robert. "Champion of Orthodoxy: The Emergence of Samson Raphael Hirsch as a Religious Leader." *AJS Review* 6 (1981): 43–60.

———. *Religious Conflict in Social Context: The Resurgence of Orthodox Judaism in Frankfurt Am Main, 1838–1877*. Westport, CT: Greenwood Press, 1985.

Lichtblau, Albert, ed. *Als hätten wir dazugehört: Österreichisch-jüdische Lebensge-schichten aus der Habsburgermonarchie*. Vienna: Böhlau, 1999.

Liebes, Yehuda. "The Author of the Book *Tsaddik Yesod Olam*: The Sabbatean Prophet Rabbi Leib Prossnitz." *Da'at* 2–3 (1978–79): 159–74.

———. *Studies in Jewish Myth and Jewish Messianism*, Batya Stein, trans. Albany: State University of New York Press, 1993.

Limm, Peter. *The Thirty Years War*. London: Longman, 1991.

Löw, Leopold. *Aron Chorin: Eine biografische Skizze*. Szegedin: Sigmund Burger, 1863.

———. *Gesammelte Schriften*, 5 vols. Szegedin: Alexander Baba, 1889–1900.

———. "Das mährische Landesrabbinat." In his *Gesammelte Schriften*, v. 2. Szegedin: Alexander Baba, 1890.

Lowenstein, Steven M. "The 1840s and the Creation of the German-Jewish Religious Reform Movement." In Werner Mosse, Arnold Paucker, and Reinhard Rürup, eds., *Revolution and Evolution: 1848 in German-Jewish History.* Tübingen: J. C. B. Mohr, 1981.

———. "Voluntary and Involuntary Limitation of Fertility in 19th Century Bavarian Jewry." In Paul Ritterband, ed., *Modern Jewish Fertility.* Leiden: Brill, 1981.

Macartney, C. A. *The Habsburg Empire, 1790–1918.* New York: Macmillan, 1969.

Maciejko, Pawel. *The Mixed Multitude: Jacob Frank and the Frankist Movement During His Lifetime.* Oxford: Oxford University Press (forthcoming).

———. "Sabbatian Charlatans: The First Jewish Cosmopolitans." *European Review of History / Revue Européenne d'Histoire* 17(3) (2010): 361–78.

Manekin, Rachel. "Herz Homberg: The Individual and the Image." *Zion* 71(2) (2006): 153–202 (in Hebrew).

Mannheimer, Isak Noa. *Predigt über Haggaj 2, 4. 5. zur Einweihung der Synagoge in Misslitz Mähren am 5ten Juni 1845.* Vienna: Franz Edlen von Schmid & J. J. Busch, 1845.

———. *Tefilat Israel: Gebete der Israeliten.* Vienna: Franz Edlen von Schmid, 1840.

Marada, Miroslav. "Zapomenutý žurnalista Sigmund Kolisch." In *Židé a Morava (Sborník příspěků z konference konané v listopadu 1996 v Kroměříži).* Kroměříž: Muzeum Kroměřížska, 1997.

Markbreiter, Moritz. *Beiträge zur Geschichte der jüdischen Gemeinde Eisenstadt, nach archivarischen Quellen bearbeitet.* Vienna: Verlag des "Humanitären Vereines der Eisenstädter in Wien," 1908.

Marton, Ernő. *A Magyar zsidóság családfája.* Kolozsvár: Fraternitas R.-T. Kiadása, 1941.

Marx, Alexander. *Essays in Jewish Biography.* Philadelphia: Jewish Publication Society, 1948.

Mayer, Bonaventura. *Die Juden unserer Zeit: Eine gedraengte Darstellung ihrer religioesen und politischen Verhaeltnisse in den drei alten Erdtheilen.* Regensburg: G. J. Manz, 1842.

Mayer, Sigmund. *Ein jüdischer Kaufmann 1831 bis 1911.* Leipzig: Duncker & Humblot, 1911.

McCagg, William O. *A History of Habsburg Jews, 1670–1918.* Bloomington: Indiana University Press, 1989.

McEwan, Dorothea. "Jüdisches Leben im mährischen Ghetto: Eine Skizzierung der Stadt-Geschichte von Lomnitz bis 1848." *Mitteilungen des Institut für Österreichische Geschichtsforschung* 99(1–2) (1991): 83–145.

Mendelssohn, Moses. *Jerusalem, or on Religious Power and Judaism,* Allan Arkush, trans. Hanover, N.H.: Brandeis University Press, 1983.

Mendes-Flohr, Paul, and Jehuda Reinharz, eds., *The Jew in the Modern World: A Documentary History,* 2nd ed. Oxford: Oxford University Press, 1995.

Mevorah, Barouh. "Ma'asei hishtadlut b'Europa l'meni'at girusham shel yehudei Bohemia ve-Moravia, 1744–1745." *Zion* 28 (1963): 125–64.

Meyer, Michael A. *Response to Modernity: A History of the Reform Movement in Judaism*. New York: Oxford University Press, 1988.

Meysels, Lucian O. "Brunos 'Roots': Die Kreiskys und Felix' zwischen Kanitz und Trebitsch." *Illustrierte neue Welt*, August–September 1999, 17.

Michelsohn, Avraham Hayim Simha Bunim. *Sefer Ohel Elimelekh*. Landsberg: Yitshaki, 1948.

Miller, Michael L. "Crisis of Rabbinical Authority: Nehemias Trebitsch as Moravian Chief Rabbi, 1832–1842." *JB* 44 (2008): 65–91.

————. "From Liberal Nationalism to Cosmopolitan Patriotism: Simon Deutsch and 1848ers in Exile." *European Review of History / Revue Européenne d'Histoire* 17(3) (2010): 379–93.

————. "Die Nationalgarde 1848: Grenzen der Emanzipation." In Emil Kordiovský, Helmut Teufel, and Jana Starek, eds., *Moravští Židé v rakousko-uherské monarchii, 1780–1918*. Mikulov: Státní okresní archiv Břeclav, 2003.

————. "Reluctant Kingmakers: Moravian Jewish Politics in Late Imperial Austria." In András Kovács and Eszter Andor, eds., *Jewish Studies at the Central European University*. Budapest: CEU, 2004, v. 3, 111–24.

————. "The Rise and Fall of Archbishop Kohn: Czechs, Germans, and Jews in Turn-of-the-Century Moravia." *Slavic Review* 65(3) (fall 2006): 446–74.

————. "Samson Raphael Hirsch and the Revolution of 1848." In András Kovács and Eszter Andor, eds., *Jewish Studies at the Central European University*. Budapest: CEU, 2002, v. 2, 223–38.

————. "Voice and Vulnerability: Vagaries of Jewish National Identity in Turn-of-the-Century Moravia." *Simon Dubnow Institute Yearbook* 5 (2006): 159–71.

Mislovics, Erzsébet. "Demographic and Socio-Economic History of Hungarian Jewry, 1700–1830." Ph.D. dissertation, Hebrew University, Jerusalem, 2008.

Mitterauer, Michael, ed. *"Gelobt sei, der dem schwachen Kraft verleiht": Zehn Generationen einer jüdischen Familie im alten und neuen Österreich*. Vienna: Böhlau, 1987.

Modena, Leone. *The Autobiography of a Seventeenth-Century Venetian Rabbi*. Princeton, N.J.: Princeton University Press, 1988.

Moses, Leopold. *Die Juden in Sudmähren*. Unpublished. Vienna, 1939.

————. *Spaziergänge: Studien und Skizzen zur Geschichte der Juden in Österreich*, Patricia Steines, ed. Vienna: Löcker, 1994.

Mosse, Werner, Arnold Pauker, and Reinhard Rürup, eds. *Revolution and Evolution: 1848 in German-Jewish History*. Tübingen: J. C. B. Mohr, 1981.

Müller, Willibald. *Urkundliche Beiträge zur Geschichte der mähr: Judenschaft im 17. und 18. Jahrhundert*. Olmütz: Laurenz Kullii, 1903.

Münz, L. *Rabbi Eleasar, genannt Schemen Rakeach*. Trier: Sigmund Mayer, 1895.

Nascher, S. *Moses Nascher: Eine exegetische Monographie*. Berlin: Friedrich Stahn, 1879.

Neubauer, Adolf. "Der Wahnwitz und die Schwindeleien der Sabbatianer nach ungedruckten Quellen." *MGWJ* 36 (1887): 201–14.

Neuda, Abraham. *Mase davar adonai: Eine Auswahl gottesdienstlicher Vorträge—Gehalten in der Synagoge zu Loschitz von Abraham Neuda, Rabbiner.* Vienna: Schmid, 1845.

Nezhodová, Soňa. *Židovský Mikulov.* Brno: Matice moravská, 2006.

Nosek, Bedřich. "Shemuel Shmelke ben Tsvi Hirsh ha-Levi Horovits: Legend and Reality." *JB* 21(2) (1985): 75–94.

Novotný, Miroslav, ed. *Letáky z roku 1848.* Prague: Nakladatelství Elk, 1948.

Nugent, Walter. "Migration from the German and Austro-Hungarian Empires to North America." In Robin Cohen, ed., *The Cambridge Survey of World Migrations.* Cambridge, U.K.: Cambridge University Press, 1995.

Ohm-Januschowsky, Georg. *Chronik der königlichen Hauptstadt Olmütz.* Olmütz: Hölzl, 1850.

Pech, Stanley Z. *The Czech Revolution of 1848.* Chapel Hill: University of North Carolina Press, 1969.

Pěkný, Tomáš. *Historie Židů v Čechách a na Moravě.* Prague: Sefer, 1993.

Petuchowski, Jakob J. "Manuals and Catechisms of the Jewish Religion in the Early Period of Emancipation." In Alexander Altmann, ed., *Studies in Nineteenth-Century Jewish Intellectual History.* Cambridge, Mass.: Harvard University Press, 1965.

———. *Prayerbook Reform in Europe: The Liturgy of European Liberal and Reform Judaism.* New York: World Union for Progressive Judaism, 1968.

Polišenský, Josef. *Aristocrats and the Crowd in the Revolutionary Year 1848: A Contribution to the History of Revolution and Counter-Revolution in Austria.* Albany: State University of New York Press, 1980.

Polonsky, Antony, Jakub Basista, and Andrzej Link-Lenczowski, eds. *The Jews in Old Poland, 1000–1795.* London: I. B. Tauris, 1993.

Porter, Roy, and Mikuláš Teich, eds. *The Enlightenment in National Context.* Cambridge, U.K.: Cambridge University Press, 1981.

Příbram, A. F., ed. *Urkunden und Akten zur Geschichte der Juden in Wien,* 2 vols. Vienna: Braumüller, 1918.

Rabbinische Gutachten über die Verträglichkeit der freien Forschung mit dem Rabbineramte, 2 vols. Breslau: L. Freund, 1842–1843.

Rabinowicz, Aharon M. K. "The Jewish Political Community: A Contribution to the History of the Legal Position of Jews in Moravia." In Moshe Auerbach, ed., *Aharon M. K. Rabinowicz Jubilee Volume.* Jerusalem: Bialik Institute, 1996.

Rabinowicz, Meir. *Beyn Peshisha le-Lublin: Ishim ve-shitot ba-ḥasidut Polin.* Jerusalem: Kesharim, 1997.

Rachamimov, Alon. "Diaspora Nationalism's Pyrrhic Victory: The Controversy Regarding the Electoral Reform of 1909 in Bukovina." In John S. Micgiel, ed., *State and Nation Building in East Central Europe: Contemporary Perspectives.* New York: Columbia University Press, 1996.

Radimský, Jiří. "Vývoj obyvatelstva na Moravě do r. 1857." *Vlastivědný věstník moravský* 1 (1946): 72–110.

———, and Milada Wurmová. *Petice moravského lidu k sněmu z roku 1848*. Prague: Archivní správa Ministerstva vnitra, 1955.

Rath, Reuben John. *The Viennese Revolution of 1848*. Austin: University of Texas Press, 1957.

Reich, Ignaz. *Beth-El: Ehrentempel verdienter ungarischer Israeliten*, 2 vols. Pest: Alois Bucsánsky, 1867.

Řepa, Milan. *Moravané nebo Češi? Vývoj českého národního vědomi na Moravě v. 19 století*. Brno: Doplnek, 2001.

Richarz, Monika. "Ländliches Judentum als Problem der Forschung." In Monika Richarz and Reinhard Rürup, eds., *Jüdisches Leben auf dem Lande*. Tübingen: Mohr Siebeck, 1997.

Richtmann, Mózes. *Landau Ezekiel prágai rabbi (1713–1793) és a magyar zsidók*. Budapest: Athenaeum, 1905.

Ritterband, Paul, ed. *Modern Jewish Fertility*. Leiden: Brill, 1981.

Robertson, Ritchie. *The "Jewish Question" in German Literature, 1749–1939: Emancipation and Its Discontents*. Oxford: Oxford University Press, 1999.

Roest, M. "Het verhaal van eene reis door eein groot gedeelte van Europa in het eerste vierde der 18de eeuw, door een Israëlit." *Israelitische Letterbode* 10 (1884–85): 148–89; 11 (1885–86): 21–38, 93–147.

Rohrbacher, Stefan. *Gewalt im Biedermeier: Antijüdische Ausschreitungen in Vormärz und Revolution (1815–1848/49)*. Frankfurt: Campus, 1993.

Rosenbloom, Noah H. *Tradition in an Age of Reform: The Religious Philosophy of Samson Raphael Hirsch*. Philadelphia: Jewish Publication Society, 1976.

Rosenbusch, Max. "Zur Statistik der Wohnungen in den Judenvierteln Österreichs vor der Revolution." *Zeitschrift für Demographie und Statistik der Juden* 9(12) (1913): 176–78.

Rosenmann, Moses. *Dr. Adolf Jellinek: Sein Leben und Schaffen*. Vienna: J. Schlesinger, 1931.

———. *Isak Noa Mannheimer: Sein Leben und Wirken*. Vienna: R. Löwit, 1922.

Rosenwasser, R. *Rabbi Mordechai Benet (Marcus Benedict 1753–1829)*. Berlin-Schönberg: S. Scholem, n.d.

Rosman, M. J. *The Lords' Jews: Magnate-Jewish Relations in the Polish-Lithuanian Commonwealth During the Eighteenth Century*. Cambridge, Mass.: Harvard University Press, 1990.

Roth, Ernest, ed. *Takkanot Nikolsburg / Constitutiones Communitatis Judaeorum Nikolsburgiensis*. Jerusalem: Sura, 1961.

Roubík, František. *Český rok 1848*. Prague: Ladislav Kuncíř, 1948.

———. "Die Judensiedlungen in Böhmen auf den Ortsplänen vom Jahre 1727." *JGGJČR* 3 (1931): 283–306.

————. "Zur Geschichte der Juden in Böhmen in der ersten Hälfte des neunzehnten Jahrhunderts." *JGGJČR* 6 (1934): 285–322.

Rozenblit, Marsha. "Jewish Assimilation in Habsburg Vienna." In Jonathan Frankel and Steven J. Zipperstein, eds., *Assimilation and Community: The Jews in Nineteenth-Century Europe*. Cambridge, U.K.: Cambridge University Press, 1992.

————. *The Jews of Vienna, 1867–1914: Assimilation and Identity*. Albany: State University of New York Press, 1983.

————. "The Struggle over Religious Reform in Nineteenth-Century Vienna." *AJS Review* 14(2) (fall 1989): 179–221.

Růžička, Leon. "Die österreichischen Dichter jüdischer Abstammung Moyses Dobruska = Franz Thomas von Schönfeld und David Dobruska = Emanuel von Schönfeld." *Jüdische Familien-Forschung* 6(3) (September 1930): 282–90.

Sadek, Vladimír. "La synagogue réformée de Prague (La 'Vielle Ecole') et les études juives au cours du 19e siècle." *JB* 16 (1980): 119–23.

Sameš, Vincenc (Čeněk). "K historii revolučního roku 1848 v Třebíči." *Ročenka musea a archivu v Třebíči* 1 (1948): 26–66.

————. "Protižidovské hnutí v Třebíči po roce 1848." *Od Horácka k Podyjí* 9 (1931–32): 110–17.

Samet, Moshe. "The Beginnings of Orthodoxy." *Modern Judaism* 8(3) (1988): 249–69.

————. "Besamim Rosh shel R. Shaul Berlin: Bibliografya, historiografya ve-ideologya." *Kiryat Sefer* 48 (1973): 509–23.

Sandler, Perez. *Mendelssohn's Edition of the Pentateuch*. Jerusalem: Rubin Mass, 1940 (in Hebrew).

Sauer, Walter. "Anton Füster—Priester der Wiener Revolution 1848." *Zeitgeschichte* 11–12 (1975): 249–56.

Scari, Hieronymus von. *Systematische Darstellung der in Betreff der Juden in Mähren und im k.k. Antheile Schlesiens erlassenen Gesetze und Verordnungen*. Brünn: L. W. Seidel, 1835.

————. *Zusätze zu der im Jahre 1835 erschienenen: Systematische Darstellung der in Betreff der Juden in Mähren und im k.k. Antheile Schlesiens erlassenen Gesetze und Verordnungen*. Vienna: J. P. Sollinger, 1841.

Schatzky, Jacob. "Jewish Ideologies in Austria During the Revolution of 1848." In Salo Baron, Ernest Nagel, and Koppel S. Pinson, eds., *Freedom and Reason: Studies in Philosophy and Jewish Culture in Memory of Morris Raphael Cohen*. Glencoe, Ill.: Free Press, 1951.

Schlesinger, A. *Biographische Skizze und feierliches Leichenbegräbniss des verewigten hochgeehrten Rabbi Nehemias Trebitsch, Oberlandrabbiner in Mähren und Schlesien*. Prague: J. Landau, 1842.

Schmidt-Hartmann, Eva, and Stanley B. Winters, eds. *Grossbritannien, die USA und die böhmischen Länder 1848–1938*. Munich: R. Oldenbourg, 1991.

Schnitzer, Armin. *Jüdische Kulturbilder (aus meinem Leben)*. Vienna: L. Beck & Sohn, 1904.

Scholem, Gershom. "Redemption Through Sin." In his *Messianic Idea in Judaism*. New York: Schocken, 1971.

———. "Review of M. J. Cohen, 'Jacob Emden, a Man of Controversy.'" *Kiryat Sefer* 16 (1939–40): 320–38 (in Hebrew).

———. *Sabbatai Sevi: The Mystical Messiah*. Princeton, N.J.: Princeton University Press, 1973.

Schopf, Alfred. *Die Revolution von 1848/49 in der Donaumonarchie und der verhinderte Ausgleich zwischen Tschechen und Deutschen in Böhmen und Mähren*. Neuried: Ars Una, 1997.

Schorsch, Ismar. "Emancipation and the Crisis of Religious Authority: The Emergence of the Modern Rabbinate." In Werner Mosse, Arnold Paucker, and Reinhard Rürup, eds., *Revolution and Evolution: 1848 in German History*. Tübingen: Mohr, 1981.

———. *From Text to Context: The Turn to History in Modern Judaism*. Hanover, N.H.: University Press of New England, 1995.

———. "Myth of Sephardic Supremacy." *LBIYB* 34 (1989): 47–66.

Schubert, Kurt. "Der Einfluss des Josephinismus auf das Judentum Österreich." *Kairos* 14(1–4) (1972): 81–97.

Schudt, Johann Jacob. *Jüdischer Merckwürdigkeiten*. Frankfurt am Main: S. T. Hocker, 1717.

Schwab, Löw. *Das Gedächtniss des Gerechten ist zum Segen: Trauerrede auf den Tod Seiner Majestät Franz I. Kaisers von Oestereich glorreichen Angedenkens, gehalten in der Synagoge zu Prossnitz*. Vienna: C. Gerold, 1835.

Schwarzfuchs, Simon. "Alsace and Southern Germany: The Creation of a Border." In Michael Brenner, Vicki Caron, and Uri R. Kaufmann., eds., *Jewish Emancipation Reconsidered: The French and German Models*. Tübingen: Mohr Siebeck, 2003.

Schwenger, Heinrich. "Die jüdische Schule in Lundenburg." *ZGJT* 1(3) (1931): 171–73.

Scott, H. M., ed. *Enlightened Absolutism: Reform and Reformers in Later Eighteenth-Century Europe*. London: Macmillan, 1990.

———. "Reform in the Habsburg Monarchy, 1740–90." In H. M. Scott, ed., *Enlightened Absolutism: Reform and Reformers in Later Eighteenth-Century Europe*. London: Macmillan, 1990.

Šedinová, Jiřina. "Alttschechische Glossen in mittelalterlichen hebräischen Schriften und älteste Denkmäler der tschechischen Literatur." *JB* 17(2) (1981): 73–89.

———. "Hebrew Historiography in Moravia at the 18th Century: Abraham Trebitsch (Around 1760–1840)." *JB* 10 (1974): 51–61.

Seibt, Ferdinand, ed. *Die Juden in den boehmischen Laendern: Vortraege der*

Tagung des Collegium Carolinum in Bad Wiessee vom 27 bis 29 Nov. 1981. Munich: R. Oldenbourg, 1983.

———. *Německo a Češi: Dějiny jednoho sousedství uprostřed Evropy.* Prague: Academia, 1996.

———, and Winfried Eberhard, eds. *Europa 1500: Integrationsprozesse im Widerstreit—Staaten, Regionen, Personenverbände, Christenheit.* Stuttgart: Klett-Cotta, 1987.

Seton-Watson, R. W. *A History of the Czechs and Slovaks.* London: Hutchinson, 1943.

Shavit, Yaacov. "A Duty Too Heavy to Bear: Hebrew in the Berlin Haskalah, 1783–1819—Between Classic, Modern, and Romantic." In Lewis Glinert, ed., *Hebrew in Ashkenaz.* New York: Oxford University Press, 1993.

Shear, Adam. "Judah Halevi's Kuzari in the Haskalah: The Reinterpretation and Reimagining of a Medieval Work." In Ross Brann and Adam Sutcliffe, eds., *Renewing the Past, Reconfiguring Jewish Culture: From al-Andalus to the Haskalah.* Philadelphia: University of Pennsylvania Press, 2004.

Shulvass, Moses. *From East to West.* Detroit: Wayne State University Press, 1971.

Silber, Michael. "The Historical Experience of German Jewry and Its Impact on the Haskalah and Reform in Hungary." In Jacob Katz, ed., *Toward Modernity: The European Jewish Model.* New Brunswick, N.J.: Transaction, 1987.

———. "On the Relationship Between Hasidism and Sabbateanism: A Geographic Exploration." World Congress of Jewish Studies, Jerusalem, 1981.

———. "Shorshei ha-pilug ba-yahadut hungariya: temurot tarbutiyot me-yamei Joseph ha-sheni ad erev mahapekhat 1848." Ph.D. dissertation, Hebrew University, Jerusalem, 1985.

———. "The Social Composition of the Pest Radical Reform Society (Genossenschaft für Reform im Judenthum), 1848–1853." *JSS* 1(3) (1995): 99–128.

Singer, Ludwig. "Zur Geschichte der Toleranzpatente in den Sudetenländern." *JGGJČR* 5 (1933): 231–311.

Šlesinger, Václav. *Zápas půl století: Boj o českou Moravu 1848–1918.* Brno: Novela, 1946.

Society for the History of Czechoslovak Jews. *The Jews of Czechoslovakia: Historical Studies and Surveys,* 3 vols. Philadelphia: Jewish Publication Society, 1968–1984.

Sofer, Moses. *Sefer Ḥatam Sofer.* Pressburg, 1818.

Sofer, Shelomo. *Igrot Sofrim: mikhteve kodesh mi-ge'one ha-dor.* Vienna & Budapest: J. Schlesinger, 1929.

Sorkin, David. *Moses Mendelssohn and the Religious Enlightenment.* Berkeley: University of California Press, 1996.

———. *The Transformation of German Jewry, 1780–1840.* Detroit: Wayne State University Press, 1999.

Sperber, Jonathan. *The European Revolutions, 1848–1851.* Cambridge, U.K.: Cambridge University Press, 1994.

Spyra, Janusz. "Židé v rakouském Slezsku (1742–1918): Nástin dějin." In Janusz Spyra and Marcin Wodzinski, eds., *Židé ve Slezsku: Studie k dějinám Židů ve Slezsku.* Těšín: Muzeum Těšínka, 2001.

Stampfer, Shaul. "The 1764 Census of Polish Jewry." *Bar-Ilan* 24–25 (1989): 41, 126–28.

Statut für den mährisch-jüdischen Landesmassa-Fond. Brünn: Rudolf M. Rohrer, 1869.

Steiner, Leo. "Das Bilbul von Gross-Meseritsch." *Hickl's Jüdische Volkskalendar* 27 (1927–28): 93–96.

Steinherz, Samuel. "Kreuzfahrer und Juden in Prag (1096)." *JGGJČR* 1 (1929): 1–32.

Steinschneider, Moritz. *Briefwechsel mit seiner Verlobten Auguste Auerbach, 1845–1849: Ein Beitrag zur juedischen Wissenschaft und Emanzipation,* Renate Heuer and Louise Steinschneider, eds. Frankfurt am Main: Campus, 1995.

Štěpán, Václav. "Die gesellschaftliche und rechtliche Stellung der Juden in Mähren in der vorhussitischen Zeit." *JB* 28(1) (1992): 3–21.

———. "Vznik židovské obce v Moravské Ostravě." In Emil Kordiovský, Helmut Teufel, and Jana Starek, eds., *Moravští Židé v rakousko-uherské monarchii, 1780–1918.* Mikulov: Státní okresní archiv Břeclav, 2003.

Streng, Karl. *Ausführliche Biographie des am 13. März 1848 in Wien gefallenen Freiheitshelden Karl Heinrich Spitzer.* Vienna: Edl. v. Schmidbauer und Holzwarth, 1848.

Sulzer, Salomon. *Schir Zion: Gottesdienstliche Gesänge der Israeliten.* Vienna: J. Schlossberg, 1840.

Tafeln zur Statistik der oesterreichischen Monarchie, Neue Folge. Vienna: K. K. Direction der Administrativen Statistik, 1828–1865.

Tal, Tobias. *Samson Raphael Hirsch: Vortrag gehaltan von Oberrabbiner T. Tal am Sonntag 12. Kislew 5652 (10 Dezember 1891) in Verein Mekor hayyim in Amsterdam.* Cologne: Bibliothek des Jüdischen Volksfreundes, 1891.

Teufel, Helmut. "Neue Literatur zur Geschichte der Juden in Böhmen und Mähren." *Aschkenaz* 4(2) (1994): 531–36.

———. "Neuere Literatur zur Geschichte der Juden in Böhmen und Mähren." *Aschkenaz* 1 (1991): 173–93.

———. "Zur politischen und sozialen Geschichte der Juden in Mähren von Antritt der Habsburger bis zur Schlacht am Weissen Berg (1526–1620)." Ph.D. dissertation, Friedrich-Alexander-Universität, Erlangen-Nürnberg, 1971.

Tietze, Hans. *Die Juden Wiens: Geschichte, Wirtschaft, Kultur.* Leipzig: E. P. Tal, 1933.

Till, Rudolf. "Zur Herkunft der Wiener Bevölkerung im 19. Jahrhundert." *Vierteljahrschrift für Sozial- und Wirtschaftsgeschichte* 34(1) (1941): 30–35.

Timmerman, Heiner, ed. *1848—Revolution in Europa: Verlauf, politische Programme, Folgen und Wirken.* Berlin: Duncker & Humblot, 1999.

Torat ha-ken'aot. Amsterdam: Props, 1845.

Toury, Jacob. *Die jüdische Press im österreichischen Kaiserreich: Ein Beitrag zur Problematik der Akkulturation 1802–1918*. Tübingen: J. C. B. Mohr, 1983.

———. "Townships in the German-Speaking Parts of the Austrian Empire Before and After the Revolution of 1848/49." *LBIYB* 26 (1981): 55–72.

———. *Turmoil and Confusion in the Revolution of 1848: The Anti-Jewish Riots in the "Year of Freedom" and Their Influence on Modern Antisemitism*. Tel Aviv: Moreshet, 1968 (in Hebrew).

Trapl, Miloslav. *České národní obrozene na Moravě v době předbřeznové a v revolučních letech 1848–1849*. Brno: Blok, 1977.

Trebitsch, Abraham. *Korot ha-Ittim*. Brünn: Josef Rossmann, 1801.

Trebitsch, Nehemias. *Kovets ʿal Yad ha-ḥazakah*. Vienna: Anton von Schmid, 1837.

———. *Sefer shalom yerushalayim*. Vienna: Anton Schmid, 1821.

———. *Sefer Shalom Yerushalayim: ḥidushim ʿal ha-Mishnah, Masekhet Zevaḥim*. Jerusalem: Machon Yerushalayim, 2000.

———. *Sefer Shalom Yerushalayim: ḥidushim u-ferushim, hagahot ve-tikunim ʿal Talmud Yerushalmi, Seder Zeraʾim*. Jerusalem: Machon Yerushalayim, 1980.

———. *Sheʾelot u-teshuvot Rabi Naḥum Trebitsch*. Jerusalem: Machon Yerushalayim, 1988.

———. *Trauerrede über das Hinscheiden weiland Seiner Majestät des höchstgeliebten, höchstseligen Franz des Ersten, Kaisers von Oesterreich*. Vienna: Anton Edlen von Schmid, 1835.

Trepp, Leo. *Die Oldenburger Judenschaft: Bild und Vorbild jüdischen Seins und Werdens in Deutschland*. Oldenburg: Heinz Holzberg, 1973.

Twersky, Isadore. "The Shulḥan ʿAruk: Enduring Code of Jewish Law." *Judaism* 16(2) (1967): 141–58.

Tykocinski, H. "Lebenszeit und Heimat des Isaak Or Sarua." *MGWJ* 55 (1911): 490–94.

Újvári, Péter, ed. *Magyar zsidó lexikon*. Budapest: A Magyar zsidó lexikon kiadása, 1929.

Urban, Otto. *Česka společnost, 1848–1918*. Prague: Svoboda, 1982.

———. *Die tschechische Gesellschaft, 1848 bis 1918*, 2 vols., Henning Schlegel, trans. Vienna: Böhlau, 1994.

Urbanitsch, Peter. "Die politischen Judengemeinen in Mähren nach 1848." In Emil Kordiovský, Helmut Teufel, and Jana Starek, eds., *Moravští Židé v rakousko-uherské monarchii, 1780–1918*. Mikulov: Státní okresní archiv Břeclav, 2003.

Válka, Josef. "Moravia and the Crisis of the Estate's System in the Lands of the Bohemian Crown." In R. J. W. Evans, ed., *Crown, Church, and Estates: Central European Politics in the Sixteenth and Seventeenth Centuries*. New York: St. Martin's Press, 1991.

———. "Die Stellung Mährens in Wandel des böhmischen Lehensstaates." In Ferdinand Seibt and Winfried Eberhard, eds., *Europa 1500: Integrationsprozesse im Widerstreit—Staaten, Regionen, Personenverbände, Christenheit.* Stuttgart: Klett-Cotta, 1987.

Verhandlungen des oesterreichischen Reichstages nach der stenographischen Aufnahme. Vienna: K. K. Hof- und Staatsdruckerei, 1849.

Vielmetti, Nikolaus. *Das österreichische Judentum: Voraussetzungen und Geschichte.* Vienna: Jugend & Volk, 1974.

Viner, Shelomo. *R. Yehezkel Landau: Toldot ḥayav u-fe'ulotav.* Jerusalem: Da'at Torah, 1961.

Wachstein, Bernhard. *Die Hebräische Publizistik in Wien.* Vienna: Selbstverlag der Historischen Kommission, 1930.

———. "Notizen zur Geschichte der Juden in Prossnitz." *JJLG* 16 (1924): 163–76.

———. "Shnei mikhtavim me'harav Mordekhai Benet 'al dat hitḥadshut ha-rabbanut b'Vina bi-shnat 5589." *Ha-tsofe* 2 (5672/1912): 94–97.

———. *Urkunden und Akten zur Geschichte der Juden in Eisenstadt und den Siebengemeinden.* Vienna: Wilhelm Braunmüller, 1926.

Walden, Aaron. *Yekhabed av.* Piotrków Trybunalski: Libeskind, 1923.

Walk, Yosef. "Benei Ziyyon le-Herz Homberg." *Bar Ilan* 14–15 (1977): 218–32.

Walzer, Tina. "Mährische Juden in Wien 1784–1874." *David—Jüdische Kulturzeitschrift* 48 (April 2001): 27–34.

Wandruszka, Adam, and Peter Urbanitsch, eds. *Die Habsburgermonarchie, 1848–1918*, v. 3, *Die Völker des Reichs*. Vienna: Akademie der Wissenschaften, 1980.

Washofsky, Mark. "Halakhah in Translation: The Chatam Sofer on Prayer in the Vernacular." *CCAR Journal* 51(3) (2004): 142–63.

Weiglová, Markéta. "Jews as a Barometer of the National Struggle in Bohemia and Moravia, 1890–1910." *JB* 43 (2007–8): 93–120.

Weiss, Isaac Hirsch. *Meine Lehrjahre.* Berlin: Schocken, 1936.

———. *Zikhronotai mi-yalduti 'ad milat li shemonim shanah.* Warsaw: Shuldberg, 1895.

Welzl, Hans. "Zur Geschichte der Juden in Brünn während des XVII. und XVIII. Jahrhunderts." *Zeitschrift des Vereines für die Geschichte Mährens und Schlesiens* 8 (1904): 296–357.

Wenzel, Rainer. "Judentum und 'bürgerliche Religion': Religion, Geschichte, Politik und Pädagogik in Herz Hombergs Lehrbüchern." In Britta L. Behm, Peter Dietrich, and Ingrid Lohmann, eds., *Jüdische Erziehung und aufklärerische Schulreform: Analysen zum späten 18. und 19. Jahrhundert.* Münster: Waxmann, 2002.

[Wertheimer, Joseph Ritter von]. *Die Juden in Österreich: Vom Standpunkte der Geschichte, des Rechts und des Staatsvortheils.* Leipzig: Mayer & Wigand, 1842.

Wieser, J. C. von. *Chronik des Hauses der Grafen Laánsky, Freiherr von Bukowa.* Brünn: Gastl, 1860.

Wilensky, Mordechai. "Hasidic-Mitnaggedic Polemics in the Jewish Communities of Eastern Europe: The Hostile Phase." In Gershon Hundert, ed., *Essential Papers on Hasidism*. New York: New York University Press, 1991.

Wininger, Salomon. *Grosse jüdische Nationalbiographie*, 7 vols. Czernowitz: "Orient," 1925–1936.

Winter, J., and Aug. Wünsche, eds. *Die Jüdische Literatur seit Abschluss des Kanons*, 3 vols. Trier: Sigmund Mayer, 1896.

Wischnitzer, Mark. "Origins of the Jewish Artisan Class in Bohemia and Moravia, 1500–1648." *JSS* 16 (1954): 335–50.

Wiskemann, Elizabeth. *Czechs and Germans: A Study of the Struggle in the Historic Provinces of Bohemia and Moravia*, 2nd ed. New York: St. Martin's Press, 1967.

Wistrich, Robert. "The Modernization of Viennese Jewry: The Impact of German Culture in a Multi-Ethnic State." In Jacob Katz, ed., *Toward Modernity: The European Jewish Model*. New York: Transaction, 1987.

Wittemann, M. Theresia. *Draussen vor dem Ghetto: Leopold Kompert und die "Schilderung jüdischen Volkslebens" in Böhmen und Mähren*. Tübingen: Niemeyer, 1998.

Wlaschek, Rudolf M. *Juden in Böhmen: Beiträge zur Geschichte des europäischen Judentums im 19. und 20. Jahrhundert*. Munich: Oldenbourg, 1990.

Wolf, Gerson, ed. *Die alten Statuten der jüdischen Gemeinden in Mähren sammt den Synodalbeschlüssen*. Vienna: A. Hölder, 1880.

———. *Ferdinand II und die Juden*. Vienna: W. Braumüller, 1859.

———. *Isak Noa Mannheimer, Prediger: Eine biographische Skizze*. Vienna: J. Knöpfelmacher, 1863.

———. *Joseph Wertheimer: Ein Lebens- und Zeitbild—Beiträge zur Geschichte der Juden Oesterreich's in neuester Zeit*. Vienna: Herzfield & Bauer, 1868.

———. *Judentaufen in Oesterreich*. Vienna: Herzfeld & Bauer, 1863.

———. "Die Versuche zur Errichtung einer Rabbinerschule in Oesterreich." *Zeitschrift für die Geschichte der Juden in Deutschland* 5 (1892): 27–53.

Wolny, Gregor. *Die Markgrafschaft Mähren: Topographisch, statistisch und historisch geschildert*, 6 vols. Brünn: K. Winiker, 1846.

Wurmová, Milada. *Soupis moravských novin a časopisů z let 1848–1918*. Brno: Krajské nakladatelství, 1955.

Wurzbach, Constantin von. *Biographisches Lexikon des Kaiserthums Österreich*, 60 vols. Vienna: Zamarski, 1856–1891.

Yerushalmi, Yosef Hayim. *The Lisbon Massacre of 1506 and the Royal Image in Shebet Yehudah*. Cincinnati: HUC Jewish Institute of Religion, 1976.

———. *Zakhor: Jewish History and Jewish Memory*. Seattle: University of Washington Press, 1982.

Žáček, Václav. "Die jüdischen Gerbereien in Mähren zu Beginn des 18. Jahrhunderts." *JGGJČR* 5 (1933): 175–98.

———. "Zwei Beiträge zur Geschichte der Frankismus in den böhmischen Ländern." *JGGJČR* 9 (1938): 370–72.

Zahra, Tara. *Kidnapped Souls: National Indifference and the Battle for Children in the Bohemian Lands, 1900–1948*. Ithaca, N.Y.: Cornell University Press, 2008.

Zinberg, Israel. *A History of Jewish Literature*, 12 vols., Bernard Martin, ed. and trans. Jerusalem: Ktav, 1977.

Zulässigkeit und Dringlichkeit der Synagogen-Reformen. Vienna: F. Edler von Schmid, 1845.

Zur Geschichte der Juden in Mähren: Ein Patent aus dem Jahre 1787. Troppau: Ernst Gieler, 1928.

Zweig, Stefan. *The World of Yesterday: An Autobiography*. Lincoln: University of Nebraska Press, 1964.

Zwergbaum, Aharon. "'Al yehudei Brno." In Moshe Auerbach, ed., *Aharon M. K. Rabinowicz Jubilee Volume*. Jerusalem: Bialik Institute, 1996.

Index